Lecture Notes in Computer Science 4397

Commenced Publication in 1973
Founding and Former Series Editors:
Gerhard Goos, Juris Hartmanis, and Jan van Leeuwen

T0223156

Constantine Stephanidis Michael Pieper (Eds.)

Universal Access in Ambient Intelligence Environments

9th ERCIM Workshop on User Interfaces for All
Königswinter, Germany, September 27-28, 2006
Revised Papers

 Springer

Volume Editors

Constantine Stephanidis
Foundation for Research and Technology - Hellas (FORTH)
Institute of Computer Science (ICS)
70013 Heraklion, Crete, Greece
E-mail: cs@ics.forth.gr

Michael Pieper
Fraunhofer Institut für Angewandte Informationstechnik (FIT)
Schloss Birlinghoven, 53754 Sankt Augustin, Germany
E-mail: michael.pieper@fit.fraunhofer.de

Library of Congress Control Number: 2007921000

CR Subject Classification (1998): H.5.2, H.5.3, H.5, H.4, H.3, D.2, C.2, K.4

LNCS Sublibrary: SL 3 – Information Systems and Application, incl. Internet/Web
and HCI

ISSN   0302-9743
ISBN-10   3-540-71024-8 Springer Berlin Heidelberg New York
ISBN-13   978-3-540-71024-0 Springer Berlin Heidelberg New York

Springer is a part of Springer Science+Business Media

springer.com

© Springer-Verlag Berlin Heidelberg 2007
Printed in Germany

Typesetting: Camera-ready by author, data conversion by Scientific Publishing Services, Chennai, India
Printed on acid-free paper   SPIN: 12023714   06/3142   5 4 3 2 1 0

Foreword

Since its establishment in 1995, the ERCIM Working Group "User Interfaces for All"[1] (WG UI4ALL) has systematically promoted the proactive realization of the design for all principles in HCI. Its activities have included the organization of a series of very successful workshops[2] that have contributed to consolidate recent work and stimulate further discussion on the state of the art in user interfaces for all and its increasing range of applications in the upcoming Information Society. Such workshops have brought together, in a new scientific community, researchers and teams working not only in the different ERCIM organizations, but also in organizations beyond ERCIM and the European boundaries, who share common interests and aspirations and contribute to the endeavors towards making the Information Society equally accessible to all citizens. This volume contains the proceedings of the last ERCIM "User Interfaces for All" Workshop.

The work of the ERCIM WG UI4ALL led in 2001 to the establishment of the International Conference on Universal Access in Human–Computer Interaction (UAHCI)[3], which takes place in the context of the HCI International Conference series[4]. UAHCI has established an international forum for the dissemination and exchange of scientific information on theoretical, methodological and empirical research that addresses all issues related to the attainment of universal access in the development of interactive software, attracting participants from a broad range of disciplines and fields of expertise.

The work of the ERCIM WG UI4ALL has also contributed to the establishment of the international, interdisciplinary refereed journal *Universal Access in the Information*

---

[1] http://www.ui4all.gr/

[2] - 1st ERCIM Workshop "User Interfaces for All", Heraklion, Crete, Greece, October 30–31,1995.
- 2nd ERCIM Workshop "User Interfaces for All", Prague, Czech Republic, November 7–8, 1996.
- 3rd ERCIM Workshop "User Interfaces for All", Obernai, France, November 3–4,1997.
- 4th ERCIM Workshop "User Interfaces for All", Stockholm, Sweden, October 19–21,1998.
- 5th ERCIM Workshop "User Interfaces for All", Dagstuhl, Germany, November 28– December 1 1999.
- 6th ERCIM Workshop "User Interfaces for All", Florence, Italy, October 25–26, 2000.
- 7th ERCIM Workshop "User Interfaces for All", Paris (Chantilly), France, October 23–25, 2002.
- 8th ERCIM Workshop "User Interfaces For All", Vienna, Austria, June 28–29, 2004.

[3] - 1st International Conference on Universal Access in Human-Computer Interaction 2001, in the context of HCI International 2001, August 5–10, 2001, New Orleans, LA, USA.
- 2nd International Conference on Universal Access in Human-Computer Interaction 2003, in the context of HCI International 2003, June 22–27, 2003, Crete, Greece.
- 3rd International Conference on Universal Access in Human-Computer Interaction, in the context of HCI International 2005, July 22–27, 2005, Las Vegas, Nevada, USA.

[4] http://www.hci-international.org/

Society (UAIS), published by Springer[5]. UAIS provides an archival publication channel for the discussion and advancement of theoretical and practical aspects of universal access in the Information Society, facilitating the rapid and wide diffusion of scientific and technological results that promote universal access in the Information Society; and stimulating cross-fertilization between the different contributing disciplines.

Many members of the ERCIM WG UI4ALL have also contributed to the edited book "User Interfaces for All – Concepts, Methods and Tools," the first book dedicated to the issues of universal design and universal access in HCI, published by Lawrence Erlbaum Associates in 2001[6]. The book is a collection of 30 chapters written by leading international authorities, affiliated with academic, research and industrial organizations and non-market institutions, providing a comprehensive overview of the state of the art in the field, and including contributions from a variety of theoretical and applied disciplines and research themes.

Furthermore, the work of the ERCIM WG UI4ALL has contributed to the establishment of the International Scientific Forum "Towards an Information Society for All" ISF-IS4ALL (1997–2000)[7], an international ad hoc group of experts which was the first one to recognize the need for a global approach towards an Information Society accessible, usable and acceptable by all citizens. Two White Papers have been published in the *International Journal of Human-Computer Interaction* and were also submitted to the European Commission, reporting on an evolving international R&D agenda in the field of HCI. Since then, the vision of an Information Society for all and the necessity for universal access to Information Society technologies have acquired widespread acceptance and importance not only at a scientific and technological but also at a European policy level, as demonstrated by the Europe "Information Society for All" initiative of the European Commission. The activities initiated by the ISF-IS4ALL have been continued in the framework of the Thematic Network (Working Group) "Information Society for All" (IST-1999-14101 - IS4ALL), which has consolidated knowledge on universal access in the context of Information Society technologies into a comprehensive validated code of design practice, leading to the publication by Springer, in 2005, of the edited book *Universal Access in Health Telematics - A Design Code of Practic*"[8], and has developed an on-line training course in design for all[9].

As a result of the 12 years of activities of the ERCIM WG "User Interfaces for All," the field of "universal access and design for all" has made significant progress towards consolidating theoretical approaches, methods, tools and technologies, as well as exploring new application domains. The ERCIM WG UI4ALL, which was the recipient of the ERCIM WG Award for the year 2000, can be considered as an example of a dedicated, prolific and successful research and development community, which has highly contributed to the establishment in Europe of a new scientific field, that of "universal access and design for all".

As of the end of 2006, after the successful ninth workshop, the time has come to consider the mission of this WG as fully accomplished. The papers presented during

---

[5] http://www.springeronline.com/journal/10209/about
[6] http://www.ics.forth.gr/hci/publications/book.html
[7] http://www.ui4all.gr/isf_is4all/
[8] http://www.springeronline.com/3-540-26167-2
[9] http://is4all-tc.ics.forth.gr

the ninth ERCIM "User Interfaces for All" Workshop and included in the present volume demonstrate that Ambient Intelligence is raising new fascinating research challenges, rapidly gaining wide attention by an increasing number of researchers and practitioners in Europe and worldwide. The notions of universal access and user interfaces for all are central to this vision, since Ambient Intelligence aims at providing implicit, unobtrusive interaction paradigms, putting people, their social situations, and the corresponding environments at the center of design considerations. These issues are now addressed by the new (established in 2006) ERCIM WG "Smart Environments and Systems for AMbient Intelligence" (SESAMI[10]). The research community established by the ERCIM WG UI4ALL will therefore continue its collaborative efforts in the context of SESAMI.

September 2006   Constantine Stephanidis

---

[10] http://www.ics.forth.gr/sesami/

Preface

The Ninth ERCIM Workshop "User Interfaces for All" was held in Königswinter (Bonn), Germany, September 27–28, 2006, building upon the results of the eight previous workshops held in Heraklion, Crete, Greece, October 30–31, 1995; Prague, Czech Republic, November 7–8, 1996; Obernai, France, November 3–4, 1997; Stockholm, Sweden, October 19–21, 1998; Dagstuhl, Germany, November 28–December 1, 1999; Florence, Italy, October 25–26, 2000; Paris (Chantilly), France, October 24–25, 2002; and Vienna, Austria, June 28–29, 2004.

The concept of "user interfaces for all" targets a proactive realization of the "design for all" principle in the field of human–computer interaction (HCI), and involves the development of user interfaces to interactive applications and e-services, which provide universal access and usability to potentially all users. In the tradition of its predecessors, the ninth ERCIM Workshop "User Interfaces for All" aimed to consolidate recent work and to stimulate further discussion on the state of the art in "user interfaces for all" and its increasing range of applications in the Information Society.

The emphasis of the 2006 event was on "Universal Access in Ambient Intelligence Environments." In the years ahead, as a result of the increasing demand for ubiquitous and continuous access to information and services, Information Society technologies are anticipated to evolve towards a new computing paradigm referred to as Ambient Intelligence. Such an environment will be characterized by invisible (i.e., embedded) computational power in everyday appliances and other surrounding physical objects, and populated by intelligent mobile and wearable devices. Ambient Intelligence will have profound consequences on the type, content and functionality of the emerging products and services, as well as on the way people will interact with them, bringing about multiple new requirements for the development of Information Society technologies. Towards this end, the notion of universal access, which, by definition, aims towards the accessibility and usability of Information Society technologies by anyone, anywhere and at anytime, is critically important. In the Ambient Intelligence environment, universal access will face new challenges posed by the pursuit of proactive accessibility and usability in the context of embedded interactivity "hidden" in a variety of interconnected, multifunctional art facts. It is therefore important to understand such new challenges, and to identify how these will affect the continuing efforts towards universal access in the Information Society. Thus, the ninth ERCIM Workshop "User Interfaces for All" focused on the new HCI challenges that Ambient Intelligence brings about under a universal access perspective, with the aim to envisage new scenarios of use of Ambient Intelligence technologies by users with diverse needs and requirements, and to identify some of the critical issues that will have to be addressed throughout all phases and aspects of the development life-cycle of interactive applications and services. The workshop offered two keynote speeches, "From Human–Computer Interaction to Human–Environment Interaction: Ambient Intelligence and the Disappearing Computer" by Norbert Streitz (Fraunhofer IPSI, Germany) and "Human Computer Confluence" by Alois Ferscha (Institut für

Pervasive Computing, Johannes Kepler Universität Linz, Austria). In all, 27 long papers and 9 posters on topics related to Ambient Intelligence and universal access were presented during the workshop, which attracted participation from all over the world.

These proceedings contain the long papers and the invited papers presented at the workshop. The volume is organized into four sections:

I. "Interaction Platforms and Techniques for Ambient Intelligence." This section includes the two invited papers of the workshop, which introduce the vision of Ambient Intelligence and present the current state of the art, with particular emphasis on interaction and on the central role of humans in the new technological environment. Other papers in this section discuss interaction in a continuously evolving technological environment, addressing issues such as gesture recognition for motor-impaired users, haptic interaction in virtual reality environments, digital TV, mirror-based interaction, avatars in ambient intelligence environments and spoken dialog with home appliances.

II. "User and Context Awareness." This section contains papers discussing the types of knowledge required for addressing user and context diversity, as well as the necessary mechanisms for exploiting such knowledge. Topics include the generation of audio interfaces, scenarios for accessible and personalized multimedia messaging services, the design of context aware eTourism systems, intelligent and adaptive tutors, user profiles for adapting speech support for disabled users, and transgenerational design of small screen device applications.

III. "Inclusive Design and Evaluation." This section presents recent advances in designing for user diversity. Topics include methodological accessibility issues, design techniques, accessibility evaluation, case studies, including defining levels of accessibility, participatory evaluation methods, and empirical experiments.

IV. "Access to Information, Education and Entertainment." This last section contains papers presenting applications and services in the domains of access to information, education and entertainment. Topics include accessible browsing, transportation assistance services, mobile messaging services, accessibility of content management systems, ambient-based learning systems, universally accessible, ambient and emotional games.

We would like to thank all the contributors and participants who made the ninth ERCIM "User Interfaces for All" Workshop a successful international event. We also wish to thank the members of the Programme Committee and all the reviewers for their dedicated efforts to maintain the high scientific quality of the event, as well as the invited speakers Norbert Streitz and Alois Ferscha for their enlightening presentations.

September 2006   Constantine Stephanidis and Michael Pieper

Ninth ERCIM Workshop "User Interfaces for All"

Königswinter (Bonn), Germany, September 27–28, 2006

Special Theme: "Universal Access in Ambient Intelligence Environments"

Workshop Chair

Constantine Stephanidis

Programme Chair

Michael Pieper

Programme Committee

- Ray Adams, University of Middlesex, UK
- Elizabeth André, University of Augsburg, Germany
- Margherita Antona, ICS-FORTH, Greece
- Markus Bylund, SICS, Sweden
- Noelle Carbonell, LORIA (CNRS, INRIA, Université de Nancy), France
- P. John Clarkson, University of Cambridge, UK
- Pier Luigi Emiliani, CNR-IFAC, Italy
- Michael Fairhurst, University of Kent, UK
- Hans W. Gellersen, Lancaster University, UK
- Dimitrios Grammenos, ICS-FORTH, Greece
- Seppo Haataja, NOKIA Mobile Phones, Finland
- Andreas Holzinger, University of Graz, Austria
- Eija Kaasinen, VTT, Finland
- Simeon Keates, IBM, USA
- Sri Hastuti Kurniawan, UMIST, UK
- John Mylopoulos, University of Trento, Italy
- Reinhard Oppermann, FhG-FIT, Germany
- Fabio Paternó, CNR-ISTI, Italy
- Thomas Rist, University of Applied Sciences Augsburg, Germany
- Boris de Ruyter, Philips Research, The Netherlands
- Anthony Savidis, ICS-FORTH, Greece
- Dominique Scapin, INRIA, France
- Christian Stary, University of Linz, Austria

- Norbert Streitz, FhG-IPSI, Germany
- Manfred Tscheligi, University of Salzburg, Austria
- Jean Vanderdonckt, Université catholique de Louvain, Belgium
- Gerhard Weber, Multimedia Campus Kiel, Germany
- Harald Weber, ITA, Germany
- Michael Wilson, RAL, UK
- Juergen Ziegler, University of Duisburg-Essen, Germany

Sponsors

- European Research Consortium for Informatics and Mathematics (ERCIM - http://www.ercim.org/)
- Institute of Computer Science, Foundation for Research and Technology - Hellas (ICS-FORTH - http://www.ics.forth.gr/)
- Fraunhofer - Institut für Angewandte Informations- technik (Fraunhofer-FIT - http://www.fit.fraunhofer.de/)

Table of Contents

Part III: Inclusive Design and Evaluation

Part IV: Access to Information, Education and Entertainment

Part I

Interaction Platforms and Techniques for Ambient Intelligence

From Human–Computer Interaction to Human–Environment Interaction: Ambient Intelligence and the Disappearing Computer

Norbert A. Streitz

Fraunhofer IPSI
Dolivostr. 15
D-64293 Darmstadt, Germany
streitz@ipsi.fraunhofer.de

Abstract. In this keynote, I argue for a transition from designing Human–*Computer* Interaction to Human–*Environment* Interaction. This is done in the context of ambient intelligence and the disappearing computer, and the resulting challenges for designing interaction in future smart environments. Our approach is based on exploiting the affordances of real objects by augmenting their physical properties with the potential of computer-based support. Combining the best of both worlds requires an integration of real and virtual worlds resulting in hybrid worlds. In this approach, the computer "disappears" and is almost "invisible", but its functionality is ubiquitously available and provides new forms of interaction. The general comments are illustrated with examples from different projects.

1 Introduction

"It seems like a paradox but it will soon become reality: The rate at which computers disappear will be matched by the rate at which information technology will increasingly permeate our environment and our lives". This statement by Streitz and Nixon (2005) illustrates how computers are increasingly becoming an important part of our day-to-day activities and determine many physical and social contexts of our life. The availability of computers is one step towards such a goal, followed by the integration of information, communication and sensing technology into everyday objects resulting in smart artefacts and smart environments.

There are a number of associated visions known as Ubiquitous/ Pervasive/ Proactive/ Ambient Computing, the Disappearing Computer, Calm Technology, Ambient Intelligence, Smart Objects, etc. All of them share some basic assumptions and predictions about how these future environments are supposed to present themselves, make themselves available for interaction and "behave" in an intelligent and smart way.

2 Ambient Intelligence

Ambient Intelligence (AmI) represents a vision of the (not too far) future where "intelligent" or "smart" environments react in an attentive, adaptive, and active

C. Stephanidis and M. Pieper (Eds.): ERCIM UI4ALL Ws 2006, LNCS 4397, pp. 3 – 13, 2007.

(sometimes even proactive) way to the presence and activities of humans and objects, in order to provide intelligent/smart services to the inhabitants of these environments. The underlying approach is based on the integration of sensing capabilities, processing power, reasoning mechanisms, networking facilities, applications and services, digital content, and actuating capabilities to be distributed in the surrounding environment.

While there are a number of different technologies involved, the goal of ambient intelligence and smart environments is also to hide their presence from the users by having the computer "disappear" from the users' perception and providing them with implicit, unobtrusive interaction paradigms. People and their social situations ranging from individuals to groups, be them work groups, families or friends and their corresponding environments (office buildings, homes, public spaces, etc) are in the centre of the design considerations.

The focus of this presentation is on the resulting challenges for designing interaction in future smart environments. Our approach is based on exploiting the affordances of real objects, by augmenting their physical properties with the potential of computer-based enrichment. Combining the best of both worlds requires the integration of real and virtual worlds resulting in hybrid worlds (Streitz et al., 1998). In this approach, the computer "disappears" and is almost "invisible", but its functionality is ubiquitously available and provides new forms of interacting with information (Russell et al., 2005; Streitz & Nixon, 2005).

3 Disappearing Computer

The notion of the 'disappearing computer' is an implication of Weiser's (1991) statement that 'The most profound technologies are those that disappear. They weave themselves into the fabric of everyday life until they are indistinguishable from it.' Weiser argues for the development of a 'calm technology' by moving technology into the background while the functionality is available in a ubiquitous fashion. We took this as a starting point for our approach (see also Streitz et al., 2001).

Computers became primary objects of our attention resulting also in a research area called 'human-*computer* interaction.' Today, however, we must ask: Are we actually interested in interacting with computers? Isn't our goal rather to interact with information, to communicate and to collaborate with people? Shouldn't the computer move into the background and disappear? Thus, we argue now that the focus should be on 'human-*environment* interaction'.

This 'disappearance' can take different forms: physical and mental disappearance. *Physical* disappearance refers to the miniaturization of devices and their integration in other everyday artefacts as, for example, clothes. In the case of *mental* disappearance, the artefacts can still be large but they are not perceived as computers because people discern them as, for example, interactive walls or interactive tables. This leads us to the core issue and questions: How can we design human-information interaction and support human-human communication and cooperation by exploiting the affordances of existing objects in our environment, i.e., designing human-*environment* interaction? And, in doing so, how do we exploit the potential of computer-based support augmenting these activities?

4 Smart Environments

The availability of information technology for multiple activities is one important step but it is not sufficient for achieving the objectives indicated above. It is to be followed by the integration of information, communication and sensing technology into everyday objects of our environment in order to create what is called 'Smart Environments'. Their constituents are smart artefacts that result from augmenting the standard functionality of artefacts thus enabling a new quality of interaction and 'behaviour' (of artefacts). Without entering into the philosophical discussion of when it is justified to call an artefact 'smart' or what we consider 'smart' or 'intelligent' behavior in general, the following distinction is useful (Streitz et al., 2005 b).

4.1 System-Oriented, Importunate Smartness

An environment is called 'smart' if it enables certain self-directed (re)actions of individual artefacts (or by the environment as a whole) based on previously and continuously collected information. For example, a space or a place can be 'smart' by having and exploiting knowledge about which people and artefacts are currently situated within its area, who and what was there before, when and how long, and what kind of activities took place. In this version of 'smartness', the space would be active (in many cases even proactive) and in control of the situation by making decisions on what to do next, and actually take action and execute them automatically (without a human in the loop). For example, in a smart home, we have access control to the house and other functions like heating, closing windows and blinds are being done automatically. Some of these actions could be importunate. Take the almost classic example of a smart refrigerator in a home analyzing consumption patterns of the inhabitants and autonomously ordering depleting food. While we might appreciate that the fridge makes suggestions on recipes that are based on the food currently available (that would be still on the supportive side), we might get very upset in case it is autonomously ordering food that we will not consume for reasons beyond its knowledge, such as a sudden vacation, sickness, or a temporal change in taste.

4.2 People-Oriented, Empowering Smartness

The above view can be contrasted by another perspective where the empowering function is in the foreground and which can be summarized as *'smart spaces make people smarter'*. This is achieved by keeping 'the human in the loop', thus empowering people to be in control, making informed decisions and taking actions. In this case, the environment also collects data about what is going on and aggregates the data, but provides and communicates the resulting information - hopefully in an intuitive way so that ordinary people can comprehend it easily - for guidance and subsequent actions determined by the people. In this case, a smart space might also make suggestions based on the information collected, but people are still in the loop and in control of what to do next. Here, the place supports smart, intelligent behavior of the people present (or in remote interaction scenarios people being away 'on the road' but connected to the space). For example in an office scenario, the smart space could recommend to those currently in the room that it would be useful to consult other people that were there before and worked on the same content, or to take a look at related documents created in this room before.

Of course, these two points of view will often not exist in their pure distinct forms. They rather represent the end points of a dimension where we can position weighted combinations of both somewhere in between. What kind of combination will be realized may be different for different cases, and depends very much on the application domain. It is also obvious that in some cases it might be useful that a system is not asking for user's feedback and confirmation for every single step in an action chain, because this would result in an information overload. The challenge is to find the right balance. The position we like to propagate here is that the overall design rationale should be guided and informed by the objective of having the human in the loop and in control as much as possible and feasible.

5 Interaction Design

Having the different kinds of technology available is one aspect of developing smart environments. Designing interaction with the different smart artefacts constituting these environments is another challenge. As one might expect, there are dependencies between both design and development strands of having the computer "disappear" and making the artefacts "smart".

As computers disappear from the scene and the perception of the users, becoming invisible (Streitz & Nixon, 2005), a new set of issues is created concerning the interaction with computers embedded in everyday objects resulting in smart artefacts: How can people interact with invisible devices? How can we design implicit interaction for sensor-based interfaces and at the same time provide for a migration path from explicit to implicit interfaces? How can we design for transparency and coherent experiences? One way of tackling these problems is described in the following examples. Our approach is mainly characterized by returning to the real world as the starting point for design and trying to exploit the affordances that real-world objects provide.

Another challenge is the shift from designing primarily interaction with information to designing experiences by being exposed to ambient displays and/or immersed in smart environments (Streitz et al, 2005 a).

6 Cooperative Buildings

Already some time ago, we introduced the concept of so called 'Cooperative Buildings' (Streitz et al., 1998). We used the term 'building' (and not 'spaces') on purpose, in order to emphasize that the starting point of the design should be the real, architectural environment, whereas 'spaces' has been used in many cases also for 'virtual' and/or 'digital' spaces. By calling it a 'cooperative' building, we wanted to indicate that the building serves the purpose of cooperation and communication. At the same time, it is also 'cooperative' towards its users, inhabitants, and visitors by employing active, attentive and adaptive components. This is to say that the building does not only provide facilities but it can also (re)act 'on its own' after having identified certain conditions. It is part of our vision that it will be 'smart' and able to adapt to changing situations, and provide context-aware information and services. The first instantiations of constituents for cooperative buildings were our Roomware components.

6.1 Roomware

We will mention the Roomware® components only in passing because we have reported about them in several places (Streitz et al., 1998, 1999, 2001) [www.roomware.de]. On the other hand, it is interesting to note that a number of design issues we addressed at that time in the context of office environments reappear now again in the context of smart home environments. Although there are differences in terms of user groups and the type of information and media content being created, processed and used, there are some generic design issues that are invariant. Examples are: designing for interacting with large vertical displays as, e.g., interactive walls, or horizontal displays as we experience them with interactive tables.

We defined Roomware® as the result of integrating information and communication technology in room elements such as doors, walls, and furniture, thus making the 'world around us' an interface to information and for the cooperation of people. Therefore, the Roomware approach moves beyond the limits of standard desktop environments on several dimensions, and extends usage into the architectural environment, as well as outside of buildings into public spaces, etc.

The design of our roomware components and the associated software exploits the affordances provided by real objects. We assume and build upon the existence of general knowledge and specific experiences people have when interacting with everyday artefacts as, e.g., a table, a wall or a pin board. This motivated also our gesture-based approach to interaction that is realized via the BEACH software (Tandler, 2003; Prante et al., 2004). It allows to throw, to shuffle and to rotate digital information objects, e.g., on the DynaWall and the InteracTable, similarly to real objects in the real world.

Fig. 1. Examples of Roomware components: DynaWall, InteracTable, CommChair, ConnecTables

Examples of the second generation of roomware components are shown in Fig. 1 and described in more detail in (Streitz et al., 2001). Specific aspects of the ConnecTable can be found in Tandler et al. (2001), and the Passage mechanism is described in Konomi et al. (1999). Passage provides an intuitive way for the physical transportation of virtual information structures using arbitrary physical objects, called 'Passengers'. The assignment is done via a simple gesture moving the information object to (and for retrieval from) the 'virtual' part of the so called 'Bridge' that is activated by placing the Passenger object on the physical part of the Bridge. No electronic tagging is needed. Passengers can be viewed as 'physical bookmarks' into the virtual world.

7   The Disappearing Computer Initiative

'The Disappearing Computer' (DC) [www.disappearing-computer.net] was an EU-funded proactive research initiative of the Future and Emerging Technologies (FET) section of the Information Society Technologies (IST) research program. The goal of the DC-initiative was 'to explore how everyday life can be supported and enhanced through the use of collections of interacting smart artefacts'. Together, these artefacts will form new people-friendly environments in which the 'computer-as-we-know-it' has no role. There were three main objectives:

- Developing new tools and methods for the embedding of computation in everyday objects in order to create smart artefacts.
- Investigating how new functionality and new use can emerge from collections of interacting artefacts.
- Ensuring that people's experience of these environments is both coherent and engaging in space and time.

These objectives were addressed via a cluster of 17 related projects under the umbrella theme of the DC-initiative. The cluster was complemented by a variety of support activities provided by the DC-Network and coordinated by the DC Steering Group, an elected representation of all projects. For more details please visit the corresponding website [www.disappearing-computer.net].

8   Ambient Agoras

The Ambient Agoras project [www.ambient-agoras.org] was one of the projects of the 'Disappearing Computer' initiative introduced above. Its overall goal was to augment the architectural envelope in order to create a social architectural space (Streitz et al., 2003) supporting collaboration, informal communication, and social awareness. Ambient Agoras aimed at providing situated services, place-relevant information, and a feeling of the place ('genius loci') to the users, enabling them to communicate for help, guidance, work, or fun, in order to improve collaboration and the quality of life in future office environments. The guiding metaphor for our work was the Greek 'agora' (market place). In line with this, we investigated how to turn everyday places into social marketplaces of ideas and information where people can meet and interact. Ambient Agoras addressed the office environment as an integrated organization located in a physical environment and having particular information needs both at the collective level of the organization and at the personal level of the worker. Although the application domain was office work, it became obvious during the project that a number of results can be transferred to similar communication situations in other application domains as well, e.g., public spaces and distributed networked home environments. This is due to the fact that we addressed rather generic issues of informal communication, awareness and social cohesion in distributed groups residing in remote sites.

For the 'Ambient Agoras' environment, we coupled several interaction design objectives (disappearance and ubiquity of computing devices) with sensing technologies (active and passive RFID, WLAN-based positioning) and smart artefacts (walls, tables, mobile devices, ambient displays), and investigated the functionality of two or more artefacts working together. In particular, we addressed the following three major issues:

- Support of informal communication in organizations, both locally and between remote sites
- Role and potential of ambient displays in future work environments
- Combination of more or less static artefacts integrated in the architectural environment with mobile devices carried by people.

8.1 Ambient Displays and Mobile Smart Artefacts

In line with our general approach, we decided that a calm ambient technology can be used to support the informal social encounters and communication processes within a cooperative corporate building (Streitz et al., 2003). Ambient displays are examples of this approach.

The **Hello.Wall** is our version of an ambient display that was developed for the Ambient Agoras environment (Streitz et al, 2005 b). It is a large (1.8 m wide and 2 m high) compound artefact with integrated light cells and sensing technology. Communication of information is facilitated via dynamically changing light patterns.

Fig. 2. Observing light patterns on the Hello.Wall and using the ViewPort to access additional information

The Hello.Wall artefact is controlled by a standard computer (somewhere hidden in the background) using a special driver interface. The design of the system is general and allows taking a range of parameters as input and mapping them on a wide range of output patterns.

In our setting, the Hello.Wall provides awareness and notifications to people passing by or watching it (see Fig. 2). Different light patterns correspond to different types of information, e.g., presence and mood of people. It is interesting to note that the use of abstract patterns allows distinguishing between public and private or personal information. While the meaning of public patterns is known to everybody and can therefore easily be interpreted, the meaning of personal patterns is only accessible to those who are initiated. Another observation is that it not only communicates information, but at the same time its appearance has also an effect on the atmosphere of a place and thus influences the mood of the social body around it.

The Hello.Wall is complemented by a mechanism by which it can 'borrow' the display of other artefacts to communicate additional information. This enables users to access information complementing the Hello.Wall (see Fig. 2) via mobile devices called '**ViewPorts**' (see Fig. 3). The ViewPort is a WLAN-equipped PDA-like handheld device based on commercially available components but integrated in and mapped to a new form factor. In addition, we integrated RFID readers and transponders. Thus, a ViewPort can sense other artefacts and can be sensed itself.

Fig. 3. The ViewPort in front of the Hello.Wall

8.2 Connecting Remote Teams

One major application for the Ambient Agoras environment was the 'Connecting-Remote-Teams' scenario (Röcker et al., 2004). It addressed the issue of extending awareness information and facilitating informal communication from within a corporate building to the connection of distributed teams working at remote sites.

Besides opportunistic chance encounters in the hallway, people sojourning in lounge areas having a coffee or tea are especially accessible for informal communication. While people's availability and current mood for a conversation are easily detectable in a face-to-face situation, it is very difficult to identify opportunities

Fig. 4. The Hello.Wall – an ambient display communicating awareness information between different locations via a range of dynamic light patterns

for similar encounters in a remote-sites setting. In order to provide equivalent information for a distributed team situation, we employed the Hello.Wall in lounge areas (see Fig. 4) in order to communicate information about presence, mood, and availability of people via defined light patterns. We evaluated this scenario in a Living Lab experiment (Streitz et al., 2005 b) with our project partners using two sites, one at Electricité de France (EDF) in France (Paris) and one at Fraunhofer IPSI in Germany (Darmstadt).

9 Conclusions

The work reported demonstrates our approach to the role of information and communication technology in future smart environments, for which the notion of the 'disappearing computer' is of central importance. While in the context of developing Roomware components the focus was on supporting more the productivity-related processes of team work and group meetings, the Ambient Agoras environment focused on informal communication and social awareness. We combined two corresponding design goals: First, to develop a smart environment that supports selected social processes as, e.g., awareness, informal communication, and coordination of team work in local and distributed collaboration settings. Second, the implementation corresponds to and is compatible with the nature and characteristics of the processes addressed by following the objectives of developing calm technology. Computers move into the background and are not considered or perceived anymore to be computers or computer-related devices. Therefore, we have argued for a transition from Human–*Computer* Interaction to Human–*Environment* Interaction.

   In our current and future work, we exploit the results gained in office environments and transfer our experiences to building intelligent user services for smart home environments, with a focus on home information and entertainment within and also between distributed but networked homes. This is done in the context of the EU-funded project 'Amigo – Ambient Intelligence in the Networked Home Environments'.

Acknowledgements

The work reported in this article was supported in various ways. The Roomware components by the 'Future Office Dynamics (FOD)' industrial R&D Consortium. The work on ambient displays and mobile devices by the European Commission as part of the 'Disappearing Computer' initiative ('Ambient Agoras' project, contract IST–2000-25134). Thanks are due to our partners in the different projects as well as to the members and students of the Fraunhofer IPSI research division AMBIENTE [www.ipsi.fraunhofer.de/ambiente] for their substantial contributions in realizing the different components and environments.

References

Konomi, S., Müller-Tomfelde, C., Streitz, N. (1999). Passage: Physical Transportation of Digital Information in Cooperative Buildings. In: N. Streitz, J. Siegel, V. Hartkopf, S. Konomi (Eds.), *Cooperative Buildings - Integrating Information, Organizations, and Architecture. Proceedings of Second International Workshop CoBuild'99* (Pittsburgh, USA). LNCS Vol. 1670. Heidelberg, Germany, Springer. pp. 45-54.

Prante, T., Streitz, N., Tandler, P. (2004). Roomware: Computers Disappear and Interaction Evolves. *IEEE Computer*, December 2004. pp. 47-54.

Röcker, C., Prante, T., Streitz, N., van Alphen, D. (2004) Using Ambient Displays and Smart Artefacts to Support Community Interaction in Distributed Teams. *Proceedings of OZCHI-2004 Conference* (Nov. 2004, University of Wollongong, Australia.)

Russell, D., Streitz, N., Winograd, T. (2005). Building Disappearing Computers. *Communications of the ACM*, Vol. 48 (3), March 2005. pp. 42-48.

Streitz, N., Geißler, J., Holmer, T. (1998). Roomware for Cooperative Buildings: Integrated Design of Architectural Spaces and Information Spaces. In: Streitz, N. Konomi, S., Burkhardt, H. (Eds.): *Cooperative Buildings - Integrating Information, Organization, and Architecture. Proceedings of the First International Workshop CoBuild '98* (Darmstadt, Germany). LNCS Vol. 1370, Heidelberg, Germany, Springer, 1998. pp. 4-21.

Streitz, N., Geißler, J., Holmer, T., Konomi, S., Müller-Tomfelde, C., Reischl, W. Rexroth, P., Seitz, P., Steinmetz, R. (1999). i-LAND: an Interactive Landscape for Creativity and Innovation. *Proceedings of ACM Conference CHI'99* (Pittsburgh, USA). pp. 120-127.

Streitz, N., Magerkurth, C., Prante, T., Röcker, C. (2005 a). From Information Design to Experience Design: Smart Artefacts and the Disappearing Computer. *ACM interactions, Special Issue on Ambient intelligence.* 12 (4) July + August 2005. pp. 21-25.

Streitz, N., Nixon, P. (2005). The Disappearing Computer. *Communications of the ACM*, Vol. 48 (3), March 2005. pp. 33-35.

Streitz, N., Prante, T., Röcker, C., van Alphen, D., Magerkurth, C., Stenzel, R., Plewe, D.A. (2003). Ambient Displays and Mobile Devices for the Creation of Social Architectural Spaces: Supporting Informal Communication and Social Awareness in Organizations. In: O'Hara, K., Perry, M., Churchill, E., Russell, D. (Eds.) *Public and Situated Displays: Social and Interactional Aspects of Shared Display Technologies*, Kluwer Publishers, pp. 387-409.

Streitz, N., Röcker, C., Prante, T., van Alphen, D., Stenzel, R., Magerkurth, C. (2005 b). Designing Smart Artefacts for Smart Environments. *IEEE Computer*, March 2005. pp. 41-49.

Streitz, N., Tandler, P., Müller-Tomfelde, C., Konomi, S. (2001). Roomware: Towards the Next Generation of Human-Computer Interaction based on an Integrated Design of Real and Virtual Worlds. In: J. Carroll (Ed.): *Human-Computer Interaction in the New Millennium*, Addison-Wesley, 2001. pp. 553-57.

Tandler, P. (2003). The BEACH application model and software framework for synchronous collaboration in ubiquitous computing environments. *The Journal of Systems & Software*. Special issue on Ubiquitous Computing. Vol. 69/3. pp. 267-296.

Tandler, P., Prante, T., Müller-Tomfelde, C., Streitz, N., Steinmetz, R. (2001) ConnecTables: Dynamic Coupling of Displays for the Flexible Creation of Shared Workspaces. *Proceedings of the 14. Annual ACM Symposium on User Interface Software and Technology (UIST'01)*, ACM Press. pp. 11-20.

Weiser, M. (1991) The Computer for the 21st Century. *Scientific American*, September 1991, pp. 66-75.

Human Computer Confluence

Alois Ferscha, Stefan Resmerita, and Clemens Holzmann

Johannes Kepler University Linz
Institute of Pervasive Computing
Altenberger Stra sse 69, 4040 Linz, Austria
ferscha@soft.uni-linz.ac.at

Abstract. Pervasive Computing has postulated to invisibly integrate technology into everyday objects in such a way, that these objects turn into smart things. Not only a single object of this kind is supposed to represent the interface among the "physical world" of atoms and the "digital world" of bits, but a whole landscapes of them. The interaction among humans and such landscapes of technology rich artifacts happens to be more confluently, rather than on a per device basis. To address the confluence among humans and computing landscapes we study we study human gesticulation and the manipulation of graspable and movable everyday artifacts as a potentially effective means for the interaction with the physical environment. In detail, we consider gestures in the general sense of a movement or a state (posture) of the human body, as well as a movement or state of any physical object resulting from human manipulation. Further, based on the tangible user interface paradigm, we propose employing intuitive tangible universal controls that translate physical motions into actions for controlling landscapes of smart things. Such intuitive "everyday"-gestures have been collected in a series of user tests, yielding a catalogue of generic body and artifact gesture dynamics. We present a systematic approach to selecting and steering using tangible artifacts by associating a flip-movement to service selection and a turn-movement to parameter steering. An implementation of this approach in a general software framework and several experiments with various fully functional artifacts and devices are described.

1 Introduction

Computing devices are pervading already now into everyday objects, in such a way that users do not notice them anymore as separate entities. Appliances, tools, clothing, accessories, furniture, rooms, machinery, cars, buildings, roads, cities, even whole agricultural landscapes increasingly embody miniaturized and wireless - thus invisible - information and communication systems, establishing information technology rich socio-economic systems with the potential of radically changing the style of how we perceive, create, think, interact, behave and socialize as human beings, but also how we learn, work, cultivate, live, cure, age as individuals or in societal settings.

Prospective advances in microprocessor-, communication- and sensor/actuator-technologies envision a whole new era of computing systems, seamlessly and invisibly woven into the "fabric of everyday life" [40], and hence referred to as

C. Stephanidis and M. Pieper (Eds.): ERCIM UI4ALL Ws 2006, LNCS 4397, pp. 14–27, 2007.

Pervasive Computing. Their services will be tailored to the person and their context of use. After the era of keyboard and screen interaction, a computer will be understood as secondary artifact, embedded and operating in the background, with its complete physical environment acting as interface (primary artifact). Pervasive Computing aims at interaction with digital information by manipulating physical real world artifacts as "graspable interfaces", by simultaneously involving all human senses, and by considering interaction related to the semantics of the situation in which it occurs.

Future pervasive computing senses and controls the physical world via many sensors and actuators, respectively. Applications and services will therefore have to be greatly based on the notions of context and knowledge, will have to cope with highly dynamic environments and changing resources, and will need to evolve towards a more implicit and proactive interaction with humans. Communication must go beyond sending information from one fixed point to another, considering situations where devices cooperate and adapt spontaneously and autonomously in the absence of any centralized control. A vast manifold of small, embedded and mobile artifacts characterize the scenarios envisaged by Pervasive Computing. The challenges are related to (*i*) their ubiquity, (*ii*) their self-organization and interoperation, (*iii*) their ability of perceiving and interpreting their situation and consequently (*iv*) adapt the services they offer, the different modes of user interaction with those services.

All the considerations above show that the traditional understanding of having an "interface" among humans and computers vaporizes both from the interaction as well as from the technology viewpoint - considering human and computer activity at a confluence appears to be a more adequate characterization. In this paper, we discuss gestural interaction with everyday artifacts as a means for interacting with services provided by the surrounding environment. In contrast to traditional Human Computer Interaction, such interaction generally comprises ensembles of devices, where each device provides certain services. The user thus interacts with a *service composite*, which is composed of the single devices' services, by using one or more graspable artifacts. As it does not make a difference from the user's viewpoint if the used services are composed of multiple devices' services or not, we just use the terms *device* and *service* without distinguishing from device ensembles and service composites henceforth, respectively.

2   Gestural Interaction

Human gesticulation as a modality of human-machine interaction has been widely studied in the field of Human-Computer Interaction. With the upcoming Pervasive and Ubiquitous Computing research field, the explicit interaction with computers with mouse, keyboard and screen in the WIMP metaphor has given way to a more implicit interaction involving all human senses. As an important part of this tendency, gestures and movements of the human body represent a natural and intuitive way to interact with physical objects in the environment.

Thus, manipulation of objects can be regarded as a means of intuitive interaction with the digital world. This paradigm underlies the research on Tangible User Interfaces (TUIs) [34]. Embodied interaction [5] [7] aims at facilitating remote control applications by providing natural and intuitive means of interaction, which are often more efficient and powerful compared with traditional interaction methods. TUIs couple physical representations (e.g. spatially manipulable physical artifacts) with digital representation (e.g. graphics and sounds), making bits directly manipulable and perceptible by people [9] [12]. In general, tangible interfaces are related to the use of physical artifacts as representations and controls for digital information [34].

We witness the advent of applications, appliances and machinery that are richer and richer in information technology, providing large palettes of services to end users. This richness brings up many challenges to the user interface designer, which must face the task of offering the user simple, natural, and intuitive interfaces to service providers, hereafter called *devices*. An important aspect of the user interface with devices is remote control, i.e., setting the inputs of services on devices. Most of today's devices come equipped with button-based remote controls. These are often badly designed, unnecessarily complicated, bound to specific devices, they tend to get misplaced, their usage is not intuitive and natural.

These issues can be addressed by the Tangible User Interface (TUI) paradigm [15], where button-based control artifacts are replaced with physical objects whose manipulation allows for intuitive and natural expression of control. In the sequel we present such an approach, based on the idea that device ensembles in physical space can be controlled by manipulating objects that reside in that space. We are interested in universal control, where the user is able to control multiple devices and device ensembles by using one or more artifacts. This tangible remote control paradigm provides an alternative to classical remote controls by using objects with multiple equilibrium states like cubes.

2.1 Discovery, Selection, Connection, Control

In order to control a certain device, the user needs to perform the following general sequence of operations:

1. **Device discovery.** Device discovery is necessary when the user is situated in a non-familiar space, as the user must know whether the desired device is available or not.

2. **Device selection.** The user must specify which device it needs to control. Alternatively, a certain device can be implicitly selected based on the user's context (i.e. information about his situation), preferences, and history.

3. **Connection.** The control artifact must be able to connect to the selected device. Thus, a communication channel must be established between the control artifact and the device such that control commands from the artifact can be relayed to the device.

4. **Device control.** A device offers a set of services, and the user manipulates the control artifact to set up input values for the services. To do so, the following steps are performed:

    (a) Service discovery. If the user is not already familiar with the device, then it needs to know the services provided by the device. In many cases, the user already knows which service it needs to control. For example, it is common knowledge that air conditioning devices have at least two services: temperature and fan power.

(b) Service selection. The user chooses one of the services to control. For example, in the air conditioner case, it chooses temperature.

(c) Parameter steering. The user sets up values for the controllable parameters of the service. For example, it sets a temperature value of $25°C$.

Considerable research and development efforts have been devoted to stage 1 ([37], [36], [39], [24], [38]), stage 2 ([37], [30], [16]), stage 3 ([24], [32], [33]), and stage 4a ([37], [24]). As for steps 4b and 4c, a combined approach for controlling the environment with physical artifacts, which allows to browse and select both devices and their services as well as to steer the input values of a selected service with simple gestures, is described in [24]. Without loss of generality, we consider only services with one parameter having a one-dimensional set of values. We assume that each device or service has a suitable user interface output which provides the user with appropriate feedback. Our approach is based on the simple but crucial observation that there exist two types of manipulations that can be intuitively associated to service selection and to steering, respectively.

In general, the geometry of objects suggests manipulation affordances in a TUI. The geometry of a physical object defines a number of stable mechanical equilibria of the object placed on a planar horizontal surface called a *flat*. A stable equilibrium of an object will be called an object *mode*. Once a control artifact is connected to a device, each service of the device is associated to a distinct mode of the object, under the assumption that the number of modes is greater than or equal to the number of services (a relaxation of this assumption will also be discussed). By a *flip-movement*, the user moves the object from one stable equilibrium to another, by changing the object's surface that touches the flat. Thus, a flip-manipulation triggers a change of the selected service. For example, a box has six stable equilibria. Hence, a box can be used to select from up to six services. A *turn-movement* is simply a rotation of an object. It is associated to steering the parameter value of the selected service. Figure 1 illustrates this assignment. Both movements are geometric rotations of objects. They can be executed with the objects in hand, without the need to place objects on actual surfaces. We shall later present experiments in a domestic setting, where objects of various shapes are employed for controlling a TV set and a music player. The artifacts are embedded with wireless orientation sensors to detect flipping and turning.

2.2 Universal Interaction

Considerable research efforts have targeted the realization of a universal interaction device, which is a mobile computing system (usually a PDA or smartphone) that can be used for interacting with multiple services, e.g. the "Universal Information Appliance" [1], the "Universal Interactor" [13], and the "Personal Universal Controller" in [18]. The main issues are discovery of devices and services [37] and composition of user interfaces [24], [18]. Discovery is supported by service oriented frameworks, communication protocols and standards such as UPnP [36], Jini [39], Bluetooth [24], URC [38]. Proposed approaches for device selection include

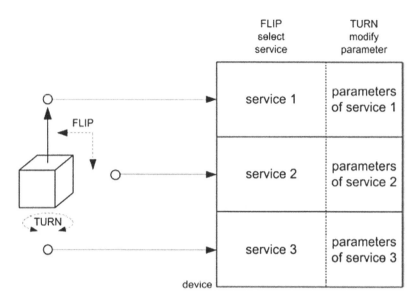

Fig. 1. The flipping and turning control actions

browsing, pointing and touching [37], [30], or automatic selection based on context clues and user history [16]. Connection is supported by wireless technologies such as Bluetooth, Zigbee [33], and WiFi [32]. In general, the universality of the control device means the ability to control multiple services, with as little a priori information as possible about the services. Such a handheld control device suffers from some of the shortcomings of today's remote controls: the device is complicated and therefore hard to use, it offers non-intuitive control means, it requires to be available at all times. In this paper, we consider several universality layers. In particular, more than one physical object can be used to control the same service. The redundancy of physical objects in the user's environment together with a dynamic mapping of objects and movements to services and parameters can ensure that a control object is always handy for any device that the user decides to control.

Tangible User Interface (TUI) research has studied the capabilities of physical objects as rich input devices. Specific movements of objects were considered for control. Tilting user interfaces [25] use the tilt of a portable device as input for the device. In [13], various artifacts and associated gestures are used for device control. Some works present objects where multiple faces are associated to different functions and flipping is used to select a function. In [9], flipbricks are described as part of graspable user interfaces. Different commands, such as "cut", "copy", "paste", are associated to each face of a flipbrick, and one of them can be activated by flipping the brick. The ToolStone device described in [26] uses also the rotation of the device, in addition to flipping, to further increase the selectable functionalities. Our paper builds on this research to investigate the use of such manipulations for remote control of devices. We do not assume particular shapes or types of objects and particular applications or services to be controlled. Thus, flipping and turning are considered here as manipulations of objects that can be generically mapped to abstract control actions.

An approach for using physical objects for home device control is reported in [17], where everyday objects and an augmented table are employed for configuring and using interfaces to applications. Objects must be placed on the table, and then they can be moved against the table. In contrast, we rely here on the geometry of the object to suggest the object's usage. As opposed to most of the papers described above, our implementation employs only orientation sensors for detecting the flip- and turn-movements (there is no sensing table or active surface on which control objects must be placed).

2.3   A Universal Remote Control

Tangible Interaction If the same artifact is used for both types of manipulation, then the turn-movement should be executed while the object is in a stable equilibrium state. This is guaranteed if the object is turned by an axis that is orthogonal to the related flat.

The association of flip- and turn-movements to service selection and respectively parameter steering is based upon the following observations:

- The service space of a device (or of an ensemble of devices) is a discrete set, with a relatively small number of services. The input space of a service can be a continuous set. On the other hand, the mode space of an object is also discrete with relatively few number of modes, while the space of the turning angle is a continuous set.
- The selected service should not change while the user is steering its parameters. This is why we are looking at stable equilibria. Thus, once a service is selected, the user is free to focus only on steering the value by turning.
- The stable equilibria can be used to disambiguate between intentional and unintentional control movements. To activate a service selection, the user must keep the artifact in a stable equilibrium for a certain amount of time (which can be heuristically determined at the design phase). If no mode is activated, then no control action is taken, regardless of the object's motion.

The artifacts that offer the flip and turn affordances can be everyday items or objects specially designed for control. Objects can have various numbers of modes, ranging from no mode (e.g. a ball), to one mode (a swivel chair), to tens of modes. (Notice that our approach is valid also when several artifacts are used to control a device at the same time. In this case, the modes of the artifact ensemble are given by all the possible combinations of modes of the component artifacts.)

The association of flip-movements to service selection and of turn-movements to steering is viable if the number of services is smaller than or equal to the number of modes of the involved artifact. If this is not the case, then a different association can be used, as follows: the turn-movement is associated to both service selection and steering, and the flip-movement is used to distinguish between the two cases. Thus, an artifact (or artifact ensemble) with at least two modes can fully deal with controlling large numbers of services.

Control types of a service. For a given service, according to the set of all possible parameter values, we distinguish two control types: *discrete control* and *continuous* *control.* For example, the TV channel selection is a service with discrete control, whereas the TV volume is a continuous control.

There are two ways by which the user can set the value of a parameter: direct and sequential. In the *direct* type, the user is able to indicate the control value in one step, without browsing intermediate values. Examples are: setting a TV channel number with a classic remote control, setting a predefined value for room temperature. In the *sequential* type, the user browses input values until the desired value is reached. Usually, the sequential mode is required by the user-centric feedback-based control. Examples are: setting TV volume, setting light levels.

Universality requirements. We seek remote control mechanisms that satisfy the following universality requirements:

1. The control artifacts should provide means for performing discrete, continuous, direct and sequential control.
2. The same device can be controlled by more than one artifact and different devices can be controlled by the same artifact. The mapping between control objects and devices should be dynamic. The user should be able to configure this mapping. In addition, the mapping can be context sensitive.
3. The mapping between artifact modes and services should be dynamic. This mapping can be context sensitive: the service that is associated to a mode can be determined ad-hoc, based on the user's context, rather than being a priori fixed or explicitly specified by the user.

Unintentional manipulations of artifacts (i.e., manipulations which are not targeted for explicit control) can be used for providing implicit control, whenever this supports the user's interaction with the device.

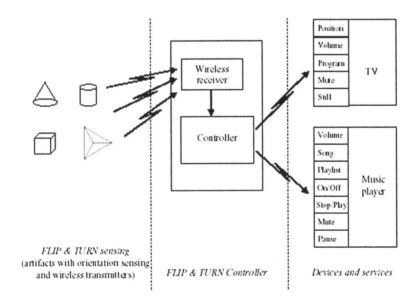

Fig. 2. The experimental setup

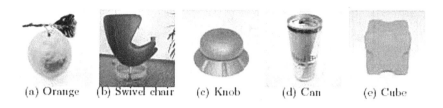

(a) Orange   (b) Swivel chair   (c) Knob   (d) Can   (e) Cube

Fig. 3. Example of control artifacts

Implementation and Experiments. We have employed the movements flip and turn for controlling devices in a domestic setting. Our experiments aimed at showing how the above universality requirements can be satisfied by our approach. In this respect, physical objects of various shapes have been embedded with orientation sensors that allowed a detection of the two manipulations. The devices to be controlled are a TV set and a music player. The experimental setup is depicted in Figure 2.

Artifacts. We have used both everyday items and specially designed objects. Figure 3 presents some of the artifacts, which have no modes (e.g. a decorative orange), one mode (e.g. a swivel chair or a knob), two mods (e.g. a beverage can) and six modes (e.g. a cube).

Sensors. We used InertiaCube3 wireless orientation sensors from Intersense [29]. The InertiaCube3 has 3 degrees of freedom (yaw, pitch and roll) with 360 degrees in all three axes. Together with a battery pack, the hardware is small enough to fit in half of a cigarette box. Figure 4 shows the embedded sensing.

Software. We developed a flexible software platform, which is able to accommodate a variable number of sensors and a variable number of applications. In this respect, we used Java and the OSCAR implementation of OSGi [31].

Devices and services. For rapid prototyping reasons, the two devices were implemented as computer applications. The TV is represented by a Java video player and Winamp is the music player. The TV screen and the Winamp graphical userinterface are projected onto adjacent walls of the same room. The controlled services of the two devices are represented in Figure 2. The position service of the TV offers the user the possibility to change the horizontal positioning of the TV screen on the TV wall. Notice that each service has one parameter, which is also called a service *input*. There are services with continuous input space (e.g., volume, position), and with discrete input space (e.g., Program, Playlist, On/Off).

The following experiments now demonstrate various usage modes of flipping and turning for remote control, addressing the universality aspects described in the previous section.

Experiment A: The chair (Figure 3(b)) and the cube (Figure 3(e)) are employed to control the TV and the music player. The chair has one mode, and the cube has six modes. When connected to the TV, the chair's mode is mapped to the position service of the TV. Thus, a rotation of the chair steers the horizontal position of the TV screen on the wall such that the screen is always facing the chair. When connected to the

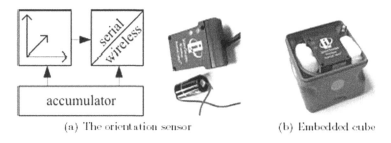

(a) The orientation sensor   (b) Embedded cube

Fig. 4. The embedded sensing

Winamp, the chair mapped to the On/Off service: if the chair faces the Winamp wall, then the player is "On" (and the Winamp skin is visible on the wall). Otherwise, the player is "Off" (and the skin is not shown). The cube modes are mapped to the other services of the two devices. Thus, when the cube is connected to the TV, the user can flip the cube to change the service and then rotate the cube to steer the input. Snapshots from this experiment are presented in Figures 5(a) and 5(b).

(a) TV position control with chair

(b) TV program control with cube

Fig. 5. Experiment A. TV control with chair (one mode), and cube (six modes).

Since in this setting at most one device is used at a time, the chair is connected to both devices at the same time. When the chair is facing neither of the two walls or the user does not sit in the chair, both devices are off and hidden. If the user sits in the chair and the chair is oriented towards the TV wall, the TV screen appears on the wall at a position corresponding to the chair's orientation. Moreover, the cube is automatically connected to the TV device. Any subsequent rotation of the chair determines a steering of the screen's position on the wall. When the chair is steered to face the Winamp wall, the music player starts out and its skin is shown on the wall. The cube is automatically connected to the Winamp.

Let us consider now the universality requirements defined in the previous section.

1. Discrete control is provided by a suitable discretization of the rotation angle, and it is performed for example when changing programs on the TV, titles and playlists on the music player. For continuous control, the rotation angle is directly mapped to the service input (possibly after a continuous transformation). For example, the distance between the left edge of the TV screen and the left edge of the TV wall is determined by a continuous nonlinear function $f : [a; b] \;!\; [0; L_w]$, where $[a; b]$ ½ $[0; 360]$ is the interval of angles for which the chair faces the TV wall and L_w is the length of the wall. Sequential control is naturally achieved by using mappings from angles to the input space that are onto and monotone. Direct control can be achieved by an unidimensional turn-movement only for two predefined input values (e.g., any clockwise rotation selects one value and any counterclockwise rotation selects the other value). More suitable for direct control is to flip the artifact, where predefined input values are defined as services and flipping is used to select one of them. Consider, for example, that a cube is used to control room temperature. By flipping the cube, the user can directly select one of six possible predefined values, while turning the cube can still be used for sequentially (and continuously) steering the temperature.

2. In this experiment, each of the two devices accepts control from the same artifact (e.g., the cube). Moreover, two artifacts are used to control the same device. The cube is dynamically connected to either the TV or the Winamp. The user determines this mapping by steering the chair. The use of context information for devices selection has been studied e.g. in [16].

3. The mapping of the chair mode is dependant upon whether the user sits in the chair or not. This context information regards the human motion activity. If the user does not sit in the chair, nothing happens when the chair is turned.

When the user sits in the chair and watches TV, chair rotations are usually not intended for establishing a certain position of the TV on the wall. They are rather triggered by factors which are external to the TV control problem (e.g., finding a more comfortable body position). Steering the TV screen such that it remains in the user's main attention is an example of implicit control.

Experiment B: A soft drink can (Figure 3(d)) is employed to control the music player. This illustrates how an object with only two modes can be used to control a device with many services by flipping and turning it. In normal position (i.e., with the top side up), turning the can selects one of the seven services offered by Winamp. To change from service selection to steering, the can is flipped. In upside down position, the can changes the input of the selected service. A snapshot of this experiment is given in Figure 6.

Experiment C: The chair (Figure 3(b)) and the knob (Figure 3(c)) are employed to control the TV. This shows how two single-mode objects can be used to control a device with multiple services. As in the previous experiment, one mode (of the chair) is used for service selection by turning and the other one (of the knob) is used for actual steering by turning. In this case, there is no flip-movement and the two turns can be executed in parallel.

The experiments described above demonstrate the potential of tangible interaction for universal remote control. Moreover, they show how combinations of control artifacts can be employed to fully control fairly complex devices.

Fig. 6. Experiment B. TV control with soft drink can (two modes).

3   Conclusions and Future Work

The vision impacting the evolution of Pervasive Computing is the claim for an intuitive, unobtrusive and distraction free interaction with technology-rich environments. In an attempt to bring interaction *back to the real world* after an era of keyboard and screen interaction, computers are being understood as secondary artifacts, embedded and operating in the background, whereas the set of all physical objects present in the environment are understood as the primary artifacts, the *interface*. Instead of interacting with digital information via traditional computing means, Pervasive Computing aims at physical interaction with digital information, i.e. interaction by manipulating physical artifacts via *graspable interfaces*. It links the "atoms of the physical world" with the "bits of the digital world" in such a way, that physical artifacts are considered as being both representation of and control for digital information. Manipulating physical artifacts in the physical world hence causes the manipulation of their respective associations in the digital world and vice versa.

Motivated by the expressive power of gestures as enablers of intuitive interaction, we have presented a general approach to remote control of devices based on TUIs.

Given that a remote control artifact is connected to a device, we proposed using a flip-movement for selecting the service of the device, and a turn-movement for steering the service's input. This approach enables the achievement of universal remote control. The concept of universality considered in this paper has a larger scope than the usual case where a single artifact is able to control multiple devices. Thus, from our viewpoint, a universal remote control must be able to provide natural and intuitive means for continuous, discrete, sequential and direct control. Moreover, the same device can be controlled by more than one artifact and different devices can be controlled by the same artifact.

The mapping from artifacts and manipulations to devices and services should be dynamic. This mapping can be determined in an ad-hoc manner, based on the user's context and preferences.

We showed how our approach can be applied to satisfy the above requirements by a series of experiments in a domestic setting. These experiments involved various objects of diverse shapes, including everyday items and specially designed artifacts. For the clarity of presentation, the unidimensional input case was considered. It should be noted that the turn-movement can be used to steer up to three dimensions. Thus, our approach is viable for most of the cases encountered in remote control of real world devices.

Clearly, to apply the proposed approach in fully mobile and ad-hoc settings, one needs suitable methods for device discovery and selection. In principle, on can employ existing solutions involving handheld devices (e.g., PDAs). Upon device selection, flipping and turning movements can be applied to the handheld object. Upon connecting a control artifact to a device, the mapping between the artifact modes and the services of the device must be automatically determined. We are addressing this issue at the device level. Thus, the artifact sends a description of itself to the device, which is then able to determine the artifact's modes. Challenging problems are how to use information about the user's context for achieving an intuitive mapping of modes to services, and how to make the user aware of this mapping.

With respected to the traditional understanding of considering an "inter- face" among humans and computers, it should have become clear, that it is rather the "confluence" among human activity and a sensitive, technology rich environment, that defines the "interaction" among humans and computers.

References

[1] Amft O., Junker H., Tröster G.: Detection of Eating and Drinking Arm Gestures Using Inertial Body-Worn Sensors. Proceedings of the 9th IEEE International Symposium on Wearable Computers (ISWC'05), pp. 160-163, 2005.
[2] Bahlmann,C., Haasdonk, B., Burkhardt, H.: On-line Handwriting Recognition with Support Vector Machines - A Kernel Approach. In Proc. of the 8th Int. Workshop on Frontiers in Handwriting Recognition (IWFHR), pp. 49-54, 2002.
[3] Benbasat, A.Y., Paradiso, J.A.: An Inertial Measurement Framework for Gesture Recognition and Applications. Gesture Workshop, LNAI 2298, pp.9-20, 2001.
[4] Burges, C.J.C., A tutorial on support vector machines for pattern recognition. *Data Mining and Knowledge Discovery 2(2):1-47*, 1998.

[5] Chang, C.-C., Lin C.-J., LIBSVM: a library for support vector machines, 2001. Software available at http://www.csie.ntu.edu.tw/ cjlin/libsvm

[6] Dourish, P.: Where the action is: the foundations of embodied interaction. MIT Press, Cambridge, 2001.

[7] K. F. Eustice, T. J. Lehman, A. Morales, M. C. Munson, S. Edlund, M. Guillen. A universal information appliance. *IBM Systems Journal*, Vol. 38, Nr. 4, pp. 575-601, 1999.

[8] Fishkin, K., Moran, T., Harrison, B.: Embodied user interfaces: towards invisible user interfaces. Proceedings of the 7th international conference on engineering for human-computer interaction (EHCI'98), Heraklion, Crete, Greece, September 1998.

[9] G.W. Fitzmaurice. Graspable user interfaces. Ph.D thesis, University of Toronto, 1996.

[10] Fitzmaurice, G.W., Ishii, H., Buxton, W.: Bricks: laying the foundations for graspable user interfaces. Proceedings of the ACM conference on human factors in computing systems (CHI'95), Denver, Colorado, May 1995.

[11] Greenberg, S., Fitchett, C.: Phidgets: easy development of physical interfaces through physical widgets. Proceedings of ACM symposium on user interface software and technology (UIST 2001), Orlando, FLorida, November 2001.

[12] Holmquist, L.E., Redström, J., Ljungstrand, P.: Token-based access to digital information. Proceedings of the first international symposium on handheld and ubiquitous computing (HUC'99), Karlsruhe, Germany, September 1999.

[13] T.D. Hodes, R.H. Katz, E. Servan-Schreiber, L. Rowe. Composable Ad-hoc Mobile Services for Universal Interaction. Proceedings of the Third Annual ACM/IEEE International Conference on Mobile Computing and Networking, pp. 1-12, 1997.

[14] C. Holzmann, S. Resmerita, M. Leitner, A. Ferscha. A Paradigm for Orientation-Based Universal Remote Control. Proceedings of the International Workshop on the Tangible Space Initiative, in conjunction with Pervasive 2006, Dublin, Ireland, May 7, 2006.

[15] Ishii, H. and Ullmer B. Tangible Bits: Towards Seamless Interface to Access Digital Information. In Extended Abstracts of Conference on Human Factors in Computing Systems (CHI '01), Seattle, Washington, USA, March 31 - April 5, ACM Press, pp.187-188, 2001.

[16] K. Kaowthumrong, John Lebsack, R. Han. Automated Selection of the Active Device in Interactive Multi-Device Smart Spaces. Spontaneity Workshop at Ubicomp 2002.

[17] C. Kray and M. Strohbach. Gesture-based Interface Reconfiguration. Workshop "AI in mobile systems" (AIMS 2003) at Ubicomp'03, Seattle, WA, USA.

[18] Koleva, B., Benford, S., Hui Ng K., Rodden T.: A framework for tangible user interfaces. Proceedings of the real world user interfaces workshop at the 5th international symposium on human-computer interaction with mobile devices and services (MobileHCI 2003), Udine, Italy, September 2003.

[19] Lementec, J.C., Bajcsy, P.: Recognition of Arm Gestures Using Multiple Orientation Sensors: Gesture Classification. 7th International IEEE Conference on Intelligent Transportation Systems, Washington, D.C., October 3-6 2004, pp 965-970.

[20] Lenman, S., Bretzner, L., Thuresson, B.: Computer Vision Based Hand Gesture Interfaces for Human-Computer Interaction. Technical Report TRITA-NA-D0209, 2002, CID-172, Royal Institute of Technology, Sweden.

[21] B.A. Myers. Using handhelds for wireless remote control of PCs and appliances. *Interacting with Computers*, vol. 17, no. 3, pp. 251-264, 2005.

[22] Nielsen, M., Störring, M., Moeslund, T.B., Granum, E.: A procedure for developing intuitive and ergonomic gesture interfaces for man-machine interaction. Technical report CVMT 03-01, 2003, Aalborg University.

[23] Orientation Sensing for Gesture-Based Interaction with Smart Artifacts. *Computer Communications*, vol. 28, no. 13, pp. 1552-1563, 2005.
[24] S.R. Ponnekanti, B. Lee, A. Fox, P. Hanrahan, T. Winograd. ICrafter : A Service Framework for Ubiquitous Computing Environments. Proceedings of Ubicomp 2001, LNCS 2201, pp. 56-75, 2001.
[25] Jun Rekimoto. Tilting operations for small screen interfaces. In Proceedings of the ACM Symposium on User Interface Software and Technology (UIST 1996), pp. 167-168, 1996.
[26] Rekimoto, J. and E. Sciammarella. ToolStone: Effective Use of the Physical Manipulation Vocabularies of Input Devices. Proceedings of ACM User Interface Software and Technology (UIST), pp.109-117, 2000.
[27] Shimodaira, H., Noma, K., Nakai, M., Sagayama, S.: Dynamic Time-Alignment Kernel in Support Vector Machine. Advances in Neural Information Processing Systems 14, NIPS2001, 2:921-928, Dec 2001.
[28] The Bluetooth specification. http://www.bluetooth.org.
[29] The InertiaCube3 orientation sensor. http://www.isense.com/products/prec/ic3/wirelessic3.htm.
[30] The Near Field Communication Forum. www.nfc-forum.org.
[31] The OSGi Service Platform. http://www.osgi.org.
[32] The Wireless Fidelity Alliance. http://www.wi-fi.org.
[33] The ZigBee Alliance. http://www.zigbee.org.
[34] Ullmer, B., Ishii, H.: Emerging frameworks for tangible user interfaces. IBM Syst 39 (3-4):915-931.
[35] Ullmer, B., Ishii, H. and Glas, D. mediaBlocks: Physical Containers, Transports, and Controls for Online Media. In Proceedings of SIGGRAPH '98, Orlando, Florida USA, ACM Press, pp. 379-386, 1998.
[36] Universal Plug and Play. http://www.upnp.org/.
[37] P. Välkkynen, I. Korhonen, J. Plomp, T. Tuomisto, L. Cluitmans, H. Ailisto, H. Seppä. A user interaction paradigm for physical browsing and near-object control based on tags. Proceedings of the Physical Interaction Workshop at Mobile HCI Conference, Udine, Italy, 2003. http://www.medien.informatik.uni muenchen.de/en/events/pi03/proceeding. htm.
[38] G. Vanderheiden, G. Zimmermann, S. Trevin. Interface Sockets, Remote Consoles, and Natural Language Agents: A V2 URC Standards Whitepaper. http://myurc.com/whitepaper. php, 2005.
[39] Jim Waldo. The Jini Architecture for Network-centric Computing. *Communications of the ACM*, July 1999, pp. 76-82.
[40] Mark Weiser. The Computer for the 21st Century. Scientific American, vol. 265, no. 3, pp. 94-104, 1991.
[41] Westeyn, T., Brashear, H., Atrash, A., Starner, T.: Georgia Tech Gesture Toolkit: Supporting Experiments in gesture Recognition. Proceedings of ICMI 2003, November 5-7, Vancouver, British Columbia, Canada.
[42] Williams A., Kabisch E., Dourish P.: From Interaction to Participation: Configuring Space Through Embodied Interaction. Proceedings of the Ubicomp 2005, LNCS 3660, pp.287-304, September 2005.

A Customizable Camera-Based Human Computer Interaction System Allowing People with Disabilities Autonomous Hands-Free Navigation of Multiple Computing Tasks

Wajeeha Akram, Laura Tiberii, and Margrit Betke

Department of Computer Science, Boston University
111 Cummington Street, Boston, MA 02215, USA
{wajeeha, ltiberii, betke}@cs.bu.edu

Abstract. Many people suffer from conditions that lead to deterioration of motor control making access to the computer using traditional input devices difficult. In particular, they may loose control of hand movement to the extent that the standard mouse cannot be used as a pointing device. Most current alternatives use markers or specialized hardware, for example, wearable devices, to track and translate a user's movement to pointer movement. These approaches may be perceived as intrusive. Camera-based assistive systems that use visual tracking of features on the user's body often require cumbersome manual adjustment. This paper introduces an enhanced computer vision based strategy where features, for example on a user's face, viewed through an inexpensive USB camera, are tracked and translated to pointer movement. The main contributions of this paper are (1) enhancing a video based interface with a mechanism for mapping feature movement to pointer movement that allows users to navigate to all areas of the screen even with very limited physical movement and (2) providing a customizable, hierarchical navigation framework for human computer interaction (HCI). This framework provides effective use of the vision-based interface system for accessing multiple applications in an autonomous setting. Experiments with several users show the effectiveness of the mapping strategy and its usage within the application framework as a practical tool for desktop users with disabilities.

Keywords: Computer-vision, assistive technology, alternative input devices, video-based human-computer interfaces, autonomous navigation.

1 Introduction

Several conditions may cause computer users to be unable to use the standard mouse. Paralysis from brain injury, stroke, multiple sclerosis, or Amyotrophic Lateral Sclerosis (ALS, also called Lou Gehrig's disease) may cause the user to have very little motor control except for limited head or eye movement. Loss of fine motor control with age and muscle injuries may also make use of the standard mouse difficult.

C. Stephanidis and M. Pieper (Eds.): ERCIM UI4ALL Ws 2006, LNCS 4397, pp. 28–42, 2007.
© Springer-Verlag Berlin Heidelberg 2007

According to the National Multiple Sclerosis Society [1], approximately 400,000 Americans and 2 million individuals worldwide suffer from Multiple Sclerosis, and about 200 people are diagnosed every week in the US. As such conditions restrict physical mobility and often speaking capability, loss of the ability to communicate is one of the most limiting problems for these individuals. Being able to use computers for common tasks such as sending email and browsing the web opens a huge avenue of possibility to improve quality of life.

A study by Forrester Research for Microsoft Corporation [2] presents statistics on the need and significance of accessible technology. It is estimated that about 17% (22.6 million) of computers users who suffer from severe impairments are very likely to benefit from accessible technology. It is also postulated that the need for accessibility devices may grow due to the increase in computer users above the age of 65 and the increase in the average age of computer users.

There has been extensive research in the domain of mouse alternatives as accessibility aids for users who have very limited movement. Broadly, these efforts can be divided into two main categories: systems that rely on specialized mechanical or electronic hardware devices and camera-based systems. Mouse-actuated joysticks, mechanical switches, breath-puffing straws, and electrodes placed on the user's face that measure movement of features are some of the strategies in the first category [3]. Many camera based systems track physical markers, for example, infrared markers placed on the user's body [4, 5] or markers on glasses. Systems that capture gaze information often rely on infrared illumination or special headgear-mounted cameras; a survey of these methods is provided by Magee et al. [6]. Most of these systems are expensive, require special devices, and may be intrusive. In addition, significant levels of technical expertise may be required to install and configure these systems. Betke et al. [7] presented a vision based solution called the camera mouse which tracks features on a user's body in a non-intrusive manner.

There has also been substantial work in developing applications for people with disabilities [8, 9, 10]. Some existing applications include on-screen keyboards [11], alternate text entry mechanisms [12, 13], games and learning aids for children [7], and tools that interact with a web browser to make the internet more accessible for camera mouse users [14, 15].

In this paper, we present a system that tracks features on the user's body, usually the face, and translates feature movement to pointer movement on the screen. Our work builds on the camera mouse presented by Betke et al. [7], which proposed a vision based feature tracking approach for pointer movement. Here, we present an improved mapping strategy that allows translation of minimal feature movement to pointer movement across the entire range of the screen. A framework for using the camera mouse to carry out common tasks, with minimal intervention from a caregiver, is also proposed. Experiments were conducted to determine how well the users were able to access and perform each of the computing tasks in the HCI framework. Test results have shown that the system successfully provides access to common tasks such as opening games, web sites, text entry, and playing music.

The system is cost effective and requires little technical expertise of the user and caregiver. Use or extension of the proposed system does not incur significant cost, because the system was developed with open source technologies such as OpenCV [16] and Java. The only additional hardware required, besides a personal computer, is a low-cost USB camera. We refer to the interface system as the camera mouse throughout this paper. However, as an alternative to the camera mouse [7], any interface system, video-based or even the standard computer mouse that provides a pointing and selection mechanism can be used with our HCI framework.

2 System Overview

The goal of our work is to provide a customizable camera-based human computer interaction system allowing people with disabilities autonomous hands free navigation of multiple computing tasks. We focus on two main aspects of the system; designing a robust feature tracking strategy and an effective interaction approach that operates optimally with a camera mouse. The following sections give an overview of the components of the system.

2.1 Tracking Features

This section describes our method to track a feature or set of features on the user's body, usually face, and convert the feature movement to pointer movement. The study by Fagiani et al. [18] gives an experimental comparison of various tracking mechanisms for use with the camera mouse and recommends either an optical flow or correlation based tracker. We found the optical flow based algorithm to be both robust and computationally efficient. Our system operates in real time on a computer with a 1.6 GHz processor, taking up on average less than 5% of processor time. This demonstrates the use of the camera mouse as a background process that does not affect the performance of other applications running on the system. Our camera mouse implementation executes as a standalone application that moves the standard windows pointer.

A USB Camera is connected to the computer and set up to capture a frontal view of the user. On starting the application, a window with the video of the user is displayed. The camera location should be adjusted so that the feature to be tracked is in clear view. Typically, the user sits within 1 m of the camera. However, if the user is very close to the camera, even a small physical movement can result in the feature falling out of the camera's field of view. Therefore, the distance from the camera should be carefully adjusted such that the feature remains within the camera's field of view throughout the session.

The caregiver selects a feature on the user's body by clicking at the desired location of the input video stream. We designed the system to automatically refine the feature location by finding an image patch with the highest brightness gradient in the 11-by-11-pixel neighborhood of the manually selected feature [16]. The feature is then tracked in subsequent frames using the Lucas-Kanade optical flow computation [17]. We used a pyramid-based implementation of the Lucas-Kanade tracker provided in Intel's OpenCV library [16].

2.2 Feature Movement to Pointer Movement

Once the feature movement in pixels is known, an effective mapping from pixels of movement in the video frames to pointer movement on the screen is required.

Pointing devices such as the standard mouse and mouse pad do not have an absolute mapping of device movement to pointer movement. The pointer is moved in a differential manner, governed by speed and acceleration parameters set by the user. Similarly, the camera mouse cannot be used with any degree of flexibility if this mapping is absolute: an absolute mapping would mean that the feature to be tracked would have to move the same distance (in pixels, as viewed by the camera) as the pointer is to move on the screen. Most users do not have such a large range of movement and even if such movement were possible, it does not complement the natural movement of a computer user as they view the computer screen. Therefore the camera mouse operates the pointer in a relative manner.

A relative scheme of pointer movement must consider how to adjust for the difference in scale of feature movement and pointer movement. The movement of the detected feature must be scaled in some reasonable manner before being added to the current pointer position. In previous systems, the scale factor is a user-customizable setting. However, adjusting the scale factor manually is a cumbersome trial and error process and requires intervention by a caregiver for manually entering scale factors. The scale factor is pertinent to the usability of the system, because if the scale factor is too low, all areas of the screen may not be reachable by the pointer. Alternatively, if it is too high the pointer may become too sensitive and thus move too quickly.

It can be observed that the scale factor is a function of the user's distance from the screen, as well as the range of possible movement of the feature in both horizontal and vertical directions. The user's range of movement may be seriously limited by motor dysfunction. The range of movement is also typically asymmetric in the vertical and horizontal directions due to the fact that vertical rotation of the head when viewing a standard computer screen is smaller than horizontal rotation.

From a usability point of view, the scaling factor should not be such that the system requires the user to move in a way that interferes negatively with the user's visual focus on the screen. In other words, during facial feature tracking with the camera mouse, feature movement and visual focus cannot be decoupled. Feature movement required for effective use of the system should not be such that it causes a strain on the visual focusing mechanism of the user.

Designing a mechanism to allow optimal setting of the scale factor by the user is therefore important towards the end of improving system performance and usability. A calibration phase was introduced to determine the optimal scale factor for individual users. Calibration is performed in advance of a usage session. After a feature is selected to be tracked, the users are lead through a calibration phase, in which they are directed to rotate their head towards distinct markers shown on the video stream, while retaining a comfortable view of the computer screen. The users successively move towards markers on the top, bottom, left and right boundaries of the screen (Figure 1). It is important to direct users to move within a comfortable range of motion, which permits clear and non stressful visual focus on the screen. Pointer movement is calibrated to the range of movement demonstrated by the user, using a linear mapping of demonstrated movement range to screen dimensions.

Fig. 1. System Calibration: The small colored disk shown in the video indicates the tip of the eyebrow has been selected as the feature to track. The larger disk on the boundary of the video display window indicates the direction the user should move her head.

After performing the calibration phase once for a particular user and a specific feature, in situations where the distance from the camera remains approximately the same across sessions, for example, for a user in a wheelchair, the scale factors found by the calibration phase may be saved in a user configuration file that can be loaded for subsequent use.

2.3 Application Framework

Applications often have to be tailored to work with the camera mouse, since the effective movement resolution of the camera mouse is not enough to navigate windows menus or operate standard windows applications. Several on-screen keyboards, educational programs, and game applications are available for use with the camera mouse. However, the user must rely on a caregiver to start the custom application before they can start using it. If the user wants to start a new application for another task, there is no means to navigate available programs autonomously without the caregiver's help. Our motivation in proposing a hierarchical framework for application navigation is to provide the camera mouse user with an autonomous experience with their computer, allowing them to perform common tasks of interest such as text entry, internet browsing, and entertainment applications in a manner that is user friendly, requires little technical expertise, and is configurable to meet the needs of individual users.

Several considerations must be kept in mind when designing an effective interface [19].

- The user should be able to clearly identify the target being selected.
- Distinguishing information should be placed at the beginning of headings.
- Clear and simple language should be used.
- The design should be consistent.
- There should be clear navigation.

Our interface opens with a main menu that is a list of common tasks (Figure 2). The main menu items configured in the test system are: *Play this Song* launches the default media player and plays the chosen song, *Text Entry* launches an on-screen keyboard, *Common Sayings* speaks saved text using a speech synthesis program, *View a webpage* launches the default browser and displays the chosen website, and *Games* launches games, such as Eagle Aliens [6], which have been developed to require only pointer movement.

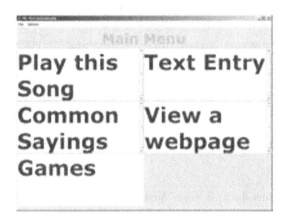

Fig. 2. Main Menu of Interface

The list of common tasks desired in the application varies depending on the interests of each user. The system is designed so that menu items can be added, removed, or modified. This allows the list to be customized for each individual user.

The user will choose the common task they desire in one of two modes, select mode or scan mode. In select mode, the user moves the pointer to an item. When the pointer reaches an item it is highlighted in blue, clearly identifying the target to be selected. In scan mode, the application scans through the list of items highlighting each item for a specified time interval. The time interval can be changed to the length of time that is reasonable for the current user.

To facilitate autonomous use, a dwell feature is available to simulate a selection command. The dwell feature acts as a timer. When an item is highlighted the timer is started. If that item stays highlighted for a specified time interval, a selection command is executed. The gray areas of the interface, shown in Figure 2, represent rest areas where the pointer can dwell without causing a selection command to occur. Gray was used to stress the inactive nature of such areas. The dwell feature can be enabled or disabled, as alternate methods may be available to simulate pointer clicks, such as blink detection [22], raised eyebrow detection [23], or use of a mechanical switch.

The font size of the menu items was also a consideration for users who are unable to sit close to the system due to wheelchairs. The system is designed so that the font size can be increased or decreased as desired. Items on the main menu are either links that directly launch programs or links that open a submenu. Every submenu has the same font type and size. The same color is used to highlight the menu items. This consistency helps maintain usability. A 'Return to Main Menu' option is always the last item in the submenu list. This feature supports clear navigation among the various menus. When a submenu item is selected the program associated with that menu item is launched. The 'Return to Main Menu' option is displayed on the screen after the program is launched so that the user can return to the system and navigate to other programs if desired. A strategy for navigation among opened programs is proposed by our framework, but has not been implemented yet.

An example of navigating through the system and selecting a song to play is shown in Figure 3.

Fig. 3. Navigation from the main menu through the 'Play this Song' submenu to launch a musicplayer that automatically begins playing the selected song

3   Experiments and Results

The system was tested to determine the performance of the tracking mechanism and to understand its limitations, as well as to determine the usability of the application framework proposed. Results from the first test provided input for the design of interface elements for the application framework.

A test group consisting of 8 subjects did the first set of experiments (Group 1). The subjects were between 14 and 60 years of age with varying levels of computer skills. The subjects did not have any functional limitations. The same set of users was asked to perform a control test, where the same sequence of steps was performed with a standard mouse (Control Group). The second test group (Group 2) consisted of two patients from The Boston Home [20]. Both subjects suffered from functional limitations that made it difficult or impossible to use the standard mouse. One of the subjects was diagnosed with muscular dystrophy more than 15 years ago. His condition causes muscle weakness and wasting in major joints and muscles, his shoulders and hips have been affected most. The other subject was diagnosed with multiple sclerosis more than 15 years ago. His condition causes muscle weakness, limiting his ability to move his arms, hands, and neck. The limitation in neck movement has resulted in a very small range of head movement.

3.1 Evaluating Tracker Performance

The tests were designed to record indicators of tracker performance. Specifically, we focused on factors pertaining to the tracker's ability to track features and translate feature movement to pointer movement on the screen. Specific factors include:

- Effective Dwell Area: the smallest region within which the user can dwell for 3 seconds. This will allow us to study the tradeoff between tracker sensitivity and dwelling ability.
- Movement patterns that cause the tracker to lose features while tracking.
- Movement patterns that affect the smoothness of the tracker's constructed pointer movement.

A movement evaluation tool was developed to analyze the above factors (Figure 4). During the test, users were asked to move the pointer from box to box. The order of movement between boxes was chosen so that we could evaluate the user's ability to move the pointer vertically, horizontally, and diagonally. The placement of the boxes on the screen was chosen to allow us to determine if there were areas of the screen that the users found difficult to reach, or were unable to reach. Different sized boxes were used to evaluate the smallest area that the user can easily dwell in for a few seconds. The size and location of the boxes was chosen so as to discern if it was easier to dwell in smaller boxes in some areas of the screen. The use of color in the boxes allows the user to recognize the area they are asked to move without having to read through the labels.

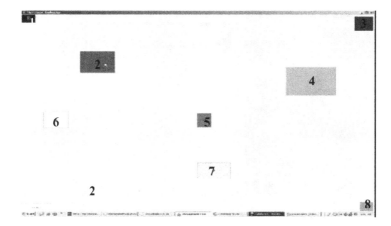

Fig. 4. Movement Evaluation Tool

The users were asked to move the pointer in the following sequence, dwelling for three seconds in each box: dark blue box labeled 3, yellow box labeled 7, green box labeled 8, red box labeled 2, light blue box labeled 4, black box labeled 1, purple box labeled 5, white box labeled 6.

Figure 5 shows a user with multiple sclerosis performing a subset of steps in the movement evaluation test. It is apparent from the test that despite being restricted to only slight movements of the head, the user was able to reach all areas of the screen, including corners, and could dwell even in small regions.

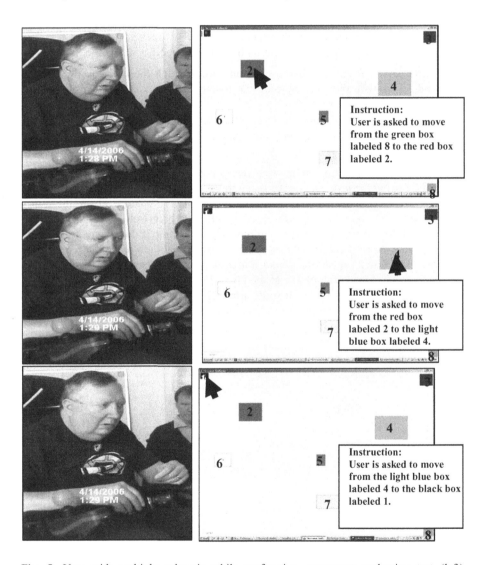

Fig. 5. User with multiple sclerosis while performing movement evaluation test (left), simultaneous screen shots depicting pointer location (center), and the instruction given (right). (Note: Pointer is shown enhanced in the figure.)

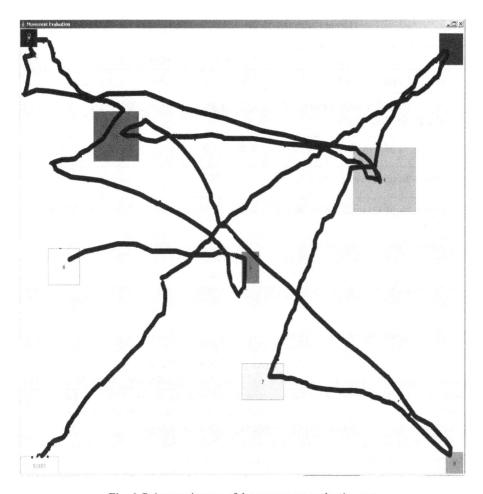

Fig. 6. Pointer trajectory of the movement evaluation test

Figure 6 shows the entire trajectory of pointer movement as a user performs the movement evaluation test.

The task in the tracker evaluation test was to move from one colored box to another (Figure 4) and then focus on the box for several seconds. The test consisted of eight tasks. The tracker evaluation tests showed that all ten users, with and without disabilities, were able to move the pointer to every location. This indicates that we were successful in designing a system that tracks features and translates feature movement to pointer movement on the screen. Table 1 categorizes three levels of movement error, no overshooting, overshooting once, and overshooting more than once. Overshooting occurs when the mouse pointer moves beyond the target on the screen. This did not prevent the user from selecting the desired target. The control experiment was done using the standard mouse.

Table 1. Results of Movement Evaluation Test

	Control	Group 1	Group 2
Average Completion Time	1.0 s	1.8 s	3.2 s*
Average % of Tasks Completed on the First Trial	8/8 = 100%	8/8 = 100%	7.5/8 = 94%
Average % of Not Overshooting	8/8 = 100%	4/8 = 50%	2/8 = 25%
Average % of Overshooting Once	0/8 = 0%	2/8 = 25%	2.5/8 = 31%
Average % of Overshooting more than Once	0/8 = 0%	2/8 = 25%	3.5/8 = 44%

* We discounted the timing result of one of the eight assigned tasks for one user in Group 2 in computing the average completion time. The reason was that, during the test, the subject was asking questions and the recorded time of 30 seconds did not reflect the actual time to move the pointer, which was on average less than 3 seconds for the remaining seven tasks performed by this user.

3.2 Evaluating Application Design

The tests in this section were designed to capture the usability of the application framework with respect to the design and layout of the interface elements. The test consisted of launching five applications in sequence, Text Entry (Keyboard application), Common Sayings (speech synthesizer), View a webpage (open browser), Games (open a game), and Play this Song (open a media player).

We were interested in determining how well users were able to navigate through the menus (average completion time), how many times the users had to try before they successfully launched the correct application (number of tasks completed on the first trial), and how often the programs were launched unintentionally (percent of unintentional launches). Table 2 presents the results.

Another consideration for the application evaluation was the degree of independent use, i.e., the degree to which the user can effectively use the application without intervention, once it has been set up. This factor is difficult to measure quantitatively. From personal observation we saw that the subjects were able to launch all of the programs independently and interact with the applications. For example, using the cascading menu selection strategy, they were able to launch and play a game, get back to the main menu by hovering above it and then launch and use a text entry application.

The users were also provided with the opportunity to use the system on their own, without a guided sequence of steps. This helped determine their opinion on the overall use of the system. During this period unexpected problems with the system could be identified. A survey was used to gather the opinions of the sample test group.

Table 2. Application Evaluation Results

	Control	Group 1	Group 2
Average Completion Time *	5.0 s	6.3 s	9.4 s
Number of Tasks Completed on the First Trial **	1	5/5 = 100% for 5 users 4/5 = 80% for 2 users	5/5 = 100% for user 1 3/5 = 60% for user 2
Percent of Unintentional Launches	0	0/5 = 0% for 5 users 2/7 = 29% for 1 user 3/8 = 38% for 1 user	0/5 = 0% for user 1 4/9 = 44% for user 2

*Actual task completion times for Group 1 and 2 were not significantly different. The computed results for Group 2 were affected by the fact that users in Group 2 showed much interest in the system; they stopped to discuss, ask questions, and give ideas. Such instances skewed the average of the recorded times.

**The users needed more than one trial to complete a task due to unintentional launches. The unintentional launches were instances where the user diverted from the test to discuss something and hence caused unintentional launching of the applications. This forced them to return to the main menu and repeat the task. This also highlights the need for a binary switching mechanism to turn off the tracker when not in active use.

Issues were determined by analysis of survey questions and by personal observation. The tests performed by Group 1 revealed several issues. It was observed that after a program was launched it was not possible to return to the application without using the standard mouse. To resolve this issue, the system was configured such that when the pointer moves over the title area of the partially occluded application, the application is brought into the foreground. This assumes that the programs opened will not take the full screen area.

Another issue noticed during preliminary testing was that the testers could not easily identify where to rest the pointer without causing a selection command to occur. As a result, programs were opened unintentionally; the Midas touch problem [21]. To resolve this issue, all areas where the pointer can rest were changed to have a gray background color distinguishing them from the areas with a white background that cause a selection command to be executed. The users of Group 2 also found that the pointer had some jitter, due to the increased sensitivity. We propose a simple averaging mechanism to solve this problem.

Users showed interest in the prospect of being able to write and save text and send email autonomously using the camera mouse. Current users rely on a separate application to enter the text and then the caregiver has to copy and paste the text into an email application to dispatch the email. Users also expressed interest in a system that allowed effective web browsing with the camera mouse.

4 Discussion

In summary, we developed a customizable camera-based human computer interaction system and showed that people with and without disabilities can complete multiple computing tasks with slight head movements. The improvements made to the camera mouse have resulted in a robust feature tracker and a calibration of feature movement to pointer movement that is specific for each individual user. Taking advantage of the features of the camera mouse, our interaction system was able to provide hands-free access to many common computing tasks. The test results show that users were able to successfully open all of the programs available in our system with only a small percentage of error. This provides evidence that we designed a user-friendly interface with an effective navigation strategy. Survey results obtained from the test subjects showed that their holistic experience of the system was positive and they especially enjoyed playing the games.

Several of the test subjects in the first group used the system more than once. Their ability to control the pointer movement and dwell in a selection area improved as quickly as the second use. This indicates that the difference in average completion time between the control experiment and the camera mouse experiment would be reduced if all subjects were given more time to become accustomed to moving the pointer with the camera mouse.

A possibility for extension is to provide automatic feature detection. This would eliminate the dependence of tracking performance on the manual selection of an appropriate feature. The type of features best suited for tracking with the camera mouse was studied by Cloud et al. [24], who suggested that the tip of the nose was a robust feature. Gorodnichy [25] also discussed the robustness of nose tracking. Our experiments with the camera mouse showed similar results. Features on the sides of the face were lost by the tracker frequently as they were occluded upon rotation of the head. The outer tips of the eyes and features on the outer boundaries of the face were similarly not suitable for tracking. Features that exhibited good contrast on the central band of the face, e.g. the inner tip of the eyebrows, the tip of the nose and the outer boundary of the top or bottom lip, were the best features to track with the camera positioned so that it has a frontal view of the person's face. Tracking a feature on the lips may however be problematic if the user speaks during use. Features on the eye were often lost during blinking. Also, experiments showed that if the user wore glasses, especially of a dark color, features on the glasses, such as the bridge of the glasses, were robust to track.

Directions for future work include:

- Providing an automatic feature detection method.
- Smoothing pointer jitter that resulted from the increased sensitivity.
- Navigation among the opened programs.
- Providing better internet browsing, text entry, and email programs.
- Designing interaction strategies that allow the camera mouse to be used with standard, non-specialized applications. For example, adding features such as generalized dwell that is decoupled from camera mouse enabled applications and operates with the desired dwell radius on the entire screen. To overcome the limitation of small interface elements found in many standard applications, screen

magnification could be used to magnify menus as the pointer hovers above them. A binary switch could then be provided to toggle to the magnified area and select menu items. A cursor lock could also be used to aid selection of small interface elements.

- Extension to usage scenarios within the ambient intelligence paradigm [26]. The computer vision strategy presented here as a pointer alternative can be applied to menu selection tasks in common appliances such as telephones, microwave ovens, web-enabled digital television (DTV) and CD players.

Acknowledgements

The authors thank David Young-Hong from The Boston Home for his help with the experiments and for sharing his insights regarding technologies needed for people with disabilities. This work was supported by NSF grants IIS-0093367, IIS-0329009, and 0202067.

References

1. National Multiple Sclerosis Society, http://www.nationalmssociety.org, accessed April 2006.
2. Microsoft Accessibility, http://www.microsoft.com/enable/research/agingpop.aspx, accessed April 2006.
3. J. Gips, P. Olivieri, and J.J. Tecce, "Direct Control of the Computer through Electrodes Placed Around the Eyes", Human-Computer Interaction: Applications and Case Studies, M.J. Smith and G. Salvendy (eds.), Elsevier, pages 630-635. 1993.
4. Synapse Adaptive, http://www.synapseadaptive.com/prc/prchead.htm, accessed April 2006.
5. NaturalPoint SmartNAV, http://www.naturalpoint.com/smartnav/, accessed July 2006.
6. J.J. Magee, M.R. Scott, B.N. Waber and M. Betke, "EyeKeys: A Real-time Vision Interface Based on Gaze Detection from a Low-grade Video Camera," In Proceedings of the IEEE Workshop on Real-Time Vision for Human-Computer Interaction (RTV4HCI), Washington, D.C., July 2004.
7. M. Betke, J. Gips, and P. Fleming, "The camera mouse: Visual tracking of body features to provide computer access for people with severe disabilities", IEEE Transactions on Neural Systems and Rehabilitation Engineering, 10:1, pages 1-10, March 2002.
8. D.O. Gorodnichy and G. Roth, "Nouse 'Use your nose as a mouse' perceptual vision technology for hands-free games and interfaces", Proceedings of the International Conference on Vision Interface (VI 2002), Calgary, Canada, May 2002.
9. Assistive Technologies, http://www.assistivetechnologies.com, accessed April 2006.
10. Apple Computer Disability Resources, http://www.apple.com/accessibility, accessed April 2006.
11. WiViK on-screen keyboard (virtual keyboard) software, http://www.wivik.com, accessed April 2006.
12. The Dasher Project, http://www.inference.phy.cam.ac.uk/dasher, accessed April 2006.
13. J. Gips and J. Gips, "A Computer Program Based on Rick Hoyt's Spelling Method for People with Profound Special Needs," Proceedings International Conference on Computers Helping People with Special Needs (ICCHP 2000), Karlsruhe, pages 245-250.

14. B.N. Waber, J.J. Magee, and M. Betke, "Web Mediators for Accessible Browsing," Boston University Computer Science Department Technical Report BUCS 2006-007, May 2006.

15. H. Larson and J. Gips, "A Web Browser for People with Quadriplegia." In Universal Access in HCI: Inclusive Design in the Information Society, Proceedings of the International Conference on Human-Computer Interaction, Crete, 2003, C. Stephanidis (ed.), Lawrence Erlbaum Associates, pages 226-230, 2003.

16. OpenCV library. http://sourcforge.net/projects/opencvlibrary, accessed April 2006.

17. B.D. Lucas and T. Kanade. "An iterative image registration technique with an application to stereo vision." In Proceedings of the 7th International Joint Conference on Artificial Intelligence (IJCAI), pages 674-679, Vancouver, Canada, April 1981.

18. C. Fagiani, M. Betke, and J. Gips, "Evaluation of tracking methods for human-computer interaction." In Proceedings of the IEEE Workshop on Applications in Computer Vision (WACV 2002), pages 121-126, Orlando, Florida, December 2002.

19. "Human-centered design processes for interactive systems," International Organization for Standardization ISO 13407, 1999.

20. The Boston Home, http://www.thebostonhome.org, accessed April 2006.

21. R.J.K. Jacob, "What you look at is what you get," Computer, 26:7, pages 65–66, July 1993.

22. M. Chau and M. Betke, "Real Time Eye Tracking and Blink Detection with USB Cameras," Boston University Computer Science Technical Report 2005-012, May 2005.

23. J. Lombardi and M. Betke, "A camera-based eyebrow tracker for hands-free computer control via a binary switch", In Proceedings of the 7th ERCIM Workshop, User Interfaces For All (U14All 2002), pages 199-200, Paris, France, October 2002.

24. R. L. Cloud, M. Betke, and J. Gips, "Experiments with a Camera-Based Human-Computer Interface System." In Proceedings of the 7th ERCIM Workshop "User Interfaces for All," UI4ALL 2002, pages 103-110, Paris, France, October 2002.

25. D.O. Gorodnichy, "On importance of nose for face tracking", In Proceedings of the IEEE International Conference on Automatic Face and Gesture Recognition (FG 2002), pages 188-196, Washington, D.C., May 2002.

26. A. Ferscha, "Contextware: Bridging Physical and Virtual Worlds." In Proceedings of the Ada-Europe Conference on Reliable Software Technologies, 2002.

Interactive TV Design That Blends Seamlessly with Everyday Life

Konstantinos Chorianopoulos

Department of Architecture
Bauhaus University of Weimar, Germany
k.chorianopoulos@archit.uni-weimar.de

Abstract. Television use does not require high skill or effort, which is ideal as a paradigm of use for ambient user interfaces. In this paper, universal access in ambient intelligence is modeled after the use of TV in everyday life. Instead of considering television only as a content medium and the focus of user activity, an alternative approach is to consider television use as a secondary function to other activities, such as socializing, domestic chores, leisure pursuits. For this purpose, the requirements for ambient user interactivity with TV are organized in a small set of design principles. The design principles have been selected, analyzed and synthesized from readings in previous works on media and ethnographic studies about television, and everyday life. It is suggested that universal access in ambient intelligence is promoted by considering design principles such as opportunistic interaction, user participation, group interactions, and multiple levels of attention to the user interface. Finally, the principles have been tested in the design of a user interface for interactive music television. This preliminary case suggests that the proposed principles facilitate the design of user interfaces that blend seamlessly with everyday life.

Keywords: Design principles, metaphors, paradigm of use, Ambient ITV, interactive TV, media studies.

1 Introduction

Television is one of the most pervasive mediums in daily life and it has traditionally occupied the largest share of domestic leisure time [33]. In sharp contrast to the also ubiquitous personal computer, television use does not require high skill or effort, which is an ideal paradigm of use for the design of ambient user interfaces. In this work, we propose that universal access in ambient intelligence applications could be modeled after TV use. Indeed, besides the ease of use, the pervasiveness of TV could be attributed to a focus on universal access. Historically, the design of TV systems has regarded all members of the society. For example, there are technical standards for closed captioning services (i.e. optional text captions for the hard-hearing people) that have been mandated by the government, in order to provide equal access to TV services for all. Traditional TV has been undergoing a process of transformation, due to digital storage, digital transmission, proliferation of alternative distribution channels, and active user participation. Therefore, developers of new interactive TV

C. Stephanidis and M. Pieper (Eds.): ERCIM UI4ALL Ws 2006, LNCS 4397, pp. 43–57, 2007.

(ITV) applications should be provided with design principles and technical standards that ensure universal access. Moreover, it is argued that the same design principles could also be employed in ambient intelligence applications that blend seamlessly with everyday life. In the rest of this article, ITV is considered as a paradigm of use and not as a technology for ambient intelligence.

Although interactivity offers additional benefits to the media audience, the introduction of interactivity in TV systems raises issues of increased complexity. Many ITV technologies and applications support the interactive display of additional information on the screen and the interactive manipulation of rich content, but without considering the design principles that could sustain ITV use as an integral part of everyday life activities. Contemporary ITV applications have been developed with traditional multimedia authoring tools that make many assumptions with regard to ITV user behavior. For example, there are some ITV applications that interrupt TV channel flow, take over the whole TV screen and do not proceed unless the user interacts with a few dialog boxes. Such a paradigm of use is very well suited for personal computer applications, when users perform highly structured tasks, but it is unsuitable for leisure or secondary activities, such as when users just want to keep an eye on TV news, or want to change the flow of the TV channel [4]. For this purpose, we investigate design principles that regard ITV as a secondary low demand activity, referred to as Ambient ITV.

Universal Access in Ambient ITV is promoted by a user interface (UI) that provides interactive access to multimedia information and communication services, but without any discount on the established uses and gratifications of traditional TV. Then, the requirement for Ambient ITV applications is to gratify entertainment needs and leisure activities in a relaxed setting. In this context, the mentality of efficiency and task completion found in traditional user interface heuristics may not be suitable. Indeed, there is a body of research work that has elaborated on the relationship between TV, viewers and daily life. The field of media studies has accumulated an extensive knowledge of TV usage and TV viewer behavior. Moreover, there are numerous ethnographic and longitudinal studies that describe the role of TV in everyday life. In the rest of this paper, media and ethnographic studies are analyzed and synthesized into a small set of design principles that facilitate the inclusive design of Ambient ITV applications. It is also expected that the same design principles apply to other types of Ambient Intelligence applications, especially in the context of leisure activities.

2 Design Principles

UI principles have played an important role in guiding the design choices of interactive computer applications, as it becomes evident by the wide acceptance and the many citations to the Macintosh Human Interface Guidelines report [1]. As a matter of fact, personal computer application developers have been accustomed to a standard set of principles (e.g. desktop metaphor, direct manipulation, etc), which are employed in computer applications. In addition, usability engineers employ the respective lists of UI heuristics to perform expert evaluations (e.g. consistency of buttons in dialog boxes, provide shortcuts, etc). Most importantly, UI principles establish an implicit conceptual framework into developers' minds with regard to usability goals. For example, efficiency is a popular UI design goal, which is pursued with an effort to minimize task execution time. Arguably, task efficiency is not a high-priority requirement for Ambient ITV applications that blend seamlessly with daily patterns of life.

Design principles are important because they facilitate the process of designing a UI for a new application, but principles are also loaded with implicit assumptions with regard to the application domain, the context of use, and the user characteristics and goals. There are generic (e.g. "know the user") and more specific (e.g. "use red for urgent items") principles that address the multitude of issues associated with UI design, such as screen design, user needs and performance, input device, etc [24]. UI design principles usually stem from the extensive experience of a few HCI experts. HCI was mainly developed alongside the desktop paradigm of use and most of the current principles reflect a productivity mentality. It has been argued that most UI design principles are catholic and apply to many categories of interactive applications, but experts admit that there might be exceptions in new usage paradigms [23]. Indeed, it is argued that user interface requirements for Ambient ITV are quite different from those for desktop computer applications.

Universal access is often seen as providing everybody with the means to get information and to perform tasks within a reasonable time-span and with a reasonable amount of effort. Compared to the traditional usability definition, universal access emphasizes the diversity in the user population, in the application domain and in the context of use [29]. Universal access methods have been applied to facilitate the accessibility of information society services for the disabled, aged, and children, and should be updated for the case of ubiquitous computing applications [10]. Interactive TV is an information society technology that is employed in a leisure context of use, is targeted to the majority of the population, and provides a terminal for diverse activities, such as e-commerce, e-learning, and games. At first sight, contemporary universal access techniques seem to be appropriate for the design of ITV applications. Still, the TV audience has been accustomed to expect much more than ease of use. In particular, the TV audience receives information and expects to be entertained, in a lean-back posture, which does not require neither high skills, nor high effort. Besides being a unique requirement for universal access in ITV, this paradigm of use is rather suitable for modeling the design of other categories of ambient intelligence applications, beyond ITV.

Related work has treated some aspects of universal access to interactive TV, such as accessibility for specific populations such as the disabled [14]. Besides accessibility, the designers of ITV should also consider the needs and gratifications of the existing TV audience. Some researchers have emphasized that ITV applications are deployed in a relaxed setting and users have entertainment goals [3] [7]. Still, there is no research available about design principles that regard the interaction with TV as an ambient UI. Then, a major research question is:

'Which design principles promote Universal Access in Ambient ITV applications?'

Table 1. Differences in user requirements for Universal Access between desktop computing and Ambient ITV applications

Requirements	Desktop computing	Ambient ITV
Users	Employed, Disabled, elderly, children	Everyday roles
Activities	Focused, primary, structured	Peripheric, secondary, unstructured
Goals	Transactions, information seeking, health, communication	Entertainment, relaxation, information exploration
Context	Work, productivity	Leisure

In summary, universal access research has to consider the design requirements for Ambient ITV (**Table 1** provides an overview of the discussion in this section). Previous research in universal access for ITV has treated some aspects of the user studies [11], multimodal interfaces [3] and affective quality evaluation [7], but there is still limited research available for the design methods, techniques and principles, which fulfill the requirement of universal access in Ambient ITV applications.

3   Methodology

In this paper, Ambient ITV applications are considered as information and entertainment applications that blend seamlessly with daily activities. Here, daily activities are defined as those that take place in public or private settings and do not necessarily involve computing activities as the primary focus of activity. Examples of this type of activities include socializing, domestic chores, leisure pursuits. Then, the challenge is to design information technology that supports daily activities, without requiring high skills or effort to learn and use. Previous research in ambient intelligence has considered computing applications that are integrated with the physical environment (e.g. sensors, public displays), or mobile applications. In these cases, the main requirement for the design of the user interface is the automation of computing tasks and the minimal user intervention, which are based on detailed user models, sensors and context adaptation [27]. Although user profile and context are important factors in the delivery of effective ambient intelligence, designers should also consider ambient applications as being of secondary priority in performing other daily life activities (e.g. socializing at home or outside, doing house chores, relaxing, etc), which might have nothing to do with any computing devices. Overall, universal access in Ambient ITV applications is treated as a requirement for UI design that blends seamlessly with everyday life. For this purpose, we examine media and ethnographic studies of TV use.

Longitudinal studies about TV and the quality of life have revealed that there is a strong correlation between TV watching behavior and several aspects of daily life [13], [17], [20]. Audience surveys and ethnographic studies have shown that viewers appropriate TV content in many ways, such as selective distraction from home activities, conversation starter, structuring of time [18], [25]. Researchers have also investigated how the domestic build environment affects TV use and found that different architectural styles of domestic space facilitate different patterns of TV use [26]. It has been also demonstrated that the introduction of electronic mediums in homes has influenced the design of architectural space [32]. Furthermore, there are studies of the use of TV in public spaces, which document the impact of TV well beyond the familiar domestic environment in to public spaces of work, commerce and leisure [20]. In brief, there is body of research work that considers TV viewing as part of daily life, instead of 1) focusing on the technical requirements, 2) analyzing only the effects of particular types of content, and 3) considering interaction with the user as if it was the main objective of user activity. Therefore, the consideration of ITV applications as part of daily life could encourage the specification of design principles for ubiquitous computing, in general.

Next, we explore the implications of media and ethnographic studies for UI design principles.

4 Design Principles for Ambient TV Interactivity

HCI research and practice has been benefited by a multidisciplinary approach to design problems. In this section, the design principles are formulated after a systematic and critical review of previous research in media and ethnographic studies. The most useful findings from each field are collected, analyzed and presented in an easy-to-use designer's checklist that should be addressed in the design and expert evaluation of an ITV application. In general, it is argued that these principles could aid the design of other ambient intelligence applications. In the description of each principle, we examine fallacies and pitfalls that should be avoided when designing for ITV. At the same time, the UI principles are formulated into short generic descriptions for ambient interactions.

4.1 Opportunistic Interaction

The introduction and wide adoption of the Web has been promoted and attributed to the interactive nature of the new medium. It often goes without much thought, that if something is interactive then it is also preferable. Interactivity with the user might seem as the major benefit of ITV, but this is a fallacy that designers with computer experience should learn to avoid. Most notably, there is evidence that in some cases interactivity may be disruptive to the entertainment experience. Vorderer et al. [30] found that there are some categories of users who do not like to have the option to change the flow of a TV story; they just prefer to watch passively. Indeed, the passive uses and emotional needs gratified by the broadcast media are desirable [18]. Still, there might be cases such as video games, in which the addition of interactive elements enhances the entertainment experience [19]. As a principle, the viewer should be empowered with features borrowed from a TV production studio. For example, ITV users could control the display of sports statistics and play along the players of quiz games. Interactivity should not be enforced to the users, but should be pervasive for changing the flow of the running program, or augmenting with additional information on demand.

4.2 Multiple Levels of Attention

A common fallacy is that TV viewers are always concentrated on the TV content, but there is ample evidence that TV usage takes many forms, as far as the levels of attention of the viewer are concerned. Jenkins [16] opposes to the popular view that ITV will support only the needs of the channel surfers by making an analogy: 'With the rise of printing, intensive reading was theoretically displaced by extensive reading: readers read more books and spent less time on each. But intensive reading never totally vanished.' Lee and Lee [18] found that there is a wide diversity of attention levels to the television set —from background noise to full concentration. For example, a viewer may sit down and watch a TV program attentively, or leave the TV open as a radio and only watch when something interesting comes-up [8]. These findings contrast 'to the image of the highly interactive viewer intently engaged with the television set that is often summoned up in talking about new possibilities.'[18]. Instead of assuming a user, who is eager to navigate through persistent dialog boxes, designers should consider that users do not have to be attentive for the application to proceed.

4.3 Relaxed Exploration

During the 90's there had been a lot of speculation about the 500 channels future of ITV. In contrast, mass communication researchers found that viewers recall and attend to fewer than a dozen of TV channels [12]. The fallacy of the 500 channels future was turned upside-down into a new fallacy, during the first decade of 2000, when researchers put forward the vision of a single personalized channel. In sharp contrast, the study of TV consumption in the home reveals that TV viewing is usually a planned activity, which is a finding that sharply contrasts with the focus on the EPG as a method to select a program to watch each time a user opens the TV. Indeed, ritualized TV viewing was confirmed by a survey, in which 63% of the respondents had watched the program before and knew it was going to be on [18]. Still, there is a fraction of the viewers that impulsively selects a program to watch, especially among the younger demographic [13]. As a consequence, designers should consider that most TV viewing starts with familiar content and happens in a ritualistic pattern (e.g. early morning news, or late evening series), but it might continue with browsing of relevant items. Therefore, interactive TV applications should support relaxed exploration, instead of information seeking. This principle becomes especially important in the age of hybrid content distribution systems, which include peer-to-peer, IPTV and mobile TV.

4.4 Structuring of Time-Schedule

Using the television as a time tool to structure activities and organize time has been documented at an ethnographic study of a STB trial [25]. The fact that most TV viewing is considered to be 'ritualistic' [18] does not preclude the exploitation of out-of-band techniques for delivering the content at user's premises. Broadcast distribution is suitable for the delivery of high-demand, high-bit rate items, which have a real-time appeal (e.g. popular sport events, news). Designers should justify the use of persistent local storage and broadband Internet connections, which are becoming standard into many ITV products (e.g. video game consoles, digital media players). Digital local storage technology takes viewer control one big step further — from simple channel selection with the remote— by offering the opportunity for conveniently time-shifted local programming and content selection. As a principle, designers should try to release the content from the fixed broadcast schedule and augment it with out-of-band content delivery. Therefore, an appropriate UI for content delivery should allow the user to customize the preferred sources of additional and alternative information and video content.

4.5 User Contributed Content

TV content production has been regarded as a one-way activity that begins with the professional TV producers and editors and ends with post-production at the broadcast station. As a matter of fact, television viewers have long been considered passive receivers of content, but a new generation of computer literate TV viewers has been accustomed to make and share edits of video content online. The most obvious example of the need for user contributions in available TV content is the increased activity of TV content forums and related web sites. There are many types of user communities from the purely instrumental insertion of subtitles in hard-to-find Japanese anime to the creative competition on scenarios of discontinued favorable TV series (e.g. Stat Trek). In any case, there are many opportunities for user contributed content, such as annotations, sharing, and virtual edits. Furthermore, the wide-availability of video capture (e.g. in mobile phones, photo cameras) and easy-to-use video editing software, opens up additional opportunities for wider distribution of home made content (e.g. peer-to-peer, portable video players, etc).

4.6 Group Viewing

Most TV sets come with one remote control, which excludes the possibility for interactivity to anyone, but the one who holds the remote control. Despite this shortcoming, TV usage has been always considered a group activity [13] and it might provide a better experience when watched with family members [17]. In contrast, PC usage is mostly solitary, partly because the arrangement of equipment does not provide affordances for group use. Then, a possible pitfall is to consider only one user interacting with the TV, because there is only one remote control. Therefore, designers should consider social viewing that might take place locally. For example, an ITV quiz game might provide opportunities for competition between family members. In the case of distant groups of synchronous viewing, there are further opportunities for group collaboration, which are discussed next.

4.7 Content Enriched Communication

Besides enjoying TV watching together, people enjoy talking about, or referring to TV content [18]. This finding could be regarded as an overlap of the previous "Group Viewing" and "User Contributed Content" principles, but in an asynchronous, or distant communication fashion. Therefore, ITV applications should support the communication of groups of people who have watched the same content item, although not on the same time (e.g. family members living in the same or diasporic households). Moreover, ITV applications should facilitate the real-time communication of distant groups of viewers, who watch concurrently TV. An additional aspect of this principle is that it poses an implicit argument against personalization. If TV content is such an important placeholder for discussion, then personalization reduces the chances that any two might have watched the same program. On the other hand, this social aspect of TV viewing might also point towards new directions for personalization, which are based on the behavior of small social circles of affiliated people.

4.8 Visual Language and Aesthetics

A difficulty in the domain of ITV UI design is the interface's inability to stay attractive over time. TV audiences have become familiar with a visual grammar that requires all programs, as well as presentation styles to be dynamic and surprising [21], which is in sharp contrast with traditional usability principle of consistency [24]. In summary, designers should enhance the core and familiar TV notions (e.g. characters, stories) with programmable behaviors (e.g. objects, actions). Then, an ITV UI might not look like a button or a dialog box. Instead, it could be an animated character, which features multimodal behaviors. Furthermore, user selections that activate scene changes should be performed in accordance with the established and familiar TV visual grammar (e.g. dissolves, transitions, fade-outs).

Table 2. Design principles for interactive television applications

Principle Name	Principle Description
Opportunistic interaction	Continuous flow of content manipulated by optional user interactivity
Relaxed exploration	Relaxed exploration, instead of information seeking
Structuring of time-schedule	Promote flexible structuring of daily life time-schedules
Group viewing	Affordances for social viewing in co-located groups
Multiple levels of attention	Attention may be on the periphery of vision or focused, or anything in between
Visual language and aesthetics	Familiar TV elements include characters and stories
User contributed content	The viewer as a TV producer could perform annotations, sharing, and virtual edits
Content enriched communication	Synchronous or asynchronous distant communication around TV content

The above table (**Table 2**) summarizes the design principles into a coherent list of principle name and the respective description for use by designers and developers of programming frameworks in ambient intelligence.

In the following section, a few of the above design principles are applied in the case of a simple ITV application for music videos.

5 Interactive Music Television

The music video is a commercially successful, popular and worldwide available format of TV content (e.g. MTV channel). Music TV channels are considered to be innovative, because they have a young and dynamic audience, so they can play the role of the Trojan horse for novel ITV applications. MTV was the first TV channel to offer information related to video-clips a while ago, and since then, there have been many followers, even in different program types. MTV has been also showing which music video comes next. Music information usually contains trivia about the artist, or biographical information and discography. Music TV channels had originally adopted the informational video-overlays, because they make viewers spend more time in front of the TV set, instead of listening to it, like a radio.

Next, music video TV is redesigned as an ITV application, by addressing the proposed design principles.

Opportunistic interaction: Music TV producers enhance the programs with song and artist related trivia, which could be inserted dynamically at the user's premise. The main objective in the design of an entertaining ITV application is to offer relaxed interactivity. In this case, relaxed interactivity is materialized in two ways: 1) music video skipping and 2) on-demand song information.

Relaxed exploration: The interactive music video application offers popular actions such as stop, play, and next, just like a normal CD player. Further navigation options could be available for music videos, such as genre, artist, mood, tempo, decade, etc. Textual information about a music video clip could be browsed sequentially, or could be organized in categories, such as biography, discography, trivia, etc.

Structuring of time-schedule: A music TV broadcaster might create an interactive complement to the existing fixed channel, or a consumer might arrange a virtual music channel by selecting the favorite music video clips from local storage and setting preference categories for pre-fetching. A virtual TV channel is created by arranging accessible content (video-clips and ancillary data on local storage and Internet resources) in play-lists and by retrieving additional content (audiovisual or textual).

Group viewing: The current application does not provide any support for group viewing. Still, music video TV offers many opportunities for computer mediated socializing. Music preferences are employed in social situations to communicate personality/interests and as discussion placeholder. Then, an ITV application could set-up ad-hoc discussion groups for viewers who listen to the same music bands, or genres.

Multiple levels of attention: The user may either just tune into the music channel and leave it playing as radio or watch attentively the related information. Unless the track-skip button is pressed, there is a continuous flow of music video clips, just like a normal music TV channel (Fig. 1). Overlay information appears automatically, but the user may navigate on demand music video information.

Fig. 1. Music video selection allows the user to direct the –otherwise– continuous flow of the program, thus supporting multiple levels of attention

Visual language and aesthetics: Static video is used only for the video clips. The rest of the elements are computer generated (animated character, overlay box). The animated character displays related information about each video clip (Fig. 2). There is also an option to display the related information with a semi-transparent overlay rectangular box, instead of the animated character. Still, the animated character offers many opportunities for further research. For example, it might react to the mood of the song, or it could play the role of an avatar for remote users.

User contributed content: The current application does not support user participation, but there are many opportunities for user-contributed content. For example, music video clips could be offered with alternative edits and visuals, thus allowing the distribution of user-edited versions of a given music video. Moreover, trivia about the music videos and the artist offer an unlimited space for content contribution by the users.

Content enriched communication: The current application does not support any means of personal communication, but it is straightforward to describe such features. One popular contemporary example is text messaging over a ticker at the screen. Such services have been already used by the majority of analog TV broadcasters and could be enhanced with instant messaging in the domain of digital TV. Besides real-time communication, interactive TV systems should allow the users to allow filter through programs that have been watched and edited by their peers, thus enhancing the sense of community.

Fig. 2. Interactive graphics are embedded into the video, thus supporting TV grammar and aesthetics

In summary, the present section demonstrated how a simple ITV application was designed by addressing the principles. Moreover, it portrays that the principles could be also used to describe the features of that application in accordance to the established uses and gratifications of the TV audience, long before any implementation, and even before an early prototype has been constructed. As a proof of concept, the interactive music TV prototype was evaluated with end-users in a natural setting [4]. Although the prototype does not address all the proposed principles, the reaction of end-users was rather positive and motivated further research in the field of Ambient ITV.

6 Discussion

Some of the findings are opposed to the contemporary ITV design practice, while other findings reveal possible pitfalls for designers with desktop and web design background. In order to assist the design of ITV applications, the results of the literature review were formulated as design principles. Although principles are also employed in expert evaluation (e.g. heuristics) and for designing the syntactic details of the UI (e.g. specific guidelines for menus, icons, dialogs, etc), in the present work, we focused on the role of principles for facilitating the process of early-stage design for user interaction with ITV applications. In future research, the refinement of the proposed principles into more specific guidelines and could also be used for heuristic evaluation, as well. It is also proposed that the same design principles apply to Ambient ITV applications, especially in the context of leisure activities.

Ambient Intelligence and ubiquitous computing research could be broadly categorized along two dimensions of interaction design: 1) tangible user interfaces and 2) support for social activities [9]. Here, the work focuses on the social analysis of established and new technologies that support user interactivity during leisure pursuits in domestic settings. In contrast, the focus of previous work in related research, such as the cooperative buildings conference, was on the organizational aspects of collaborative work [28]. In this context, the concept of Ambient ITV was proposed as a metaphor for the design of UIs that are not work-related and do not require any training to use. Instead Ambient ITV UIs are seamless and a secondary part of daily life activities that are not related to computing. Indeed, the proposed design principles were elaborated from previous work in ethnographic and media studies research about TV and daily life, so they concern the use of electronic media technologies as a peripheric element of daily activities and thus, they are rather suitable for modeling ambient intelligence interaction design.

The design principles were conceptualized in the context of universal access in Ambient ITV applications, but there are some findings that could be applicable for other categories of ambient intelligence applications, as well. For example, television producers have an expertise in producing content that does not require any effort to use, to get informed and to get entertained (e.g. "relaxed exploration" principle). This type of experience could be very suitable for the design of private or domestic displays of information. In addition, some principles (e.g. "multiple levels of attention" and "opportunistic interaction" principle) promote a calm interaction paradigm with information technology [31]. This type of design support could aid the developers of ambient intelligence and ubiquitous information systems. Finally, the majority of the population is rather familiar with the presentation of information on TV (e.g. "TV grammar and aesthetics" principle), which could be exploited by graphic and video professionals for the design of presentation mechanisms in ambient intelligence applications.

Existing work in universal access in ambient intelligence has highlighted the user interface requirements for people with disabilities in various domains such as health and safety [10]. The latter are complimented by the suggestion for inspiration from the TV paradigm of use (**Table 3**). Previous work on Ambient TV has focused only on the impact of public space traditional TV in everyday life [20], but it has not considered the additional challenges and opportunities introduced by interactive technology, such as opportunistic interaction, user-contributed content and content enriched communication. The study of interactive music TV has been an informative and feasible experience, but further research should also consider other types of ambient multimedia applications, in order to test the applicability of the proposed design principles.

Table 3. Issues for Universal Access and potential contributions from the TV paradigm of use

Issues	Desktop computer	TV as a paradigm of use
Physical Context	Domain specific (office)	Generic
Users	Computer literate	Low skill and effort
Goals	One user-one computer, information and transactions	Group activities, leisure time, socializing
Tasks	Application tasks is the focus of the user	TV is of secondary focus to main user activity

The intuition and the experience of each UI designer may translate the same design principles into different solutions, depending on other factors, such as business and technical requirements. In this research, the design principles were explicitly addressed in an ITV prototype that has been tested with users. It has been argued that the design based on human considerations is not enough because design can rarely be detached from implementation and that the UI development tools implicitly give shape to the final application [2]. Accordingly, the proposed principles have been implemented in a UI programming toolkit, which was exploited to develop the example interactive music video application [5]. Test users evaluated the application very positively, when compared with traditional fixed music video TV [6]. Further research will consider enhancements to the music TV prototype and consideration of other types of TV content, or novel ITV formats.

The proposed set of design principles was presented as a list of high-level and generic design factors, which define the design space of ITV applications that blend seamlessly with everyday life. Still, there might be design principles, which are specific and concern particular parts of the interaction, such as video overlays, transitions etc. Indeed, there are guidelines, which are quantitative reformulations of principles. For example, the generic principle 'respond fast to user commands' may be transformed to 'respond in 1sec to user commands' as a guideline for a specific system. Then, the high-level ITV UI principle for 'multiple levels of attention' may be transformed to a more specific UI principle, such as 'remove a video overlay, if the user does not interact with the TV system', or transformed to a guideline such as 'remove a dialog box, if the user does not interact with the TV system after 5 seconds.' Therefore, further research should refine the proposed set of design principles into longer lists of more specific principles and guidelines for particular types of ITV applications.

Overall, the proposed principles facilitate the design process of early interactive prototypes. In particular, they facilitate the description of the design rationale, thus making the alternative, or progressive design decisions easily traceable and comparable. Most importantly, designers might use them to make decisions that regard important aspects of the interaction with Ambient Intelligence. In summary, the proposed UI principles consider the ITV user as a TV viewer and exploit IT in the home for seamless blending with patterns of daily life.

7 Conclusion

The following points summarize the contribution of this research with regard to ambient user interfaces:

- The TV is one of the most pervasive and familiar electronic mediums. TV content and viewers are continuously evolving, but there exists a small set of TV-related patterns of daily life that remain unchanged.
- The multiple uses of TV in daily life offer many insights for the design of Ambient ITV applications that facilitate the actual needs of users, instead of transferring paradigms of use from incompatible mediums (e.g. personal computer, web).
- The design of ambient user interfaces could be informed by the paradigm of use with TV. Universal access in ambient intelligence could be regarded as a seamless integration with daily activities and the consideration of the above principles could enhance user interface design.

Further research will investigate the translation of the design principles into technological requirements for the development of ambient intelligence systems that blend seamlessly with everyday life. Of particular interest would be the "content enriched communication" principle and the respective applications in domestic and public spaces, with the objective to facilitate sociability and to enhance public participation.

Acknowledgements. Parts of this work have been supported by the MEDIACITY project (http://www.mediacity-project.com), which is sponsored by the European Commission Marie Curie Host Fellowships for Transfer of Knowledge (MTKD-CT-2004-517121).

References

1. Apple Computer. Macintosh Human Interface Guidelines. Addison-Wesley, Reading, Mass., 1992
2. Baecker, R. M., Grudin, J., Buxton, W. A., and Greenberg, S. Human-Computer Interaction: To-ward the Year 2000, Second Edition. Morgan Kaufmann Publishers, 1995
3. Berglund, A., Berglund, E., Larsson, A., and Bang, M. Paper remote: an augmented television guide and remote control. Universal Access in the Information Society, 4(4): 300-327, 2006
4. Chorianopoulos, K. Virtual Television Channels: Conceptual Model, User Interface Design and Afective Quality Evaluation. Unpublished PhD Thesis. Athens University of Economics and Business, 2004
5. Chorianopoulos, K. and Spinellis, D. User interface development for interactive television: Extending a commercial DTV platform to the virtual channel API. Computers and Graphics, 28(2):157–166, 2004a
6. Chorianopoulos, K. and Spinellis, D. Affective usability evaluation for an interactive music television channel. ACM Computers in Entertainment, 2(3):14, ACM Press 2004b
7. Chorianopoulos, K. and Spinellis, D. User Interface Evaluation of Interactive TV: A Media Studies Perspective. Universal Access in the Information Society, 5(2):209-218, Springer, 2006.
8. Clancey, M. The television audience examined. Journal of Advertising Research, 34(4):2–11, 1994
9. Dourish, P. Where the Action Is: Foundations of Embodied Interaction. MIT Press, 2002.
10. Emiliani, P.L. and Stephanidis, C. Universal access to ambient intelligence environments: Opportunities and challenges for people with disabilities. IBM Systems Journal, 44(3): 605-619, 2005
11. Eronen, L. Five qualitative research methods to make iTV applications universally accessible. Universal Access in the Information Society, 5(2): 219-238, Springer, 2006
12. Ferguson, D. A. and Perse, E. M. Media and audience influences on channel repertoire. Journal of Broadcasting and Electronic Media, 37(1):31–47, 1993
13. Gauntlett, D. and Hill, A. TV Living: Television, Culture and Everyday Life. Routledge, 1999.
14. Gill J, Perera S. Accessible universal design of interactive digital television. In Proceedings of the 1st European Conference on Interactive Television: from Viewers to Actors? pp 83–89, 2003.
15. Herigstad, D. and Wichansky, A. Designing user interfaces for television. In Proceedings of the conference on CHI 98 summary : human factors in computing systems, pages 165–166. ACM Press, 1998
16. Jenkins, H. TV tomorrow. MIT Technology Review, May 2001
17. Kubey, R. and Csikszentmihalyi, M. Television and the Quality of Life: How Viewing Shapes Everyday Experiences. Lawrence Erlbaum, 1990
18. Lee, B. and Lee, R. S. How and why people watch tv: Implications for the future of interactive television. Journal of Advertising Research, 35(6):9–18, 1995
19. Malone, T. W. Heuristics for designing enjoyable user interfaces: Lessons from computer games. In Proceedings of the 1982 conference on Human factors in computing systems, pages 63–68. ACM Press, 1982
20. McCarthy, A. Ambient Television: Visual Culture and Public Space. Duke University Press, 2001

21. Meuleman, P., Heister, A., Kohar, H., and Tedd, D. Double agent—presentation and filtering agents for a digital television recording system. In CHI 98 conference summary on Human factors in computing systems, pages 3–4. ACM Press, 1998
22. Mountford, S. J., Mitchell, P., O'Hara, P., Sparks, J., and Whitby, M. When TVs are computers are TVs (panel). In Conference proceedings on Human factors in computing systems, pages 227–230. ACM Press, 1992
23. Nielsen, J. Traditional Dialog Design Applied to Modern User Interfaces. Commun. ACM, 33(10):109-118, 1990
24. Nielsen, J. Usability Engineering. Morgan Kaufmann, San Francisco, 1994.
25. O'Brien J, Rodden T, Rouncefield M, Hughes J. At home with the technology: an ethnographic study of a set-top-box trial. ACM Transactions on Computer-Human Interaction (TOCHI) 6(3):282–308, 1999
26. Pardun, C. and Krugman, D. How the architectural style of the home relates to family television viewing. Journal of Broadcasting and Electronic Media, 38(2):145-162, 1994
27. Schmidt, A. Implicit Human Computer Interaction Through Context. Personal Technologies, 4(2), 2000.
28. Streitz, N.A., J Gei ler, T. Holmer. Roomware for Cooperative Buildings: Integrated Design of Architectural Spaces and Information Spaces, Lecture Notes in Computer Science, Volume 1370, pp 4 – 21, 1998
29. Stephanidis C, Akoumianakis D. Universal design: towards universal access in the information society. In CHI '01: CHI '01 extended abstracts on Human factors in computing systems, pp 499–500, 2001
30. Vorderer, P., Knobloch, S., and Schramm, H. Does entertainment suffer from interactivity? the impact of watching an interactive TV movie on viewers' experience of entertainment. Media Psychology, 3(4):343–363, 2001
31. Weiser, M. and J. S. Brown. The coming age of calm technology. Technical report, Xerox PARC, 1996.
32. Wildman, M. Plugged-in: homes in the information age. Unpublished MSc thesis. McGill University, Montreal, Canada, 2001
33. Zillmann, D. The coming of media entertainment. In Zillmann, D. and Vorderer, P., editors, Media entertainment: The psychology of its appeal, pages 1–20. Lawrence Erlbaum Associates, 2000

Hybrid Knowledge Modeling for Ambient Intelligence

Porfírio Filipe[1,2] and Nuno Mamede[1,3]

[1] L²F INESC-ID – Spoken Language Systems Lab, Lisbon, Portugal
{porfirio.filipe, nuno.mamede}@l2f.inesc-id.pt
[2] ISEL – Instituto Superior de Engenharia de Lisboa, Lisbon, Portugal
[3] IST – Instituto Superior Técnico, Lisbon, Portugal

Abstract. This paper describes our research in enhance everyday devices as a solution to adapt Spoken Dialogue Systems (SDS) within ambient intelligence. In this context, a SDS enables universal access to ambient intelligence for anyone, anywhere at anytime, allowing the access to any device through any media or language. The main problem that we want to address is the spontaneous configuration of SDS to deal with a set of arbitrary plug and play devices. Such problem is resumed as a portability feature and is a critical research issue. We propose a hybrid approach to design ubiquitous domain models to allow the SDS to recognize on-the-fly the available devices and tasks they provide. When a device is activated or deactivated, a broker's knowledge model is updated from device's knowledge model using a knowledge integration process. This process was tested in the home environment represented by a set of devices.

Keywords: Ambient Intelligence, Spoken Dialogue System.

1 Introduction

Ambient Intelligence (AmI) [1] is a vision that expresses a recent paradigm in information technology. It can be defined as the fusion of two important trends: ubiquitous computing and social user interfaces. It is supported by advanced networking technologies, which allow robust, ad-hoc networks to be formed by a broad range of mobile devices. These context aware systems combine ubiquitous information, communication, and entertainment with enhanced personalization, natural interaction and intelligence. This kind of environment is characterized by the following basic elements: ubiquity, awareness, intelligence, and natural interaction.

Ubiquity refers to a situation in which we are surrounded by a large amount of interconnected embedded systems, which are invisible and moved into the background of our environment. Awareness refers to the ability of the system to locate and recognize objects and people, and their intentions. Intelligence refers to the fact that the digital surrounding is able to analyze the context, adapt itself to the people that live in it, learn from their behavior, and eventually to recognize as well as show emotion. Natural interaction finally refers to advanced modalities like natural speech and gesture recognition, as well as speech synthesis, which will allow a much more human like communication with the digital environment than is possible today.

C. Stephanidis and M. Pieper (Eds.): ERCIM UI4ALL Ws 2006, LNCS 4397, pp. 58 – 77, 2007.
© Springer-Verlag Berlin Heidelberg 2007

Ubiquitous computing [2] or pervasive computing are emerging disciplines bringing together elements from distributed systems, mobile computing, embedded systems, human computer interaction, computer vision and many other fields. This means integration of microprocessors into everyday devices like household appliances, furniture, clothing, toys and even paint. Networked computing devices will proliferate in this landscape, and users will no longer be tethered to a single computing device. People on the move will become networks on the move as the devices they carry network together and with the different networks around them.

The nature of devices will change to form augmented environments in which the physical world is sensed and controlled in such a way that it merges with the virtual world [3]. This massive use of such devices will fill the gap between the cyberspace and the real world.

Typically, within a pervasive computing environment two key concepts are designated by: "*device*" and "*service*". Devices include conventional computers, small handheld computers (PDAs), printers, and more specialized network devices, such as a thermometer or a household appliance. Services include any sort of network service that might be available. In fact, most devices are represented on the network by one or more services. Furthermore, a single network attached device may implement several services, e.g., a network printer may provide printing and fax (and who knows what else), all in a single device. In this context, devices and services are considered essentially equivalent and interchangeable. Together, these will be termed "*entities*" or "*resources*" on the network.

Ideally, entities should interoperate with other entities without pre-existing knowledge. This is a key aspect of spontaneous configuration.

A pervasive computing environment offers us an interesting starting point of discussion regarding the goal of achieving Plug and Play (PnP) functionality and its subsequent application to manage and control devices. There are several imaginable levels of PnP, which can be summarized in the following possibilities:

(i) No PnP – The environment can handle a fixed set of devices that are always connected;

(ii) Weak PnP – The environment can handle a fixed set of devices that can be connected to or disconnected from the network;

(iii) Medium PnP – The environment can handle a fixed set of device classes and only new instances of these device classes can be plug and played;

(iv) Strong PnP – The environment can handle completely new devices of previously unknown classes.

2   Spoken Dialogue Systems

A Spoken Dialogue System (SDS) should be a computational entity that allows access to any device by anyone, anywhere, at anytime, through any media or language, allowing its users to focus on the task, not on the tool.

The user's request is captured by a microphone, which provides the input for the Speech Recognition component. Next, the Language Understanding component receives the recognized words and builds the related speech acts. The Dialogue Manager processes the speech acts and then calls the Response Generation component to generate a message. Finally, the message is used by the Speech Output component to produce speech. The response of the SDS is final or is a request for clarification. When everything is acceptable, a final answer is produced based on an external data source, traditionally a relational database.

Fig. 1 shows the logical flow associated to the management of a user's request.

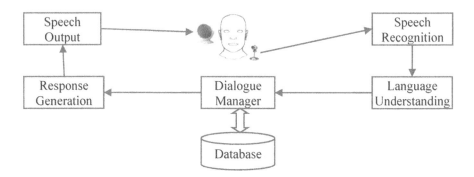

Fig. 1. Logical flow through SDS components

The origins of SDSs can be traced back to Artificial Intelligence (AI) research in the 1950s concerned with developing conversational interfaces. However, it is only within the last decade or so, with major advances in speech technology, that large-scale working systems have been developed and, in some cases, introduced into commercial environments. The integration of components into a working system is still a key issue [4]. The use of SDS within AmI can only worsen the former problems transforming them into a major challenge.

Since the first SDSs, developed under American and European research projects, issues on portability, extensibility, scalability and reusability still remaining as active research issues. Typically, these issues are addressed through architectures that allow the integration of reusable components. Nevertheless, there is still significant work required to build a new SDS. In practice, most of the work is due to large difficulties in the integration and reutilization of resources or components even when porting from a similar application domain.

Many implementations of dialogue managers perform input interpretation, output generation, and domain specific tasks. These tasks are usually domain dependent because their designs consider particular requirements of each domain. This approach may easily lead to situations in which the dialogue manager is a monolithic component. Monolithic components make it harder to build modular, distributed systems, and reusable components [5]. Some progresses can be seen in [6], [7], [8], [9], [10], [11].

3   Spoken Dialogue Systems at Home

In this paper, we consider a SDS as a computational entity that allows universal access to AmI. Under the major topic that is AmI, we are mostly interested in home environments as a particular example of other spaces such as the office, the car or public spaces. Devices throughout the house can be in constant contact with each other, making the AmI home responsive to its inhabitant's needs. These devices must be easily installed and personalized according to the user's wishes. The AmI home is also energy-conscious, able to intelligently manage the use of heat, light and other resources depending on the occupant's requirements.

The exponential drop in microprocessor cost over time has enabled appliance manufacturers to pack increasingly complex feature sets into appliances such as video recorders, refrigerators, washing machines, air conditioners, and more. As household appliances grow in complexity and sophistication, they become harder and harder to use, particularly because of theirs tiny display screens and limited keyboards. In fact, this can be seen in the growing amount of information on manuals and inscriptions or symbols on the appliance itself. SDSs provide an opportunity to handle this amount of technical information and help users to directly invoke tasks as a way to solve the interface problems in an effortless style.

According to [12] it is demonstrated that interactions with computers and new technologies are similar to real social relationships and to the navigation of real physical spaces. In this context, it is reasonable to disclose, for instance, that people will talk naturally with a microwave oven.

At the moment, it is unrealistic to consider the existence of an autonomous SDS embedded into each device, due to hardware limitations. While the coordination and collaboration between a set of autonomous SDS is, per se, another challenge.

The use of a SDS admits non-technical users, i.e., with no a priori knowledge of the environment. During the interaction, the SDS has to define the devices that have to be operated, and must inform the user about the tasks and options he/she has available.

The use of simulated characters is frequent in multimodal SDSs [13], [14]. Nevertheless, we believe that in an increasing number of cases, these characters will be replaced by real devices with intelligent behavior.

Dealing with isolated devices is a first important step, but we consider that the real challenge is to deal with tasks involving the collaboration between several devices. Within a very sophisticated home environment, "*turning on*" the light through a voice command is not an important feature, since the lights will be turned on just by the user's presence. However, it will be very useful to control the room's luminosity, when the order "*more light*" is given, as the SDS (automatically at day) may change the transparency of the window, built with electrochromic materials [15], instead of acting over an artificial source of light. The SDS might also take the initiative: asking if the user wants the lights on when leaving home.

We think that a mixed-initiative dialogue will emerge not only from the isolated devices but also from their collaboration. For instance, a sensor in a window sends an alarm "*open window*", simultaneously to the security system, to the sound system and to the control environment system (to turn off the room air conditioner). In this context, the SDS must be aware of any alarm, measure (i.e. temperature, wind) or command that may determine the behavior of any device (or peripheral system) in order to suggest actions (adding not predicted content to the discourse) or just to provide answers when asked.

4 Hybrid Approach

We use a hybrid approach, which was introduced by Filipe and Mamede in [16], for modeling the Domain Knowledge (DK), combining a top-down approach applied to acquire Global Knowledge (GK) and a bottom-up approach applied to acquire Local Knowledge (LK). Both approaches, applied at design time, converge to reach middle-level concepts directly associated to the device interface.

Fig. 2 shows a schema of hybrid approach, where X_n represents a generic device. This schema represents the DK that includes the GK and LK under a device-centered perspective.

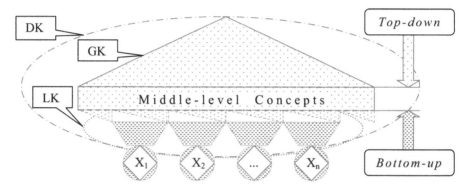

Fig. 2. Schema of the hybrid approach

The SDS deals with two kinds of knowledge (GK and LK), that are viewed at runtime as a single centralized knowledge model, which is managed by a broker.

Our proposal is not about plug and play environments but about an important issue around them: "*the agree on meaning*". The main question is: "*Is it possible for a SDS to deal with a device that was not previously known?*".

In this scenario, the SDS does not know which capabilities will be found on a device. In order to address this problem, the capabilities of the device must be described at knowledge or conceptual level [17]. Each device, provided with its own knowledge model, will assist the dialogue manager to understand its functional and structural features.

4.1 Local Knowledge Modeling (Bottom-Up)

The LK (local knowledge) is defined considering all the available devices (belonging to the surrounded environment) and is modeled using a bottom-up approach applied to adapt the native device interface.

The integration process of a device in a SDS is prepared building a set of three layers, which would potentially cover all the relevant device features:

(i) Communication layer: provides an elementary abstraction of the device expressing its primitive capabilities. For instance, if the device is a door we must be able, to open or to close the door and to ask about its state (opened/closed);

(ii) Adaptation layer: transforms the first layer into a more convenient interface, considering the device class. For instance, the adapter might transform labels into infrared command codes;

(iii) Operation layer: includes particular features of the device, bearing in mind, for instance, variations of the device commercial model. This layer is personalized to cover the SDS needs. For each capability of this layer, we must define a correspondent descriptor in device knowledge model.

Fig. 3 shows the layers involved in device adaptation. This adaptation allows the SDS to manipulate the device. However, this is not for exclusive use of the SDS because it can be also freely use by other concurrent systems.

Fig. 3. Device adaptation layers

According to the presented knowledge model, the knowledge about a device includes concept declarations, class declarations, and task declarations.

A local concept declaration can be about a completely new concept or is a forward declaration, in other words, is a reference to a concept globally (and previously) declared, that is a middle-level concept (see Fig. 2). Therefore, a forward concept declaration is realized indicating only a concept identifier.

When we are filling a task descriptor, using concept identifiers, if we do not know the identifier of a concept (because it is not previously declared as global) it must be declared as local in order to obtain the needed identifier.

4.2 Global Knowledge Modeling (Top-Down)

The GK (global knowledge) is modeled using a top-down approach. Knowledge modeling is a creative process. We can consider many ways to model the knowledge of a device or either of a domain. The best solution usually depends on the application that we have in mind and the extensions that we anticipate.

Before we start to represent a domain, we have to decide the use of the knowledge will have and, consequently, how detailed or general the model is going to be. We need to determine which representation would simplify the algorithms, be more intuitive, more extensible, and more maintainable.

Fig. 4 shows an example of a type hierarchy.

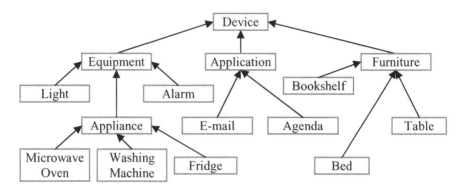

Fig. 4. Example of a type hierarchy

Following a top-down approach, we start modeling the global knowledge by defining its scope or domain, for instance, the home environment.

Therefore, we have to decide about the important classes and subclasses of devices that we should consider. Then, we have to identify which are the collections of concepts (middle-level concepts) associated with the selected device classes.

At the end, we can sketch a list of competency questions such as *"Does the model contain enough knowledge to cover the relevant SDS needs?"* or *"Do we have the needed detail level for a particular case study?"*.

5   Knowledge Model

In order to support the knowledge representation we propose a *Knowledge Model* composed by three independent components: a *Discourse Model*, a *Task Model*, and a *World Model*. These components encapsulate the descriptors of the entities that can be mentioned by the user.

A general class diagram of the Knowledge Model is presented in Fig. 5.

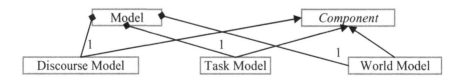

Fig. 5. Knowledge model main components

The design of this model was adapted from Unified Problem-solving Method Development Language (UPML) [18].

Fig. 6 presents an illustration of the knowledge that can be represented in the proposed knowledge model.

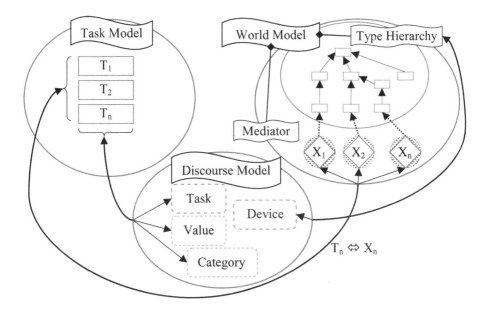

Fig. 6. Knowledge representation illustration

5.1 Discourse Model

The *Discourse Model* defines a conceptual support, grouping a set of concept definitions used to describe devices and the tasks they provide. A *Concept* is an atomic knowledge unit that has a unique identifier (*ID*). Concepts are not included for complex terms (word root or stem) unless necessary.

a) Concept Declaration
In order to guarantee the existence of the vocabulary needed to designate a concept the concept declarations include linguistic resources. This approach tries to reach the ubiquitous essence of natural language. Although, the coverage of handmade resources such as WordNet [19] in general is impressive, coverage problems remain for applications involving specific domains or multiple languages.

The vocabulary is organized by language, allowing a multi-lingual definition of concepts. Each concept declaration has its own linguistic resources included into a *Linguistic Descriptor*. For example, an item, such as "*kitchen light*", should be modeled as an instance of a "*light*", having the location "*kitchen*" without creating a new concept "*kitchen light*". A linguistic descriptor holds a list of terms, or more generically a list of *Multi-Word Unit* (MWU), referring linguistic variations associated with the concept, such as synonymous or acronyms. Each *Word* (or term), has a part of speech tag, such as a noun, a verb, an adjective or an adverb; a language tag, such as "pt", "br", "uk" or "us"; and some phonetic transcriptions. For instance, if the language tag of a word is "pt" its phonetic transcription is encoded using the Speech Assessment Methods Phonetic Alphabet (SAMPA) for European Portuguese [20].

Fig. 7 shows the relations between the classes involved in a concept declaration.

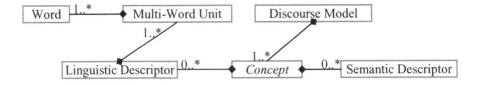

Fig. 7. Concept declaration

Optionally, each concept can also have semantic resources references represented by a *Semantic Descriptor*. A *Semantic Descriptor* has references to other external knowledge sources, for instance, an ontology [21] or a lexical database, such as WordNet. The knowledge sources references in the knowledge model must be unique.

The references to knowledge sources must be encoded using a data format allowing a unique identification of the concept in the knowledge source. The syntax of the knowledge source references do not need to be universal it is enough to keep the same syntax for a particular knowledge source. We recommend the use of a generic Uniform Resource Identifier (URI) format to encode the knowledge sources references. In particular, could be used a Uniform Resource Locator (URL) or a Uniform Resource Name (URN). For instance, the declaration of the concept *"device"* could have the reference *"URN:WordNet21:device:noun:1"* meaning: the concept *"device"* is linked to the first sense of the noun *"device"* in WordNet 2.1, where it is described by *"an instrumentality invented for a particular purpose"* (in WordNet 2.1 this noun has five senses).

The *Discourse Model* organizes the concepts by classes and subclasses as shown in Fig. 8. The most relevant classes are *Device* and *Task*. The other classes are used to represent task roles.

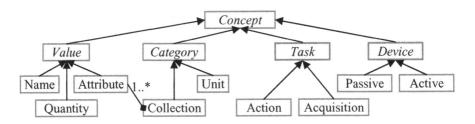

Fig. 8. Classes of concepts

b) Device and Task Representation

A concept, representing a *Task* name, can be an instance of two subclasses: *Action*, when the task can modify the device state; or *Acquisition*, when it never modifies the device state. A device name is a concept of the class *Name*. A device class can be an instance of two subclasses of *Device*: *Active*, when providing at least one action task; or *Passive*, when providing only acquisition tasks. For instance, an oven is an active device and a thermometer is a passive device. These device and task classifications are important to prevent task execution conflicts.

c) Representation of Task Roles
The representation of task roles involves two different aspects: role default *Value* and role *Category* used to establish the role range. The default value can be an instance of two subclasses: *Quantity*, to represent default numbers, for instance, zero; or *Attribute*, to represent default attributes, for instance, the black color. The role category can be an instance of two subclasses: *Collection*, when a role has a limited set of attributes, for instance, the rainbow colors; or *Unit*, when a role represents a physical dimension, for instance, the distance in meters, miles or inches.

5.2 Task Model

The *Task Model* represents the set of available tasks provided by existing devices. Typically, before performing a task, it is necessary to express the argument values or parameters that establish the execution conditions. It is mandatory for these values to be represented in the *Discourse Model*. The *Task Model* is also used to check the state of the world before and after a task execution.

a) State of the World
The state of the world is represented by the set of individual states of each device. The state of each device is obtained by calling the adequate acquisition tasks. For instance, when the task is "*switch on the light*", we have to check if the "*light*" is not already "*switched on*" and after the task execution, we have to check if the "*light*" has really been "*switched on*".

b) Task Descriptor
A *Task Descriptor* is used to represent a task in the *Task Model* and is composed by a unique identifier (*ID*), a name (*Acquisition, Action*), two optional lists (*In List, Out List*) of roles that describe in and out task parameters and two optional rules (*Final, Initial*) applicable to the state of the world.
    Fig. 9 shows the class diagram of the *Task Descriptor*.

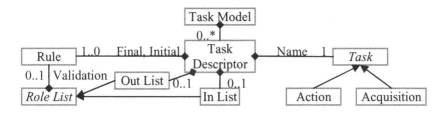

Fig. 9. Task representation

    The *Initial* rule is checked before the task call and must produce the logical value true before the task execution. The *Final* rule is checked after the task execution and must produce the logical value true when a successful task execution occurs. A rule is expressed using relational operators ('<', '>', '=', '<>', '<=', '>=') and logical operators ('Or', 'And'). When we need to specify a task argument value in a rule expression, the ID, of the concept that is the role *Name*, must be between square parenthesis ('[',']'). When we need to specify a concept, its ID must be between braces ('{','}'). For instance, we can write the rule "{1} > [2]" to denote that. Each task argument is represented in its *Task Descriptor* by a *Role* that is associated with other classes (see Fig. 10).

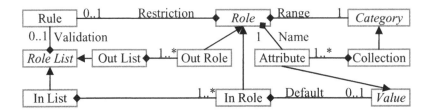

Fig. 10. Task role representation

A role describes the possible values that can be used to instantiate a task argument. An *In Role* describes the values that can be used as input parameters. An *Out Role* describes the values that can be used as output parameters. All roles have a name (*Attribute*) and a range (*Category*). Each role has an optional *Restriction* rule to check the parameters, for instance, the parameter must be positive. An *In Role* may have an optional *Default Value* (*Quantity*, *Attribute*).

When the *Default Value* is not present, the task parameter is mandatory. Task roles are organized in two role lists (*In Role* and *Out Role*) that have a *Validation* rule to check its parameters. The validation rule of an *In Role* list is evaluated before the task execution. The validation rule of an *Out Role* list is evaluated after the task execution.

5.3 World Model

The *World Model* represents the devices that are part of the world and integrates two components: a *Type Hierarchy* and a *Mediator*.

Figure 11 presents a class diagram of the World Model components.

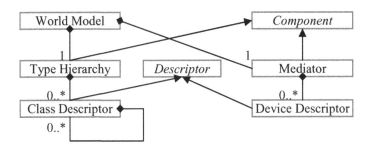

Fig. 11. World model components and descriptors

5.4 Coupling the Descriptors

The knowledge representation is essentially based on descriptors (*Task Descriptor*, *Device Descriptor*, *Class Descriptor*) that are coupled using bridges. After the definition of the needed concepts belonging to the *Discourse Model*, we can fill the descriptors without obligation to follow a predefined sequence. Then, we can introduce the instances of the *Bridge* class that associate task descriptors to device descriptors (*Bridge T*) and device descriptors to class descriptors (Bridge C).

Figure 12 shows the knowledge model descriptors and bridges involved in the knowledge representation.

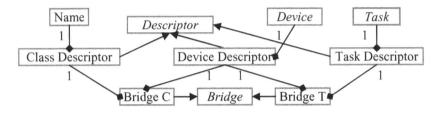

Fig. 12. Model descriptors and bridges

A device knowledge model has only one device descriptor that describes the device itself and must have at least one task descriptor. The broker's knowledge model does not include any device descriptors, because the device descriptors are added only at runtime.

6 Knowledge-Based Broker

The broker is a proposed SDS component that assumes two responsibilities: performs the domain knowledge management and maintains the predefined global knowledge. This component allows the customization of the principal SDS component, the dialogue manager, which should only be concerned with phenomena related to the user's dialogue. Fig. 13 shows the SDS reference architecture with a broker, where X_n is a generic device and A, B, C, and D are other components of the SDS.

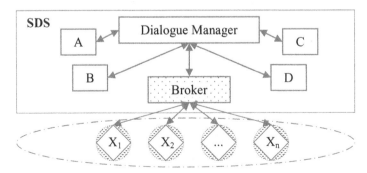

Fig. 13. Adaptation of the SDS to AmI

The main goal of the broker is to support the communication interoperability between the SDS and the devices in the pervasive application domain. The use of a broker allows successive improvements of the global knowledge by including concepts earlier defined as local.

The basic idea is that the global knowledge can evolve, considering that, the improvement of the global knowledge leads to a better and efficient domain model that is able to continue operational with the former devices.

6.1   Broker's Knowledge Integration Process

The goal of the Knowledge Integration Process (KIP) is to update automatically the DK (Domain Knowledge), integrating the GK (Global Knowledge) included in the broker and the LK (Local Knowledge) included in the domain's devices.

Two other processes compose the KIP: the device attachment process and the device detachment process.

a)   Similar Concepts

We consider that two concepts are similar when: its identifiers are equal, one of its semantic descriptors is equal or its linguistic descriptors are equal. In special cases, two concepts can be considered as similar by other convenient similarity criteria. In this context, two similar concepts cannot exist in the same *Discourse Model*.

At its starting point, KIP puts side by side the concept definitions in DK and the concept definitions in LK, which are going to be merged. KIP uses a Conversion Concept Table (CCT), linked to each *Device Descriptor*, to switch identifiers of similar concepts.

b)   Device Attachment Process

When a device is attached (activated), it searches for the broker component of the SDS. After establishing the initial communication, the broker leads the device attachment process following the next nine steps, in order to update its *Knowledge Model*:

(i) A new *Device Descriptor* is added to the broker's *Mediator*;

(ii) An empty CCT is linked to the new *Device Descriptor*;

(iii) The concepts in the device's *Discourse Model* fill the first column of the CCT;

(iv) Each concept in the first column of the CCT, with a similar concept in the broker's *Discourse Model*, is associated with its similar, filling the second column of the CCT;

(v) Other concepts in the first column of the CCT (without a similar concept in the broker's *Discourse Model*) are added to broker's *Discourse Model*;

(vi) Each new device *Task Descriptor* is added to the broker's *Task Model* and its concepts identifiers are replaced by the existing similar concepts identifiers, using the CCT;

(vii) Each *Class Descriptor* in the device's *Type Hierarchy* is integrated in the broker's *Type Hierarchy* and its concepts identifiers are replaced by the existing similar concepts identifiers, using the CCT;

(viii) The new *Device Descriptor* is associated with its *Class Descriptor* using the appropriate bridge (Bridge C);

(ix)The new *Device Descriptor* is associated with its *Task Descriptors* using the appropriate bridge (*Bridge T*).

c) Device Detachment Process

When the broker detects that a device has been detached (deactivated), it follows the next five steps, in order to update its Knowledge Model:

(i) *Task Descriptors* exclusively associated with the current (detached) *Device Descriptor* are removed from the broker's *Task Model*;

(ii)*Class Descriptors* exclusively associated (in a *Bridge* or in a CCT) with the current *Device Descriptor* are removed from the broker's *Type Hierarchy*;

(iii)Concepts that appear only in the CCT are removed from the broker's *Discourse Model*;

(iv)*Bridges* associated to current *Device Descriptor* are removed from the broker's Knowledge Model;

(v) Current *Device Descriptor* is removed from broker's *Mediator*.

6.2 Broker's Recognizer

This section describes the broker's recognizer service, proposed to recognize the domain's concepts from a natural language request.

The recognizer service receives a request and split its words into groups, trying to obtain a match against the linguistic descriptors in the broker's *Domain Model*. The words in the request are grouped from the left to the right. Each group of words is processed in several interactions.

First iteration uses a group of W words. Second iteration uses a candidate group of W-1 words, and so on. The maximum length of a group of words, represented in the *Domain Model*, determines the value of W.

When a group of words matches a MWU (multi-word unit) in a concept *Linguistic Descriptor*, the concept is recognized and these words are removed form the original request. When the candidate group as only one word this word is removed form the request. The recognition process ends when the request is empty.

An improved version of the recognizer service can also accept annotated natural language requests, including part of speech tags and specific phonetic transcriptions of some words, in order to solve potential linguistic ambiguities.

The list of recognized concepts can be directly used by the SDS *Dialogue Manager* to fill the list of pivot concepts indicated as input to the broker's advisor service. However, the *Dialogue Manager* can remove or add other concepts into the pivot concept list, according to its own dialogue strategies.

6.3 Broker's Advisor

This section describes the broker's advisor service, proposed to suggest the best task-device pairs to satisfy a request formalized in a list of domain's concepts. The ideas behind this service are based on the relative weight of each concept that figures in the request.

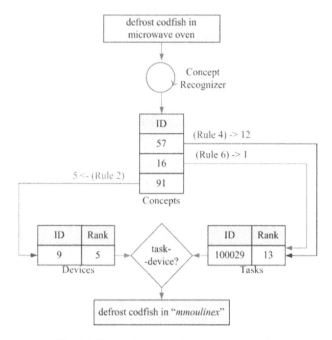

Fig. 14. Illustration about the recognizer service

Fig. 14 illustrates the processing of the request "*defrost codfish in microwave oven*" that combines the use of the recognizer service with the use of the advisor service.

In Fig. 14 example, the concept recognizer service identifies a list with three concepts: ID=57: "*defrost*", ID=16: "*codfish*", and ID=91: "*microwave oven*". In order to determine the best task-device pair, the advisor service applies its rules to each one of the pivot concepts. Rule 4 applied to concept, with the ID=57, adds 12 points to the rank of the task, with the ID=00029. Rule 6 applied to concept, with the ID=6, adds 1 point in the rank of the same task. Finally, Rule 2 applied to concept, with the ID=91, adds 5 points in the rank of the device, with the ID=9. The reference to the device class "*microwave oven*" becomes a reference to the device with the name "*mmoulinex*", because we have only this microwave oven represented in the *Domain Model*.

Two independent ranking, for tasks and devices, support the suggestion for the best task-device pairs. The ranking points are determined considering three heuristic values: *nABase*, *nTBase*, and *nTUnit*. The *nABase* value is determined by the maximum height of the domain model type hierarchy plus (1) one. The *nTBase* value is determined by the maximum number of task roles (arguments) plus (1) one. The *nTUnit* value is constant and equal to 3 (three) that are the number of ways to reference a task role (by *name*, *range*, or *value*).

The advisor service uses as input a list of pivot concepts. The pivot concepts references, about tasks and devices, are converted following the next six rules into points that are credited to the respective device or task rank.

The rank of a device is modified according to the rules:

(i) If the pivot concept refers a device name, the value $nABase*2$ is credited in the respective device rank;

(ii) If the pivot concept refers a device class name, the value $nABase$ is credited in the respective device rank;

(iii) If the pivot concept refers a device super-class name, the value $nABase-n$ is credited in the respective device rank, where n is determined by the number of classes (in the *Type Hierarchy*), between the device class and the referred super-class.

The rank of a task is modified according to the rules:

(iv)If the pivot concept refers a task name, the value $nTBase*nTUnit$ is credited in the respective task rank;

(v)If the pivot concept refers a task role name or a task role range, the value $nTUnit/2$ is credited in the respective task rank;

(vi)If the pivot concept refers a task parameter, the value $nTUnit/3$ is credited in the respective task rank.

Finally, the task-device pairs are composed selecting the tasks with the best rank and the devices, which provide the tasks, also with the best rank.

7 Experimental Evaluation

Our work is based on an environment simulator in which we are testing the proposed approach considering a set of common home devices, described in Table 1, that are normally present in the kitchen.

Table 1. Devices in the environment simulator

Device Name	# (Concept) (Task) (Argument)	# (Adjective) (Noun) (Verb) => (Term)
Air Conditioner	(63) (24) (25)	(8) (44) (8) => (63)
Freezer	(96) (13) (20)	(19) (79) (3) => (106)
Fryer	(92) (23) (36)	(18) (64) (10) => (96)
Light Source	(62) (20) (21)	(9) (39) (10) => (61)
Microwave Oven	(167) (26) (44)	(17) (117) (18) => (159)
Kitchen Table	(48) (13) (17)	(10) (28) (4) => (44)
Water Faucet	(63) (24) (25)	(8) (44) (8) => (63)
Window	(44) (13) (17)	(8) (26) (4) => (41)
Window Blind	(65) (22) (23)	(10) (39) (10) => (62)
Total	**(700) (178) (228)**	**(107) (480) (75) => (695)**

The 9 (nine) devices are using a total of 700 concepts. Initially the GK (that is equal to DK at design time) is using 261 concepts.

After the attachment of all devices, DK retains 360 concepts (at runtime).

The knowledge integration rate is $360/700*100 = 51\%$.

Each one of the knowledge models for devices and broker is supported by a relational database with 19 (nineteen) tables.

Fig. 15 shows a screenshot of the environment simulator, developed originally for Portuguese users. On the bottom of the screen, we can see the electrochromatic Table device simulator.

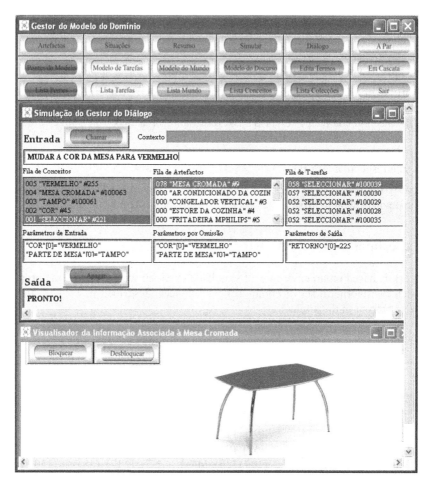

Fig. 15. Screenshot of the environment simulator

The environment simulator allows the debugging of KIP and the simulation of the interaction made by the dialogue manager. We can attach and detach devices, do requests of tasks, obtain the answers and observe the devices behavior. We can also consult and print data about the several knowledge models and about the task execution progress.

Figure 16 shows the screen of the microwave oven simulator after the execution of the request: "*defrosting carrots*". This picture shows the automatically select power (300 watts – see symbol) and duration (8 minutes) of the defrosting process.

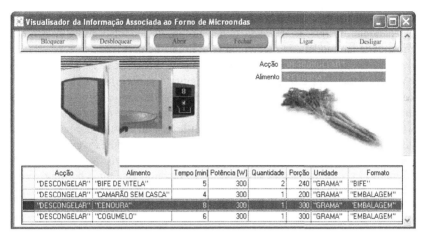

Fig. 16. Screenshot of the microwave oven simulator

Fig. 17 shows the screen of the freezer simulator after the execution of the request: "*asking the amount of carrots*". Table in the picture shows the selected type of food. However, the domain simulator also returns the answer "*1 package with 300 g*" in a text window.

We can also execute requests that evolve relational operators, for instance: "*asking the type of food with amount less than five*".

Fig. 17. Screenshot of the freezer simulator

The "*carrot*" concept is shared by the microwave oven and by the freezer. We have only one declaration of the "*carrot*" concept in the broker's knowledge model.

8 Discussion

The growth in pervasive computing will require standards in device communication interoperability. These devices must be able to interact and share resources with other existing devices and any future devices across the network.

Our proposal tries do improved the flexibility of the SDSs architectures allowing the independent design of devices. Other proposals are also using a centralized domain knowledge model complemented with linguistic parts [22].

However, our knowledge model, supported by the broker, can be unfilled at design time. We are proposing KIP (knowledge integration process) to update, at runtime, this knowledge model dealing from completely new devices of previously unknown classes and trying to achieve "*Strong PnP*". In addition, we propose the recognizer and advisor services to provide a broker's high-level and easy to use small interface, instead of a conventional interface with several remote procedures/methods.

Current technologies require human interventions to solve environment reconfiguration problems. We believe that these technologies must be improved with more human like ways of interaction that should include spoken natural language support.

9   Concluding Remarks and Future Work

This paper describes our research in enhance everyday devices to be dynamically managed by a SDS. Essentially, we are dealing with a reconfiguration problem that can be seen also as a portability issue [23].

We have described an approach to deal with communication interoperability between a SDS and a set of heterogeneous devices within AmI vision. We have presented a knowledge-based broker component to adapt the SDS to the environment, which provides the recognizer and advisor services to simplify and support the dialogue manager needs.

We have also present a broker's knowledge integration process, trying to reach the ubiquitous essence of natural language, because the coverage of handmade lexical resources is limited, coverage problems remain for applications involving specific domains or involving multiple languages.

The hybrid knowledge modeling approach, supported in the field by a knowledge-based broker, is a significant contribution to improve the flexibility, and simultaneously the robustness, of the SDS being developed in our lab.

The presented ideas have been applied, with success, in a set of devices that represents a home environment.

As future work, we expect to explore, more deeply, the knowledge integration perspective working with simulated and real devices. In order to include real devices we expect to extend the *Device Descriptor* to support specific data about the different kinds of device access network protocols.

We believe that in the near future, SDSs are not only useful but also easy to use and accommodating, such that users will prefer them over alternative means of managing their needs.

Acknowledgments. This paper was partially supported by project POSI/PLP/41319/2001.

References

1. K. Ducatel, M. Bogdanowicz, F. Scapolo, J. Leijten, and J-C. Burgelman: Scenarios for Ambient Intelligence in 2010. ISTAG 2001. IPTSSeville (Institute for Prospective Technological Studies) (2001)
2. Weiser, M.: The Computer for the Twenty-First Century. Scientific American (1991)
3. Henricksen, K., Indulska, J., Rakotonirainy, A.: Infrastructure for Pervasive Computing: Challenges. Workshop on Pervasive Computing Informatik 01, Viena (2001)
4. McTear, M.: Spoken Dialogue Technology: Enabling the Conversational Interface. ACM Computing Surveys, Vol. 34 (2002)
5. O'Neill, I. and McTear, M.: Object-Oriented Modelling of Spoken Language Dialogue Systems. Natural Language Engineering 6, Cambridge University Press, Cambridge (2000)
6. Bohus, D. and Rudnicky, A.: RavenClaw: Dialog Management Using Hierarchical Task Decomposition and an Expectation Agenda. Eurospeech 2003, Geneva, Switzerland (2003)
7. O'Neill, I., Hanna, P., Liu, X. and McTear, M.: An Object-Oriented Dialogue Manager. Eurospeech 2003, Geneva, Switzerland (2003)
8. Pakucs, B.: Towards Dynamic Multi-Domain Dialogue Processing. Eurospeech 2003, Geneva, Switzerland (2003)
9. Polifroni, J. and Chung, G.: Promoting Portability in Dialogue Management. ICSLP 2002, Denver, Colorado, USA (2003)
10. Neto, J., Mamede, N., Cassaca, R., Oliveira, L.: The Development of a Multi-purpose Spoken Dialogue System. Eurospeech 2003, Geneva, Switzerland (2003)
11. Turunen, M., Hakulinen, J.: JASPIS^2 – An Architecture for Supporting Distributed Spoken Dialogues. Eurospeech 2003, Geneva, Switzerland (2003)
12. Reeves, B., Nass, C.: The Media Equation: How People Treat Computers, Television and New Media Like Real People and Places. Cambridge, Mass: CUPress (1996)
13. Gustafson, J., Lindberg, N., Lundeberg, M.: The August Spoken Dialogue System. Eurospeech 1999 (1999)
14. Gustafson, J., Bell, L., Beskow, J., Boye, J., Carlson, R., Edlund, J., Granström, B., House, D., Wirén, M.: AdApt - A Multimodal Conversational Dialogue System. ICSLP 2000, (2) 134-137, Beijing, China (2000)
15. Wigginton, M.: Glass in Architecture. Phaidon Press Ltd, London (1996)
16. Filipe, P., Mamede, N.: Towards Ubiquitous Task Management. Interspeech 2004, Jeju Island, Korea (2004)
17. Newell, A.: The knowledge level. Artificial Intelligence, 18(1) (1982)
18. Fensel, D.; Benjamins, V.: Motta, E.; Wielinga, B.: UPML: A Framework for Knowledge System Reuse, IJCAI 1999 (1999)
19. Fellbaum, C., (editor): WordNet: An Electronic Lexical Database. MIT Press (1998)
20. SAMPA (Speech Assessment Methods Phonetic Alphabet), Spoken Language Systems Lab (L2F), http://www.l2f.inesc-id.pt/resources/sampa/sampa.html
21. Gruber, T.: Toward Principles for the Design of Ontologies Used for Knowledge Sharing. International Workshop on Formal Ontology, Padova, Italy (1992)
22. Montoro, G., Alamán, X., Haya, P.: A Plug and Play Spoken Dialogue Interface for Smart Environments. CICLing 2004: 360-370 (2004)
23. Zue, V., Glass J.: Conversational Interfaces: Advances and Challenges. IEEE (2000)

Setup Consistent Visual Textures for Haptic Surfaces in a Virtual Reality World

Wanhua Hu, Tao Lin, Kazuo Sakai, Atsumi Imamiya, and Masaki Omata

Graduate School, University of Yamanashi
Takeda 4-3-11, Kofu, Yamanashi Prefecture, 400-8511, Japan
g04dh102@ccn.yamanashi.ac.jp, lintao@hci.media.yamanashi.ac.jp,
k-sakai@yamanashi.ac.jp, imamiya@yamanashi.ac.jp,
omata@hci.media.yamanashi.ac.jp

Abstract. In the real world, interactions with objects are typically multimodal, involving two or more sensory modalities. To simulate the real world in virtual environments, it is thus important to provide multisensory input. Haptics are increasingly being employed as an input channel. However, different modal interfaces are artificially created in a virtual reality world. Does the visual information we provide about surfaces need to be consistent with their haptic representation? In this paper, we present the results of a haptic texture cognition experiment in which subjects judged the haptic size of regular dots. We found that visual texture information that was consistent with haptic information lead to a higher percentage of correct answers and shorter judging times. Furthermore, we found that participants relied on visual information as judgments became more difficult, even though they were asked to make decisions using haptic stimuli only.

Keywords: multimodal human-computer interfaces, virtual reality, haptics, textured surfaces.

1 Background

Universal access in the context of human-computer interaction refers to the conscious and systematic effort to practically apply principles, methods, and tools of universal design in order to develop high-quality user interfaces, accessible and usable by a diverse user population with different abilities, skills, requirements, and preferences, in a variety of contexts of use and through a variety of different technologies [19]. Universal access implies the accessibility and usability of information by anyone, anywhere, anytime [20]. It is obvious that no single interaction mode will satisfy all potential users or computer-mediated human activities. Thus, multimodality, the simultaneous or alternate use of several modalities, advances the implementation of universal accessibility.

Also, in the real world, most of our interactions with objects are multimodal, involving two or more sensory modalities. In a virtual human–computer interface environment, which is designed to simulate the real world, it is thus important to

C. Stephanidis and M. Pieper (Eds.): ERCIM UI4ALL Ws 2006, LNCS 4397, pp. 78–87, 2007.

provide multisensory input. Durlach and Mavor [3] have stated that a virtual environment with multisensory input would likely enhance the realism of the experience and be perceived as more realistic than a unisensory one, even if the unisensory environment employed more advanced rendering. Lederman et al. [7] found that participants were more confident of their judgments in a bisensory environment than a unisensory one.

Among multimodal interfaces, haptic human–computer interaction is considered to be a promising approach, with its potential for bidirectional stimuli, as compared with unidirectional visual and auditory interfaces. More and more haptic devices have been developed [2] [13] [14], and their usefulness has been demonstrated [13] [1]. Studies on haptic related multimodal interfaces have mainly focused on the relative contributions of the different modalities [21] [15] [22]. Wang and MacKenzie [21] investigated the surrounding role of haptic and visual information on object manipulation in a visual environment. They found that contextual haptic constraints— for example, a physical table surface—dramatically increased object manipulation speed compared to free space, but slightly reduced spatial accuracy. Contextual visual constraints, such as the presence of a checkerboard, actually impaired object manipulation speed and accuracy. Poling et al. [15] investigated the role of multisensory visual–haptic feedback in the perception of surface roughness. Their results suggested that the threshold for distinguishing roughness was determined by haptic input at low surface amplitudes, and by visual input at high surface amplitudes. At intermediate amplitudes, it appeared that observers were able to combine visual and haptic information to achieve greater sensitivity than with either modality alone. Weisenberger and Poling [22] examined the ability of observers to use information from three sensory modalities (visual, auditory, and haptic) in a virtual texture discrimination task. Results indicated better performance for two- and three-modality conditions for some stimuli but not for others, suggesting that the interactions of haptic, auditory, and visual inputs are complex and dependent on the specifics of the stimulus condition.

In a virtual world with multimodal interfaces, each modality is artificially created. When we deploy haptic interfaces, do we need to consider how to setup proper visual information for haptic surfaces? Or, does textures' visual setup influence perception of haptic texture? Previous studies [9] [10] [11] in our laboratory have found color, an important component of visual information, influences haptic perception and recognition memory for haptic textured surfaces and color presentation mode affects human haptic memory, as well. Our subsequent studies [5] [4] have found that haptic textured surfaces are easier to perceive when they are visually presented as lighter, and that it is better to use different visual setups to indicate different rough haptic surfaces and the same visual setup to indicate the same rough haptic surfaces.

Surface texture is considered fundamental for the accurate identification of an object [6]. For visual and haptic multimodal interfaces, a surface has both visual and haptic texture attributes. Do we need to create consistent visual information according to the surface's haptic texture attributes? To answer the question, we conducted a haptic texture cognition experiment in which subjects judged the size of regular dots, which are spheres in shape.

2   Experiment Method

2.1   Participants

Twenty full-time students, 11 female and 9 male, ranging in age from 21-35, took part in the experiment. All participants had normal or corrected to normal vision and reported normal tactile function.

2.2   Apparatus and Stimuli

The hardware setup for our rendering is shown in Figure 1. It was composed of a PHANToM Premium EW 6-degree-of-freedom force feedback device (SenseAble Technologies), a computer monitor for visual representation (Reachin Technologies AB), a dual–Pentium III computer operating on a Windows 2000 Professional platform, and a set of headphones. The PHANToM Premium EW has a workspace of 19.5 cm x 27.0 cm x 37.5 cm. The Reachin 3.0 API (Reachin Technologies AB) [16] for PHANToM was used to program the haptic experimental environment. The programming languages used for creating the three-dimensional experimental environment were C++ (Borland C++ Builder 5.0), VRML (The Virtual Reality Modeling Language), and Python. Through PHANToM, participants can hold a stylus or put their finger into a "thumb stall" to explore a virtual haptic textured surface under a half-mirror that reflects the monitor. In our study, the thumb stall was used.

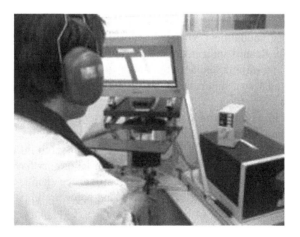

Fig. 1. The hardware setup for the virtual roughness rendering

Stimuli used in the experiment were surfaces consisting of matrices of regular dots with different radii (Figure 2). Each surface had two layers: The lower matrix layer was created with Reachin 3.0 API with visual and haptic attributes. The upper matrix layer, 1.5 mm above the lower layer, was programmed with VRML and had visual attributes only. The upper layer was totally opaque, so that participants could only see the upper layer but could touch the lower layer. Previous studies [11] [5] [4] from our

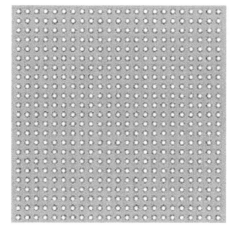

Fig. 2. Sample matrix of regular dots

laboratory have indicated that yellow or lighter surfaces permit better perception, so an RGB (Red, Green, and Blue) value of (1, 1, 0.6) was used in the experiment.

2.3 Procedure

We created nine combinations of surfaces with dot radii of 0.8 mm, 1 mm, and 1.2 mm in the lower layer and in the upper layer: $S_{H0.8V0.8}$ (a surface with haptic dot radius 0.8 mm and visual dot radius 0.8 mm), $S_{H0.8V1}$, $S_{H0.8V1.2}$, $S_{H1V0.8}$, S_{H1V1}, $S_{H1V1.2}$, $S_{H1.2V0.8}$, $S_{H1.2V1}$, and $S_{H1.2V1.2}$. The distance between dots was 5 mm in both layers. Participants were presented with the interface of two textured surfaces with a left–right layout (that a left-right haptic textured surface layout is recommended when using PHANToM is a result of our previous research [5] [4]) and asked which one they perceived, by haptics only, as having the larger size or if they were the same. Participants' judgments, as well as judging times, were recorded. The selected radii were chosen to make the task neither too easy nor too difficult so that the influence of visual texture on haptic perception would be most manifest. If the left–right order of the two textured surfaces is ignored, there were 45 ($2C_9+9$) pairs for participants to judge. Usually, a participant could complete these 45 comparisons in 20 minutes, including initial time for training. The sequence of the 45 pairs of textured surfaces and left–right order of a pair were randomly presented.

3   Results and Conclusions

We scored a participant's judgment as correct when his answer was consistent with the haptic size of the dots in a pair. In other words, we scored a participant's judgment as correct when the left surface's haptic size of the dots was larger than that of the right surface's, his answer was also the left; or when the left surface's haptic size of the dots was the same as that of the right surface's, his choice was also they were the

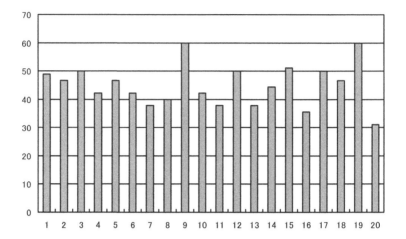

Fig. 3. Percentage of correct answers (vertical axis) for participants (horizontal axis)

same size; or when the left surface's haptic size of the dots was smaller than that of the right surface's, his answer was also the right. Overall, 45.1% of responses were correct (range: 31.1-60%, Figure 3).

We calculated perceived size score for $S_{H0.8}$ (including $S_{H0.8V0.8}$, $S_{H0.8V1}$, and $S_{H0.8V1.2}$), S_{H1} (including $S_{H1V0.8}$, S_{H1V1}, and $S_{H1V1.2}$), and $S_{H1.2}$ (including $S_{H1.2V0.8}$, $S_{H1.2V1}$, and $S_{H1.2V1.2}$) by adding 1 point to their perceived size score if they were perceived as larger and 0.5 point to each of a pair if they were perceived as the same size (a similar way as in papers [5] [4]). The perceived size score tells us whether participants can really distinguish between textures or not. Figures 4 and 5 show that textured surfaces with dot of radii of 0.8 mm, 1 mm, and 1.2 mm were distinguishable ($F = 36.37 > F_{0.01}(2, 57) = 5.02$).

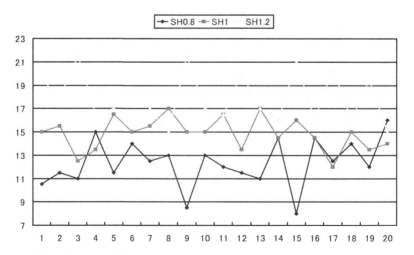

Fig. 4. Perceived size score (vertical axis) for participants (horizontal axis)

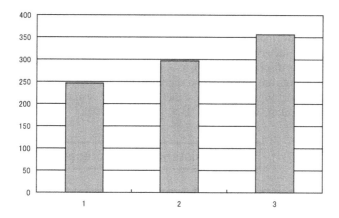

Fig. 5. Total perceived size score (vertical axis) for $S_{H0.8}$ (*1*), S_{H1} (*2*), and $S_{H1.2}$ (*3*)

We draw the following four conclusions from our experiment:

(1) The surface's visual texture influences haptic texture perception, even if participants were asked to make their judgments by their haptic feeling only.

Figure 6 shows perceived size scores for the different surfaces. We can see that visual texture influences haptic texture perception, even when participants were asked to make their judgments by their haptic feeling only. If there were no influence of surface's visual texture, $S_{H0.8V0.8}$, $S_{H0.8V1}$, and $S_{H0.8V1.2}$ (1-3) should have the same score, as should $S_{H1V0.8}$, S_{H1V1}, and $S_{H1V1.2}$ (4-6), and $S_{H1.2V0.8}$, $S_{H1.2V1}$, and $S_{H1.2V1.2}$ (7-9). However, ANOVA analysis indicates that perceived size scores are quite different for $S_{H0.8}$ (F = 11.49 > $F_{0.01}$ (3, 57) = 5.02), S_{H1} (F = 11.93), and $S_{H1.2}$ (F = 26.05). It can also been seen that, because the influences of visual textures, the score for $S_{H0.8V1}$ (2) was larger than $S_{H1V0.8}$ (4), and the score for $S_{H0.8V1.2}$ (3) was larger than $S_{H1V0.8}$ (4) and S_{H1V1} (5), etc.

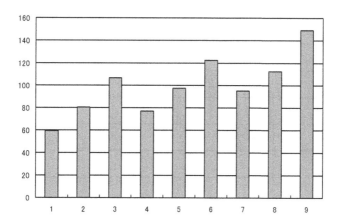

Fig. 6. Perceived size score (vertical axis) for $S_{H0.8V0.8}$ (*1*), $S_{H0.8V1}$ (*2*), $S_{H0.8V1.2}$ (*3*), $S_{H1V0.8}$ (*4*), S_{H1V1} (*5*), $S_{H1V1.2}$ (*6*), $S_{H1.2V0.8}$ (*7*), $S_{H1.2V1}$ (*8*), and $S_{H1.2V1.2}$ (*9*)

(2) Consistent visual texture information can lead to more correct answers.

Visual texture information is consistent with haptic information when, for each modality, the same surface has larger dots or the two surfaces are the same. When visual information is discrepant, the visual and haptic comparisons do not agree (i.e., the surface whose dots are larger in one modality has smaller or the same size dots in the other modality). Figure 7 shows that consistent visual texture information produces more correct answers (t = 20.03 > $t_{0.01}$ (19) = 7.40).

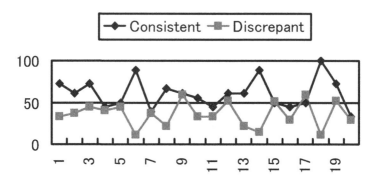

Fig. 7. Comparison of consistent or discrepant visual texture for participants (horizontal axis) and percentage of correct answers (vertical axis)

(3) Consistent visual texture information can lead to shorter judging time.

Figure 7 shows that consistent texture information allowed participants to spend less time (t = 1.79 > $t_{0.05}$ (19) = 1.73) judging dots size. This may be because participants had more confidence and less hesitation time was spent when the visual information supported their haptic perceptions.

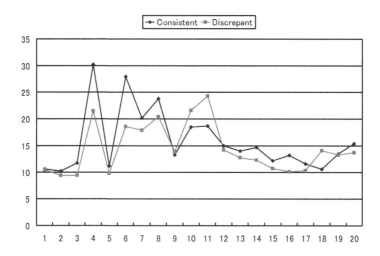

Fig. 8. Comparison of consistent or discrepant visual texture for participants (horizontal axis) and mean judging time (seconds, vertical axis)

(4) Participants depend more on visual information when judgments were harder.

We created two number sequences: one for the visual texture of surfaces and the other for the judgments of participants. For the visual texture number sequence, we scored a trial as 0 if the left surface's dot radius is smaller than the right surface's, 0.5 if they have the same size, or 1 if the left surface's dot radius is larger than the right surface's. For the judgments of participants number sequence, we scored a trial as 0 if the participant judged the right surface dots as larger, 0.5 if they were judged to be the same size, or 1 if the left surface dots were judged as larger, and the according number value in the number sequence is the mean value of the 20 participants' scores.

We can then find to what extent participants depended on their visual texture information by calculating the correlation coefficient of the two number sequences. A correlation coefficient of 1 would mean that participants make their judgments totally depending on visual information.

There were three kinds of visual radius, 0.8 mm, 1 mm, and 1.2 mm, in the experiments. For all trials, the visual radius differences were 0, 0.2, or 0.4 mm. Table 1 shows the mean percentage of correct answers and correlation coefficients for radius differences 0, 0.2, and 0.4 mm. It indicates that the smaller the difference in radius, the more difficult it was for participants to answer correctly and the more they depended on visual information.

Table 1. Mean percentage of correct answers and visual correlation coefficient for radius difference 0, 0.2, and 0.4 mm

Radius difference	Mean percentage of correct answers	Correlation coefficient
0 mm	35%	0.994
0.2 mm	49.2%	0.745
0.4 mm	61.1%	0.669

4 Discussion and Future Work

Spence et al. [18] gave a neural substrate explanation for multisensory perception by referring to the concept of *multisensory binding*, by which the brain uses spatiotemporal coincidence to determine which sensory stimuli are bound together to create a multimodal perceptual object. In their explanation, an observer considers stimulation from different sensory modalities to refer to the same perceptual event if they occur in close spatial and temporal proximity. The cells in the brain involved in multisensory integration typically have fairly broad temporal windows, which permit the integration of stimuli that are not exactly simultaneous. This latitude of the temporal windows is necessary because of the differing neural conduction rates for stimuli arriving via different sensory modalities.

About whether observers can ignore sensory input, some researchers [17] argued that subjects might choose either to ignore or to combine inputs from any set of modalities in making perceptual judgments. The *modality appropriateness* hypothesis [8] suggest that in any particular sensing situation, the modality whose capabilities are best suited to the task will be weighted most heavily in making a perceptual judgment. While others [12] found that it was difficult to ignore additional sensory input even when it was unnecessary or misleading with an example that an observer is presented with one speech sound while simultaneously viewing a talker on a TV monitor speaking a different speech sound. The typical observer response is a fusion of the two stimuli even when the observer is told the nature of the conflict.

The present study examined whether the presence of additional sensory inputs changed the nature of other percept with a haptic texture perception experiment, and our conclusions seem to support the later opinion. Experiment parameters with dots radii of 0.8 mm, 1 mm, and 1.2 mm and dot distance 5 mm were purposely selected by our preparatory experiments. They were chosen to make the task neither too easy nor too difficult. If the task is too easy, participants can make right judgments easily with their haptic perception only, and the influence of visual texture on haptic perception will not be manifest. If it is too difficult, participants completely can not make judgments by their haptic perception, so haptic texture stimuli in the experiments will lose their meaning. Final results showed proper task difficulty with overall percentage of correct answers of 45.1% and distinguishableness of haptic surfaces with dot of radii of 0.8 mm, 1 mm, and 1.2 mm. We think our findings are important in creating visual and haptic multimodal human–computer interfaces, because in a virtual reality world all modalities can be independently created, and it has to be made clear how different modal interfaces interact, and how different factors in different modal interfaces interact, especially how different modal textures, fundamental for the accurate identification of an object, interact.

The present study was under a visual-haptic environment, and audio sensory, another main information input channel for us, is not considered. Further work may be done with visual, auditory and haptic sensory inputs to find more design guidelines for multimodal interfaces.

References

[1] Basdogan, C., De, S., Kim, J., Muniyandi, M., Kim, H., Srinivasan, M.A.: Haptics in minimally invasive surgical simulation and training. Special issue on Haptic Rendering-Beyond Visual Computing, IEEE Computer Graphics and Applications, 24(2) (2004) 56-64

[2] Campbell, C., Zhai, S., May, K., Maglio, K.: What you feel must be what you see: adding tactile feedback to the TrackPoint. In: Proc. INTERACT '99 of Human-Computer Interaction. Edinburgh, UK (1999) 383-390

[3] Durlach, N.I., Mavor, A.S.: Virtual Reality: scientific and technological challenges. National Academy Press, Washington, D.C. (1994)

[4] Hu, W., Lin, T., Sakai, K., Imamiya, A., Omata, M.: Visual and Haptic Interaction on Virtual Haptic Roughness Perception with Different Lightness. In: Proc. IASTED-HCI 2005. Phoenix, USA (2005) 126-131

[5] Hu, W., Sakai, K., Imamiya, A., Omata, M., Lin, T.: Lightness Influence on Virtual Haptic Roughness Perception. Information Technology Letters, Vol. 4 (2005) 249-252

[6] Katz, D.: The world of touch. (Translated by Krueger LE) Erlbaum, Hillsdale, NJ, USA (1989)

[7] Lederman, S.J., Klatzky, R.L., Hamilton, C. Morgan, T.: Integrating Multimodal Information about Surface Texture via a Probe: Relative contributions of haptic and touch produced sound sources. In: Proc. 10th Annual meeting of Haptic Interfaces for Teleoperator and Virtual Environment Systems, Satellite meeting of the Annual IEEE VR '02 meeting (2002) 97-104

[8] Lederman, S.J., Martin, A., Tong, C., Klatzky, R.: Relative performance using haptic and/or touch-produced auditory cues in a remote texture identification task. In: Proc. IEEE Haptics Symposium. Los Angeles, CA (2003) 151-158

[9] Luo, Z., Imamiya, A.: Color presentation mode affects human haptic memory for rough surfaces. In: Proc. the 2003 IEEE International Conference on Information Reuse and Integration (IRI2003). Las Vegas, Nevada, USA (2003) 345-353

[10] Luo, Z., Imamiya, A.: Do colors affect our recognition memory for haptic rough surfaces? In: Proc. The International Workshop on Interactive Visualization and Interaction Technologies. Krokow, Poland (2004) 897-904

[11] Luo, Z., Imamiya, A.: How do colors influence the haptic perception of textured surfaces? Universal Access in the Information Society (UAIS), Special Issue "Multimodality: a Step towards Universal Access", 2(2) (2003) 160-172

[12] McGurk, H., MacDonald, J.: Hearing lips and seeing voices. Nature, 264 (1976) 746-748

[13] Murayama, J., Luo, Y., Akahane, K., Hasegawa, S., Sato, M.: A haptic interface for two-handed 6DOF manipulation-SPIDAR-G&G system. IEICE Trans. on Information and Systems, E87- D (6) (2004) 1415-1421

[14] Nam, C.S., Di, J., Borsodi, L.W., Mackay, W.: A Haptic Thermal Interface: Towards Effective Multimodal User Interface Systems. In: Proc. IASTED-HCI 2005. Phoenix, AZ, USA (2005) 13-18

[15] Poling, G.L., Weisenberger, J.M., Kerwin, T.: The Role of Multisensory Feedback in Haptic Surface Perception. In: haptics of 11th Symposium on Haptic Interfaces for Virtual Environment and Teleoperator Systems (HAPTICS'03) (2003) 187-194

[16] Reachin API 3.0 programmer's guide. Reachin Technologies AB, Sweden (1998-2001)

[17] Rock, I., Victor, J.: Vision and touch: An experimentally created conflict between the two senses. Science, 143 (1964) 594-596

[18] Spence, C., Baddeley, R., Zampini, M., James, R., Shore, D.I.: Multisensory temporal order judgments: when two locations better than one. Percept Psychophys., 65 (2003) 318-328

[19] Stephanidis, C. (ed) (2001): User Interfaces for All-Concepts, Methods and Tools. Lawrence Erlbaum Associates, Mahwah

[20] Stephanidis, C. (2001). IS4ALL: promoting universal design in healthcare telematics. In: Stephanidis, C. (ed.): Universal Access in HCI: Towards an Information Society for All, vol 3. Lawrence Erlbaum Association, London (2001) 50-54

[21] Wang, Y., MacKenzie, C.L.: The role of contextual haptic and visual constraints on object manipulation in virtual environments. In: Proc. CHI 2000. The Hague, The Netherlands (2000) 532-539

[22] Weisenberger, J.M., Poling, G.L.: Multisensory Roughness Perception of Virtual Surfaces: Effects of Correlated Cues. In: haptics of 12th International Symposium on Haptic Interfaces for Virtual Environment and Teleoperator Systems (HAPTICS'04) (2004) 161-168

Alice Through the Inter-face
Electronic Mirrors as Human-Computer-Interface

Daniel Michelis[1,2] and Florian Resatsch[1]

[1] Institute for Media and Communications Management, University of St. Gallen
[2] Institute of Electronic Business, University of the Art Berlin
{michelis,resatsch}@ieb.net

Abstract. This article describes the multi-media installation Magical Mirrors with which the tradition of the mirror, as an interface between real and virtual worlds is carried over into the world of digital mediums. Long before the development of the computer, mirrors were used as a medium for visual simulation and with them virtual worlds have already been simulated for hundreds of years. The ability to capture the real world and reflect it back in a true to life or even distorted way was for a long time the sole privilege of the mirror. Today this ability is emulated via digital media technologies, such as the installation Magical Mirrors.

1 Introduction

"I know I should have to get through the Looking-glass again--back into the old room--and there'd be an end of all my adventures!", Alice said, "I'm NOT going in again yet."

(Alice through the Looking-Glass, Lewis Carroll, 1872)

Mirrors exert an almost magical fascination on the viewer. Ones own image and the world "behind" the mirror have for hundreds of years given rise to intense debate and wild speculations. Children, teenagers, and adults all observe their mirror image with great curiosity and experience themselves and their surroundings from new perspectives.

This paper describes the multi-media installation MAGICAL MIRRORS with which the tradition of the mirror not only as a metaphor but as natural Human-Computer-Interface, is carried over into the world of digital mediums. The installation follows in the tradition of the magical mirror found in palaces or amusement parks. Like their predecessors they awaken the curiosity of the viewer and invite him or her on a trip into virtual worlds.

2 Remediation Theory

The theoretical foundation for the installation MAGICAL MIRRORS presents the concept of remediation by Jay David Bolter and Richard Grusin [3], who define

C. Stephanidis and M. Pieper (Eds.): ERCIM UI4ALL Ws 2006, LNCS 4397, pp. 88–98, 2007.
© Springer-Verlag Berlin Heidelberg 2007

remediation as the representation of a prior medium in a newer one. Remediation is for them, following Paul Levenson, the developmental logic of media, according to which traditional media are always advanced through new technologies.

In the theory by Bolter and Grusin, remediation is based on hypermediacy and immediacy, two oppositional developmental tendencies that are often encountered in tandem. Whereas for hypermediacy the viewer is explicitly reminded of the existence of the actual medium, the goal of immediacy is to make one forget this existence. On the one hand the viewer should be fully cognizant of the existence of the medium (hypermediacy), on the other hand he or she should have the impression of being directly immersed in the medially simulated content (immediacy).

Hypermediacy is based on a fascination with the medium as representational technique, one that is consciously pointed out: "Hypermediacy makes us aware of the medium or media". This desire for hypermediacy is clearly shown in connection with "mediated spaces" such as amusement parks or street fairs: "In the highly mediated spaces of amusement parks and theme parks, the logic of hypermediacy predominates. The parks themselves are full of sights and sounds from various media, and the attraction recall and refashion the experience of Vaudeville, live theatre, film, television, and recorded music". [3]

In contrast, immediacy should shape the interaction with the computer as 'naturally' and intuitively as possible, and create an "interfaceless" interface, through which the user can interact with objects as in the physical world. [3]

As an overarching process remediation links the developmental tendencies of hypermediacy and immediacy with one another. In defining remediation, Bolter and Grusin reference McLuhan who already in the 60's in his book, "Understanding Media" postulated: "The content of any medium is always another medium. The content of writing is speech, just as the written word is the content of print, and print is the content of the telegraph". [McLuhan (1964), Pp. 23 – 24, quoted from: Bolter/Grusin (2000), P. 45] Bolter and Grusin take on this conceptual overview and supply additional examples for their theory: photography is for them the remediation of painting, film the remediation of theatre.

According to Schumacher [13] the word remediation can be traced back to the Latin "remedium" which is similar to the English word "remedy", an agent for something, denoted as a cure or aid. Schumacher's view incorporates this root and corroborates Bolter and Grusin's definition. For him remediation is a process of recasting and reshaping older mediums, through which the inadequacies of prior media forms are resolved and optimized media forms are developed.

In the remediation theory of Bolter and Grusin a distinction is made between four variants of remediation: transparent remediation, translucent remediation, refashioning remediation and absorbing remediation [3].

1. In transparent remediation, prior media forms are reproduced in new media forms that stay true to the original as much as possible. "The digital medium wants to erase itself, so that the viewer stands in the same relationship to the content as she would if she were confronting the original medium."

2. If the difference between prior and new media forms is consciously present as a result of additional features, then it is a matter of translucent remediation. In this

way some multimedia encyclopaedias adopt the features of their analogue predecessors, but also offer the user additional possibilities through images, sounds, and videos.

3. Refashioning remediation is "more aggressive". New technologies completely do away with a prior media form, but their original existence still remains visible in the sense of hypermediacy.

4. The forth type of remediation is designated as absorbing remediation in that a media form is completely assimilated by another one. According to the general principle of remediation, the original source is also in this case not entirely lost since the new media form continues in the tradition of its predecessor and incorporates a considerable amount of basic features.

Through the process of remediation digital media forms are always in dialog with prior media forms. The newness of digital media forms lies in the strategies with which they advance the long tradition of media forms. Within the transformation of mirrors into today's world, the emphasis needs to be on the remediation and its implication. Furthermore, an historical point of view helps in understanding the relevance of mirrors as visual interface.

3   Developmental History of the Mirror as Interface

Long before the development of the computer, mirrors were used as a medium for visual simulation and with them virtual worlds have already been simulated for hundreds of years. The term 'virtuality' originally indicated the opposite of reality: the virtual distinguishes itself from the real and denotes a fictional world. The mirror was the central instrument for the creation of a virtual world. The creation of illusion was and is its inherent function. The images that arise through the reflections on its surface exist only apparently. They reflect back another real image fictionally [11].

3.1   From Optical Magic to Visual Entertainment

After the possibility arose to produce glass mirrors in larger numbers, they became a frequently used means of simulating visual illusions. The mirror was a wonder of immediate and perfect reflection; a symbol of the unchanged view on things. For a long period of time, the mirror was the only instrument to show people their physical appearance, their taints and their perfection. While showing an absolutely exact picture of the reality to the viewer, it could also be an instrument of transfiguration with alienation. Reality is no longer virtually recreated, but deconstructed in pieces and pieced together again [1]. The viewer could not explain these delusive and apparently magical visions and interpreted them as an illusion [6].

The European mythology awarded the mirror itself with transcendental powers of soothsaying. [5] The fascination of mirrors is also in the centre of the story "Alice in Wonderland" by Lewis Carroll, one of the best known novels in English literature. Back from Wonderland, Alice explores the sequel "Through the Looking-glass", the world behind a mirror, in which the known regularity of our world is lost [3].

In modern times, the interest on visual illusions flows into the scientific "optical magic", which was characterized as "artful science" [13]. Followers of the "optical magic" strived for solutions to the enigmas of nature and impart theoretical knowledge through artful solutions.

During the age of enlightment, research on "optical magic" received an algebraic-logical direction. The artful research as before was trivialized and existed for the solely purpose of recreation and amusement. Out of an optical magic algebraic logic arose: visuals weren't anymore magical visions, but optical tricks that were calculated with the usage of mirrors. Different from followers of optical magic, who were in the discourse of science, the "Récreátion mathématique" was not interested in research at all. The goal wasn't the quest for solving Mother Nature's secrets, but enjoyable education.

Fig. 1. Mirror Hall in Versailles (Source: Houghton Mifflin)

3.2   The Simulation of Virtual Worlds

Purchasing mirrors was a sign of wealth and reserved to nobleness and the wealthy bourgeoisie who used mirrors for prestigious purposes. With the simulation of visual illusions, courtly peers satisfied their needs for fascination, curiosity and manipulation [6]. Mirror cabinets and halls were initially built in castles. Through the placement of the mirrors, daylight should be allocated as best as possible in the rooms including a visual extension of the hall. The most famous mirror hall is in the castle of Versailles.

Especially concave or convex mirrors were a great attraction with their ability of deforming and distorting the viewers' picture. The mirror was a medium of an intelligent way to spend time and to satisfy the demand for visual entertainment.

After the prestigious usage of mirrors, annual fairs and amusement parks followed. In mirror halls, fully equipped with mirrors, the people were guided through a labyrinth of mirror walls.

3.3 Electronic Mirrors as Human-Computer-Interface

The ability to capture the real world and reflect it back in a true to life or even distorted way was for a long time the sole privilege of the mirror. Today this ability is emulated via digital media technologies. Through the development of photography, film, radio, television and computers today's world is inundated with images that imitate the virtuality of the mirror's image. [11] With the introduction of new mediums, according to Murray not only the mirror but all forms of representation developed by man in the last five thousand years have been translated into digital form. As a consequence a variety of digital techniques for visual simulation have taken root that operate within the tradition of past mediums. They consistently fulfil the same goal: they satisfy the needs of the viewer and meet his or her desire for visual simulation. The content and purpose of the presentation haven't changed, rather the technique and form have. Through the use of digital technologies new opportunities arise to satisfy man's age-old desire for experiencing fictional worlds. Independent from content and fictional histories the desire for immersion is at the fore: in striving to experience fictional worlds we are searching for an experience similar to that of jumping into a swimming pool or into the ocean. The experience of being completely submerged in another reality. We enjoy leaving our familiar world behind and exploring the characteristics of the new environment. We want to swim around and see what new possibilities arise. The feeling of experiencing virtually a fictional place is according to Murray "pleasurable in itself". [9]

As an example for a working approach of new media applying the experience of immersion, Murray describes the ALIVE project of the MIT Media Lab. Core component of the project is a "magic mirror", in which the viewer finds himself next to a comic character who directly interacts with the user. The figure follows any movement of the user, appearing to have a live on its own within the mirror [1]. The digital mirror of the ALIVE project is the interface that reflects the picture of the user in a virtual world. The function of the mirror is implemented in the hardware, in this case the camera that records the picture and the screen that visualizes the user next to the comic figure. In the development of new media is the camera the central interface for users and the screen the visualization component.

The production of illusion in the 20th century was primarily overtaken by mass media photography, film and video, which were then displaced by the computer with its screen that Manovich also designates as "illusion generator". In the digital age analogue glass mirrors are displaced as a medium of visual production. In its place stands the digital screen as the dominant interface between man and computer. [8]

In the developmental history of the screen Manovich differentiates between three essential phases that he designates as classic screen, dynamic screen, and real-time screen. During all three phases the screen is characterized by the existence of another virtual place, a three-dimensional world enclosed within its frame. Via this frame two totally different worlds are separated from one another, and yet exist simultaneously parallel to one another. The classic screen phase begins with painting on canvas and lasts until today: elements of the classic screen can be found on modern computers. As a flat, four-cornered surface, the screen simulates a special reality. Approximately one hundred years ago with the development of the moving image, the dynamic screen phase began. While in its new form it still retains all the characteristics of the classic screen, one central function is widened: the dynamic screen can display images that change with the passing of time. Manovich also designates the dynamic screen as the screen of cinema, televisions and video. With the spread of the dynamic screen the relationship between screen and viewer is altered. A new viewing regime takes hold: since the image of the dynamic screen simulates a possible total reality, the viewer identifies with the image and gives into the illusion. Hence in the new viewing regime the screen takes on the active roll, insofar as it makes possible much of the filtering out and blending out of what takes place outside its frame. The third phase, the phase of the real-time screen that also corresponds to the introduction of the computer screen, amounts to a fundamental reordering of the relationship between viewer and screen. With the introduction of the real-time screen, the viewer is pulled out of his passivity and becomes an active user. Thus, the computer screen isn't limited to the display of a single image. The display of windows arranged on top of one another with an entire range of diverse images becomes a basic principle of the real-time screen. The arrangement of different images and compositions take the user over. One no longer focuses on the single image, instead one steers the simulation on the screen independently and takes an active roll in the construction of one's subjective reality. While from the passive viewer a more active, more reflective and goal-oriented user has developed, all three forms of the screen still exist side by side. Each screen simulates accordingly the manner inherent in it and its specific reality and makes possible a determined spectrum of interactions. With a view toward virtual reality and ubiquitous computing, Manovich asserts that the screen in the future gradually disappears. When the simulated and the real world fuse together the screen connecting the two becomes redundant. The virtual world was in the past simulated by painting or film, now it becomes increasingly integrated into the actual, physical world itself [8]. With the apparent disappearance of the screen, traditional principles of reality simulation and typical patterns of reception are lost. In a world of constant digital networks, in which the computer increasingly eludes visual perception, new forms of interaction will develop. [8]

4 Installation Magical Mirrors

The idea of the installation is based on the attempt of establishing tried and proven interactions in public space into the world of digital media. As a result, the idea of the distorting mirrors, as used in man many fairs during the turn of the century and later, was as chosen the interaction component. These distorting mirrors pleased many people because their functional principle can be discovered intuitively and playfully

Fig. 2. Media Façade Rosenthaler Straße

with the whole human body. Magical mirrors were considered as potentially interesting interaction components for passers-by. The installation aims at encourage the debate on digital media and the research on technological interaction possibilities and limits.

The media façade located on Rosenthaler Strasse in Berlin Mitte becomes a world of mirrors, through witch the viewer can enter into a virtual reality. The installation follows the tradition of the magical mirror found in palaces or amusement parks. Like its predecessors it awakens the curiosity of the viewer and invites him or her on a trip into virtual worlds.

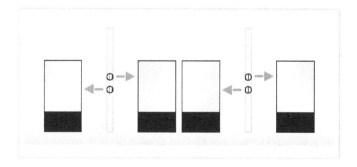

Fig. 3. Outline Life-size Screens

MAGICAL MIRRORS uses all possible projection spaces on the media façade. In the centre of the installation are digital mirrors for an interaction with passers-by. The major elements of the installation are four live-size displays in the casino, three projectors in the foyer, as well as background projectors in the so-called tower, the foyer and the casino.

4.1 Life-Size Screens

Magical Mirrors invites passers-by to play before and with the following mirrors: Aura, Progression, Luminary, Flexibility.

Aura – The mirror is loaded with virtual energy. An aura of this energy develops around the viewer in front the mirror. It reacts to his movements with flame-like clouds that surround him like polar light.

Progression – Fast growing flowers follow the movement of the viewer and grow over the entire mirror. Once the viewer gets out of sight the plants shrink and disappear.

Luminary – The building is covered by a pulsating star from bright zeros and ones. Once the viewer steps before the mirror a current of zeros and ones develops around his body. The numbers react to his movements, so he can direct the cloud of number in the mirror.

Flexibility – A magic ribbon moves over the mirror. The viewer can take it in his hands and write artful figures on the mirror and his mirror image.

Fig. 4. Mirror Luminary

Fig. 5. Mirror Flexibility

Fig. 6. Foyer Projections

4.2 Projections in the Foyer

The faces above the main entrance of the building act as a picture gallery of momentary photos taken in front of the mirrors. The aim of the picture gallery is the creation of an initial component to arrest attention of people from far away. The pictures shown build a colourful contrast against the colour gradient in the building.

4.3 Background Projections in Tower, Foyer and Casino

Additional projector faces show a colour gradient in and in front of the building. The colour gradient depends on the interaction level of passers-by.

Fragments of text are projected on the facade and in the various projection faces. The underlying text is not shown connected but in single words. The meaning of the text can not be decoded by a close look into the subject as a whole; background knowledge is needed about the text to recognize it.

5 Conclusion

As the history of development of visual simulation shows, the basic functions of the installation are in the long standing tradition of distortion mirrors placed in the digital world. Using advanced camera and software technologies the functionality of the classic mirrors is remediated with more different functionality. The viewer does not only see his own reflection moreover he can enter a virtual world and directly interact with it.

The installation MAGICAL MIRRORS carries over the tradition of simulation of the magical mirror into the world of digital media. The media facade is a representative "Mediated Space" to attract passers-by and motivate them to interact with the mirrors. The interaction with the digital mirrors is designed as much as possible unstudied and natural, tied up to learned interactions. The interface itself – the front end of the screen – is not perceived by the viewers, the movements are intuitive and natural.

Digital illusion generators can meet the demands of fascination, curiosity and manipulation more than static mirrors and cabinets could ever have. Only the possibilities of technology are something new, the desire of human mind to travel into fictitious worlds via visual illusions is the same.

The installation MAGICAL MIRRORS showed that not only the interaction action itself can be transferred from an old tradition, furthermore the acceptance can be brought forward as well.

References

[1] ALIVE Project, http://vismod.media.mit.edu/vismod/demos/smartroom/
[2] Baltrusaitis, Jurgis (1986), Der Spiegel: Entdeckungen, Täuschungen, Phantasien, Giessen
[3] Bolter, Jay David/Grusin, Richard (2000), Remediation. Understandig New Media, MIT Press, Cambridge, Mass.

[4] Carroll, Lewis (1872), Through the Looking-glass, http://www.gutenberg.org/dirs/etext91/lglass19.txt

[5] Gebrüder Grimm, Schneewittchen und die sieben Zwerge, http://gutenberg.spiegel.de/grimm/ maerchen/sneewitt.htm

[6] Gronemmeyer, Nicole (2004), Optische Magie: Zur Geschichte der visuellen Medien in der frühen Neuzeit, Bielefeld

[7] Heinz-Mohr, Gerd (1992) Lexikon der Symbole: Bilder und Zeichen der christlichen Kunst, München

[8] Manovich, Lev (2001), The Language of New Media, MIT Press, Cambridge, Mass.

[9] Murray, Janet (1998), Hamlet on the Holodeck, MIT Press, Cambridge, Mass.

[10] Pausanias, Description of Greece, http://classics.mit.edu/Pausanias/paus.1.html

[11] Ryan, Marie-Laure (2001), Narrative as Virtual Reality: Immersion and Interactivity in Literature and Electronic Media, John Hopkins, Baltimore, London

[12] Sachs, H., et al (2004), Wörterbuch der christlichen Ikonographie, Regensburg

[13] Schumacher, Eckhard, et al (2004), Einführung in die Geschichte der Medien, Fink, Paderborn

[14] Stafford, Barbara Maria (1998), Kunstvolle Wissenschaft. Aufklärung, Unterhaltung und der Niedergang der visuellen Bildung, Amsterdam, Dresden

[15] Stephan (2001) Denken am Modell - Gestaltung im Kontext bildender Wissenschaft in: Bernhard E. Bürdek (Hrsg.): »Der digitale Wahn«, Frankfurt/M.

Elderly Users in Ambient Intelligence: Does an Avatar Improve the Interaction?

Amalia Ortiz[1], María del Puy Carretero[1], David Oyarzun[1],
Jose Javier Yanguas[2], Cristina Buiza[2], M. Feli Gonzalez[2], and Igone Etxeberria[2]

[1] VICOMTech Research Centre. Graphical Conversational Interfaces Dept.
Paseo Mikeletegi 57, 20009 San Sebastian, Spain
`aortiz@vicomtech.es`
[2] Ingema. Matia Gerontological Institute Foundation
Usandizaga 6 2002 San Sebastian, Spain
`ietxeberria@fmatia.net`

Abstract. In order to examine the effect of an avatar in natural interaction with elderly users in ambient intelligent environments, we performed an empirical study with elderly people (normal aging, mild cognitive impairment and Alzheimer's patients) not only on subjective but also on objective measures. The data supports the following: 1) The subjects followed some instructions much better when interacting with the avatar. 2) The presence of the avatar has neither any positive nor negative effect on the recall of elderly people and it has a positive effect only on the subjective measures. 3) We found that elderly people both with and without cognitive impairment are capable of recognizing emotions in the facial expressions of the avatar and 4) they found the experience of having an emotional avatar in the interface a pleasant one. Thus, we conclude that virtual characters could improve the interaction between elderly people and machines, but this would depend greatly on the request task.

1 Introduction

Ambient Intelligence (AmI) builds on three recent key technologies: Ubiquitous Computing, Ubiquitous Communication and Intelligent User Interfaces. The last field, Intelligent User Interface, enables the inhabitants of an AmI environment to control and interact with the environment in a natural (voice, gestures) and personalised way (preferences, context).

Hence, Ambient Intelligence assumes that the interaction between humans and the ambient should be based on the natural communication between people. Moreover, according to Nijholt [12] most of the research on ambient intelligence does not take into account the fact that perhaps people would become confused by ambient intelligence, wouldn't know who to talk to and would not be able to build some kind of social relationship with the anonymous environment that nevertheless supports them, observes them and keeps track of their activities. People speak, gesticulate and feel in human interactions. Therefore, the interaction should be totally different to the present desktop paradigm based on keyboard, mouse and screen.

C. Stephanidis and M. Pieper (Eds.): ERCIM UI4ALL Ws 2006, LNCS 4397, pp. 99 – 114, 2007.
© Springer-Verlag Berlin Heidelberg 2007

To achieve natural communication, communication channels between people and the ambient should be the same ones which people use in human communication. People usually communicate with other people through the following communication elements, based on:

1. The use of the senses of sight and hearing in order to interpret the input data of the communication.
2. The use of corporal and oral language in order to communicate the data of the communication.

A natural interface should be capable of understanding the user input data and reproducing the corresponding output through the same communication channels. Hence, as is shown in Figure 1, in order to achieve a natural interaction our approach is to include the following systems in the ambient:

1. A speech recognition system in order to interpret the user's oral language.
2. A gesture recognition system in order to interpret the user's corporal language.
3. A text to speech system in order to communicate through voice.
4. A facial and corporal animation system in order to communicate through corporal language.

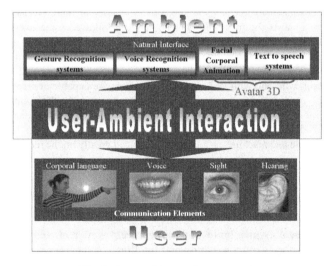

Fig. 1. A natural interaction approach

We have focused our research on the communication from the ambient to the user, that is, on the corporal and verbal language produced by the natural interface. Our approach is based on the use of avatars in simulating this kind of communication. Avatars are virtual characters which make communication between user and machine more natural and interactive. The role of the avatar depends on the application; it can act as a guide or assistant, as an information presenter and can even represent the user in a virtual environment. The character's appearance can be anthropomorphical or cartoon type, 2D or 3D, depending on the end user and on the executing device

(PC, PDA, cell phone, digital television, ...). The main advantage of using avatars within interfaces is to enable the user to interact intuitively with the system by giving him/her the illusion of communicating with a real human. This illusion is obtained by mimicking human communication, i.e. giving the avatar the ability to express emotions through facial and body gestures.

While significant progress has been made in the individual aspects of the "life-likeness" of animated agents, such as their graphical appearance or the quality of their synthetic voice, evidence of their positive impact on human-computer interaction is still rare [13].

In section 2 we will examine the reasons that make us think that using an avatar could improve the interaction between elderly people and the ambient. Then, in section 3 the focus of this research is outlined. The methodology followed is contained in the evaluation and the results are explained in section 4 and in section 5. At the end of this paper, in section 6, we will describe the discussions and conclusions produced by this research.

2 Avatars in Ambient Intelligence

A growing number of research projects have begun to investigate the use of animated life-like characters in natural user interfaces because they present *a priori* a lot of advantages, which have also been validated by many authors:

1. Social Interaction: In 1994, Nass [11] carried out five experiments which provide evidence that individual interactions between human and machine are fundamentally social. More recently, Prendinger et al [16] reached the same conclusion following another evaluation using a novel method based on tracking users' eye movements. His research also shows that users interact with life-like interface agents in an essentially natural way. He also realized that users follow the verbal and non-verbal navigational directives of the agent and mostly look at the agent's face. Human-like behavior occurs during interaction with the computer and human-like behavior is expected of the computer. Computer users turned out to be sensitive to flattery and humor; moreover, they were very much influenced by the properties of the synthesized voice in text to speech synthesis when assigning personality characteristics to a computer [12].
2. User attention: Animated characters are capable of capturing users' attention, engaging users in active tasks, and entertaining them [4]. This is very important for learning environments where a virtual character can have a positive effect on the learning process, more so if it can show affective responses [5].
3. Naturalness: Whether the virtual character is believable or not, the illusion of life is generated and [17] the user has the illusion of interacting with a real person.
4. More information in the transmitted message: in the transmitted message: In communication, facial expressions provide a lot of information. This was demonstrated by Mehrabian [8], who shows in his research, that the 93% of our messages are transmitted through non-verbal language. 55% is mainly based on facial and corporal motions, whilst 38% is based on the use of the voice.

5. Trustworthiness and believability: Generally the agents act when the user authorizes them. If the user has to delegate some tasks to the agent, he/she should trust it. It is believed that the level of trustworthiness is increased by the personification of the agent. Due to this, the design of the avatar is very important. Koda [6] found that a realistic face is rated as more intelligent, engaging, and likable than the less realistic faces.

In agreement with the above findings, Nijholt [12] concluded that embodied agents allow the development of affinitive relationships with their human partners and can therefore help to fulfill the need of affiliation in ambient intelligence environments.

Moreover, Bartneck [1] considered that to be able to employ the full range of dialogue control acts and to amplify the meaning of a message with emotional expression, the ambient intelligent environment needs an anthropomorphic entity to execute facial expressions and gestures.

In spite of these advantages, there is still great controversy about whether the best way to interact with the ambient is through mimicking human communication using virtual characters. A lot of authors have tried to answer this question through real users evaluations. For example, Koda and Maes [6] realized a quantitative analysis of subjects' impressions about a personified interface. They concluded that having faces and facial expressions is considered likable and engaging and that they also require more attention from the user. Walker [21] also argued that the virtual character occupies the users' attention but in a negative way. She compared subjects who answered questions presented via a text display on a screen, with subjects who answered the same questions spoken by a talking face. The subjects who responded to questions presented by text spent more time on the task, made fewer mistakes, and wrote more comments. From these results he concluded that adding human characteristics could make the experience for users worse rather than better, because it would require more effort and lower performance. However, Prendinger et al. [16], using a novel method for evaluating interaction with life-like interface agentsbased on tracking users' eye movements, found that the believability of the agent can be conceived as its ability to effectively direct the user's focus of attention to objects of interest.

Most studies have concentrated on subjective measures such as acceptance and believability. Other authors, such as Mülken et al. [10] and Okonkwo et al. [14] have performed an empirical study in order to examine the effect of the avatar not only on subjective but also on objective measures. All of them reached the same conclusion, that the presence of an avatar neither has a positive nor a negative effect but it may have a positive effect on the subject's impression, as the user's experience may be perceived as less difficult and more entertaining.

Motivated by the advantages of having an avatar in natural user interfaces and due to the previous evaluations that underline the positive aspects over the negatives, we decided to integrate a virtual character into an interface for elderly people. However we did not find any previous evaluations using elderly users, so first of all we designed and implemented some prototypes in order to evaluate the effect of an avatar on elderly people.

3 Natural User Interfaces for Elderly People

The use of virtual reality as an evaluation and rehabilitation tool in cognitive impairments has experienced a great peak in recent years. However, as pointed out by Gaggioli [19] there is a lack of discussion about the role that such autonomous virtual humans could have in VR-aided psychotherapy. Their group realized an evaluation of the interaction characteristics required for a successful relationship between the patient and the virtual human. There is also some research taking place concerned with the use of avatars with autistic people [9] however we did not find any work related to avatars and elderly people.

Ogozalek [13] developed some research focused on elderly people and multimedia computer interfaces. In her experiment 64 elderly participants, with an average age of 71, used a text only or multimedia computer interface. She found that a multimedia presentation was better than a text-only screen or printed leaflet in both performance and preference measures. We did not find any research with virtual characters but Ogozalek's evaluation made us think that avatars can improve the interaction between machine and elderly people.

Since we did not find any information about which kind of interface best suits the needs of elderly people and whether elderly people are capable of interacting with avatars, we centered our research on these issues. Another interesting field is concerned with the abilities of elderly people in the area of emotion recognition. Many studies underline the fact that elderly adults are poor at recognising certain emotions. Overall the existing results provide support for an age-related decline in the recognition of some emotions that it is independent of changes in perceptual or cognitive abilities [20]. Hargrave's study [3], examined facial emotion matching, facial emotion labelling and same/different emotion differentiation in Alzheimer's disease patients, healthy elderly volunteers, and elderly non-demented psychiatric outpatients. Compared with both control groups, Alzheimer's patients were significantly impaired in all three measures.

Like Mülken [10] we consider it to be very important to realize an evaluation not only on subjective measures, as with most evaluations, but also on objective measures, above all when we are working with users with cognitive impairment, who cannot fluently express themselves.

In our research, we were mainly interested in the following aspects:

1. Finding out which kind of interface best suits the needs of elderly people both with cognitive impairment and without it.
2. Analyzing whether this kind of user is capable of interacting with avatars.
3. Discovering if the virtual character enhances the performance of users during a specific task .
4. Investigating if the presentation of information by a virtual avatar helped in recalling it.
5. Analyzing whether elderly people with and without cognitive impairment are capable of recognizing emotions in the facial expressions of the avatars.

4   Method

4.1   Subjects

The sample consisted of 15 elderly people distributed in three different groups. The first (n=5) was composed of elderly people without cognitive impairment, in short, those experiencing normal aging. The second group (n=5) was made up of elderly people with mild cognitive impairment, which means that a person has memory problems greater than expected with normal aging, but does not show other symptoms of dementia, such as impaired judgment or reasoning. Finally the third group (n=5) consisted of elderly people in the moderate stage of Alzheimer's disease. These patients suffered from moderate cognitive impairment, behavioural disturbances and needed support in the Activities of Daily Living (ADL). All the subjects were recruited through the Ingema data base.

All of them passed through the same experimental conditions. Before the trial they underwent a neuropsychological assessment with the double aim of objectively measuring their memory status, and of sorting the subjects into the different groups. With respect to the Alzheimer's patients, these subjects had been previously diagnosed by a neurologist according to NINCDS-ADRDA criteria [7].

The socio demographical characteristics of the participants were the following: there were 9 females and 6 males taking part in the study. The average age was 72.33 years and the range oscillated between 61 and 80 years. All the subjects were Spanish speaking. Concerning the experience of the participants with TIC'S, we found that the device they most-used was the mobile phone (50%), while the 25% had ever used the computer.

As usual in this kind of research, each participant or by default their guardian, was requested to voluntarily sign the informed consent form demonstrating their willingness to participate in the study. In addition, each participant signed a consent form which allowed us to video record the trial. These recordings were analyzed in order to obtain the qualitative data.

4.2   The Design of the Experiment

In order to answer all the questions mentioned above we divided the experiment into two parts. The first part focused on evaluating which kind of interface best suits the needs of elderly people and on discovering the effect of the virtual character on the interaction. The second part was centred on the capacity of elderly people to recognize the emotions of the avatar.

4.2.1   Part One: Evaluation of Interfaces for Elderly People

In this experiment we presented three kinds of interfaces to each subject individually. For each kind of interface the subject had to perform two tasks. The first task was to write on a sheet of paper the answer to a question posed by the interface. The second task was to visualize some images presented by the interface. These images were organized into three different kinds of objects (daily, non-daily and pictograms). They were presented in sequences of three items at a time. Each interface worked as follows:

1. Conversational Virtual Character interface: The request to write the users name on a sheet of paper was made by the virtual character in full screen. Afterwards, the virtual character also showed and named each of the nine objects in the half screen. The features of the avatar used for this interface are explained in section 4.2 and its appearance is shown in Figure 3.
2. Text and speech interface: The request to write the user's favourite colour on a sheet of paper was made by a voice and written text in full screen. Afterwards, the voice and the text also showed and named each of the nine objects in the half screen. The appearance of this interface is shown in Figures 4 and 5.
3. Text interface: The request to write down the name of the city where the user lived on a sheet of paper was made by written text in full screen. Afterwards, the written text presented the name of the nine objects. The appearance of this interface is shown in Figures 4 and 5.

4.2.2 Second Part: Evaluation of Emotion Recognition

In this experiment we presented an interface composed of six buttons and the avatar zone to each subject individually. First of all, the avatar showed a neutral expression. When the experimenter clicked a button, the avatar showed one of the basic emotions: joy, sadness, angry, disgust, surprise or fear. The features of the avatar used for this interface are explained in section 4.2 and its appearance is shown in Figure 2.

4.2.3 Features of the Avatar

In order to design the virtual character, in line with mentioned in section 2, we created the avatars for this experiment with the following characteristics: gender, appearance, speaking capability and believability (natural behavior and facial expressions capability).

Oknown [14] found out that there are some gender-based and individual differences in the user's perception of a life-like character, which need to be taken into account when designing the virtual characters. For this reason, we used two avatars for the experiment. Both of them had anthropomorphic appearance. The first was a young woman with red hair as shown in Figure 3. This avatar was capable of reproducing text synchronized with lip movements.

The second avatar (used in the emotional interaction interface) was a young man (Figure 2) with the ability to express emotions. The animation techniques used were based on morphing and they were developed in a previous work by Ortiz et al. [15].

In order to achieve natural behavior, both, non-verbal and verbal behavior is essential. We integrated the following rules into the system:

1. Non-verbal behavior is automatically given to the avatar. This behavior is mainly based on an undulating head motion until speech is continued. The virtual character is never motionless, giving the illusion that it is alive and waiting for user feedback.
2. Eye motion is randomly directed towards both sides and is very smooth. The pupils are dilated and contracted giving the illusion that it is watching different points of light.
3. The avatar blinks randomly.
4. The eyebrows are raised with changes of *tone* and *pitch*

5. We have to take into account differences in *tone* and *pitch* in order to understand that there is a specific stress for semantic reasons. The facial animation is strengthened by raising the eyebrows and making the head nod.
6. A long pause between words or sentences makes the avatar blinks.
7. The blinks are also synchronized with the open vowels (a,e,o).

Regarding the emotional features, several research papers have focused on defining how humans express the emotions they are experiencing. Darwin was one of the pioneers in this field. His studies resulted in an emotional theory which has been followed by researchers such as Ekman [2]. Ekman's theory is perhaps the most successful and most followed for representing facial expressions. In 1978 he developed a system for coding facial actions called FACS (The Facial Action Coding System). FACS is a comprehensive, anatomically based system for measuring all visually discernible facial movement. FACS describes all visually distinguishable facial activity on the basis of 44 unique action units (AUs), as well as several categories of head and eye positions and movements. In our work, shown in Figure 2, we transfered these studies to the emotional dramatization of the avatars.

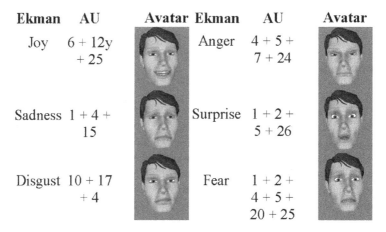

Fig. 2. Avatar expressing emotions following Ekman's AUs

4.3 Questionnaires

Each participant was administered a neuropsychological assessment in which several questionnaires were given to them before the beginning of the trial. First of all a participant form was distributed in order to collect personal data and register their experience with TICS. Concerning the neuropsychological tools, two scales were used, the Rey Auditory Verbal Learning Test [18] and the stories of the Weschler Memory Scale-R Logical Memory [22]. The first test evaluates the ability of people to learn word lists. It is the forerunner of other testsconcerning verbal learning using lists of words. The second scale evaluates the ability to recall logical stories.

Finally, with the goal obtaining information related to the interfaces two questionnaires were specifically developed for both parts of the experiment (Ïnterfaces for Elderly People" and Ëmotion recognition"). These questionnaires were designed following the conclusions obtained by state of the art technology. Like Mülken, we divided both questionnaires into two parts. In the first part we assessed the effect of the avatar on the objective measures with respect to the required task (feedback, recall and emotions recognition). In the second part, we were interested in the influence of the avatar on subjective assessments of the interface (in terms of its likeability, pleasantness, entertainability, ease and complexity).

4.4 Apparatus

The experiment was run on a Pentium IV PC with Windows 2000 Professional SO. The information was presented to the subjects on a TFT 19" color monitor. The text reproduced by the virtual character or by the audio-text interface was synthesized by Scan Soft RealSpeak Solo v4.0 with a female voice. We also used a Webcam, speakers, paper and pens to perform the experiment.

4.5 Procedure

As explained earlier, the subjects were found through The Ingema (Matia Gerontological Institute Foundation) database and contacted by telephone. Each participant signed a consent form and afterwards was enrolled in the neuropsychological assessment. The next step was the performance of the research. The study was carried out in Ingema's laboratories. During each experimental session, a psychologist was present in order to answer any possible questions and to ensure that everything proceeded as intended. The subjects were informed that in the first part of the experiment some information would be presented in three different ways; with a virtual character, with text and voice and finally only with text. They were also informed that in the second part of the experiment they should say which emotion was represented by the virtual character. The procedure was as follows:

1. The virtual character asked the user to write their name on a sheet of paper as shown in Figure 3.
2. The virtual character showed three daily objects as is shown in Figure 3.

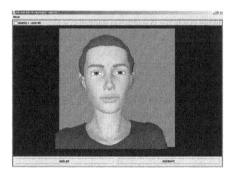

Fig. 3. Appearance of Virtual Character

Table 1. Questionnaire 1

Questionnaire 1
Which objects do you remember?
On a scale of 1 to 10, which presentation did you like more?
On a scale of 1 to 10, how do you rate the pleasantness of each presentation?
On a scale of 1 to 10,how do you rate the entertainability of each presentation?
On a scale of 1 to 10, how do you rate the easiness of each presentation?
On a scale of 1 to 10, how do you rate the complexity of each presentation?

Fig. 4. Appearance of Text and Speech Interface

3. The text and speech interface showed three daily objects.
4. The text interface showed three daily objects.
5. The user filled out the questionnaire 1 (Table 1).
6. The text and speech interface asked the user to write down their favourite color on a piece of paper.
7. The virtual character showed three non-daily objects.
8. The text and speech interface showed three non-daily objects.
9. The text interface showed three non-daily objects.

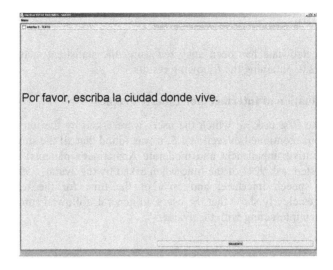

Fig. 5. Appearance of Text Interface.

Table 2. Questionnaire 2

Questionnaire 2
On a scale of 1 to 10, how do you rate the ease of each emotion identification?
On a scale of 1 to 10, how do you rate the realism of each emotion?
Which of the avatars did you like more, the woman or the man?
Did you like that this virtual character appears in another applications?
Would you like it if this virtual character appeared in other applications?

10. The user filled out the questionnaire 1 (Table 1).
11. The text interface asked the user to write down the name of their city on a piece of paper as shown in Figure 5.
12. The virtual character showed three pictograms.
13. The text and speech interface showed three pictograms.
14. The text interface showed three pictograms.
15. The user filled out the questionnaire 1 (Table 1).
16. Each avatar emotion was shown to the user, who then described the emotion they were seeing (Figure 2).
17. The user filled out the questionnaire 2 (Table 2).

5   Results

The collected data has been analyzed using the statistical analysis software SPSS version 12.0, obtaining the following results.

5.1   Evaluation of Interfaces for Elderly People

During the first task, in which the users were asked by the interfaces to follow the instructions mentioned in section 4.5, it was found that all the subjects (normal aging, mild cognitive impairment and moderate Alzheimer's patients) correctly performed the requested task 92% of the time when asked by the avatar, 75% of the time for the text and speech interface, and 66% of the time for the text interface. These percentages clearly show that the users, in general, followed some instructions much better when interacting with the avatar.

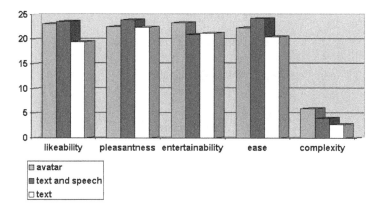

Fig. 6. Normal ageing results

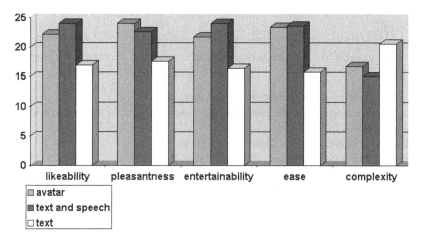

Fig. 7. Mild impairment results

Statistical analysis was performed using the Kruskal-Wallis test to establish differences, using a level of significance of less than 0.05. Values are the mean and the standard deviation. Some important results obtained during the evaluation are the following: in the second task, where each interface shows the user different objects which they have to remember later, quite significant results ($p < .05$) were obtained with the group of subjects with mild cognitive impairment, since these users were able to remember the objects better when presented by the text rather than by the other interfaces. However, within this collective these results could also be due to the recency effect because this interface was presented last.

Some other important results obtained during the evaluation are the following:

1. Every interface was evaluated in terms of its likeability, pleasantness, entertainability, ease and complexity. The interface which obtained the highest scores for the first four variables, was the text and speech interface, followed by the avatar and the text interface. In the complexity evaluation the order was inverted, with the text interface being the most complex, followed by the avatar and the text and speech interface. It was not possible to administer the questionnaires to Alzheimer's disease patients as they did not understand the questions or they answered without criteria. The results for subjects with normal aging are shown in Figure 6 and the results for subjects with mild cognitive impairment are shown in Figure 7.

2. At the end of the questionnaire there were two questions regarding the willingness of the subject to have the virtual character appear in other computational applications. The total groups' average was 8.1. This was higher for subjects with mild cognitive impairment than for subjects with normal ageing (8.4 and 7.8 respectively).

5.2   Evaluation of Emotion Recognition

The ease and rate of the emotional reality created by the avatar were the variables taken into account for the evaluation of this part of the experiment.

Table 3. Emotions recognition: Success percentage

Group	Joy	Anger	Sadness	Disgust	Fear	Surprise
Normal ageing	100%	60%	80%	20%	20%	60%
Mild impairment	100%	40%	60%	0%	20%	80%
Alzheimer patients	50%	0%	100%	0%	0%	50%

It was not possible to distribute the questionnaires to Alzheimer's patients because they did not understand the questions or they answered without criteria. For the other two groups the average for the ease variable was very similar (41, the range being, from 0 to 60). For the reality rate we obtained 44.8 in the normal ageing group and 42.6 in the mild cognitive impairment group. The results are shown in Table 3.

6 Discussion and Conclusions

We performed an empirical study with elderly people (normal aging, mild cognitive impairment and Alzheimer's patients) to examine the effect of the avatar not only on subjective but also on objective measures. The first objective measure we took into account was user feedback to the avatar questions. The data obtained supports the fact that subjects followed some instructions much better when interacting with the avatar. 92% of the subjects performed the requested task correctly when asked by the avatar but only 66% answered correctly when the questions were asked by the text interface. This result contradicts the conclusion reached by Walter [21], who wondered why subjects who answered the same questions posed by avatars required more time. As he argued, this could be because the presence of another person usually serves to increase arousal and motivation on the part of someone asked to perform a task. However, this fact can also lead to an improvement in performance if the task is not very complex but to a degraded performance if the task is complex. Our questions were very simple due to the kind of users participating in the experiment.

The second objective measure was concerned with recall. We found that users were better able to remember objects when they were presented by the text interface rather than by the other interfaces. These results were found in users with mild cognitive impairment but this data could be explained by the recency effect, which means that they could better recall the last information presented. We did not find any significant statistical differences in the other groups.

According to these results and following on from Mülken's [10] conclusion, we deduced that the presence of the avatar has neither any positive nor negative effect on recall. Mülken obtained a positive effect only through assessing the subjective measures, that is, on the subject's impression of the presentation. Our results are consistent with this conclusion assuming that the results of the mild cognitive impairment group were due to the recency effect. However, when we asked the users about whether they would like this virtual character to appear in other computational applications, we obtained an average result of 8.1.

If the recency effect were not the reason, these results may have been obtained because the users were not used to interacting with virtual characters and therefore their attention was focusing on the particular characteristics of the avatar and not on the presentation itself. Hence, the avatar plays a distracter role in the recall task, something frequently found in people with cognitive impairment. If the users were to become accustomed to the avatars, the distraction effect could be decreased.

However, Walker [21], Prendinger [16] and Hongpaisanwiwat [4], reached the conclusion that avatars did not lead to a poorer performance through distracting people and that they are capable of capturing users attention and engaging them in active tasks. We opt for the reason stated above, that the presence of the avatar neither has neither any positive nor negative effect on the recall of elderly people and that it has a positive effect only on the subjective measures.

Regarding the capacity of elderly people, with or without cognitive impairment, to recognize emotions, we observed that joy and sadness were the emotions identified best and also that the subjects scored them as being the most realistic. By contrast, the most difficult to recognise and the least was disgust. A great deal of consistency is apparent in this regard and many studies underline that elderly adults are poor at recognising certain emotions. Hargrave [3] developed an evaluation with Alzheimer's disease patients, healthy elderly volunteers, and elderly non demented psychiatric outpatients. Compared with both control groups Alzheimer's patients were significantly impaired on all three measures. Those results are consistent with our study in the sense that Alzheimer's patients have deficits in recognizing facial emotions.

We found that healthy elderly people and elderly people with mild cognitive impairment are capable of recognizing the emotions in the facial expressions of the avatar and that they found the experience of having an emotional avatar in the interface as pleasant.

During the process of designing a natural interface for ambient intelligent environments for elderly users we decided to mix text, speech and virtual characters depending on the request task. According to this research, if it is desired that a user carry out a task, the user will perform better if the avatar makes the request. However, if it is required that the user remember some information, having an avatar in the interface is something that should be considered carefully because the effect of an avatar does not affect objectively and, if the user is not used to interacting with an avatar, it wouldplay a distracter role. Moreover, we consider it to be very important to give emotional capacities to the avatar as elderly people can recognize them and they also make the interface more pleasant. However, when designing the avatar's emotions, it is important to consider which emotions are best recognized by each group. The least recognized emotions were anger, disgust and fear, so the avatar should use these emotions very carefully and less frequently.

In the future, we will plan to expand this evaluation with subjects ranging from 22 to 40 years old and we also plan to compare these results with those obtained with elderly subjects. This would resolve the issue of the unknown nature of some of these results which may have been due to the users having little experience with computers.

References

[1] Bartneck, C.: eMuu - An Embodied Emotional Character for the Ambient Intelligen Home. PhD thesis, Technische Universiteit Technische Universiteit Eindhoven (2002)

[2] Ekman, P.: Facial expression and emotion. American Psychologist **48** (1993) 384-392

[3] Hargrave, R., M.R.J., Stone, V.: recognition of facial expressions of emotion in alzheimer's disease. Journal of Neuropsychiatry and Clinical Neuroscience **14** (2002) 64-71

[4] Hongpaisanwiwat, C., Lewis, M.: Attentional effect of animated character. In: INTERACT. (2003)

[5] Kim, Y.: Pedagogical agents as learning companions: the effects of agent affect and gender on student learning, interest, self-efficacy, and agent persona. PhD thesis, Tallahassee, FL, USA (2004) Major Professor-Amy L. Baylor.

[6] Koda, T., Maes, P.: Agents with faces: The effects of personification of agents. In: 5th IEEE International Workshop on Robot and Human Communication, Tsukuba, Japan (1996)

[7] McKhann G, Drachman D, F.M.K.R.P.D.: Clinical diagnosis of alzheimer's disease. Technical Report 34: 939-944, NINCDS-ADRDA Work Group under the auspices of Department of Health and Human Services Task Force on Alzheimer's Disease (1984)

[8] Mehrabian, A.: Communication without words. Psychology Today **2** (1968) 53-56

[9] Moore, D., C.Y.M.P.y.P.N.: Avatars and autism. In Knops, A.P..H., ed.: Assistive technology from virtuality to reality, Lille - France (2005)

[10] Mülken, S., A.E., Mü ller, J.: The persona effect: How substantial is it? In Johnson, L.N., (eds.), C.R., eds.: The British HCI Group, Springer, Sheffield, UK (1998) 53-66

[11] Nass, C., Steuer, J., Tauber, E.R.: Computers are social actors. In: CHI '94: Proceedings of the SIGCHI conference on Human factors in computing systems, New York, NY, USA, ACM Press (1994) 72-78

[12] Nijholt, A.: Disappearing computers, social actors and embodied agents. In Kunii, T., Hock, S.S., Sourin, A., eds.: 2003 International Conference on CYBERWORLDS, Singapore, IEEE Computer Society Press Los Alamitos (2003) 128-133 ISBN=0-7695-1922-9.

[13] Ogozalek, V.Z.: A comparison of the use of text and multimedia interfaces to provide information to the elderly. In: CHI '94: Proceedings of the SIGCHI conference on Human factors in computing systems, New York, NY, USA, ACM Press (1994) 65-71

[14] Okonkwo, C., V.J.: Affective pedagogical agents and user persuasion. In (ed.), C.S., ed.: Universal Access in Human - Computer Interaction (UAHCI), New Orleans, USA (2001) 397-401

[15] A. Ortiz, D. Oyarzun, I.A.I.A., J.Posada: Three-dimensional whole body of virtual character animation for its behavior in a virtual environment using h-anim and inverse kinematics. In Press, I.C.S., ed.: Institute of Electrical and Electronics Engineers (IEEE), Los Alamitos, CA (2004) 307-310

[16] Prendinger, H., Ma, C., Yingzi, J., Nakasone, A., Ishizuka, M.: Understanding the effect of life-like interface agents through users' eye movements. In: ICMI '05: Proceedings of the 7th international conference on Multimodal interfaces, New York, NY, USA, ACM Press (2005) 108-115

[17] Reilly, W.S.N.: Believable Social and Emotional Agents. PhD thesis (1996)

[18] Rey, A.: Léxamen clinique en psychologie. París : Presses universitaires de France. (1964)

[19] Riva, A.G.F.M..G.C.B.W.G.: Avatars in clinical psychology: A framework for the clinical use of virtual humans. CyberPsychology & Behavior: The Impact of the Internet, Multimedia and Virtual Reality on Behavior and Society **6(2)** (2003) 117-125

[20] Sullivan, S., Ruffman, T.: Emotion recognition deficits in the elderly. Journal of Neuroscience. **114(3)** (2004) 403-32

[21] Walker, J.H., Sproull, L., Subramani, R.: Using a human face in an interface. In: Human factors in computing systems, New York, NY, USA, ACM Press (1994) 85-91

[22] Wechsler, D.: Wechsler memory scale revised manual. San Antonio, CA: Psychological corporation. (1987)

Part II

User and Context Awareness

Barriers of Information Access in Small Screen Device Applications: The Relevance of User Characteristics for a Transgenerational Design

Katrin Arning and Martina Ziefle

Department of Psychologie, RWTH Aachen University,
Jägerstr. 17-19, 52066 Aachen, Germany
{Katrin.Arning, Martina.Ziefle}@psych.rwth-aachen.de

Abstract. The proliferation of ubiquitous computing is accompanied by the development of devices, which promise to facilitate the daily living activities of people. However, the question if mobile devices address the usability demands of older users is still unsettled. This paper reports the findings of a series of studies that examined the performance of younger and older adults when using personal data management software applications of a PDA. In order to learn about the ageing impact, the influence of user characteristics like spatial and memory abilities, the subjective technical confidence and computer-expertise on performance outcomes were analysed. Beyond quantitative performance measurements, the major shortcomings in interface design were identified. Results showed that older users reached lower performance outcomes. Even young adults did not reach a perfect performance level, hinting again at shortcomings in the design of PDA applications. Overall, the findings demonstrate the need to include user characteristics in interface design.

Keywords: experimental, older adults, spatial ability, expertise, menu navigation, personal data management applications, PDA.

1 Introduction

Imagine the following scenario [1]:
An old couple, Old Bird and Gramps wants to visit relatives on the canary island La Palma. Unfortunately, traveling is no „walk in the park" for them any more, because of sight and hearing losses and problems to find their way in unfamiliar surroundings. Coincidentally, they come across a new offer of the travel agency „Charly's Magic Travel", which particularly addresses the travel demands and needs of older or disabledpeople. Charly Magic Travel offers informational support while traveling about timetables, traveling routes, means of travel, etc. via mobile devices. On the day the journey starts, Old Birds PDA lets the couple know, when they have to leave their home. At the bus station it informs the seniors in how many minutes the bus will arrive and at which platform they will have to wait. The PDA also gives notice about the length of the journey and the arrival time, so that Old Bird and Grampy have enough time to prepare for leaving the bus. During their journey the PDA offers information about restaurants, accommodations and attractive sights. (...) The device is

C. Stephanidis and M. Pieper (Eds.): ERCIM UI4ALL Ws 2006, LNCS 4397, pp. 117–136, 2007.
© Springer-Verlag Berlin Heidelberg 2007

context-aware, adaptive and able to save the individual user settings. Based on this user profile the PDA offers Old Bird and Grampy convenient services, e.g. it informs Grampy at the next day around noon, that an excellent café close to their hotel offers the best café latte of the whole island. Charly's Magic Travel concept and Old Birds PDA allow the old couple to travel independently and to take care for themselves.

This scenario does not describe visionary dreams of the future, but gives an example how intelligent computational systems may accompany our lives. The rapid proliferation of ubiquitous computing and continuously accessible information and services refers to the development of a new computing paradigm known as ambient intelligence (AI). AI-systems will provide embedded, sometimes even invisible computer applications, which are supposed to support and facilitate the daily living activities of people. As target population of ambient intelligence not only young people and those interested in technology are addressed. Ambient computing aims at a broader and more heterogeneous group of users. Especially for older adults, who represent the fastest growing group in western societies, pervasive and adaptive devices can offer an enormous benefit in various areas of application. Ambient computing does not only provide information similar to the scenario mentioned above, it also enables the ageing population to have an independent and unrestricted life. A typical field of future standard applications is the "intelligent house", in which technical facilities (e.g. heating) and service features (drawing the curtains, shopping of food, etc) are operated by mobile computers like PDAs. In the aforementioned example "Old Bird" and "Granny" also use a PDA in order to retrieve relevant information for their journey. Further applications, which are currently developed especially for older adults are for example medical monitoring, wayfinding aids for blind or deaf people, communication or memory aids, as well as personal data management applications (e.g. a diary with a reminder for medical appointments or birthdays).

The utilisation of ambient computing devices is supposed to happen "along the way", i.e. the user does not have to pay much attention to it. In a typical user scenario, users are expected to integrate the utilisation of computer devices into their daily life, while being engaged with other activities. However, the benefit depends on the ease of use while interacting with those devices. Therefore, beyond feasibility demands of technology and mobile services, one of the most important aspects in the development of ambient computing devices is the ergonomic aspect.

Ambient computing devices should be developed in a way that users want to use it, not only "for technologies sake" [2]. However, it is important to take a step forward: technology has to be created in a way that users want to use it – and that they are able to use it. As long as interface designs are not easy to use and learn, the technical innovations will not have sustained success. Thus, users' needs and cognitive demands have to be carefully studied and considered. Even though the interaction of users with desktop computers is well studied, little is known about the ability of users to interact with small screen devices, like mobile phones, pagers, communicators and PDAs. The mobile character of these devices represents a higher cognitive demand compared to conventional computer work. Many different problem areas might hamper the successful interaction with these devices: The first problem refers to the utilisation in a multiple task environment. Ambient computing devices will be used in a context, where several actions can be executed simultaneously, e.g. retrieving information from the PDA while watching out for traffic. Second, problems of understanding can arise, because the interaction with a device requires a understanding of technology, which is not present in every user. Computers in the AI-paradigm do not resemble the conventional desktop computers any more, they will become physically and mentally invisible, e.g. when they are embedded in furniture or walls [3]. Third, a major problem is concerned with the interaction with menu-based software applications. As the complexity of functions implemented in devices is increasing, it is important to ensure that users are able to accomplish the navigation in a complex menu. Due to a limited screen size, the majority of menu functions is not visible. Thus, users are urged to memorize, a) which functions are implemented and b) at which location in the menu [4, 5], which imposes considerable cognitive load. The described problems do not affect all users in the same way, but especially aged users or those with little computer-related experience are disadvantaged. Therefore, it is necessary to obtain knowledge about specific usability demands of those user groups.

2 The Older User and Technology

For at least two reasons it is necessary to focus on the specific characteristics and requirements of older users when designing ambient computing systems. The first one is the rapidly growing number of senior citizens in western societies. The second reason comes from the increasing proliferation of technology into professional and private areas. Applications like word processor programs, web browser, ATMs, ticket vending machines or online library catalogues are deeply integrated into daily life. Although these technologies are supposed to be accessible to everyone, a gap between those, who are "computer-literate" and those who are not (predominantly older users) is emerging. Although the knowledge about the older user and the utilisation of ambient computing devices is rather limited, the literature shows that older users usually face larger difficulties than younger adults in learning and using new computer applications [6, 7, 8]. Contrary to current stereotypes, older users are in fact interested in the acquisition of computer skills [9, 10]. Up to now, new applications are often designed without considering the demands of this user group. In order to include the potential user group of older adults, a transgenerational design is needed, which is supposed to allow users of all age groups and ability levels to interact with new technical applications. To achieve this goal, interface designers need to know about age-related changes and how they may affect the interaction with computer systems.

2.1 Characteristics of the Older User

Several different factors account for age-related differences in computer utilisation and performance. A first important factor is computer experience. Studies have shown that older adults possess a lower computer experience compared to younger users [11, 12]. This "experience-gap" can be explained by cultural factors and a different upbringing. Furthermore, when people have retired, they no longer keep in intensive contact with new technology for work purposes and the acquisition of new computer applications becomes less attractive. As a result, computer-related knowledge and concepts or models about how to operate technical devices is limited in the older group. This might increase the difficulty of computer-related tasks and therefore accounts for differences in computer-based performance. But the pure factor computer experience alone is not sufficient to explain age differences in computer performance [6]. A further explanation for age-related computer performance differences is the decline in cognitive, psychomotor and sensory functioning over the lifespan [13, 14, 15, 16, 17]. Age-related changes in the cognitive system lead to a decline in working-memory capacities, a slowing-down in processing speed and a reduced ability to distinguish relevant from irrelevant information [18]. As a result, older learners face greater difficulties in extracting relevant information from user manuals or they are overwhelmed with displays with a high information density. A reduced working memory capacity becomes critical when task demands are high, e.g. when using novel or complex technical devices. The reduced processing speed is often considered as an additional decline, but it also serves as an explanation for the age-related reduction in other cognitive abilities [19]. This "slowing-down" results in longer execution times of single steps, especially in complex tasks [16, 20]. Another profound decline over the life span concerns spatial abilities [21, 22, 23] as well as spatial memory [24, 25]. Older users with reduced spatial abilities experience disorientation and the feeling of "getting lost" while navigating through the menu of software applications [26, 27, 28]. Regarding changes in sensory functioning, the auditory and visual abilities of older adults decline. Changes in the auditory system comprise an increase in the auditory threshold (especially for high-frequency tones), difficulties in the perception of speech and in the discrimination and the spatial location of tones [29]. Apart from an ongoing decrease in visual acuity, the eyes' ability to accommodate and adapt to light changes declines and the sensitivity to glare and reflections increases [30,31]. Finally, the ability to execute fast and accurate movements is also declining over the life span [32].

In the present experimental study, the focus was laid on the interaction of older users with personal data management software of a PDA. In order to learn about the age-specific impact, a group of young adults was examined as well. Thus, we wanted to find out if "typical" users of different age groups are able to successfully use the personal data management software. In order to find out, which specific demands have to be considered for a transgenerational design, users were surveyed with respect to their age, spatial ability, verbal memory, the technical self-confidence and the extent of computer experience. Furthermore, user ratings regarding usability problems while interacting with the device were assessed. The outcomes are not only important for the identification of age-related factors that should be considered in interface design, but also with respect to their impact on performance when working with software applications of a PDA-device. In general, the study aimed at two objectives:

1. The identification of user characteristics, which underlie the age-related differences and should be considered in a transgenerational design approach.
2. The identification of typical "barriers" in the interface design.

3   Method

3.1   Variables

As independent variable, user age was examined, contrasting the performance of older and younger participants. As dependent measures the effectiveness and efficiency were analysed according to the standard measures for usability [33]. For task effectiveness, the percentage of successfully solved tasks was summed up. As efficiency measure the time needed to process the tasks was measured. As user characteristics, spatial ability, verbal memory, technical self-confidence (STC) and the reported experience with computers were surveyed. Additionally, the perceived ease of use concerning the interaction with the PDA and the usefulness as well as usability problems were surveyed.

3.2 Participants

A total of 96 participants took part in the study. As three typical PDA applications were experimentally examined, three samples of 32 users were selected. They were balanced by age (16 adults per age group) as well as by gender (16 females and 16 men per group). The younger group had a mean age of 23.2 years (s = 2.4), the older group of 58.2 years (s = 6.0). There were no age differences in the groups of the three samples (see Table 1). A benchmark procedure was pursued regarding the recruitment of older adults: we aimed at the "younger and healthy older adults". All of them were active parts of the work force, mentally fit and not hampered by stronger age-related sensory and psychomotor limitations. The younger group consisted of students of different academic fields (engineering and social sciences).. Within their age group the three samples did not differ in their educational background (see Table 1)[1]. Contrasting the educational background of younger and older adults across the three samples, the younger adults were found to possess a significantly higher educational degree than older adults ($M_{young} = 4.1$ $M_{old} = 3.2$, t = 3.5, p < 0.05).

Younger participants were recruited at the university and fulfilled a course requirement; older participants were reached by an advertisement in a local newspaper. The older adults came from different professions (engineers, administrative officers, secretaries, (high school) teachers, nurses, architects, physiotherapists, physicians and psychiatrists). Ruling out further confounding variables, a careful screening of

Table 1. Mean and standard deviations of age and educational background for both age groups in the three experimental samples

		Diary		To-Do-List		Directory		
		M	SD	M	SD	M	SD	p
Age (in years)	Young adults	23.8	2.8	23.4	2.0	22.2	2.0	0.13
	Older adults	56.4	6.8	59.9	5.9	58.2	5.0	0.26
Educational level	Young adults	4.1	0.4	4.0	0.9	4.1	0.5	0.86
	Older adults	3.0	1.5	3.3	1.8	3.3	1.4	0.81

[1] The educational background was assessed on the following scale: 1 = ger. "Haupt/Volksschulabschluß" (6-8 years of school), 2 = ger. "Realschulabschluß" (10 years of school), 3 = ger. "Fachhochschulreife" (12 years of school), 4 = ger. "Abitur" (13 years of school), 5 = ger. "Hochschulabschluß" (academic degree).

participants' abilities was undertaken. All participants were in good physical and mental health conditions. Visual acuity was normal or corrected to normal and no history of eye-illnesses was reported.

3.3 Experimental Tasks

The experimental tasks simulated standard software applications, implemented in commercially available PDAs: the digital diary of a PDA, the to-do-list and, as a third application, the digital directory. Participants had to accomplish four prototypic PDA tasks, where they had to create a new entry or change an existing one.

A flowchart of the task procedures for the two task types ("create a new entry" and "change an existing entry") can be seen in Figure 1 on the following page. Participants had a time limit of five minutes per task.

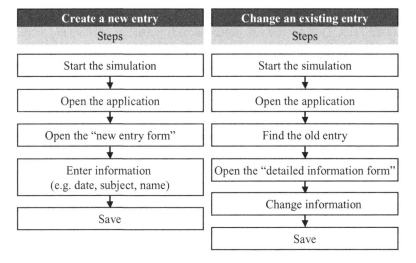

Fig. 1. Flowchart of the task procedure for a "new entry" and a "change entry" task

3.4 Apparatus

The PDA (iToshiba Pocket PC e740, system software Windows CE) was simulated as a software solution and run on a Dell Inspiron 8100 notebook PC that was connected to an LCD-screen (Iiyama TXA3841, TN, 15'', with a display resolution of 1024 x 768 Pixels). The software emulation exactly corresponded to the real device, in size (chassis 80 x 125 mm), display size (3.5''), font size (9 pt for functions, and 11 pt (bold) for category headers), menu structure and operational keys.

3.5 Procedure

Before participants started to work on the tasks, they completed a computer-based questionnaire. In order to familiarize participants with the experimental setting and to control that older adults were able to handle the computer mouse, the questionnaire had to be filled in by using the mouse. Participants were instructed to use the mouse with their preferred hand (all were right-handed). All participants, even the older group, were highly familiar in using the mouse. The questionnaire assessed demographic variables (age, profession) and experience with computers by requesting the length of computer use, the frequency and the ease of use. The length of computer utilisation ("For how long have you been working with …?") was measured in years, the frequency ("How often do you use / work with …?") was rated on a 4 point scale (1 = less than once a week, 2 = once a week; 3 = 2-3 times a week, 4 = daily). Regarding the valid assessment of computer expertise, different facets of computer experience (length of computer use, frequency and perceived ease of computer use) have to be taken into consideration. Therefore, a total measure was built by comprising all of the three facets. The ratings of length of computer use, frequency and reported ease of computer use were aggregated multiplicatively to build the variable "computer experience". After completing the computer-based questionnaire, the handling of the PDA-simulation was explained by the experimenter. All participants worked on four experimental tasks in each study. The order of tasks was kept constant and was presented in the following sequence: (1) create a new entry, (2) change an existing entry, (3) create a new entry, (4) change an existing entry. Finally, the ease of use ("Using the PDA is … for me") was assessed on a scale with four answering modes (1= very easy, 2 = quite easy, 3 = quite difficult and 4 = very difficult) in a computer-based questionnaire. Participants were also asked to rate usability-problems they encountered during the interaction with PDA. Participants sat on a height-adjustable chair in a comfortable seating position. In order to optimize viewing conditions, participants were allowed to individually adjust the viewing distance and the inclination of the TFT-monitor, where the PDA-emulation was displayed. Corrective lenses, if necessary, were worn throughout the experiment.

3.6 Materials

In order to measure *spatial ability*, participants completed the Paperfolding-test, a spatial visualisation test [34]. Each item shows successive drawings of two or three folds made in a square sheet of paper. The final drawing shows a hole punched in the folded paper. Participants had to select one of five drawings to show how the punched sheet would appear when fully opened . The maximum score to be reached was 20.

To assess *verbal memory abilities*, a verbal memory test as used in earlier experiments [35] was conducted. In order to diminish semantic processing of the stimuli and further elaborative processes, participants had to memorize Turkish nouns, which are completely unfamiliar to native speakers of the German language. The stimuli were presented successively for three seconds on a computer screen. Immediately after the presentation of the 20 nouns (delay < 0.5 sec), participants had to recognize each target word among three phonologically and visually similar distractors. Here, the maximum score that could be reached was 15 (Figure 2).

tatil

☐ tafil   ☐ tarak   ☐ tital   ☐ tatil

Fig. 2. Item example of the verbal memory test

The *subjective technical confidence* (STC) measures the subjective confidence of a person regarding his/her competency when using technology [34]. Participants were given the short version of the test containing eight items (e.g. "Usually, I cope with technical problems successfully"), which had to be rated on a five-point scale, ranging from 1 (totally disagree) to 5 (totally agree). The maximum score to be reached was 100. The reliability of the STC short version is high (Cronbach's alpha = 0.89). Several studies assessing the validity of the STC showed satisfactory results and proved the construct of STC as a technology-related personality trait [36].

For the assessment of *ease of use* and *usefulness* the original items of Davis' Technology-Acceptance-Model were used [37]. The validity and reliability of the items has been proven by Davis et al. and by a multiplicity of other empirical studies [38]. For each item, a 5-point Likert-scale was used and participants were asked to give a response ranging from 1 (strongly disagree) to 5 (strongly agree).

To get insights into sources of usability problems when working with the PDA applications, participants rated items, which referred to navigational disorientation, menu complexity, icon-design (pictorial transparency), icon-meaning (semantic transparency) and icon-naming (labeling). The items had to be answered on a 5-point Likert-scale ranging from 1 (strongly disagree) to 5 (strongly agree).

4   Results

Results were analysed by bivariate correlations, multivariate and univariate analysis of variance and multivariate regression analysis, with a level of significance set at 5%. The significance of the omnibus F-Tests in the MANOVA analyses were taken from Pillai values. In order to determine associations between performance outcomes and user characteristics, correlations were carried out (Pearson values for interval-scaled, Spearman-Rho values for ordinal-scaled and Eta values for nominal-scaled data).

As the experimental tasks share the same semantic context, the performance in the four tasks of an application was comprised and the means for the performance in the diary, to-do-list and directory are reported.

4.1   User Characteristics of the Sample

A 3x2 MANOVA was conducted in order to find out if the samples and the two age groups differed according to their cognitive abilities (spatial visualisation and verbal memory), their STC and computer expertise. No differences were found ($F_{(8, 174)} = 0.7$, $p = 0.7$), therefore we regard the three samples as comparable and merge them for an overall-analysis of performance.

With respect to the main effect "age", highly significant age differences were found (F (4,87) = 33.9, p = 0.000). Younger adults scored higher in spatial ability, verbal memory, STC and computer-expertise (see Table 2). No interaction between sample and age group was found.

Table 2. Cognitive abilities , STC and expertise for younger and older adults

	Spatial ability [max = 20]		Verbal memory [max = 15]		STC [max = 100]		Expertise [max = 160]	
	M	SD	M	SD	M	SD	M	SD
Young adults	14.3	2.7	11.4	3.0	76.3	14.7	95.1	48.5
Older adults	6.7	3.6	8.1	3.5	61.2	17.2	63.6	56.3

Controlling for gender effects it was found that male participants reported a significantly higher STC than female participants (F (1, 95) = 13.5, p = 0.000). Male participants reached an average score of 74.3, while female participants scored lower with 63.1 out of 100 points. No other effects of gender or interactions with age or sample group were found.

In order to find out how the cognitive variables, STC and expertise were associated, bivariate correlations were carried out for both age groups separately. In the younger group the cognitive variables were not strongly related. The only significant association was found for the STC and expertise (r = 0.39, p < 0.05), according to which younger adults with a high STC also reported to have a high computer experience.

A different pattern can be seen in Table 3 or the older group: Older participants with high spatial abilities also show higher scores in verbal memory, STC and expertise. Similar to the correlation pattern in the group of younger adults, higher reports of expertise of older adults correlated positively with STC-ratings.

Table 3. Correlations between cognitive variables, STC and expertise for older adults (n = 48), an asterisk indicates a significant relationship (p < 0.05)

	Spatial ability	Verbal memory	STC	Expertise
Spatial ability	1	.35*	.34*	.36*
Verbal memory		1	-.17	-.01
STC			1	.35*
Expertise				1

4.2 Performance of Younger and Older Adults Using a PDA

The performance of younger and older adults in the three software applications was compared by multivariate analysis. A 2 (age group) x 3 (application) MANOVA revealed a highly significant effect of age (F (2, 180) = 72.4, p = 0.000). The task effectiveness of older adults was nearly 50% lower than performance of younger adults when working with standard software applications (see Figure 4). Older adults solved only 47.9%, whereas younger adults accomplished 94.3% of the tasks. Older adults also needed more than twice as much processing time than younger adults (M_{young} = 337.4 sec, M_{old} = 812.5 sec).

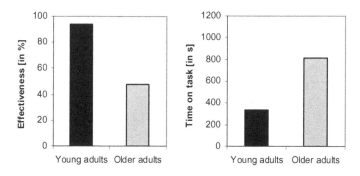

Fig. 3. Effectiveness (left) and time on task (right) for young and older adults

Furthermore, it is insightful whether older participants differ in their judgments with respect to the perceived ease of use and the perceived usefulness. These judgments were collected after the participants had completed the PDA tasks (see Figure 4).

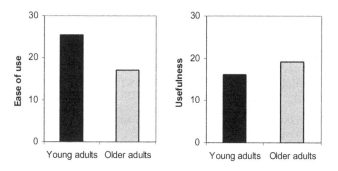

Fig. 4. Ease of use (left) and usefulness (right) for both age groups

As found, older participants reported significantly lower values with respect to the perceived ease of use and the perceived usefulness after working with the PDA (F (2, 180) = 30.5, p = 0.000). Older adults reported an ease of use of on average 17 (out of 30 points), whereas younger adults gave a rating of 25.5 points. The age group differences were less pronounced in the ratings of perceived usefulness: older adults gave an average rating of 16.1; the rating of the younger group was 19.2.

Comparing the performance of the two age groups in the three software applications, significant differences were found (F (2, 180) = 12.9, p = 0.000). The highest task effectiveness was reached in the digital directory application, where 84.4% of the tasks were solved, followed by the to-do-list with 66.4% and the diary with 62.5%.

Participants worked the fastest in the diary (M = 514.2 s), followed by the directory (M = 532.2 s) and the to-do-list (M =687.4 s). No differences between the three applications were found in the ratings of ease of use and usefulness. Furthermore, there was no interaction between the factors age and application.

Table 4. Performance in the three PDA-software applications

	Diary		To-Do-List		Directory	
	M	SD	M	SD	M	SD
Effectiveness in %	62.5	40.2	66.4	39.5	84.4	27.5
Efficiency	514.2	301.2	687.4	364.2	523.2	259.9

In a next step we analysed the learnability regarding task effectiveness, i.e. if performance improved in the second trial of a task in comparison to the first trial (see Figure 5). A 2 (age group) x 2 (trials) x 3 (application) ANOVA with repeated measurement revealed that effectiveness increased in the second trial (F (1, 90) = 10.0, p = 0.02).

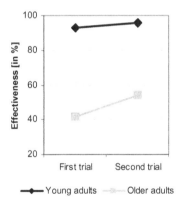

Fig. 5. Learnability effects in task effectiveness for both age groups

The task effectiveness increased from 67% in the first trial to 75% in the second trial. Interestingly, the learning progress was more pronounced for the older age group (from 41.7% in the first trial to 54.2% in the second trial) as compared to the younger group (from 92.7% to 95.8%), although this interaction missed statistical significance (F (1, 90) = 3.5, p = 0.06). It is remarkable, that not even the younger group was able to reach a "perfect" performance in the second trial, especially because the examined PDA tasks referred to standard applications. Apparently, the personal data management applications were not easy to use, even for a technology-prone student user group. Nevertheless, the high variances in task effectiveness indicate the effect of differential factors. Therefore the following section focuses on user characteristics, which might explain the sources of variability.

4.3 User Characteristics and Performance

In order to find out, which user characteristics are associated with a successful interaction with the PDA software applications, bivariate correlation analyses with performance variables and user characteristics were conducted (see Table 5). In the group of younger adults a successful performance was accompanied by high computer expertise (for task effectiveness) and high spatial abilities (for time on task). This means that young computer-experienced users were able to solve the tasks more effectively and those with high spatial abilities are able to accomplish the task more efficiently. The missing relationship between effectiveness and spatial ability might by explained by the high task performance by younger adults, i.e. the low variability in task effectiveness.

Table 5. Bivariate correlations between performance measures and user characteristics for younger adults. An asterisk indicates a significant relationship ($p < 0.05$).

Younger adults (N = 48)	Spatial abil-	Verbal mem-	ST	Exper-
Effectiveness in %	-.01	.05	.19	.30*
Efficiency	-.35*	.02	-.23	-.16

A similar pattern for the relationship between performance measures and user characteristics was found for the group of older adults, but here the associations were even stronger. Older participants with high spatial abilities were able to complete the tasks more effectively and efficiently. In contrary to the correlation pattern of younger adults, where expertise and effectiveness were positively related, in the group of older adults expertise was related with efficiency. This finding indicates that older adults' expertise did not enhance the success of interacting with the software applications, but was related to the time, which users needed to process the tasks.

Table 6. Bivariate correlations between performance measures and user characteristics for older adults. An asterisk indicates a significant correlation ($p < 0.05$), two asterisks a highly significant relationship ($p < 0.01$).

Older adults (N = 48)	Spatial abil-	Verbal mem-	ST	Exper-
Effectiveness in %	.33*	.23	.19	.25
Efficiency	-.31*	-.16	.27	-.41**

The results of the correlational analyses show that a successful interaction with the PDA is strongly associated with two user characteristics: spatial ability and computer experience. Participants of both age groups, which showed high levels of spatial ability and expertise, were able to work more successful with the personal data management software.

Summarising the findings of the user-centered analysis we found that the very same user characteristics (i.e. spatial abilities and expertise) are related to a high performance in both age groups, even though the young adults performed much better. However, the present study was not limited to a user-centered approach, that aimed on the identification of "optimal user characteristics", which promote a successful interaction with a device or which might compensate for suboptimal interface design. We also pursued a "device-centered" approach, in order to analyse the interface-design-factors, which account for performance decrements. Therefore, participants' ratings of usability problems were related to performance measures (see 4.4) and a qualitative analysis of interface shortcomings (see 4.5) was conducted.

4.4 Usability Problem Ratings

In a next step we wanted to explore the reasons for the performance differences between younger and older adults from the "device-perspective". First insights came from the ratings of usability problems. Nonparametric tests showed that older adults faced significantly higher usability problems regarding navigational disorientation ($M_{old} = 4.0$, $M_{young} = 3.0$; $z = -3.7$, $p = 0.00$) and a hampered memorization of functions in the menu ($M_{old} = 3.5$, $M_{young} = 2.5$; $z = -3.0$, $p = 0.00$). Older participants reported larger disorientation problems when navigating through the PDA menu and also higher difficulties to remember the location of functions. Interestingly, the size of font or buttons was not seen as a severe usability problem in the older group. No age differences occurred in nonparametric t-Tests for usability topics like icon-design, icon-meaning, font- or button size or naming of functions (see Table 7).

Table 7. Bivariate correlations between usability problem ratings and performance measures for older adults. An asterisk indicates a significant correlation ($p < 0.05$), two asterisks a highly significant relationship ($p < 0.01$).

Older adults (N =	Dis-orientation	Memoriza-tion of func-	Icon-Design	Icon-Meaning	Font- / Button size	Nam ing
Effec-tiveness in %	-.449**	-.356*	-.245	-.193	.183	.064
Effi-ciency	.306*	.384**	.247	.232	-.044	.112

The reports about usability problems were correlated with performance measures in order to find out, which of the problem domains accompanied low task effectiveness and longer processing times. In the group of younger adults a reduced efficiency was related to navigational disorientation ($r = -.31$, $p < 0.05$), further significant associations were not present. However, in the group of older adults stronger associations were found: low task effectiveness and efficiency were accompanied by high navigational disorientation and problems in the memorization of the location of functions in the menu. The other usability problem domains like icon-design, icon-meaning, font- or button size and the naming of functions showed only weak relationships with performance measures. Accordingly, these aspects did not account for a lower performance in the group of older adults. The main problems, which occurred when participants reached low task effectiveness, were disorientation in the menu and difficulties in memorizing the location of functions in the menu.

4.5 Qualitative Analysis of Usability Problems

Based on participants' navigational path, which was recorded online in logfiles, and participants' comments while interacting with the PDA, an analysis of frequent user errors was carried out. A phenomenon-based description of the main user errors and their possible reasons is follow in the next section:

Choosing the right application: Especially older participants had great difficulties to decide, which application to choose in order to accomplish the experimental tasks (see Figure 6). Even though the task instructions contained hints about the correct application, participants sometimes chose the wrong one. This especially occurred in the to-do-list application and the diary application, e.g. when participants opened the diary in order to enter a new task or vice versa. We assume that the participants were guided by a inappropriate mental model and were confused by the similar semantic context of the applications. From participants' commentaries it was derived, that they have a mental model that does not differentiate between a "diary" and a "to-do-list".

Fig. 6. Scaled-down screenshot of the date sheets in the digital diary (left) and the to-do-list-application

Participants reported to usually write their to do's or tasks into their diaries. Therefore, the differentiation between a diary and a to-do-list in the data management software was not comprehensible for them. Moreover, the interface-design features in both applications might have contributed to the difficulties in choosing the right application. Both, the to-do-list application and the diary application contain entry-fields where data information can be filled in by choosing the data from a date sheet (see Figure 6). Participants assumed that the calendars of both applications were linked and that information would automatically be transferred and exchanged between the two applications. In this case, the design-guideline to present operating elements like the date sheet across different software applications in a consistent way caused wrong assumptions about connections between the two applications. In order to overcome the described difficulties, users of personal data management applications should learn (e.g. in manuals or trainings) about the two different applications and their separate functioning.

Differentiation between "Create a new entry" and "Change an existing entry": Interestingly, in the experimental tasks where an existing entry had to be changed, participants tended to create a new entry instead of changing the given one. Based on our data we cannot interpret if participants could not find the "change"-button in order to edit the information in the already existing entry or if they did not know about the conceptual differences between creating a new entry and changing an existing one. Again, participants' commentaries about their mental model when changing an existing entry were highly insightful. When paper-based diaries or directories are used, an existing entry is "changed" by writing in the new one and by crossing out or erasing the old entry. When participants pursued the familiar procedure they knew from paper-based data management, they "only" created a new entry. In order to avoid double entries, which unnecessarily waste storage capacity and might cause confusion (e.g. when the warning signal rings for an old and a new appointment), the user manual should contain information about the location (in the menu and on the screen) and design of the "change"-button. Moreover, users should be informed about the two different concepts of creating a new entry and changing an existing entry in a training or user manual.

Opening the "new-entry form": Many participants had difficulties when they wanted to click on the "New-Button" in order to open the "new-entry form". Instead of clicking on the "new"-button they clicked on the "extras"-button, which was located right next to the "new"-button (see Figure 7).

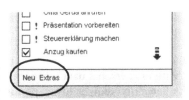

Fig. 7. Missing visual contour between the buttons "Neu" (left, engl. new) and "Extras" (right, engl. extras)

Based on the analysis of logfiles we assume that participants did not recognize that two separate buttons were implemented, because there was no visual contour between the two buttons. Instead of this, they perceived the field as one big button. The two buttons in the lower bar of the display should be re-designed, e.g. by encircling the icons or colouring the background.

Saving the entries: The most frequent error, which occurred in the group of older adults as well as in the group of younger adults, was the failure to save new entries or changes in given entries. At least two interpretations are possible to explain this error. First, we assume that participants were not acquainted with the concept of "saving", at least in the context of using a PDA device. Users of desktop computers are supposed to be acquainted to the fact that any data input has to be saved. However, users do not necessarily transfer this knowledge to software applications of mobile devices like a PDA. Instead, it was assumed that the digitally based management of personal data in digital diaries or directories activated a mental model of conventional paper-based personal data management. The personal data management software on the PDA shares conceptual and semantic features with the conventional way to organise personal data, but it also features considerable differences. Whenever new data is entered in a conventional paper-based directory, diary or to-do-list, people are used to simply write it down, and the writing process itself is – from a cognitive point of view – the concluding and confirming action. Especially older adults reported that they were sure that the information was saved after entering it in the PDA, because it was "written" on the PDA-display. Again, participants were misguided by a model or procedure, which was derived from the traditional paper-based data management, but not transferable to the utilisation of software applications. Another less probable explanation is that "saving" as the final step in the sequence of action was simply forgotten, because the motivation to finish the task and to reach the task goal was so high. In both cases, an automatic feedback, which reminds the user to save the entries before closing the application, seems to be appropriate. Interestingly, feedbacks like "are you sure that you want to close the document without saving" are highly common in desktop computers, but this feature was not applied to the design of the PDA-interface.

Summarising the findings in this section so far, the majority of usability problems found in the qualitative analysis stem from a mismatch between the users' models and the design of the software application. On the one hand, the knowledge and expectations of users about how the device may work is not appropriate and on the other hand, the device is not addressing these expectations. The implications for interface-design will be discussed in the following section.

5 Discussion

The present study surveyed the performance and usability ratings of 96 younger and older adults, which worked with the personal data management software of a PDA. It was found, that older adults generally show a lower performance in comparison to younger users. But it is noteworthy, that even younger users, which are much more familiar with computers and software applications, were not able to handle the software applications error-free. These findings clearly demonstrate that applications of current small screen devices like the PDA, which might be implemented in ambient computing devices, are not as "easy to handle" as they are considered to be. Even the "best" users of both age groups, i.e. healthy and comparably young older adults in the older group and students of a technical university in the younger group faced usability problems and were not able to perfectly solve the experimental tasks. However, we assume that the current findings still underestimate the "real" performance level of older users with age-related illnesses and constraints.

Transgenerational Design: Critical voices claim that a transgenerational interface design is not necessary, because usability-problems will become extinct, when the current generation of technology-experienced young users becomes older (cohort-explanation). From our point of view there are at least two arguments, which contradict this perspective. First, the cycles of technical innovations become faster and faster and lead to a development of novel and more complex devices, which might even be a problem for the current technology-prone generation. Second, the young generation will also grow older will be subject to cognitive ageing processes, which happen cohort-independently. This underlines the importance of research activities, which contribute to a transgenerational design, where even the "weakest" user is able to handle a technical device successfully.

Ageing Impact: However, we found strong evidence, that chronological age alone is not very informative for the deduction of guidelines for a transgenerational design. Hence, chronological age must be regarded as a "carrier-variable". Based on our results the underlying reasons for performance differences are lower spatial abilities and a lower computer expertise. This finding has important implications for the interface design of ambient computing devices. Referring to current interface solutions, an effective interaction is restricted to user groups, which possess high levels of spatial abilities and / or computer expertise. However, it is highly improbable that these "optimal" characteristics are pronounced in broader and diverse user groups (e.g. as present in "old old adults"). On the one hand, "spatial abilities" decline with increasing age; therefore older adults need extra-support in order to diminish disorientation when navigating through menu-based applications.

Typical barriers: Beyond age-related performance differences, a final consideration is concerned with typical barriers, which hamper a proper handling of PDA personal data management applications. The detailed qualitative analysis showed that the majority of user errors could be ascribed to a lack of transferability between different mental models of the user and /or a lack of cross-platform consistency between traditional desktop computers and mobile devices. In this context, many pitfalls are present when the relation between the users' model of the task procedure (represented as procedural knowledge) and the task structure implemented in different devices is not cognitively compatible. Nowadays, similar applications are implemented in different technical devices (e.g. personal data management applications can be found in mobile phones, smartphones, PDAs, desktop computers). Although the semantic content and the field of application are the same, the data structures or interaction rules of these technical devices are different. The user is urged to learn the similarities and differences to handle these applications in a tedious "trial and error"-way. This is especially problematical for the older user group. According to our experience, older users are highly motivated to use new technologies (Ziefle & Bay, in press), but they have immense difficulties to change over to new operating routines and they are very sensitive to a suboptimal interface design. According to Richter, Nichols, Gajos & Seffah, "we cannot expect to easily transfer our digital activities from one platform to another as our interaction context changes. The challenge for user interface design is to ensure that users can seamlessly move between interfaces and continue to accomplish their tasks, even when the interfaces are presented on devices with considerably different display and interaction mechanisms" [38]. Especially older users weigh up the costs and benefits before accepting and utilizing new technologies, and a low perceived ease of use and usefulness due to suboptimal interface design might lead to a rejection of these devices [39]. Therefore it is important that AI-research activities take the user-perspective into consideration. This refers to the identification and development of innovative areas of application but also to the inclusion of user abilities, which affect the interaction with ambient computing devices.

Limitations of the Study: Some final remarks deal with potential limitations of the study, with respect to methodological aspects and the generalizability of our findings. A first point refers to the dependent variables in our study. The binary definition of task effectiveness (task solved or not solved) might lead to an underestimation of performance. As observed in our study, younger and older adults did not execute the final "saving"-step. Although the task accomplishment was completely correct up to this final step, the task was assessed as "not solved", which completely ignores the performance in the rest of the task. Therefore, more sensitive measures should be applied, which more gradually assess task effectiveness. One possible solution is to analyse users' problem-solving activities while working on the tasks and to define sub goals, which have to be reached by the user. This allows a more sensitive assessment of performance on the hand and gives insights into more or less difficult elements (~sub goals) of the task. These elements can be addressed in an ergonomic redesign- or the support of users.

A second point deals with the assessment of computer expertise. In our study, computer expertise was assessed by subjective user ratings of frequency, ease and length of computer use, which were aggregated multiplicatively. However, subjective ratings are often biased by social desirability, fear of failure and misinterpretation of ones own performance. Furthermore, the items used to measure computer experience in this study (frequency and length of computer utilisation) might lack content validity. The items refer to quantitative aspects of computer utilisation and do not necessarily reflect qualitative aspects of computer expertise, i.e. computer-related knowledge. Therefore, the correlation between STC and computer-expertise in our study might be traced back on a method (self-report)-bias. In future studies, instead of using ratings of temporal aspects of computer utilisation, the knowledge of task-relevant concepts should be assessed.

In this study, we comprised the results of the three applications of the PDA, because they represent common standard applications of a PDA. Thus, the described usability problems or barriers are valid for the three application types. However, a more detailed analysis of the three applications should be carried out in future studies in order to explore performance differences in the three application types and to optimize the interface design of the three applications.

One could critically object that the PDA interface itself was not "intelligent", because it contains more inconsistencies and "logical" errors than other devices. However, in the huge number of studies dealing with shortcomings in interface design of desktop computers and mobile devices, it was consistently shown that the presence of cognitive incompatibilities is not specific for a certain device type, but for devices, which are developed without considering the human factor. The present study clearly shows that the gap, which still exists between technological genius and usability demands, might represent a serious obstacle for the acceptance of technology by broader user groups. However, if the knowledge of both, the technological and the human factors is incorporated into current design, the devices may meet the demands of users, of designers and manufacturers at the same time.

A last point refers to the experimental laboratory setting. Working with software applications in a laboratory is certainly less demanding than the utilisation in a real environment, where the workload is typically higher. Therefore, when compared to the demands of a multitasking context, the findings might be an underestimation of usability problems occurring in the real world.

References

1. Christoph, U., Krempels, K.-H., Spaniol, O.: Automatic mapping of information service interfaces on operational elements of mobile devices. Unpublished Master Thesis, RWTH Aachen University, Germany (2006)
2. Wyeth, P., Austin, D. & Szeto, H.: Designing Ambient Computing for use in the mobile healthcare domain. In: Online-Proceedings of the CHI 2001, (2001) http://www.teco. edu/chi2001ws/17_wyeth.pdf, 01.05.2005
3. Streitz, N.A.: The Disappearing Computer: From Human-Computer Interaction to Human-Artefact Interaction (Opening Keynote). In: M. Khalid, M. G. Helander, A. W. Yeo (Ed.): Proceedings of the 7th International Conference on Work With Computing Systems (WWCS 2004), Kuala Lumpur, Malaysia (2004)
4. Ziefle, M., Arning, K. & Bay, S.: Cross-platform consistency and cognitive compatibility: How important are users` mental models for the performance when interacting with mobile devices. In: The Many Faces of Consistency, Workshop CHI 2006, http://www. multipleu.org (2006) 1-5
5. Ziefle, M. & Bay, S.: How older adults meet complexity: Ageing effects on the usability of different mobile phones. Behaviour and Information Technology (2005) 375-389
6. Czaja, S.J. & Sharit, J.: The influence of age and experience on the performance of a data entry task. Proceedings of the Human Factors and Ergonomics Society 41st Annual Meeting, Santa Monica, Human Factors and Ergonomics Society (1997) 144-147
7. Kelley, C. L. & Charness, N.: Issues in training older adults to use computers. Behaviour & Information Technology (1995) 107-120
8. Westermann, S.J.: Individual Differences in the Use of Command Line and Menu Computer Interfaces. International Journal of Human Computer Interaction (1997) 183-198
9. Arning, K. & Ziefle, M.: What older users expect from mobile devices: an empirical survey. In: Proc. IEA 2006 (2006)
10. Morrell, R. W., Mayhorn, C. B. & Bennett, J.: A survey of World Wide Web use in Middle-aged and older adults. Human Factors (2000) 175-182
11. Czaja, S.J. & Sharit, J.: Age Differences in the Performance of Computer-Based Work. Psychology and Ageing (1993) 59-67
12. Mead, S.E., Sit, R.A., Rogers, W.A., Jamieson, B.A. & Rousseau, G.K.: Influences of general computer experience and age on library database search performance. Behaviour & Information Technology (2000) 107-123
13. Birren J.E, & Fisher L.M.: Ageing and speed of behavior: possible consequences for psychological functioning. Annu. Rev. Psychol. (1995) 329-353
14. Salthouse, T. A.: The processing-speed theory of adult age differences in cognition. Psychological Review (1996) 403-428
15. Fisk, A. D. & Rogers, W. A.: Handbook of Human Factors and the Older Adult. CA, Academic Press San Diego (1997)
16. Park, D.C. & Schwarz, N. Cognitive Ageing. Philadelphia, Buchanan (1999)
17. Ziefle, M.: Ageing, visual performance and eyestrain in different screen technologies. Proceedings of the human factors and ergonomics society 45th annual meeting (2001) 262-266

18. Welford, A.T.: Practice effects in relation to age: A review and a theory. Developmental Neuropsychology (1985) 173- 190
19. Salthouse, T. A., & Babcock, R. L.: Decomposing adult age differences in working memory. Developmental Psychology (1991) 763-776
20. Vicente, K. J. Hayes, B. C. & Williges, R. C.: Assaying and isolating individual difference in searching a hierarchical file system. Human Factors (1987) 349-359
21. Stanney, K. & Salvendy, G.: Information Visualisation: Assisting low-spatial individuals with information access tasks through the use of visual mediators. Ergonomics (1995) 1184-1198
22. Downing, R.W., Moore, J.L. & Brown, S.W.: The effects and interaction of spatial visualisation and domain expertise on information seeking. Computers in Human Behaviour (2005) 195-209
23. Cherry, K.E., & Park, D.C.: Individual differences and contextual variables influence spatial memory in young and older adults. Psychology and Ageing (1993) 517-525
24. Park, D. C., Cherry, K. E., Smith, A. D., & Lafronza, V. N.: Effects of distinctive context on memory for objects and their locations in young and older adults. Psychology and Ageing (1990) 250-255
25. Edwards, D.M. & Hardman, L.: Lost in hyperspace: Cognitive mapping and navigation in a hypertext environment. In R. McAleese (Ed.), Hypertext: theory into practice. Oxford: Intellect limited (1989) 105-125
26. Ziefle, M. & Bay, S.: How to overcome disorientation in mobile phone menu. A comparison of two different navigation aids. Human Computer Interaction (2006)
27. Kline, D.W. & Scialfa, C.T.: Sensory and perceptual functioning: Basic Research and Human Factors Implications. In: A. D. Fisk & W. A. Rogers (Eds.). Handbook of Human Factors and the Older Adult San Diego: Academic Press (1997) 27-54
28. Craik, F.I.M. & Salthouse, T.A. (Ed.): Handbook of Ageing and Cognition. Hillsdale, N.J.: Lawrence Erlbaum Associates (1992)
29. Haegerstrom, T. Portnoy, G., Schneck, M.E. & Brabyn, J.A.: Seeing into old age: vision function beyond acuity. Optom. Vis. Science (1999) 141-158
30. Vercruyssen, M.: Movement Control and Speed of Behavior. In A.D Fisk and W.A. Rogers (Eds.), Handbook Human Factors and the Older Adult. San Diego: Academic Press (1997) 55-86
31. EN ISO 9241-11: Ergonomic requirements for office work with visual display terminals. Part 11: Guidance on usability. Berlin, Germany: Beuth (1997)
32. Ekstrom, R. B., French, J. W., Harman, H. H, & Dermen, D.: Manual for the Kit of Factor-Referenced Cognitive Tests. Princeton, NJ: Educational Testing Service (1976)
33. Bay, S., & Ziefle, M.: Design for All: User Characteristics to be Considered for the Design of Devices with Hierarchical Menu Structures. In H. Luczak and K. Zink (Eds.) Human Factors in Organisational Design and Management Santa Monica: IEA. (2003) 503-508
34. Beier, G.: Kontrollüberzeugungen im Umgang mit Technik. [Locus of control in the interaction with technology] Report Psychologie (1999) 684-693
35. Davis, F.D.: Perceived usefulness, perceived ease of use, and user acceptance of information technology. MIS Quarterly (1989) 319-340
36. Adams, D.A., Nelson, R., & Todd, P.A. Perceived usefulness, ease of use, and usage of information technology: A replication. MIS Quarterly (1992) 227-247
37. Richter, L., Nichols, J., Gajos, K., Seffah, A. The Many Faces of Consistency in Cross-Platform Design. In: Extended Proceedings of CHI'2006 (2006)
38. Arning, K. & Ziefle, M.: Cognitive and personal predictors for PDA navigation performance. Human Factors (submitted)

Designing Intelligent Tutors to Adapt Individual Interaction

Andrina Granić, Slavomir Stankov, and Jelena Nakić

University of Split, Faculty of Natural Sciences, Mathematics and Education
Nikole Tesle 12, 21000 Split, Croatia
{andrina.granic, slavomir.stankov, jelena.nakic}@pmfst.hr

Abstract. Present-day efforts in designing technologies to serve and adapt to human needs rather than forcing humans to adapt, embrace intelligent user interfaces as one of ambient intelligence key technologies. This paper elaborates on the design of an adaptive individual interaction in a type of computer-based educational system whose operation is supported by intelligent methods, an emulation of human teacher in the process of learning and teaching. In order to design interaction simple and effortless as well as to adjust learning process and teaching material to individual student, a mechanism for monitoring student's interaction and generating related adaptive interface based on student model is developed. Furthermore, a classification of adaptive hypermedia systems with regard to employed adaptation technology is offered.

1 Introduction

The vision of ambient intelligence (AmI) puts the user, the individual at the center of all developments for a knowledge-based society for all [24], stressing the importance to design technologies for human needs and not forcing humans to adapt. With the growth of Internet, the World Wide Web and computer usage in general, users with a wide variety of background, skills, interests, expertise and learning styles are using computers for quite diverse purposes. For that reason no single user interface, though designed to be both easily learnable and highly efficient, will satisfy every user. Users have different needs as they learn to use an interface, which change as they use a computer and become more familiar with its capabilities as well as the task domain. They have their own preferences and interests as well. This can be seen in some popular web sites which integrate personalization features (to some degree) based on user profiles (for example, Amazon.com, MyNetscape, myCNN and a like).

The emergence of adaptive interface, an interface that dynamically modifies itself during the run-time has provided a satisfactory framework for taking into account users' heterogeneity, by adapting the interface behavior to a user's individual characteristics. Adaptive system generally relies upon user model to adaptively shape its behavior – it collects data about the user (personal characteristics, proficiencies, preferences, interests, attitudes and/or goals (cf. [38]) and then processes them in order to create a model on which to perform the adaptation process. Running a history login allows it to

C. Stephanidis and M. Pieper (Eds.): ERCIM UI4ALL Ws 2006, LNCS 4397, pp. 137–153, 2007.
© Springer-Verlag Berlin Heidelberg 2007

keep a history of the communication and to build inferences over the interaction between users and the system during run-time. Within the area of adaptive interfaces a distinction is being made between adaptive and adaptable systems [30], [34]. Adaptable systems allow the user to control the interface customization and adapt their behavior accordingly, while adaptive systems monitor a user's interaction and automatically make adjustments based on the system's assumptions about user needs.

In today's emerging knowledge society for all, knowledge is considered as a foundation of all aspects of society and economy in general and the need for rapid knowledge acquisition is more important then ever. Furthermore, the number of users of computer-based educational systems rapidly grows. Current research efforts mainly address adaptive educational hypermedia systems (AEHSs), hence emphasizing a particular kind of adaptivity that encompasses adaptive presentation, adaptive navigation support and adaptive content selection [6]. However, it can be noted that these techniques still haven't been applied in everyday learning and teaching environments, apart from their development surroundings [3], [25].

Focusing on computer-based educational systems which emulate human teacher in the process of learning and teaching, it is an accepted opinion that their interaction mechanisms have been given inadequate consideration [9], particularly because the majority of existing systems simply predefine the respective interface, without means for its adaptation [28]. Intelligent tutoring systems (ITSs) are computer-based educational systems which attempt to mimic the behavior of a human teacher in order to support the process of learning and teaching in arbitrary domain knowledge [8]. ITSs provide individualized instruction for students, attempting to adjust the contents and the way of domain knowledge perception. Despite the fact there are still only few ITSs in practical use [41], it has been claimed that starting from the 1970's when the first system was developed, ITSs undoubtedly have improved the process of learning and teaching for arbitrary domain knowledge [16], also taking into account individuality of the person being taught. In fact, ITSs still represent the best way to enable one-to-one instruction, since they provide the student her/his own "computer teacher" [32]. This viewpoint is supported by our research concerning ITSs and their generators, authoring shells (ASs) [28] as well, as exemplified in a series of developed systems based on TEx-Sys model [19], [33], [35], [36]. These systems are employed in the process of learning and teaching a number of real subject matter and have been continually evaluated concerning their efficiency of a learning process as well as usability of their user interface (e.g. [18], [20]). Nevertheless, regardless of our expertise and experience as well as the fact that those systems have unquestionably enriched the process of knowledge acquisition, we are still facing difficulties that have to be taken into consideration.

The remainder of the paper is structured in the following way. Section 2 explains our motivation and need for the research on adaptive hypermedia technology with the intention of its appliance in our systems. Section 3 discusses adaptive hypermedia systems (AHSs), highlighting those implementing the most frequently used and evaluated adaptation techniques. A classification regarding implemented adaptation technology completes the presentation of the systems. In order to design adaptive interaction in systems which emulate human teachers, an employment of AHSs adaptation technology is elaborated in Section 4. After a short primer on intelligent tutoring systems and authoring shells, a concept of a student model and adaptation mechanism to be engaged in our systems is presented. Finally, Section 5 provides concluding remarks and outlines further research as well.

2 Motivation

In order to design interaction simple and effortless as well as to adjust the TEx-Sys model founded systems to fit the needs and individual characteristics of all students, we have considered adaptive educational systems, especially those Web-based developed in the last decade. Most of the computer-based educational systems available today could be classified either as intelligent tutoring systems or adaptive educational hypermedia systems. Although ITSs' development started from the seventies, first adaptive hypermedia systems (AHSs) were developed in the early nineties by involving user modeling and adaptation into static "one-size-fits-all" hypertext and hypermedia. They adapt the content or presentation of the system to some relevant characteristics of the user on the basis of a dynamic understanding of each particular user. These systems, with interfaces that look and feel like typical hypermedia documents, became a very natural way of delivering adaptive e-learning courses to the Web, often presented as electronic textbooks or hyperbooks (see classification of AHSs in section 3.1). Consequently, education still remains the widest AHS application area.

Each of these two categories of systems has developed its own adaptation mechanisms, almost independently from each other. Only a curriculum sequencing technology has originally been developed in intelligent tutoring systems and later successfully applied in many adaptive educational hypermedia systems. ITSs also developed an intelligent analysis of student's solutions, interactive problem solving support, example-based problem solving support and later, with the growth of Internet, an adaptive collaboration support. On the other hand, emerging adaptation techniques from AHSs, related to the system's layout as hypertext or hypermedia, appeared to be very effective [12]. Recently, a growing number of ITSs which have accepted and successfully implemented some of the adaptive hypermedia techniques can be found [2].

We aim to design intelligent tutors for students and not make students adapt to the systems. Specifically, in order to improve student's interaction and knowledge acquisition in the family of systems based on TEx-Sys model, we incorporate a number of adaptive hypermedia techniques. To facilitate examination of AHSs' adaptation functionalities, various systems mostly applied in the field of education are analyzed. In the following a cross section of our research in adaptive hypermedia is presented, without pretending to give an overview of all existing systems, but an extraction of AHSs which implement the most frequently used and evaluated techniques. All presented systems are elaborated on the basis of their "live" versions (when possible) instead of relevant elaboration papers.

3   Background Research on Adaptive Hypermedia

In order to be called an adaptive hypermedia system (AHS) the system must satisfy following criteria: (i) it should be based on hypertext or hypermedia, (ii) have an explicit user-model which reflects some features of the individual user and maintains them dynamically, (iii) have a domain model which is a set of knowledge items and relationships between them and (iv) be capable of modifying some visible or functional part of the system on the basis of information stored in the user-model [14]. Few years after developing first single purposes AHSs, their authors began to generalize them into authoring tools for simplifying the development process of new AHSs, usually in the same application area (see Table 1). The creation of the course is usually high level process based on the construction of topics hierarchy in domain model, but some tools go even further and let the authors write some specific adaptation rules, consequently directly involving in adaptation functionality of the system. These authoring tools are commonly used in educational domain but recently authoring tools for the development of on-line information systems, on-line help systems and information retrieval hypermedia can be found.

3.1   Adaptive Hypermedia Systems

Although all adaptive systems are designed to adjust their presentation and functionality to individual needs, wishes and abilities of the user, they significantly differ in (i) what individual characteristics of the user they consider as relevant for the adaptation process, (ii) how do they observe user's actions and gather those information and finally (iii) how do they employ these characteristics to perform adaptation. In the following we present a number of adaptive hypermedia applications distinguishing authoring tools from concrete systems. The majority of them are educational systems, not only selected because of our particular interest in education, but also because of the fact that education is still leading application area of adaptive systems.

AHA![1] [11] is the Adaptive Hypermedia Architecture, a complex but powerful tool for creating adaptive Web-based applications intended to serve many different purposes. Regardless the fact that is mainly used for developing distance learning applications, but in order to preserve generality, adaptation decisions are based exclusively from observing the user's browsing actions, not considering browsing as a learning process.

InterBook[2] [5] is free authoring tool for creating and delivering adaptive electronic textbooks on the Web, not necessarily learning courses. Textbooks written as a word documents are annotated and converted to the HTML documents. Reading material is presented in different windows consisting of several frames, but they all are considered as multiple views on the same page.

KBS Hyperbook system [21] provides a framework for developing and maintaining open, adaptive hypermedia systems in the Internet. It is intended to serve for creating distance learning applications and implements project-based learning. Students are free to choose their own learning goals and the adaptation techniques are based on a goal-driven approach.

---

[1] http://aha.win.tue.nl
[2] http://www.contrib.andrew.cmu.edu/~plb/InterBook.html

ELM-ART[3] [7] is one of the first Web-based ITSs, aimed to support learning programming in Lisp. It presents all course materials (topics introductions, examples, problems and tests) in hypermedia form, integrating features of an electronic textbook, of a learning environment and of an intelligent tutoring system. Observations about the user are made by monitoring the problem solutions and by considering test results.

NetCoach [39] is an authoring system that allows creation of adaptive and individual course modules using a simple Web-based interface. Authoring includes creation of the learning material, composition of tests, definition of learning goals, adaptation of a layout and behavior of the interface as well as management of access rights for students and tutors. NetCoach is derived from ELM-ART, so courses that have been developed with NetCoach are ELM-ART alike: all of them are adaptive, adaptable, interactive and communicative.

AdaptWeb [17] is an adaptive environment application for Web-based learning used in a Numerical Methods course. Adaptation mechanism considers three aspects as relevant: the student's current knowledge, the student's program, and the student's navigation preferences.

INSPIRE [31] is an adaptive educational hypermedia system. It allows the learner to select her/his own learning goal and dynamically generates lessons sequence that guides the user toward that goal. System's adaptive behavior exploits student's knowledge state and learning style.

AVANTI [37] is a Web browser which addresses the interaction requirements of individuals with diverse abilities, skills, requirements and preferences (including disabled and elderly people), using Web-based multimedia applications and services. The design and development of the AVANTI browser's user interface supports the concept of User Interfaces for All. Adaptations include the selection of different interaction styles as well as a selection of those attributes of physical interface objects that are appropriate for a given user (e.g. font size, colors, speech parameters).

Table 1. Authoring tools for AHS development

Adaptive Hypermedia Authoring Tool	Adaptive Hypermedia Systems	Publicly Available
AHA! [11]	2L690	Free download
InterBook [5]	ACT-R bookshelf [4]	Free download
KBS Hyperbook [21]	CS1	No
NetCoach [39]	HTML-Tutor, ELM-ART, Peugeot Germany,...	Demo
AdaptWeb [17]	Numerical Methods course	Free download

---

[3] http://www.psychologie.uni-trier.de/projects/ELM/elmart.html

As a result of our research in adaptive hypermedia we have classified the above systems with regard to their general characteristics, distinguishing authoring tools for creating as well as delivering adaptive systems to the Web (presented in Table 1) from the systems themselves (given in Table 2).

Table 2. General characteristics of a number of AHSs

Adaptive Hypermedia System	Application Area	Title	Publicly Available	Learning Strategies
2L690 [10]	Education	"Hypermedia structures and Systems"	Free access	None
CS1 [21]	Education (Programming)	"Introduction to Java Programming"	No	Project-based learning
ELM-ART [7]	Education (Programming)	"Programming in Lisp"	Free access	Example-based learning
INSPIRE [31]	Education	"Computer Architecture"	No	Experimental learning
AVANTI [37]	Web browser	Domain dependent	Case studies	—

3.2 User Modeling in Adaptive Hypermedia Systems

According to the definition of adaptive hypermedia system stated at the beginning of this section, it is clearly understood that adaptation process heavily relies on individual characteristics of each particular user encompassed in her/his user model, as the necessary prerequisite for the adaptation success [40]. Adaptation mechanisms of present AHSs are usually based on following user features: knowledge, user goals, preferences, background and experience [1]. Although clearly identified as essential requirements for adaptation functionality, some of these features may not be stable over time or easy to deduce from the interaction with a user. Therefore the reliability of the inferred features may vary [23].

User's *knowledge*, although changeable and unreliable, is the most important feature for adaptivity in many adaptive systems and especially in educational systems. User's knowledge is usually represented as an attribute in an overlay user model. This means that the system stores user's current knowledge level about each concept from the domain model and then dynamically updates these values according to observations of the user's browsing actions (AHA!, InterBook, ELM-ART, INSPIRE), passed tests (AHA!, ELM-ART, INSPIRE) and possibly solved problems (ELM-ART) or designed projects (KBS Hyperbook). Throughout her/his interaction with a system, user usually aims to accomplish certain task or goal. In educational systems the user can ask and get *user's goal* from the system. Although user's goal is the most volatile of all her/his features, it is extremely important for adaptation and that's why many systems employ goal–driven approach (INSPIRE, KBS Hyperbook). Adaptive systems often accept some *preferences* of the user, mainly concerning the mode of content presentation. In most cases it is impossible to deduce user's preferences from her/his navigation manners so the user has to directly inform the system about them, thus leading the system towards adaptability (AHA!, ELM-ART). Concerning adaptive educational systems, *learning styles* are also considered as relevant for the success of students' learning process (INSPIRE). AHSs distinguish users according to their *experience* in using hyperspace, meaning how familiar they are with its structure and navigation capabilities (InterBook, ELM-ART). An experience in computer usage in general can be considered too. Similarly, a user's *background* describes her/his previous knowledge about the domain or related topics but acquired outside the system. User's experience and background are usually modeled through the stereotypes. Stereotype user model is sometimes employed for modeling other user's features (AVANTI, AdaptWeb), but the best results in adaptation are achieved by combining these two approaches in such a manner that stereotype user model serves as initiation component of the overlay model (AVANTI, InterBook).

Besides storing the user's individual characteristics, user model is very suitable for storing information about history of user's navigation through the system that is relevant for adaptation, e.g. status of the pages, time the user spent on reading the page, the last visited page in previous session and some other information in respect to content of the page.

3.3 AHS Adaptation Technology

The first issue in the development of any adaptive system is the identification of its adjustable parts, meaning the parts that will look differently or act differently for different users. Due to the fact that hypermedia systems are basically sets of pages connected by links, adaptation of the presented page content, called adaptive presentation and adaptation of links to other pages, called adaptive navigation support is usually enabled [1]. Present AHSs implement various techniques to perform adaptation, often developed especially to fulfill the purpose of the particular system. In the last decade these techniques have grown into very powerful technology that is commonly used in the majority of recent AHSs.

Adaptive Presentation. Although content of a page may be text and multimedia as well, most of existing systems use adaptive presentation techniques to perform text adaptation only (AHA!, INSPIRE, KBS Hyperbook). A main goal of adaptive presentation is to provide different content of the page for each individual user respecting her/his user model. In order to accomplish an idea of providing additional explanation to certain users according their knowledge and interests, AHSs usually use a conditional text technique. Text representing information about some domain concept is presented according to respective user's knowledge level. This simple but quite successful technique sometimes is called inserting/removing fragments (AHA!). To adapt page content, an AHS may store several different explanation variants for the same topic in form of fragment of even whole page. Considering the user model (e.g. category of the user or user's learning style) the system decides which variant to present (INSPIRE). Another way for storing different explanation variants is a frame-based technique. Some newer systems use dimming fragments for adaptive presentation, where less relevant parts of the page content are dimmed or shaded but are still visible.

Adaptive Navigation Support. In an educational hypermedia system there is usually a learning goal for each student representing the knowledge that the student has to learn. To provide adaptive guidance the system has to know not only the student's goal, but also her/his current knowledge level. The *curriculum sequencing technique* is very useful to build the shortest, individually planed trail of learning units leading to the specified learning goal. This technique was originally developed in ITSs but then successfully adjusted and employed in most present AEHSs.

A very simple technique for implementing user's guidance called *direct guidance* can be found in most AHSs in all application domains. It is provided through the "next" button leading the user to the next most suitable page considered user's goal and other parameters represented in the user model (particularly knowledge level in educational hypermedia). *Adaptive link sorting* is another helpful technique for supporting user's navigation. It encompasses ordering the links available from the particular page according to their relevance for the user. Sorting is typical for information retrieval systems, but also successfully used in some educational hypermedia systems (InterBook, ELM-ART).

The basic idea of *link hiding* is simplifying the navigation and supporting the user's orientation by restricting the navigational space (AHA!). Links that are not relevant or not yet ready to be read are disabled (visible but inactive), hidden (transferred to normal text) or even removed from the page content. The goal of *link annotation* technology is to indicate the current state of pages or fragments behind annotated links. It is usually used simultaneously with link hiding techniques. Adaptive link annotation is especially useful in educational hypermedia to indicate the student's knowledge level on particular topics. *Map adaptation* concerns adapting graphical presentation of global and local hyperspace link structure using any of the techniques listed above or their combination.

Classification of AHS Adaptation Technology. In order to review presented adaptation technology, a classification of previously introduced AHSs according to the implemented adaptation techniques is given in Table 3. As shown, numerous

Table 3. Application of adaptation technology in AHSs

Adaptation technology	AHA!	InterBook	ELM-ART	INSPIRE	KBS Hyperbook
Content adaptation	x			x	x
Direct guidance		x	x	x	x
Link annotation	x	x	x	x	x
Link hiding (removing, disabling)	x				
Link sorting		x	x		
Curriculum sequencing			x	x	

reviewed systems apply adaptive navigation support as dominant adaptation technology. Due to the fact that content adaptation is not so frequently used, as most of the systems use one or no adaptive presentation technique at all, the table brings adaptive content presentation as a general technology, not specifying any particular related technique.

First AHSs have been developed independently from each other and usually even unaware of each other. Therefore existing systems considerably differ in their architecture and even more in their functionality, especially adaptation. That makes comparison of existing AHSs very difficult, especially because each of them has been elaborated in a different manner. In the field of adaptive hypermedia there are only few isolated efforts in formal description of systems architecture and adaptation mechanisms as well. We stress the importance of AHAM reference model [13] and a characterization of systems, observations and adaptivity rules in first-order logic [22].

4 Designing Interaction with AHS Adaptation Technology

Since adaptive hypermedia is quite new direction of research within the area of adaptive and user-model based interfaces, many of the systems have not been evaluated to date considering their adaptation functionality. There is still a lack of methodology for adaptivity evaluation [27] and a limited amount of empirical evaluations of adaptive systems has been performed thus far [40]. Nevertheless, they do report the effectiveness of presented adaptation techniques [12], [40] and therefore justify our intention for their employment in our systems.

A brief introduction on intelligent tutoring systems and authoring shells is followed with an outline of adaptive interaction design in the TEx-Sys model based systems.

4.1 Intelligent Tutoring Systems

Intelligent tutoring systems (ITSs) are computer-based educational systems that emulate the human teacher in order to support the process of learning and teaching in arbitrary domain knowledge. The emulation process attempts to mimic the behavior of a human tutor, teaching individually in a one-to-one relationship [15]. ITSs are built on a fairly well established architecture, which relies on four interconnected modules: (i) expert module acting as the domain knowledge unit, (ii) student module comprehending the generated student model based on the learning and teaching process in the domain knowledge, (iii) teacher module guiding the learning and teaching process and (iv) communication module realizing the interaction among student, teacher and knowledge [8]. ITSs provide individualized instruction for the users and accordingly such systems must be intelligent, attempting to adjust the contents and the way of domain knowledge perception. When considering adaptivity, the most important part of a student model is the information which system maintains about the student's relation to the concepts of the domain knowledge, gathered by observing the student's interaction pattern.

As the need to cover a variety of different domain knowledge have arisen since, instead of having a number of particular ITSs for the domains of interest, authoring shells (ASs) [28] have been developed, which are intended to act as generators of specific domain knowledge ITSs. ASs are meant to accommodate to the teachers as well as to the students within an interactive learning environment by supporting teachers in the development of a series of ITSs for arbitrary domain knowledge and conversely, by enabling students to learn, test themselves and be advised on further work. Because of their ability to express the cognitive model of human memory and reasoning [29], in some ITSs and ASs knowledge representation is based on semantic networks, whose basic components are nodes representing domain knowledge objects and links showing relations between objects.

In order to make interaction simple and "transparent" as well as to improve the learning experience, user interface design in these systems plays a fundamental role. Hence the interest is to make ASs and ITSs more acceptable (and usable!) to the users by applying adaptation in order to implement a more intelligent interaction.

Due to an inadequate consideration given to their interaction mechanisms in general, we have developed Adaptive Knowledge Base Builder (AKBB) that supports the communication through interaction styles' adaptation. AKBB supports teachers in the development of specialized ITSs for particular domains of education [19]. Its self-adaptive interface, conformant to individual user interaction, provides three diverse types of interfaces (command, mixed and graphical) with appropriate interaction styles.

Currently we are employing AHS adaptation techniques in order to design adaptive interaction in systems which emulate human teachers in the learning and teaching process, enabling students to learn, test themselves and be advised on further work.

4.2 Designing Individual Interaction in an Intelligent Tutor

In contrary to the classic hypertext pages, which mainly present textual content, user interface of systems based on TEx-Sys model offers nodes representing domain knowledge objects (concepts to be learnt) as well as links showing relations between objects. Each concept is additionally described by its structural attributes that may be text, pictures, presentations and a like. Within the text describing a concept we do not perform content adaptation on individual level, but adaptability in regards to students' university program and for younger pupils respecting their age.

Central part of the interface presents hierarchy of nodes containing teaching material that students are supposed to learn. We consider that on the nodes structure level a high level of adaptivity to individual students can be reached. Engaged technology is essentially adaptive navigation support applied on the nodes instead of classic hyperlinks. Nodes will be adaptively annotated on the basis of recording student's navigation through the nodes structure as well as tests results, aiming to lead the student toward her/his learning goal.

Student Model. We have accepted the methodology of user modeling from the field of AHSs but kept the term 'student model' from previous generations of TEx-Sys model founded systems because users of intelligent tutoring systems are indeed the learners. The student model as the basis of system's adaptivity is an overlay user model. Each student is described by a set of attributes with associated values. We use

Table 4. Student model attributes and their role in interface adaptation of an intelligent tutor

Attribute	Value	Adaptation role
knowledge	%	student's knowledge about a concept
selected	true / false	currently selected node
traversal	[0,2]	visited node and/or its children
relevance	true / false	the next suitable node to select

four attributes, namely *knowledge, selected, traversal* and *relevance*. For each node from the teaching material structure the system calculates and stores values of those attributes. Student model attributes are listed in Table 4, together with their possible values and short description of their role in system's adaptation.

The *selected* attribute directly detects student's interaction with the system. When a student selects a node, system adaptively annotates selected node by changing node color into purple and then updates the student's model accordingly, that is changes attribute values for selected node and for all nodes directly related to the selected one.

Traversal attribute enables the system to continuously keep record of student's actions that include navigation through the node hierarchy and visiting structural attributes of the nodes as well. For each node traversal value is calculated in the following way: if the student visits the node, traversal value of the node becomes "1", and as the student keeps reading children of that node, traversal value increases in a smaller amount dependent on the number of the children. Maximum traversal value the student can reach reading a content of a lesson is "2". As student usually passes the nodes in the parent-child direction, selection of a child causes the propagation of traversal values of its parent. Traversal attribute is very important for adaptation since a student can access the test at the end of each teaching unit only if she/he has read 70% of presented material expressed in total traversal values of all nodes within that unit.

Recent systems from this ITS family keep tracking the time a student spends on learning particular node, but we argue that time spent on learning can not be consider as a reliable indicator of student's knowledge. The system updates the *knowledge* attribute only on the basis of test results. The test is offered at the end of each teaching unit and consists of dynamically generated questions. This provides trustful information about student's current knowledge level of tested concepts. After test analysis is done, knowledge values propagate through the network of nodes in a way similar to propagation of traversal values.

For presentation of new teaching unit of domain knowledge the system considers student's knowledge tested in previous chapter in the following way. Before presenting new content the system initially increases traversal values of those nodes that have been mentioned in previous units or directly related in the knowledge base to some of the previously mentioned nodes. This improves students learning process by simplifying her/his access conditions for taking the next test.

Respecting the student's learning goal, we use a *relevance* attribute to suggest the most suitable concept for the student to be learned next. Consequently the direct guidance technique is implemented to create an individual learning trail for each student.

Adaptation Mechanism. System performs adaptivity process in four phases: initialization, reconstruction, inference and adaptation (meaning a generation of an interface adapted to individual student). Each phase is realized through its own set of rules.

- The first set of rules operates in initialization phase. When a new student is registered and logged on the system for the first time, the system reacts in running these rules to create her/his student model, assigning default values to its attributes and generating the initial layout of the system's interface.
- Instead of initialization rules (if it is not the first time that a student logs on the system) the second set of rules is executed to perform the phase of reconstruction. Considering previously stored values in the student model, the system reconstructs the state of the user interface from the last student's session.
- The third set of rules concerns inference mechanism. Inference rules define the ways of observing student's actions while she/he is logged on the system and record those actions by updating the user model accordingly.
- In the last phase the system generates an interface adapted to individual learner on the basis of current state of her/his student model. This phase is realized through the fourth set of rules called adaptation rules.

Inference rules as well as adaptation rules are being executed in alternations after each student's action (e.g. selection of a node or a structural attribute of the node) thus providing continuous dynamic update of the student model and generation of a user interface adapted to its new state.

The design is just a high-level outline of the adaptivity mechanism (which hasn't been implemented yet) and consequently its rules are expressed in pseudo-code. As an illustration of the inference phase a rule for monitoring student's navigation and updating traversal values is provided:

```
if node.selected then
    node.traversal := node.traversal + 1;
    n := node.parent.count;
    node.parent.traversal := node.parent.traversal+(1/n);
```

Subsequent to an update of the user model, the system performs adaptation rules to derive new interface features and generate their presentation to the student. In the following the rule for adaptive annotation of nodes is given. All nodes with *traversal>0* are assumed to be visited or known, accordingly being colored blue. Currently selected node is purple-colored. Nodes that have not been visited or learned yet (according to tests results) remain yellow as colored in the initial phase, except the relevant node which is being colored green to suggest the student to selected it next.

```
if node.traversal > 0 then
  node.colour := blue;
if node.selected then
  node.colour := purple;
if node.relevance then
  node.colour := green;
```

We claim that these sets of rules provide a very dynamic and flexible interface adaptation of systems built on TEx-Sys model. Although traversing the nodes in order to learn particular domain knowledge cannot be actually concerned as knowledge, we expect that proposed combination of learning and testing will significantly enhance the process of student's knowledge acquisition. Student's knowledge is evaluated only through tests, with different dynamically generated questions. Therefore, tests are reliable indicators of student's knowledge. Accordingly, immediately after student receives her/his first test, the system gets a trustful base for interface adaptation which simplifies student's learning in further interaction. Nevertheless, the student model initialization, which particularly includes assessment of student's starting knowledge level, remains an open issue. Two approaches are considered; first imposing an entry tests on each course and second using a short introductory lesson ending with a test. Both options have certain limitations so the selection of an appropriate approach will depend on the implementation of particular ITS.

5   Conclusion

Ambient intelligence places the individual at the heart of the development of future Information Society Technologies (IST), emphasizing the need to design technologies for human needs, making interaction simple and effortless. Furthermore, knowledge is the most important resource in such context, hence also dubbed the knowledge society, and the need for its rapid acquisition is more important then ever. On the other hand, although computers are being used at different levels of a teaching process (as subject of teaching as well as tool for supporting the teaching process) despite decades of research their use for tutoring (as the teacher itself) in everyday teaching environment has been quite limited. Intelligent tutoring systems (ITSs), as computer-based educational systems which emulate one-to-one human tutoring process, must consider a student as an individual just like a human teacher would do. In order to improve the effectiveness of a learning process, ITSs have to be adaptive, adjusting the teaching material and the way of its presentation to the student's needs, wishes and abilities. Recently, development in the field of adaptive hypermedia (AH) produced a number of possibly effective adaptivity techniques that could be applied in ITSs to improve their interaction mechanisms.

Despite our expertise and experience in the conceptualization and development of systems based on TEx-Sys model and the fact that they have unquestionably enriched the process of knowledge acquisition at our Department, we are still facing some difficulties. Systems still do not employ any intelligence in the presentation of teaching material but only in the generation of test questions. Consequently, in order to adjust the learning process and teaching material to an individual student, a mechanism for monitoring student's actions and generating adaptive user interface based on those observations is developed and presented in this paper. Adaptation process relies on student model as well as on dynamic updating of its attribute values during the individual interaction. A system mainly performs adaptive navigation support, adjusting the adaptive hypermedia techniques to its own interface. Student's knowledge deduced from tests, is simplifying student's further interaction, consequently improving the process of knowledge acquisition. In order to have better insight in applied AH adaptive technology, background research is summarized in two classifications, first based on user modeling methods applied in a number of recent systems, as well as a second one based on commonly used adaptivity techniques.

Future work will be focused on the employment of such adaptation mechanism in authoring shells (ASs) facing the possibility that such approach has to be refined in order to fit existing architecture. A series of experiments will follow to examine the effects of adaptivity on learning process, as well as to obtain results concerning evaluation of efficiency, accessibility and usability of developed solution. Additional work will also encompass a research of Kolb's learning theory [26] as well as the possibility of learning styles consideration in the interface adaptation on the TEx-Sys model founded systems.

References

1. Brusilovsky, P.: Methods and Techniques of Adaptive Hypermedia. User Modeling and User-Adapted Interaction, Vol. 6 (1996) 87-129 (Reprinted in Adaptive Hypertext and Hypermedia. Kluwer Academic Publishers (1998) 1-43)
2. Brusilovsky, P.: Adaptive hypermedia: From intelligent tutoring systems to Web-based education. (Invited talk) In: Gauthier, C., Frasson, C., Van Lehn, K. (eds.): Intelligent Tutoring Systems. Lecture Notes in Computer Science, Vol. 1839. Springer-Verlag, Berlin (2000) 1-7
3. Brusilovsky, P.: A Distributed Architecture for Adaptive and Intelligent Learning Management Systems. 11th International Conference on Artificial Intelligence in Education. Workshop Towards Intelligent Learning Management Systems, Vol. 4. Sydney (2003)
4. Brusilovsky, P., Anderson, J.: ACT-R electronic bookshelf: An adaptive system for learning cognitive psychology on the Web. In: Maurer, H., Olson, R.G. (eds.): Proceedings of WebNet'98, World Conference of the WWW, Internet, and Intranet. Orlando, FL, AACE (1998) 92-97
5. Brusilovsky, P., Eklund, J.: InterBook: an Adaptive Tutoring System. UniServe Science News, Vol. 12 (1999)
6. Brusilovsky, P., Maybury, M.: From Adaptive Hypermedia to the Adaptive Web. Communications of the ACM, Vol. 45, No. 5 (2002) 31-33
7. Brusilovsky, P., Schwarz, E., Weber, G.: ELM-ART: An intelligent tutoring system on World Wide Web. In: Frasson, C., Gauthier, G., Lesgold, A. (eds.): Intelligent Tutoring Systems. Lecture Notes in Computer Science, Vol. 1086. Springer-Verlag, Berlin (1996) 261-269

8. Burns, H., Capps, C.: Foundations of Intelligent Tutoring Systems: An Introduction. In: Polson, M., Richardson, J. (eds.): Foundations of Intelligent Tutoring Systems. Lawrence Erlbaum Associates Publishers, Hillsdale, NJ (1998) 1-18

9. Collins, A., Neville, P., Bielaczyc, K.: The role of different media in designing learning environments. International Journal of Artificial Intelligence in Education, Vol. 11, No. 1. (2000) 144-162

10. De Bra, P.: Hypermedia structures and systems. (2006) [Available On-line] http://wwwis.win.tue.nl:38080/aha/2L690

11. De Bra, P., Calvi, L.: AHA! An open Adaptive Hypermedia Architecture. The New Review of Hypermedia and Multimedia (1998) 115-139

12. De Bra, P., Brusilovsky, P., Houben, G.J.: Adaptive hypermedia: from systems to framework. ACM Computing Surveys, Vol. 31 n.4es, December 1999, [Available On-line] http://www.cs.brown.edu/memex/ACM_HypertextTestbed/papers/25.html

13. De Bra, P., Houben, G.J., Wu, H.: AHAM: A Dexter-based reference model for adaptive hypermedia. In Proceedings of ACM Conference on Hypertext and Hypermedia, Hypertext' 99, Darmstadt, Germany (1999) 147-156

14. Eklund, J., Sinclair, K.: An empirical appraisal of adaptive interfaces for instructional systems. Educational Technology and Society Journal, Vol. 3 (2000) 165-177

15. Fleischmann, A.: The Electronic Teacher: The Social Impact of Intelligent Tutoring Systems in Education. (2000) [Available On-line] http://wwwbroy.informatik.tu-muenchen.de/~fleischa/papers/its.html

16. Fletcher, J.: Evidence for Learning From Technology – Assisted Instruction. In: O'Neil, H., Perez, R., (eds.): Technology Applications in Education: A Learning View. Lawrence Erlbaum Associates (2003) 79-99

17. Freitas, V., Marcal, V.P., Gasparini, I., Amaral, M.A., Proenca, M.L., Brunetto, M.A.C., et.al.: AdaptWeb: An Adaptive Web-based Courseware. In Proceedings of the International Conference on Information and Communication Technologies in Education (ICTE). Badajoz, Spain (2002) 20-23

18. Granić, A.: Human-centred Design in Intelligent Tutoring: a Key Role of Usability Evaluation. In Proceedings of the 3rd Cambridge Workshop on Universal Access and Assistive Technology (CWUATT 06). Cambridge, United Kingdom (2006) 121-129

19. Granić, A: Foundation of Adaptive Interfaces for Computerized Educational Systems. Ph.D. Diss., Faculty of Electrical Engineering and Computing, University of Zagreb, Croatia (2002) (in Croatian)

20. Granić, A., Glavini , V, Stankov, S.: Usability Evaluation Methodology for Web-based Educational Systems. In Adjunct Proceedings of 8th ERCIM Workshop "User Interfaces for All" (UI4All). Heraklion (Crete), Greece: ERCIM - The European Research Consortium for Informatics and Mathematics (2004) 28.1-28.15.

21. Henze, N., Nejdl, W.: Adaptivity in the KBS Hyperbook System. In 2nd Workshop on Adaptive Systems and User Modeling on the WWW. Toronto, Banff (1999) Held in conjunction with the WorldWideWeb (WWW8) and the International Conference on User Modeling.

22. Henze, N., Nejdl, W.: Logically characterizing adaptive educational hypermedia systems. In International Workshop on Adaptive Hypermedia and Adaptive Web Based Systems, AH 2003, Budapest, Hungary (2003)

23. Höök, K.: Steps to take before intelligent user interfaces become real. Interacting with computers, Vol. 12 (2000) 409-426

24. ISTAG, Information Society Technologies Advisory Group: Scenarios for Ambient Intelligence in 2010. Final Report (2001) EC 2001. [Available On-line] ftp://ftp. cordis.europa.eu/pub/ist/docs/istagscenarios2010.pdf
25. Kinshuk: Does intelligent tutoring have future! In Kinshuk, Lewis, R., Akahori, K., Kemp, R., Okamoto, T., Henderson, L., Lee C.-H. (eds.): Proceedings of the International Conference on Computers in Education, Los Alamitos, CA: IEEE Computer Society (2002) 1524-1525
26. Kolb, A.Y., Kolb, D.A.: Learning styles and learning spaces: A review of the multidisciplinary application of experiential learning in higher education. In Sims, R., Sims, S. (eds.): Learning styles and learning: A key to meeting the accountability demands in education. Hauppauge, NY. Nova Publishers (2006)
27. Magoulas, G.D., Chen, S.Y., Papanikolaou, K.A.: Integrating Layered and Heuristic Evaluation for Adaptive Learning Environments. In Weibelzahl, S., Paramythis, A. (eds.): Proceedings of the Second Workshop on Empirical Evaluation of Adaptive Systems, held at the 9th International Conference on User Modeling UM2003, Pittsburgh (2003) 5-14
28. Murray, T.: Authoring Intelligent Tutoring Systems: An Analysis of the State of the Art. International Journal of Artificial Intelligence in Education, Vol. 10 (1999) 98-129
29. Nute, D.: Knowledge Representation. In Shapiro, S. (ed.): Encyclopedia of Artificial Intelligence. John Wiley & Sons, Inc. (1992) 743-869
30. Oppermann, R., Rashev, R., Kinshuk: Adaptability and Adaptivity in Learning Systems. In Behrooz, A. (ed.): Knowledge Transfer, volume II, pAce, London (1997) 173-179
31. Papanikolaou, K.A., Grigoriadou, M., Kornilakis, H., Magoulas, G.D.: Personalising the Interaction in a Web-based Educational Hypermedia System: the case of INSPIRE. User-Modeling and User-Adapted Interaction, Vol. 13, Issue 3 (2003) 213-267
32. Rickel, J.: Intelligent Computer-Aided Instruction: A Survey Organized Around System Components. IEEE Transactions on System, Man and Cybernetics, Vol. 19, No. 1 (1989) 40-57
33. Rosi , M.: Establishing of Distance Education Systems within the Information Infrastructure. M.Sc. Thesis. Faculty of Electrical Engineering and Computing, University of Zagreb, Zagreb, Croatia (2000) (in Croatian)
34. Schneider-Hufschmidt, M., Kühme, T., Malinowski, U. (eds.): Adaptive User Interfaces: Principles and Practice. North-Holland, Elsevier Science Publishers B.V. (1993)
35. Stankov, S.: Isomorphic Model of the System as the Basis of Teaching Control Principles in the Intelligent Tutoring System. Ph.D. Diss., Faculty of Electrical Engineering, Mechanical Engineering and Naval Architecture, University of Split, Split, Croatia (1997) (in Croatian)
36. Stankov, S.: Principal Investigating Project TP-02/0177-01 Web-oriented Intelligent Hypermedial Authoring Shell. Ministry of Science and Technology of the Republic of Croatia (2003-2005)
37. Stephanidis, C., Paramythis, A., Karagiannidis, C., Savidis, A.: Supporting Interface Adaptation: the AVANTI Web-Browser. 3rd ERCIM Workshop on User Interfaces for All (UI4ALL 97), Strasbourg, France (1997)
38. UM 97 Reader's Guide: User Modeling. Proceedings of the Sixth International Conference, UM97, On-line proceedings (1997) [Available On-line] http://www. um.org

39. Weber, G., Kuhl, H.C., Weibelzahl, S.: Developing adaptive Internet based courses with the authoring system NetCoach. In Proceedings of the Third International Workshop on Adaptive Hypermedia, Sonthofen, Germany (2001) [Available On-line] `http://wwwis.win.tue.nl/ah2001/papers/GWeber-UM01.pdf`

40. Weibelzahl, S. Weber, G.: Evaluating the Inference Mechanism of Adaptive Learning Systems. Pedagogical University Freiburg, Germany (2003)

41. Woods, P.J., Warren, J.R.: Rapid Prototyping of an Intelligent Tutorial System. ACM SIGCSE Bulletin, Vol. 30, No. 3 (1998) 69-73

User Profiles for Adapting Speech Support in the Opera Web Browser to Disabled Users

Jan Heim, Erik G. Nilsson, and Jan Håvard Skjetne

SINTEF ICT
Norway
{jheim,egn,janhs}@sintef.no

Abstract. In this paper we describe results from our work on adapting speech support in the Opera web browser to disabled users, through using available gross categories of equipment feature (screen presentation and program control) to categorize user and usage characteristics in user profiles. Allocation of users to equipment is based on characteristics of user and equipment, rather than on diagnostic categories. We have combined a number of approaches to investigate how users with different kinds of disabilities may benefit from speech support in the Opera web browser, and how the speech support may be adapted to enhance their utility of this support. After an introduction, we present the method used, the user profiles, and how different types of voice support may be adapted to different (combinations of) profiles. The latter includes both general requirements and suggestions for presentation formats and commands (voice or keyboard) for the profiles. The main conclusions from the work are that the voice support in the version of the Opera web browser that was used in the study is most suitable for people who have reading and writing disorders and that further development of voice support should focus on better adaptation for persons with motor disabilities. Most blind and visually impaired people in Norway already have access to specialized support, and do not need the voice support in Opera.

1 Introduction and Related Work

From the early days of computing, new technology has been associated with a lot of possibilities, but it has also introduced new barriers for end-users. Today we can use computers to conduct all our banking tasks, read up to date news and do remote work, but these different solutions are not accessible to all end-users and have introduced new barriers to many of them. Many new Internet based applications do not meet the minimum requirements to accessible design, e.g., the Web Accessibility Initiative (WAI) guidelines – priority 1 [1]. Also, it is not clear how new mobile services and interactive TV can be made fully accessible.

This paper focuses on how to design technology which supports development of web-based services with design for all qualities. "Design for all" is defined by ETSI in a model with three levels [2]:

1. Mainstream products designed according to good Human Factors practice, incorporating considerations for people with impairments, that can be used by a broad range of users.

C. Stephanidis and M. Pieper (Eds.): ERCIM UI4ALL Ws 2006, LNCS 4397, pp. 154 – 172, 2007.
© Springer-Verlag Berlin Heidelberg 2007

2. Products that are adaptable to permit the connection of assistive technology devices
3. Specially designed or tailored products for very disabled users

We will describe a method on how to develop accessible web-based applications with integrated support and use of standard speech technology, supporting developers in making applications with level 1 qualities.

Through the history of computer people with a disability have always struggled to keep up with the development and to get access to computers and applications which have been offered. At all times there has been a race against time to develop specialized solution to make these applications accessible to disabled people, but usually the next cycle of technology development started when adapted technology and applications have been finalized [3]. To meet this challenge, many initiatives have been established, e.g., in USA legislation has been successfully introduced, and is acting as an incentive for the industry to focus on solutions that can be used by all. Politicians have backed these developments because the populations grow older and therefore will be more diverse in abilities and needs. Application developers have also seen a need for technology which may easily be targeted to different technology platforms, because users today do not only use a PC, but also mobile phones, PDAs and interactive TV. This variation in client terminals demands some of the same technical solutions as solutions with design for all qualities.

W3C is the main contributor to the development of specifications to the technology for the web. The Web Accessibility Initiative (WAI) has been working to make web services and applications accessible to as many as possible. WAI was established in 1996 and the first set of guidelines was published in 1999. Today, there is a requirement in USA and Europe that Internet services should follow the priority 1 level within a few years [4, 5].

1.1 Speech and Sound Based Web Clients

There has been conducted development and research on how to use speech and sound to present and operate information and functions for people with different types of disabilities for many years [6-14]. It is however not evident that it is possible to develop a service, which could both have a good visual presentation and at the same time be usable with speech and sound based systems. Nielsen has stated that it is not possible to design a good and usable solution, which is universal – for use by vision and by sound [15]. The requirements are too far apart to make a good unified solution.

The approach this paper presents is to describe different groups of users to make it easier to develop applications and to make the necessary tailoring to the target group. This approach is also supported by Gregor et al. in their work on developing speech applications used by elderly people [16, 17]. Their conclusion is that developers need to seek out diversity in the target group instead of focusing on the typical user group. They have called this new design method "User sensitive inclusive design" instead of the traditional "User centred design".

This paper is specifically addressing the Opera Web browser and its speech and sound interface. The suggestions put forward are therefore specific to this browser.

1.2 Solutions Today

Today, there are specialized software for blind and visually impaired users which give the users access to all programs running on a PC by reading the content and status in documents and applications. There are also products that let the user control a PC only using voice.

There are three different methods to develop applications for speech and sound-based web applications. One solution is to develop a speech and sound interface at the operating system level. This makes it possible to have general access to all applications. The benefit of this solution is that it is application independent. The drawback of it is that web applications, which are multi-modal, will not operate well together with this general solution. A second method is to develop specialized web clients designed for speech control and sound output. The disadvantage of this is that the clients are not optimal for handling all the different types of web pages and applications existing. The third method, which this paper describes, is to make the sound output and the speech control a part of the standard web client and server system. By using XHTML+VoiceXML, CSS2 Speech module and voice navigation (C3N - Command, Control and Content Navigation) in the applications, the developer can make special adaptations to different types of terminals and still reuse most of the contents and functionality [18-21].

2 Method

In this research, we have combined a number of approaches to investigate how users with different kinds of disabilities may benefit from speech support in the Opera web browser, and how the speech support may be adapted to enhance their utility of the speech support. This is an attempt to define the user requirements for the speech and sound interface of the Opera browser. Once implemented, traditional user testing should be applied in order to evaluate the usability of the solution.

2.1 Reference Group

Six experts on the different user groups in question constituted the group. They were appointed on the expectation that people with dyslexia, motor and visual disabilities would benefit from a voice and sound interface. Three were teachers for pupils with special needs: Dyslexia, vision and motor disabilities. Two were working at, and appointed by, user organizations: Norwegian Federation of Organizations of Disabled People (FFO) and The Norwegian Association of the Blind and Partially Sighted. One was working at and appointed by The Delta Centre, a governmental unit working for the promotion of Universal design.

They participated in an interview, two workshops, and evaluated the project at the end. Two participants gave written input after the last workshop.

2.2   Interview of the Participants in the Reference Group

The interview was given in advance of the first meeting in the reference group. It started with a brief introduction to the project and the role of the reference group. The following template was used as a guide to the semi-structured interview.

Which user group does the interviewee represent?
Are there any general characteristics for this group regarding disability, age, experience with ICT equipment, etc?

Tools:
What kind of ICT tools are use among the user group?
Are there any tools utilizing sound for interaction?
Which tools are most common?
What decides which tools that are used?
What is the best, according to your opinion?

What is the most important functionality?
What are the problems?
What is missing?

Who in the user group are benefiting most from using the tools?
Who are benefiting least?

Do you have any opinion about integrating sound interaction in web browsers?

The results from the interviews were used as input to the first meeting in the reference group.

2.3   Workshops

The project had two workshops with participation of the reference group, two developers from Opera Software, and two researchers. The workshops reviewed preliminary results, gave input and suggested solutions and further work. Main goals were to define an optimal set of commands and presentation formats for the different user groups, as well as defining user groups that would benefit from the technology.

2.4   Walkthroughs

The product was presented for three potential users in a semi-naturalistic setting. Participants were videotaped during the walkthroughs. The participants were recruited on the assumption that they were representative for the user groups under study. However, no claim is made that the users are representative in a statistical sense.

Participant 1. Girl 14 years, diagnosis AMC (Arthrogryposis Multiplex Congenitia), this involves inability to lift the arms, resulting in problems when using the keyboard and the mouse, normally she uses some assistive devices like roller mouse and moth stick to operate her PC. During the walkthrough she used her own computer with standard input and output devices in addition to the voice/sound features being tested. She used a headset for voice input. She had a printed page describing the 24 voice commands that could be used during the walkthrough. The walkthrough was carried through at her home, with one facilitator and one observer. Her father was present throughout the whole session.

Walkthrough. The overall user task was to navigate to a web page about The Beatles, a topic she was working with in a project at school. A facilitator guided her through the necessary steps, asking her to perform a variety of input actions along the way; however, she had to come up with the actual commands herself.

Commands used in the walkthrough:
- Back/ Forward
- Home
- Full screen
- Next page/Previous page
- New page
- Quit application
- Zoom in/out
- Zoom normal
- Top/Bottom
- Up/Down/Left/Right
- Next/previous link
- Open link
- Next/previous heading
- Read
- Speak

A short interview was taken at the end of the session.

The user had few problems identifying the correct commands; however she confused Back and Previous page (which are two different commands in Opera). The browser misinterpreted Up, Top, Down, Zoom in, and Home, at least once.

She doubted that she would use voice input in an actual user situation, positively not if she was in a classroom situation.

Participant 2. Boy, 17 with dyslexia. He is used to the Internet and uses it more than eight hours per day, reading English pages daily. He uses English and Norwegian speech synthesis all the time. He was accompanied by his mother.

The speech synthesis part of Opera was activated during the whole session. He was asked to read eight paragraphs in English, from five to ten lines of text, from the computer. The texts were about Eminem and Britney Spears. After each paragraph he was asked to reproduce the content in his own words. The difficulty of each task was indicated on a five point scale from "Very difficult" to "Very easy". Half of the paragraphs were read with speech synthesis the other half was read without, starting without. In both cases the participant read silently.

All four paragraphs with speech synthesis were rated "Very easy", while the 3 paragraphs read without were rated as "Difficult" and one as "Neither easy nor difficult". He used about half the time to read paragraphs when utilizing speech synthesis. In all cases his oral reproductions were satisfactory. He reported that he uses earphones while reading in the class. He found the voice in Opera a little more blurred than the one he was used to (on Apple Macintosh).

Participant 3. Male, 50, congenitally blind, teacher and IT-expert at a competence center for blind people.

During the walkthrough the participant used his own computer with Braille display. He is used to a standard synthetic speech program (JAWS[1]), which he use together with a Braille display. A headset was used when the speech input was tested. 21 keyboard commands and 24 speech input commands were presented aurally before the relevant walkthrough. The commands were repeated whenever the participant asked for it.

The participant was first asked to demonstrate how he usually uses his equipment by reading from newspapers, telephone directory and an information page from WAI (http://www.w3.org/WAI/). Then he was asked to navigate around the WAI page using only the Opera speech synthesis. He commented that the voice used in Opera also is available in JAWS. He used the Braille display together with the synthetic speech. There were a few instances of interference between what he was used to in JAWS and the functionality in Opera (e.g., the enter key did not always work as expected). He tested the speech input also using the WAI pages, and the pages for a vendor of assistive technology. The software interpreted almost all speech commands that were used correctly. There were some troubles hitting the "Scroll Lock" button that were used as the switch for inputting speech. He was not used to giving a separate commando for having the text read. He could not see that speech input would be an improvement compared to the functionality he usually had available.

2.5 Expert Review

Two experts on user interface design (researchers from SINTEF) had a preliminary review of the command set that was implemented at the time. They gave a separate written report on this review.

3   User Profiles

3.1 Background

The idea behind defining a user profile is to offer users a version of the functionality of the browser that is adapted to their particular needs and wishes. It is important that

---

[1] http://www.freedomscientific.com/fs_products/software_jaws.asp

the same version of Opera should be capable of alternating among various user profiles, so that a helper, for example, can enter the application in the way that she is used to.

In the following paragraphs, "function" means "what Opera does", while "command" refers to "what the user does in order to have a function carried out". There are three types of command in Opera: voice commands, mouse commands (including "Basic mouse usage" and "Mouse gestures"), and keyboard commands.

It will be possible to implement adaptations via the use of one or more of these mechanisms.

- **Redefining the command set.** This is a matter of defining new commands. For voice control, new combinations of phonemes; for keyboard commands, new keyboard combinations; and for mouse control, new mouse movements and mouse clicks. The necessity for this operation may be due to a wish that the commands should be easy to remember, easy to pronounce or easy to perform. Some users may have a limited vocabulary at their disposal, while others may be able to reach only some of the keys on their keyboard.
- **(Re)defining how commands are mapped onto functions.** This process will always be necessary after redefinition of the command set, but it can also be performed on the basis of an existing command set.
- **Defining "command macros".** This process will lead to a command automatically triggering a sequence of functions, e.g., read = Highlight next block & Speak selection.
- **Limiting the number of commands.** This is partly a matter of limiting the number of commands that are capable of performing the same function, and partly of limiting the number of functions that can be performed. This process may be useful in making a set of commands easier for a user to learn, and it may also help to improve success rates when using voice control and "Mouse gestures".
- **Defining standard functionality.** This may be a matter of how the pages are presented, or whether some particular action is performed when a new page is opened, when the cursor is at the bottom of the page, and so on. For switch control, one type of function will consist of the cursor moving automatically from element to element until a switch is pressed. For speech synthesis, it could be useful to customize reading speed, voice (male/female), and how cursors for headings, font sizes, links, etc., are sound-coded. Much of this can be dealt with via style-sheets.

3.2 The Profiles

The user profiles are defined on background of which user groups that will benefit from different combinations of content presentation and interaction. Here we present the user groups in some details, giving some general considerations regarding their need for speech control. Table 1 (at the end of this section) sums up the profiles. In the next section, we look more closely into how different types of speech support may be adapted to different combinations of these user groups.

3.3   Group 1 - Blind and Partially Sighted Persons Who Wish to Use Voice Control

In Norway, this group largely consists of persons who have become blind or partially sighted as adults. Blind and partially sighted children and young people will normally receive special training and equipment, and they are capable of using keyboards, Braille readers and speech synthesis: see the group "Blind and partially sighted persons who wish to use keyboard control".

Norwegian users in this group are extremely heterogeneous in terms of their experience of computer technology and the Internet. We can not assume that all users are capable of using the keyboard according to the touch-typing method, i.e., not looking at the keyboard while they type. For these people, therefore, entering web addresses and filling in forms is not an option. If current versions of Opera (which only support English speech synthesis) are to be of interest to this group, we will need to assume that they wish to read English-language pages.

3.4   Group 2 - Blind and Partially Sighted Persons Who Wish to Use the Keyboard

In Norway, this group largely consists of people who have been blind or have suffered visual impairment since birth or from an early age. They have been given suitable training and equipment, and can make use of keyboard commands, Braille readers and speech synthesis, skills that in many cases will make Opera's speech functions superfluous. In other countries, however, the situation will be quite different, and Opera will be capable of being a good, reasonably priced alternative.

3.5   Group 3 - Persons with Motor Disabilities[2] Who Wish to Have Speech Synthesis

Users with this profile will experience problems in dealing with standard input media such as the mouse and keyboard, may be blind or partially sighted, or may wish to have the text read out for other reasons, for example if they are unable to read.

3.6   Group 4 - Persons with Cognitive Disabilities or with Reading and/or Writing Disorders, Who Wish to Have Speech Synthesis

Users with this profile have the sensory and motor abilities needed to handle the mouse and keyboard, but wish to have the text read out. This desire may be due to poor reading skills, or it may be based on pedagogical grounds such as a need for practice in English. For users with reading disorders, experiences show that once the user has become accustomed to the voice, the reading speed can be set for example to 300 words per minute or more if the user can simultaneously see the text and he/she will still be able to grasp its content.

---

[2] In this context, "motor disabilities" refers to having problems with using the standard input devices as mouse and keyboard.

3.7 Group 5 - Partially Sighted Persons Without Proficiency of Keyboard Control or With Motor Disabilities

For this group, the need for speech commands may primarily be due to their difficulty in seeing the mouse pointer, or because they cannot use the mouse for other reasons. Searching, typing and completing forms are basically all problematic for this group, who should be able to see well enough to prefer visual to auditory presentation. In general, the same commands as suggested for those who use both voice control and synthetic speech should be usable in this case, but they will need to be supplemented by commands for zooming and moving around the screen image. It should also be possible to utilize both buttons and menus. For this group, it would be useful to include simple mechanisms for entering name and address into forms by means of previously completed fields that can easily be related to the information in a form.

3.8 Group 6 - Persons with Motor Disabilities

The possibilities of repeating voice commands and of using an extra visible cursor should be considered for this group too, as this would make it easier for them to deal with error situations and would simplify navigation. It would also be useful for this group to include simple mechanisms for entering a name and address into forms by means of previously completed fields that can easily be related to information in a form. The possibility of spelling out words when entering URLs, searching and completing forms is also important.

"Push to talk"/"Hold in", an option in the voice control in Opera, is not a good solution for people with severe mobility problems. Special keyboards and switch-boxes allow a key-press or a mouse-click to be transferred to a switch that can subsequently be configured according to the needs of the individual (location and/or design, e.g., a sound-actuated switch or a suck/blow switch). An alternative would be to implement a "Wake up" voice command to start and stop voice control. This is a function which is implemented in commercial voice recognizers. It should be possible to configure the browser in such a way that it is receptive to voice commands until the function is turned off again: i.e., an "On/off" function as well as a "Hold in" function. This would be similar, but not identical, to Opera's "Key not required to talk". A half-way solution might be that in "Key not required to talk" mode, Opera would require a wake-up word (e.g., "Browser") to be given before all commands, i.e., that what is currently an option would become a requirement in this mode.

Many persons with motor disabilities need a combination of means of operating a computer. One and the same user, for example, may have a need for both keyboard control and voice commands. For certain diagnostic groups, their illness may have a negative prognosis (i.e., they are likely to become worse in the course of time), which may mean that using the keyboard will gradually have to be replaced by switch control and voice control. Pronunciation abilities can also gradually deteriorate.

The cell for group 1 also covers persons with both visual and motor disabilities and all users who, due to their context of use, have a need for both voice control and auditory presentation. The cell for group 6 also covers all users who wish to employ speech control because of the context of use, motorists, machine operators, etc.

Table 1. Summary of the chosen user profiles

Content presentation / Interaction	Speech synthesis	Magnified screen image	Normal screen image
Voice control	**Group 1** - Blind and partially sighted persons who wish to use voice control	**Group 5** - Partially sighted persons without proficiency of keyboard control or with motor disabilities	**Group 6** - Persons with motor disabilities
Keyboard control	**Group 2** - Blind and partially sighted persons who wish to use the keyboard		
Key control and alternative input mechanisms, etc.	**Group 3** - Persons with motor disabilities who wish to have speech synthesis		
Ordinary mouse pointer (and keyboard)	**Group 4** -Persons with cognitive disabilities		
	Group 4 - Persons with reading or writing disorders who wish to have speech synthesis		

4 Adapting Different Types of Speech Support to User Profiles

4.1 Presentation

For the given user profiles, there are four main presentation formats that are applicable:

1. Spoken output as implemented in Opera (group 4 & 3 (partly))
2. Adapted spoken output (group 1, 2 & 3 (partly))
3. Standard visual presentation (group 6)
4. Simplified visual presentation (group 5)

Spoken Output as Implemented in Opera (group 4 & 3 (partly)). This presentation format is applicable for Group 4 and users in Group 3 that can see. These users do not require different types of sound markers ("earcons") for different types of content to enable them to identify individual types of element. The most important thing is that the text should be read out as naturally as possible. They must be given the possibility of highlighting text and having it read out, via a keyboard or mouse command. At present, when text is marked in Opera it stays highlighted when speech is turned on. This function is important, as it allows the user to see just where he or she is in the text.

It is also important that it should be possible to highlight the text word by word while it is being read out, as an aid for grasping the content or understanding what is being read. In some browsers, text from the Internet can be copied over to another document or window in order to allow access to this type of function. However, the best solution would be if such functions were directly available in the text on the web-page. Reading speed also needs to be modifiable in order to match the requirements of individual users in different situations. When a text continues over a number of columns, it is important that only a single column should be highlighted at a time. If several columns of text are highlighted simultaneously, this will influence the reading process negatively. Users with reading and/or writing problems often suffer from reduced memory capacity. The simultaneous use of auditory and visual channels will give such users the special support they need.

Adapted Spoken Output (group 1, 2 & 3 (partly)). This presentation format is applicable for Group 1 & 2 and users in Group 3 that are blind or partially sighted.

The number of headings, links, images, frames and tables should be read aloud automatically every time a new page is opened. This would also function as an auditory signal that the page had been downloaded completely. It is important that this feature can be toggled on and off, and that it can be linked to pages that the user already knows. Reading aloud takes a long time and is not always necessary if one is already familiar with the page. It should also be an option to have the name of the page read out when it is opened.

An auditory signal should be given every time a new window is opened (typically when following a link; when the screen cannot be seen this is important information).

Suggestions for Presentation Format. When text is being read aloud, a distinction should be made between image/graphic elements with and without text, links, headings and body text. All text should be read by male voice unless otherwise indicated. Text relating to images and graphic elements should be read by a female voice. Different earcons should be used to mark images and graphic elements, empty elements, and before and after a link text. For links without text, the URL should be read, with a supplementary mechanism to break off the reading if the address is very long. Headlines should be read with "Formal speech", i.e., a combination of slightly reduced speed, heavy "voice stress" and low "voice pitch". The possibility of having different presentation formats for different levels of headlines should be considered. Ordinary body text will not have a different presentation format from that which is set directly in Opera, partly because it may be appropriate for members of this user group to vary the speaking rate as they gradually become familiar with speech synthesis. Handling figures is difficult to do well in a general way. As a point of departure, figures that indicate quantities or numbers should be read as complete numbers, while telephone numbers, serial numbers, etc., should be read one figure at a time, or possibly in groups of three or four. An alternative would be to read all numbers as complete numbers, and after any number consisting of more than e.g., four figures has been read out, the user would be given the opportunity to request the figures to be read individually. If forced to choose whether figures should be read as a single continuous number or figure by figure, we recommend reading all numbers one figure at a time.

Not all user groups will benefit by text being read out using different voices and sound effects. As an alternative presentation format, it should be considered offering the possibility of purely verbal signals as providers of information about different types of element before they are read: e.g., "Link", "Heading level 1", "Body text", "Image", etc., followed by a pause before the elements themselves are read out.

Standard Visual Presentation (group 6). This user group may utilize the standard visual presentation, possibly adapted to personal preferences using standard tailoring mechanisms in Opera.

Simplified Visual Presentation (group 5). When using this presentation format, each page should be opened with a minimum number of panels and graphic elements. The most commonly used short-cuts (Print, Home) should be shown, but search fields and any inessential text at the top of the page should be eliminated. If possible, the user should be able to set the cursor to provide an extra clear visual signal in order to simplify navigation and orientation on the page.

The user should be given an automatic audio "echoing" of all keyboard commands understood by Opera, in order to make it easier for the user to deal with error situations, or that it is provided an explicit command to repeat the last command given, as it was interpreted by Opera.

4.2   Commands, Navigation and Text Entry

For the given user profiles, there are four schemes that are applicable:
1. Voice control (group 1, 5 & 6)
2. Reduced keyboard command set (group 2)
3. Standard interaction using mouse and/or keyboard (group 4)
4. Adapted to individual users (group 3)

When presenting these schemes below, we divide between navigation within a single page, and navigation between pages.

Voice Control (group 1, 5 & 6). The users should be given an automatic "echo" of all spoken commands understood by Opera, or that it is provided an explicit command to repeat the last command given, as it was interpreted by Opera. There should also be an option to use a simple "beep" to tell the user that the command has been understood.

As these user groups either are blind, have problems reading or can read from the screen, the commands needed for navigation within a single page vary a bit between the groups. Also, there are some special considerations for some of the groups.

Navigation and Presentation within a Single Page. There should be a simple command set for navigating within a page and selecting text. For group 1, reading should start automatically when the cursor is moved to a new element. This also applies, for example, to the bookmark panel. Reading or other form of sound coding of tags for headline level, links, tables, frames, figures, images, etc. should also be included.

Table 2 lists the voice commands that are considered most important for these user profiles (texts in square brackets are not part of the command, but are included to explain the command):

For Group 1 it should also be considered including a command that will pause the reading process. A "Stop" command could be supplemented by a "Continue" command. When text is being read continuously, a "Skip" command would be useful for jumping to the next element. There is a need for mechanisms that would enable text to be inserted letter by letter, for example in performing searches (within a page and in Google, for example) and in dialogue boxes and forms. Voice commands for configuring the presentation format should also be included. It is particularly important to be able to adjust the speed, but the other features are also important. It ought to be possible to give a command to follow a link before the name of the link has been fully read out. If a command has been misinterpreted, it is important that a command should be available that returns the user to where she or he was before the error occurred.

Table 2. Suggested voice command sets

Command	Group 1	Group 5 & 6
Quit application	X	X
Reload page	X	X
Go to top [of page]	X	X
Go to bottom [of page]	X	X
Select all	X	
Stop [reading]	X	
[Highlight] Next link	X	X
[Highlight] Previous link	X	X
[Highlight] Next heading	X	X
[Highlight] Previous heading	X	X
[Highlight] Next element	X	X
[Highlight] Previous element	X	X
Zoom in		X
Zoom out		X
Zoom normal		X
[Scroll] Right		X
[Scroll] Left		X
[Scroll] Down		X
[Scroll] Up		X
Tab [to next widget]		X
Back tab [to previous widget]		X
[Enter or leave] Full screen		X
Click [button]		X
Check [or uncheck checkbox]		X

Navigating Between Pages. There should be provided a list of bookmarks of WAI-compatible English-language web-pages as standard. All these pages should have good "nicknames" for direct access. For managing the bookmarks, we recommend avoiding the use of folders, instead offering only a long list to which bookmarks can be added (from the currently open page) and deleted. This will simplify the set of commands necessary to navigate in the set of bookmarks.

The voice commands that are considered most important for these user profiles are (texts in square brackets are not part of the command, but are included to explain the command):

- Forward
- Back
- Next page
- Previous page
- Home
- Open link
- Open link in new [page]
- Go Up [to previous item in bookmark list]
- Go Down [to next item in bookmark list]
- Go to bookmark <nickname>
- Voice help
- Voice commands
- Open bookmark panel
- Add bookmark
- Delete [bookmark]

Forms Management. We suggest including speech commands for this purpose in Opera. It would then also be useful to spell out the content of text fields. It would also be useful to include simple mechanisms for entering a name and address, for example, in forms by means of previously completed fields that could easily be related to the information in a form. If this is done, commands that enable users to use check-boxes, radio buttons and push buttons, should be available.

Reduced Keyboard Command Set (group 2). For this group, the need for a reduced command set is primarily based on the desire to make it easy to learn. There ought to be a "basic" command set that users will learn first, before they have the possibility of accessing more advanced functions. For this user group it may be useful to be able to alternate between a limited command set (in order to reduce the chances of typing errors) and a full command set.

Navigation and presentation within a page. There should be a simple command set for navigating within a page and selecting text. Reading should start automatically when the cursor is moved to a new element. Reading or other form of sound coding of tags for headline level, links, tables, frames, figures, images, etc. should also be included.

The functions that are considered the most important to be supported by keyboard commands for this user profile are (we present just the functions, not the actual keyboard commands):

- Exit
- Reload
- Go to start
- Go to end
- Select all
- Stop reading
- Highlight next URL
- Highlight previous URL
- Highlight next heading
- Highlight previous heading
- Highlight next element
- Highlight previous element

Navigating Between Pages. This scheme should include the same bookmarks mechanisms that were suggested above for the scheme "Voice control (group 1, 5 & 6)", but the command set for navigating between pages is slightly different.

The functions that are considered the most important to be supported by keyboard commands for this user profile are (we present just the functions, not the actual keyboard commands):

- Forward
- Back
- Switch to next page
- Switch to previous page
- Go to homepage
- Go to bookmark <nickname>
- "Focus panel, "bookmarks""
- Add to bookmarks
- Delete (from bookmarks)
- Open link
- Open link in new page
- Previous item in bookmark list
- Next item in bookmark list

Forms management. To the extent that they have mastered touch-typing (i.e., writing without looking at the keyboard) this user group will relatively simply find it useful to be able to use forms. Meaningful auditory feedback for elements such as check-boxes, radio buttons, command buttons and fields to be completed in forms will have to be provided. It would also be useful to include simple mechanisms for entering a name and address, for example, in forms by means of previously completed fields that could easily be related to the information in a form.

Standard interaction using mouse and/or keyboard (group 4). This user group may utilize standard interaction mechanisms, possibly adapted to personal preferences using standard tailoring mechanisms in Opera.

Adapted to individual users (group 3). For persons who utilize other input mechanisms, the problem as far as commands are concerned will largely be related to the specific form taken by such mechanisms, and how Opera can integrate them into its set of functions. It is beyond the scope of this paper to investigate the possibilities and limitations of this area.

5 Discussion

The version of the Opera browser with speech support used in this study is most suitable for people who have reading and writing disorders. Apart from its lack of support for Norwegian speech synthesis, the present-day product could be used by very many persons in this group who can read English.

Many people with motor disabilities would benefit by being able to control an Internet browser via spoken commands. Many people in this group would require individual adaptations of the browser (special commands) as well as other equipment such as switch control, and Opera would have to function along with such equipment. It should also be pointed out that at present there are few or no voice-control products on the market that have been adapted to the needs of this group.

Most blind and visually impaired people in Norway already have access to modified equipment and software such as screen interpreters, speech synthesis and Braille readers. They use the keyboard and have no need for voice control. If Opera is to be an alternative for them, its speech synthesis must be on a level with the best available Norwegian speech synthesizers.

Both voice control and speech synthesis are capable of providing useful support in specific contexts of use such as driving, when the hands are needed for other purposes, in the dark, when one's attention is elsewhere or when wearing gloves or mittens.

Our recommendation is that Opera should continue to develop voice support for disabled persons according to the following set of priorities:

1. Better adaptation for persons with motor disabilities, partly because such modifications could be implemented fairly easily, but also because the benefits to this group would be great relative to the amount of effort involved.
2. Voice control for people with poor vision, for the same reasons as above.
3. Norwegian speech synthesis and more advanced adaptations for dyslexic persons and those with motor disabilities.
4. Adaptations for blind persons.

These recommendations are based on user requirements and on solutions that are already available on the Norwegian market.

5.1 Design for All or Design for Special Needs?

The position taken in this paper is that each individual has its own requirements for all pieces of equipment. However, these requirements will change dynamically with the context of use, and the with the user's experience. It is also true, that many different individuals in many different usage contexts will have very similar requirements. The reason why people can not see a computer screen, may, for example, vary from conditions due to the person's sight, characteristics of the screen and keyboard, the position of the equipment in relation to the user or the lightning conditions. However, all these users may have the same requirements to input/output mechanisms. We have therefore followed an approach where gross categories of equipment feature (screen presentation and program control) are used to categorize user and usage characteristics. This results in allocation of users to equipment that is based on characteristics of user and equipment, rather than on diagnostic categories.

In doing this we will support the development of design for all, which is especially interesting in the area of ambient technology where interaction with equipment with sound interfaces plays an important part. Generalizing this, there are clear connections between the needs of users that benefit from utilizing speech support when using a web browser and the needs of all users in an ambient intelligent environment, as such environments may exclude both traditional interaction devices like mouse and keyboard and display screens.

6   Conclusions and Future Research

In this paper we have described results from our work on adapting speech support in the Opera web browser to disabled users, through using available features as a main means for categorization. We have presented the method used, the user profiles, and how different types of voice support may be adapted to different (combinations of) the profiles. The main conclusions from the work are that the voice support in the version of the Opera web browser that was used in the study is most suitable for people who have reading and writing disorders and that further development of voice support should focus on better adaptation for persons with motor disabilities. In Norway blind and partially blind people will normally have an option to use other kinds of assistive technology that is more efficient that the voice and sound interface offered by Opera.

"Mainstream users" has not been the central focus of this discussion; however such users will experience situations where the voice and sound interface will be valuable. Further work remains to be done here.

For further development, it is important the one and the same version of Opera should be capable of alternating among various user profiles, so that a helper, for example, can enter the application in the way that she is used to. For speech synthesis, it should be possible to customize reading speed, voice (male/female), and how cursors for headings, font sizes, links, etc., are sound-coded. It is also important that Opera should support Norwegian and that it should be possible to choose among different languages.

The main requirements for voice control are:

- It should be easy to implement pre-configured command sets for specific user groups.
- It should be easy to configure individual spoken commands.
- The system should minimize the speech recognition errors through designing a robust dialog system [22].
- It should be possible to get auditory feedback on own spoken commands.
- There should be good opportunities to undo and escape from error situations.

The main requirements for synthetic speech are:

- It should be possible to get information on content before page is read (number of links, headings, paragraphs etc)
- It should be possible to turn on automatic reading of selected text.
- There should be aural coding (voice or earcon) of different page elements.
- It should be possible to get a visual cue on what word of the text that is read at the moment.
- It should be functionality for easy and flexible justification of reading speed.

The research presented in this paper has drawn conclusions on status, suggested direction and requirements for further development of voice support in the Opera web browser. Including the suggested enhancements and features in future versions of the Opera web browser is mainly an issue for Opera Software. The chosen approach of coupling available features to user groups and using this for finding typical user profiles which are fairly uniform in their needs for functionality should be generalized and further developed on new and different cases.

Acknowledgements. The work on which this paper is based is supported by the projects *Making Internet accessible by using speech, FAMOUS and FLAMINKO,* all funded by the Norwegian Research Council (the first by the IT Funk programme). SINTEF's research has been conducted in cooperation with Opera Software and the participants in the reference group. The following individuals from Opera Software have contributed to the work: Lillian Medbye, Olav Mørkrid, Ola Peter Kleiven and Claudio Santambrogio. The following individuals from the reference group have contributed to the work: Haakon Aspelund (Deltasenteret), Tone Finne (Bredtvet Kompetansesenter), Anne Kathrine Halvorsen (SIKTE), Randi Kvåle (Huseby kompetansesenter), Øyvind Skotland (FFO) and Arild Øyan (Blindeforbundet).

References

1. *Web Content Accessibility Guidelines 1.0.* 1999 [cited 2006 May 12]; Available from: http://www.w3.org/TR/WCAG10/.
2. *ETSI EG 202 116 Human Factors (HF): Guidelines for ICT products and services; "Design for all".* 2002.
3. *The Web: Access and Inclusion for Disabled People.* 2004, Disability Rights Commission: London.
4. European Commission, *eEurope 2005 : an information society for all : an action plan to be presented in view of the Sevilla European Council 21/22 June 2002.* Documents / Commission of the European Communities. 2002, Luxembourg: Office for Official Publications of the European Communities.
5. Norwegian Ministry of Trade and Industry, *E-Norge 2005.* 2002, Oslo: Norwegian Ministry of Trade and Industry.
6. Zajicek, M., A. Lee, and R. Wales, *Older adults and the usability of speech interaction,* in *Proceedings of the Latin American conference on Human-computer interaction.* 2003, ACM Press: Rio de Janeiro, Brazil.
7. McTear, M.F., *Spoken dialogue technology: Enabling the conversational user interface.* ACM Computing Surveys, 2002. **34**(1): p. 90-169.

8. Massof, R.W. *Auditory assistive devices for the blind.* in *International Conference on Auditory Display.* 2003. Boston, MA, USA.

9. James, F. *Presenting HTML Structure in Audio: User Satisfaction with Audio Hypertext.* in *International Conference on Auditory Display (ICAD).* 1996.

10. Deng, L. and X. Huang, *Challenges in adopting speech recognition.* Commun. ACM, 2004. **47**(1): p. 69-75.

11. Bronstad, P.M., K. Lewis, and J. Slatin. *Conveying Contextual Information Using Non-Speech Audio Clues Reduces Workload.* in *Technology And Persons With Disabilities Conference.* 2003: Center On Disabilities.

12. Zajicek, M., *Patterns for encapsulating speech interface design solutions for older adults*, in *Proceedings of the 2003 conference on Universal usability.* 2003, ACM Press: Vancouver, British Columbia, Canada.

13. Gregor, P. and A. Dickinson, *Cognitive difficulties and access to information systems: an interaction design perspective.* SIGACCESS Access. Comput., 2005(83): p. 59-63.

14. Furui, S. *Automatic speech recognition and its application to information extraction.* in *37th conference on Association for Computational Linguistics.* 1999. College Park, Maryland, USA: Association for Computational Linguistics.

15. Nielsen, J. *Alertbox - Alternative Interfaces for Accessibility.* 2003 [cited 2004 May 5]; Available from: http://www.useit.com/alertbox/20030407.html.

16. Gregor, P., A.F. Newell, and M. Zajicek, *Designing for dynamic diversity: interfaces for older people*, in *Proceedings of the fifth international ACM conference on Assistive technologies.* 2002, ACM Press: Edinburgh, Scotland.

17. Newell, A.F. and P. Gregor, *"User sensitive inclusive design"— in search of a new paradigm*, in *Proceedings on the 2000 conference on Universal Usability.* 2000, ACM Press: Arlington, Virginia, United States.

18. Cross, C., et al. *XHTML+Voice Profile 1.1.* 2003 [cited 2004 May 10]; Available from: http://www-306.ibm.com/software/pervasive/multimodal/x+v/11/spec.htm.

19. *W3C Recommendation: Voice Extensible Markup Language (VoiceXML) Version 2.0.* 2004 [cited 2004 May 10]; Available from: http://www.w3.org/TR/2004/REC-voicexml20-20040316/.

20. *W3C Working Draft: CSS3 Speech Module.* 2003 [cited 2004 May 10]; Available from: http://www.w3.org/TR/2003/WD-css3-speech-20030514/.

21. *W3C Recommendation: XHTML™ 1.0: The Extensible HyperText Markup Language.* 2000 [cited 2004 May 10]; Available from: http://www.w3.org/TR/2000/REC-xhtml1-20000126/.

22. Marc, C., *An empirical study of speech recognition errors in a task-oriented dialogue system*, in *Proceedings of the Second SIGdial Workshop on Discourse and Dialogue - Volume 16.* 2001, Association for Computational Linguistics: Aalborg, Denmark.

A Context Model for Context-Aware System Design Towards the Ambient Intelligence Vision: Experiences in the eTourism Domain

Federica Paganelli, Gabriele Bianchi, and Dino Giuli

Electronics and Telecommunications Department, University of Florence, v. S. Marta 3
Florence, Italy
federica.paganelli@unifi.it,
gabriele.bianchi@gmail.com,
dino.giuli@unifi.it

Abstract. The Ambient Intelligence (AmI) vision implies the concept of "smart spaces" populated by intelligent entities. While most implementations focus strictly on local applications of "AmI", we think of an AmI scenario as a federation of instances of local and application AmI domains. In order to deal with distributed context handling in AmI domains, we propose a context model suitable for distributed context acquisition, reasoning and delivery to applications. We propose a hybrid approach, which aims at combining the advantages of object-oriented models for distributed context handling and those of ontology-based models for context reasoning. We have applied this model to the development of a context-aware eTourism application. This application aims at providing tourists with context-aware services supporting communication and knowledge exchange. It integrates already available location-based content delivery services with a context-aware instant messaging service and a provider reputation service. Here we describe main design issues and prototype implementation.

Keywords: context-awareness, context modeling, ontology, eTourism.

1 Introduction

Context-awareness is a major issue for realizing the Ambient Intelligence vision: "AmI implies a seamless environment of computing, advanced networking technology and specific interfaces. This environment should be aware of the specific characteristics of human presence and personalities" and "...adapt to the needs of users..." [8].

The AmI vision proposed by ISTAG [14] includes the notion of "AmI Spaces", populated by smart intelligent objects and environments (e.g. home, vehicle, public spaces, and so forth), which are provided with computational resources and decision and communication capabilities. They are also capable of seamlessly interoperating and adapting their behavior to their surrounding environment.

While most contributions of context-awareness focus on strictly "local applications" of AmI (e.g. smart homes, smart meeting rooms, etc.), some authors have recently

C. Stephanidis and M. Pieper (Eds.): ERCIM UI4ALL Ws 2006, LNCS 4397, pp. 173 – 191, 2007.

begun to extensively analyze AmI issues. Lee et al. [21] distinguish three categories of ubiquitous services: proximity, domain, and global services. The proximity services are found through the closest service registry, while the domain services are discovered within an administrative domain boundary. The global services include any other services from the Internet. Da Rocha [5] distinguishes a local context domain, containing context information provided by a device and used by applications running on that device, and non-local domain containing information from another context provider, requiring at least one hop through the network.

Our approach is based on the definition of two types of AmI domains, according to geographical and application-dependent criteria, rather than on coverage [21] and network topology issues [5]:

- a Local domain, where applications should adapt to the context of entities which do not move or have delimited mobility, circumscribed by geographical boundaries (e.g. smart homes, offices, museums).
- An Application domain, where applications should adapt to the context of entities which move in non-predefined environments; instead, organizational/application boundaries are defined (e.g. tourist guides, or application for mobile workers).

Each domain instance is characterized by a certain level of autonomous behavior. However, in a real AmI deployment scenario, we can imagine a federation of heterogeneous AmI domains, rather than a set of "AmI islands". It is likely to imagine that an application domain could use services provided by local domains, therefore different AmI domains would need to mutually exchange context knowledge.

In order to deal with distributed context handling in AmI domains, a proper context model approach should be defined. Here we propose a context model that supports distributed context acquisition, reasoning and delivery to applications. Our work uses a hybrid approach, aiming at combining the advantages of two models: an object-oriented model, which is better suited for distributed context handling and exchange, and an ontology-based model, which provides better support for reasoning, but cannot be efficiently managed in a mobile environment (e.g. local inference engines cannot be deployed on resource constraint mobile devices).

According to that model, we also describe the logical architecture for a context-aware system. This architecture has been implemented in the framework of the KAMER Project for the development of a context-aware system supporting knowledge-intensive human activities.

Kamer (Knowledge Management in Ambient Intelligence: technologies enabling the innovative development of Emilia Romagna) is an Italian regional project that involves two universities and one industry. The main objective of the Kamer project is to define novel models and technologies of Ambient Intelligence and context-awareness supporting knowledge exchange and collaboration among individuals in mobility. The scenario that has been identified for testing out knowledge processes focuses on tourists visiting a cultural city (Piacenza) and its points of interest.

Well-known examples of context-aware e-tourism services are location-based content delivery services. Our approach differs from previous ones as we consider a tourist not only as a target for content delivery, but also a source of valuable information, useful for other tourists and service providers as well. In order to address these issues, an eTourism context-aware application prototype has been developed providing tourists on the move with proper context-aware services to support communication and knowledge exchange. The application integrates already available location-based content delivery services with a context-aware instant messaging service and a tourist service provider reputation service, which supports tourists during decision-making processes. The context management architecture deployed for this scenario includes one application domain (tourism in Piacenza), and one local domain (a museum of the city). Here we describe main design issues and prototype implementation.

This paper is organized as follows: in Section 2 we discuss state of the art approaches for context modeling. In Section 3 we describe the proposed hybrid context model. Section 4 provides an overview of the logical architecture of a Context-Aware System. Section 5 describes design and implementation issues of the Kamer eTourism application. Section 6 concludes the paper with insights into future work.

2   State of the Art

In the literature several context modeling approaches can be found. Most relevant ones have been classified by Strang & Linhoff-Popien [30] according to scheme of data structures which are used to exchange contextual information: key-value models, markup scheme models, graphical models, object-oriented models, logic-based and ontology-based models. Ontology-based modeling is considered as the most promising approach, as they enable a formal analysis of the domain knowledge, promoting contextual knowledge sharing and reuse in an ubiquitous computing system, and context reasoning based on semantic web technologies [9].

Gu [10] divides a pervasive computing domain into several sub-domains (e.g. home domain, office domain etc.) and defines individual low-level ontologies in each sub-domain to reduce the complexity of context processing.

The Context Ontology Language (CoOL) [29] uses the Aspect-Scale-Context (ASC) model. Each aspect is a set of scales defining the range of valid context information. The model includes a set of quality aspects (e.g. minError, timestamp), which may be assigned to context information using the hasQuality property.

In Gaia [24] context is represented through predicates, such as Context (<ContextType>, <Subject>, <Re-later>, <Object>), written in DAML+OIL [11]. The Context Type refers to the type of context the predicate is describing, the Subject is the person, place or thing with which the context is concerned, and the Object is a value associated with the Subject.

Each of the above mentioned models is also associated to a context-aware framework. The most common design approach for distributed context-aware frameworks is an infrastructure with one or many centralized components [1]: whereas sensors, mobile devices are distributed components, context management features (e.g. storage, reasoning, etc.) are in most cases centralized in a so called "context manager". This approach is useful to overcome resource constraints on mobile devices, but it introduces a single point-of failure [1]. Most frameworks supporting ontology-based context models have a centralized component for context reasoning and ontology management. In particular, Gaia [24] provides a middleware enabling distributed reasoning, but a centralized ontology server characterizes each ubiquitous computing environment.

Some middleware solutions aiming at providing distributed context storage and processing exist: for instance the MoCA middleware [5], the Strathclyde Context Infrastructure (SCI) [9] and the Hydrogen framework [12].

The MoCA's Context Service Architecture is based on an object-oriented model for distributed context handling, instead of ontology-based models, because at present limited resource devices do not allow the usage of local ontology engines. Two main context domains are distinguished: a local context domain and non-local context domain.

The Strathclyde Context Infrastructure (SCI) is a middleware infrastructure for discovery, aggregation, and delivery of context information. It is organized in two layers: the upper layer, named SCINET, is a network overlay of partially connected nodes. The lower layer concerns the content of each node, consisting of Context Entities (People, Software, Places, Devices and Artifacts) producing, managing and using contextual information. A Context Entity is a lightweight software component which communicates by means of producing and consuming typed events.

The architecture built in the Hydrogen project distinguishes between a remote and a local context: remote context is information another device knows about, local context is knowledge our own device is aware of. When the devices are in physical proximity they are able to exchange these contexts in a peer-to-peer manner. The project adopts an object-oriented context modeling approach.

As discussed by da Rocha and Endler [5], context modeling and middleware design are strongly interrelated: the complexity of a context model determines the complexity of a middleware context handling capability. In the previous state-of-the art analysis we have highlighted two main trends: object-oriented models are usually supported by middleware architectures providing distributed context handling and storage, and ontology-based models, which offer reasoning features, are usually coupled with middleware characterized by a centralized context management component.

Our work aims at combining the advantages of both models, by proposing a hybrid approach, described hereafter.

3   A Model for Context Distribution and Reasoning

The design of a context model should take into account several requirements.

First of all, a context model should provide a representation of context information, in order to enable context data acquisition from heterogeneous providers, delivery to heterogeneous context-aware applications, and processing (e.g. aggregation, inference) in order to obtain high-level context information from raw context data.

The model should enable the context description related to users as well as to other entities relevant to application purposes and should also be easily extended with new context data types in order to cope with specific requirements of application domains.

As context data are usually interrelated, the model should be able to represent such relations and dependencies in order to enable reasoning and inference processes to produce further context information from sensed context data.

Context items are often obtained from uncertain data. Many context data are sensed by physical devices with constant finite precision and often in difficult environmental conditions (noise, working in motion, frequent changes, etc..). As a consequence, context items have to be characterized in terms of time and quality properties for their proper interpretation and management.

In order to address these issues, most current research focuses on the use of ontology-based models [10], [24], [29]. However, this approach does not take into account AmI environments' heterogeneity: pervasive environments are mainly characterized by device heterogeneity, with different capabilities and computational resources [5]. Resource-limited devices cannot proper handle ontology context models.

In order to accommodate these requirements, we propose a model for Context Distribution and Reasoning (ConDoR), consisting of two sub-models: a Context Acquisition and Delivery Data Model (CADDM), which defines the format for data exchange among distributed components (e.g. sensors and applications); a Context Reasoning Data Model (CRDM), which is a semantically rich model, enabling reasoning on context data.

For each sub-model we distinguish two representation levels:

1. a *conceptual level,* which provides an abstract representation of main concepts and relations, independently from implementation details. We adopted the conceptual UML class diagram notation [2], because it is a standard providing a visual modeling notation valuable for designing and understanding complex systems. This level provides a uniform representation format of both CADDM and CRDM models.

2. a *physical level,* which adopts specific technological standard and modeling paradigms. The CADDM is represented in the XML Schema notation. We chose XML Schema as it provides standard instruments for defining grammars for data exchange among distributed components and it supports object-oriented concepts, such as polymorphism and inheritance. Several tools for XML data parsing and validation are also available for mobile devices. The CRDM is based on the OWL language [33]. We chose OWL as it is a W3C recommendation and it is more expressive than other RDF-based languages [10].

The conceptual representation of CADDM and CRDM models is shown in Figures 1 and 2 respectively. Hereafter, we explain the main concepts underlying both models.

Our work moves from the widely accepted definition of context, provided by Dey & Abowd in [7]: "Context is any information that can be used to characterize the situation of an entity. An entity is a person, place or object that is considered relevant to the interaction between a user and an application, including the user and applications themselves". Based on this seminal contribution, we use a more operative definition:

Entity is a person, place, computational entity, or object which is considered relevant for determining the behavior of an application.

Context is the minimum set of information that can be used to characterize a situation of an entity according to the application purposes.

The model described hereafter is populated by entities and attributes representing basic concepts of context. In order to represent concepts relevant to specific application fields, the model can be further extended by adding sub-models. Both CADDM and CRDM provide standard extension mechanisms (thanks to the modeling primitives provided by XML Schema and OWL, respectively).

3.1   CADDM

As shown in the conceptual level representation of the CADDM, in Figure 1, the context of an entity is composed of one or more Context Items. A Context item describes a specific characteristic of the entity context. Context items are classified into five general categories:

Location: The position of the entity. It can be represented in terms of geographical coordinates and/or symbolic location (for instance "home" and "museum").

Environmental Data: Data describing the physical features of the environment surrounding the entity (e.g. temperature, light, noise).

Activity: Activity which can be referred to the entity (e.g. meeting). According to our model, activity is not only referred to users, as intended in some works [20], but also to other entities, more precisely places and computational objects. As a matter of fact, a place can also be described in terms of activities which can be performed in that location (e.g. visit or film projection in a museum), and computational resources can be described in terms of their activity status (active, stand-by, etc.).

Instrumental Context: Software and hardware resources (e.g. PDAs) which surround the entity and are potentially relevant to provide instrumental support for computation, connectivity, and so forth.

Social Context: This item describes the social aspects of the entity context, in terms of individuals or groups which have a physical relation of proximity to that entity at a certain instant of time. It is also possible to define a social context for a "place" entity in terms of the users located in that place.

This set of categories aims at being general enough to accommodate different application purposes, but could be extended by adding other appropriate item categories, or by refining the existing ones.

As the Context structure is based on an aggregation of Context Items, these items can be exchanged between entities like "cookies", according to specific dependency rules, permitting fusion or aggregation of context data between entities.

3.1.1   Context Quality

Quality of context data is characterized by the following properties:

– *Reliability*: probability of the information being true.
– *Accuracy*: difference between the encoded and actual value of an attribute.

- *Precision*: the smallest measurable element.
- *Source*: source of information, e.g. GPS.
- *Lineage*: processing steps that data have undergone, described in terms of the following labels: *static* for rarely changing data; *pre-defined* for scheduled data; *sensed* for data captured from the external environment; *processed* for data which have undergone some processing steps.
- *AcquisitionTime* and *ValidityTime* provide the temporal reference of the information associated to the context item.

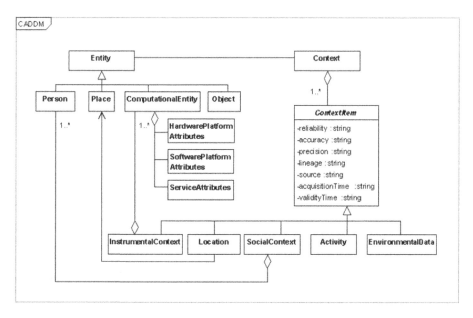

Fig. 1. Context Acquisition and Delivery Data Model – conceptual level representation

3.2 CRDM

Figure 2 shows an excerpt of the Context Reasoning Data Model. The class Entity is specialized by four subclasses: User, Place, Computational Entity and Object. This model aims at highlighting semantic relations among ontological classes, while the CADDM represents mainly syntactical relations. Each context item, which describes the context of an entity according to the syntactical rules defined in the CADDM model, is here translated into an ontology property.

OWL distinguishes two types of properties: an "object property" linking a resource to a resource, and a "datatype property" linking a resource to a literal.

For instance, an entity can be characterized by the "hasActivity" property (an owl datatype property), corresponding to the Activity context item in the CADDM model. In order to express the social context related to a place or a person, specific properties (owl object properties) are defined in the CRDM: a "Place" "isPopulatedBy" some "Persons" and a "Person" has other "Persons" as "SocialMembers" ("hasSocialMember" is an object property).

These facts are expressed as a set of OWL statements in order to be analysed and processed by inference engines. More details about reasoning mechanisms are provided in the following section.

The CRDM instances can be mapped into the CADDM XML-based representation by means of XSL Transformations (XSLT).

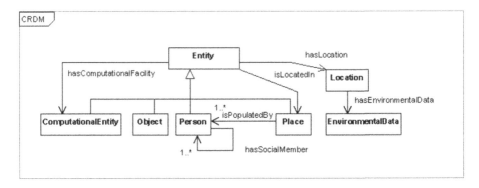

Fig. 2. Context Reasoning Data Model – conceptual level representation

4   Context-Aware System Logical Architecture

According to a widely accepted logical abstraction [10], [24], a context-aware system is made of three types of components: context provider, context manager, and context consumer.

Context Providers: distributed sensors that gather context data (e.g., temperature, light, location).

Context Manager (CM): a component that collects data from heterogeneous context providers, and processes them in order to make a context interpretation available to applications in a format which is understandable for application purposes. It consists of the following components: a data acquisition block which acquires raw data coming from heterogeneous context providers, converts them into a uniform format and labels them with quality and time attributes; a knowledge base, which stores the context ontology and related instances; a reasoner, which processes context information in order to obtain further information by performing several reasoning steps: aggregating and inferring context information, handling dependencies among the context of different entities and checking data consistency against the model; a context delivery component, which makes context information available managing queries from applications and/or notifying interested applications when the context has changed.

Reasoning is distinguished in:

-   ontology reasoning. As OWL-DL has its foundation in Decription Logics, DL reasoners can be used in order to determine concept satisfiability, class subsumption, consistency and instance checking [3].
-   rule-based reasoning. It provides more flexible mechanisms to infer high-level context by means of user-defined rules.

Context Consumers are components such as software applications, hardware controllers, and even end users, which use context information in order to properly adapt their behavior according to their application purposes.

5   eTourism Context-Aware Application

In order to prove the feasibility of the proposed context modeling approach, we have developed a context-aware application for eTourism.

Tourism is a key scenario for context-aware applications. As a matter of fact, a tourist during a journey demands a set of services in a manner often depending on the current situation. Our original contribution resides in considering a tourist not only as a target for commercial promotion and cultural content delivery, but also as a source of valuable information, which can be shared with other tourists and tourist service providers as well. We believe that seeing tourists not just as individuals, but as members of communities is a key concept for the design of innovative eTourism applications. We intend tourist communities as groups of tourists with common interests, where communication should be enabled and knowledge should be formalized and exchanged for the benefit of all members.

The context aware system developed for the Kamer project is a prototypal eTourism context-aware application, providing tourists on the move with proper services to support the above mentioned aspects of community building based on communication and knowledge exchange, together with already available location-based con-tent delivery services. This section aims at describing the first set of these services developed in their prototypal version:

- Instant messaging service, supporting the creation of tourist communities, exchanging comments about common interests and accessed services.
- A service provider reputation manager, supporting tourists during decision-making processes.

Here, context awareness means not only awareness of user location, but also awareness of user preferences, current activity, closeness to points of interest and physical proximity to other tourists, especially those with similar preferences and itineraries.

Prior efforts to develop context aware applications in the tourism application domain are numerous. Early work includes the GUIDE system [4], which provides tourists with context-aware information about a city by accessing a PDA. The focus of the system is on providing location-based services. COMPASS [34] is an application providing tourists with context-aware recommendations and services. Gulliver Genie [23] is a prototype of a context-aware application, delivering proactive information services to tourists based on their location and preferences. Another example of a city guide is Sightseeing4U [26], which delivers location-based information services via a multimodal user interface on a mobile device.

PALIO (Personalized Access to Local Information and service for tourist) is a framework for the development of location-aware information systems for tourist. It is capable of delivering adaptive information to a wide range of devices, including mobile ones [28].

The above mentioned applications represent relevant contributions to the field of tourist context-aware service development. However, some issues are still not addressed. Regarding assistance provided to tourists, these applications mainly provide location-based content delivery and the social dimension of tourism is not sufficiently supported. In fact, in most applications context data include user location, user device characteristics, user profile and environmental context (e.g. weather), but social awareness is not supported.

A first attempt to investigate a new approach about mobile technologies for tourist service delivery, considering tourists as knowledge units, not only as content consumers, has been done in History Unwired [12]. At present, project results focus mainly on designing mobile solutions for enhanced interactivity, both between tourists and mobile media and tourists and locals, in order to improve knowledge exchange between tourists and locals.

Furthermore, with the exception of PALIO, most of the above mentioned context-aware tourist applications ([4], [34], [23]) do not offer mechanisms to extend pre-defined context data, they store data in proprietary formats and are designed as strictly vertical applications [27].

Our contribution proposes a novel approach for tourist community building, aiming at improving communication and knowledge exchange between tourists, leveraging on context-aware service delivery. Moreover, our design approach of context-aware applications aims at coping with requirements of extensibility, reuse and interoperability, by means of open formats for context data representation (XML Schema and OWL) and standard interfaces based on Web Services, as detailed hereafter.

5.1 Scenario

In this paragraph we describe a scenario illustrating Kamer eTourism Application functional requirements.

Tom, the tourist, equipped with a PDA, starts his visit in the Piacenza city-centre. When Tom is near a tourist point of interest, the eTourism application proactively shows the description and multimedia contents related to the monument. The application also provides an IM service. Tom's contact list is dynamically updated by the system to show the list of other Kamer tourists currently located close to him. For each contact in Tom's list, the IM client displays some context data: the current physical location, profile data (e.g., age, nationality, preferences, tourist path) and current activity (e.g., relax, indoor visit). Tom can choose which tourists to contact according to these data. He decides to send a message to Julia, who is relaxing in a café nearby. A conversation about Piacenza is established.

It's lunch time, the eTourism application alerts Tom that he is near a typical restaurant which fits his meal preferences. When Tom is prompted with this notification (e.g. "you are close to the restaurant..."), he can ask for the reputation of the restaurant and read textual comments left by other tourists. Optionally, he can contact feedback authors if still present on site (through instant messaging). He contacts Julia again to suggest a meeting in front of the restaurant. After lunch, he can insert his comment about the service.

5.2 Kamer eTourism Application Technology Description

The context-aware Kamer eTourism application is based on the Kamer system, which provides basic services for the development of context-aware applications.

According to the logical architecture described in Section 4, the Kamer system is composed by the following logical parts:

- Context Providers are represented by GPS, RFID tags and a weather web service.
- The Context Manager is implemented by a Context Management Middleware, which takes care of context data acquisition, data representation and reasoning and delivery to context-aware applications.
- A Kamer eTourism application acting as a Context Consumer.

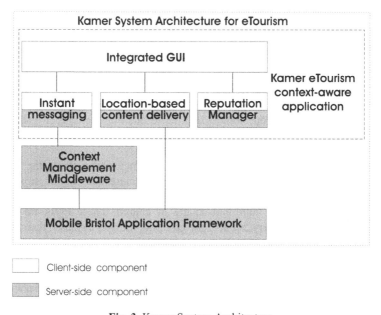

Fig. 3. Kamer System Architecture

The implementation of this architecture is based on the service infrastructure provided by the Mobile Bristol Application Framework (MB) [22]. MB offers basic services and development tools intended to facilitate the rapid development and deployment of pervasive mobile applications. It offers modules for data acquisition from sensors (such as GPS and RFID for user's location) and services for location-based content delivery (context consumers), thus providing the main skeleton of the Kamer eTourism application.

Figure 3 represents the main blocks of the architecture: the above mentioned MB, the Context Management Middleware (described below), and the eTourism context-aware application. The eTourism context-aware application provides tourists with an integrated access to the following services: location-based content delivery, instant messaging, provider reputation management. The first one is provided by the MB and will not be described here, as it is out of the scope of this paper. The other two services are described hereafter. A Graphical User Interface (GUI) has been designed in order to provide tourists with an integrated access to these context-aware services via a Web browser on a PDA.

5.2.1 Context Management Middleware

The Kamer System Architecture explicitly separates context management components from application logic. This choice aims at facilitating the design and development of context-aware applications and promotes reuse and extensibility of context management modules.

The Context Management Middleware acquires data coming from heterogeneous sources (e.g. GPS, RFID, Web services, etc.) and processes them for data aggregation, inference of higher-level context data and delivery to applications. This middleware is based on the deployment and co-ordination of Context Management nodes (in short Context Manager, CM) in distributed physical locations, each monitoring the surrounding environment.

Each CM is a J2EE module which takes care of context data acquisition from context providers, data representation, reasoning and delivery to context-aware applications, managing queries from applications and/or notifying them when context has changed (Fig. 4).

As previously described, our context data representation includes two sub-models: an object-oriented data model (CADDM), encoded in XML Schema and an ontology-based model (CRDM) encoded in OWL syntax.

The OWL ontology model represents data relevant for describing the context of entities populating the tourist scenario. Entities of interest for application purposes are, of course, tourists, but also places, more especially Points Of Interest (POI). For instance, a POI can be an important square or church. These POIs are useful for location-based content delivery but also for grouping tourists based on their reciprocal physical proximity, as described below.

Entity context is described in terms of context items organized in five categories: location, activity, environmental data (e.g. weather), social context and instrumental context. For the Kamer eTourism application, we divided the centre of Piacenza into a set of areas, each corresponding to a POI. User location is provided by MB, via a GPS receiver and an RFID reader mounted on the user PDA. Geographical coordinates and RFID readings are mapped into POIs' symbolic positions. Weather information is provided by an external web service. Description of device characteristics (instrumental context) is provided manually by the user at application start-up. Other items (tourist activity and social context) are inferred via deductive reasoning. With the term user "social context" we mean the set of tourists who are located close to the user himself, or more precisely in the same POI area.

Context reasoning and management features implementation is based on Jena [19], a Java framework for building Semantic Web applications. Rules can be written in the Semantic Web Rule Language [31] and then transformed, via XSLT, in the Jena textual rule format. The Context model representation is stored in a relational database (MySQL).

Communication between CM and context-aware applications for context data delivery is based on Web Services standards and on a Publish & Subscribe (P&S) service notifying changes of context data items to subscribed applications.

As mentioned above, this architecture allows the deployment of a distributed set of CMs. When a user moves from a place monitored by a CM to another place monitored by a second CM, user context data management "moves" consequently. In order to co-ordinate distributed CMs' activities each CM exposes a set of Web Services to exchange the current context of a tourist or the entire representation of the CM context model with another CM.

The P&S service is managed transparently to applications: applications subscribe once to user context items and these subscriptions can be transmitted from one CM to a second one.

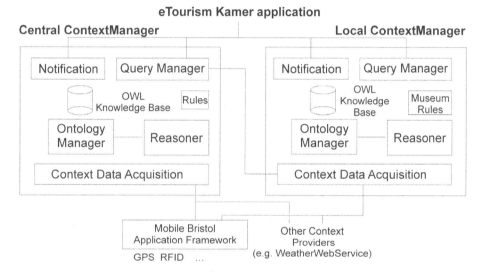

Fig. 4. Context Management Middleware Architecture

The configuration already implemented for the Kamer eTourism application scenario includes two CMs: a central CM acting as default context manager and managing the contexts of all tourists in the system; a local CM deployed in a museum (Palazzo Farnese in Piacenza) responsible for tourist context there. During the tour, tourist context data are managed by the central CM, except when he/she visits the museum.

While in most context-aware tourism applications user context data are entirely managed on user PDA, our approach aims at distributing context data acquisition and management features, assuming a permanent connection. Main advantages of this approach are:

- the possibility of exploiting context data consistency check and reasoning capabilities of ontology-based technologies, which at present cannot be deployed on mobile devices;
- the extensibility of the system: each local CM can be configured with ad-hoc reasoning rules, related to the kind of place in which it is deployed (e.g. a museum or a theatre).

5.2.2 Kamer Reputation Manager

The tourist service provider reputation management system, in short Reputation Manager (RM), provides features for creation, updating and visualization of a tourist service provider reputation. The system is based on a knowledge base fed by tourists' feedbacks after having used services on site (e.g. restaurants, hotels, and so forth).

Users can express their degree of satisfaction by means of feedback submission. Feedbacks are structured in terms of service quality attributes (e.g. service quality, kindness, etc.). Users can assign a rating choosing between three types of values: positive, neutral, negative. Users can also leave a short textual comment, in order to build a history of comments and user interactions. The application logic of the Kamer Reputation Manager aggregates the collected feedbacks and applies a statistical computation in order to calculate the global rating which supplies the service provider reputation. Positive, neutral and negative feedback are converted into integer values (+1, 0, -1, respectively). Missing reports are also taken into account as slightly positive feedback (+0,2), by applying an optimistic policy (no news is good news) [6].

The application publishes a provider reputation profile, structured as follows: an average rating for each quality attribute; a global rating (in the range 0:10), which is the weighted average of attribute ratings; a statistical report of the positive, neutral and negative feedbacks over a pre-defined interval of time; a history of textual comments.

The RM is implemented as a J2EE module. The Reputation knowledge base is stored in a relational database (MySQL).

5.2.3 Kamer Instant Messenger

The Kamer Instant Messenger aims at promoting knowledge exchange and collaboration between tourists, by enhancing traditional communication and presence features of instant messaging with user context awareness to promote the creation of tourist communities.

This system provides users with additional information (i.e. current activity and location) about personal contact list members, in addition to all instant messaging basic features. Personal contacts also include tourists on site which are currently located close to the user. These contacts are organized in a dynamic group called "TouristsNearby". This group changes ac-cording to the composition of the user social context, which is continuously updated by the Context Management Middleware. The composition of tourists groups can be related to the user location, as in our scenario, but also to other kinds of context-based data items (e.g. common interests, nationality, current activity, etc.). This approach, based on the Context Management Middleware, is thus more flexible than other strictly proximity-based approaches (e.g. those using Bluetooth).

The system architecture is composed by an IM client, an IM server enhanced with two plugins for context data management and a module (CClient) managing the communication with the CM (Fig. 5). Among existing IM protocols, we chose the Jabber Protocol [17], as it is an open XML-based standard and a wide community is working on upgrading the protocol and adding new features, including context-awareness [15], [16]. The IM server implementation is based on Wildfire [34], a Java server which supports most Jabber features and can be easily extended with custom plugins. The IM client is based on webJabber [18], a J2EE client running on a Tomcat server and using a web browser GUI. In order to maintain a light configuration on the PDA, we decided to deploy the IM client at the server side. Dynamically generated HTML pages are sent to the PDA and displayed by the web browser.

The CClient manages the interaction between the IM server and the CM. It subscribes to the CM in order to be notified when IM user context changes. Notification content is sent to the IM server in a Jabber XML stream (XML Stanza in the Jabber standard) with a custom namespace.

At present we are developing two server plugins for context data management: one for user activity and location data, another for user social context. The first one is a Jabber XML stanzas handler which processes Stanzas with the above-mentioned custom namespace. When a change of a user's location or activity occurs, the IM client of that user and those of his/her contact list members are notified of the change, according to the standard Jabber protocol [25]. The second plugin is responsible for the social context updating. This plugin manages the composition of the "TouristsNearby" group for each IM user, according to the user social context composition.

Regarding the IM client implementation, management of the "TouristsNearby" group has not required additional features. On the contrary, Activity/location data management and presentation will require ad-hoc application logic development.

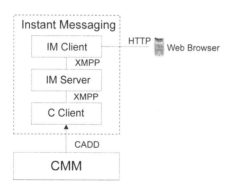

Fig. 5. Kamer Instant Messaging Architecture

5.3   Implementation and First Experiences

At present we are implementing the prototype system in order to test the Kamer eTourism application with tourists visiting Piacenza. The Context Management Middleware, the Reputation Manager module and the content-delivery application have been already implemented, while the IM system is under development.

During the design and development of Kamer eTourism application we are facing several issues related to the user interaction with a mobile tourist application. As a matter of fact, tourists are generally not accustomed to using PDAs, and they do not want to be over-whelmed by the amount of effort required to interact with technological devices during a tour. In order to make the interaction as pleasant as possible we chose the HP iPAQ hx4700 PDA, which is characterized by higher resolution display (640x480) with respect to similar devices.

Moreover, the application allows users to configure the content delivery service behavior: contents are proactively delivered without any interaction with the user, or the option "view content" or "skip" is shown before content delivery. The first choice requires a minimal user interaction, while the second one allows the user to control the information flow.

Introducing context-awareness features in the IM system requires the display of additional information in a clear and non invasive way. In common IM clients for desktop environments, contact list and contact presence information can be displayed on the main page and events are notified with alerts. This approach is not satisfactory for a context-aware IM system for a PDA, where additional context information has to be displayed on a small size screen and alerts to notify context changes could be too invasive. We decided to show context information in a separate ad-hoc contact details page, which can be reached from the main page, and to let the user choose for what context data type he/she should be alerted.

We are planning two stages of testing in Piacenza, aiming at evaluating user acceptance of implemented features and interface design solutions. The city centre has WiFi coverage and tourists will be provided with PDAs, equipped with GPS receiver and RFID reader. For these tests some RFID tags will be disseminated in indoor environments (mainly in the Palazzo Farnese museum) in order to detect user physical proximity to points of interest.

The testing environment includes a main server and a secondary one. The MB framework, the main instance of CM (central CM), the eTourism web application, the Kamer Instant Messaging system and the Reputation Manager are deployed on the main server. The other server, located in Palazzo Farnese, contains the secondary CM instance, which manages con-text data of tourists inside the museum. On the PDA, the client-side part of MB is deployed for context data acquisition (i.e. user's current location), while the eTourism application is accessible via Web browser.

The first stage (planned at the end of July) will be conducted in group sessions, involving groups of young Italians, namely students. These students, equipped with a PDA, will visit the centre of Piacenza along predefined tourist itineraries. This stage will be useful to test the usability of our application with users who are usually quite accustomed to using technological devices. A second stage will involve older age groups from different foreign countries. These kinds of users will probably have more heterogeneous technology skills and consequently usability tests could be more interesting. Moreover, users with different nationalities will provide useful feedback for improving the RM profiling mechanisms, for example introducing filters related to user nationality in the service reputation management. Test results will be reported in the conference presentation.

6   Conclusions

In this paper we have outlined a context model, named Context Distribution and Reasoning (ConDoR) based on a hybrid approach aiming at combining the advantages of object-oriented and ontology-based modeling. The ConDoR model consists of two sub-models: the object-oriented Context Acquisition and Distribution Data Model (CADDM) and the ontology-based Context Reasoning Data Model (CRDM).

We have applied this modeling approach in order to develop a context-aware eTourism application prototype based on a widely accepted logical architecture of context-aware systems.

As further contribution of the paper, the context aware eTourism application integrates instant messaging and service provider reputation management services for promoting the concept of tourists as content producers and consumers and members of a community, communication and knowledge exchange. The originality of this contribution resides in augmenting these services with context-awareness and offering them to users on the move together with location-based content delivery.

As part of our future work, we will continue our activity on developing the eTourism application, taking into account the results of the first stage of testing.

Context awareness requires an extensive use of data about individuals. At present, we have not yet tackled the issues of privacy. In order to adequately address these issues, we will investigate solutions for privacy policy specification and enforcement. Based on the context model, privacy policies should specify the "owner" entity of context items (ownership of context data) and permission of other entities to access and use such context items. For what especially concerns the Kamer eTourism application, we will investigate more sophisticated mechanisms for allowing users to choose what kind of context items and profile data can be shared with other tourists, mainly via the IM system and the provider reputation management system.

References

1. Baldauf, M., Dustdar, S.: A survey on context-aware systems. Technical Report TUV-1841-2004-24, Technical University of Vienna (2004)
2. Booch, G., Rumbaugh, J., Jacobson, I.: The Unified Modeling Language User Guide. Addison-Wesley, Reading Massachusetts (1998)
3. Bunningen, A.H.: Context aware querying – Challenges for data management in ambient intelligence. In: CTIT Technical Report TR-CTIT-04-51. University of Twente, Enschede, The Netherlands (2004)
4. Cheverst, K., Davies, N., Mitchell, K., Friday, A.: Experiences of developing and deploying a context-aware tourist guide: the GUIDE project. In: Proceedings of the 6th annual international conference on Mobile computing and networking, Boston, Massachusetts, United States (2000)
5. da Rocha, R. C. A., Endler, M.: Evolutionary and Efficient Context Management in Heterogeneous Environments. In: Proc. of the 3rd International Workshop on Middleware for Pervasive and Ad-Hoc Computing - Middleware'2005. Grenoble (2005)
6. Dellarocas, C.: Sanctioning Reputation Mechanisms in Online Trading Environments with Moral Hazard. MIT Sloan Working Paper No. 4297-03. (July 2004)
7. Dey, A.K., Abowd, G.D.: Towards a Better Understanding of Context and Context-Awareness. In: Proc. Of Workshop on The What, Who, Where, When, and How of Context-Awareness, as part of the 2000 Conference on Human Factors in Computing Systems, The Hague, The Netherlands (2000)
8. Ducatel, K., Bogdanowicz, M., Scapolo, F., Leijten J., Burgelman, J.C.: Scenarios for Ambient Intelligence in 2010. In: ISTAG 2001 Final report, Seville (2001)

9. Glassey, R., Stevenson, G., Richmond, M., Nixon, P., Terzis, S., Wang, F., Ferguson R. I.: Towards a Middleware for Generalised Context Management. First International Workshop on Middleware for Pervasive and Ad Hoc Computing, Middleware (2003)

10. Gu, T., Wang, H., Pung, H. K., Zhang, D. Q.: An ontology based context model in intelligent environments. In: Proceedings of Communication Networks and Distributed Systems Modeling and Simulation Conference (2004)

11. Harmelon, F.: Reference Description of the DAML+OIL ontology markup language. http://www.daml.org/2001/03/reference.html (Visited 7.3.2005)

12. History Unwired. Project Web Site. http://web.mit.edu/frontiers/ (Visited 6.4.2005)

13. Hofer, T., Schwinger, W., Pichler, M., Leonhartsberger, G., Altmann, J., Retschitzegger, W.: Context-Awareness on Mobile Devices - the Hydrogen Approach Proceedings of the 36th Hawaii International Conference on System Sciences (HICSS'03)

14. IST Advisory Group: Ambient Intelligence: from vision to reality. In: ISTAG 2003 consolidated report (2003)

15. Jabber Enhancement Proposal 0108 – User Activity. http://www.jabber.org/jeps/jep-0108.html (Visited 6.4.2005)

16. Jabber Enhancement Proposal 0112 – User Physical Location. http://www.jabber.org/jeps/jep-0112.html.

17. Jabber Software Foundation. http://www.jabber.org (Visited 6.4.2005)

18. Jabber Web Browser Client. http://webjabber.sourceforge.net/ (Visited 6.4.2005)

19. JENA: A Semantic Web Framework for Java.

20. Kaenampornpan, M., O'Neill, E.: Integrating History and Activity Theory in Context Aware System Design. In: proceedings of the W8 ECHISE 2005 - 1st International Workshop on Exploiting Context Histories in Smart Environments, Munich (2005)

21. Lee, C., Helal, S.: A Multi-tier Ubiquitous Service Discovery Protocol for Mobile Clients. International Symposium on Performance Evaluation of Computer and Telecommunication Systems (2003)

22. Mobile Bristol Application Framework. http://www.mobilebristol.com (Visited 6.4.2005)

23. O'Grady, M. J., O'Hare, G. M. P.: Gulliver's Genie: agency, mobility, adaptivity. In: Computers & Graphics, V. 28(5) (2004)

24. Ranganathan, A., Campbell, R. H.: An Infrastructure for Context-Awareness based on First Order Logic. In: Personal and Ubiquitous Computing, Vol. 7. Issue 6 (2003)

25. RFC 3921: Extensible Messaging and Presence Protocol (XMPP). http://www.ietf.org/rfc/rfc3921.txt (Visited 6.4.2005)

26. Scherp, A., Boll, S.: mobileMM4U - framework support for dynamic personalized multimedia content on mobile systems. In: Proceedings of Techniques and Applications for Mobile Commerce Track of Multi Conference Business Informatics 2004, Essen, Germany (2004)

27. Schwinger, W., Grün, C., Pröll, B., Retschitzegger, W., Schauerhuber, A.: Context-awareness in Mobile Tourism Guides - A Comprehensive Survey. In: Technical Report (2005)

28. Stephanidis, C., Paramythis, A., Zarikas, V., Savidis, A.: The PALIO Framework for Adaptive Information Services. In A. Seffah & H. Javahery (Eds.), Multiple User Interfaces: Cross-Platform Applications and Context-Aware Interfaces. John Wiley & Sons, Ltd, Chichester UK (2004) 69-92

29. Strang, T., Linnhoff-Popien, C., Frank, K.: CoOL: A Context Ontology Language to enable Contextual Interoperability. Proceedings of 4th IFIP WG 6.1 International Conference on Distributed Applications and Interoperable Systems (DAIS2003)

30. Strang, T., Linnhoff-Popien, C.: A Context Modeling Survey. In: Workshop on Advanced Context Modelling, Reasoning and Management (UbiComp 2004), Nottingham (2004)
31. SWRL: A Semantic Web Rule Language Combining OWL and RuleML http://www.w3.org/Submission/2004/SUBM-SWRL-20040521/ (Visited 6.4.2005)
32. Van Setten, M., Pokraev, S., Koolwaaij, J.: Context-Aware Recommendations in the Mobile Tourist Application COMPASS. In: Proceedings of Adaptive Hypermedia and Adaptive Web-Based Systems, Third International Conference, Eindhoven, The Netherlands (August 23-26 2004)
33. Web Ontology Language. http://www.w3.org/TR/2004/REC-owl-guide-20040210 (Visited 7.3.2005)
34. Wildfire server, JiveSoftware. http://www.jivesoftware.org/wildfire/ (Visited 6.4.2005)

Applying the MVC Pattern to Generated User Interfaces with a Focus on Audio

Dirk Schnelle and Tobias Klug

Telecooperation Group
Darmstadt University of Technology
Hochschulstrasse 10
D-64283 Darmstadt, Germany
{dirk,klug}@tk.informatik.tu-darmstadt.de

Abstract. Mobile users can interact with devices in the environment either by operating them directly or through personal devices carried by the users. This requires an adaption of the user interface to the device used. Declarative markup languages are considered to be a solution for single authoring user interfaces for different devices and modalities. This is a challenging task, since each device has its own characteristics. We present in this paper a novel architecture to support the creation of user interfaces based on a declarative markup language and a UI-independent task model. This architecture is based on the Model-View-Controller pattern (MVC) to generate user interfaces from declarative markup languages. We introduce a clear border between a modality independent task model and UI design. We also show how the development of smart environments can benefit from the workflow engine underlying our architecture.

1 Introduction

Ubiquitous computing poses new challenges to human-computer interfaces. One of them is the use of input devices that are available in the environment or which the user carries with her. As a consequence it is necessary to adapt the interaction with the user to the current device. This implies also the use of different communication channels, or *modalities*, which are used to interact with the user [3]. The development of multimodal applications is complex and time-consuming, since each modality has unique characteristics [12]. Research and modern development approaches try to solve this by means of declarative markup languages, mostly XML-based.

They promise that the same model can be reused for different modalities and output devices [20]. The reusability concerns mainly the so called *business logic* of the application. We understand business logic as a specification of the concept: Who (roles) does what (task) when (process) and how (environment). The main requirements in business logic are reusability and the independence of the user interface. But the community of authors and users of generated

C. Stephanidis and M. Pieper (Eds.): ERCIM UI4ALL Ws 2006, LNCS 4397, pp. 192–210, 2007.
© Springer-Verlag Berlin Heidelberg 2007

interfaces have already discovered the limits of this approach. "Using the same user interface for all devices means that the thinnest device will set the limits for the user interface, and unless the user interface is extremely simple, some device categories necessarily will be excluded" [15]. Gerd Herzog et al. [8] come to the same conclusion that "it is impossible to exclude all kinds of meaningless data from the language and the design of an interface specification will always be a sort of compromise" [8].

One of the modalities for which such a compromise has to be found is audio. Its invisible and transient nature poses many challenges to the interface designer [19]. Due to the fact, that multimodal applications are often considered to have both, graphical and audio in- and output capabilities, it is astonishing, that audio-only applications seem to be considered with lower priority.

Lingam [10] first seems to ignore this fact by stating that the "[...] day the limitations of voice recognition and Natural Language processors are overcome [...]" [10], but he also argues that not all limitations can be overcome. He sees a solution in a complementary use of all available modalities. This is also the common tenor, that voice can only be used as a complementary modality, but not on it's own. Because humans are more visually-oriented than aural, there is much more research being done with a focus on graphical rendering, i.e. layout of forms, than on audio-based interfaces.

Shneiderman names the example of a stock market where a survey result showed, that although trading is done by voice, the visual approach is 10 times more attractive to users [19]. The limits of audio are not well understood and are therefore replaced by the approach to use audio as a complementary modality. However, under some circumstances audio is a first class medium. Especially for visually impaired people or for workers who do not have their hands and eyes free to interact with the computer.

In this paper, we introduce a novel architecture to support the creation of user interfaces based on a declarative markup language and a UI-independent task model. This architecture satisfies all requirements in a reusable business logic and combines it with the advantages of generated user interfaces.

The architecture applies the MVC pattern to generated user interfaces using existing standards i.e. workflow engines and XHTML. Our main goal is to remove all implementation details from the model by separating the application into a modality- or implementation-independent part executed by the workflow engine and a modality-dependent part executed by a renderer for each supported modality. Using a workflow engine as the central building block allows us to easily integrate backend systems, user interfaces and other services like sensors and actuators to the environment via a standardized API.

The rest of this paper is structured as follows. In the motivation section we name shortcomings of existing solutions for UI generation. The next chapter takes a closer look at existing comparable solutions. Then we give an overview about our architecture and the way from the task model to the UI in section 4. Two use case scenarios for voice-based user interfaces and graphical user interfaces are given in section 5 to demonstrate how our approach can be applied to different modalities. Finally we conclude this paper with a short summary and an outlook to further enhancements.

2   Motivation

Declarative markup languages use the MVC pattern [6] to decouple model and business logic from representation and user interaction. Luyten [11] concretizes this with his model-based approach. He distinguishes between *task model* $\mathcal{M_T}$, *presentation model* $\mathcal{M_P}$ and *dialog model* $\mathcal{M_D}$. These can be directly mapped to *model, view* and *controller* of the MVC pattern [6]. From the MVC's perspective, controller and view are responsible for the presentation. The model can be reused for alternative representations. Some UI generators for declarative languages also reuse the controller. But since the controller is tightly coupled with the view, it is debatable if this approach can be successful for different modalities. Others try to generate the dialog model out of the task model [11]. Luyten in fact tries to generate a mapping

$$\mathcal{M_T} \rightarrow \mathcal{M_D} \tag{1}$$

From the MVC point of view the controller serves as a mediator between task model and presentation model, but we doubt that it can be generated from the task model. Since the model contains no clues about the interface, this attempt will result in basic interfaces that need further editing. An example for that is the form generator of Microsoft Access, that creates a basic form UI from a table. However, the MVC approach seems to be promising, but we still need different dialog models for different modalities. These approaches, like the ones of Paterno and Luyten, are widespread in academic research but not in industry. One reason, besides the known limitations of generated interfaces, is that they primarily focus on the interaction with the user and only some even consider integration into back-end systems, which is a requirement for the business case.

Consider a brokerage application, where the system *displays* a huge list of stock market values. This is no problem for visually-oriented modalities, even on small displays. The one-dimensional and transient nature of audio makes the delivery of large amounts of data nearly impossible. Audio requires different interaction strategies. Another problem is caused by the accuracy of recognizers. Since speech is not detected with an accuracy of 100%, additional steps are necessary to confirm the entered data. A big advantage of speech, to provide also out of focus information items remains unexploited by existing UI generators. This feature can be used in mixed initiative dialogs with the requirement:

Say what you want at any time you want to.

Mixed initiative dialogs allow for overloading, which means, that the user is able to provide information that is not in the focus of the current dialog step. This is not possible in graphical UIs or with task based generators collecting this information from the user sequentially.

It is obvious, that the reuse of the dialog model is not suitable to satisfy the needs of different modalities, which is probably also a reason, why this model is the one least explored [16]. Olsen's statement is still true as Luyten points out in [11].

This becomes clearer in the following example. Consider a shopping task, where the customer first has to select the items to buy and then proceeds to entering the billing address. Fig. 1 shows, how the task *Shopping* is decomposed into the sub-tasks *Select an item* and *Purchase the items*. This is exactly the way as it is proposed by Luyten et al. [11]. According to Luyten, a task t can be recursively decomposed into a set of sub-tasks:

$$t \xrightarrow{d} \{t_1, \ldots, t_n\}_{n \geq 2} \tag{2}$$

We concentrate on the purchasing task, which is further decomposed into the sub-tasks *Enter address information* and *Enter credit card information*.

Fig. 1. Shopping Task

The designer of a graphical interface would stop modelling at this stage, since these are tasks, which can be handled by a single view in the user interface. Note that it is also possible to expand these tasks, but it is not necessary. An example implementation of the address entry from Amazon is shown in Fig. 2.

The same level of expansion would not work in audio, since each input field of the address entry is a complex operation in audio and has to be treated separately.

Apart from the problem, that free-form voice entry of names is still an unsolved problem, several other challenges inherent to the medium have to be considered. Since speech cannot be recognized with an accuracy of 100%, users need feedback about the entered data. Another problem is, that speech is invisible, so users might forget what they entered a few moments ago. As a consequence, the task *Enter address information* must be expanded for voice as shown in Fig. 3. Stopping decomposition is no longer an option.

Another problem deals with the selection from lists, i.e. selecting the country. Since speech is one-dimensional, it is unacceptable for users to listen to a list with dozens of items. This requires special interaction techniques, like scripted interaction [18].

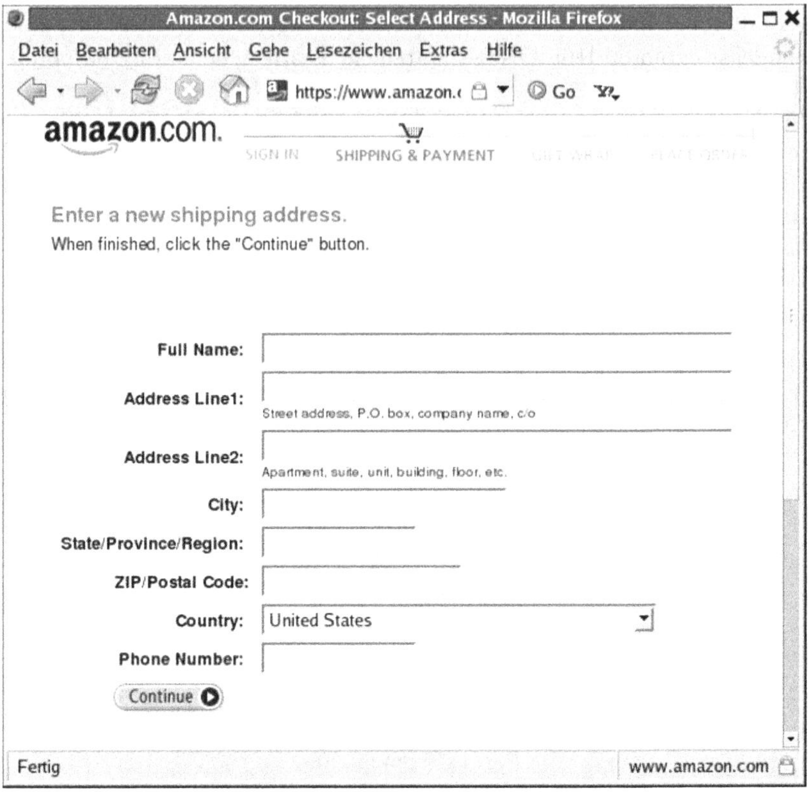

Fig. 2. Amazon: *Enter address information* form

Fig. 3. Expansion of *Enter address information* for voice

This means, that a task decomposition d may have modality dependencies M, where M is a set of targeted modalities $m_1, \ldots, m_k$. Moreover, the task t itself supports only a set of modalities M, expressed by t_M.

Equation (2) has to be extended to:

$$t_M \overset{d_{M'}}{\to} \{t_{1,M'}, \ldots, t_{n,M'}\}_{n \geq 2} \tag{3}$$

where M' is a set of supported modalities of the decomposition with

$$M' \subseteq M \tag{4}$$

The decomposition $d_{M'}$ decomposes the current task into subtasks supporting all modalities of M'. As long as $M' = M$ we do not loose a modality. Decomposition starts in $\hat{t}_{\hat{M}}$ with $\hat{M}$ being a set of all known modalities, which means modality independence.

In this paper, we introduce an approach that splits a set of tasks into a task model and a dialog model. The task model is highly independent of the modality whereas the dialog model captures modality specific aspects. This approach is used to create higher quality UIs and satisfies all requirements in a reusable business logic. Task decomposition stops at a point where we loose a modality, which means $M' \subset \hat{M}$. All these tasks $t_{M'}$ must not be part of $\mathcal{M}_\mathcal{T}$ but part of $\mathcal{M}_\mathcal{D}$. More mathematically

$$\{t_{M'} | M' \subset \hat{M}\} \notin \mathcal{M}_\mathcal{T} \tag{5}$$

In other words: Tasks with a modality dependency are treated as a modality dependent view on the corresponding modality independent task.

3   Related Work

Chugh et al. have reviewed the influence and advantages of voice technologies on existing web and enterprise applications [4]. They introduce an architecture built upon a centralized application server providing services through a CORBA API. One of the supported UIs is a phone-based access via a VoiceXML interpreter.

This architecture has the business logic in CORBA services. These services are more or less decoupled. The order in which they are used depends on the logic implemented in the client. This means, that parts of the business logic are shifted from the model to the controller. What is missing, is a structured way to separate real business logic from presentation logic. Our approach uses a workflow engine for sequencing service calls.

In [23] Vantroys et al. describe an architecture of a learning platform with a centralized workflow engine. The targeted platforms vary from desktop PCs to mobile phones and their focus is to transform XML-formatted documents stored in the learning database into a suitable format for the current device. This is achieved by XSL transformations. Since they use their own proprietary format for the documents this approach is strongly limited. They consider neither a general approach nor the way how users can access the documents. The main disadvantage is that they do not consider user input at all. In addition the approach takes no respect to special limitations of the used device. They stop at transforming into a format that is supported by the target device.

In [13] Mori et al describe an approach called TERESA, where the *Task Model* is being used as a common basis for platform dependent *System Task Models*. In contrast to our approach their task model contains a mix of modality dependent and modality independent tasks. By filtering they then generate a *System Task Model* for each modality. Because of that, the main *Task Model* needs to be a compromise between different modalities. We believe that this approach does not support the design of efficient modality specific dialog models. Mori's Task Model allows the designer to specify targeted platforms and even allows to store dependencies among these platform descriptions. This becomes evident in their discussion of a demo implementation. The VoiceXML-enabled system plays a *grouping sound*, which makes only sense in visual environments. This sound does not provide any information to the user of audio-only interfaces, but is transferred directly from the visual interface without questioning its sense. This is not compliant with our understanding of a model. We store only abstract task descriptions without any relation to possible implementations.

One of the main problems when dealing with (semi-)automatically generated user interfaces is the mapping problem defined by Puerta and Eisenstein [17]. The mapping problem is characterized as the problem of "linking the abstract and concrete elements in an interface model". However, our approach does not deal with the mapping problem as the creation of modality dependent dialog models is left to the designer.

4 Architecture

4.1 General

Today, the established term of *workflow systems* comes back as *business process modelling* systems. The **W**orkflow **M**anagement **C**oalition, WfMC [21], has defined *workflow* as the automation of a business process, in whole or part, during which documents, information or tasks are passed from one participant to another, according to a set of procedural rules. Workflows are established in industry and provide methods to describe and access process definitions. They help to coordinate multiple applications with the defined activities. The sequence in which these activities are performed is controlled by a workflow engine. It also defines who (roles) does what (task), when (process) and how (environment). An advantage of process descriptions for workflows is that they do not consider UI components by definition. We have an independence of media. Thus they fulfill equation (5).

User interfaces for workflow engines have been considered to be graphically-oriented desktop PC applications only. The MOHWAS [14] project extended this approach to mobile users using heterogeneous devices. Moreover it tried to integrate contextual information from the environment into workflows. However, research in this project concentrated on graphical devices. Our approach tries to fill the gap between the world of workflow engines and the world of voice-based UIs.

4.2   Workflow Process Description

Our basic architecture is shown in figure 4.

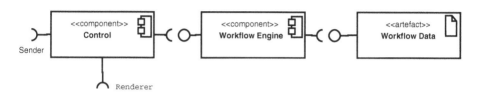

Fig. 4. Core architecture

The task model is stored as *Workflow Data* and is accessed by the *Workflow Engine.* The *Controller* reads the current activity from the workflow engine and asks the *Renderer* for the next UI. Currently the output of the Renderer is limited to markup languages. But this is only a minor issue, since markups for Swing-based Java user interfaces and others exist [1] and are well explored.

The workflow engine uses the XPDL format [22] to describe processes and their activities. We will explain the architecture using a shopping process example shown in Fig. 5.

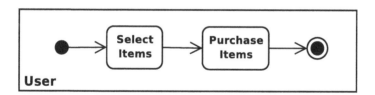

Fig. 5. Shopping task

To author processes in XPDL, we use JaWE [5]. The following listing in XPDL format shows the activity *Add to cart* from the *Select Items* block activity shown in Fig. 6 to select the items to buy.

```
<Activity Id="question" Name="Add to cart">
    <Implementation>
        <Tool Id="SendData" Type="application">
            <ActualParameters>
                <ActualParameter>user</ActualParameter>
```

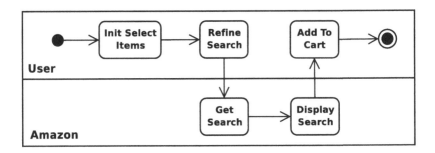

Fig. 6. Shopping task: Select Items

```
            <ActualParameter>booklist</ActualParameter>
            <ActualParameter>cart</ActualParameter>
        </ActualParameters>
    </Tool>
    <Tool Id="ReceiveData" Type="application">
        <ActualParameters>
            <ActualParameter>user</ActualParameter>
            <ActualParameter>booklist</ActualParameter>
            <ActualParameter>cart</ActualParameter>
        </ActualParameters>
    </Tool>
</Implementation>
...
</Activity>
```

Parameters of the task are *user* (the user's identification), *booklist* (a list of books, which has been obtained from a database) and *cart* (the items, which the user selected). The *Control* component is attached as a so called *ToolAgent* and exchanges the data with the UI.

In the example, we concentrate on voice-based user interfaces. We use VoiceXML to handle speech input and output. Other modalities can be supported by other markup languages, see section 5.1. Fig. 7 shows the architecture of the VoiceXML renderer.

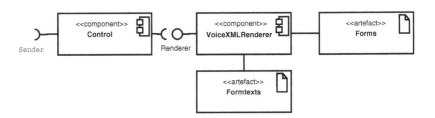

Fig. 7. VoiceXML Renderer based on XForms

The *VoiceXMLRenderer* implements the *Renderer* interface of the *Control* component. The renderer transforms XForms [24] forms, stored in the correspondent artefact into the targeted markup language, i.e. VoiceXML.

Each activity of the workflow engine can have multiple forms. This enables a modality dependent decomposition into sub-tasks as shown in figure 3. In fact the *Control* component is a state machine, that handles all interactions belonging to a single activity. The process designer can concentrate on her task to establish a workflow and has little stimulation to over design the workflow, since she need not care about the UI.

4.3   Modelling of Data

XForms is based on an `<xfm:model>` element. The following listing shows the model for the book list:

```
<xfm:model>
    <xfm:instance id="booklist">
    <data>
        <title>
            Harry Potter and the halfblood prince
        </title>
        <author>J. K. Rowling</author>
        <review>
            The long-awaited, eagerly anticipated, arguably
            over-hyped Harry Potter...
        </review>
        <price>17.99</price>
        <quantity/>
    </data>
    </xfm:instance>
    ...
</xfm:model>
```

We use the workflow engine to retrieve the data. In our case the data is obtained from a database in the *Get Data* activity and stored in the *booklist* parameter of the shopping process.

4.4   Definition of Forms

Next we have to define that the title and price should be read to the user, before she is prompted for the quantity. This is shown in the next listing.

```
<xfm:output id="title" ref="instance('cart')/data/title"/>
<xfm:output id="author" ref="instance('cart')/data/author"/>
<xfm:input id="quantity"
    ref="instance('cart')/data/quantity">
```

Besides simple input and output for the default data types known from XPDL, we also implemented support for selections from lists and complex data types like structures.

The ref attributes indicate, that the text resides outside this document. This can be used i.e. for internationalization. It is defined in its own document. This makes it possible to write texts independently of the XForms data model and the workflow activity. The following listing shows the text for the shopping task.

```
<Item isa="text">Do you want to buy</Item>
<Item isa="output" id="title"/>
<Item isa="text">from</Item>
<Item isa="output id="author"/>
<Item isa="text">for</Item>
<Item isa="output id="price"/>
```

In addition, a form can have internal variables which are used to control the selection of the next form or to transfer data from one form to another.

4.5   The Form State Machine

Next we have to define how to process the data. An action to perform such a processing step is defined by the `<xfm:action>` tag. The XForms specification defines elements like `<xfm:trigger>` or `<xfm:submit>` to activate certain actions like `<xfm:setvalue>` or `<xfm:insert>`. Some of these action elements do not have a meaningful implementation in voice-based UIs. One of them is `<xfm:setfocus>`. In our prototype, the voice renderer simply ignores these tags. Again it is noteworthy that the weakest medium limits the expressions of a UI markup language. Current implementations ignore this or are just able to produce UIs with limited capabilities [8].

An action to perform such a processing step is defined by the `<xfm:action>` tag. The following listing shows how this action is defined in our example to add a book from the booklist to the shopping cart.

```
<xfm:action>
    <xfm:insert at="1" ref="instance('cart')/cart/order"
        position="before"/>
    <xfm:setvalue ref="instance('cart')/cart.../@amount"
        value="'1'"/>
    <xfm:setvalue ref="instance('cart')/cart.../@price"
        value="instance('booklist')/books/..[...]/@price"/>
</xfm:action>
```

We look upon the forms as a description of input and output elements, linked with the actions. Each activity defined in the workflow engine can have multiple assigned forms. The logic to *display* a certain form is then comparable to a state machine. This is where we enhance XForms with the `<Transition>` tag. After submission of a form, the state machine decides, whether there is another form to display or if the activity is complete. In the latter case, control is returned to the workflow engine. A transition can be defined like in the following example:

```
<Transitions>
    <next to="bookinfo">
        <test var="todo" op="eq" value="n"/>
    </next>
    <next to="booklist_again"/>
</Transitions>
```

Checking for the next next transition is done by the **eq** attribute of the `<next>` tag. Currently we are able to check data for equality in combination with logical operators `<and>` and `<or>`, which can surround the `<next>` tags. An empty `<next>` tag is the default value, where control is returned to the workflow engine.

Some media may require certain renderer parameters, like fonts and colors for XHTML or voice for VoiceXML. These parameters depend on the renderer. They can be defined in a `<RendererParam>` node. They are delivered to the renderer without further evaluation.

The benefit from using a state machine is that the UI tasks are separated from the business process. We gain a separation of concerns. The business process is defined in the workflow engine without any information of the display medium. UIs are defined in an independent repository with all the specific parameters that are required for rendering.

4.6 VoiceXML Frontend

The Renderer can be defined via a plug-in architecture. As an example implementation, we show a VoiceXML renderer based on XForms (Fig. 8).

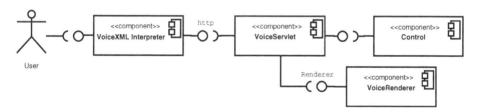

Fig. 8. VoiceXML Frontend

The VoiceXML renderer is implemented using an XSLT transformation. We use the Saxon [9] implementation, since this implementation satisfies all our needs and is fast enough.

The user communicates with the VoiceXML interpreter over the phone. The VoiceXML documents are retrieved from the VoiceServlet, stored on a Tomcat servlet container. The VoiceServlet communicates with the Controller, using Mundo [2,7], a communication middleware developed at the Telecooperation Group of the Technical University of Darmstadt.

5   Scenarios of Use

To illustrate how this architecture can be applied to ease the development of ubiquitous computing systems, we will discuss how it could be used in two exemplary scenarios.

The first scenario is a ticket machine which overcomes the bottleneck of its single graphical user interface by allowing different modes of access depending on the resources available to the user.

The second scenario highlights the usefulness of the workflow capabilities introduced by the architecture. This example demonstrates how user input and information gathered from sensors in the environment can be easily integrated into a single application.

5.1   Ticket Machine Scenario

We all know the situation. We have been rushing to the station to catch a specific train. As we arrive at the platform, the train is already pulling into the station. Unfortunately we still need to buy a ticket and the queue in front of the ticket machine kills any thought of taking that train.

The bottleneck in this situation is the ticket machine. More specifically it is the fact that there is only a single, sequential working user interface to the ticket machine which has to be shared by all users. Imagine a ticket machine, that is able to extend its user interface to external devices like PDAs, mobile phones or bluetooth headsets. A user that wants to use the ticket machine can connect to it wireless with her device. The machine determines the capabilities of the mobile device and renders an appropriate user interface.

The first activity asks the customer which service she wants to use. Depending on her selection, the *Get Schedule Information* or *Edit Ticket Details* tasks are

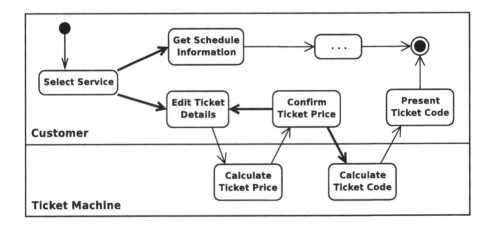

Fig. 9. Ticket Machine workflow example (bold arrows indicate conditional transitions)

executed. For simplicity the remainder of the *Get Schedule Information* work-flow has been omitted. *Edit Ticket Details* presents default ticket details to the customer and gives her the opportunity to change them. When she finishes this activity, the values are transferred to the *Calculate Ticket Price* activity which calculates the final fare for the ticket. Next, the calculated amount is presented to the customer who can decide to make further adjustments or confirm the purchase. If she confirms, the ticket machine computes a ticket code as a re-placement for a *real* ticket. This code is again presented to the customer. Once this is done, the workflow finishes.

Although different interaction techniques (e.g. VoiceXML, XHTML) are sup-ported, they all share the same basic workflow to determine the overall structure of the application and how information is exchanged between different activities. This scenario demonstrates key strengths of the architecture provided. By de-coupling the business logic from the implementation of the user interface, the implementation of different modalities is greatly simplified while still providing enough flexibility for the UI designer to build the interface most appropriate for a specific interaction technique. Also by having the same workflow beneath all variants, the user does not have to relearn the logic behind the application when switching devices.

Voice-Only Interface. The voice-only interface can be used when no visual interface is available. Low-end mobile phones, or wireless headsets would be examples of devices using this mode of access. This is also true when visual user interfaces are not an option as for visually impaired people.

Sample Dialog:

System: Which Service can I provide? Say 1 for buying tickets and 2 for schedule information.
User: 1

System: Do you want an adult ticket for zone 1? Say 1 to change the ticket type, 2 for another zone and yes to confirm.
User: 1
System: Name the number of the destination zone.
User: 1
System: Say 1 for adult, 2 for student and 3 for child.
User: 2
System: Do you want a student ticket for zone 1? Say 1 to change the ticket type, 2 for another zone and yes to confirm.
User: yes

System: The student ticket for zone 1 costs € 1.20, buy that ticket?
User: yes

System: Your ticket code is ABZ723S. Shall I repeat the code?
User: yes
System: Your ticket code is ABZ723S. Shall I repeat the code?
User: no

System: Good bye and thank you for using our service.

Notice that the architecture is flexible enough to accommodate UI patterns specific to the voice-based nature of the interface. I.e. repeating important information is one of these aspects that is not necessary with visual interfaces, but which is required in audio-based interfaces due to it's transient and invisible nature.

The task model could also be used for a hand crafted mixed initiative dialog.

System: What can I do for you?
User: I need a ticket for zone 1
System: Do you want to buy an adult, a student or a child ticket for zone 1?
User: student

System: Do you want to buy a student ticket for zone 1 for € 1.20?
User: Yes

System: Your ticket code is ABZ723S. Shall I repeat the code?
User: No.
System: Good bye and thank you for using our service.

This dialog is only hand crafted, but demonstrates the flexibility of our approach. It is even possible to generate user interfaces like that with another type of renderer

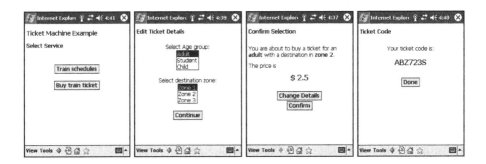

Fig. 10. Ticket Machine Example XHTML Interface

XHTML Interface When a PDA or smartphone is available, the architecture uses a different renderer with its own repository of UI forms to deliver the service to the customer. Fig. 10 shows sample screenshots from an XHTML renderer.

The forms for this renderer are been optimized for PDA and smartphone interfaces to improve the user experience. At the same time, the overall business process and associated links into the backend system are reused. Therefore the user interface designer can concentrate on the user experience and is not concerned with backend integration.

5.2   Maintenance Scenario

This example implements a maintenance task for a complex machine, that involves opening the machine, using a manoscope to measure a pressure, adjusting a valve to regulate that pressure, and closing the machine again. The worker uses a wearable device to get instructions on the task and record its performance. The manoscope is connected to this device and can transfer measurements directly into the application. Task execution starts, when the wearable device detects that the worker is close to the machine.

Again the central part of this application is a workflow definition, that connects and orchestrates the different components of the software. These components are the user interface to give instructions to the user, a component to detect the user's proximity to the machine and a component that communicates with the pressure tool.

The workflow starts with an action for the proximity component. This task is finished as soon as the user is close to the machine to be maintained. Next the worker is instructed to open the machine and confirm this step. The system then documents this step of the maintenance task for future reference. Now the worker is instructed to measure the pressure using the pressure tool. Once the measurement is taken and confirmed by the user, the system retrieves the measure from the tool and stores it for documentation. Depending on the pressure measured, the user is instructed to adjust a valve and measure the pressure again. This is repeated until the pressure is within a certain range, at which point the user is asked to close the machine again, which concludes this maintenance task.

If the wearable system was able to detect the open and close machine tasks by analysing further sensors in the environment, these steps could also be automated.

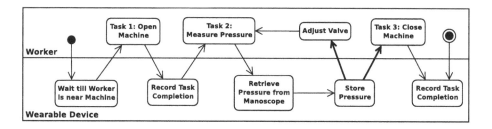

Fig. 11. Maintenance example workflow (bold arrows indicate conditional transitions)

This scenario shows how smart devices and context information can be integrated into applications. By using the workflow as a basic structural model of the application, the code for smart devices, context detection and user interface can be separated.

6 Conclusion

In ambient intelligence environments, multiple devices are used to interact with the environment. Each device has it's own characteristics, depending on the modalities used. Declarative markup languages are considered to be a solution for single authoring user interfaces targeting different devices and modalities. In this paper we introduced a novel architecture to combine model-based UI generation from declarative markup languages with a modality independent task model.

We showed that current approaches of task models are not modality independent and pointed out, that this is the main reason, why these approaches for UI generation are not yet widely adopted in industrial settings. Our approach is a generalization of the MVC pattern to model-based architectures as proposed in [11].

We identified modality-dependent components of the task model and moved those to the dialog model. As a positive consequence, the business logic, which is stored in the remaining task model, is fully reusable for different modalities. This makes it also possible to integrate other systems or trigger events.

We implemented our architecture and showed, that it is possible to generate higher quality user interfaces which take respect to the current modality. The current implementation focuses on voice interfaces. Other markup languages like XHTML are currently being implemented (see section 5.1).

In the near future we will explore the quality of these generated interfaces in user studies. Furthermore the current approach is restricted to markup languages. We need to find a way, how to overcome this limitation and find a way to generate more flexible UIs i.e. mixed initiative dialogs.

Another problem to solve is the need to figure out which device to use to interact with the user by means of the ambient intelligence environment.

Acknowledgments

Thanks a lot to Dr. Michael Lipp from danet GmbH `http://www.danet.com` for his patient support and troubleshooting our problems with the workflow engine WfMOpen `http://wfmopen.sourceforge.net`.

References

1. Abstract User Interface Markup Language Toolkit. `http://www.alphaworks` ibm.com/tech/auiml, March 2006.
2. Erwin Aitenbichler, Jussi Kangasharju, and Max Mühlhäuser. Experiences with MundoCore. In *Third IEEE Conference on Pervasive Computing and Communications (PerCom'05) Workshops*, pages 168–172. IEEE Computer Society, March 2005.

3. Jürgen Baier. Beschreibung von Benutzerschnittstellen mit XML. Master's thesis, Fachhochschule Karlsruhe, Fachbereich Informatik, 2001.
4. J. Chugh and V. Jagannathan. Voice-Enabling Enterprise Applications. In *WET-ICE '02: Proceedings of the 11th IEEE International Workshops on Enabling Technologies*, pages 188–189, Washington, DC, USA, 2002. IEEE Computer Society.
5. Enhydra. Open Source Java XPDL editor. http://www.enhydra.org/workflow/jawe/. accessed on 05/08/2006.
6. Erich Gamma, Richard Helm, Ralph E. Johnson, and John Vlissides. *Design Patterns: Elements of Reusable Object-Oriented Software*. Addison-Wesley, 1992.
7. Andreas Hartl, Erwin Aitenbichler, Gerhard Austaller, Andreas Heinemann, Tobias Limberger, Elmar Braun, and Max Mühlhäuser. Engineering Multimedia-Aware Personalized Ubiquitous Services. In *IEEE Fourth International Symposium on Multimedia Software Engineering (MSE'02)*, pages 344–351, December 2002.
8. Gerd Herzog, Heinz Kirchmann, Stefan Merten, Atlassane Ndiaye, and Peter Poller. Multiplatform testbed: An integration platform for multimodal dialog systems. In Hamish Cunningham and Jon Patrick, editors, *HLT-NAACL 2003 Workshop: Software Engineering and Architecture of Language Technology Systems (SEALTS)*, pages 75–82, Edmonton, Alberta, Canada, May 2003. Association for Computational Linguistics.
9. Michael Kay. http://saxon.sourceforge.net/. accessed on 05/12/2006.
10. Sumanth Lingam. UIML for Voice Interfaces. In *UIML Europe 2001 Conference*, March 2001.
11. Kris Luyten. *Dynamic User Interface Generation for Mobile and Embedded Systems with Model-Based User Interface Development*. PhD thesis, transnational University Limburg: School of Information Technology, 2004.
12. J. Terry Mayes. *Multi-media interfaces and learning*, chapter The 'M-word': multimedia interfaces and their role in interactive learning. Springer-Verlag, Heidelberg, 1992.
13. Giuli Mori, Fabio Paternò, and Carmen Santoro. Design and Development of Multidevice User Interfaces through Multiple Logical descriptions. *IEEE Transactions on Software Engineering*, 30(8):507–520, August 2004.
14. Mowahs project. http://www.mowahs.com/, 2004.
15. Stina Nylander. The ubiquitous interactor - mobile services with multiple user interfaces. Master's thesis, Uppsala: Department of Information Technology, Uppsala University, November 2003.
16. Dan Olsen. *User Interface Management Systems: Models and Algorithms*. Morgan Kaufman Publishers Inc., 1992.
17. A. Puerta and J. Eisenstein. Towards a general computational framework for model-based interface development systems. *Proceedings of the 4th international conference on Intelligent user interfaces*, pages 171–178, 1998.
18. Dirk Schnelle, Fernando Lyardet, and Tao Wei. Audio Navigation Patterns. In *Proceeding of EurPLoP 2005*, 2005.
19. Ben Shneiderman. The Limits of Speech Recognition. *Communications of the ACM*, 43(9), 2000.
20. Jonathan E. Shuster. Introduction to the User Interface Markup Language. *CrossTalk*, pages 15–19, January 2005.
21. The Workflow Management Coalition. Woorkflow Management Coalition - Terminology & Glossary. Technical Report Technical Report WMFC-TC-1011, The Workflow Management Coalition (WfMC), February 1999.

22. The Workflow Management Coalition. Workflow Process Definition Interface – XML Process Definition Language (XPDL). Technical Report WFMC-TC-1025, The Workflow Management Coalition (WfMC), October 2005.
23. Thomas Vantroys and José Rouillard. Workflow and mobile devices in open distance learning. In *IEEE International Conference on Advanced Learning Technologies (ICALT 2002*, 2002.
24. W3C. `http://www.w3.org/TR/xforms11/`. accessed on 05/09/2006.

Scenarios for Personalized Accessible Multimedia Messaging Services

Thorsten Völkel, Gerhard Weber, and Philipp Eichelberg

Multimedia Campus Kiel, Human-Centered Interfaces Research Group
Westring 431-452, 24118 Kiel, Germany
phone +49 431 7097641, fax +49 431 7097632
{t.voelkel, g.weber}@hci-research.de

Abstract. In this paper we present usage scenarios for accessible multimedia messaging services (MMS) including scenarios for public transportation and information services for spas. Results of a survey are presented which was conducted to analyse the interest of potential users in services described by the scenarios. Additionally, the concept of media transformation for the realization of accessible multimedia messaging services and a basic architecture for the server side generation of multimedia messages based on user profiles are introduced. In this context, the problem of coherence of time-dependent media is discussed which occurs when information is presented using alternative media.

Keywords: Accessibility, Personalization, Multimedia Messaging Services, Usage Scenarios.

1 Introduction

In 2001, nearly a quarter of the German population (24%) will be aged 60 years or older. The German Federal Institute for Population Research at the Federal Statistical Office predicts that in 2020 the number of 60 years and older will increase up to 29% and in 2050 up to 37% respectively [4]. Consequently, elderly people will play an even more important role within society compared to our actual situation. The expectancy of life increased continually during the last decades and the average is nearly 80 years in Germany [7]. As more and more people are getting older, restrictions such as visual impairment or an increased obliviousness become more frequent among the population.

As the impact of mobile telephony upon society increased significantly within recent years and will continue to do so, disabled and elderly people can benefit and carry out an independent life if appropriate services are available [1]. Recent surveys reveal that 85% of the German population aged 14 to 64 and 72% of the 50 to 64 year olds are using mobile phones frequently [2]. Concerning the group of people aged from 50 to 64 years, half of them (48%) use short messaging services (SMS) regularly. Consequently, services based on SMS and its successor multimedia messaging service (MMS) have the potential to support in particular the abovementioned user groups in managing their daily life more autonomously. This usage pattern stands in

C. Stephanidis and M. Pieper (Eds.): ERCIM UI4ALL Ws 2006, LNCS 4397, pp. 211–226, 2007.

contrast to the lack of usability of most mobile phone services due to small keys and small display size as well as interference with hearing aids.

State-of-the-art mobile phones offer a broad range of various output facilities on large displays supporting different media, i.e. sound, text, video, and vibration. The combination of the multiple media permits a multimodal presentation of information. Consequently, elderly people and especially print-disable people can benefit from personalized presentations of information rendered using different media types [12].

However, content delivered via multimedia messaging services is not well accessible nor personalized regarding special needs of the recipient. This paper therefore focuses on accessibility issues concerning MMS. After a brief introduction of the main concepts of multimedia messaging services at the end of the first chapter, usage scenarios are presented in section 2. The survey and its results are presented in section 3, followed by a description and discussion of the architecture used for the realization of accessible multimedia messaging services in section 4. Finally, a conclusion is given in section 5.

1.1 Multimedia Messaging Services

The Synchronized Multimedia Integration Language (SMIL) is a markup language for authoring interactive multimedia presentations and is recommended by W3C (version 2.1; see [18]). SMIL can be used to author multimedia presentations containing text, audio, video and graphics content. Different media elements can be synchronized regarding space and time.

The Multimedia Messaging Services standard is a subset of the original SMIL standard considering the limitations of mobile phones' output facilities [5]. Consequently, MMS SMIL is identified to meet the "minimum set of requirements and guidelines for end-to-end interoperability" [10]). A MMS document is a succession of pages containing at most two regions. One of the regions contains either an image or a video clip whereas the other region contains text. Fig. 1 shows a simple scheme of the structure of a multimedia message.

To guarantee the broadest possible interoperability, Open Mobile Alliance published the MMS Conformance Document defining different content classes ranging

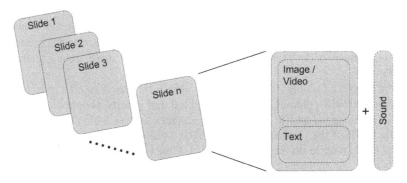

Fig. 1. Basic structure of a multimedia message

from pure plain text support (Text) to multimedia content classes, i.e. Video Basic and Video Rich. The later supports messages up to 300 kb of size, plain text, baseline JPEG, GIF, and WMBP images as well as video in H.263 and MPEG4, and sound in AMR-NB, and SP-MIDI format. We will focus on the Video Rich content class during the following discussion as this content class is supported by most of the actual mobile phones.

2 Scenarios

Multimedia messaging services make use of mobile phones' ability to present information by using different media. This key feature leads to the possibility of presenting information in an accessible way within mobile scenarios. We are currently working on two public funded projects which make extensive use of the concepts presented in this paper. Within the following sections, scenarios concerning the use of accessible multimedia messaging services are described.

The mAIS (mobile automatic information assistance system) project deals with public transportation scenarios. Our main objective is to support disabled people when using public transportation. More precisely, we aim at overcoming barriers imposed by traditional printed forms and up-to-date electronic displays used for presenting timetable data. Partners within this project include public transportation companies in Flensburg, Neumünster, and Kiel, as well as local engineering companies.

Project MEAD (Multimedia E-Healthcare Services in Schleswig-Holstein, translated from German) deals with accessible information services for spas as have been introduced in [17]. The services are intended to support the rehabilitation process of patients and tourists by enabling better planning of the daily routine as well as improving navigation throughout the area of the spa. The scenarios presented here are based on a first requirements analyses which is the results of interviews conducted with physicians and therapists of two spa carriers in Northern Germany.

Recently, many activities have been started in the area of location based services and services to support the mobility of impaired people. Examples include the Ask-It project [3] which concentrates on an ambient intelligence system of agents for knowledge-based and integrated services for mobility impaired people. Still, multimedia messaging services are not included within present concepts.

Sendero Group [15] is a California located company developing assistive technologies for visually impaired people. One of its main products, the Sendero GPS, combines a Braille and speech personal digital assistant with a GPS receiver to enable blind pedestrians to navigate in an unfamiliar area. The device is small enough to be carried easily, still, only few services are offered besides navigation including some points of interest such as bus stops, or train stations.

The Movípolis system [14] developed by Rigel Mobile Solution Provider, a Madrid based software company, aims at creating a smart environment around sensory impaired people and provides relevant information related to the surrounding objects and places in an appropriate format. The service can be accessed using a mobile phone which must connect to beacons installed at strategically important places.

These beacons are then responsible for tracking and for the provision of the desired information. The system requires proprietary client software for the communication in contrast to MMS based services which rely on standardized protocols supported by most mobile phones. Additionally, systems which rely upon the distribution of beacons are not available without major investments.

2.1 Public Transportation

Amongst others, the group of mobility impaired people includes sensory disabled people and elderly people, i.e. partially sighted, blind, and deaf people. People with restricted mobility are at least partially excluded from carrying out an autonomous daily life as they are faced with multiple barriers when covering distances. For example, visually impaired and blind people are not able to drive a car and thus rely on public transportation for distances longer than what is affordable for pedestrians. In addition to structural barriers of bus or tramway stops, the retrieval of schedule information imposes additional barriers.

Considering street based public transportation and its frequency, timetables play an important role for deciding which means of transportation to use. For example, choosing appropriate bus routes if the complete itinerary is not known in advance is only possible by observing timetables. To avoid long waiting periods, a good knowledge of departure times is particularly important very early in the morning and late in the afternoon when the frequency of transportation means decreases.

In most cases, timetables are provided as printed information posted on a wall within display cabinets. Because of the static nature of printed information, schedules can only provide target data and planned departure times. Recently, also electrical timetable displays have emerged providing actual departure times and are consequently more up-to-date compared to printed information.

For people with disabilities, the readability of information presented in the described manners is far from optimal. The German organization for the blind and visually impaired (DBSV) has developed criteria for the readability of timetable data [6]:

1. The printed timetable must not be presented above eye level.
2. The font must be big and with a high-contrast such as black on white background. The font type must be sans-serif.
3. The presentation should avoid reflection and glare.
4. The printed timetable must be plane without any jitter corrugation.
5. Visually impaired passengers must be able to position assistive devices such as magnifiers close to the timetable within a distance of a few millimetres.
6. The printed form should be presented in landscape format as the change of position of the observer might not be possible in vertical direction.
7. The use of unusual and hardly distinguishable icons and signs should be avoided. In any case, icons and signs should be presented in a way and size such that an interpretation will be facilitated for visually impaired passengers.
8. Currently available electrical timetable displays should be mounted on eye level and provide large and high-contrast presentation of fonts.
9. As a principle, any presentation of timetable information should be presented for the reception by at least two senses.

Fig. 2 shows a common printed timetable and a digital display at a bus stop in Kiel as it is found in many other European cities. The timetable is organized into five columns whereas the first one denotes the full hour followed by the minutes for days from Monday to Friday (second row), Saturday (third row), and Sunday (fourth) row. The fifth row presents following stops until the end of the line together with the time necessary to reach them. The digital display in Fig. 2 presents the timetable data organized into three columns. Listed are the numbers of the bus routes, the final destination of the route, and finally either the relative time (i.e. 8 Min) until the arrival of the bus or an absolute time (for example 13:45).

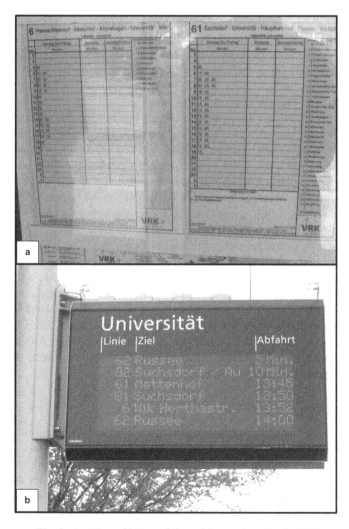

Fig. 2. a) static and b) actual timetables at a bus stop in Kiel

Although most of the criteria are fulfilled by the timetables, some important points are missing. Criteria 2 is only partly fulfilled as the font size requires the usage of magnifiers, glasses, or other visual aids. The usage of visual aids is difficult as criteria 6 is not met because adult observers using magnifiers need to adjust the face level and people using wheelchairs are not able to reach the timetable. Concerning the electronic display, criteria 8 is not met as it is well above face level. Observers using visual aids will thus face difficulties reading the timetable data. Regarding criteria 9, both the printed timetable and the electronic display offer only visual access to the information. Consequently, many sensory disabled people are excluded from autonomously gathering necessary information. For example, partially sighted and blind people rely on the assistance of other people, deaf people or dyslexic might also face reading problems. At this point, services based on accessible multimedia messaging services can enable impaired people to use public transportation more independently which will be underlined by the following usage scenarios.

2.1.1 Scenario 1: Timetable Data at Bus Stop

This scenario assumes that the passenger already reached the bus or tramway stop of departure. By using the information service, the passenger can retrieve timetable data for the desired bus route by using one of the short keys of his mobile phone. The mobile phone establishes a Bluetooth connection to the electronic display which includes a beacon. Based on the profile of the user, the mobile phone then queries for a personalized multimedia message containing the actual timetable data for the requested bus route and renders it using large font size and audio.

2.1.2 Scenario 2: Route Investigation Before Departure

Before reaching a bus or tramway stop, the passenger has to decide when to prepare for departure and which route to take for which stop. In this scenario the passenger needs to select a bus stop and submit it together with his profile data to the service. The route and the nearest bus or tramway stop will then be calculated based on the submitted destination and the current location of the passenger. As in the first scenario, the service generates and delivers the requested information within a personalized multimedia messaging service. Acceptance of the service is not as dependent on fast response times as in the previous scenario.

2.2 Information Services for Spas

Visitors of spas can be divided into two main groups namely patients and tourists. Patients stay for treatment or therapy at the spa for at least two weeks and eight weeks at maximum whereas tourists normally prefer to stay between a weekend, one week, and three weeks. In Germany, the health insurance company of the patient decides about the treatment at a spa within relative short notice, that is between one week and up to six weeks in advance. Depending on the time span left until the beginning of treatment, preparation time for patients is very short.

The residence of patients and tourists can be temporally divided into two main phases: an initial orientation phase followed by a routine phase. During the first two to four days patients and tourists must orientate themselves searching places where therapies and treatments are to be attended. This may become very difficult for many patients and tourists as they do not have any previous knowledge about the spa site and may be walking only slowly and probably using walking aids. Currently, printed information about places where treatments take place are handed out at the very first day which is normally the day of arrival. As patients must also attend a first medical examination and receive specific information about their daily treatments, diets, etc. patients become overwhelmed by the information provided. The combination of lack of knowledge about the daily routine and the information overload at the day of arrival imposes immense mental pressure upon patients and in some weaker form upon guests as their daily schedule typically only includes treatment for relaxation such as mud baths or massages.

After gaining some routine with the daily schedule, patients and tourists seek to spend their spare time more actively within the second phase, looking for events and leisure facilities within the near environment. As information provided is only available in printed form, patients and guests have reported difficulties in acquiring essential information particularly important for their actual situation. Because many patients and visitors of spas are elderly people and hence are possibly afflicted with certain kinds of visual impairments, printed information might not be accessible. Consequently, information services based on accessible MMS and the actual situation of the patient / tourist can deliver timely and essential information accessible for each individual user. This potential is underlined by the scenarios described in the following sections.

2.2.1 Scenario 1: Assistance for Timing and Orientation

This scenario covers both phases of patients' and tourists' residence. Within the first phase, information about the treatment schedule and locations will be generated and delivered. Two use cases are possible. The time of delivery can either be controlled by the recipient, that is the user requests information by sending a SMS and receives a MMS (pull service), or the delivery of information is controlled using temporal constraints (push service).

Considering the first case, the user must request the information explicitly. A personalized multimedia messaging service will then be generated containing the requested information. However, this request imposes barriers dependent on the impairment of the user. For example, the usage of SMS for transmitting a key word to a service number is not possible for some deaf and especially illiterate people. Additionally, deaf people cannot gain access via automatic speech dialogs as they rely upon the provision of short keys and are thus only able to request a predefined set of information.

For the pull service, certain triggers are responsible for firing an event to initiate the generation of multimedia messaging services. For example, such an event might be fired half an hour before the very first treatment of a patient. The generated MMS will then include the time of the treatment as well as a location plan which depends on the actual location of the patient. The triggers are set by staff members of the spa or the computer-based scheduling service. To facilitate the usage, specific patterns can be used which include certain kinds of triggers. The associated points of time for each trigger is then adjusted automatically to fit the duration of the patient's stay.

2.2.2 Scenario 2: Planning Leisure Activities

After the initial orientation phase, resident patients and tourists focus upon spending their spare time on additional activities. At this point two kinds of problems must be solved: firstly, the problem of which information is important to whom and secondly, the presentation of information in a way which is accessible for the specific recipient.

Although information about events and leisure activities within the near environment is available in printed form, not all information desired by patients and tourists actually reaches all interested people. Additionally, due to the static nature of printed information, it is not possible to address people personally regarding the presentation format.

To provide individual and adequate information, preferences about the user must be available. The information is gathered by enabling the user to provide his preferences via a web based interface before her / his arrival at the spa. Additionally, onsite possibilities for providing such preferences must be provided.

2.2.3 Scenario 3: Supporting Therapy and Aftercare Activities

The third scenario covers both phases of the patients' and tourists' residence and also includes the period after departure as it supports the entire therapy process and aftercare activities. Support for therapy is realized by providing information about relevant topics, i.e. many patients are supposed to learn to keep a specific diet. Although patients attend special courses ranging from theory to practical cooking, many people face immense difficulties in keeping their newly learned daily routine after leaving the spa. Our service therefore offers personalized information about dietary sheets such as specific recipes useful for the patient's therapy.

Another service that has the potential to support therapies is the building and maintaining of communities. During their therapy, patients do not exclusively attend individual treatments but may also attend group therapies with other patients facing similar problems. The information service can be extended in a way that leads to increased therapeutic success by building a strong link between the members of the therapy group. For example, group members may share their problems by phone. Consequently, patients will have fewer problems in changing their daily routine when encouraged by other patients.

After building a community within the duration of patients' residence, many people have difficulties in continuously following newly learned principles when getting back into their familiar surroundings. Aftercare thus plays an important role within a holistic approach to therapy.

3 Survey

A survey was undertaken to investigate the interest of potential users in information services based on messaging services regarding our first scenarios (public transportation).

3.1 Goals

Questions were related to the general usage of mobile phones and in particular the usage by people suffering visual impairments. One additional point was to investigate how much money people would spend for a service that could improve autonomy within their daily life. Besides gaining a deeper understanding of actual requirements, a better justification from the financial point of view seems possible. This becomes increasingly important when developed prototypes lead to real systems which need to be financed by third party organizations.

3.2 Subjects and Procedure

A total of fifty persons participated in this research. 29 persons were interviewed at the central bus station, 5 at a residential home for the elderly, and 16 at a local school for partially sighted and blind. As shown in Table 2, respondents represent a broad range of different ages.

Table 1. Age of Participants

Age	<25	26-45	46-65	66-75	>75
Participants	18	11	10	8	3

A total of 16 respondents or 32% were partially sighted and 6 respondents or 12% were blind. All other participants did not declare any impairment which would restrict their access to information based on multimedia messaging services.

Respondents were asked to answer a total of ten questions. Firstly, respondents were asked about their age and possible visual impairment. The next four questions dealt with the respondents' usage of mobile phones and short messaging service as well as their usage of public transportation and timetables respectively. After these more general questions, the MMS service was described and some example screens were presented to the respondents. Respondents were asked about the maximum acceptable amount of charge they might be willing to pay for the service. Additionally, respondents were asked if they would consider any advantages of audio enhancements provided by MMS. Finally, respondents were asked about their usage of the Internet and electronic mail.

3.3 Results

As our target group mainly includes people with disabilities and elderly people, different evaluations have been conducted. The results were analysed regarding different groups of participants, in particular partially sighted (22 participants) and people without any impairment restricting their mobility (28 participants). Results are organized in the following way (for appropriate questions): value for partially sighted respondents separated by the sign "|" from the value for respondents without impairment.

Table 2. Results of the Survey

Question	Answer				
1 Age	< 25	26-45	46-65	66-75	>75
	15 | 3	1 | 10	3 | 6	3 | 6	0 | 3
2 Impairment	Part. Sighted		Blind		No Impairment
	16		6		28
3 Mobile Phone Usage	Often		Seldom		Never
	95% | 61%		5% | 18%		0% | 21%
4 SMS Usage	Often		Seldom		Never
	82% | 57%		13% | 18%		5% | 25%
5 Pub. Transport. Usage	Never	Yearly	Monthly	Weekly	Daily
	0% | 0%	0% | 7%	23% | 14%	55% | 29%	22% | 50%
6 Timetable Usage	Never	Yearly	Monthly	Weekly	Daily
	5% | 14%	5% | 21%	36% | 18%	45% | 29%	9% | 18%
7 Service Charge	Free of Charge	SMS Charge	0,50 €	1,00 €	1,50 €
	0% | 14%	73% | 46%	27% | 40%	0% | 0%	0% | 0%
8 Internet Usage	Yes		No		
	91% | 57%		9% | 43%		
9 Mail Usage	Yes		No		
	100% | 54%		0% | 46%		
10 Audio Description	Yes		No		
	86% | 32%		14% | 68%		

3.4 Discussion

Concerning the results, most interesting interpretations can be derived by comparing the results of the two user groups. The percentage of people with visual impairments using mobile phones is significantly higher than the one of people which declared no impairment. Additionally, respondents of the first group stated higher usage of short messaging services. Concerning the six blind participants, all reported frequent usage of SMS. The accessibility problem is solved by using screen reader products for mobile phones such as the aforementioned Nuance Talks.

Regarding the questions about the usage of public transportation, the majority of respondents with visual impairment (77%) makes frequent use of buses, that is weekly or more often. The percentage determined for respondents without impairments (79%) is similar, although a higher percentage of daily usage is reported. The frequency of usage of timetables is significantly lower than the one of public transportation. One reason seems obvious as people using public transportation daily do not need to consult a timetable by the same frequency. Still, people make intensive usage of timetables to verify the exact time of departure.

The answers given for the questions about acceptable charges for a messaging based timetable service revealed that most respondents would basically accept a charge within the range of the charge for a SMS (0,19 €) up to 0,50 €. Consequently, the costs for providing such a service can be refinanced easily if a sufficient quantity of users can be acquired.

The results regarding the questions about the internet usage revealed that visually impaired people make more use of this medium than people who did not declare any impairment. Concerning the six blind respondents, all make extensive use of the internet as well as of electronic mail. Finally, concerning our last question about possible benefits of audio representation of the delivered content, almost all visually impaired participants (including 100% of the blind) agreed about the advantages. The majority of participants without visual impairments did not recognize any positive effects from audio enhancements.

4   Accessible Multimedia Messaging Services

4.1   Realising Accessibility: The Scope of Personalization

Multimedia messaging services inherently make usage of multiple media to present information. Normally, MMS use different media carrying complementary parts of information. Instead, our approach uses different media as alternative channels and enrichment [13] for the presentation of content.

In contrast to accessibility issues regarding Web based content, additional problems occur when dealing with the generation of accessible MMS. For example, authors of Web content can assume that visually impaired users take usage of assistive client side technologies such as screen readers or screen magnifiers. This assumption does not hold for multimedia messaging services. Although screen readers for mobile phones such as Nuance Talks [9] have reached product quality and are widely used among visually impaired users, they do not offer support for MMS. Additionally, different software is used to render multimedia messaging services dependent on the phone manufacturer and the used operating system.

Client side adaptation is not possible without developing individual software for a broad range of different mobile phones. The application at server side thus offers many benefits for the realization of accessibility of multimedia messaging services. The personalization must be based on user profiles which provide rules for choosing appropriate media for the presentation of information [13]. The generation process of accessible MMS (see next section for details) is thus based on identifying possible alternatives for media types included within the original MMS. As an example, we will discuss the media selection for the profiles of blind and deaf users. Fig. 3 presents the usage of alternative media dependent on the user profile and the original media type.

Regarding the profile for blind users, alternative text based descriptions are necessary for pictorial elements and video sequences. These descriptions are the basis for generating audio descriptions (using for example synthetic speech) and must be provided by authors as they cannot be generated automatically. An additional description is also necessary for video content as the information presented visually is not

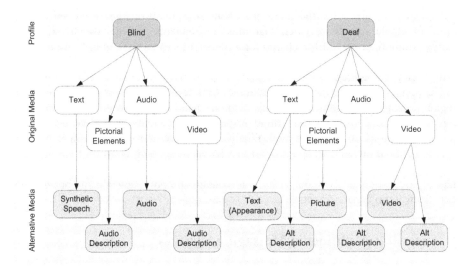

Fig. 3. Two Examples of Profile-based Media Substitution

accessible. Regarding the profile for deaf users, mainly audio based media have to be substituted by alternative representations. Additionally, as people who are deaf by birth might read very slowly, alternative representations must also be provided for text based information. Possible solutions include an enrichment of the appearance of the text or an alternative video clip containing sign language which itself can be generated using recently developed technologies for the provision of avatars [8].

4.2 The Generation Process for Accessible MMS

As already mentioned within the previous section, accessibility of multimedia messaging services must be realized through personalization. Fig. 4 presents a general architecture for the generation of accessible MMS. The main component of the system is the MMS Assembly Engine shown at the centre. The engine receives the basic MMS as an input, that is the MMS how it would be prepared for people with no impairments. Additionally, the profile of the specific user is provided from which the rules for media selection are derived. We thus follow the one-document-for-all approach as the presented architecture clearly separates content from presentation.

Based on the original specification of the MMS and the user profile, appropriate documents are selected from an underlying storage. These documents serve as a replacement for inappropriate media of the original multimedia messaging service. For example, if a MMS should be generated for a partially sighted user, the appearance of text content must be modified regarding font size and contrast.

The actual Video Rich content class does only support plain text, changes to the appearance of text content cannot be realized by simply choosing a different stylesheet. Instead, our architecture introduces a transformation engine which generates a bitmap representation of the adapted text. In a first step, the appearance of the text is realized using Scalable Vector Graphics [16]. Because SVG is not (yet) supported by actual content classes, the engine will thus transform the SVG document into a bitmap representation (gif format) while applying an appropriate stylesheet. The second step might become obsolete as future content classes for MMS are supposed to support at least a subset of SVG. Such requirements have also been identified by dyslexic and deaf users [11].

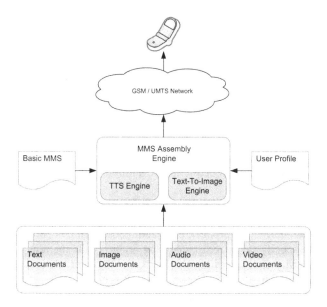

Fig. 4. General Architecture for Generating MMS

Regarding the media substitution for blind users, text content will be replaced by synthetic speech. Additionally, alternative text based descriptions of pictorial elements will also be rendered as audio. Transformation is realized by a text-to-speech (TTS) engine which is part of the assembly engine. The simple rule of providing alternative speech based descriptions for all visual content imposes one serious problem. If a slide of the original MMS contains a pictorial element in the first region and text within the second region, the two alternative audio representations must be rendered one after another because multimedia messaging services only allow for rendering one audio stream at the same time. Consequently, the rendering order for the audio representations must be determined.

The problem of determination of the rendering order of time-dependent media within multimedia messaging services is a problem of linearization. It mainly occurs when information available via different media must be represented by the same time-dependent media. We refer to this problem as the problem of coherence of time-dependent media:

Temporal coherence is a quality mark applicable to interactive systems for their ability to replace multiple time-dependent or time-independent media with other time-dependent or time-independent media at different levels of temporal granularity [13].

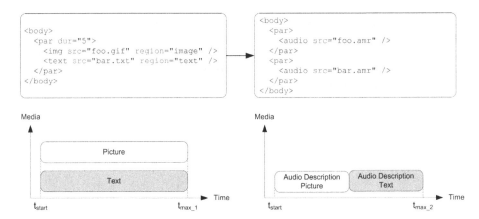

Fig. 5. Linearization problem of time-dependent alterative media

Fig. 5 shows the linearization of alternative audio representations of two previously synchronous media.

Picture and text are presented within two different regions within the given example and are thus referenced from within one par tag denoting a synchronous presentation. After the transformation process, each audio description is embedded within one single par tag to specify the specific rendering order. While the temporal intervals of the presentation fully overlap within the first case, the intervals are disjunctive after media transformation. In general, the time interval necessary for rendering alternative media will differ from the original time interval specified for the original presentation, thus $t_{max\_1} \neq t_{max\_2}$.

Besides the basic two regions normally containing image data and text, MMS can also include audio content as a third media imposing additional constraints concerning the coherence of time-dependent media. For example, regarding the profile for blind users, three audio documents must be synchronised and ordered in a way which does not interfere with the original relationship of picture and text. Consequently, additional information must be gathered during the authoring process to enable correct rendering of the MMS content after transforming to alternative media.

5 Conclusion

In the first part of this paper, usage scenarios for accessible multimedia messaging services are introduced. Our first scenarios are currently implemented in the mAIS project dealing with public transportation. Basic services for the retrieval of actual timetable data using mobile phones and beacons located at specific bus stops are introduced. A simplified interaction with the service is realized by enabling the people to use a short key on their mobile phone to retrieve the desired information if a beacon is in the range of the Bluetooth emitter. Otherwise a connection is built over standard GPRS or UMTS channels. In contrast to the area of public transportation, the actual location of the user plays an even more important role for the generation of the messages as the service is also intended to assist people in navigation throughout the area of the spa. All presented scenarios have been developed in co-operation with our partners, they thus rely on practical background. A survey including patients and tourists at two spa carriers is planned in the late summer this year to verify our current results and to gather additional requirements.

Results of our first survey concerning the acceptance of the described scenarios for public transportation are presented in the second part. Regarding the results, most respondents and in particular the group of visually impaired showed significant interest in the described service. Consequently, personalized information services based on accessible multimedia messaging services have the potential to be deployed widely as a wide acceptance of possible users is probable.

Basic technical concepts for the generation of accessible MMS are introduced in the third part of this work. Accessibility is realized by presenting information with the means of different media dependent on the profile of the specific user. Due to restrictions of mobile phones, personalization cannot be performed at client side, hence our architecture includes personalization at server side. Generated messages are then rendered using different media while presenting the same information. Consequently, the one-document-for-all approach is followed which includes a clear separation between content and presentation.

References

1. Abascal, J., Civit, A. Universal access to mobile telephony as a way to enhance the autonomy of elderly people. In WUAUC'01: Proceedings of the 2001 EC/NSF workshop on Universal accessibility of ubiquitous computing. New York: ACM Press, 93-99, 2001.
2. ACTA. Institut für Demoskopie Allensbach: Allensbacher Computer- und Technikanalyse. Partly published in: w&v-Compact 03/2006.
3. Ask-It. Ambient Intelligence System of Agents for Knowledge-based and Integrated Services for Mobility Impaired People. Retrieved May, 9, 2006. http://www.ask-it.org/index.php, 2006.
4. BiB. German Federal Institute for Population Research at the Federal Statistical Office. http://www.bib-demographie.de/index2.htm, 2006.
5. Bulterman, D. C. A., Rutledge, L. SMIL 2.0 – Interactive Multimedia for the Web and Mobile Devices. Berlin: Springer, 2004.
6. DBSV. Kriterienkatalog für eine blinden- und sehbehindertengerechte Gestaltung von Bahnanlagen und Reisezugwagen. Retrieved May, 2, 2006. http://www.dbsv.org/dbsv/download/GFUV/Kriterienkatalog%20zur%20barrierefreien%20Bahn%20Stand%20Dez.%202004.rtf, 2004.
7. DSW. Deutsche Stiftung Weltbevölkerung. Soziale und demographische Daten zur Welbevölkerung 2005. Retrieved May, 9, 2006. http://www.weltbevoelkerung.de/publikationen/dsw-datenreport.shtml?navid=51, 2006.
8. Elliot, R., Glauert, J.R.W., Kennaway, J.R., Marshall, I. The development of language processing support for the ViSiCAST project. In ASSETS'00: Proceedings of the fourth international ACM conference on Assistive technologies, New York: ACM Press, 101-108, 2000.
9. Nuance Talks. Convenient Audio Access to Mobile Phones. Retrieved March, 17, 2006. http://www.nuance.com/talks/, 2006.

10. Open Mobile Alliance. MMS Conformance Document 1.2. Retrieved March, 10, 2006. http://www.openmobilealliance.org/release_program/mms_v1_2.html, 2005.

11. Petrie, H., Langer, I., Weber, C., Fisher, W., Gladstone, K., Rundle, C., Pyfers, L. Universal Interfaces to Multimedia Documents. In ICMI `02: Proceedings of the 4th IEEE International Conference on Multimodal Interfaces, Washington: IEEE Computer Society, 319, 2002.

12. Petrie, H., Weber, G., Fisher, W. Personalization, interaction and navigation in rich multimedia documents for print-disabled users. IBM Systems Journal, 44 (3), 629-636, 2005.

13. Petrie, H., Weber, G., Weimann, K., Langer, I., Fisher, W. Personalization of multimedia eBooks for a diversity of print-disabled readers. In Lazar, J. (Edt.): Universal Usability – Designing Information Systems for Diverse Users. John Wiley & Sons, in print, 2006.

14. Rigel Mobile Solutions: The Movípolis System. Retrieved May, 07, 2006. http://www.rigelmsp.com/esp/movipolis.html, 2006.

15. Sendero Group LLC. Retrieved May, 10, 2006. http://www.senderogroup.com/, 2006.

16. SVG. Scalable Vector Graphics 1.1 Specification. Retrieved May, 5, 2006. http://www.w3.org/TR/SVG11/, 2006.

17. Völkel, T., Weber, G. Location-based and Personalized Information Services for Spas. In INTERACT'05: Workshop Space, Place & Experience in Human-Computer Interaction, Rome, Italy. http://infosci.cornell.edu/place, 2005.

18. W3C SMIL. Synchronized Multimedia Integration Language (SMIL 2.1). Retrieved March, 8, 2006. http://www.w3.org/TR/2005/REC-SMIL2-20051213/, 2005.

Part III

Inclusive Design and Evaluation

Lessons from Ambient Intelligence Prototypes for Universal Access and the User Experience

Ray Adams and Clive Russell

CIRCUA
Collaborative International Research Centre for Universal Access
Middlesex University, School of Computing Science,
Ravensfield House, The Burroughs, Hendon, London NW4 4BT
r.g.adams@mdx.ac.uk

Abstract. A cognitive evaluation of a sample of first wave of ambient intelligent prototypes was used to identify key implications for universal access in ambient intelligence environments, using a simple model of cognitive factors (Simplex Two). Emotional aspects of the user experience were the least well developed. A study of user experience, with two intelligent prototypes, one less intelligent and irritating showed a substantial impact of negative emotions on user performance that was independent of age. Surprising, performance changed significantly but ratings of perceived difficulty did not, suggesting caution in their uses. Finally, a case study of the user-participative development of a PDA for use with ambient intelligence confirmed the importance of emotional factors in inclusive design. Clearly, well structured and systematic methodologies (e.g. UUID) can consider the users' emotional experience and inform the construction of ambient intelligence prototypes and systems.

Keywords: cognition, smart systems, prototypes, emotion.

1 Introduction

Universal access and ambient intelligence are now bringing new perspectives to HCI in particular and to the future of mainstream computing science in general. Universal access provides some key concepts that include; inclusive design, context-orientation, diversity of user requirements, and adaptable / adaptive interactive dialogues as a framework for new methodologies and technologies [19]. Salvendy [17] captures the essence of universal access by saying "In order for these new technologies to be truly effective, they must provide communication modes and interaction modalities across different languages and cultures, and should accommodate the diversity of requirements of the user population at large, including disabled and elderly people, thus making the Information Society universally accessible, to the benefit of mankind".

The fundamental nature of ambient intelligence can also be captured by its key concepts that include; context awareness, personalization, immersiveness and adaptivity (on the Philips website; www.research.philips.com). To paraphrase Philips

C. Stephanidis and M. Pieper (Eds.): ERCIM UI4ALL Ws 2006, LNCS 4397, pp. 229–243, 2007.

A vision of 'Ambient Intelligence' is to enable people living well in digital environments where the systems are sensitive to people's needs, personalized to meet their requirements, able to anticipate their behavior and able to respond to their presence. Putting the two sets of key concepts side-by-side provides a striking demonstration of the degree of relatedness of the two fields of work, ambient intelligence and universal access, as follows.

Key concepts	Ambient intelligence	Universal access
1	Context awareness	Context orientation
2	Personalization	Diverse user requirements
3	Adaptive	Adaptable / adaptive
4	Immersive*	Inclusive design

There is clearly a substantial degree of semantic overlap between universal access and ambient intelligence. Only immersiveness* stands out as semantically distinctive. Immersiveness conveys the notion that ambient intelligence should enable users to immerse themselves in the user experience, to heighten their experiences by reflecting or invoking their moods and by controlling their environment, a concept is not at odds with those of universal access. The point to be taken here is that both universal access and ambient intelligence are conceptually compatible, based on the shared concepts identified in the above table.

Clearly, there is considerable potential for substantial synergy between ambient intelligence and universal access, but, paradoxically, there may also be the distinct likelihood that the two fields could continue to develop as independent subjects with different populations of experts providing different solutions to the same problems or even the same solutions described in incompatible terms. There are a number of emerging prototypes of new systems that have implications for both ambient intelligence and universal access. If so, then analyses of samples of ambient intelligence prototypes should be able to identify some important lessons for the development of new methodologies.

2 Cognitive Analysis

Before reporting the prototype analysis, the cognitive factors used in the analysis are introduced. Based upon an ongoing research programme, nine (human) cognitive factors have been identified as relevant to cognitive technologies. These factors are based on a range of case studies and meta-analyses and are detailed elsewhere [1] [2] [3] [4] [5] [6] [7] [14]. The nine factors identified so far as; input, feedback, output, complex output sequences, working memory, emotions and motivation, mental models, long term memory and executive functions. These factors have been validated by two meta-analyses [3] and based initially on the research of Broadbent [10] [11]. They are intended both as a (simplistic) model of human cognition and as a simple checklist for use by practitioners. Their application to the results of the present studies is described below.

Whilst a literature review is beyond the scope of this paper, specialists in other aspects of universal access may require background briefing at this point. The definition of a simplistic model or theory was introduced by Adams, Langdon and Clarkson [7]), defined as the ability to be powerful enough to capture important research findings but simple enough to guide good practice. It was educated by the model human processor (MHP) by Card., Moran and Newell, [12] and Broadbent's Maltese cross [11]. The latter provided an architecture of five factors; input, output, working memory, long term memory and executive functions. Adams, Langdon and Clarkson [7] presented Simplex One which contained the same five functions as the Maltese cross but in a more modular design [16] Simplex Two, with the nine factors listed above, was presented by Adams and Langdon [4]. The nature of each of the nine modules of Simplex Two is described in more detail in Adams [2].

3   Prototype Analysis

A random sample of prototypes was selected using Google Scholar and the key words "ambient intelligence prototype". This produced a sample of twenty prototypes, from which five prototypes were selected here, as a prerequisite to a new experiment. The above table identifies four pairs of related concepts of universal access. These concepts are also used to evaluate the selected sample of prototypes below along with the nine concepts of Simplex Two. The approach was very simple. An expert user of Simplex worked through each system, applying simple heuristic questions derived from Simplex Two [4] and was instructed to use these questions to derive an overview of the issues that each system had tackled reasonably well and those issues where substantially more work was required. Whilst this is a simple approach, current work is aimed at developing more powerful and incisive methods [4] [9].

3.1   COMIC

The first prototype is provided by den Os and Boves [13]). As part of COMIC, an FP5 project, two prototypes were produced, one dealing with intelligent, pre-sales bathroom design support for non-experts and the other for human-human problem solving. Focusing on the first prototype, it was designed to provide a "conversational multi modal interaction with computers" which the researchers saw as a future cornerstone for eCommerce and eWork. The prototype provides two screens, one screen on a small pad on which allows the users to sketch their requirements with a pen and a second screen which displays a human-like avatar to provide information and feedback to the non-expert, system users.

3.2 Ozone

The ozone project (see final report referenced below) aimed to generate a framework for supporting "consumer oriented ambient intelligence applications". The objective is to supply information and information based services to anyone, anytime and anywhere, thus improving quality of life. The framework itself was made up of three architectural levels (i) context awareness to adapt content and interface parameters by non-experts to reflect user interests and requirements. (ii) The middle level is the software domain including, amongst other things, task and data migration between platforms. (iii) The third level is the powerful computing platform that supports high performance for low energy demands. This program has produced three prototypes / demonstrators.

3.3 Seamless Content Access

The "Seamless Content Access" demonstrator (SCA) provides direct delivery of external content delivery from an external content provider (server), to enable user to access personalized video contents on a variety of screens around the house through a network with dynamic varying conditions. The system is intended to be responsive (adaptation of content) to the presence of people and to show awareness of the context of use (adaptation to context). The demonstrator is underpinned by an infrastructure of different interconnected networks to provide access to content.

3.4 In-Home Content

The "In-Home Content" demonstrator provides an electronic television programme guide (EPG) with a programmable remote control (PRC) and a touch sensitive design. The system provided both reminders and suggestions with adaptive consideration of the context of use. Detection of human proximity provided a basis to enable members of a family to watch the same content at different locations at the same time within the house.

3.5 Away Demonstrator

The "Away" demonstrator provides intelligent resources for nomadic use based in a motor vehicle, through "invisible" technology to achieve access and privacy.

4   Emerging Issues from Prototypes

A number of issues emerge from a consideration of the COMIC prototype. COMIC is a prototype of an intelligent presales system to enable non-expert customers in a presales context to work out their ideas for remodelling a bathroom with the support of expert advice. In the context of pre-sales, there is no lack of data, quite the reverse. Customers often face input data overload. What is needed is the expert selection and provision of relevant information in a constructive and helpful manner that is intuitively acceptable and comprehensible. There are also user output problems such that a customer might refer to a "thing like this" rather than its formal name. The designers also need to consider the enormous amount of overt and tacit knowledge ([8] long term memory and cognitive models) that people bring to a task. All parties need the ability to deal with errors of speech recognition and understanding during interactive conversations. The researchers also identified problems with standardisation, logistics and business issues, as well as a need to produce better understanding of human perceptual and cognitive processes involved in interactive dialogues. This prototype also emphasises the importance of strategies of interaction (executive processes?) for effective and acceptable dialogues, as well as support for user responses by the system. Adaptation of style, interface and interaction strategies can now be achieved on the basis of validated cognitive models of the users.

Whilst COMIC raises a number of important implications, an important subset of issues deals with cognitive factors of the human user. Such factors include input processes, output processes, memory limitations, executive functions and feedback.

The researchers used a range of methods to develop this prototype, including expert input and experimental studies with human participants to identify the better design options. They observed that the potential volume of experimental work that could be done was dauntingly large and that the development of design guidelines based on cognitive models would enable designers to narrow the range of options to be considered.

4.1 Ozone

There are a number of important lessons to be learned from the Ozone prototypes. Content interface adaptation in a context sensitive manner can be achieved. Non-experts can adapt the systems to match better their preferences and requirements. New interfaces can now be produced that are more intelligent, multi-modal and interactive. New portable, light-weight technology improves the user's experience of accessibility. New users will experience the same content differently on different devices in different contexts i.e. "one content for many devices". The researchers concluded that "the intervention of a human factors specialist and users in a more premature phase of the project (participatory design) . . . could avoid several problems". Issues of information (cognitive overload and human memory), security and trust as well as understanding human perception of speech and visual input are all raised by these prototypes. Information for the users should be carefully filtered to avoid input overload. User responses should be supported by the system to avoid output overload, attempting to do too many conflicting actions at once. User feedback was positive about all three prototypes, including: overall appreciation, the freedom, completeness and consistency afforded by the systems, the central role of the television as a family friendly setting and the retention of familiar features and services (supporting their current mental models and response habits?) e.g. a pause function. On the other side, users were concerned about complexity of installation, use and management of the systems as well as cost implications even when cost issues were not raised. They also liked the bundling together of new and existing resources.

The Ozone project aims to put the user in the centre of technological design and implementation through improved functionality, acceptability, usability and accessibility. To do so effectively calls for expertise in both ambient intelligence and universal access.

In this project, a range of research methods including prototyping, user needs analysis; expert human factors input have been deployed. The researchers have identified the need to development of powerful new methodologies with which to create an effective platform architecture and supporting tools. The requirements for the systems were developed on the basis of demonstration scenarios that provided a basis for the investigation and validation of the main features of the prototypes. An inventory of relevant technologies and open research issues was also produced at the same time. The next stage was to produce a first draft design of the overall Ozone architecture. At the end of the project, gap analyses were conducted between requirements and actual achievements, in order to identify recommendations for further work in the creation of future universal access systems for ambient intelligence environments. For context awareness, an entity-relationship based framework was produced to model the contexts in which the prototypes were used. The system was designed to cope with data or sensor errors.

5 An Overview of Implications

This paper forms part of an ongoing study in which prototypes are analysed for their implications for universal access in ambient intelligence environments. First, the concepts of universal access and ambient intelligence identified above are related to these prototypes. First, all five prototypes supported context awareness and orientation, personalization, meeting diverse user requirements, adaptivity and adaptability, immersive user experience and inclusive design.

Cognitive factors have a major role to play in this emerging field. Despite their obvious importance in this context, it is also clear that their intrinsic complexity creates real problems for the appreciation of their important implications for theory and practice. For this reason, the cognitive user model Simplex Two ([2] [7]) has been developed to support researchers and practitioners in universal access. This approach identifies nine aspects of the human users of information society technology and provides a simple framework within which to evaluate the implications of ambient intelligence prototypes for universal access, as shown below. Of course, there are many other implications of such prototypes and equally there are many implications of universal access methods for the production of better prototypes, however, these are beyond the scope of this paper and will be considered at a later date. For now, the following table sets out the nine, validated components of human user cognition and reports the extent to which they are satisfied by emerging prototypes.

Human User Cognitive Function	Dealt with by prototypes
Input and perception	Usual perceptual experiences augmented
Output and responses	Supported by familiar features
Feedback	Superior feedback now possible
Working memory	Potential cognitive overload avoided
Emotions *	MORE WORK REQUIRED
Mental models	Current models supported, new models facilitated
Executive functions	Supported by familiarity and data selection
Complex response skills	Supported by familiarity and usability
Long-term memory	Memory load reduced by intelligent support

Of the above cognitive factors, eight of the nine show substantial lines of development. However, the most recent and perhaps the most complex is the role of user emotions* and feelings. User emotions need more work, but are a difficult area to study. On the whole, users tend to be polite and restrained in their comments and often encounter prototypes in relatively protective laboratory environments rather than the more stressful conditions of everyday life. Designers are often more focussed upon the functionality, usability and accessibility of prototypes systems, since they often focus on them themselves, tacitly underplaying the dimension of the user emotions.

6 Definitions

To investigate the role of the human emotions in universally access to ambient intelligence, the above definitions of universal access and ambient can be set out, based upon some of their key concepts. Universal access is defined by the aspiration to achieve e-accessibility to information society, by anyone, anywhere, anytime [19] Ambient intelligence is defined by context awareness, personalization, adaptiveness and immersion. It is said to be "a step beyond Ubiquitous Computing" [15]. It has the following components at least; ubiquity of computing devices, mobile users who are electronically identifiable, context sensitive environments can detect the users and can provide relevant resources and information on a suitably intelligent basis. The following two studies consider two types of prototype within the dual framework of universal access and ambient intelligence.

7 Experiment: Emotions, Stress and the User Experience

To explore the user experience, two intelligent, on-line banking prototypes for a PDA were created with the aim of being used anywhere and anytime, by anyone, drawing upon smart, ambient resources. They were identical in design and functionality, differing only in the quality of the user experience provided. The first prototype (R indicating "relaxed") provided a simple interface and few options for the user to remember and required a minimal amount of user input. The second prototype (S indicating "stressful") was essentially designed to be the same, except for one feature, users must enter their password at every page and for every request. Any mistake is rewarded by being asked to begin the whole process again. The dependent variable was time on task corrected by the time required to for participants to enter their passwords.

The prototypes were produced to be smart interactive systems, in two senses. First, they would have the capability to answer user questions in a constructive and helpful way. Second, the S prototype behaved less intelligently as compared with the R prototype, in as much as it required the participants to enter their password without any intelligent reason to do so. The link between smartness and user emotion is that unintelligent systems are often more irritating.

7.1 Methods

The two prototypes were used by ten participants (two of the participants were significantly older i.e. over 60 years of age than the other participants who were all less than 50 years of age), counter-balancing for order, such that half the participants received S (stressful) prototype first and half received the R (relaxed) prototype first. For each website prototype, three tasks were required; logging in, checking a balance and withdrawing cash. Performance was measured by the time to complete each task. Time taken to log in was subtracted from these times. Though the participants were not given time limits, where the time taken reached thirty seconds, the task was terminated. Participants were asked to work at their own pace and all reported that they did not feel to be under undue time pressure. Thus any stress felt by the participants would be most readily ascribed to the websites themselves and not pressure from the experimenters.

7.2 Results and Analysis

No significant effects were found for order of presentation of prototypes, either as a main effect or as an interaction. Log in times were significantly better for the R website than for the S website (Wilcoxon, $T=0$, $p <0.01$). . The difference between the two websites found above was confirmed by analysis of variance ($F=12.84$, d f $=$ 1.8, $p <0.01$). Two of the participants were significantly older (over 60 years of age) than the other participants (all less than 50 years of age). The older participants were very clearly slower than the other participants ($F=37.16$, d f $= 1, 8$, $p <0.001$) but the interaction between these two factors was not significant ($F=1.65$, $p>0.05$), the difference between the two websites was the same for older and younger participants. Equally, the influence of age is the same for both types of website.

Balance check times were significantly better for the R website than for the S website (T=0, p <0.01). Analysis of variance confirmed the difference between the two types of website (F=14.87, d f = 1.8, p <0.01). The older participants were very clearly slower than the other participants (F=13782.70, df = 1, 8, p <0.0001). The interaction between these two factors was also significant (F=10.25, p<0.05), the difference between the two websites was bigger for the older than the younger participants. Equally, the influence of age was greater for the R website than the S website, due mainly a floor effect in the performance data of both groups declining substantially when using the S website.

The third analysis was based on the times to withdraw cash via the two websites. Withdrawal times were significantly better for the R website than for the S website (T=0, p <0.01). The difference between the two websites found above was confirmed by analysis of variance (F=4.0, d f = 1.8, p <0.08), though it did not reach conventional statistical analysis. (This is almost certainly a statistical anomaly, as ANOVA is usually more powerful than the Wilcoxon). The older participants were very clearly slower than the other participants (F=299.53, d f = 1, 8, p <0.0001). The interaction between these two factors was not significant (F=0.18, p>0.05), the difference between the two websites was the same for older and younger participants. Equally, the influence of age is the same for both types of website. The above age related differences were also confirmed by the Mann Whitney test.

In addition to the analyses of participant performance, ratings of perceived difficulty and perceived pleasantness of the two websites. Using the Wilcoxon text, it turns out that perceived difficulty of logging in or difficulty of checking was not rated differently for the two websites (p> 0.05). Perceived difficulty of withdrawing cash was seen as significantly more difficult for the S website than the R website (T = 0, n=8, two ties, p < 0.05).

Turning to ratings of perceived pleasantness / appearance, for all three tasks, the S website was rated as better (p<0.05, p<0.05, p<0.01). Comparing the older participants (over 60 years of age) with the younger participants (under 50 years of age) on their ratings of the two websites. The older participants rated the R website as perceptible easier when withdrawing cash (Mann Whitney U = 16, p < 0.05). None of the other older / younger comparisons were statistically significant.

Clearly, the frustrating and stressful nature of the interactions between the users and the S (stressful) prototype caused real problems over and above those related to functionality, usability and accessibility. If so, it is important to begin to identify the features of a website that produce debilitating levels of frustration and stress. To do so, after the tasks were completed, the participants were asked four questions about commonly found aspects of typical websites found on the Internet these days:

1. Do you find persistent pop up advertisements annoying?
2. Do you find it annoying when an Internet link takes you somewhere you don't want to go?
3. Does spam email annoy you?
4. Do you find lots of images on a web page confusing/annoying?

These questions were asked as these features are often reported as particularly irritating. The questions were structured in such a way as to inspire and encourage the respondents to proffer any comments they may have, not only about the programs they had just tested but also any other general annoyances and irritations that they might have.

Of the ten participants;

Question 1,   10 / 10 answered yes
Question 2,   10 / 10 answered yes
Question 3,   10 / 10 answered yes
Question 4,   7 / 10 answered yes

Participants responded that persistent pop up advertisements, Internet link misdirection and spam emails were annoying but did not impair performance or intimidate them. Generally, it was found that they were able to continue with what they were doing, but all participants found them particularly annoying or irritating. For pop up windows, it is not simply a case of closing the offending window. Although invariably the action of closing the window triggers another window to open, all respondents had a problem with closing them. The odd pop – up window seemed to be acceptable to the respondents, but the persistent nature of some pop – ups was found to be annoying and irritating. This, of course leads to frustrations and ultimately to resentment of the application being used.

With question 2 "Do you find it annoying when an Internet link takes you somewhere you don't want to go?" all ten respondents answered yes. It was commented that because there was a 'back' button on every web page, this did not present any of the respondents with any significant problems, but it was considered a major irritation by all respondents.

Question 3 "Does spam email annoy you?", again all the respondents answered yes. Spam email fills up their mail boxes and is usually for products that most of the respondents would not even consider purchasing. It is the persistent nature of spam email that respondents found most irritating. The fact that as soon as they have deleted the offending mail, another email with a similar or sometimes identical address would be delivered.

Question 4 asks "Do you find lots of images on a web page confusing/annoying?" seven of the ten respondents answered yes, while three answered no. Of those who answered yes, the general consensuses was that the pictures, particularly moving pictures and scrolling marquees, were a distraction and many blamed the amount of pictures as the reason for slow loading web pages.

Whilst any impressions drawn from these brief interviews and questions can be only tentative, the results have at least two important implications that can be explored in further work. First, it is relatively easy to identify common features of many websites that are seen to be frustrating and stressful. If so, it would be relatively easy to avoid them with real world ambient intelligence systems. Second, there seem to be at least two factors involved in the nature of such system irritants. The first factor involves the sheer introduction of unwanted elements like uninvited emails, pictures etc. The second factor involves reduction in the performance that these unsolicited items can cause. If so, both factors will be unpopular for different reasons and will require different solutions.

7.3 Summary of Results

Factors	Task	Measures	Results
Website difference (W)	Log in	Time taken	R website better
Age (A)	Log in	Time taken	Older slower
Interaction (W x A)	Log in	Time taken	No interaction
Website difference (W)	Check balance	Time taken	R website better
Age (A)	Check balance	Time taken	Older much slower
Interaction (W x A)	Check balance	Time taken	Age difference less on S
Website difference (W)	Withdraw cash	Time taken	R website better
Age (A)	Withdraw cash	Time taken	Older much slower
Interaction (W x A)	Withdraw cash	Time taken	No interaction
Website difference (W)	Log in	Rated difficulty	No difference
Website difference (W)	Check balance	Rated difficulty	No difference
Website difference (W)	Withdraw cash	Rated difficulty	R rated better
Website difference (W)	Log in	Rated pleasant	R rated better
Website difference (W)	Check balance	Rated pleasant	R rated better
Website difference (W)	Withdraw cash	Rated pleasant	R rated better
Age	Log in	Rated difficulty	No difference
Age	Check balance	Rated difficulty	No difference
Age	Withdraw cash	Rated difficulty	Older - more difficult (S website only)
Age	Log in	Rated pleasant	No difference
Age	Check balance	Rated pleasant	No difference
Age	Withdraw cash	Rated pleasant	No difference

8 Case Study: Ambient Friend

Having established the importance of user-emotion elicitation in working with ambient intelligence prototypes for on-line banking, the next study looked at the involvement of emotions in user-participative prototype design. In this study, a single participant (over 50 years of age, female) was asked to select design options for a portable computer device, the aim of which is to provide information wherever the user is and whatever their needs. The user was given a number of options to consider, including six overall design options, seven types of avatar interface, twelve technical options (e.g. testing software) and twelve function options (e.g. email function). She was encouraged to select those options that met her requirements and to explain such selections as they were made. Instructions emphasised that the choices were entirely up to her and no attempts were made to influence decisions or explanations.

Of the twelve technical options, only two were selected. Of the twelve functional options, ten were selected. Using a chi-squared test, these frequency differences were found to be statistically significant in favour of functional requirements over technical requirements ($\chi^2 = 10.67$, $p < 0.05$, two tailed). This participant was interested in the provision of an anthropomorphic agent or onscreen avatar to improve the user interface. It was interesting to note that this person preferred a head and torso to a talking head. The final choice was based on selected on the basis of emotional rather than functional criteria i.e. the most friendly, human-like avatar of the same gender. Aesthetic aspects were judged to be important for the overall design. Finally, of the thirty explanatory explanations generated, only two related to technical matters, but the remaining 28 statements were divided almost equally between emotive (e.g. preventing irritating adverts or unwanted messages) and functional factors (e.g. display a clock), though avatars generated a significant proportion the emotive statements. This was a much higher incidence of emotive issues than prior expectations would have predicted.

9   Applications of Current Results

The present results have important implications for both theory development and good practice in universal access, including the evaluation of user requirements, the development of new prototypes through use-participative design, the evaluation of new systems and the refinement of new methods of research and development. In particular, Simplex Two [4] provides a structure and checklist questions for accessible design, develop, evaluation and prototyping [2] It provides nine vital areas where cognitive overload and other problems can occur ([3]. Thus design questions [5] and user-centred design heuristics can be generated for specific projects. For example, [4] and [9] provided case studies of universal access heuristics for blind and visually impaired people who use ICT. Simplex can also be used to construct user models [2] as an important contribution to the UUID (unified user interface development) methodology for accessible systems [18].

10   Discussion

The consideration of emerging ambient intelligence prototypes demonstrates that a number of important lessons need to be learned if ambient intelligence products and services are to contribute substantially to universal access in the emergent Information Society. However, the scale and complexity of the issues and methods to be accommodated can be daunting, even given the multidisciplinary research and development underway. Focussing on cognitive factors at this stage, Simplex Two [2] provides a simplistic but validated framework of nine related human user cognitive processes with which to assess progress in access to cognitive technologies. Of the nine cognitive processes, the feeling and emotions of users have been identified as a difficult area in which more work is required.

The present evaluation of two on-line banking prototypes showed that, over and above considerations of functionality and usability, the quality of the user experience made a very significant impact on the performance of a set of participants, though their ratings of the perceived difficulty of the two prototypes were hardly different at all. This contrasted with the ratings of pleasantness which distinguished sharply between the two prototypes. The older participants worked significantly more slowly than the younger participants, though there were no indications of any meaningful interactions between age and type of prototype except for one interaction that is best explained by floor effects in the data. If so, then the age-related differences are not due to the same factors as the prototype-related differences. Surprisingly, all participants said that they would be willing to work with either prototype in the future, indicating a high level of tolerance that is not reflected in their performance. These results were supported by the above case study of use-participative prototype design of a smart, portable PDA. It is important to pint out that we are not equating the negative impact of prototype S with the whole of the human emotional spectrum. Certainly, our participants found S to be irritating and stressful, due to its rather unintelligent interaction style. However, on a positive note, they also rated R as significantly more pleasant. Of course, other work should look at positive implications of human emotion, like pleasure, fun, joy etc. There is indeed more to emotion than stress.

There are many ways to explore the best ways to design a new intelligent system and to establish the best possible match between the system and requirements / preferences of the intended users. These methods include; evaluating the technology for effective functionality, consulting experts, comparing system deliverables against accurate user models or profiles, asking intended users for their views and observing their performance. It is very noticeable in the present data that there are discrepancies between two of these methods, namely user performance and user perceptions / stated opinions. Whilst user performance was substantially impacted by the different natures of the two website prototypes, ratings of difficult showed no such pattern. Whilst it is not clear whether this was due to a reluctance to admit to difficulties or to a lack of insight is not clear. However, in practice, this means that performance and verbal reports cannot be simply equated. This is not an isolated finding, since similar results are reported by [6] and [1], however, it is a very important result for methodologies for universal access and for ambient intelligence.

These results demonstrate substantially how the user experience, including the feelings and emotions they experience, can have a substantial influence on user performance, underlining the importance of these factors for the construction of universally accessible prototypes for ambient intelligence environments. There is also a major but different influence of age on performance. More surprising, the results show a major divergence between user performance with the prototypes and user perceptions of the prototypes. Clearly, it can be dangerous to rely on stated user preferences when building successful smart prototypes, or any prototypes for that matter. If so, then greater attention should be paid to well structured and systematic methodologies for developing prototypes and consequent systems for universal access and ambient intelligence. For many prototypes, the methodologies are assumed or not specified well. In contrast, there is now the opportunity to use structured methodologies like UUID, Unified User Interface Development, as set out by Stephanidis, Paramythis, Sfyrakis and Savidis [20] for implementation with interface management systems like the I-GET UIMS [18]). Whatever the chosen methodologies and the details of their development, it is clear that the emerging methodologies can inform the construction of ambient intelligence prototypes and vice versa.

Finally, it may be concluded that there a number of cognitive factors that can be identified in the development of universally accessible systems in ambient intelligence environments. In particular, it is clear that human feelings and emotions can have substantial influences of user performance and the perceived attractiveness of new websites, though not necessarily of ratings of perceived difficulty. If so, the influence of human emotions when working with accessible and intelligent systems will need more research and development in the future.

Acknowledgement. Thanks are due to the referees and to Dr. Dr. Norbert Streitz for useful advice to guide our completion of this paper.

References

[1] Adams, R.G. (2004).Universal access through client-centred cognitive assessment and personality profiling. Lecture Notes in Computer Science, 3196, 3-15. Stary, C. and Stephanidis, C. (Eds.)

[2] Adams, R.G. (2005). Natural computing and interactive system design. Essex, UK: Pearson Education.

[3] Adams, R. (2006).Decision and Stress: Cognition and e-Accessibility in the Information Workplace. Universal Access in the information Society. In press

[4] Adams, R.G. and Langdon, P.M. (2003a). SIMPLEX: a simple user check-model for inclusive design. In Stephanidis, C. (Ed.).Universal Access in HCI: inclusive design in the information society. Mahwah, NJ: LEA.

[5] Adams, R. and Langdon, P. (2003b). Principles and concepts for information and communication technology design. Journal of Visual Impairment and Blindness, 97, 602-611.

[6] Adams, R.G. and Langdon, P.M. (2004). Assessment, insight and awareness in design for users with special needs. In Keates, S., Clarkson, J., Langdon, P. and Robinson, P. (Eds.). Designing a more inclusive world. London: Springer.

[7] Adams, R., Langdon, P., and Clarkson, P.J., (2002) a systematic basis for developing cognitive assessment methods for assistive technology. pp 53-62. In Keates, S., Langdon, P., Clarkson, P.J., and Robinson, P. (Eds.) Universal Access and Assistive Technology. London: Springer.

[8] Adams, R. G. and Whitney, G. (2003). Accessibility for all and tacit knowledge requirements of systems at work. Published proceedings of CEN / CENELEC / ETSI. Nice, France. 2003.

[9] Adams, R.G., Whitney, G. and Langdon, P. (2003). Universal access heuristics for blind and visually impaired people who use ICT. In Stephanidis, C. (Ed.).Universal Access in HCI: inclusive design in the information society. Mahwah, NJ: LEA.

[10] Broadbent, D. E. (1971) Decision and stress. London: Academic Press.

[11] Broadbent, D. E. (1984) The Maltese cross: A new simplistic model for memory. The Behavioral and Brain Sciences, 7, 55-94.

[12] Card, S.K., Moran, T. P. and Newell, A. (1983). The psychology of human-computer interaction. Hillsdale, NJ: LEA.

[13] den Os., E. and Boves, L. (2003). Towards ambient intelligence: multimodal computers that understand our intentions. Proceedings, eChallenges e2003. Ozone IST Project (2005). Final report. www.hitech.projects.com/euprojects/ozone/public_docs/ozone-phr-19Jan05-project-jg.pdf.

[14] Simeon Keates, Ray Adams, Cathy Bodine, Sara Czaja, Wayne Gordon, Peter Gregor, Emily Hacker, Vicki Hanson, Mark Laff, Clayton Lewis, Michael Pieper, John Richards, David Rose, Anthony Savidis, Greg Schultz, Paul Snayd, Shari Trewin, Philip Varker (2006). Cognitive and learning difficulties and how they affect access to IT systems. Universal Access in the information Society. In press.

[15] Latta, J. (2005). EUSAI (Ambient Intelligence) 2004 WAVE 0503 1/21/05 . http://www.wave-report.com/conference_reports /2004/AmbientIntelligence2004.htmViewed 7/22/2006.

[16] Pinker, S. (1998). How the mind works. London; Penguin.

[17] Salvendy, G. (2001). Foreword. In Stephanidis, C. (Eds.). User interfaces for all: concepts, methods and tools. Mahwah, NJ: Lawrence Erlbaum Associates.

[18] Savidis, A. and Stephanidis, C. (2001). Development requirements for implementing unified user interfaces. In Stephanidis, C. (Eds.). User interfaces for all: concepts, methods and tools. Mahwah, NJ: Lawrence Erlbaum Associates.

[19] Stephanidis, C. (2001). User interfaces for all: new perspectives into human-computer interaction. In Stephanidis, C. (Eds.). User interfaces for all: concepts, methods and tools. Mahwah, NJ: Lawrence Erlbaum Associates.

[20] Stephanidis, C., Paramythis, A., Sfyrakis, M. and Savidis, A. (2001). A case study in unified user interface development: The AVANTI web browser. In Stephanidis, C. (Eds.). User interfaces for all: concepts, methods and tools. Mahwah, NJ: Lawrence Erlbaum Associates.

Automatic Evaluation of Mobile Web Accessibility

Myriam Arrue, Markel Vigo, and Julio Abascal

Laboratory of Human-Computer Interaction for Special Needs, Informatika Fakultatea,
University of the Basque Country, Manuel Lardizabal 1, 20018 Donostia, Spain
{myriam,markel,julio}@si.ehu.es

Abstract. Nowadays there is a growing trend towards using web based applications and web browsers in mobile devices such as cellular phones, PDAs, smart phones, and so on. However, interacting with these web interfaces tends to be a frustrating and unsatisfactory experience due to the existing accessibility barriers. Developing accessible web interfaces for mobile devices is a step towards user satisfaction in these environments. "Mobile Web Best Practices" are being discussed so that developers can have a valid reference when creating these web interfaces. However, since they do not have to be experts in the mobile web field, they need tools which automatically evaluate their applications and give them guidance during the development lifecycle. In this paper, EvalAccess, a polyvalent and flexible evaluation tool, has been transformed into a mobile web accessibility evaluation tool, EvalAccess *MOBILE*.

1 Introduction

Mobile access to Internet services, such as the World Wide Web (WWW), is becoming more and more usual in recent years. In fact, due to the improvement of mobile devices features and connection speeds, the group of users using them for WWW access is speedily increasing. This new access mechanism emphasizes the importance of Universal Access concept as it facilitates access to the information in the World Wide Web by anyone, anywhere, and at any time [19].

This modality of access widens the different technologies used, the diverse situations, and the different objectives of users accessing the WWW. However, mobile access to the WWW might present some drawbacks due to the device physical characteristics such as the lack of a pointing device, the limited size of keypads, keys and screens. In addition, there are other features and factors that browsing the WWW can turn into an unsatisfactory experience. For example, the limited bandwidth, the cost of connections, the use of browsers with limited functionalities, and so on.

Nowadays, web sites are commonly designed for desktop computers. This lack of foresight when developing web content can lead to usability and accessibility problems and as a result to unpleasant browsing experiences for users of mobile devices. Consequently, this modality of access requires significant changes in the traditional development process of web sites where Universal Access should be one of the main objectives.

C. Stephanidis and M. Pieper (Eds.): ERCIM UI4ALL Ws 2006, LNCS 4397, pp. 244–260, 2007.

Designers usually have to face a lack of knowledge and experience on design of web sites accessible by mobile devices. Therefore, methods, tools and guidelines are needed to help them in this task. Guidelines have frequently been used to collect design knowledge and experience. Even if they may present problems, such as incoherence and unreliability, and be difficult to handle (when the set of guidelines is too large) they nevertheless prove to be the best method in order to transmit satisfactory design experiences within large design groups or for the external world [1]. Web Content Accessibility Guidelines 1.0 (WCAG 1.0) [5] have been successfully applied [5] and have become such a widespread practice that some accessibility legislations rely on them [11]. However, WCAG guidelines evaluation is not enough to ensure the accessibility of a Web system. It is helpful to remove many accessibility barriers and it is complementary to other evaluations such as expert evaluation and evaluations with users.

Mobile Web Initiative [http://www.w3.org/Mobile/] aims at improving browsing experience by means of recommendations for mobile web content and device description. This initiative is working in the development of a set of best practices for the development of good quality web sites for the mobile web, the Mobile Web Best Practices (MWBP). A draft version of this document, which includes a subset of WCAG 1.0 and more specific mobile focused recommendations, can be found currently at the MWBP web site [12]. Therefore, some research studies carried on web accessibility could be adapted to the new access modality.

This is useful for ambient intelligence scenarios since they rely on ubiquitous devices. In these scenarios, ubiquitous devices play an important role as users interact with the system by using them [18]. According to Hansmann [12] these devices are classified in four main groups:

- Smart controls (smart cards, smart labels, home controls...)
- Intelligent appliances (kiosks, medical monitoring, white goods...)
- Entertainment systems (TV, digital cameras...)
- User access devices (cellular phone, PDA, smart phones...)

User access devices evolve rapidly and currently, many of them support web browsing. In addition, since several light web servers do run on embedded devices [6] the access to ad-hoc web services via web interfaces is becoming a generalized practice. Due to these features, the web browser has the potential to be the main user interface in ambient intelligence scenarios [14]. The use of web interfaces is justified due its lightweight software requirements, its ability to work locally and either on a global scale [13] and its platform independent nature.

In this paper, a tool for automatic evaluation of mobile web accessibility is presented. It is the result of an adaptation process where an automatic evaluation tool for web accessibility based on WCAG guidelines have been successfully converted into a prototype of mobile web accessibility evaluation tool. This work allows us to predict the applicability of traditional web accessibility research in mobile web area.

2 Automatic Accessibility Evaluation

Mobile Web Best Practices are contributing to a more accurate definition of mobile accessibility. This will lead to a situation where developers will be able to systematically implement accessible web products for mobile environments. However, the manual evaluation of guidelines on the whole is an extremely hard task, as the information amount tends to be unmanageable in many web sites. In the traditional web developing context, automatic accessibility evaluation tools are useful so that accessible content could be verified and developed. These tools evaluate web pages according to sets of guidelines and return reports in order to help correcting the detected accessibility errors. Despite their similarities, each tool has some features that make it different from others so they can be classified according to different criteria. For instance, by location or type of service offered.

- Location - when classifying the tools according to their location, it is necessary to discriminate whether they run on a web server (on-line) or on the local computer (off-line).
- Type of service offered - a tool can either offer an analysis service (returns a report of encountered errors) or either analysis and repair service (also guides the user in the reparation task).

On the other hand, it is possible to classify the tools according to their facility for incorporating new guidelines or new versions of existing accessibility guidelines. Regarding this classification, an accessibility evaluation tool can be:

- A tool which has built-in guidelines, so that updating the set of guidelines implies modifying the code.
- A tool where the specification of guidelines is separated from the validation code, so that guidelines can be easily updated. For instance, using this type of tools an organization can define its own guidelines and validate documents according to them [18].

WebXACT [http://webxact.watchfire.com/], and A-Prompt [http://www.aprompt. ca] are well-known automatic accessibility evaluation tools which belong to the group of tools which have built-in guidelines. The current version of A-Prompt works only off-line whereas WebXACT works on-line. Regarding the service they provide, WebXACT offers an accessibility analysis service returning very detailed and complete report while A-Prompt also provides assistance for the error reparation task.

EvalAccess [1], WebKing [21] and DESTINE [6] have a structure where the specification of guidelines is separated from the validation code. Even if each one specifies guidelines in different way, both of them return a detailed report of found errors after validating the accessibility of web content.

An analysis of different web accessibility automatic evaluation tools can be found in Brajnik (2000) [8] and Brajnik (2005) [9].

Due to the fact that several checkpoints can not be automatically tested, these tools are not enough to ensure web accessibility and manual evaluations must be performed. In addition, evaluations with users should be done to find out specific problems and usability issues. However, there is a tendency in the web industry to develop accessible sites only by means of automatic tools. Manual evaluations and evaluations with users are seldom performed and this lack of good practices influences negatively in the obtained accessibility levels. These evaluations should rely on accepted usability techniques such as the proposed by Nielsen and Mack (1994) [15] and Rubin (1994) [18].

Developing automatic evaluation tools for the mobile web area will be very helpful for web sites developers in order to perform automatic evaluations and removing any accessibility error during the development lifecycle. To our best knowledge, there is not currently any framework for automatic evaluation of mobile web accessibility. The main reason for the lack of tools in this area could be that Mobile Web Best Practices are still a draft version. In this paper, a prototype for mobile web accessibility evaluation tool, which have been developed by reusing a previous automatic accessibility evaluation framework, is presented. Specifically, we have taken advantage of the type of tools that have the specification of guidelines separated from the code, so adapting its specification of guidelines is sufficient to perform a completely different evaluation process.

3   EvalAccess Evaluation Tool

The Laboratory of HCI for Special Needs developed EvalAccess, a Web Service for web accessibility automatic evaluation. The main objective when developing this service was to provide a tool which could automatically evaluate any set of web accessibility guidelines specified using a particular XML schema [3]. Therefore, the main characteristics of this Web Service are the following:

- A machine-understandable flexible accessibility guidelines implementation. This ensures an easy integration of new accessibility guidelines into the evaluation tool.
- An evaluation module able to automatically evaluate web sites according to the defined accessibility guidelines. This module is independent of the accessibility guidelines to evaluate, which means that the guidelines are not built-in the evaluation module.
- An accessibility guidelines management module which provides the functionalities in order to define and modify accessibility guidelines.

The architecture of EvalAccess which fulfils the requirements described above is shown in the Fig. 1.

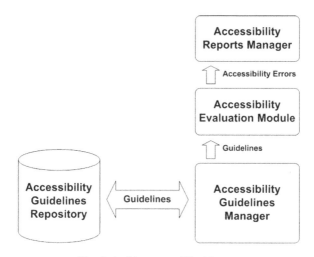

Fig. 1. Architecture of EvalAccess

3.1 Accessibility Guidelines Manager

The function of this module is to manage the different accessibility guidelines existing in the system. This module obtains the accessibility guidelines to evaluate for the current design from the Accessibility Guidelines Repository (AGR). After that it processes this information for making it available to the Accessibility Evaluation Module.

The AGR is a native XML database which contains all the accessibility guidelines accordingly formatted for their easy management. The accessibility guidelines are formatted following a specific XML Schema [http://www.w3.org/XML/Schema]. This schema allows the specification of accessibility guidelines in a language based on XML which is called GXML (Guidelines in XML). This language aims at being a general purpose pattern to define different guidelines and rules. This objective is successfully achieved as it can be observed in the following sections. The Fig. 2 shows the XML schema used for the specification of accessibility guidelines.

All the accessibility guidelines are specified in terms of HTML elements and attributes using the presented XML schema. Table 1 presents an accessibility guideline defined in the WCAG formatted in this language. Concretely, this definition refers to the checkpoint 5.5: *"Provide summaries for tables"*.

Due to this feature, it is possible to easily define new accessibility guidelines or update the existing ones. To this end, an application has been developed by the Laboratory of HCI for Special Needs in order to facilitate the definition of accessibility guidelines in GXML. This application can be locally executed by experts and the XML file generated is manually integrated into the database. An on-line and public version of this application is currently under development.

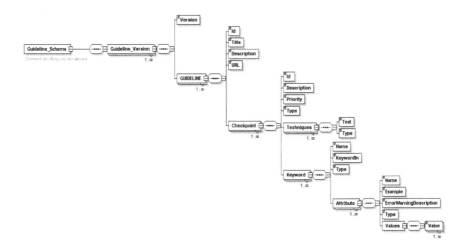

Fig. 2. XML Schema for guidelines specification

Table 1. GXML specification of an accessibility guideline

Element	Description	Example
GuidelineID	Guideline identifier	*5*
Title	Guideline title	*Create tables that transform gracefully*
Description	Guideline description	*Ensure that tables have necessary mark-up to be transformed by accessible browsers and other user agents*
URL	URL where more information is provided	*http://www.w3.org/TR/WCAG10/#gl-table-markup*
CheckpointID	Checkpoint identifier	*5*
CPDescription	Checkpoint description	*Provide summaries for tables*
Priority	Checkpoint priority	*3*
EvalType	Type of evaluation to apply to the checkpoint: automatic or manual	*Automatic*
Keywords	HTML element to validate	*TABLE*
KevType	Validation type for the HTML element	*AnalyseAttributes*
Attribute	HTML element attribute to validate	*SUMMARY*
AevType	Validation type	*NoEmpty*

3.2 Accessibility Evaluation Module

This module evaluates the web sites according to available accessibility guidelines in the Accessibility Guidelines Repository.

The evaluation process is performed as follows:

1. Retrieve the HTML code of the web page to evaluate.
2. Analyse the HTML code detecting all the different HTML elements.
3. Request accessibility information regarding the different HTML detected in the previous step to the Accessibility Guidelines Manager (AGM).
4. Evaluate the HTML code according to the accessibility guidelines returned by the AGM.
5. Return the accessibility errors and warnings detected in the evaluation process to the Accessibility Reports Manager.

Not all accessibility guidelines can be automatically evaluated. For instance, the following guideline: "Use the clearest and simplest language appropriate for a site's content" can not be validated by automatic tools since it requires human judgment. Therefore, these type of guidelines have to be evaluated manually. EvalAccess tool allows defining this type of guidelines using the GXML format and setting the *EvalType* element as *Manual*. Then, information regarding these guidelines can be returned to the Accessibility Reports Manager labeled as *general warnings*.

In addition, there is another type of guidelines that can not be automatically evaluated but can be triggered by content. For instance, one of these guidelines is:

"Organize documents so they may be read without style sheets. For example, when an HTML document is rendered without associated style sheets, it must still be possible to read the document". An automatic tool can detect that a web page is associated with a style sheet but up to date it is not possible to automatically validate if the web page is well organized. Since this type of issues can be triggered by the content, they are known as semi-automatic guidelines. This type of guidelines can be defined using the GXML format and EvalAccess will produce a *warning* if detects that the content regarding a semi-automatic guideline exists in the HTML code.

For the rest of automatically evaluable guidelines the Evaluation Module of EvalAccess tool will produce *errors*. Therefore, *errors*, *warnings and general warnings* are returned to the Accessibility Reports Manager.

3.3 Accessibility Reports Manager

The main objective of this module is to gather all the accessibility *errors*, *warnings* and *general warnings* detected by the Accessibility Evaluation Module and produce a structured report. The resulting report is defined following a specifically produced XML Schema RXML (Report in XML). Due to the use of this XML language for the report, it is possible to create machine readable and customized reports for users. Currently, the Evaluation and Repair Tools Working Group from the WAI is working on a standard evaluation and report language called EARL [15] which is based on XML/RDF. Since the latest version is still being discussed (EARL 0.95) and a beta version of the language has been published, the transformation from RXML into EARL is postponed until a stable version is specified. Note that this future adaptation will be quite straightforward and will not affect to the EvalAccess framework. Table 2 shows a report example in RXML.

Table 2. An example of an accessibility evaluation report in RXML

Element	Description	Example
Guideline ID	Identifier of the guideline which is not fulfilled	*1*
CheckpointID	Identifier of the checkpoint which is not fulfilled	*1*
CPTitle	Checkpoint title	*Provide a text equivalent for every non-text element (e.g., via "alt", "longdesc", or in element content).*
Priority	Checkpoint priority	*1*
URL	URL where more information is provided	*http://www.w3.org/TR/WAI-WEBCONTENT/#gl-provide-equivalents*
Lines	HTML code lines where the same error is repeated	*2, 18, 56*
Keyword	HTML element to be reviewed in order to repair the error	*IMG*
Attribute	HTML attribute which encloses the error	*ALT*

4 Development of Mobile Web Accessibility Evaluation Tool

EvalAccess Web Service was the basis for the development of a mobile web accessibility evaluation tool, EvalAccess *MOBILE*. The main reason for selecting EvalAccess has been its independence between the guidelines to evaluate and the code, since these guidelines are not built-in. Therefore, as mentioned before, it is enough to change the content of the guidelines repository for developing a completely different evaluator. In addition, other features of EvalAccess have been taken into account:

- It is developed as a Web Service, this means that it can be easily integrated into other software applications. This feature also makes easy developing different user interfaces for the same service which is sometimes very useful.
- Its easily understandable guideline format in XML facilitates the task of any research group who wants to validate some proposed guidelines. For example, currently integrated mobile best practices are a draft version but when new versions are launched it will be not difficult to update the repository in order to perform the evaluation according to new guidelines.
- The current locally executed application for guidelines definition facilitates the creation of new guidelines following the proposed XML schema.

The development process of EvalAccess *MOBILE* has consisted of two main phases:

1. Adapting the Accessibility Guidelines Repository
2. Developing a user interface for the new tool

4.1 Adapting the Guidelines Repository

The XML schema used for specification of web accessibility guidelines in EvalAccess is based on WCAG set of guidelines. Therefore, it has been necessary to locate similarities to WCAG in MWBP document, in order to accommodate mobile web best practices into the Accessibility Guidelines Repository. Due to the flexibility of GXML, the codification of MWBP into GXML has not been a hard task.

In WCAG, accessibility information is organized in guidelines and each guideline has a number of checkpoints which contain specific data for performing the evaluation process. The same structure can be implied from the MWBP document, as it can be considered that the information is organized in 5 groups which can be understood as principal guidelines:

- Guideline 1: Overall Behavior
- Guideline 2: Navigation and Links
- Guideline 3: Page Layout and Content.
- Guideline 4: Page Definition
- Guideline 5: User Input

For example, the necessary data in the XML schema regarding the guideline 1 can be completed as showed in the Table 3.

Table 3. Specification of guideline information for MWBP 1.0

Element	Example
Guideline ID	*1*
Title	*Overall Behaviour*
Description	*There are some general principles that underlie delivery to mobile devices.*
URL	*http://www.w3.org/TR/mobile-bp/#bpgroupgeneral*

Each guideline in MWBP consists of a number of tests or checkpoints. For instance, the guideline 5 contains the following checkpoints:

- Checkpoint 5.1: Keep the number of keystrokes to a minimum.
- Checkpoint 5.1: Avoid free text entry where possible.
- Checkpoint 5.1: Provide pre-selected default values where possible.
- Checkpoint 5.1: Specify a default text entry mode, language and/or input format, if the target device is known to support it.
- Checkpoint 5.2: Create a logical tab order through links, form controls and objects.
- Checkpoint 5.3: Label all controls appropriately and explicitly associate labels with controls.
- Checkpoint 5.3: Position labels so they lay out properly in relation to the controls they refer to.

These checkpoints have to be specified in terms of HTML elements and attributes according to the XML schema used. For instance, checkpoint 4.6 defines the next statement: "Specify the size of images in markup, if they have an intrinsic size". This statement can be redefined by terms of HTML elements and attributes as: "Determining a value for the *height* and *width* attributes is necessary for *IMG* HTML element".

The specification of this checkpoint in GXML can be appreciated in the following table, Table 4.

Thus, all the checkpoints in the MWBP have been specified using GXML following the process described above. However, not all of them could be redefined in terms of HTML elements and attributes. For example, there are some checkpoints that can not be automatically evaluated: "Checkpoint 1.3: *Take reasonable steps to work*

Table 4. Specification of checkpoint information for MWBP

Element	Example
CheckpointID	*6*
CPDescription	*Specify the size of images in markup, if they have an intrinsic size.*
URL	*http://www.w3.org/TR/mobile-bp/#ImageSize*
EvalType	*Automatic*
Keyword	*IMG*
KevType	*AnalyseAttributes*
Attribute	*HEIGHT, WIDTH*
AevType	*NoEmpty*

around deficient implementations". As mentioned in a previous section this type of checkpoints will create a *general warning* for any evaluated web page.

In addition, there are other type of checkpoints that could be automatically evaluated but require minor changes in the GXML, for example: "Checkpoint 3.3: *Limit scrolling to one direction, unless secondary scrolling cannot be avoided*". This checkpoint could be easily defined by terms of *width* attribute and testing if it specifies a value less than 120 pixels (for the default delivery context). Currently, GXML does not support this kind of testing case so this checkpoint has been specified as semi-automatic creating *warnings* when width attributes are detected. This specification problem could be solved only performing minor changes to the current GXML.

Moreover, there are some checkpoints in MWBP document that could be automatically evaluated but it can not be redefined in HTML elements and attributes, for example: "Checkpoint 3.2: *Divide pages into usable but limited size portions*". This could be automatically evaluated checking that the page does not exceed 10Kbytes (for the default delivery context). However, this test can not be specified in GXML, so it is defined as a manually testable checkpoint and a *general warning* will be created.

The following table, Table 5, indicates the number of checkpoints defined using GXML classified by their type. As it can be appreciated in this table, checkpoints defined in MWBP can be divided into two main groups: manually testable checkpoints (they will create *general warnings*) and automatic/semi-automatically testable checkpoints.

Table 5. Number of checkpoints classified by their type

Number of Checkpoints classified by type		
Manually testable checkpoints (***General Warnings***)	**Automatic/semi-automatically** testable checkpoints	
	Produce *Errors*	15
27	Produce *Warnings*	17
	Total	32
Total number of checkpoints		59

Test cases are those issues that must be evaluated for determining the conformance of a checkpoint. For example checkpoint 5.2 (*Create a logical order through links, form controls and objects*) is defined by 5 different test cases:

- *INPUT* requires *tabindex* attribute.
- *TEXTAREA* requires *tabindex* attribute.
- *A* requires *tabindex* attribute.
- *SELECT* requires *tabindex* attribute.
- *OBJECT* requires *tabindex* attribute.

The following table, Table 6, shows the number of test cases that have been defined using GXML for the automatic/semi-automatically testable checkpoints, as well as, the number of these test cases producing *errors* and *warnings*.

Table 6. Number of test cases by guideline

Number of implemented Test Cases by Guideline		
Guideline Id	No. Checkpoints	No. Test Case
1	0	0
2	6	18
3	4	10
4	16	36
5	6	19
		Errors *Warnings*
		44 29
Total	32	73

As it can be appreciated in the previous table, guideline 1 of MWBP could not be defined by automatic or semi-automatic checkpoints. But the rest of guidelines could be defined by a mean of 2 test cases for each checkpoint.

4.2   Development of the User Interface

Since the automatic evaluation tool is implemented as a Web Service, a graphical client is necessary so that it can be accessed from a web browser. The implemented architecture (Fig. 3) transforms the RXML document into a browser friendly format. A new user interface has been developed for this new evaluation tool. It is based on the one designed for EvalAccess accessibility evaluation tool. EvalAccess interface was designed taking into account the results of a usability study where guidelines reviews and heuristic evaluations were carried out by five usability experts [1]. This allows us to predict an acceptable usability level of the user interface developed for the new service.

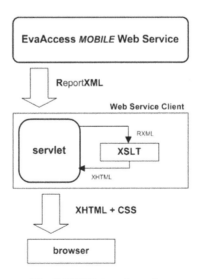

Fig. 3. RXML transformation

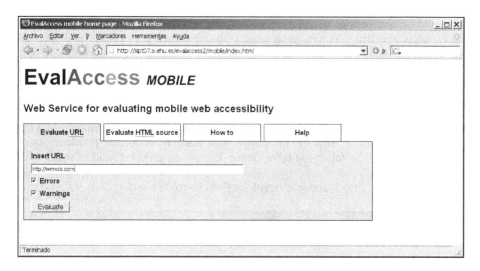

Fig. 4. EvalAccess *MOBILE* interface

It differs in some ways from the original user interface of EvalAccess as in this case the forms have been simplified and all the references to different level of priority deleted, since MWBP document does not assign any priority to the checkpoints. The following figure, Fig. 4, shows the user interface for EvalAccess *MOBILE*.

As it can be observed in Fig. 4, EvalAccess *MOBILE* evaluates a single web page either inserting its URL or its source code. In addition, the user can select the guidelines to evaluate: automatically testable guidelines and/or guidelines that require manual evaluation. Currently, this service is available at http://sipt07.si.ehu.es/evalaccess2/mobile/index.html

After performing the evaluation process, the EvalAccess *MOBILE* Web Service returns a report (see Fig. 5) containing all the detected errors in a XML format, RXML, created by the Accessibility Report Module. This feature makes easy to display customized web reports by applying specific style with XSLT. In this case, a web page for displaying this report has been developed which divides the reported items into three different sections. Firstly, a table with *errors* discovered is listed and further information such as the HTML element and attribute which have caused the

Table 7. Examples of reported items

Type	Example	HTML element, attribute	lines
Error	4.6: Resize images at the server, if they have an intrinsic size.	IMG, WIDTH	x, y, z
Warning	3.3: Limit scrolling to one direction, unless secondary scrolling cannot be avoided.	TABLE, WIDTH	i, j
General Warning	2.4: Provide consistent navigation mechanisms.	independent from content	no line

error and the line of code where it has occurred is reported. Secondly, if evaluation of checkpoints requiring human judgement (those producing *warnings* and *general warnings*) has been previously requested, another two tables are displayed. The first one shows the potential errors (*warnings*) and they are listed in the same format than *errors*. However, they have to be checked manually. The second one shows a list of *warnings* which do not depend on the content and also require manual verification, *General Warnings*. Since they do not depend on the content no HTML element and attribute nor line are provided. Every reported item links to its corresponding MWBP checkpoint in order to help the developer with possible doubts or problems more comprehensively. The following table, Table 7, explains different kind of items with some examples.

The next figure, Fig. 5, shows a report for [http://wrmob.com].

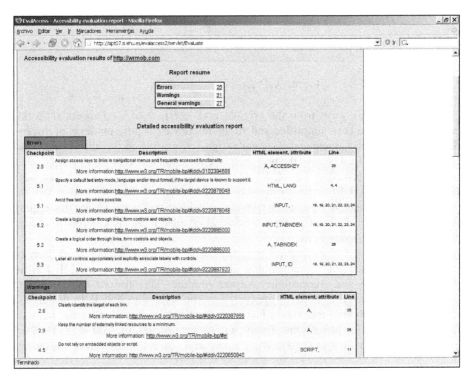

Fig. 5. EvalAccess *MOBILE* evaluation report

5   Results

In order to test EvalAccess *MOBILE*, a specific site designed for mobile devices has been chosen. WordReference is an online multilingual dictionary [http://www. wordreference.com/] which has recently launched a mobile device service. At first sight (see Fig. 6), some good practices are observed: its user interface is simpler and the URL is shorter [http://wrmob.com] as recommended in MWBP, section 5.2.

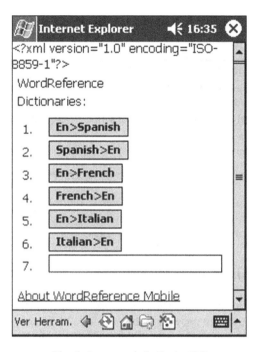

Fig. 6. An example in Pocket PC

Table 8. Reported errors and warnings at http://wrmob.com

Checkpoint	Description	HTML element, attribute	Line
Errors			
2.5	Assign access keys to links in navigational menus and frequently accessed functionality.	A, ACCESKEY	26
5.1	Specify a default text entry mode, language and/or input format, if the target device is known to support it.	HTML, LANG	4
5.1	Avoid free text entry where possible.	INPUT	18, 19, 20, 21, 22, 23, 24
5.2	Create a logical tab order through links, form controls and objects.	INPUT, TABINDEX	18, 19, 20, 21, 22, 23, 24
5.2	Create a logical tab order through links, form controls and objects.	A, TABINDEX	26
5.3	Label all controls appropriately and explicitly associate labels with controls.	INPUT, ID	18, 19, 20, 21, 22, 23, 24

Table 8. (*continued*)

Warnings			
2.6	Clearly identify the target of each link.	A	26
2.9	Keep the number of externally linked resources to a minimum.	A	26
4.5	Do not rely on embedded objects or script.	SCRIPT	11
5.1	Specify a default text entry mode, language and/or input format, if the target device is known to support it.	INPUT, TYPE	24

However, once EvalAccess *MOBILE* evaluates it, the following errors and warnings are reported (See Table 8). Therefore, this proves the usefulness of this kind of tools for the development of mobile web accessible sites.

6 Conclusions and Future Work

The developed evaluation tool, EvalAccess *MOBILE,* is useful when web sites are to be developed for target user groups with mobile devices. Moreover, general purpose web sites might be developed with the help of this tool in order to expand their business as more users will access the services offered. These web sites require a more specific accessibility aware design which focuses on mobile web guidelines in order to obtain satisfactory browsing sessions.

This new evaluation tool is a result of an adaptation process where previous knowledge on traditional accessibility and its related frameworks have been successfully transformed into mobile web paradigm. Due to the flexible architecture of the original framework, this adaptation process has been quite straightforward and obtained results are promising. Therefore, it can be concluded that previous knowledge and tools are useful for this new access technology if they are appropriately designed in the first stages. Due to the flexibility of GXML, future versions of guidelines will be easily specified and a prompt adaptation to them is assured.

Future work will focus on trying to include more guidelines to evaluate automatically. The current XML schema, GXML, will be extended in order to maximize the number of guidelines to evaluate. As previously mentioned, these minor changes in GXML will efficiently improve the performance of EvalAccess *MOBILE.*

In addition, a module to analyze HTTP content will be incorporated into the framework so that guidelines related with HTTP traffic data can be also evaluated. Taking these measures, a more complete tool will be achieved and comprehensive reports will facilitate the development of accessible mobile web systems.

The adaptation process performed by some web servers when delivering web content to mobile devices has to be also considered in next EvalAccess *MOBILE* versions. The current version does not simulate this adaptation process and the only alternative is to gather the adapted content manually and evaluate this code by "Evaluate HTML Source" functionality.

As far as ambient intelligence is concerned, the need for a MWBP evaluation tool is justified since the use of web interfaces for ubiquitous computing will considerably grow thanks to new concepts such as Ajax or Web 2.0. Using these techniques will make mobile web interfaces more usable and interactive. In other words, more powerful and attractive ambient intelligence applications will be developed.

Including new features such as a device profile manager will make possible to evaluate the MWBP according to specific device characteristics. This will improve the evaluation process since it will be focused on the particularities of the device such as its screen size, bandwidth, etc.

References

[1] Abascal, J., Arrue, M., Fajardo, I., Garay, N: An Expert-Based Usability Evaluation of the EvalAccess Web Service, HCI Related Papers of Interacción 2004, in Navarro-Prieto, R. and Lorés, J, Springer, Netherlands (2006) 1-17

[2] Abascal, J., Arrue, M., Fajardo, I., Garay, N., Tomás, J.: Use of Guidelines to automatically verify web accessibility. International Journal on Universal Access in the Information Society (UAIS), Springer Verlag, 3(1), (2004) 71-79

[3] Abascal, J., Arrue, M., Garay, N., Tomás, J.: A Web Service for Automatic Accessibility Analysis of Web Pages Based on the Use of XML Structures, in Proceedings of 10th International Conference on Human-Computer Interaction, Lawrence Erlbaum Associates, (2003) 925-929

[4] Abascal, J., Nicolle, C.: Inclusive Design Guidelines for HCI, Taylor & Francis, (2001)

[5] Abascal, J., Nicolle, C.: Moving towards inclusive design guidelines for socially and ethically aware HCI, Interacting with Computers, Elsevier, 17(5), (2005) 484-505

[6] Bereikdar, A., Keita, M., Noirhomme, M., Randolet, F., Vanderdonckt, J., Mariage, C.: Flexible Reporting for Automated Usability and Accessibility Evaluation of Web Sites, in Proceedings of 10th IFIP TC 13 International Conference on Human-Computer Interaction, INTERACT 2005, M.-F. Costabile, F. Paternò (Eds.), Lecture Notes in Computer Science, Vol. 3585, Springer-Verlag, Berlin, (2005) 281-294

[7] Borriello, G., Want, R.: Embedded Computation Meets the World Wide Web, Communications of the ACM, 43(5), (2000) 59-66

[8] Brajnik, G.: Automatic Web Usability Evaluation: What Needs to be Done? in Proceedings of 6th Conference on Human Factors and the Web Conference, (2000)

[9] Brajnik, G.: Comparing accessibility evaluation tools: a method for tool effectiveness, International Journal on Universal Access in the Information Society (UAIS), Springer Verlag, 3(3-4), (2004) 252-263

[10] Chisholm, W., Vanderheiden, G., Jacobs, I. (Eds.): Web Content Accessibility Guidelines 1.0, (1999, May 5), retrieved from http://www.w3.org/TR/WAI-WEBCONTENT/

[11] eEurope 2005 Action Plan, An Information Society For All (2005), retrieved from http://europa.eu.int/information_society/eeurope/2005/index_en.htm

[12] Hansmann, U., Merk, L., Nicklous M.S., Stober, T.: Pervasive Computing Handbook, 2nd edition, Springer, (2003)

[13] Kindberg, T., Barton, J.: A Web Based Nomadic Computing System, Computer Networks, 35(4), (2001) 443-456

[14] Kindberg, T., Barton, J., Morgan, J., Becker G., Caswell, D., Debaty, P., Gopal, G., Frid, M., Krishnan, V., Morris, H., Schettino, J., Serra, B., Spasojevic, M.: People, Places,

Things: Web Presence for the Real World, in proceedings of the 3rd Annual Wireless and Mobile Computer Systems and Applications, (2000)

[15] McCathieNevile, C., Abou-Zahra, S. (Eds.): Evaluation and Report Language Schema 1.0, (2005, September 9), retrieved from http://www.w3.org/TR/EARL10-Schema/

[16] Nielsen, J., Mack, R: Usability Inspection Methods, John Wiley & Sons, (1994)

[17] Rabin, J., McCathieNevile, C. (Eds.): Mobile Web Best Practices 1.0, Basic Guidelines, (2006, April 12), retrieved from http://www.w3.org/TR/mobile-bp/

[18] Rubin, J.: Handbook of Usability Testing, John Wiley & Sons, (1994)

[19] Stephanidis, C., Savidis, A.: Universal Access in the Information Society: Methods, Tools, and Interaction Technologies, International Journal of Universal Access in Information Society (UAIS), Springer Verlag, 1(1), (2001) 40-55

[20] Takata, Y., Nakamura, T., Seki, H.: Automatic Accessibility Guideline Validation of XML Documents Based on a Specification Language, in Proceedings of 10th International Conference on Human-Computer Interaction, Lawrence Erlbaum Associates, (2003) 1040-1044

[21] Web Site Load and Testing & Web Application Testing: WebKing. http://www.parasoft.com/jsp/products/home.jsp?product=WebKing&itemId=86

[22] Weiser, M.: The Computer for the 21st Century, Scientific American, (1991) 94-104

A Participatory Evaluation Method of Graphic User Interface Storyboards: FAST AIDE

(Function Annotated Storyboards Targeting Applicability, Importance, Design, Elaborations)

Gisela S. Bahr[1], Beth F. Wheeler Atkinson[2], and Melissa M. Walwanis Nelson[1]

[1] NAVAIR Orlando Training Systems Division
12350 Research Parkway, Orlando, FL 32826 USA
[2] Jardon and Howard Technologies, Inc.
13501 Ingenuity Drive, Suite 300, Orlando, FL 32826 USA
{Gisela.Bahr,Beth.Atkinson.Ctr,Melissa.Walwanis}@navy.mil

Abstract. The FAST AIDE (Function Annotated Storyboards Targeting Applicability, Importance, Design, Elaborations) method was developed to capture qualitative and quantitative feedback from highly specialized, expert end-users during the storyboarding stage of new software applications. Unlike traditional approaches, FAST AIDE does not rely on the generation of walk-through scripts or scenarios, but is focused on software features and functionalities. Our rationale is based on the cognitive concept of spreading activation. Spreading activation is hypothesized to occur within knowledge structures similar to organized networks of words or concepts (i.e., nodes). FAST AIDE taps into experiential background of specialized users by utilizing feature dimensions and functionality characteristics to trigger relevant memory. In addition to presenting an approach to knowledge solicitation, FAST AIDE employs a combination data collection questionnaire tool in order to facilitate data evaluation. The paper provides a background and a guide to the implementation of the FAST AIDE method.

Keywords: GUI design - GUI Evaluation Method - GUI mock-up storyboard testing - participatory method - scenario-free - subject matter experts - schema - spreading activation - context memory.

1 Motivation for FAST AIDE Method

The need to develop the FAST AIDE (Function Annotated Storyboards Targeting Applicability, Importance, Design, Elaborations) method arose from a usability challenge that required the merging and integrating of existing methods: Our Human Factors team was tasked to conduct usability testing on a highly specialized graphic user interface (GUI) in development. The GUI was to serve a population of military aviation instructors in virtual training environments. (Live training involves real assets or "entities", such as planes or tanks, while virtual training environments are populated by simulators and computer generated forces.) The challenge was fourfold:

C. Stephanidis and M. Pieper (Eds.): ERCIM UI4ALL Ws 2006, LNCS 4397, pp. 261–272, 2007.
© Springer-Verlag Berlin Heidelberg 2007

(a) Involve the end-users (b) as early as possible, (c) iteratively in the design process and (d) generate quantifiable data that are meaningful to the relevant stakeholders (usability team, end-users, GUI designers and GUI engineers).

1.1 Challenge Background

The involvement of the targeted user groups is regarded as a critical element of the GUI design process, in particular during the development of highly specialized GUIs in unique domains (e.g., health care, emergency management). A primary reason to engage end-users as participatory subject matter experts during the design process is to control the risks associated with financial and schedule uncertainties [1]. In order to optimize control, testing requires iterative administrations which enable a meaningful dialogue between the usability team, end-users, GUI designers and GUI engineers. A concern when choosing an iterative method is the cumulative cost of necessary testing materials as a result of a somewhat aggressive testing schedule. This issue is potentially magnified by the need involve the end-users as early as possible in the design process [2]. Nonetheless, the early diagnosis of potential problems contributes positively to avoid escalating costs and schedule slippage resulting from *unanticipated redesigns* and is not negotiable from a risk management perspective. While schedule and cost concerns are major motivating factors in usability testing, the main benefit of early and iterative involvement of the end-user population is to empower the end-users to shape their future GUI in line with their needs.

1.2 Relevant Methods

The objective to employ an iterative, early-stage, cost efficient evaluation method that supports communication between the usability team, end-users, GUI designers and engineers, narrows the choice of appropriate methods. A relevant solution for GUI evaluation should employ GUI visualizations, such as storyboards, mock-ups and two-dimensional (2-D) paper-prototypes.

Storyboards are generally a series of low fidelity sketches that are not taken to the end-user and primarily support the dialogue between GUI designers and GUI engineers [3]. More "finished," high fidelity storyboard visualizations are referred to as mock-ups and act as a literal representation of the design idea [4]. They may be presented to the end-users by usability teams, to provide an overview of the GUI system, to illustrate its functionalities or to demonstrate navigation schemes [3], [4].

Within the traditional static dimensions of GUIs, i.e. the computer screen, the use and benefits of mock-ups overlaps with that of non-interactive 2-D prototypes: They can be generated and tested early in the development process and require minimal resources [3], [5], [6]; They can be refined quickly to support rapid design iterations driven by an aggressive schedule [3], [6]; They foster communication between end-users and GUI designers, and, most importantly usability testing with 2D-mock-ups generally identifies the majority of usability issues [3], [5].

While the development of 2-D mock-ups compared to functional prototypes is less time and resource consuming, the preparation demanded by the data collection techniques may require a disproportionate amount of time. For instance, a well documented and popular approach to data collection is the 'walkthrough'. Guiding the tester/user through a possible use case requires a scenario and a script generated by expert end-users, i.e., individuals who are highly familiar with the application domain and the tasks to be supported by the GUI in development. In highly specialized domains, the expert end-users act as the testers. Further contributions on their part, as scenario or script developers, may be beneficial but require additional time and validation of the scenarios. (Another, implicit concern regarding scenario-bounded testing is addressed in the next section, *Solution Background*.)

In addition to the need for development of plausible scenarios for testing, Smith [7] puts forth another possible disadvantage of 2-D mockup testing. He suggests that visualization based approaches in general lack formality and do not generate quantifiable data. The later is a desirable trait of data in order to facilitate feedback analysis and to simplify the evaluation report. The types of data that can be generated in participatory testing involving non-functional 2-D mock-ups are qualitative and potentially quantitative. Qualitative data generally captures responses to open-ended questions, end-user (tester) comments or other elaborations. The marking-up of the mock-up stimuli by the testers' annotations also falls into the category of qualitative data. Still, several data reduction techniques may lend themselves to categorize such data to yield descriptive and summary statistics [8].

2   FAST AIDE Solution Background

The difficulty of extracting knowledge from subject matter experts has earned a certain degree of notoriety among psychologists and human systems scholars [9]. The "expert" paradox conceptualizes the researcher's (and expert's apprentice) dilemma when collecting data and learning from experts: Experts in any area are highly skilled and exhibit superior performance; however, they are also likely to lack the ability to articulate their knowledge and explain their performance to a novice. To elicit such knowledge, usability testing has borrowed scenario-focused techniques from the training research communities [10]. From a cognitive perspective, scenarios provide templates that activate schemas and scripts [11], [12], [13]. Schemas and scripts tend to be dependent on context and affect memory retrieval. For instance, during a game of volleyball, individuals are less likely to recall an algebra formula than during an algebra exam.

To test highly specialized GUI's early in development, scenario-focused testing appears unsuitable for scientific and practical reasons. The former refers to the scripted nature of experimenter-designed scenarios. Their benefits include structure and face validity during data collection. At the same time, the strength of scenario context is likely to weaken the activation of related, but not scenario-specific information in the subject matter domain. Thus, scenario-driven feedback appears vulnerable to the suppression of relevant knowledge not obvious within a specific scenario. In addition to their cognitive limitations, traditional scripted approaches require time-consuming development and validation (as mentioned above). Thus, for the expeditious assessment of features and functionalities during the prototype stage, scenario-stimulated or script-driven user feedback appears costly and unsuitable.

Access to expertise relevant to the interface function in question, without being privy to the depth and breadth knowledge space commanded by the specialized user, may be facilitated by taking a constructivist approach rooted in cognitive psychology. For instance, the principle of spreading activation [14], [15], [16] is hypothesized to occur within knowledge structures similar to organized networks of words or concepts (i.e., nodes). Related nodes are connected through associative and semantic pathways. Thus, activation of one node triggers activation of pathways and related nodes. Likewise, a non-scenario method can tap into specialized users' experiential backgrounds by using feature dimensions and functionality characteristics to trigger spreading activation. Once related nodes are activated, memory searches of relevant knowledge networks are in progress.

Activation may be accomplished by identifying functionalities on 2-D mock ups of the GUI in development. An example of how static GUI representation can be

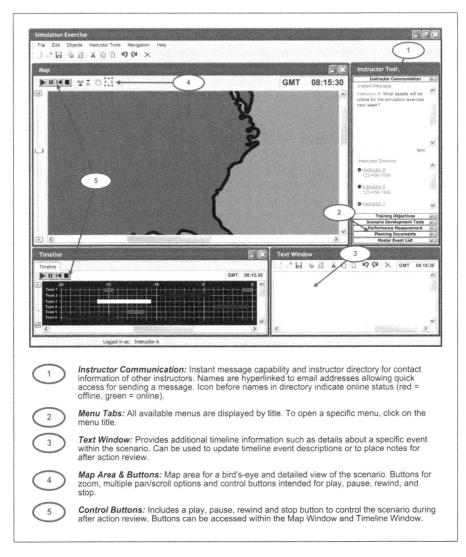

Fig. 1. Example of Annotated Storyboard

annotated is seen in Fig. 1. The figure illustrates an annotated GUI storyboard or "mock screen shot" for an instructor GUI used in simulation exercises. The features that require evaluation are identified by call-outs. Each call-out describes the feature and explains the functions to be coded into the feature. Call-outs are used to pinpoint functions within the design of the GUI screen and provide direct links to clarifying information.

We suggested that scenarios may be unnecessarily restrictive and bound feedback inappropriately; however, placing some limitation on the spread of activation appears reasonable. To direct the expert end-user (tester), a general *frame* of reference or a larger context must be established [17]. This can be accomplished by identifying overarching goals and objectives of the product in development. Feedback is thus bounded by the established frame of reference without being limited by scenario plots or scripted activities. (For a notional representation see Fig. 2.) The notion of contextually exciting and controlling feedback, similar to bounding activation by context, has been successfully implemented in non-storyboard usability techniques, most notably in the *contextual inquiry* technique [1].

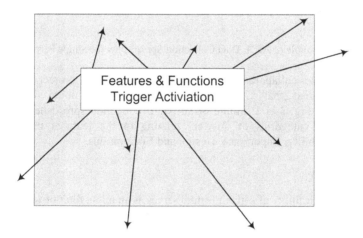

Fig. 2. Representation of Frame of Reference bounding with knowledge activation beyond the relevant context (*external arrowheads*)

In addition to framing the scope of the feedback to include the end-users' relevant knowledge space that was stimulated by the 2-D mock-ups, the knowledge that is expressed requires capture. Discussing the various approaches, such as *think-aloud* protocols, is beyond the scope of this paper [1]. Suffice it to say, that the transcription and coding of qualitative data require considerable amount of time and human resources. Simplification may be accomplished by establishing a priori, conceptual factors that reflect the GUI functionalities in question. These a priori factors can be composed of multiple dimensions that address the various concerns of the stakeholders. The end-users' responses to these dimensions can quantified by providing scale based measurement, i.e., providing a questionnaire with a rating scheme along with the 2-D mock-up stimuli.

14 April 2006				SME-1
A = APPLICABILITY: Yes, No I = IMPORTANCE LEVEL: 1=Low, 2=Medium, 3=High D = DESIGN EXECUTION: 1=Complete Redesign, 2=Can be improved, 3=Do not change E = ELABORATIONS: open-ended entries				
Feature	A	I	D	E
1. Instructor Communication	Yes	3	1	No comment
2. Menu Tabs	Yes	1	1	Separate training/scenario tools from communication tools
3. Text Window	No	-	-	Seems irrelevant
4. Map Area & Buttons	Yes	2	3	Nice design
5. Control Buttons	Yes	3	2	Add time-slider and replay control

Fig. 3. Example of AIDE Data Collection Spreadsheet for Single Participant

Based on close collaboration with GUI engineers and project managers we identified four areas that yield conceptual factors to facilitate the harvest of quantitative data. Fig. 3 is a sample of an AIDE collection spreadsheet for a single participant. Four categories of answers relating to the features in question are depicted: Applicability, Importance, Design and Elaborations.

2.1 Applicability

Assessing the applicability of a given feature serves as an initial filter of whether the GUI goals are in line with the need of the users. A negative answer ("not applicable") serves as an indication to reassess the motivation to initially include that feature and to consider elimination of that feature and its functions. Applicability is a binary category (yes/no).

2.2 Importance

Rating the importance of a particular feature provides an estimate of how critical that feature may be for optimal functionality of the software in development. Three levels of importance ratings allow developers and designers with limited resources to prioritize their time and allocate their budget to develop those features and functionalities rated as highly important.

The three levels of importance that can be assigned are low, medium, and high which can be coded 1, 2 and 3 respectively to facilitate data summary. Higher scores indicate greater perceived importance. Low describes features and functions which are not likely critical or essential. Medium refers to preferred features and functions which could potentially become essential. High is reserved for essential features and functions critical to the software. Translated into the language of the users, low, medium, and high stand for the following: "I don't see why I might need that feature or function but seems nice enough"; "It would be nice to have this feature or function but I can do without it"; and "I cannot operate the software without this feature and its functions." The possible rating of "no importance" is not available because the applicability filter already identified irrelevant features.

2.3 Design

A feature's desirability to a specialized user is likely based on the value added by its functionality. Regardless of the desirability of the proposed functions, the user must be able to access them in a reasonably simple, usable manner. Generally, GUIs serve as the access points to features and functions. Because good functionality does not necessarily translate into good GUI design, the Design category allows expert users to rate the envisioned GUI. Three ratings are available: Completely redesign, improve existing design, do not change current design, which can be coded 1, 2 and 3 respectfully to facilitate data summary. Lower scores indicate greater need for redesign. The possibility exists that expert users critical of the proposed design may wish to contribute their own ideas and visions. The next category (elaborations) captures such input.

2.4 Elaborations

This feedback category serves as a "catch-all" for general remarks, comments, ideas, suggestions, sketches and drawings. As an open-ended call for feedback, the data generated are considered qualitative (i.e., no previously designed scale can be applied to summarize the data across participants). However, the informational value of this category cannot be overemphasized. It provides designers and engineers with a direct view into the users' minds. While the other three categories provide data that can be tracked, summarized and compared easily, elaborations can be very user-specific and require one-by-one evaluation and potential follow-up. Common or recurring themes may emerge during evaluation that point towards a new feature development or approach.

In summary, FAST AIDE may be described as an end-user participatory, contextually-based, 2-D mock-up evaluation method and data collection technique. When designing FAST AIDE, we chose to develop a paradigm that supports (a) engagement of the expert end-user prior to the availability of functional prototypes, i.e., early in the design process, (b) iterative testing, (c) elimination of scenario and script development, (d) quantifiable data that are meaningful to the relevant stakeholders (usability team, end-users, GUI designers and GUI engineers).

3 Guide to FAST AIDE

3.1 Practitioners and Testers

Primarily three groups are involved with a FAST AIDE: Usability teams, expert end-users and the GUI software development team consisting of designers and engineers. The usability team (experimenters or practitioners) prepare, administer and evaluate the FAST AIDE. The expert end-users of the envisioned product participate in the FAST AIDE as testers. Last but not least, designers and engineers utilize the FAST AIDE data and results to evaluate and enhance the software and GUI development.

3.2 FAST AIDE Procedures

At the base level, FAST AIDE can be implemented as paper-and-pencil testing. The minimum sufficient materials to generate scenario-free data consist of a script for the frame of reference (Fig. 2), at least one annotated GUI storyboards (Fig. 1) and a data collection spreadsheet in the AIDE (applicability, importance, design and elaborations) format (Fig. 3). Once these necessary materials are in place, the usability team should observe the following steps for data collection in order:

Step 1. The usability team (or individual) briefs the testers (expert end-users) on the "frame of reference" (see Tips for Materials).

Step 2. The usability team (or individual) administers the annotated 2-D mock ups to the testers and uses the AIDE spreadsheet for data collection.

Step 3. Evaluate FAST AIDE data to guide ("tweak") GUI development plan.

As in any data collection effort, one has to coordinate the participant pool. Specialized end-users are not necessarily readily available, thus flexible administration of the testing must be supported. With this in mind, we kept the procedure for administering FAST AIDE relatively simple and the arrangement for data collection very flexible. The FAST AIDE can be conducted in any of the following configurations:

- One-on-one FAST AIDE: An interview can be conducted between researchers and expert users.
- Group FAST AIDE: Session with multiple expert users and a single researcher is held on site or as a virtual meeting.
- Self-administered FAST AIDE: Paper-and-pencil materials, including the frame of reference brief are supplied to the participant in the form of a self-guided workbook.
- Web-based FAST AIDE: Web-based materials, structured correctly, and prepared for data collection are made available to be accessed at the leisure of the expert user for examination and feedback (non-paper and pencil methods increase preparations outlined in *Tips for Materials*).

In summary, the basic FAST AIDE procedure is configuration independent. First, the participants are briefed on the frame of reference. Second, they receive the materials and instructions. The instructions include an introduction to the GUI designs and an explanation of the AIDE data collection spreadsheet. In addition to entering their assessment and feedback into the AIDE sheet, participants are encouraged to mark up (draw on) their storyboard GUIs. When administering the one-on-one FAST AIDE, the researcher is at leisure to assist the participant with any data recording.

3.3 FAST AIDE Timing

The length of each administration varies with the number of GUIs and features to be assessed. As a rule of thumb, based on the experience of the authors, sessions or interviews exceeding an hour should be avoided due to fatigue. Depending on the degree of engagement of the participant, one can expect to FAST AIDE between 15 and 45 features and their functionalities within a 1-hour window.

3.4 Tips for Materials

The frame of reference should encompass the overarching goal of software development and how it applies to the specialty area of the expert user. This step is critical to create the necessary context for feedback activation (see Fig. 2). The researcher may supply a prepared (replicable) statement that outlines the long-term objective of the GUI as well as the current goal of involving the users early in the design process. In line with the sample annotated screenshot and the AIDE table in Fig. 2 and Fig. 3 respectively, the FAST AIDE frame of reference brief would explain, for instance, that the envisioned software is supposed to provide features and functions that allow instructors to collaborate over time and space and that it supports planning, actual training and debriefing. In addition, as a motivational factor, the researcher would explain that the main FAST AIDE goal is to involve the specialized users as early as possible into the design process, and to incorporate their expert feedback and contribution.

Annotated Screenshots depict static GUI interfaces (screenshots) annotated with functionalities and written explanations of these functions. High fidelity 2-D mock-ups and clearly worded descriptions are critical to the success of the data collection. The informational value of these materials in conjunction with the frame of reference allows the expert end-users to explore the GUI design and relate its envisioned functionality to their own experience. Poor or sketchy designs create ambiguous, confusing stimuli which lead to compromised feedback.

3.5 FAST AIDE Data Analysis

A number of descriptive statistics can be computed from the data. This section makes some suggestions based on the authors' FAST AIDE experience, but new researchers are encouraged to add their own ideas. Care should be taken to report the number of expert user participants and to provide descriptive statistics for individual participants as well as overall averages and totals. The following are potentially useful summary statistics:

- Total number of items tested,
- Total number of items rated not applicable/applicable,
- Breakdown totals for high, medium, low importance ratings,
- Breakdown totals for design ratings 1-3 ("redesign" - "no change").

The elaboration category generates qualitative data (i.e., a previously designed scale applicable to summarize the data is not available). Researchers are advised to carefully study comments and GUI mark-up for additional information from the participants. Ambiguous data require follow-up or need to be eliminated. All other data should be logged. It is possible that during data inspection and logging, common or recurring themes begin to emerge. Such observations, like trends or commonalities, should also be documented and it may be useful to group the log entries into meaningful, easy to search categories.

3.6 FAST AIDE Results' Presentation

In order to present the collected and analyzed data to the stakeholders (design, usability and engineering teams), the AIDE format of the data collection can be used in a slightly modified format (see Fig. 4). The AIDE summary table includes identifying information on the mock-ups evaluated (i.e., title and version), the FAST AIDE administration employed (e.g., single session, group, on-line), the number of participants (Subject Matter Experts) as well as the experimenter and the time(s) and date(s) of data collection. Furthermore, the number of features tested is reported. Based on this number, the following summary statistics are provided having an immediate impact on development schedule and planning: Number of features and functions rated as non-applicable, number of features and functions rated as very important, and number of features and functions that require follow-up.

GUI MOCK-UPS TESTED: Instructor GUI Version 1			
METHOD: FAST AIDE, single session interview			
PARTICIPANTS: 2 subject matter experts (SME-1, SME-2)			
EXPERIMENTER & DATES: Bahr, 14 April 2006 1400-1630 (SME-1); Bahr 16 April 2006 0830-1100 (SME-2)			
NUMBER OF FEATURES TESTED: 5			
NUMBER OF FEATURES RATED VERY IMPORTANT: 3	Color Code: Green		
NUMBER OF FEATURES RATED NON-APPLICABLE: 1	Color Code: Red		
NUMBER OF FEATURES THAT REQUIRE FOLLOW-UP: 2	Marked with Asterisk		
Code	SME Summary Ratings & Comments		
Green = "High/3" Importance Red = Not Applicable * = Follow-Up Required	A = APPLICABILITY: Yes, No I = IMPORTANCE LEVEL: 1=Low, 2=Medium, 3=High D = DESIGN EXECUTION: 1=Complete Redesign, 2=Can be improved, 3=Do not change E = ELABORATIONS: open-ended entries		

Feature	A	I	D	E
1. Instructor Communication *(Redesign)	Yes	3	1	SME-1: No comment
				SME-2: Provide shortcut, maintain overall design
2. Menu Tabs *(SME Disensus)	*	1	1	SME-1: Separate training/scenario tools from communication tools
				SME-2: Already present in drop-down
3. Text Window	No	-	-	SME-1: Seems irrelevant
				SME-2: Not sure I understand
4. Map Area & Buttons	Yes	2.5	2	SME-1: Nice design
				SME-2: Remove redundant, buttons already in timeline display
5. Control Buttons	Yes	3	2	SME-1: Add time-slider and replay control
				SME-2: Add PREVIEW function

Fig. 4. Example of Results' Presentation in AIDE Summary Format

The remainder of the table is similar to Fig. 3. A list of the feature is met with the average AIDE input. In addition, a code is proposed to quickly identify the features that contribute to the summary statistics: Red identifies items rated non-applicable and thus likely candidates for elimination from development; green indicates a 'very important' rating and criticality of implementation; an asterisk marks items that require follow-up (please contact FASTAIDE@gmail.com for color figure). The need for follow-up can arise for a number of reasons. For instance, participants may disagree on applicability ratings or generate conflicting design recommendation. Thus, clarification is required to eliminate contradictory or ambiguous inputs. As seen in Fig. 4, it is possible that participants may rate a feature as very important but give the design low grades without suggesting solutions. In this case, the design and usability teams are required to generate and validate new mock-ups, respectively, without causing significant schedule delays for critical feature implementation.

4 Conclusions

FAST AIDE is a flexible method designed for capturing and evaluating feedback of specialized users early in the development of new, specialized GUIs. Prototype analyses may benefit from the use of the FAST AIDE approach to data collection, but the use of annotated prototype GUIs does not replace traditional, interactive usability and heuristics testing. Instead, FAST AIDE acts as an early diagnostic to establish whether the development team is on the right track and to provide direct user input and guidance for design and implementation.

The FAST AIDE method has several characteristics that support the ease of data collection and analysis: It can be administered to individuals or groups, with paper-and-pencil materials, and does not require presence of a researcher. In addition, the range of the scales for ratings of applicability, importance level and design execution are limited to three points. (Simple scales limit overanalyzing the stimuli and facilitate scoring.) The fourth FAST AIDE measure, the elaborations category, has the inherent challenges of all open-ended, unscaled entries. For ease of FAST AIDE usage, this category is made optional. However, the effort of evaluating comments and suggestions of subject matter experts can deliver valuable insight into the perception and interpretation of GUI storyboards.

As indicated, FAST AIDE can be conducted with minimal resources, but the concept is ready for implementation as a computer-assisted or web-based usability test. Thus, the procedure and the materials described in this paper could be developed into a software application that enables researchers to quickly build FAST AIDE materials and to take advantage of automated data collection and analysis. Such software would be in line with the main goal of FAST AIDE, which is to involve the targeted user group as early as possible, during the storyboarding phase, to enhance the envisioned GUI's performance and credibility while controlling development cost. Interested individuals or those using FAST AIDE are encouraged to contact the authors at FastAide@gmail.com.

References

1. Courage, C., & Baxter, K. (2005). *Understanding your users: A practical guide to user requirements.* San Francisco, CA: Morgan Kaufmann Publishers.
2. Nielsen, J. (1993). *Usability engineering.* San Diego, CA: Academic Press.
3. UsabilityNet. (2006). *Methods table.* Retrieved March 24, 2006, from http://www.usabilitynet.org/tools/methods.htm
4. Newman, M. W., Lin, J., Hong, J. I., & Landay, J. A. (2003). DENIM: An informal web site design tool inspired by observations of practice. *Human-Computer Interaction, 18,* 259-325.
5. Hall, R. R. (2001). Prototyping for usability of new technology. *International Journal of Human-Computer Studies, 55,* 485-501.
6. Säde, S., Nieminen, M., & Riihiaho, S., (1998). Testing usability with 3D paper prototypes – Case Halton system. *Applied Ergonomics, 29,* 67-73.
7. Smith, C. D. (1998). Transforming user-centered analysis into user interface: The design of new generation products. In L. E. Wood (Ed.), *User interface design: Bridging the gap from user requirements to design.* Boca Raton, FL: CRC Press.
8. Kelley, D. L. (1999). *Measurement made accessible: A research approach using qualitative, quantitative, and quality improvement methods.* Thousand Oaks, CA: Sage Publications, Inc.
9. Hoffman, R. R., Shadbolt, N. R., Burton, A. M., & Klein, G. (1995). Eliciting knowledge from experts: A methodological analysis. *Organizational Behavior and Human Decision Processes, 62,* 129-158.
10. McClelland, I., & Suri, J. F. (2005). Involving people in design. In J. R. Wilson & N. Corlett (Eds.), *Evaluation of human work* (pp. 281-333). Boca Raton, FL: Taylor and Francis Group.
11. Ericsson, K. A., & Kintsch, W. (1995). Long-term working memory. *Psychological Review, 102,* 211-245.
12. 12.Groen, G. J., & Patel, V. (1988). The relationship between comprehension and reasoning in medical expertise. In M. Chi, R. Glaser, & M. J. Farr (Eds.), *The nature of expertise* (pp. 287-310). Hillsdale, NJ: Erlbaum.
13. Kimball, D. R. & Holyoak, K. J. (2000). Transfer and expertise. In E. Tulving & F. I. M. Craik (Eds.), *The Oxford handbook of memory* (pp.109-124). New York, NY: Oxford University Press.
14. Anderson, J. R. (1983). A spreading activation theory of memory. *Journal of Verbal Learning and Verbal Behavior, 22,* 261-295.
15. 15.Collins, A. M., & Loftus, E. F. (1975). A spreading-activation theory of semantic processing. *Psychological Review, 82,* 407-428.
16. Quillian, M. R. (1967). A theory and simulation of some basic semantic capabilities. *Behavioral Science, 12,* 410-430.
17. Lehrer, A., & Kittay, E.F. (1992). Frames, Field and Contrasts: New Essays in Semantic and Lexical Organization. Hillsdale, NJ: Lawrence Erlbaum Publishers.

Addressing the Challenges of Inclusive Design: A Case Study Approach

Hua Dong[1], Julia Cassim[2], and Roger Coleman[2]

[1] School of Engineering and Design
Brunel University, Uxbridge, Middlesex, UB8 3PH,UK
Hua.Dong@brunel.ac.uk
[2] Helen Hamlyn Research Centre, Royal College of Art,
Kensington Gore, London SW7 2EU, UK
{julia.cassim, oger.coleman}@rca.ac.uk

Abstract. The challenges for inclusive design include: education of designers; communication of the importance of inclusive design to the public; business rationale for inclusive design to industry; evaluation of the impact of inclusive design.

We believe that a case study approach to inclusive design would help answer these challenges. Based on a design research methodology and a guide for scientific writing, we have developed a template that allows us to write up inclusive design case studies in a systematic way and eventually to build a case study 'bank'. A matrix is presented to explain how this has helped in addressing the challenges of inclusive design. Two examples drawn from the case study 'bank' are presented to illustrate the approach in detail. The template proves an effective means of structuring the case studies and communicating them in a manner that is relevant to a diverse audience.

Keywords: Inclusive design, case studies, challenges, template, matrix.

1 Introduction

Elaine Ostroff, the co-founder of Adaptive Environments[1], and the co-editor of the Universal Design Handbook, mentioned the following three areas as challenges for universal design [1]:

1. Education of design professionals
2. Evaluation of the impact of universally designed products and environments
3. Communication about universal design to the general public

The combined efforts in the three areas will, as is hoped, lead to a wider adoption of universal/inclusive design. However, there is no well-established literature, formal or informal, on the business benefits to be derived from inclusive design [2].

---

[1] A 27 year old educational non-profit organization committed to advancing the role of design in expanding opportunity and enhancing experience for people of all ages and abilities. http://www.adaptiveenvironments.org/index.php?option=Content&Itemid=1.

C. Stephanidis and M. Pieper (Eds.): ERCIM UI4ALL Ws 2006, LNCS 4397, pp. 273–286, 2007.

There are inclusive design case studies for educational purposes, such as [3, 4]; for evaluation purposes, such as [5, 6]; for communication purposes, such as the DBA Inclusive Design Challenge case studies [7]. There are also design case studies focusing on the business benefits brought by design, such as the Design Management Institute's case studies. This has inspired us to build an inclusive design case study bank to fulfil the educational, evaluation and communication purposes; it is also hoped that the synthesis of the case studies in the bank will give us a better understanding of the business benefits of inclusive design.

At the pilot stage, we selected a number of inclusive design projects from the DBA Inclusive Design Challenge (http://www.hhrc.rca.ac.uk/events/DBAChallenge/) and the Helen Hamlyn Research Centre (HHRC)'s Research Associates Programme (RAP) (http://www.hhrc.rca.ac.uk/programmes/ra/how_to_partner.html). We made a template for writing the case studies based upon these projects. Two examples, the Alloy case study from the DBA Inclusive Design Challenge and the B&Q case study from the RAP are presented here to illustrate our approach. The synthesis of these case studies shows that the case study bank has the potential to offer insights into the business benefits of inclusive design, in addition to answering the challenges Ostroff outlined.

2   Case Study Template

To help write up the case studies and to facilitate the synthesis of the case studies, a template was developed. The key components of the template were extracted from two sources, i.e. a design research methodology [8, 9] and a general guide for research paper writing [10, 11].

The design research methodology (DRM) divides the research process into four stages [8, 9]:

- Stage 1. Criteria Formation: identification of the criteria for success (e.g. profit) and the measurable criteria (e.g. time-to-market).
- Stage 2. Descriptive Study I: analysis of the existing design process aiming to discover relations between the measurable criteria and the design process.
- Stage 3. Prescriptive Study: insights gained in Descriptive Study I are used to develop design support.
- Stage 4. Descriptive Study II: the design support is tested experimentally to determine whether it works as intended and whether it actually impacts the measurable criteria.

Although it would not be appropriate to treat the DBA and RAP projects as design research projects, as most of them are short term design projects (typically three months for DBA projects and one year for RAP projects); it is helpful to analyse them using the DRM framework.

A useful tool to structure the case studies is found in Ashby [10, 11], known as the 'concept sheet' (Figure 1). On an A3 sheet of paper in landscape orientation, devise a tentative title and write it at the top. Then jot down section headings, each in its own box. Sketch in anything that is relevant to a section and put them in bubbles near the box. The orders of the sections can be adjusted by adding arrows indicating the new order.

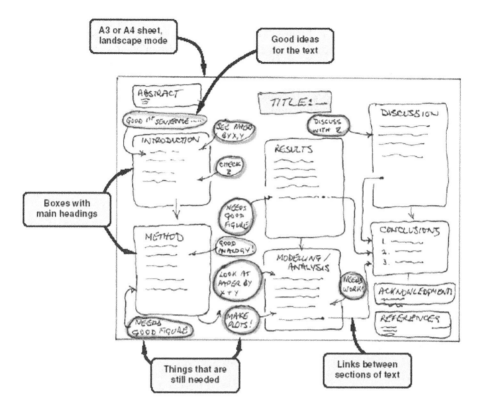

Fig. 1. The concept sheet [11] – a useful tool for structuring the case studies

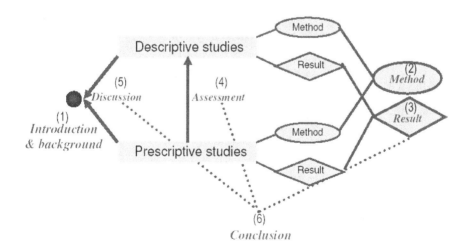

Fig. 2. Rationale of the case study template

The template we developed is a combination of the DRM and the concept sheet. The rationale is illustrated in Figure 2. The starting point (1) for any design project, be it a design problem, or a novel design concept, can be written up as an introduction to, or the background of, the case study. Typically the designer will have to investigate the problem (descriptive studies), using certain methods and obtaining certain results; and then find solutions to address the problem (prescriptive studies), using certain methods and obtaining certain results. For scientific writing, it is good practice not to

Abstract (150 words)
Keywords (4-8 in total)
Project period

Overview (300-400 words)
Introduction
- Problem statement (100 words)
- Previous work in the field: result of the literature review – 200 words
- The design brief; the research objectives – 100 words

Background (optional)
- The industry partner and the research associate – their roles in the project
- Project dates and duration

Methods (300-400 words)
- The approach to the problem, in particular methods used in the 'explore' stage and the 'focus' stage

Results/design outcomes/ solutions (500-600 words)
- Results from the 'explore' stage
- Results from the 'focus' stage
- Concepts developed (with figures illustrating the concepts)
- Selection of the concepts
- Details of the selected concepts/design outcomes

Assessment (150-400 words)
- What was the feedback – industry partners, end users?

Discussion (150-400 words)
- How did the design solution respond to the design brief?
- The challenges of the project
- How was the success measured?
- What were the constraints of the project?
- What is repeatable / transferable, and what could be done differently?

Conclusions and future work (200-300 words)
- Main conclusions drawn from 'results', 'assessment', and 'discussion'.
- What insights were gained?
- What are the next steps?

Acknowledgements and References (around 150 words in total)

Fig. 3. Case study template

Table 1. Matrix: matching the case study components to the challenges of inclusive design

Challenges	Key components of the case studies				
	Overview (project background information)	*Method* (user research & design approach)	Results (user research findings and design solutions)	*Assessment* (inclusivity evaluation, feedback from users & industry)	Discussion (issues raised, follow-up development, learning)
Education of design professionals		Designers can learn from effective user research methods and different design approaches.	Designers can be inspired by user research findings and other designers' creative solutions to certain problems.	This will help designers to be more aware of different evaluation criteria.	Designers will learn from others' success and lessons.
Evaluation of the impact of inclusive design				The impact is reflected by user comments and industry feedback.	Project follow-ups are also indicators of the impact of inclusive design.
Communication to the General Public	This will give the general public a broad view of the inclusive design projects in the UK.	This will show the general public how inclusive solutions are developed.	This will show the general public a range of inclusive solutions.	This will show the general pubic how inclusivity is evaluated.	This will show the general public what was learned and what happened afterwards.
Business benefits of inclusive design			How to build inclusive features into products to improve design.	What benefits has inclusive design bring to the users and industry.	What lessons have been learned to improve future performance.

mix methods with results, so the method used in the descriptive studies and the prescriptive studies are brought together to form a method section (2); and the results obtained from the descriptive studies and the prescriptive studies are brought together to form a result section (3). It is important to assess whether the solution has addressed the problem (4); and to discuss whether the right problem has been addressed and whether the right solution has been found (5). By drawing key points from (3) 'Result', (4) 'Assessment', and (5) 'Discussion' together, we can draw a conclusion (6).

The final template for the RAP case study is shown in Figure 3, where suggestion on the length of each section is also made. This is to keep the case studies in 'a manageable size' to communicate to a wide range of audience. A similar template is also developed for the DBA case studies. In Table 1, the key components of the template are matched to the challenges of inclusive design, in a matrix format. Based on the authors' general knowledge about inclusive design and specific knowledge about the case studies, correlations are identified, as explained in the cells. Stronger correlations are highlighted with bold borders.

It is hoped that the synthesis of the case studies would offer insights into inclusive design. For example, the synthesis of *Method* sections of the case studies would help designers learn how to conduct user research and how to design inclusively; the *Results* sections how to design inclusive features into products; and *Assessment* sections how to evaluate the inclusivity of the final design solution.

So far, the template has been used to reporting case studies in the product design (domestic appliances, DIY tools, mobility aids), information design, packaging design, workplace design and wayfinding system design. It is easy to adapt the template for different types of design projects and design research projects.

3   Case Study Examples

In this section, two abbreviated case studies are presented to illustrate the application of the templates to the DBA projects and the RAP projects. In these short case studies, only part of the content in the 'Discussion' section, i.e. 'follow-up', is covered. Readers interested in the full case studies can refer to the Helen Hamlyn Research Centre's website (http://www.hhrc.rca.ac.uk/research/i-design2/) to which the full case studies are linked (Figure 4).

3.1   Example 1: B&Q Case Study

Overview. DIY (Do It Yourself) is among the top ten leisure activities for the post retirement sector but this activity tends to decline with age. This is due to the physical demands of DIY tools and the increasing impairments relating to the ageing process.

B&Q, Europe's largest home improvement retailer, planned to develop own brand age-friendly DIY power tools. It approached the Helen Hamlyn Research Centre and participated in the Centre's Research Associate Programme. Matthew White was recruited as the Research Associate, who then worked with B&Q to develop a new range of DIY tools. The one-year RAP project was divided into four stages, namely: 'explore', 'focus', 'develop', and 'deliver'.

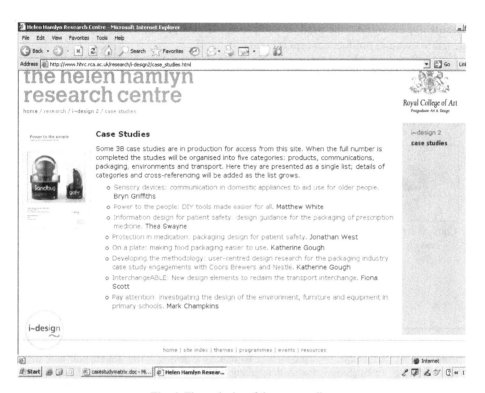

Fig. 4. The web site of the case studies

Method. The 'explore' stage involved a range of activities (Table 2).

Table 2. Activities involved in the 'explore' stage

Activities	Aims
Store visits and product audit	To understand B&Q from the viewpoint of its customers and staff.
	To try out products and make a visual record of them.
In-store interviews	To ascertain why customers were there, what they thought of B&Q and their age and background.
Analysing marketing data (competitor evaluation)	To obtain general knowledge of the nature and size of the B&Q's customer base.
Desk research (library and Internet search)	To find relevant user study methodologies.
	To obtain information about innovations and new products from brand leaders.

User testing was carried out throughout the development, including focus groups and observation during the concept creation stage, short-term tests during the concept selection/initial development stage and long-term tests throughout the process.

Result. By combining the product audit with the findings from the user tests, White generated several product concepts (Figure 5):

A cordless screwdriver: existing tools are long, unwieldy and difficult to grip and activate. A redesign made the shape easier to fit into the palm of the hand while its foreshortened design allowed it to be used in corners that were inaccessible to screwdrivers of conventional length. The tool is automatically activated as soon as the screw bit locks into the screw.

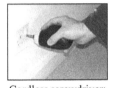 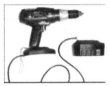  

| Cordless screwdriver: easy to grip | Cordless drill: Reducing weight | Reciprocating saw: ergonomic rethink | Palm-sized sander: hand strap innovation |

Fig. 5. Design outputs

Table 3. Evaluation against user needs

Concepts	Problem to address	User needs	User testing results
Cordless screwdriver	Current products available are not ergonomic and difficult to use in corners.	To make the device compact. To eliminate the switch.	The automation and size are beneficial, desirable and offer considerable advantages over current cordless screwdrivers.
Cordless drill	Users cannot pick up heavy tools. About 1/3 of a drill's weight is the battery alone.	Remove the battery and lighten the weight of tools by at least a third: using a retrofit device.	By relieving a third of the weight alone, the results were overwhelmingly positive.
Reciprocating saw	The current design demands the user to hold it in a position 90 degrees opposed to a natural grip with the other hand in a similar awkward placement; a difficult battery clipping system.	The ergonomics were to be changed to allow a natural strong two -handed grip. To design a better battery clipping method.	Comfort and a natural feel for the hand positioning. Battery clipping method – potentially easy.
Palm-sized sander	Noticeable vibration that became uncomfortable after prolonged use.	Allow the user to exert the force without needing to rigidly grip it, by simple addition of a hand strap.	The sander is immediately attractive to consumers who feel it would make a good tool and a great gift!

A cordless drill: Conventional drills are heavy to use due to their battery weight. By attaching the battery via belt clip to the waist and connecting it to the drill with a short power cord, the freedom of cordless drills could be preserving whilst simultaneously relieving battery weight.

A reciprocating jigsaw: By changing the angle of application and totally redesigning the handle and battery case, the ergonomics of the jigsaw is improved.

A palm-sized sanders: Conventional sanders are generally uncomfortable to hold, as the user is expected to press and hold a sander against a surface to re-create a sanding motion while it vibrates. The prototype was redesigned to 'cup' the hand while a hand strap eliminates the need to grip it firmly.

Assessment. All design concepts generated were reviewed against user needs, market compatibility and their development potential. Table 3 summarises the evaluation result against user needs.

Follow-up. B&Q patented and evaluated the prototypes and chose two to take to market – the cordless screwdriver (Gofer) and the palm-sized sander (Sandbug) (Figure 6). The tools have been among B&Q's best sellers since their launch in 2002 and were named as 'must have' products in the national press for Christmas 2004. A second iteration of the screwdriver with significant restyling and refinement was launched in 2005.

Fig. 6. Easy to use DIY power tools

After the successful one-year RAP project, Matthew White was employed directly by B&Q as a design consultant. He then spent the next 12 months making his designs production-ready by refining components and producing engineering drawings. In the following year, B&Q worked with a second Helen Hamlyn Research Associate in the area of garden power tools, and developed company guidelines for inclusive design.

3.2 Example 2: Alloy Case Study

Overview. Making a cup of tea is a basic daily activity and crucial to maintaining an independent life for older people. Unfortunately it can be dangerous because kettles, cups/mugs, and teapots are among the items most likely to cause accidents in the home. A study on the difficulties disabled people have when using everyday consumer products suggests that 273,000 people in the UK would have difficulties in manipulating and gripping a kettle while 615,000 would have difficulties in lifting and transporting it [12]. This estimate does not take into account the number of people who are excluded from using a kettle because of impaired vision.

Recognising that "kettles are something that everybody has to use, but many are struggling to use them", Alloy Total Product Design participated in the 2001 DBA Design Challenge, an annual inclusive design competition in the UK organised by the Helen Hamlyn Research Centre and tried to find a safe and inclusive way of boiling water.

Method. The design team first assessed a number of kettles themselves. They realised that many on the market relied on the use of two hands. They also found that the centre of gravity of many kettles was far from the handle, requiring the user to have high levels of strength in their hands. Moreover, most kettles were far too large for users who would typically only require one or two cups of boiled water. Alloy then ran a focus group of users with mobility, dexterity and visual impairments (so-called critical user forums) and found the concerns and preferences of these users.

Results. The design solution was Kettlesense – a 'no-pour' kettle concept (Figure 7). To remove as much of the carrying weight as possible, cold water is poured into a lightweight, two-handed plastic jug, which is slotted into the Kettlsesense Tower. With no electronics in the jug and a one-litre capacity, the jug is as light as possible. A leak-proof water connection is set into the base of the location ramp. The user

Fig. 7. Kettlesense – a no-pour kettle (photo credit: Alloy Total Product Design)

pushes the jug into place and the connection is automatically made. Then a valve allows the cold water to flow out of the jug when it is secure. The user switches it on and water is lifted by an element similar to those in coffee makers. It passes into a double-walled internal tank, where an upper element raises it to boiling point. When a fail-safe panel is pushed, the water is dispensed. The no-pour kettle also has a number of inclusive features such as the tactile handle, audio alert, tactile water indicator, and larger switch etc.

Assessment. To assess the inclusivity of the no-pour kettle, Dong made a quantified assessment of a range of kettles, using updated population data similar to those used in the DTI study [12]. Kettlesense excludes far fewer users compared with others (Table 4).

Table 4. Number of users excluded based on dexterity and vision demand

Exclusion by dexterity demand	2,105,000	2,727,000	1,135,000	945,000
Exclusion by vision demand	198,000	319,000	>137,000	137,000

The users involved in the focus group also liked the no-pour kettle concept as it eliminates the difficult *lifting* and *pouring* tasks.

Follow-up. For Alloy the Kettlesense project "did a lot to raise awareness of inclusive design issue within the company...It is something that we think we can take further." While approaching potential manufacturers to take Kettlesense to market, Alloy has

Fig. 8. BT Freestyle 6000 [13]

been applying inclusive design principles to its specialist areas, i.e. information technology (IT) and communication products. It has developed a number of inclusive telephone handsets for major suppliers of telephones in the UK and Europe, for example, BT's Freestyle 6000 (Figure 8). Alloy also helped SunCorp, a cordless telephone supplier, to increase their market share in Europe from 5% to over 25% [13]. In a recent survey, Alloy strongly believes that inclusive design could effectively help achieve a number of commercial benefits, especially as a source of innovation and differentiation.

4   Discussion

The two projects are from different programmes, hence have different backgrounds and emphases. However, they can be written up as case studies using exactly the same template. The template also proves effective in structuring other types of case studies [14]. The advantage of this approach lies in its adaptability and flexibility. It also makes comparison across case studies easy and straightforward, such as shown in Table 5, where industry initiatives (drawn from *Overview*), user research methods (drawn from *Methods*), key element of success (drawn from *Results*), assessment methods (drawn from *Assessment*), and business cases (drawn from *Follow-up*) are seen at a glance – synthesis based on more case studies in the bank would be even more useful.

Table 5. Synthesis of the two case studies

	Overview	Methods	Results	Assessment	Follow-up
B&Q	Retailer's initiative can be the start point of an inclusive design project.	Useful methods for inclusive design: product audit, interview, observation, focus group, user testing.	Simple changes can make a significant difference: inclusive design does not need to be complicated.	Useful methods for evaluation: evaluate against user needs and market compatibility.	RA projects lead to commercial success and corporate guidelines o inclusive design.
Alloy	Design consultancy's motivation leads to an inclusive design project.	Useful methods for inclusive design: designers' self assessment, critical user forums.	Radical change resulted from problem analysis (rethink the means of boiling water): inclusive design helps innovation.	Useful methods for evaluation: exclusion estimate and task analysis.	Experience of a DBA project leads to success in mainstream market.

While more and more case studies are being written up based on the past DBA and RAP projects by us designer researchers; we are also helping designers to write up their projects in a more accessible format. The template has been given to the HHRC research associates, together with a writing guide [15]. We shall modify the template using the feedback received from designers. It is hoped that the template will be adopted by more and more design researchers and practitioners, who can help us build up the inclusive design case study bank and make a stronger argument for the business case of inclusive design.

5 Conclusion

To conclude, we have developed a template for writing up case studies of inclusive design, aiming to build an inclusive design case study bank. We hope that by synthesising the case studies in the bank, we can find answers to the challenges of inclusive design regarding education, evaluation, communication and the business case.

Acknowledgements. We would like to thank the Engineering and Physical Sciences Research Council in the UK for funding the research project, and the Cambridge Engineering Design Centre for supporting the work.

References

[1] Ostroff, E.: Universal Design: the New Paradigm. In: Preiser, W.F.E., Ostroff, E. (eds.) Universal Design Handbook. McGraw-Hill (2001) 1.3-1.12.
[2] Underwood, M.J., Metz, D.: Seven Business Drivers of Inclusive Design. In: Proceedings of Include2003, Royal College of Art, London (2003) 1:39-1:44.
[3] Hewer, S. (eds.) DAN Teaching Pack, RSA, Waterloo printing company, London, (1995)
[4] Goldberg, L., Jolly, E., Mellor, J.P., Moeller, B., Rothberg,M., Stamper, R., Wollowski, M.: Teaching Diversity through Inclusive Design Case Studies, In: Proceedings of the 32nd ASEE/IEEE Frontiers in Education Conference, Boston (2002). Available from http://fie.engrng.pitt.edu/fie2002/papers/1480.pdf.
[5] Manley, S.: Creating the Universally Designed City, In: Preiser, W.F.E., Ostroff, E. (eds.) Universal Design Handbook. McGraw-Hill (2001) 58.3-58.21.
[6] Dong, H., Keates, S., Clarkson, P.J.: Inclusive Design Diagnosis Based on the ONS Scales. In: Proceedings of CWUAAT'02, Trinity Hall, Cambridge (2002), UK.
[7] Cassim, J., Innovate/Challenge, Helen Hamlyn Research Centre, Royal College of Art, London (2001-2006)
[8] Blessing, L., Chakrabarti, A., Wallace, K.: A Design Research Methodology. In: Hubka, V. (eds.) Proceedings of the 10th International Conference on Engineering Design (ICED95), August 22024, 1995, Praha (1995) 50-55
[9] Blessing, L., Chakrabarti, A.: DRM: A Design Research Methodology. In: Proceedings of Les Science de la Conception, March 15-16, 2002, INSA de Lyon, Lyon (2002) 1-15
[10] Ashby, M.: How to Write a Paper (version 5), Department of Engineering, University of Cambridge (2000). A PDF version is available from http://www-users.cs.york.ac.uk/~tw/phd/ashby.pdf

[11] Ashby, M.: How to write a paper (version 6), Department of Engineering, University of Cambridge (2005). A PDF version is available from http://www-mech.eng.cam.ac.uk/mmd/ashby-paper-V6.pdf

[12] DTI: A Study on the Difficulties Disabled People Have When Using Everyday Consumer Products, Government Consumer Safety Research, Department of Trade and Industry, London (2000)

[13] Warburton, N.: Mainstream Inclusive Success. In: Proceedings of Include2005, Royal College of Art, London (2005)

[14] Dong, H., Bobjer, O., McBride, P., Clarkson, P.J.: Inclusive Product Design: Industrial Case Studies from the UK and Sweden. In: Proceedings of Ergonomics 2006, Cambridge (2006) 338-342

[15] Ashby, M., Dong, H.: How to Write a Report: Communicate Your Work Effectively (version 1).Engineering Design Centre, Department of Engineering, University of Cambridge (2004). (A PDF file is available upon request)

Defining Acceptable Levels of Accessibility

Simeon Keates

IBM T.J. Watson Research Center
19 Skyline Drive, Hawthorne, NY 10532
lsk@us.ibm.com

Abstract. This paper examines the issues facing companies when designing products and services for equitable access, particularly in view of the legislated requirements that they have to meet. The concepts of acceptability and accessibility are discussed and a framework proposed for establishing whether a product or service is acceptably accessible. Relevant case studies are referenced, where appropriate, to support the arguments presented.

1 Introduction

A range of legislation over the past decade or so has forced many companies to consider the need to design for accessibility. This legislation includes the 1990 Americans with Disabilities Act [1] and the 1995 UK Disability Discrimination Act [4]. Section 508 of the 1973 Rehabilitation Act was amended in 1998 in what became the Reauthorized Rehabilitation Act (confusingly also known as the Workforce Investment Act – [12]). This legislation prohibits the US Federal government and all of its agencies from purchasing, using, maintaining or developing any electronic and information technology products that are not deemed fully accessible.

Underlying most of this legislation is the principal that all products and services offered to the public should also offer all possible reasonable accommodations to allow users with disabilities to access them. However, except in rare circumstances, the legislation has been drafted specifically to avoid prescriptive descriptions of precisely what a "reasonable accommodation" is, to avoid the culture of minimum compliance, where companies aim to offer the bare minimum that they can get away with, without getting sued. The aim of the legislation is to encourage companies to adopt the spirit of the laws, rather than simply trying to meet the letter of the law.

However, the flip-side of this situation is that companies do not know exactly how far they have to go in terms of the final accessibility of their products and services. One of the ideas proposed is to ensure that "equitable access" is available to all users. However, this term needs to be defined explicitly as it can be interpreted as simply equitable access to a product or service's functionality – in other words, whether someone can use the product to accomplish the desired task. This can be thought of as the minimum compliance interpretation. At the other end of the spectrum is the more idealistic interpretation of offering accessibility to the functionality in the same time as all other users. In practice, most companies fall somewhere between the two extremes shown in Figure 1.

C. Stephanidis and M. Pieper (Eds.): ERCIM UI4ALL Ws 2006, LNCS 4397, pp. 287 – 303, 2007.

Fig. 1. Different interpretations of what is meant by "equitable access"

2 Understanding Acceptability

In his book on usability engineering, Nielsen [10] identified two principal attributes of successful products, namely social acceptability and practical acceptability.

2.1 Social Acceptability

Social acceptability is achieved when the product meets the expectations and aspirations of the end-user. These can be thought of as the "user wants". Social acceptability addresses issues such as:

- Does the product look nice?
- Do I trust this product?
- Does this product stigmatize me in any way?
- Do I want this product?

This list is indicative of the type of attributes associated with social acceptability. When considering in particular the design of assistive products, it is also important to add non-stigmatizing to the list of attributes. In other words, a socially acceptable product must be one that the user is happy or content to use. Some commentators go so far as to suggest that the only successful products are those that the users want to use [3]. While this may be true for most so-called mainstream commercial products, it does not necessarily apply to so-called assistive or rehabilitation products, which are often bought on behalf of the user by an intermediary, such as a health authority.

Designing for social acceptability is what most product designers try to achieve. It requires that the designers be provided with information about what constitutes a socially acceptable product for the users and then using a suitable design approach that is responsive to those requirements. Obtaining and interpreting those requirements needs specialized approaches. As would be expected, it is not possible to provide a single definition of what a user wants from a product or service. For example, some people want a product that draws attention to itself, such as a memory aid or prompt to take medication, while others would prefer something more discreet, especially for a product to be used in public. Consequently, it is often necessary todedicate some effort to finding those wants for at least each product domain, and sometimes for each product variant.

2.2 Practical Acceptability

Nielsen's definition of practical acceptability is divided into:

- cost;
- compatibility;
- reliability; and,
- usefulness.

Of these, usefulness is subdivided further into:

- utility – the provision of the necessary functionality by the product to perform the desired task; and,
- usability – defined as including:
  - ease of learning;
  - efficiency of use;
  - ease to remembering; and,
  - low (user) error rates.

All of these attributes of practical acceptability appear eminently sensible. However, in practice, with limited time and resources allocated to the design of a new product, perhaps the ones most commonly considered the top priorities are cost and utility (also frequently referred to as functionality). After all, there is no point designing a product that is either going to cost too much to succeed in the marketplace or simply does not do what is needed of it.

It is clear to see that the ultimate cost of the product will affect its success in the marketplace; otherwise everyone would drive a Ferrari, Aston Martin and the like. Functionality is also clearly important. A product that does not do what it is supposed to is not fit for purpose. However, functionality in certain product areas, especially computing, is in danger of becoming all-consuming. There are an increasing number of new versions of products offering essentially the same basic interface as older versions. The principal differences between the new versions and the older ones are additional functions, many of which the users may never even use. This trend to offer increasing levels of functionality simply for the sake of doing so, is known as feature creep.

Of the other attributes of practical acceptability, many are not normally considered top priorities when designing a new product, but often only middling priorities at best. Designing for reliability, for example, is a balancing act for many companies. Consumers typically would prefer to see the products that they purchase last as long as possible without breaking down. However, it does seem that many products are designed to last the least amount of time beyond the warranty period, as possible – this is known as designing for obsolescence. Companies typically design products to last the least amount of time that they think the consumers will accept, especially in circumstances where the underlying technology is fairly mature and evolving slowly, for example white goods such as refrigerators and washing machines.

Among those middling priorities is designing for usability. The reason for usability not being considered a top priority is that when consumers are purchasing a new product they often only consider the functions it offers and the cost of it. Usability is a property that consumers are usually only able to assess after owning the product for a period of time, after which it is usually too late to return it. After all, there are very few products, especially high-tech ones, that are readily available in a shop to try out thoroughly before actually making a purchase. When purchasing products on-line, where one or two photographs of the product are available, the situation gets even worse for consumers who are trying to decide how easy a product may be to use.

Consequently, consumers try to reduce the amount of information that they have to process to: "How much does it cost?" and "What are the main functions it offers?" Features and price are much easier to identify and compare quickly. When buying a digital camera, for instance, customers are more likely to look for the number of megapixels and price rather than how easy it is to delete an image or put in a new memory card.

Therefore, on the whole, improved usability often will not lead directly to increased sales of a product. Thus many companies do not regard it as a top design priority. After all, even after 30 years, there is still a lack of really usable VCR interfaces.

However, this is often a very short-sighted view. Returning to the issue of "cost" – this has many facets. There is the cost to the company to design, build, market and support the product. There is also the cost to the consumer to buy it, the cost to maintain it and ultimately to dispose of it. A truly usable product may cost slightly more to design, but will generally cost less to support and maintain. In addition, once consumers have used a genuinely usable product, they are much more likely to remain faithful to that product's brand, rather than switch to another.

One of the best examples of this phenomenon is OXO's GoodGrips brand. Since the company was founded in 1989, its revenues have grown by over 35% year on year and it now boasts a range of over 500 products. This is impressive growth for a company whose products are based almost exclusively around the original concept of a usable, well-constructed handle made of durable rubber, with flexible rubber fins for improved grip. Those same distinctive fins also mark the products out on the shelf as belonging to a particular range and brand. The company attributes its success entirely to its devotion to understanding the customers' needs and practicing user-centred design [7].

Consumers are becoming increasingly sophisticated and often appreciate when a company takes that extra bit of time and trouble to ensure that a product is usable. After all, the company is effectively saying that it thinks that its customers are genuinely important people and that it is going out of its way to make sure that they are happy. Accessibility is very similar to usability in this respect.

3 Understanding Accessibility

Accessibility is broadly about the ability to access the functionality or utility of the product or service and usability is about the ability to use it. There is then a question of how the ability to access the product / service differs from the ability to use it.

Many of the techniques used for designing products to be accessible are basically amended or altered versions of standard usability practices. In theory, a product that is designed using user-centred design techniques and usability practices should, by default, be accessible. However, many are not accessible. There are several ways to think about how accessibility differs from usability, but first it helps to understand the process of interacting with a product and how the user's functional capabilities (e.g. sight, hearing, memory, hand-eye coordination, etc.) affect that. Figure 2 (adapted from the Center for Research and Education on Aging and Technology Enhancement's model of ageing and technology) shows a basic map of the different possible interactions involved when using a product to accomplish a task within a given environment.

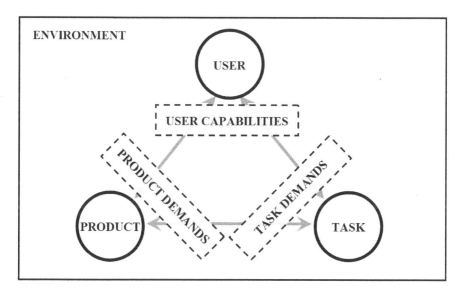

Fig. 2. A map of the different possible interactions involved when using a product to accomplish a task

For an arbitrary task, say, moving from point A to point B, the user may attempt to accomplish that task without the use of a technological product. Walking to point B would be one possible option. However, if the task demands are too excessive for the user's capabilities, it may be necessary to employ a product to help accomplish the task. In this example, the product could be a car, a bus, a train or even just a walking stick. The product will have been designed to meet the demands of the task. However, the product itself will have its own set of demands that it places on the user. If those demands do not exceed the capabilities of the user, then the user is still able to accomplish the task, but if those demands exceed the user's capabilities, then the product is inaccessible and the user will not be able to perform the task.

Building on this need to balance a product's demands and the user's capabilities, consider that any design specification contains implicit assumptions about the users. It will assume their age range, level of experience with similar products or technologies, knowledge about the product and also their functional capabilities. If these properties are not defined, then the designers will typically substitute themselves as the target users – often on the basis that they are users, so why not design for the product for themselves? This is a surprisingly common attitude among designers and is what Cooper [3] referred to as "designers design for themselves" unless directed to do otherwise.

Once the usability trials of the product start, the assumptions about who the users are often get even more entrenched into the product's operation. Any usability trial focuses on the problems and successes identified by the particular users recruited for the trials. Any solution developed should therefore be usable and accessible by those users. Further, anyone who has similar levels of experience, knowledge and functional capabilities to those users involved in the usability trials should be able to use the product.

However, the users recruited will often be very similar to those on whom the design specification was based. This, in itself, is not necessarily a bad thing. It means that the designers will be able to verify that the product is usable by the intended users, which is surely a good thing.

The problems arise when the assumptions about the users are examined, both for the design specification and the subsequent usability trials. Unless the assumption was framed explicitly to recognize the full range of potential user needs and capabilities it is highly likely that only a subset of needs and capabilities will be considered – typically young males in perfect health.

Thus, not all users will be similar to those involved in the user trials and those who are not, will most likely be unable to use the resultant product. There is a need to recognize those users and take steps to ensure that their needs are not overlooked. The term used to describe that need is accessibility. In other words, accessibility can be thought of as the set of additional user needs not covered by the usability practices employed in the design of a particular product.

4 Defining "Acceptable Accessibility"

An "acceptable" level of accessibility can be defined in many ways. Perhaps the most persuasive is to interpret it in terms of overall productivity of the user. Productivity is, in turn, often expressed in terms of minimizing the time to complete a task, often combined with keeping errors and unnecessary (i.e. repetitive or redundant) actions to a minimum.

It is often argued that for a product to be "acceptably accessible" it should represent no differentiation between users solely because of their functional capabilities and, furthermore, that the overall productivity of each user should be identical. In other words, a user with a disability should be able to complete a task with as few errors, and in the same amount of time, as someone who is nominally able-bodied. After all, it is no good claiming that a product is accessible based principally on whether someone can complete a task. For example, a task that takes an able-bodied only five minutes to complete using the product, but takes someone who is blind five hours to complete cannot realistically be considered acceptably accessible. Thus, a simplification of this argument is that all users should be able to complete a specified task using the product in the same amount of time. Any product that fails to meet this target is deficient in some way. However, this argument is an over-simplification of the issue.

For example, while the goal of equal time to complete a task may be the "ideal", it is likely to be of little use when considering whether the level of accessibility provided by a particular product is acceptable. The reason for this is that it is unlikely that the same time to complete a task is achievable for people with disabilities as for nominally able-bodied users, unless the task is a very simple (i.e. straightforward) one. Someone with a visual impairment is unlikely to be able to perform a visual task rendered aurally in the same time as a sighted person could accomplish the task. Similar levels of task completion times may be possible for a highly sequential task (e.g. listening and answering a linear series of questions), but not for more randomly organized tasks (such as seek-and-find).

4.1 Differences in User Performance

An example of how different users behave fundamentally differently can be found in a simple set of experiments based around a basic user model, the Model Human Processor (MHP – [2]). The Model Human Processor states that the time to complete a task is described by the following equation:

$$Time\ to\ complete\ =\ [x\ \times\ T(p)]\ +\ [y\ \times\ T(c)]\ +\ [z \qquad (1)$$
$$\times\ T(m)]$$

where:

- $T(p)$ is the time for one perceptual cycle, i.e. the time required for the user's senses to recognize that they have sensed something.
- $T(c)$ is the time to complete one cognitive cycle, i.e. the very simplest decision-making process in the brain. This can be thought of as being effectively akin to a "yes/no" question, such as "did I see something?" which would take one cognitive cycle to answer. A more complicated question would take several cognitive steps because it needs to be broken down into a series of either "yes/no" questions or other simple classification steps.
- $T(m)$ is the time to produce a single, simple motor movement, e.g. a downward stab of a finger onto a key. Releasing the key would require a second motor movement.
- Finally, x, y and z are all integer coefficients (1, 2, 3, etc.) that represent how many of each component cycle are required.

Card, Moran and Newell [2] describe a number of basic tests that can be performed to calibrate this model. Although the tests they describe are paper-based, they are straightforward to implement within a computer program. Such a program can be used to screen potential user trial participants as the results it generates provide a useful indication of the level of severity of motor impairment of a particular user. For an able-bodied person, the typical observed times of each cycle from such a program are as follows [6]:

- $T(p) = 80$ ms
- $T(c) = 90$ ms
- $T(m) = 70$ ms

For users with moderate to severe motor impairment, the observed $T(p)$ is typically 100 ms - close to the 80 ms seen for the able-bodied users, but still 25% slower. The observed $T(c)$ for the same users is usually 110 ms – compared with 90 ms for the able-bodied users. Note that even though the observed times are somewhat slower for the users with motor impairments, they are still close enough that the differences are not particularly important when considering the interaction as a whole.

However, the results for $T(m)$ are quite complicated and provide an informative insight into how functional impairments can fundamentally change a person's behaviour. The observed results for users with motor impairments typically fall into one of 3 bands: 100-110 ms, 200-210 ms, or 300-310 ms – all of which are significantly slower than the 70 ms observed for the able-bodied users.

The reason for the different bands is suggested by the 100 ms time differences between them. That difference is the same magnitude as either additional $T(c)$ cycles or $T(m)$ steps. If it is additional $T(c)$ cycles that are present, then that implies that more cognitive effort is required of the user to perform each "simple" motor function than for able-bodied users. The likely cause of the $T(c)$ cycles is the extra cognitive effort required to produce carefully controlled movements, for example, by having to try to suppress spasms or tremor. This extra cognitive effort has a knock-on implication that so-called "automatic" responses are not achievable for those particular users. Alternatively, if additional $T(m)$ steps are present then that implies any supposedly "simple" action, such as pressing down on a key, is not performed as a single movement, but actually several (usually) smaller ones.

Irrespective of the cause of the different bandings, the net effect is that some users simply cannot perform basic physical actions as quickly as other users can. The data presented here has been derived from users with motor impairments. Similar results are also seen in much of the literature on ageing research, showing that, for example, increasing age is strongly correlated with slower response times on simple reaction tasks. However, in the case of ageing in particular, older adults are often able to compensate to some degree for their increasingly slower response times through their increased experience and knowledge, acquired over the years. A direct consequence of this user variability in the performance of "simple" tasks is that trying to design a product to meet the requirement that all users be able to complete a task in the same time, whether nominally able-bodied, older or functionally impaired, would be almost impossible for many products.

4.2 The Difficulty of Moving Goalposts

Studies comparing the time taken for users with motor impairments to complete a task compared with the time for "able-bodied" users have shown very few instances where the users with motor impairments matched the performance of their able-bodied counterparts (e.g. [6]. In those instances where similar performance is observed, they were usually when the performance of the able-bodied users was being compromised in some way. Some of those tasks were simple comparisons of unmodified systems and so such differences would be expected. However, many of the studies were based on tests involving systems that had been modified to compensate for the impairments and so should, in theory, have minimized or mitigated the effects of the particular impairments being investigated.

Additionally, it has to be remembered that any useful compensation that can be offered to users with motor impairments usually also benefits the able-bodied users. Thus, while it may be possible for a particular form of assistance to improve the overall time to complete a task (or whatever metric is being used to measure "productivity") for a user with a motor impairment, it is likely that the time for an "able-bodied" user would also improve when using the same assistance. In other words, the goalposts are prone to moving.

An example of the goalposts moving is the use of haptic gravity wells to assist users with motor impairments perform "point-and-click" tasks on a graphical user interface [5]. A Logitech Wingman force-feedback mouse was used for input. The Wingman is capable of generating a wide range of force-feedback effects, including both translations and vibrations. The physical implementation of a gravity well is straightforward and intuitive. When the cursor enters the gravity well, a spring force pulls the mouse toward the centre of the target until the target is selected. Implementations of gravity wells vary in where the gravity effect terminates internally, typically either just inside the outer edge of the target or alternatively at the centre of the target.

Experimental participants performed a series of multidirectional "point and click" tasks, based on ISO 9241-9 [9]. Cursor movement data were collected from five motion-impaired users with a range of impairment types and severities. Although the users had predominantly the same clinical diagnoses, the severity of impairment ranged from mild to severe. The symptoms exhibited by the users included spasm, tremor, poor co-ordination, and reduced strength. Table 1 summarises the conditions of each of the motion-impaired users. For comparison, data from three able-bodied participants (CU1-3) were also collected.

Table 1. The study participants from and their medical conditions

User	Condition
PI2	Athetoid/ ataxic Cerebral Palsy, wheelchair user
PI3	Athetoid Cerebral Palsy, spasm, wheelchair user
PI5	Athetoid Cerebral Palsy, deaf, non-speaking
PI6	Athetoid Cerebral Palsy
PI7	Friedrich's Ataxia, tremor, wheelchair user

In line with the methodology outlined in ISO 9241-9, throughput was used as the principal measure of overall user productivity. As defined in ISO 9241-9 [9], throughput can be calculated from:

$$Throughput = \frac{ID_e}{MT} \tag{2}$$

where MT is the movement time and ID_e is the effective index of difficulty, based on the effective width, We and the initial distance to the target, D:

$$ID_e = \log_2\left(\frac{D}{W_e} + 1\right) \tag{3}$$

Figure 3 shows the throughput obtained by the motor impaired and able-bodied users with and without haptic assistance. It can be seen that without assistance, the respective mean throughputs obtained were 1.77 and 4.88 bits/s respectively, i.e., the able-bodied users generated slightly over twice the throughput of the motor impaired ones.

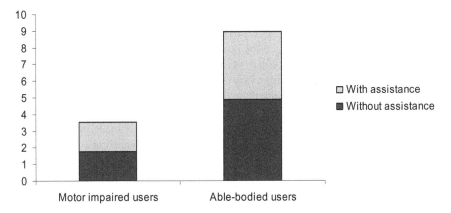

Fig. 3. The respective throughputs from the motor impaired and able-bodied users with and without gravity well assistance

When the motor impaired users were assisted by gravity wells, their mean throughput increased to 3.54 bits/s, much closer to the 4.88 bits/s of the able-bodied users. However, when the able-bodied users were provided with the gravity well assistance, their mean throughput increased to 8.95 bits/s, effectively restoring the discrepancy in throughput between the two users groups that had been seen in the unassisted condition. This means that if the gravity well assistance is offered to both user groups, they both improved by throughput by a very similar proportion (2× for the motor impaired users and 1.83× for the able-bodied users). In other words, while the throughput of the motor impaired users has improved, so has the throughput of the able-bodied users. Thus, unless the gravity well assistance was only to be offered to the motor impaired users, they have moved only very slightly closer to the throughput achieved by the able-bodied users. Thus, the throughput goalposts that the motor impaired users are trying to meet have been moved. This, in turn, means that any framework for defining acceptable levels of accessibility needs to allow for such moving goalposts.

5 A Framework for Defining Acceptable Accessibility

The most pragmatic definition of an acceptable level of accessibility for a particular product is one that allows all user groups to perform a series of tasks within an acceptable level of tolerance on an agreed range of metrics. The metrics will most likely be focused around productivity measures, such as time to complete a task, throughput and error rates [9]. It is also likely that there will be no single, universal tolerance that can be implemented across the entire range of a company's products. Instead, the best that can probably be considered is a framework for defining what levels of tolerance are acceptable for the particular product being evaluated. Table 2 shows such a framework.

Table 2. A framework for deciding whether a product is "acceptably accessible"

STAGE	ACTION
1	• Identify each target user group (or persona) to be considered
2	• Identify component steps in the interaction for each target user group and for the base-line, datum user group (most likely younger, able-bodied users)
3	• Compare number of steps for each group
DECISION GATEWAY – 1	Are there the same or very similar numbers of steps for each user group? *– If not - significant differences have to be justified to senior management or remedied.*
4	• Perform user studies with the baseline user group – calculate times to complete tasks and sub-tasks and error rates
5	• Perform user studies with each target user group – calculate times to complete tasks and sub-tasks and error rates
DECISION GATEWAY – 2	Could all of the target users complete the tasks? *– If not - the causes of difficulty need to be removed or re-designed and remedied.*
6	• Compare the error rates for each group
DECISION GATEWAY – 3	Are the error rates the same or very similar between the target user groups and the baseline group? *– If not – significant differences have to be justified or remedied.* *[Note: this should be extremely hard to justify]*

Table 2. (*continued*)

7	• Compare the times to complete tasks and sub-tasks modified by the following factors: a. the number of component steps (if it has been agreed that notable differences are OK in this case) b. the proportion of component steps affected by each group's particular disability (sight, hearing, etc.) c. the relative "importance" of the step (high, medium, low) d. the level of severity of the disability (high, medium, low) [note - this is likely to be an inverse factor] e. any additional latencies (whether innate in the user, or arising from the AT used, e.g. the time taken for a screen-reader to read out the text on-screen)
DECISION GATEWAY – 4	Are the modified times to complete tasks and sub-tasks the same or very similar? – *If not – significant differences have to be justified or remedied.* *[Note: this should also be extremely hard to justify after making the modifications to the times listed in stage 7 above]*

The framework also needs to recognise the level of severity of the user's impairment. Someone with a minor tremor will most likely be able to complete a task faster than someone with a frequent major spasm. No assistive technology exists at the moment that could level that particular playing field. Equally, the framework would also need to look at error rates. Errors are a major source of delay and increased time on task for all user groups, but especially older adults and those with disabilities. If a person's rate of interaction with a product is already slowed by the presence of functional impairments, then it is imperative that errors be kept to an absolute minimum. Continual errors affect the user's perception of a product and thus the willingness to keep using the product diminishes. In addition, the time to correct any errors is increased for these users, and so they are, in effect, paying a double penalty for errors.

6   Implementing the Framework

The framework begins with a step-by-step task analysis, breaking down the interaction into its component steps. This should be done for each of the user groups being considered - including the role of the particular assistive technologies that are required to enable access. For example, if someone using a screen-reader needs to perform fifty actions to complete a task, whereas everyone else need only do five actions, then clearly there is a problem with the model of interaction for the use of a screen-reader. Under such circumstances, the onus should be placed squarely on the shoulders of the product/service designers to explain why their interaction model for users who are blind appears to be so poor.

Similarly should any of the user groups be unable to complete any of the tasks, then the product or service clearly does not offer equitable access.

6.1 Identifying the User Capabilities of Interest

The easiest way of identifying which users may be affected is to break down the interaction into its common component steps and think about what the user has to be able to do to complete each step, e.g.:

6.2 Software Scenario Example

A user is using a word processor and decides to print the document being worked on. The "Print" dialogue box has popped up on the screen and the user needs to select the "OK" button. The interaction steps are thus:

1. Recognize that a dialogue box has appeared - either see it (vision) or hear the notification sound (hearing)
2. Find the available buttons to choose between (vision)
3. Distinguish between the buttons to choose correct one (vision, cognitive/learning)
4. Decide which one to activate (cognitive/learning)
5. Activate it (vision, motor)

6.3 Hardware Scenario Example

A user is trying to withdraw cash from an ATM. The ATM is prompting the user to answer the questions "Which account do you wish to withdraw your cash from?" The user has to press the relevant (hardware) button to proceed. The interaction steps are:

1. Read the prompt - (vision, cognitive/learning)
2. Find the available buttons to choose between (vision, maybe motor)
3. Distinguish between the buttons to choose correct one (vision, cognitive/learning)
4. Decide which one to activate (cognitive/learning)
5. Activate it (vision, motor)

The similarities between software and hardware activation of a button are obvious. Note that each of the principal impairment classifications (sensory, motor and cognitive) could potentially encounter a "showstopper" accessibility difficulty in these scenarios. Also note that the use of assistive technology requires these steps to be gone through again and amended accordingly. For example, the use of screen-reader software in the software scenario removes the vision demands on the user, but replaces them with hearing ones.

Clearly considering the needs of just one user group will only identify the issues for other users of that same group. If resources are only available to work with one or two users, one option is to find users with a range of impairments. Older adults, for example, may have limited dexterity (motor impairment) through arthritis, as well as low vision from age-related macular degeneration and slight hearing loss. It should also be borne in mind that some users may require highly specialized or customized solutions to meet their needs. Such solutions may not necessarily be applicable or beneficial to users with lesser impairments. It is preferred practice to find users who should be able to use the product but are experiencing, or are likely to experience, unnecessary difficulties in doing so.

Note that while the above discussion is focused on capabilities, it is eminently plausible, and indeed reasonable, to extend the user characteristics to include anthropometric details of the user. For example, when considering a product designed for older adults it is worth noting that the average height of someone over 65 is over 2 inches less than the average height of younger adults [11]. If such differences are overlooked when deciding, for example, on the viewing height of a screen, then older users may find themselves unable to use the final product. An example of this phenomenon was an information point designed for use in post offices in the UK, shown in Figure 4.

Fig. 4. The concept information point

The information point was designed such that the input was achieved via the six buttons either side of the screen. The output was via the screen, which was set at 1610mm high and inclined backwards, and the telephone handset. Output was not duplicated between the two output channels, i.e. unique information was provided by both the handset and the screen. The height of the screen was such that a half of all women over the age of 65 would not be able to see the contents of the screen. The combined sensory and motor demands placed on the users by the initial design of the information point meant that approximately 45% of all target users were likely to experience significant difficulty using it [8].

6.4   Deciding on Acceptable Levels of Accessibility

Central to the implementation of the framework is the notion that the times achieved by users with functional impairments should be adjusted in view of fundamental differences in user performance and/or the latencies associated with using particular assistive technologies. It is those adjusted times that should be compared with the target times, which are typically those of able-bodied users.

For example, consider a user with a severe motor impairment attempting to perform a simple reaction task compared with an able-bodied user trying to accomplish the same task. The results obtained from the experimental calibration of the MHP described earlier imply that the time taken to press and release a button in response to a simple stimulus should be:

$$Time\ to\ complete\ =\ T(p)\ +\ T(c)\ +\ [\ 2\ \times\ T(m)] \tag{4}$$

For an able-bodied user, the predicted time to accomplish this task would be:

$$(80\ +\ 90\ +\ 2\times70)\ =\ 310\ ms \tag{5}$$

The results for the motor impaired users imply that the predicted times to complete this task would range from:

$$(100\ +\ 110\ +\ 2\times105)\ =\ 420\ ms \tag{6}$$

to

$$(100\ +\ 110\ +\ 2\times305)\ =\ 820\ ms \tag{7}$$

Short of eliminating the need to press a button in response to the stimulus, it is hard to envisage how an interface designer could overcome this fundamental difference in user response time. Thus, for every button press in a task's interaction sequence, a tolerance of up to 0.5 sec per button press should be factored in when comparing the overall time to complete the task. All stages of the interaction sequence can be similarly calibrated to give a more complete comparison between the performance of the able-bodied users and those with functional impairments.

Similarly, the time delays and latencies associated with individual assistive technologies need to be estimated. For instance, if there is a 5-second delay in generating the speech output for a screen reader and there are 10 such outputs, then a total latency of 50 seconds should be factored in to the tolerance calculation. If a sighted person can read at (say) 150 words per minute, but a blind person can only listen at (say) 100 words per minute, then a tolerance of 3/2 should be factored in.

7   The Implications for Companies

The framework shown in Table 2 recognizes that directly comparable performance is unlikely because of a whole range of factors, but tries to identify what should be achievable in a more constrained fashion than simply "target users can or cannot complete the tasks." Of course, it may be that even with the modifications in overall time factored in, there is still a discrepancy in the times taken to access the functionality and complete the tasks. If the discrepancy is small, a company may decide to accept the difference unless there are obvious areas in which the interaction and product/service can be improved.

If the discrepancy is large, then the company needs to re-examine the design of the product or service and the interaction. This is not to say that the product or service should necessarily be shelved, simply that if the company decides to go ahead with it, then the company needs to be prepared to justify why there is such a discrepancy in time to access the functionality between different user groups, possibly in a courtroom.

However, there is a question as to how big a difference is acceptable. As discussed earlier, a difference in access to the functionality, i.e. whether a user group can use the product or service to complete the task, is likely to be unacceptable except in extremely extenuating circumstances. A difference in time to complete the task is a more intriguing question. Most companies may decide that a 5% difference between the adjusted times is acceptable. A 50% difference is probably not acceptable. The question then arises as to where exactly the line should be drawn between the difference being acceptable or not.

That is a question that will most likely be decided by each company individually and will be a compromise between the effort and cost of reducing the discrepancy versus the perceived risk of being sued.

8 Summary

This paper has examined the issues facing companies as they struggle with the need to design their products and services to be more accessible. The framework proposed for assessing whether the level of accessibility offered by a specific product or service has been structured to be as generic as possible and to be applied in a wide range of circumstances with a minimum of adaptation.

At some point, the level of accessibility required to meet the demands of current legislation will have to be defined through litigation and courtroom precedents. In the meantime, the framework proposed here, if used judiciously, should help companies avoid such courtroom battles.

References

[1] ADA (1990). Americans with Disabilities Act (US Public Law 101-336). Available at: http://www.usdoj.gov/crt/ada/pubs/ada.txt.
[2] Card, S.K., Moran, T.P. and Newell, A. (1983). The psychology of human-computer interaction. Hillsdale, NJ: Lawrence Erlbaum Associates.
[3] Cooper, A. (1999). The inmates are running the asylum. Indianapolis, IN: SAMS Publishing.
[4] DDA (1995). Disability Discrimination Act 1995 (c. 50). Available at: http://www.opsi.gov.uk/acts/acts1995/Ukpga_19950050_en_1.htm.
[5] Keates, S., Langdon, P., Clarkson, J., and Robinson, P. Investigating the use of force feedback for motion-impaired users. In: Proceedings of the 6th ERCIM Workshop (Florence, 2000), 207-212.
[6] Keates, S., Langdon, P., Clarkson, P.J., and Robinson, P. (2002) User models and user physical capability. User Modeling and User-Adapted Interaction (UMUAI). 12(2-3), 139-169.
[7] Keates, S., and Clarkson, P.J. (2003) Countering design exclusion: An introduction to inclusive design. London, UK: Springer-Verlag.

[8] Keates, S., Langdon, P., Clarkson, P.J., and Robinson, P. (2001) A practical approach to design for Universal Access: the Information Point case study. Proceedings of the 1st Int'l Conference on Universal Access and HCI (UAHCI), New Orleans, 18-22, Mahwah, NJ: Lawrence Erlbaum Associates.

[9] ISO (1998) ISO/DIS 9241-9 Ergonomic requirements for office work with visual display terminals, non-keyboard input device requirements. Geneva, Switzerland: IOS.

[10] Nielsen, J. (1993) Usability engineering. San Francisco, CA: Morgan Kaufman Publishers.

[11] Smith, S. Norris, B., and Peebles, L. (2000) Older Adultdata: The handbook of measurements and capabilities of the older adult – data for design safety. London, UK: Department of Trade and Industry.

[12] WIA (1998) Workforce Investment Act (US Public Law 105-220). Available at: http://www.doleta.gov/usworkforce/wia/wialaw.txt.

Combined User Physical, Physiological and Subjective Measures for Assessing User Cost

Tao Lin, Atsumi Imamiya, Wanhua Hu, and Masaki Omata

Department of Computer Science and Media Engineering, University of Yamanashi
Takeda 4-3-11, Kofu, Yamanashi Prefecture, 400-8511, Japan
{Lintao,Imamiya,Hu,Omata}@hci.media.yamanashi.ac.jp

Abstract. New technologies are making it possible to provide an enriched view of interaction for researchers using multimodal information. This preliminary study explores the use of multimodal information streams in evaluating user cost. In the study, easy, medium and difficult versions of a game task were used to vary the levels of the cost to user. Multimodal data streams during the three versions were analyzed, including eye tracking, pupil size, hand movement, heart rate variability (HRV) and subjectively reported data. Three findings indicate the potential value of multimodal information in evaluating usability: First, subjective and physiological measures showed significant sensitivity to task difficulty. Second, different user cost levels appeared to correlate with eye movement patterns, especially with a combined eye–hand measure. Third, HRV showed correlations with saccade speed. These results warrant further investigations and take an initial step toward establishing usability evaluation methods based on multimodal information.

1 Introduction

The last decade has witnessed an unprecedented development in user interface and human–computer interaction (HCI) technologies. These new technologies, such as eye tracking and physiological sensing, are making a range of novel HCIs possible and are narrowing the gap between the human and the machine. In some research communities, we no longer even speak of users and machines as separate entities, but rather of collaborative systems, integrated human–machine systems and joint cognitive systems [1]. More often than not, the user is now the central component of system design. These developments also present a new need for evaluating usability, shifting focus from productivity environments to user analysis when evaluating usability.

Traditional usability studies in the HCI field have been rooted in ergonomics and interface guidelines, which emphasize productivity of systems. Their evaluation for user experience is often neglected or mainly based on subjective data from questionnaires and interviews. Although subjective data yield valuable quantitative and qualitative results, when used alone, they do not provide sufficient information [2]. Some drawbacks are that questionnaires are not conducive to finding complex patterns and that subjects may not correspond to the actual experience. Knowing that

C. Stephanidis and M. Pieper (Eds.): ERCIM UI4ALL Ws 2006, LNCS 4397, pp. 304–316, 2007.
© Springer-Verlag Berlin Heidelberg 2007

answers are being recorded, subjects will sometimes answer what they think the investigator wants to hear, without even realizing it. Further, subjective ratings are cognitively mediated, and may not accurately reflect what is occurring [3]. Thus, objective methods that assess the user experience are needed.

The ultimate goal of our study was to develop a new method of evaluating usability based on multimodal information. The present study focused on assessing the user cost during interactions. The term user cost has been presented in usability studies. User cost refers to the level of investment required to achieve and maintain high levels of the usability indicators such as task performance and satisfying. The cost to the user may be demonstrated in terms of level of physical and /or mental effort or stress/anxiety incurred [4]. Several recent studies reported by Wilson and Sasse also revisited the usability evaluation framework of task performance, satisfaction and user cost. In their studies, physiological responses to degradations in media quality (audio and video) are taken as an objective measure of user cost. They found significant increases in galvanic skin response (GSR) and heart rate (HR), and significant decreases in blood volume pressure (BVP) for video shown at 5 frames per second versus 25 frames per second even though most subjects didn't report noticing a difference in media quality. Another main finding of this research is that subjective and physiological results do not always correlate with each other [5].

In this study, easy, medium and difficult versions of a game task were used to vary the levels of user cost. We analyzed multimodal information streams during the three versions, including subjective data, heart rate variability (HRV) data, pupillary responses data, eye tracking data and hand movement data. The study showed potential of multimodal information streams in usability evaluation. These multimodal data can not only objectively assess user cost, but also provide cues for explaining why users experience different levels of user cost. This contributes to deeper understanding human factors during interaction.

2 Physiological Measures

Physiological measures (e.g., skin conductance, heart rate, pupil size, respiration and blood volume pressure) have been reported to reflect involuntary autonomic nervous system reactions, controlling, among others, arousal level [6]; therefore, physiological measurements can provide a continuous measure of the state of the user [7]. Investigators in Human Factors have used physiological measures as indicators of mental effort and stress [8, 5]. Psychologists have used physiological measures as unique identifiers of human emotions such as anger, grief and sadness [9]. In HCI evaluation, physiological measures have also been widely studied. For example, physiological responses were used to measure multimedia quality and indicate presence [5, 11], and also were shown to correlate with performance levels [10]. The advantages of using physiological measures are manifold. They are high-resolution time series, and objectively responsive to user experience. Further, physiological measures are inherently multi-dimensional and can provide a number of views of user states [12].

2.1 Heart Rate Variability

HRV refers to the variability in the interval between consecutive heartbeats. Spectral analysis methods of HRV have gained widespread acceptance as a measure of mental load. They provide information on how power (or variability) distributes as a function of frequency, and yields a measure of how the heart rate fluctuates as a result of changes in the autonomic nervous system [13]. Spectral components of the heartbeat interval reflecting short-term changes in HRV fall into three frequency ranges: very low frequency (VLF) (0-0.04 Hz), low frequency (LF) (0.04-0.15 Hz) and high frequency (HF) (0.15-0.40 Hz). The physiological explanation of the VLF component is poorly defined and the existence of a specific physiological process underlying these heart rate changes might even be questioned [14]. Thus, it is recommended that VLF assessed from short-term recordings not be used [14].The HF component reflects momentary respiratory influences on the heart rate. It is decreased by tilting and by parasympathetic blocking drugs, and is increased by sympathetic blocking drugs and controlled respiration. Therefore, the HF component has been thought to provide a quantitative and specific index of vagal modulation [14,15,16]. The LF component has been interpreted as an indicator mainly of sympathetic influences (especially when expressed in normalized units). Many studies under laboratory conditions have shown that increasing mental load and attention cause a decrease in both time and frequency domain estimates of HRV, especially in the LF component of spectral analysis [17,18,19,20,21]. Fox example, in Vicente's study, the validity of the spectral analysis of HRV as a measure of mental workload was investigated using a psychomotor task. The results demonstrated the existence of a strong relationship between the subjective ratings of effort and the LF component of the HRV power spectrum [8]. In another study, the demands of dynamic monitoring and fault diagnosis for flight engineer trainees were examined. The results indicated that the LF component of the HRV power spectrum systematically decreased as mental demands increased [22]. In addition, HRV was also explored in an air traffic management (ATC) task as an indicator of user states. HRV showed significant discriminatory sensitivity to the manipulation of the difficulty variable on basis of the ATC domain experience. Another finding of this study was that HRV appeared able to indicate the point at which user capacity was exceed [12].

2.2 Pupillary Response

Researches have reported that the magnitude of pupillary dilation appears to be a function of processing load, or the mental effort required to perform the task [23,24,25,26,27], where increases in pupil size correlate with increase mental workload. For example, Beatty reviewed a large body of experimental data and concluded that pupillary response is a reliable indicator of mental workload for a task, and that the degree of pupillary response correlates with the workload [28]. User interface researchers are already using pupil size to evaluate the mental workload imposed by user interface designs. Iqbal et al. showed that pupillary responses correlate with the workload of interactive tasks and discovered that changes in workload seem to align well with the hierarchical model of the task being performed

[29]. Several other sources of pupil size variation have also been documented, including light and various stimulus parameters (e.g., visual and chemical) [30]. In our experiment, we controlled as many of these variables as possible.

3   Eye Tracking Methods

Eye tracking data are thought to provide an indication of the amount of cognitive processing a display requires, and hence can indicate how easy it can be processed [31]. Because of the structure of the human visual system, with high-resolution vision in only a small region, it is necessary for people to orient their gaze to the location where visual information is needed at any given moment. Thus, a record of a person's eye movements provides information about location of attention and the nature, sequence and timing of cognitive operations that are being carried out.

Several eye measures have been widely used in the study of eye behaviors, including fixation, saccade and scanpath. Fixation is generally defined as a relatively motionless gaze that lasts for 200-300 ms, in which visual attention is aimed at a specific area [31]. Fixation has been linked to intense cognitive processing. For example, fixation duration indicates the amount of information processing. Longer fixation durations indicate that more time is needed to interpret the data. The number of fixation is also related to the amount of processing. Saccades are continuous and rapid movements of gaze between fixations with a velocity of 500 degrees or more. They direct a viewer's eyes to a visual target. Information processing is suppressed during a saccade, though some peripheral information may be available [31]. Scanpath is defined as a habitually preferred eye movement path when a subject is re-exposed to a visual stimulus. The term has also been accepted as a sequence of fixations and saccades, reflecting the movement of attention and cognitive load [32, 33].

4   Experimental Design

In the study, we first focused on assessing user cost levels incurred by game tasks with heart rate variability (HRV), pupillary responses and subjective measures. Then we investigated eye and hand movements at the different user cost levels.

4.1   Participants

Nine male and one female university students, aged 18 to 30, participated in the experiment. All subjects used computers daily and were adept at using a mouse. Before the experiment, they filled out a background questionnaire about their health and experience with games, average game times and personal information such as gender and handedness. All subjects were right handed with normal vision. They were paid for participating in the study.

4.2 Tasks

We choose an action–puzzle game called *Luxor: Amun Rising* (Game House®) as the experimental task. Players move their mystical winged scarab by moving the mouse and launch spheres by left-clicking the mouse. The objective is to create matches of same colored spheres with the moving target spheres. The matches of three or more spheres will be destroyed. Player must destroy all spheres before they enter the pyramids at the end of the path. The game challenges players to think quickly and aim carefully. Fig. 1 shows a screenshot of the game.

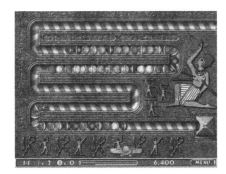

Fig. 1. Screenshot of video game used for experimental task

In the experiment, several game features were limited (e.g., no swapping between the current and next spheres in scarab). Sound effects were switched off because built-in music could influence some physiological reactions, such as heart rate and breathing responses [34]. Subjects were required to play the beginner, intermediate and expert levels of the game. The difficulty of the game increased with variations of spheres' speed and direction. Each game task lasted 10 minutes. During tasks, subjects were encouraged not to talk because speaking would affect the EKG (electrocardiogram) signal.

4.3 Experimental Setup and Procedures

The experimental setting was shown in Fig. 2. While a subject played the game tasks on the task monitor, his/her eye movements were tracked by a headed mounted tracker (NAC EMR-HM8, NAC Inc.) with the resolution of 30 frames per second, and his/her EKG signals were collected using Procomp Infiniti System and Cardiopro2.0 Software from Thought Technologies™ at 256 Hz. EKG electrodes were placed in the standard configuration of two electrodes on the chest and one on the abdomen. Additionally, game out was recorded. The EKG signal, eye tracking data and the game out were synchronized later. The experiment was divided into four phases: a welcome phase, a practice phase, a game phase, and a debriefing phase. During the welcome phase, all participants were required to sign a consent form with a detailed description of the experiment, its duration, and its research purpose, and fill out the background questionnaire. During the practice phase, instructions were read to each subject describing the game rules, and each was given a brief tutorial on how to complete the tasks. Experimenter then completed calibration of eye tracking after subjects were fitted with the physiological sensors. At the outset of the game phase, 10-minute baseline pupil size and EKG signals were recorded. Subjects then completed the three game tasks randomly. After each task, participants had about 5 minutes to rest and complete a questionnaire rating mental workload to that game difficulty level using NASA Task Load Index (NASA-TLX) rating scales [35].

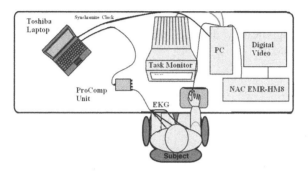

Fig. 2. Toshiba laptop computer collects the EKG signals from ProComp. Eye movements on the task monitor and game out are respectively recorded by the PC and the digital video.

4.4 Data Acquisition

Subjects' hand movements were monitored by recording the cursor motion length and the time and locations of mouse clicks into a log file. Pupil size and eye movement data (e.g., fixation and gaze coordinates) were gathered by eye tracking equipment and these data were preprocessed using the built-in software in the eye tracking equipment.

Noisy EKG data may produce HR data where two beats have been counted in a sampling interval or only one beat has been counted in two sampling intervals. We inspected the HR data and corrected these erroneous samples. The spectral analysis of HRV was conducted following the method described by Vicente [8]. First, the inter-beat interval (IBI) was computed for each 10-minute trial. The first and last IBIs were dropped to avoid start- and end-related effects. Then, IBI data were transformed into equidistant time series by cubic spline interpolation and resampled at 512 Hz. Once the interpolation was completed, the data were smoothed using the Hanning window. Finally, the data were transformed into power spectra with fast Fourier transfer analysis. This value was normalized by dividing it by the baseline for that subject taken during the rest states then subtracting this result from 1. Thus, a value between 0 (no effort) and 1 (maximum effort) was obtained. These normalized values were used in the statistical analysis. In addition, subjective data evaluating mental workload were collected by an online NASA-TLX questionnaire system.

5   Results

5.1   Subjective Assessment of User Cost

The subjective ratings of user cost were assessed by NASA-TLX. The NASA-TLX score ranges from 0 (no effort) to 100 (maximum effort). The subjects reported progressively higher task demands from the beginner, to intermediate, to expert levels of the game task. ANOVA showed significant effects in ratings across the three levels (F = 13.67, P <0.05) (see Fig. 3). Post hoc analysis using the student Newman-Keuls method indicated the three means of the subjective ratings for beginner, intermediate and expert levels significantly differed from each other. Moreover, all subjects demonstrated this pattern.

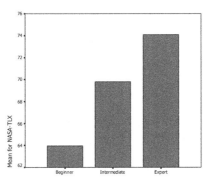

Fig. 3. Mean NASA-TLX score for beginner, intermediate and expert task levels

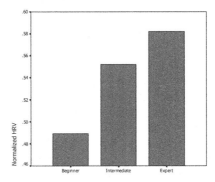

Fig. 4. Mean HRV for beginner, intermediate and expert task levels

5.2   Physiological Measures of User Cost

HRV was used to objectively distinguish different user cost levels. Statistical analysis showed that the LF range between 0.04 and 0.15 Hz was sensitive to changes in user cost. As shown in Fig. 4, the normalized values in LF range displayed a progressive increase across the beginner, intermediate and expert levels. ANOVA showed the differences among three levels were significant (F = 7.82, P <0.05). Post hoc analysis using the student Newman-Keuls method indicated that the normalized HRV of the three levels significantly differed from each other.

We also investigated the pupil size changes across the three task levels. ANOVA showed that differences in pupil size change from baseline were not significant. However, the differences in pupil size change between beginner and intermediate levels and between beginner and expert levels were significant (Fig. 5).

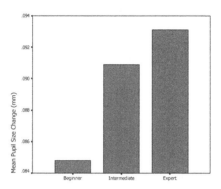

Fig. 5. Mean change in pupil size for beginner, intermediate and expert task levels

In addition, we examined correlations between HRV, pupillary responses and subjective measures (Table 1).

Table 1. Correlation coefficients of NALA-TLX, pupil size changes and HRV across three task levels

	Beginner	**Intermediate**	**Expert**
NASA vs. pupil size	0.51*	0.43	0.42
NASA vs. HRV	0.61*	0.51*	0.49*
Pupil size vs. HRV	0.33	0.35	0.39

(* P <0.05)

The correlation between HRV and NASA-TLX was significant across the three levels. Changes in pupil size also showed a significant correlation with NASA-TLX in the beginner levels. However, there was no significant correlation between HRV and change in pupil size. To sum up, both subjective reporting and objective physiological measures (HRV and pupil size changes) were sensitive to the variation of the user cost levels. As we expected, the expert level incurred the greatest user cost, followed by the intermediate and beginner levels. HRV showed higher sensitivity than pupillary responses.

5.3 Eye-Hand Movement and User Cost

The above results suggest that the beginner, intermediate and expert levels of the task led to low, middle and high use cost levels. In order to better understand the relationship between eye movements and user cost, we investigated the following measures at the three different user cost levels: fixation number (FN), fixation duration (FD) and scanpath length (SPL). In addition, we also examined hand behaviors using number of mouse clicks (MCN). ANOVA was used to examine differences in these measures at the three levels. The results are shown in Table 2.

Table 2. Mean FN, FD (sec), SPL (cm), MCN and EML (cm, defined in the next section) for beginner, intermediate and expert levels of the task (* p < 0.05)

	Beginner	Intermediate	Expert	P
FN	945.5	1105.4	1280.3	0.043 *
FD	299.4	299.5	314.6	0.32
SPL	15972.4	17027.8	19945.9	0.039*
MCN	248.7	258.9	278.5	0.29
EML	17606.2	18779.3	22159.4	0.021*

Only SPL and FN showed significant difference across the three levels of the game task. However, post hoc pairwise comparisons of them using the student Newman-Keuls method suggests the differences between the beginner and intermediate levels and between the beginner and expert levels are significant, while the difference between the intermediate and expert levels is not significant. The results suggest that eye movements showed sensitivity to variations in user cost, but this sensitivity weakened as the task difficulty increased.

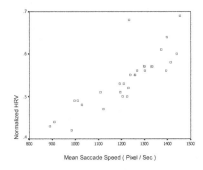

Fig. 6. Mean saccade speed correlated with normalized HRV in the LF band (0.04-0.15 Hz)

As the above results suggest, the LF band (0.04–0.15 Hz) of HRV was highly sensitive to changes in user cost levels. We examined the correlation of eye movement and HRV in the frequency band for all 30 trials (10 subjects x 3 levels) and found that mean saccade speed was significantly correlated with normalized HRV (R= 0.67, P < 0.05) (see Fig. 6).

Subjects usually followed two steps to perform a search-shoot action. The first step was to choose the target spheres, during which eye movements reflected the users' cognitive strategies and attention allocation. The second step was to move and click the mouse to launch the spheres to create the matches with the spheres chosen in the first step, which is the result of the cognitive process and were the physical action. Therefore, we defined eye-mouse length (EML)——the sum of scanpath length and cursor motion length—as a composite index representing the whole cognitive–action process of performing tasks. We analyzed the EML across beginner, intermediate and expert levels of the task. The mean EML of the expert level was longest, followed by the intermediate and the beginner levels. ANOVA showed the difference among them was significant (see Table 2). Furthermore, post hoc pairwise comparisons of the EMLs also suggest the difference between any two levels was significant.

6 Discussion

In this study, user cost was manipulated by varying the difficulty of the task. The subjective ratings of user cost measured by NASA-TLX showed good correlation with the level of task difficulty. Physiological measures—HRV and pupil size—were also studied. HRV in the LF band showed a clear correlation with the difficulty of the task. This result supports the finding that an increase in mental effort was typically related to a reduction in the power associated with the LF band in the HRV power spectrum. However, subjects' pupillary response did not show good sensitivity to changes in task difficulty. For example, there were no significant differences in pupil size changes for medium and difficult task levels. We also examined the correlations among NASA-TLX, HRV and pupillary responses. The significant correlations of HRV and NASA-TLX in all three levels also indicated that HRV is an effective objective indicator of user cost. However, HRV did not correlate well with pupil size changes, and pupillary response did not show good sensitivity to user cost in the experimental tasks. Other than environmental factors such as lightness and light reflection, there are explanations from the multiple resource views of workload, which holds that resources are specific to certain processing activities. Thus, the processing measured by HRV may be different from the processing measured by pupil size changes. Our results suggest that a single physiological measure may not provide sufficient information to assess a subject's entire user cost and it is therefore necessary to create a combined measure for evaluating the complete user cost.

It is generally accepted that eye movements are a reflection of cognitive processes, while physical actions are the result of such processes [37]. In order to examine the effects of eye and hand movements on user cost, we investigated both of these movements among easy, medium and difficult levels of the task. Although ANOVA showed there were significant differences in fixation number and scanpath length according to difficulty, post hoc pairwise comparisons showed the difference between medium and difficult levels were not significant. These results suggest that using eye movement measures alone may not reflect users' complete interaction behaviors.

Therefore, we combined eye and hand movement into the EML measure to represent the whole interaction session. The measure significantly indicated user cost levels of medium and difficult tasks, while the difference between them could not be indicated by eye measures alone. These results show that the combined eye–hand movement measure provides more complete information on user cost.

In addition, we also investigated the correlation between eye movements and HRV. A positive correlation of saccade speed and HRV in the LF band was found. This suggests that HRV in the LF band appears to be sensitive to eye saccade movements. These results may provide partial explanation for why user cost differs from person to person and contribute to deeper understanding human factors in human computer interactions.

7 Future Work

Our ultimate goal is to create a methodology for evaluating usability. This paper presents initial research testing the efficacy of multimodal information in evaluating user cost. More steps are required, however, to create the methodology for usability evaluation.

We measured the cost to user using HRV and pupillary response. The results suggest that a combined physiological measure should be developed, because physiological measures are specific responses to certain processing activities. If multiple measures of workload are obtained and correlated with one another, it may be possible to represent them as a combined measure using different weight coefficients by means of factor analysis [36].

For the next step, tools will be developed to help researchers synchronize multiple data streams, such as eye tracking data and HRV. Current software packages fall short of what researchers need to analyze a complete interaction session. New tools may better support the process of analyzing interactions and make it possible to evaluate usability at a more detailed level.

We will also further explore the use of multimodal information in evaluating usability. For example, by synchronizing eye tracking data and physiological data, we could measure attention. Eye tracking could provide a direct measure of attentional distribution, while physiological data could be used to indicate the degree of attention engagement.

As a study of methodology, more subtle experimental manipulations need to be explored. Tasks from various domains must be tested, as well as using a larger sample size to increase the statistical power.

Acknowledgments. We thank the members of the HCI group at the University of Yamanashi for their support of this research. This study was also supported in part by the Grants-in-Aid for Scientific Research of the Japan Society for the Promotion of Science, and by the RIEC of Tohoku University awarded to A. Imamiya.

References

1. Hollnagel, E.: From human factors to cognitive systems engineering: Human–machine interactions in the 21st century. In Kitamura, M., and Kimura, I. (eds.), Anzen-no-Tankyu (Researches on Safety). ERCPublishing, Tokyo, (2003).
2. Marshall, C. and Rossman, G.B.: Designing qualitative research, 3rd Edition, Sage, Thousand Oaks, CA (1999).

3. Wilson, G.M. and Sasse, M.A.: Investigating the impact of audio degradations on users: Subjective vs. objective assessment methods. In the Proceedings of OZCHI 2000: Interfacing Reality in the New Millennium. Sydney, Australia (2000) 135–142.
4. Sweeney, M., Maguire, M., and Shackel, B.: Evaluating user-computer interaction: a framework. International Journal of Man-Machine Studies, vol. 38, (1993) 689-711.
5. Wilson, G.M.: Psychophysiological indicators of the impact of media quality on users. In the Proceedings of CHI 2001 Doctoral Consortium, ACM Press (2001) 95-96.
6. Andreassi, J.L.: Psychophysiology: Human Behavior and Physiological Response, 4th Edition. Lawrence Erlbaum Associates, Mahwah, NJ, (2000).
7. Picard, R.W.: Affective Computing. MIT Press, Cambridge, MA, (1997).
8. Vicente, K.J., Thornton, C. and Moray, N.: Spectral analysis of sinus arrhythmia: A measure of mental effort. Human Factors (1987) 29, 171-182.
9. Ekman, P., Levenson, R.W. and Friesen, W.V.: Autonomic nervous system activity distinguishes among emotions. Science (1983), 221 (4616), 1208–1210.
10. Lin, T., Hu, W.H., Omata, M. and Imamiya, A.: Do physiological data relate to traditional usability indexes? In the Proceedings of the Australian Conference on Computer Human Interaction OZCHI'05, Canberra, Australia, November 21–15, (2005).
11. Meehan, M., Insko, B., Whitton, M. and Brooks, F.: Physiological measures of presence in stressful virtual environments. In the Proceedings of the 29th Annual Conference on Computer Graphics and Interactive Techniques (2002).
12. Rowe, D.W., Sibert, J. and Irwin, D.: Heart rate variability: Indicator of user state as an aid to human–computer interaction. In proceedings of the CHI (1998), 480–487.
13. Hopman, J.C.W., Kollee, L.A.A., Stoelinga, G.B.A., Van Geijn, H.P. and van Ravenswaaij-Arts, C.M.A.: Heart rate variability. Annals of Internal Medicine (1993) 118, 436–447.
14. Malik, M.: Heart rate variability. Circulation (1996) 93, 1043–65.
15. Pomeranz, B., Macaulay, R.J.B., and Caudill, M.A., et al.: Assessment of autonomic function in humans by heart rate spectral analysis. Am J Physiol Heart Circ Physiol (1985) 248, 151–H153.
16. Pagani, M., Lombardi, F., and Guzzetti, S.: Power spectral analysis of heart rate and arterial pressure variabilities as a maker of sympatho-vagal interaction in man and conscious dog. Cir Res (1986) 59, 178–93.
17. Ettema, J. and Ziclhuis, R.L.: Physiological parameters of mental load. Ergonomics (1971) 14, 137–44.
18. Luczak, I.I. and Lauring, W.J.: An analysis of heart rate variability. Ergonomics (1973) 16, 85–97.
19. Hyndman, B.W. and Gregory, J.R.: Spectral analysis of sinus arrhythmia during mental loading. Ergonomics (1975) 18, 255–70.
20. Boutcher, S.H., Naugent, F.W. and Mclaren, P.F.: Heart period variability of trained and untrained men at rest and during mental challenge. Psychophysiology (1998) 35, 16–22.
21. Hyde, C. and Izard, C.E.: Cardiac rhythmicities and attention in young children. Psychophysiology (1997) 34, 547–52.
22. Tattersall, A.J. and Hockey, G.R.J.: Level of operator control and changes in heart rate variability during simulated flight maintenance. Human Factors (1995) 37, 682-698.
23. Hess, E.H. and Polt, J.M.: Pupil size in relation to mental activity during simple problem solving. Science (1964) 132, 11901-1192.
24. Hoecks, B. and Levelt, W.: Pupillary dilation as a measure of attention: A quantitative system analysis. Behavior Research Methods, Instruments, & Computers (1993) 25, 16–26.

25. Juris, M. and Velden, M.: The pupillary response to mental overload. Physiological Psychology (1977) 5 (4), 421–424.
26. Kahneman, D.: Pupillary responses in a pitch-discrimination task. Perception & Psychophysics (1967) 2, 101–105.
27. Nakayama, M. and Takahashi, K.: The act of task difficulty and eye-movement frequency for the oculo-motor indices. In the Proceedings of the Eye Tracking Research and Application (2002) 37–42.
28. Beatty, J.: Task-evoked pupillary responses, processing load and the structure of processing resources. Psychological Bulletin (1982) 91 (2), 276–292.
29. Iqbal, S.T., Zheng, X.S. and Bailey, B.P.: Task-evoked pupillary response to mental workload in human–computer interaction. In the proceeding of CHI (2004), 1477–1480.
30. Hess, E.H. and Petrovich, S.B.: Pupillary behavior in communication. In Siegman, A.W., and Feldstein, S. (eds.), Nonverbal Behavior and Communication. Erlbaum, Hillsdale, NJ (1987) 327-348.
31. Rayner, K.: Eye movements and information processing: 20 years of research. Psychological Bulletin (1998) 124 (3), 372–422.
32. Noton, D. and Stark, L.W.: Scanpath in saccadic eye movements while viewing and recognizing patterns. Vision Research (1971) 11, 929–942.
33. Goldberg, H. and Kotval, X.P.: Computer interface evaluation using eye movements: Methods and constructs. International Journal of Industrial Ergonomics (1999), 24, 631–645.
34. Hébert. a.b., Renée. A.b., Odrée Dionne-Fournelle. a., Martine Crête. a, and Lupien. S. J.: Physiological stress response to video game playing: The contribution of built-in music. Life Sciences (2005) 76, 2371–2380.
35. Hart, S.G. and Staveland, L.E.: Development of NASA-TLX (task load index): Results of experimental and theoretical research. In Hancock, P.A., and Meshakati, N. (eds.), Human Mental Workload. North-Holland, Amsterdam (1988) 39-183.
36. Hair, J.F., Anderson, R.E., Tatham, R.L., and Black, W.C. Multivariate Data Analysis, 5th Edition, Prentice-Hall, Englewood Cliffs, NJ (1998).
37. Lin, Y., Zhang, W. J. and Koubek, R. J.: Effective Attention Allocation Behavior and its Measurement: A Preliminary Study, Interacting with Computers, (2004) Vol. 16, Issue 6, 1195-1210.

User Interfaces for Persons with Deafblindness

Sara Rutgersson[1] and Mattias Arvola[2]

[1] Antrop
Åsögatan 140
SE-116 24 Stockholm
sara.rutgersson@antrop.se
[2] Department of computer and information science
Linköpings universitet
SE-581 83 Linköping, Sweden
matar@ida.liu.se

Abstract. This paper examines the problems persons with deafblindness encounter when using computers, and what can be done to avoid the problems in the design of a communication tool. A qualitative study was conducted with 12 participants. The results show that a system needs to resolve issues of simplicity, flexibility, and feedback. In our redesign of the communication tool we employ what we call a screen reader use flow with precursor cues, to aid the user in getting an overview of the program and its functions. This is very difficult when using a Braille display. The screen reader use flow with precursor cues is one means to satisfy the demands of both users who use a visual display and users who use a Braille display.

Keywords: Deafblind, accessibility, usability, inclusive design, total communication.

1 Introduction

Persons who are deafblind often experience difficulties in handling their daily life in an independent way. Computer applications constitute a great opportunity for them to live more independently. Applications are, however, usually designed for persons who can use vision and/or hearing. Persons who cannot fully use any of those senses have to adjust themselves to applications that are not developed with their needs in focus. To create a good design-for-all the designer has to carry out a detailed analysis of what a broader range of people need and involve users in every stage of decision making [10]. In this article, the focus is on persons who are deafblind. We examine the problems computer users with deafblindness encounter in their usage and what can be done to avoid these problems. A design example of how a communication program can be redesigned to fit the needs of this user group is also provided. It focuses primarily on users who are either totally deafblind, or users who are totally deaf and visually impaired. The research reported here does therefore not cover persons who use speech synthesis.

C. Stephanidis and M. Pieper (Eds.): ERCIM UI4ALL Ws 2006, LNCS 4397, pp. 317–334, 2007.

1.1 Deafblindness

According to a definition of deafblindness agreed to by the Nordic countries in 1980, deafblindness is a severe combination of hearing and visual impairment. Some persons who are deafblind are both deaf and blind, while others have remains from both seeing and hearing. A common misunderstanding is that deafblindness can be seen as a combination of deaf- and blindness and that deafblind persons therefore can gain from services designed for deaf and blind persons. However, deafblind people are unable to use one sense to fully compensate for the impairment of the other, the way a deaf person can compensate with vision and a blind person can compensate with hearing. The two sensory impairments intensify the impact of each other, creating a severe disability that is unique.

One cause for deafblindness is the genetic disease Usher syndrome. Persons with Usher syndrom constitute approximately half of all deafblind persons in the world. Persons with Usher are born deaf or with impaired hearing, with or without balance signals from the ears. Later in life, persons with Usher get the eye disease retinitis pigmentosa (RP), which causes night-blindness, limited field of vision and in some cases total blindness.

1.2 Communication and Deafblindness

Persons who are deafblind can find their disability handicapping in many social situations. When it comes to communication, persons who are deafblind can, according to the Swedish association for persons with deafblindness (FSDB), roughly be divided in three different language groups: sign language users, spoken language users, and persons without language. Not very many are without language, but there are some who cannot use any language due to senility or an intellectual disability. The spoken language users are usually born blind and become hearing impaired or deaf later in life. Some of them learn sign language as a second language.

For persons who are born deaf, visual sign language is a natural way to communicate even when the vision is reduced. When using sign language with a person with impaired vision it is important to create high contrast between hands and background.

Persons with deafblindness who do not have enough vision to see signing, perceive the sign language tactually. When using tactile sign language, there are two different conversation positions: monologue and dialogue. In the monologue position both signers' hands are held under the hands of the listener. In the dialogue position both participants hold the right hand under the other person's left hand and the left hand on top of the other person's right hand [9].

According to FSDB, persons who become deafblind as adults, and are used to written and spoken language, can have difficulties learning tactile sign language. In those cases communication with hand alphabet can be an alternative. The hand alphabet is a part of the sign language, is much easier to learn, but is slow to use. Another possibility is to be accompanied by a contact person who assists with guiding and communication.

1.3 Communication Tools and Deafblindness

For persons who are deafblind, communication poses challenges that often are too high, which can produce anxiety [1]. Communication tools can however strengthen their skills. Below follows a list of such tools:

- *Braille* is blind persons' alphabet that can be used in most languages. The Braille code is physically presented as raised dots, usually arranged in cells with up to six dots.
- *A contact machine* is a computer connected to a Braille display. The contact person/interpreter writes what is said and the deafblind person can read it on the Braille display.
- *Text telephony* makes it possible for people with hearing impairment, deaf- or deafblindness or speech impairment to call and receive phone calls using text. Via a relay service users can communicate with hearing.
- *Video telephony* offers a possibility to use sign language, lip reading, and facial expressions.
- *Instant messengers* (ICQ, MSN Messenger, AOL Instant Messenger, Jabber, Yahoo! Messenger etc.) can be useful for persons with deafblindness.
- *Total conversation* is a multi-modal concept in which video, text and speech can be used simultaneously. In other words this service combines the functionalities of text, video and ordinary telephony in one program. The International Telecommunication Union has also defined the concept in a standard [6].

1.4 Special Input and Output Devices

When it comes to input and output, persons who are deaf but have enough residual vision to read large print, can make use of large font displays.

Another alternative is to use a Braille display, which is a device for displaying Braille one line of text at a time. While scanning a text, the Braille display uses small pins that are raised or lowered to form the Braille characters. There are usually 40, 65, or 80 characters per line of text, depending on the device. In general, deafblind and blind people use keypads, with or without tactual indicators on the keys. To present information in large font or Braille there must be a translation between information on the screen and the different ways of presenting the information. A screen reader does this.

1.5 User Interfaces and Deafblindness

Persons with deafblindness, who are unable to use a computer, mostly communicate and receive information via their contact person or interpreter [3]. This means computer technology can open up new doors for this user group and make them less isolated and dependent on others.

Designing any user interface, there are some basic usability considerations that we mostly take for granted. Considerations such learnability, effectiveness, attitude, flexibility, relevance, efficiency, and satisfaction are necessary for an application to be usable [11, 8, 5]. A designer should always have the user's perspective when designing a user interface. Design principles like suitability for the task, self-descriptiveness, controllability, conformity with user expectations, error tolerance, suitability for individualization, and suitability for learning may also have differing relative importance in different situations [5]. Furthermore, the tradeoffs involved will also vary with the situation of use. For users with special needs this is especially important to consider.

User interfaces for persons with deafblindness need to be simple so that there are few things to memorize to be able to use the system [7]. Many deafblind users do not possess strong skills of written language, why pictures and icons could be an alternative for some. However, this is not an option for those who use Braille, since it is a textual medium where graphical images are not easily presented. For those users with deafblindness who rely on tactile output there is an additional problem. They receive information from their hands, which they also use to type information. This means they cannot receive and type information at the same time. With the hands doing both input and output special care must be taken to allow the user to correct mistakes.

Following the considerations above, Ladner et al. [7] built a system called DBNet. The system is extensive including an email client, possibilities to read news and to chat with others. The user interface is based on a simple hierarchal model, which allows its users to perform hundreds of distinct tasks by taking just a few actions. The conceptual model of the system is a hierarchical list with entries that can themselves be lists. Each entry in the list has a text label associated with it.

After implementing the DBNet system, Ladner et al. tested it on six persons with deafblindness. They wanted to test how easy the conceptual model was to grasp and how easy the system was to use. Their conclusion is that five out of six participants understood the conceptual model in less than an hour. Thus, the hierarchal model of the DBNet system is well within the conceptual grasp of deafblind people and can be learned with very little teaching effort.

A similar study was carried out more recently by Fisher and Petrie [3]. In their study, thirteen persons with deafblindness were interviewed about their current use of communication and information tools. Their results are similar to the results of Ladner's et al. [7]. They found that systems designed for this user group should be easy to use. The user needs to be able to access different functionalities with the minimum of steps, and at each step the user should receive the appropriate feedback of the system status. Vibration tools are a common form of alerting for doorbells and telephones and this could be used as feedback from the system. The researchers also pinpoint the urgent need of portable systems including Braille displays, large print and hearing loops for this user group.

1.6 Focus of Current Study

The focus for the research project reported in this paper is appropriate and usable communication tools for people with deafblindness. The approach of total communication has not been researched in relation to user interfaces for persons with deafblindness while it seems promising and it is therefore worthwhile exploring further. The specific aim is to describe the problems persons who are deafblind encounter in their usage of computer-based communication tools and to find ways of avoiding them in the design of a total communication tool.

2   Method

An interview and observation study was conducted with 9 deafblind persons and 3 informants with experience from working with persons who are deafblind. Semi-structured interviews and e-mail interviews were conducted to get a deeper understanding of how persons with deafblindness use computer applications, what problems they encounter in their usage and what can be done to avoid those problems.

Semi-structured interviews were chosen because of the flexible design of this method, which allows the interviewed person to suggest new approaches to a given topic. E-mail interviews were used in two cases when face-to-face interviews were not possible. Observations were used to complement the information gained from the interviews.

2.1   Design Case

The design case in this study is a re-design of the total conversation program Allan eC. The name is an acronym for "All Languages electronic Conversation" and the system is developed by Omnitor AB in Sweden. Total conversation is a standardized concept in which video, text and speech can be used simultaneously (see Figure 1).

Allan eC can be used in different ways depending on how the users communicate. Persons who are sign language speaking can communicate with other sign language speaking persons in their own language. Hearing persons can make use of the advantages that video telephony brings and persons who have impaired hearing can

Fig. 1. The total conversation program Allan eC

use lip reading to understand the other person. Allan eC can also be used as a text telephone, where the two users have a real-time text conversation. This is a good way to communicate if one of the users is deaf and the other does not speak sign language. It can also be used to support voice or sign language communication. A deaf person who wants to contact a hearing person, who does not have a total conversation terminal, can call the IP-video interpreter service. Then an interpreter dials the number asked for and then translates the conversation.

2.2 Participants

Twelve participants have taken part in this study and nine of them have some degree of deafblindness. The remaining three has experience from working with persons who are deafblind. Of consideration for the participants they are presented by numbers and not by names.

Participants who are Deafblind. Participant 1 was born deaf and uses sign language to communicate. He has a visual impairment that narrows his field of vision to around 10 degrees. He has Retenitis Pigmentosa and will in the future totally loose the vision. He works with education and lives an active life. He has a large interest in computers and uses it for mail communication and also for MSN video communication. He uses an enlargement program. The participant was interviewed at his work with help from two interpreters.

Participant 2 has the Usher syndrome. She was born deaf and has sign language as first language. Her visual impairment was discovered when she was young and today she has tunnel vision and is dependent on good lighting conditions. The participant works at a small company and uses different computer programs such as Allan eC and ICQ to communicate per distance. She uses an enlargement program and both mouse and keys. She is also learning to use Braille and sometimes uses it to interact with the computer to rest her eyes. The interview was carried out at her work with help from an interpreter.

Participant 3 was born deaf and has sign language as first language. He has a visual impairment that slowly gets worse. The participant works with computers at a company and uses an enlargement program to his computer. To see better what is on the screen he has a special lamp behind the computer. He is an expert user of the Allan eC program and the interview was carried out via the text function in Allan eC. No interpreters needed.

Participant 4 was born deaf and has sign language as her first language. Eight years ago she went totally blind and now she communicates with tactile sign language. She runs her own company and is often out travelling. She uses Allan eC and SMS on a mobile phone with a 20-character Braille display. Two interviews were carried out; one interview was made via the text function in Allan eC and one interview was made in her home. The participant was also observed when using Allan eC in her home. The second interview and the observation were made with help from an interpreter.

Participant 5 is both deaf and blind and has sign language as her first language. She uses tactile sign language. She writes on computer with a Braille display and uses a text telephone program for communication per distance. The interview was made at her school with her assistant interpreting.

Participant 6 is deaf and blind and has Swedish as her first language. She communicates through talking and tactile sign language. She uses the computer with Braille display for mail and for searching for information on the Internet. An interview and an observation were carried out. She looked at the interface of a, for her, new program for text telephony. Her assistant helped with interpretation during the interview/observation.

Participant 7 is born deaf with a visual impairment. He has a large interest in computers and uses them for surfing the Internet and communication via an e-mail program. An enlargement program makes it possible for him to see information on the computer screen. The interview was carried out through e-mail contact.

Participant 8 has hearing and vision impairment. He uses speech synthesis and enlargement when using the computer. He also learns how to use Braille, to be able to use a Braille display in the future. He is used to computers and uses both total conversation and mail to communicate. He can also use telephone to communicate.

Participant 9 was born with a hearing impairment and speaks Swedish as her first language. She also knows sign language. Today, she is blind and hearing impaired and uses a hearing devise. At her work she uses the computer to write and to communicate via mail. She is familiar with Allan eC, but due to technical problems she does not use it. She uses Braille display and speech synthesis with a hearing device connected. The interview was carried out at the work of the participant. No interpreter was needed.

Participants who are Not Deafblind. Participant 10 works as a teacher at a school for persons with deafbindness. Among other things he teaches his students how to use computers, Braille displays and different computer-based programs.

Participant 11 works with accessibility on websites. He has experience from working with disabled persons in general, such as persons with deafblindness.

Participant 12 works with persons with deafblindness and among other things she teaches them how to work with different computer programs. Allan eC is one of the programs that she teaches.

2.3 Procedure

When interviewing participants who are deafblind every interview was adjusted to that specific user and situation. In two cases that meant interviews via e-mail, and in two other cases it meant communication via Allan eC. The rest of the interviews with the deafblind participants were conducted with help from an interpreter. The participants were asked general questions about their situation, how they communicate with others, what is difficult when using computers and what they wish for in future products. Every interview became a specific example of how the everyday life can be for a person with this disability. A majority of the participants have experience from using Allan eC and in those cases more specific questions about this program were asked. In those cases where the participant did not have experience from using Allan eC, questions about other communication programs such as mail and text telephone programs were asked.

The three interviews with persons with great experience from working with persons who are deafblind gave information about how people with this disability communicate, what can be problematic with the tools for communication today and what can be improved in future products. The persons interviewed looked at, and tested the Allan eC program, commented the interface and possible problems.

A problem when designing programs for people who use Braille display is to understand how they actually use it and what kind of information they receive in this interaction process. This can be difficult to explain in an interview and therefore two observations with two persons who use Braille display to interact with the computer were conducted. One of the participants was observed when using a mail program and a text telephone program, and the other participant when using Allan eC. During the observations the participants were given tasks to perform and they were commenting everything that happened in the interaction between them and the computer. The situations were filmed and the observer and the participants communicated with help from an interpreter.

2.3 Analysis

The gathered material was categorized to analyze information and to create meaning (see for example [2] for further information on categorization). Categories were identified by asking: "What categories can help me organize the most important aspects of what my interviews have given me?"

The analysis was iterative and the first step was to learn about the material. The interviews and observations were transcribed. All quotations concerning the research question were organized under different categories, which focus on how the users interact with computers. The different possible input and output methods are: Braille, short keys, enlargement program, mouse and keys.

The next step in the process was to re-organize the material and to create new categories. This time the information was structured under categories describing different issues deafblind users encountered in the usage of communication tools. Altogether it became a list of seven categories (simplicity, flexibility, adjustment, feedback, independence, motivation and information. These were considered in the redesign of the Allan eC user interface. The core categories focused on in this paper are: simplicity, flexibility, and feedback.

2.4 Prototyping

The results from the interviews and observations were put to use in prototypes showing what consequences the encountered usage issues have on the Allan eC interface and how it can be re-designed to manage those issues. Having the issues in mind, possible ways to create the prototypes were explored. In total, three prototypes were developed. The prototyping started with a stated problem, for example how to give enough feedback to persons using Braille. Different alternatives were put together and carefully considered. Many of them were thrown away and the design was changed many times.

2.5 Use Flow Diagramming

In the design of one of the prototypes, a variant of the use flow diagram technique [4] was used. For each function, all choices possible are shown, leading to a good overview of the program's functionalities. This method also gives a good picture of how a person using Braille will perceive the program functions. The Braille only shows information one row at a time, and cannot present graphic information. The use-flow diagram presents the information exactly as it will be presented on the Braille display, making it possible for the designer to construct a usable flow. The visual prototype was designed after the use flow diagram, resulting in a prototype usable for both persons using Braille and vision.

3 Results

The results show that for a system to fulfil the needs of this group, usage issues of simplicity, flexibility, and feedback need to be resolved. Below, we describe what these issues mean in the specific situation of user interfaces to communication tools for users who are deafblind. The quotations are translated from Swedish to English by the authors. Every quotation in the results is marked with a number that refers to a specific participant.

3.1 Simplicity

For a person who is deafblind it takes an enormous amount of time and effort to learn a new computer program or system. No matter what combination of deafblindness the user has, it will take a long time to learn how to navigate, where to look for information and how to use different functionalities. Participants express their experience of this complicatedness:

> "One must know what it looks like. I haven't really figured that out. What does the information look like, where to walk, where to go? Get the entire picture. It's really hard to know. It takes time to learn." #9

The observations clearly show the significance of reduced complicatedness in a program for this user group. One of our participants was asked to start a program, which she has very limited experience from. The most difficult thing for the user was to get an understanding for possibilities in the interface and she had trouble knowing what actions to perform. This shows both the importance of having information logically structured and to have an interface with less complicated functionality.

Many participants report that pictures and graphics are disturbing when using Braille display. The display only shows one row at a time and is therefore unable to interpret graphics. This means that the user misses the information presented and it makes it hard to navigate. Graphics can also be disturbing for persons who use enlargement programs. The pictures get too big to be seen in a context and that makes it confusing and hard to navigate for those users.

According to several of our participants, many persons who are deaf and deafblind have difficulties to fully understand complicated written text, and therefore it is important that information is presented in simple language. Also text lines with more then 40 characters cause trouble since they do not fit into a Braille display.

The observations indicate that for persons who have a narrow field of vision, it is important that information is not spread out over the screen. Then the user does not have to search a big area to find the right information.

Some of the participants use keys to navigate, either as input for a Braille display or as an alternative to the mouse. An interface, where important functions are placed late in the hierarchy, can be frustrating for the user to use.

3.2 Flexibility

Persons with deafblindness is a diverse user category. It would therefore be impossible to create one interface that is perfect for all those persons. Instead, possibility to adjust and individualize the interfaces is important. The most important features that have to be adjustable are size and colour on objects at the interface. Most of our participants with impaired vision want a high-contrast interface. Suitable colours also vary between persons. Sometimes you also need to make adjustments depending on the situation. For example, our participants say:

> "I use a lager interface and when I get tired I make it even bigger. It's good to be able to vary." #1

> "I think is good with both because sometimes it is hard to use vision too much and then it can be relieving to use Braille, but then it goes very slowly and that becomes another problem." #2

Another thing that varies is whether our participants find text preferable to icons or not. For persons using Braille, information definitely has to be text based and some persons who use their vision find it easier with text as well. Others think icons are preferable and easier to handle.

For persons with deafblindness it is quite common that the vision gets worse and worse until it disappears and blindness occurs. To support the user in this process the program interface should have the flexible features described above.

3.3 Feedback

A problem for persons who have impaired vision, and especially for those who are blind, is to get feedback and to know what should be done in every step. Sometimes information presented on the screen does not show on the Braille and this can be extremely frustrating for the user:

> "A problem for deafblind persons who use computers is: How do I know that the computer is on? That I don't know until the Braille program has started and you can read what's on the screen. If there is for example a floppy disk in the computer when it starts and information shows on the screen and tells the user to take out the floppy disk, the person using Braille can't see this. The person doesn't know what's wrong. It could be something wrong with the Braille display or something else." #10

During the observations it happened that the user gave a command and the program gave feedback visually but not on the Braille display. The user waited for information, without knowing when or even if the right information would appear. In one occasion during the observations information about the system status was shown visually in the middle of the screen, and this information was not translated into Braille. The user tried over and over again to use the call function, which was out of function at the time. Frustrated not knowing what to do, the user restarted the computer. The problem still remained and the user was still not given any information on what to do.

In some cases we observed that feedback was given, but not in a way that was self-descriptive. When starting Windows one of the users waited for the clock in the Windows program to show on the Braille display. When it did, the user knew it was okay to continue. When using the calling function in Allan eC the users must wait for the program to connect. While doing this the information "close" is shown on the Braille display. This may not be the best way to tell the user to wait while a connection is made. The users, however, looked satisfied because both have learned what the different feedback information stands for. They are used to illogical feedback and they are happy to receive information telling them that something is happening. However, receiving irrelevant information makes the program hard to learn and more complicated to use.

Sometimes it was also hard for our participants to know what to do in a certain part of the program. Using vision a person can get a quick overview of what possibilities the program offers. The blind person cannot get this kind of overview. To handle this, the participants have somewhat different strategies.

One of the participants has learned the order of some keyboard commands by heart, and follows it strictly. If she for example wants to check for her mail she presses the Window-button to go into the menu, presses the down arrow three times to find the mailing program and presses enter etc. She tends to start the process from the beginning, rather than start in the middle. If she for example wants to send a new e-mail when finished with reading old ones, she does so by pressing the Window-button, use the down arrow and so forth. It is like if she follows a path and has learned how many steps to take before making a turn. If she is not sure on how far she has got on the path and where to turn, the easiest thing is to start at the beginning. This strategy may very well work for basic tasks, but it soon become hard to learn many steps by heart for example when surfing on the Internet.

Another participant has a slightly different strategy when navigating. She has a phenomenal memory that she uses to learn short keys by heart. This strategy gives more freedom than the strategy described above, but the user has also in this case trouble navigating in new areas. She also has to depend on standards in short key commands, which are not always followed. This is a usable strategy when doing relatively simple actions, but for more complicated actions all the short keys can be difficult to remember.

Both strategies clearly show the importance of feedback and information in a program. If the user is informed of what actions are possible and in every step knows what happens, the user can be freer to explore the program.

4 Design Case

Given the three core usage issues we identified for this user group, we set out to re-structure Allan eC, to provide an example of how a total communication application can be designed to meet the needs of deafblind users. The principle idea is to design the user interface to be readily used with a visual display by users who have some vision, while being equally optimised to a Braille-display and screen reader used by users who have no vision at all. Given this objective the conceptual design was driven by a use flow diagram. The design work has, however, only begun. We have not yet put our design to test. The design case provided here should therefore be seen as an example of how the results from our field studies can be put to use.

4.1 Screen Reader Use Flow with Precursor Cues

The method used is a variant of the use flow diagram method described in the method section. Here it is used in a slightly different way and we denote it the screen reader use flow method. Inspiration to this method was also taken from Ladner et al. [7].

The need for feedback in the interaction process was evident in interviews and observations. It is also important to get an overview of the program to know its possibilities and limitations. When using vision to navigate, a person can rather quickly get an overview of a program and its functions. Even if the information is spread out over the screen, the seeing user can take in information without much problem. The interviews and observations show that feedback and navigation is a complicated matter for persons using Braille. The difference between navigating with vision and with a Braille display is enormous. The Braille display presents information one row at a time, which makes it more difficult for the user to get an overview of the program and its functions. Only getting one row of information at a time can result in difficulties in finding the right information and knowing where to look for it. This problem mainly occurs because the programs are designed for persons who can see.

Today visual interfaces are created first, and the Braille users have to try to navigate in them as well as they can. This process makes it difficult for the designer to assure that correct and sufficient information is provided to the blind users. To create a program usable for blind users, the designer must think about the consequences of information being presented one row at a time. One way of doing this is for the designer to start the design process by figuring out how the program should work. A flow model of the program's functions and interaction flow should be created.

To give the user information about when to expect functions in the interface, our approach includes what we call 'precursor cues' since their function is to announce or indicate the coming information. The precursor cues are described in Table 1. Using those cues the user does not have to look for non-existing features in the interface.

Table 1. Explanation of the precursor cues

Precursor cue	Explanation
<	Marks the beginning of a set of functions.
>	Marks the end of a set of functions.
&	Is placed after an information text or a function when there are more information or functions following.
Bold text	Commands made by the user are printed in bold letters.
(text)	Text written in parenthesis describes what happens in the computer.

The visual design is created based on the flow model. If the flow model is wisely created, the designer can feel safe knowing the program will be usable for Braille users. The designer can then concentrate on making the visual design usable for the seeing users.

One part of the redesign of Allan eC is presented below in Figure 2. In the flow model, which follows, the adjustment-function is expanded. Every part in this model can be seen in isolation, without risking the user to be confused about what actions to do. Each level contains information of what should be done, and what actions the user can choose from. Following the flow in the model should be like following a path with different forks. The user chooses the wanted path and then a new fork appears. This creates a hierarchical menu-based dialogue.

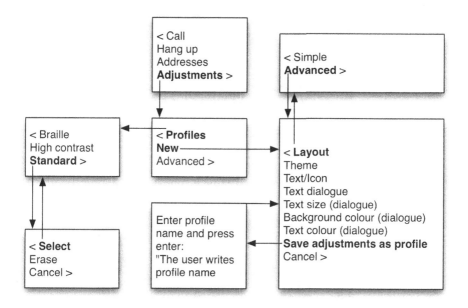

Fig. 2. A screen reader use flow model with the adjustment-function expanded

Using the screen reader use flow model as a guide, user interfaces usable for both persons using Braille and visual displays can be made. The visual design below is such an example where the screen reader use flow model is visualised in a prototype.

4.2 Visual Design

This prototype is designed for two purposes; to follow the restrictions that were decided in the use flow diagram (Figure 2) and to give an example of how an interface can be made easy to use for users with impaired vision. In other words the prototype is an attempt to design an interface usable for both persons using Braille and vision. Below, the prototype is analyzed from both views. In the prototype, the precursor cues from the use flow diagram are presented visually, to give the reader of this paper an understanding of the relation between the visual user interface and the Braille-based user interface (see Figure 3 and 4).

The interface is similar to the original Allan eC interface, but it is much less complicated. The area for text conversation is placed at the bottom of the interface. The user can choose between text presented in one window, or in two separate windows as in the original interface. The user can choose between four different functions and here the adjustment function will be expanded.

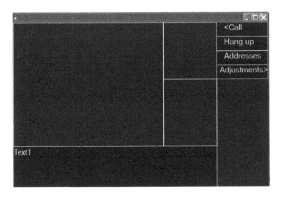

Fig. 3. Main window

As seen in Figure 4, there is a new function for saving adjustments called Profiles. This makes the program flexible without making it complicated.

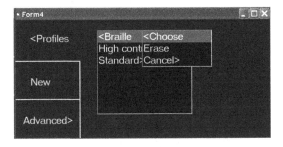

Fig. 4. Choices for the different Profile-alternatives in the adjustment window

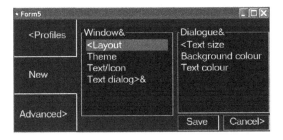

Fig. 5. The New-function

Choosing New, different adjustments can be made and saved as a new profile. Figure 5 shows how the adjustment function can be changed.

4.3 Braille Users

This interface follows the conceptual model set up in the use flow and is therefore intended to be more usable for persons using Braille. The different precursor cues from the use flow model can also be found in this prototype. Among other things the precursor cues inform the Braille user when to expect and look for functions. The interface has reduced complicatedness, which is anticipated to make the time for learning relatively short. Having only one text window also supports the usability for a person using Braille.

Choosing the "<Profiles"-alternative the user gets presented to different profiles including adjustments already made. This function makes the program flexible. A person, who wants to use Braille one day and vision another, may want to change adjustments in an easy way. The adjustments are then saved under different profiles and the user can easily change between for example the "Braille"- and the "High contrast"-profile. This function makes the program both simple and flexible.

To make the program even more flexible short keys are connected to each profile. Profiles can be changed directly from the main window using those short keys.

Choosing the New-alternative in the Adjustment-window the Braille user will be presented to a list starting with "Window&". This is not a function but information that the following functions will be connected to the window. The &-sign informs the user that a set of functions will follow. After the last function in the column, there is another &-sign indicating that there is more information below. The user continues to the next column and receives information that the following functions will be connected to the dialogue.

4.4 Visual Display Users

The prototype is not very complicated for persons with impaired vision, following the demand for simplicity from the results section. The functions in the main window are located at the right hand side in the interface. The buttons are placed just beside the window border, leaving no space in between. In this way the user with impaired vision can find the buttons by following the border of the window with the mouse. This presupposes a window that fills the whole computer screen.

The interface leaves space for bigger text, which is needed for many users. The Profile-alternative in the Adjustment-window is useful for a person using vision. Take for example a person with a vision varying from one day to another. Sometimes this person wants the text to be bigger and sometimes it is enough with a smaller text. The user can have two different profiles saved making it easy to change between the two alternatives.

5 Discussion

We set out to describe the problems persons who are deafblind encounter in their usage of computer-based communication tools, and to find ways of avoiding them in the design of a total communication tool. Our interviews and observations show that the overarching usage issues have to do with issues of simplicity, flexibility and feedback.

The unique user requirements that stem from deafblindness have to do with output methods and a high demand on flexibility in terms of suitability for individualization and adjustment. As interface designers, we have to make do with only tactile and haptic output, in some cases in combination with limited visual output. This means that it is advisable to start out with designing for the Braille display. With this in mind we designed our prototype, which shows that it is possible to design an interface suitable for both Braille users and persons using vision. The key to that is a structured screen reader use flow of the Braille interface with precursor cues.

5.1 Experts As Well As Novices Benefits from Simplicity

It is interesting to compare the result from this study with other research in the same area. Both Ladner et al. [7] and Fisher and Petrie [3] discuss the importance of simple interfaces, which is one of the main results in this study as well. Ladner et al. says simplicity is important when designing for this group because most of them are computer novices. This study complements this picture with the statement that simplicity is not important just for novice computer users, but for all persons who are deafblind. The computer is designed for persons who use vision, and vision impairment makes the usage very difficult. It takes a lot of time and effort for persons with deafblindness to learn to use a computer program. As shown in the analysis, simplicity is a key to make this process easier.

In terms of the dialogue principles in ISO 9241 [5], the reduced complicatedness will lead to increased suitability for learning. The simplicity will also provide a sense of control for the users since they can overview the complexity of the tool. Making the communication tool simpler may however increase the depth of the interface and this may cause less efficiency and hence hamper the suitability for task. However, the suitability for learning and the suitability for individualization are here relatively more important than suitability for task.

We also wish to note that flexible individualization of a tool may work against the simplicity of the user interface. Many settings can be made, and this can, if not carefully designed, increase the complicatedness.

5.2 Structuring Use Flow for Feedback

Ladner et al. underline the importance of a clear conceptual model in a program that is easy for the user to understand. This statement is closely connected to the discussion of feedback in this study. The DBNet System [7] is hierarchically structured and the user can easily navigate and receive information. The screen reader use flow with precursor cues in the design section is slightly different design, but is built by the same concept. In both prototypes the user quickly gets an overview of the program structure. The difference is that the screen reader use flow with precursor cues gives the user information of what information to expect in each step.

If we once again use the terms of dialog principles in ISO 9241 [5], the clear feedback on what the system does and what actions that are available is a means for controllability. It helps the user maintain direction towards the goal and it allows users to abort and undo actions. The flexibility of making individualizations in the system is also a means for control, since it allows users to change the format and type of presentation.

One problem of feedback still remains in our system design. Since we have focused on how to make individual adjustments to the interface we have not a clear picture on how to provide feedback on what the communication partner is doing. In a chat with another person the deafblind user does not know if the communication partner have started to write something. Therefore, one should consider using somekind of indicator to facilitate turn-taking.

5.3 Future Research

The suitability of our design remains to be tested. Neither the visual design, nor the Braille display design, or the conceptual model in the use flow has been verified. The choice of precursor cues can be further developed. A standard would be interesting to develop. Better use of tactile and haptic feedback can potentially enhance total conversation tools for persons who are deafblind.

Technically, user interface programming has a number of issues to deal with to aid the development of usable interfaces for users with different kinds of impairments. For example, it may be possible to listen when a screen reader starts, as an event. Then an application can listen for it and present appropriate user interface. Another alternative would be to design a different way to start the screen reader so that it sets a state or a flag when it is turned on and off. Applications can then check that flag to see which user interface to present. Today the most pragmatic solution may be to use special characters that are invisible to the eye in the visual display but readable for the screen reader and accordingly presented on the Braille display.

There is also a need for smarter enlargements programs and adjustment functions in operating systems that chooses what user interface objects to enlarge and what objects not to change. The development of such functions is an interesting venue for future research.

6 Conclusion

The present study show that much can be done in the area of user interface design for persons with deafblindness, and that knowledge about and cooperation with the users are crucial for a successful result. To make an interface usable for persons with deafblindness, three issues must be resolved: simplicity, flexibility, and feedback. The method of screen reader use flows with precursor cues is one means to satisfy the demands of both users who use a visual display and users who use a Braille display.

The most important learning that we bring from this design case is that creating interfaces for persons with deafblindness is a challenging, exciting and most of all a very important mission, which indeed is not impossible.

Acknowledgements

We wish to thank Gunnar Hellström and the others at Omnitor, as well as our participants. Wi would also like to thank Jonas Lundberg and Magnus Bång for comments on earlier drafts of this paper. This work has been sponsored by the program for ICT Implementation at the Swedish Governmental Agency for Innovation Systems (VINNOVA).

References

1. Csikszentmihalyi, M.: Flow: The psychology of optimal experience. Harper & Row, New York (1990)
2. Ely, M.: Kvalitativ forskningsmetodik i praktiken: Cirklar inom cirklar. Lund, Sweden: Studentlitteratur. Original title: Doing qualitative research: Circles in circles, 1991. The Flamer Press, New York (1993)
3. Fischer, W., Petrie, H.: User requirements for technologies for personal communication and information use for deafblind people. In K. J. Miesenberger, & W, Zagler (Eds.), Proceedings of Computers Helping People with Special Needs, 8th International Conference, ICCHP 2002, Lecture Notes in Computer Science, Vol. 2398. Springer Berlin Heidelberg, New York (2002) 583-584
4. Hackos, J. T., Redish, J. C.: User and task analysis for interface design. John Wiley & Sons, New York (1998)
5. ISO 9241: Ergonomic requirements for office work with visual display terminals (VDTs). International Standards Organisation, Geneva (1998)
6. ITU-T F.703: Multimedia conversational services. International telecommunication union, Geneva (2000)
7. Ladner, R., Day, R., Gentry, D., Meyer, K., Rose, S.: A user interface for deaf-blind people (Preliminary Report). In Proceedings of the SIGCHI/GI conference on Human factors in computing systems and graphics interface. ACM Press, New York (1987) 81-92
8. Löwgren, J.: Human-computer interaction: What every systems developer should know. Studentlitteratur, Lund (1993)
9. Mesch, J.: Tactile Swedish sign language: Turn-taking in signed conversations of deaf-blind people. In M. Metzger (Ed.), Bilingualism and identity in deaf communities. Gallaudet University Press, Washington DC. (2000) 187-203
10. Sandhu, J. S.: What is design for all. In European Telematics Conference: Advancing the Information Society, (1998) 184-186
11. Shackel, B.: Ergonomics in design for usability. In M. D. Harrison and A. F. Monks (Eds.), People and computers: Designing for usability. Cambridge University Press, Cambridge (1986)

Part IV

Access to Information, Education and Entertainment

Display Characteristics Affect Users' Emotional Arousal in 3D Games

Tao Lin, Atsumi Imamiya, Wanhua Hu, and Masaki Omata

Department of Computer Science and Media Engineering, University of Yamanashi, Takeda
4-3-11, Kofu, Yamanashi Prefecture, 400-8511, Japan
{Lintao,Imamiya,Hu,Omata}@hci.media.yamanashi.ac.jp

Abstract. Large computer screens are becoming more and more popular among users, and field of view and physical screen size are important considerations for users and manufacturers. In this study, we investigated the impacts of visual angles and physical screen size on users' emotional arousal using subjective and physiological measures. The results suggest that larger visual angles cause greater galvanic skin responses (GSR), and the GSR data are mirrored in the subjective ratings of emotional arousal. We also found that physical screen size causes significant effects in subjective ratings. This study contributes to our understanding of how users interact with large displays and helps refine the requirements for what constitutes effective and desirable human–computer interaction (HCI).

1 Introduction

The past decade has witnessed an unprecedented growth in user interface and human–computer interaction (HCI) technologies. These technologies are making a range of novel HCIs possible and are narrowing the gap between the human and the machine at the human–computer interface. The increased focus on the user—such as on their often idiosyncratic characteristics and reactions and their changing needs—characterizes these developments [1]. For example, researchers have suggested that affect and emotion are important to consider when designing interfaces, especially when the primary goals are to challenge and entertain the user [2]. This focus on the user has also shifted the focus of usability studies from analyzing productivity environments to analyzing the human experience. In addition, advances in technologies such as eye tracking and physiological measures have made it possible to objectively measure users' inner states in real time.

Studies of user interactions with large computer displays are becoming commonplace. Researchers have realized that when a display exceeds a certain size it becomes qualitatively different, and interface design for large displays will require new ways of thinking about HCI [3]. Although the gains provided by large displays, such as positive impacts on performance and the subjective sense of presence for the user, have been explored in detail, little is known about how large displays affect the physiology and emotion of the user. The goal of this study was to determine if correlations between emotional experience and display characteristics exist. The

C. Stephanidis and M. Pieper (Eds.): ERCIM UI4ALL Ws 2006, LNCS 4397, pp. 337 – 351, 2007.
© Springer-Verlag Berlin Heidelberg 2007

results contribute to our knowledge of how users interact with large displays and may help refine the requirements for what constitutes effective and desirable HCI.

1.1 Related Studies on Large Displays

Many researchers have studied the usability issues and benefits of large displays. When Robertson et al. reviewed a series of studies about large-display use, they identified six broad categories of usability problems: losing the cursor, bezel problems, distal information access problems, window management problems, task management problems and configuration problems [4]. They suggested that these issues inhibit the potential for even greater productivity (although, as discussed below, mounting evidence illustrates that large displays increase user productivity and aid user recognition memory). To solve these problems, they also presented research prototype techniques.

In terms of benefits, Patrick et al. found that users performed significantly better at remembering maps when using a large projection display as compared to a standard desktop monitor [5]. They attributed part of this effect to higher level of presence afforded by the large projection display, which may have provided better cues for map formation.

Tan et al. studied the use of peripheral projection displays to show pictures that serve as memory cues. They reported that the greater the sense of presence invoked by the display, the better the memory for learned information [6]; however, the researchers did not offer explanations for the increased sense of presence on large display. In later studies, they compared a reading comprehension task to a spatial orientation task at equivalent visual angles. They found that reading comprehension did not depend on display size, but the participants performed 26% better on the orientation task with a large display. They explained this difference as due to a sense of presence induced by the large display, which allowed users to employ an egocentric strategy for the orientation task, rather than an exocentric strategy [7]. They also provided strong evidence that users more effectively perform 3D navigation tasks involving path integration on larger displays than on smaller ones, even when the same environments were viewed at equivalent visual angles [8].

Czerwinski et al. documented productivity benefits from large-display use. Their study suggested that subjects accomplished a mix of typical office productivity tasks 12% faster when using a large display, and users were more satisfied with large displays than small displays. In addition to productivity benefits, the large displays improved users' recognition memory and peripheral awareness [9].

Large-display use might also reduce or eliminate gender bias, at least in some tasks related to 3D navigation of virtual worlds. Many researchers have observed that male users are significantly more effective than female users at navigating 3D virtual space [10], [11]. Tan et al. showed that while large displays typically increase performance for all users, females improved so much that males and females performed equally well in virtual 3D navigation on large displays [12].

When exploring the benefits from display size, two factors are often examined: FOV (field of view), which is also referred to as visual angle, and physical display size. Researcher suggested that the large displays' wider field of view can increase users' ability to process optical flow cues during navigation [12]. In the field of virtual environment, research have shown that restricting FOV may lead to negative impacts on perceptual, visual, and motor abilities, possibly because users have difficulty in transforming real-world experience into a virtual environment [13]. In contrast, larger visual angles and physical screen size may afford users a greater sense of presence, which benefits performance. Researchers in the entertainment industry have also reported that large displays filling a wider FOV can increase the level of involvement experienced by users [14].

Related studies exploring large-display use have been focused mainly on the gains in productivity; however, the effect of large displays on the emotional experience of users is virtually unknown. Thus, in this study, we examined how visual angles and physical screen size of large displays affect users' emotional arousal.

1.2 Emotions and Physiology

Emotional experience is an important aspect of user experience. Most psychologists agree that three factors constitute emotions—subjective feeling, expressive behavior, and physiological arousal—and others add motivational state or action tendency and/or cognitive processing [15], [16]. To better analyze emotions, researchers also use various emotion modes [17], [18]. For example, an arousal-valence mode holds that all emotions can be located in a two-dimensional space of valence and arousal. The valence dimension reflects the degree to which an affective experience is negative (unpleasant) or positive (pleasant). The arousal dimension indicates the level of activation with the emotional experience and ranges from very excited or energized at one extreme to very calm or sleepy at the other. Historically, researchers have used physiological data to try to identify emotional states, and recent evidence suggests that physiological data can differentiate among some emotions [19]. Although researchers disagree on whether emotion can be classified into discreet, specific emotions [20] or whether emotions exist along multiple axes in space [15], [21], it has been generally accepted that physiological arousal is an important property of emotions.

In this study, we examined physiological arousal rather than trying to recognize specific emotions during user interaction with large displays. Based on previous research, we chose the physiological properties of galvanic skin response (GSR) and heart rate (HR) to measure emotional arousal. The GSR signal is an indicator of skin conductance and can indicate arousal as follows: When emotional arousal increases, the accompanying activation of the sympathetic nervous system (SNS) results in increased sweat gland activity and skin conductance. In 1956, Seyle has linked GSR to stress and arousal [22]. Recent research also showed that skin conductance varies linearly with the overall level of arousal and increases with anxiety and stress [23], [24]. The validity of GSR as a measure of emotional arousal was established in a study showing that GSR varies linearly with self-reported arousal when viewing emotional pictures [25]. Additionally, HR is also a good indicator of overall activity levels: A high HR is associated with an anxious state and a low rate with a relaxed state [26].

1.3   Related Studies on Using Physiology as a Metric of HCI Evaluation

To provide an introduction for readers unfamiliar with physiological measures, we briefly introduce the related studies on using physiology as metrics of HCI Evaluation. Several studies reported by Wilson and Sasse show a novel method for assessing multimedia quality in the context of networked applications: physiological responses to degradations in media quality (audio and video) are taken as an objective measure of user cost [27]. They found significant increases in GSR and HR, and significant decreases in blood volume pulse (BVP) for video shown at 5 frames per second versus 25 frames per second [28], even though most subjects didn't report noticing a difference in media quality. Another main finding of this research is that subjective and physiological results do not always correlate with each other [29]. These discrepancies between physiological and subjective assessment support the argument for a 3-D approach to evaluating multimedia quality and other HCI evaluation areas.

Ward et al. used several physiological measures (HR, BVP, and GSR) to assess users' responses to well-designed and poorly designed web pages. No significant differences were found between users viewing the two types of web pages, in part due to large individual differences. However, distinct trends were seen between the groups when the data were normalized and plotted. Participants using the poor interface showed higher levels of arousal [30], [31]. Their study also provides an example of how physiological data can be fit into usability evaluation.

Meehan et al. used physiological measures (GSR, HR, skin temperature) to evaluate presence in stressful virtual environments. The experiments found that the change in HR can satisfy the requirements for a reliable, objective measure of presence, and that change in GSR does to a lesser extent; change in skin temperature does not [32].

In the domain of entertainment technology, an experiment was conducted to test the efficacy of physiological measures as evaluators of collaborative entertainment technology [33].Their results suggest that there are different physiological responses when a user is playing against a computer than when playing against a friend. These results are mirrored in the subjective reports provided by the participants. Ravaja et al. examined phasic psychophysiological responses indexing emotional valence (i.e., facial electromyography) and arousal (i.e., inter-beat intervals and GSR) to different game events in a video game and suggested that information on the emotion responses elicited by game events and event pattern may be applied in the game design [34].

Affective computing is one of the active areas in HCI field, whose research are aimed at giving machines skills of emotional intelligence, including the ability to recognize, model, and understand human emotion, to appropriately communicate emotion, and to respond to it effectively. The new developments in the HCI field are narrowing the gap between the human and the machine and machines are increasingly to sense, or infer user attributes. To the extent that distinct emotions prepare the organism for distinct behaviour (e.g. approach vs. avoid, and fight vs. flee at the most fundamental level), they ought to be reflected in distinct physiological signatures. This is the basis for using specific signatures along these signatures to recognize a particular affective state. While debate continues regarding the specificity of these signatures for particular emotions, and the degree of affective differentiation possible, particularly when only ANS signals are considered, some research has suggested that with sufficient data, appropriate baseline and normalizing procedures, and subsequent pattern recognition algorithms, it is possible to differentiate among a number of emotions [35], [36]. Scheirer et al. applied a pattern-recognition strategy known as Hidden MarKov Models to GSR and BVP data to detect states of frustration deliberately induced by a slow computer game interface [37].

1.4 Research Overview

The goal of our study was to investigate whether large-display characteristics (FOV and physical screen size) have impacts on emotional arousal using physiological and subjective methods. In the experiment, we used a highly interactive 3D game as the experimental task because our previous research showed emotional arousal can be easily elicited from the game [38]. Our experimental hypotheses were:

Hypothesis 1: Participants will report greater subjective ratings of arousal when playing on a larger physical screen or at a larger visual angle.
Hypothesis 2: Participants will experience higher physiological responses when playing at a large visual angle than at a small angle, due to greater arousal.
Hypothesis 3: The difference in the participants' physiological signal at different visual angles will correlate to the difference in their subjective responses of arousal.

2 Experimental Design

In this experiment, Emotional arousal elicited by a 3D video game was measured by subjective methods and physiological measures (GSR and HR). We first measured heart rate with a convenient finger-mounted BVP sensor, but the noise generated by the sensor moving on the finger made the signal unstable and unusable. We then went to more cumbersome chest-attached three-electrode electrocardiogram (EKG). This gave a good signal.

2.1 Participants

Twenty male and four female university students aged 18 to 30 participated in the experiment in return for 500 JPY. Before the experiment, all subjects were required to fill out a background questionnaire about their experience with large displays and game, average game time and personal information such as sex and handedness. Twenty of the 24 subjects were experienced with game, while the other 4 subjects were somewhat experienced or completely inexperienced. In addition, all subjects reported that they were somewhat experienced or completed inexperienced with large displays.

2.2 Tasks

The experimental tasks were performed in an HCI laboratory. A large display (*Sanyo SlimView*, 100 cm x 76 cm) and a small display (desktop monitor, 36 cm x 28.5 cm)

(a)   (b)

Fig. 1. (a) Large display and desktop monitor. (b) Screen shot of the task.

were used (see Fig. 1 (a)). We chose a popular 3D video game called *Super Mario 64®* (NINTENDO®) as the experimental task. The subjects' task was to run all regulated paths, defeat a monster, and obtain two red stars as quickly and accurately as possible. Fig. 1 (b) shows a screen shot of the task.

The game was played on a NINTENDO[64] and was viewed in three conditions: on the large display at 80° and 20° horizontal visual angles and on the small display at 80° horizontal visual angle (see Fig. 2).

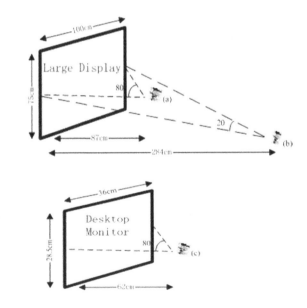

Fig. 2. Subjects played the game on the large display at 80° visual angle (a) and at 20° visual angle (b), and on the desktop monitor at 80° visual angle (c)

Subjects played a same game session for 5 minutes in each condition in random order. We collected GSR signal at 64 Hz and EKG signal at 128 Hz using Biofeedback System (ProComp Infiniti System and Cardiopro™2.0 Software from

Thought Technologies[TM]). GSR sensors were placed on the two left fingers and EKG electrodes were placed in the standard configuration of two electrodes on the chest and one on the abdomen [39].

2.3 Experimental Protocol

The experiment was divided into four phases: a welcome phase, a practice phase, a game phase, and a debriefing phase. During the welcome phase, all participants were required to sign a consent form with a detailed description of the experiment, its duration, and its research purpose. Each participant also filled out the background questionnaire.

During the practice phase, instructions were read to each subject describing the game rules, and each was given a brief tutorial on how to complete the tasks. Participants were then allowed to practice for about 10 minutes on the large display to reduce short-term physiological responses to the novelty of the large display.

At the outset of the game phase, a 5-minute baseline GSR and EKG signal were recorded. Participants then completed the game session in each condition. After each session, participants had about 10 minutes to rest and complete a questionnaire rating their emotional arousal to the game session using a 9-point pictorial scale. The scale consists of graphic characters varying from a state of low visceral agitation to that of high visceral agitation. The scale resembles Lang's Self-Assessment Manikin [40]. During the course of playing the game, participants were neither encouraged nor discouraged to talk. At the end of game, participants discussed their impressions of the experiment. An experimental trial was shown in the Fig 3.

Fig. 3. An experimental scene

3   Results

3.1   Subjective Ratings of Emotional Arousal

An ANOVA statistic was used determine whether players' game scores were influenced by the order of presentation of conditions. No significant difference was

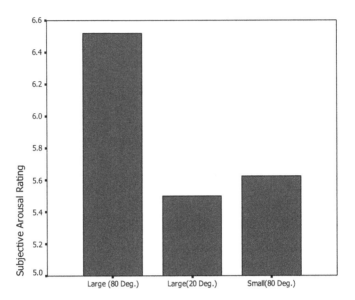

Fig. 4. Subjective arousal rating when playing on the large display at 80° and 20° visual angles and playing on the small display at 80°

found. From the subjective reports, we found a significant difference between 80° and 20° visual angles when playing on the large display (t_{24} = 2.97, p < 0.05). As shown in Fig. 4, playing at 80° visual angle elicited higher arousal compared to playing at 20° visual angle; Only one subject reported that playing at 20° visual angle led to greater arousal.

There was also significant difference between the large and small displays at equivalent 80° visual angles (t_{24} = 2.5, p < 0.05). The large display led to higher arousal as compared to the small display (see Fig. 4). The results confirmed our hypothesis one.

3.2 Physiological Measures to Emotional Arousal

Means for the physiological data were compared using independent sample t-tests. Our second hypothesis was that emotional arousal is greater when game playing at larger visual angles compared to smaller visual angles. As a result, we expected that changes in HR and GSR from baselines (HR and GSR) would be greater when playing at the larger visual angles. Overall, mean GSR was significantly higher when playing at 80° visual angles as compared to the 20° visual angle (t_{24} = 4.31, p < 0.05). We also investigated the difference in GSR between the large display and small display at the equivalent 80° visual angles. Although the large screen showed greater GSR compared to the small one, the results were not statistically significant (see Fig. 5).

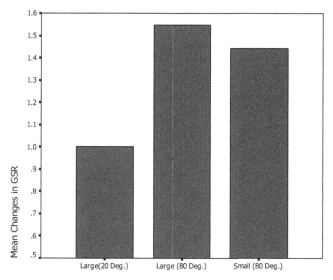

Fig. 5. Mean changes in GSR when playing on the large display at 20° and 80° visual angles and playing on the small display at 80° visual angle

We also compared the HR among the conditions. Sixteen of 24 subjects showed greater HR when playing at 80° visual angles compared to playing at the 20° visual angle, but means for all subjects did not reach statistical significance.

3.3 Correlations Between Subjective Data and Physiological Data

As we expected, the GSR and subjective rating were influenced by visual angles when playing on the large display. We examined the correlation of the two measures in the following way. To permit comparison of the time-series physiological data with one-time subjective data, we normalized the measures, transforming them into dimensionless numbers between negative one and one. The normalized method has been used to test the efficacy of physiological measures with collaborative entertainment technologies [33]. For each individual, the difference between the two visual angles was divided by the maximum range of that individual's response. The time-series GSR data were normalized using the following formula:

$$\text{Physiological}_{\text{normalized}} = \frac{\text{MeanL} - \text{Mean S}}{\text{MAX}\{\text{PeakL} - \text{MinL}, \text{PeakS} - \text{MinS}\}} \qquad (1)$$

where L refers to playing at the large visual angle and S refers to playing at the small visual angle. The corresponding normalizing equation for the one-time subjective data was:

$$\text{Subjective}_{\text{normalized}} = \frac{L - S}{8} \qquad (2)$$

These normalized measures were then correlated across all individuals using the bivariate Pearson correlation. A positive correlation of the two normalized measures showed that the amount by which subjective rating of arousal increased when playing at the large visual angle was proportional to the amount to that GSR increased during that condition (R = 0.65, p < 0.01, see Fig. 6).

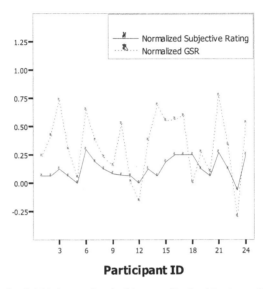

Participant ID

Fig. 6. Normalized GSR is correlated with normalized subjective ratings of arousal

4   Discussion

In this study, we examined the emotional arousal elicited by a 3D game using physiological measures and subjective ratings. The subjective results showed that both visual angles and physical screen size significantly affect the feeling of arousal: Large visual angles and large screen size caused higher arousal level. During the post-gaming interviews, subjects were asked why the arousal experience was impacted by the two factors. They felt that the 3D game world became more realistic with larger visual angles and physical screen size. Moreover, they felt that they were less distracted by outside activity because they were closer to the displays and because of the large physical screen size. Therefore, they tended to feel a stronger emotional experience.

The GSR was greater for users at 80 degrees compared to users at 20 degrees when playing on the large display. Furthermore, subjective reports of emotional arousal showed the same pattern. In contrast, although most subjects (67%) showed an increased HR when playing at 80° visual angles vs. the 20° visual angle, the difference was not statistically significant. The physiology of the measures may explain the discrepancy between the GSR and HR results. The cardiac activity resulting in HR is dually innervated by both the SNS and the parasympathetic nervous system [41]. Increased cardiac sympathetic activity is related to emotional arousal and causes the heart to speed up, whereas increased cardiac parasympathetic activity is related to information intake and attentional engagement and causes the heart to slow down [42]. Our experimental game might elicit both emotional arousal and attentional engagement, thus HR may not an optimal measure of emotional arousal in the study. In contrast, GSR is innervated entirely by the SNS [43], thus it is an unambiguous indicator of arousal levels. We also compared the physiological data between the large display and the small one at an equivalent visual angle and found no significant difference. Physical screen size seemed to affect users' emotional arousal to a lesser extent compared to visual angles.

In summary, we found that visual angle influences users' emotional arousal, as measured by both methods; in contrast, physical display size significantly affected subjective ratings but not physiological measures. This discrepancy between subjective and physiological measures may be due to the subjects' cognitive mediation. As Wilson and Decamps suggested, subjective measures may not be reliable when used in isolation, and contextual variables may influence users' assessment. For example, users rate video quality lower when performing a difficult task than when performing an easier one [44]. Moreover, reward and pacing are important features in game design. Utilizing a single subjective rating can wash out this variability, since subjective ratings provide researchers with a single data point representing an entire condition. In our experiment, the pre-questionnaires and post-interviews suggested that most subjects had little experience in using large displays, thus the novelty of large displays may have caused greater arousal rating. On the other hand, the novelty also could have caused short-term physiological responses that may have faded away during the 10-minute practice session on the large display.

One limitation of this study is that it did not consider emotional valence. Examination of valence-related physiological responses to specific game events would help us better understand how visual angles and physical screen size affect the user's emotional experience. Another limitation is that we did not keep FOV constant: When investigating the effects of FOV, we kept the horizontal visual angle constant, but the vertical visual angles were not equivalent due to the difference in display shape, thus the FOV of the two screens was not exactly same.

5 Future Work

Large displays offer users significant benefits and usability challenges. The ultimate purpose of our research is to establish a new evaluation method to investigate the large-display user experience based on subjective data and physiological data. This paper presents an initial examination of the correlation between user experience (subjective and physiological data) and display characteristics. We need more rigorous experimental conditions and analytical methods to understand the correlation in next study.

First, we need to investigate the impacts of display characteristics on users' emotional valence besides emotional arousal. Phasic physiological responses indexing emotional valence and arousal to different game events, such as anger, sadness, happiness, frustrating events, will be examined. Additionally, facial electromyography (EMG) and heart rate variability (HRV) will also be used to explore users' emotional experience.

Facial EMG provides a direct measure of the electrical activity associated with the facial muscle contractions related to emotional expression. Increased activity over corrugator supercilii is associated with negative emotions, whereas increased activity over zygomaticus major is associated with positive emotions. In additional, increased activity at the orbicularis oculi (periocular) muscle areas has been associated with both positive and high-arousal emotions during affective imagery and media viewing [45] [46]. HRV will also be analyzed in next step. HRV refers to the oscillation of the interval between consecutive heartbeats. It has been used as an indicator of the extent of task engagement in information processing requiring significant mental effort [47] [48], and has been used to detect rapid transient shifts in mental workload [49].

Second, visual details should also be investigated in the different conditions of display characteristics. The use of eye tracking enables our evaluations of emotional experience to be conducted at a more detailed level, indicating how visual angle and physical screen size affect user's eye movement. Furthermore, eye tracking has potential to help explain the impacts on performance caused by display characteristics. For example, the number of fixations overall is thought to be negatively correlated with search efficiency, and longer fixations are an indication of difficulty in extracting information from a display [50]. It also has been found that pupil diameter decreases with fatigue [51], and pupil diameter changes are related to positive effects (pupil dilation) and negative effects (pupil constriction) [52].

Finally, more subtle experimental manipulations should be explored. For instance, experiments should be extended to different domains, a variety of tasks and detailed display characteristics. This will help us testify whether the results depend on the nature of tasks and which display characteristics can enhance users' emotional experience.

6   Conclusions

The experimental results confirmed our hypotheses. Visual angles significantly affect user's emotional arousal. As measured by subjective rating and physiological responses, larger visual angles cause greater emotional arousal. Moreover, physiological measures are correlated with subjective rating. In addition, subjective ratings also reported that a large physical screen size causes higher emotional arousal compared to a small one at an equivalent visual angle, although physiological measures did not.

The study takes an initial step toward investigating user interaction with large displays. It contributes to understanding how large-display attributes affect a user's emotional experience and refines the requirements for what constitutes effective and desirable HCI. The study has also practical implications for helping game player and game manufacturers maximize the entertainment value of games.

Acknowledgements. We thank the members of the HCI group at the University of Yamanashi for their support of the research. This study was supported in part by the Grants-in-Aid for Scientific Research of the Japan Society for the Promotion of Science and by the RIEC of Tohoku University awarded to A. Imamiya.

References

1. Hudlicka, E.: To feel or not to feel: The role of affect in human–computer interaction. International Journal of Human–Computer Studies, 59, (2003)1-32.
2. Norman, D.A.: Emotion and design: Attractive things work better. Interactions, 9(4) (2002).
3. Swaminathan, N. and Sato, S.: Interaction design for large displays. Interactions, 4(1), (1997) 15-24.
4. Robertson, G., Czerwinski, M., Baudisch, P., Meyers, B., Robbins, D., Smith, G. and Tan, D.S.: Large-display user experience. IEEE Computer Graphics and Applications, 25(4), (2005) 44-51.
5. Patrick, E., Cosgrove, D., Slavkovic, A., Rode, J., Verratti, T. and Chiselko, G.: Using a large projection screen as an alternative to head-mounted displays for virtual environments. Proc. CHI 2000, ACM Press (2000).
6. Tan, D. S., Stefanucci, J. K., Proffitt, D. R. and Pausch, R.: The infocockpit: Providing location and pace to aid human memory. Workshop on Perceptive User Interfaces (2001).
7. Tan, D.S., Gergle, D., Scupelli, P. and Pausch, R.: With similar visual angles, larger displays improve spatial performance. Proc. CHI 2003, ACM Press (2003).
8. Tan, D. S., Gergle, D., Scupelli, P. and Pausch, R.: Physically large displays improve path integration in 3D virtual navigation tasks . Proc. CHI 2004, ACM Press (2004) 439-446.
9. Czerwinski, M., Smith, G., Regan, T., Meyers, B., Robertson, G. and Starkweather, G.: Toward characterizing the productivity benefits of very large displays. Proc. Interact 2003, IOS Press (2003) 9-16.
10. Kimura, D.: Sex and cognition. Cambridge, MA: MIT Press, (1999) 1-66.
11. Cutmore, T.R.H., Hine, T.J., Maberly, K.J., Langford, N.M. and Hawgood, G.: Cognitive and gender factors influencing navigation in a virtual environment. International Journal of Human–Computer Studies, 53, (2000) 223-249.
12. Tan, D.S., Czerwinski, M. and Robertson, G.G.: Women go with the optical flow. Proc. CHI 2003, ACM Press (2003), 209-215.
13. Czerwinski, M., Tan, D.S. and Robertson, G.G.: Women take a wider view. Proc. CHI 2002, ACM Press (2002) 195-202.
14. Childs, I.: HDTV—putting you in the picture. IEE Review, 34(7), (1988) 261–265.
15. Lang, P.J.: The emotion probe. Studies of motivation and attention. American Psychologist, 50, (1995) 372-385.
16. Scherer, K.R.: Neuroscience projections to current debates in emotion psychology. Cognition and Emotion, 7, (1993) 1-41.
17. Larsen, R.J. and Diener, E.: Promises and problems with the circumplex model of emotion. In M. Clark (Ed.), Review of personality and social psychology, Vol. 13, Newbury Park, CA: Sage, (1992) 25-59.
18. Gray, J.A.: The neuropsychology of temperament. In J. Strelau and A. Angleitner (Eds.), Explorations in temperament: International perspectives on theory and measurement, New York: Plenum Press (1991) 105-128.
19. Levenson, R.W.: Autonomic nervous system differences among emotions. American Psychological Society, 3(1), (1992) 23-27.
20. Ekman, P.: Basic emotions. In Handbook of cognition and emotion, T. Dalgleish and M. Power (Eds.), Sussex: John Wiley & Sons, Ltd. (1999).
21. Russell, J.A., Weiss, A., and Mendelsohn, G.A.: Affect grid: A single-item scale of pleasure and arousal. Journal of Personality and Social Psychology, 57(3), (1989) 493-502.
22. Seyle, H.: The stress of life. New York: McGraw-Hill, (1976).

23. Healey, J.A.: Wearable and automotive system for affect recognition from physiology. Doctoral dissertation, Massachusetts Institute of Technology, Cambridge, MA, (2000).

24. Picard, R.W.: Affective computing. Cambridge, MA: MIT Press, (1997).

25. Lang, P.J. Greenwald, M.K., Bradley, M.M., and Hamm, A.O.: Looking at pictures: Affective, facial, visceral, and behavioral reactions. Psychophysiology, 30, (1993)261-273.

26. Frijda, N.H.: The emotions. Cambridge, MA: Cambridge University Press (1986).

27. Wilson, G.M. Psychophysiological indicators of the impact of media quality on users, Proc. CHI 2001 Doctoral Consortium, ACM Press (2001) 95-96.

28. Wilson, G.M. and Sasse, M.A.: Do users always know what's good for them? Utilizing physiological responses to assess media quality, Proc. CHI 2000, Sunderland, UK: Springer (2000) 327-339.

29. Wilson, G.M. and Sasse, M.A.: Investigating the impact of audio degradations on users: subjective vs. objective assessment methods. Proc. OZCHI (2000) 135-142.

30. Ward, R.D., Marsden, P.H., Cahill, B. and Johnson, C.: Physiological responses to well-designed and poorly designed interfaces, Proc. CHI 2002 Workshop on Physiological Computing, Minneapolis, MN, USA.

31. Ward, R.D. and Marsden, P.H.: Physiological responses to different WEB page designs, International Journal of Human-Computer Studies, (2003)59(1/2), 199-212.

32. Meehan, M., Insko, B., Whitton, M. and Brooks, F.: Physiological measures of presence in stressful virtual environments. ACM Transactions on Graphics (2002) 21(3) 645-652.

33. Mandryk, R.L. and Inkpen, K.: Physiological indicators for the evaluation of co-located collaborative play. Proc. CSCW 2004.

34. Ravaja, N., Saari, T., Laarni, J., Kallinen, K. and Salminen, M.: The psychophysiology of video gaming: Phasic emotional responses to game events, Proc. DiGRA (2005).

35. Davidson, R.J., Ekman, P.: Afterward: is there emotion specific physiology. In:Ekman, P.,Davidson, R.J. (Eds.), The Nature of Emotion. Oxford University Press, Oxford (2004).

36. Picard, R.W., Vyzas, E., and Healey, J.: Toward machine emotional intelligence: analysis of affective physiological state. IEEE PAMI, 23 (10), (2001)1165-1174.

37. Scheirer, J., Fernandez, R., Klein, J. and Picard, R.: Frustrating the user on purpose: a step toward building an affective computer. Interacting with Computers, 14(2), (2002) 93-118.

38. Lin, T., Hu, W.H., Omata, M. and Imamiya, A.: Do physiological data relate to traditional usability indexes. Proc. OZCHI2005, ACM Press (2005).

39. Thought Technology: Cardiopro^{TM}, version 2.0 installation and user's manual (2001).

40. Lang, P.J.: Behavioral treatment and bio-behavioral assessment: Computer applications. In J.B. Sidowski, J.H. Johnson, and T.A. Williams (Eds.), Technology in mental health care delivery systems, Norwood, NJ: Ablex, (1980) 119-137.

41. Ravaja, N.: Contributions of psychophysiology to media research: Review and recommendations. Media Psychology, 6, (2004) 193-235.

42. Turpin, G.: Effects of stimulus intensity on autonomic responding: The problem of differentiating orienting and defense reflexes. Psychophysiology, 23, (1986) 1-14.

43. Dawson, M.E., Schell, A.M., and Filion, D.L.: The electrodermal system. In J.T. Cacioppo, L.G. Tassinary, and G.G. Berntson (Eds.), Handbook of psychophysiology (2nd ed). New York, NY: Cambridge University Press, (2000) 200-223.

44. Wilson, F. and Descamps, P. T.: Should we accept anything less than TV quality: visual communication, Proc. International Broadcasting Convention, 1996.

45. Ravaja, N.: Contributions of psychophysiology to media research: Review and recommendations. Media Psychology, 6, (2004)193-235.

46. Ravaja, N., Saari, T., Kallinen, K. and Laarni, J.: The role of mood in the processing of media messages from a small screen: effects on subjective and physiological responses. Manuscript submitted for publication (2004).
47. Sirevaag, E. J., Kramer, A. E, Wickens, C. D., Reisweber, I., Strayer, D. L., and Grenell, J. F.: Assessment of pilot performance and mental workload in rotary wing aircraft. Ergonomics, 36, (1993)1121-1140.
48. Tattersall, A. and Hockey, G.: Level of operator Control and Changes in Heart Rate. Variability during Simulated Flight Maintenance. Human Factors 37(4), (1995) 682-698.
49. Kramer, A. F.: Physiological metrics of mental workload: A review of recent progress. In D. L. Damos (Ed.), Multiple-Task performance. London: Taylor and Francis (1991) 279-328.
50. Goldberg, J.H. and Kotval, X. P.: Computer interface evaluation using eye movements: methods and constructs. International Journal of Industrial Ergonomics 24, (1999)631–645.
51. Hess, E.H.: Pupillometrics. In Greenfield, N.S., and Sternbach R.A. (Eds.), Handbook of psychophysiology, New York: Holt, Rinehart and Winston (1972) 491-5310.
52. Partal, T., Maria, J. and Surakka, V.: Pupillary Responses to Emotionally Provocative Stimuli. In Proceedings of ETRA 2000, Eye Tracking Research and Applications Symposium 2000, Palm Beach Gardens, FL, ACM Press, November 2000, 123-129.

User Interfaces for Pervasive Games:
Experiences of a Formative Multi-method Evaluation
and Its Implications for System Development

Carsten Röcker[1], Carsten Magerkurth[1], and Maral Haar[2]

[1] Fraunhofer IPSI, AMBIENTE
Dolivostrasse 15
64293 Darmstadt, Germany
{roecker, magerkurth}@ipsi.fraunhofer.de
[2] Experience Park
Rahlstedter Strasse 108b
22149 Hamburg, Germany
maral@experience-park.com

Abstract. This paper presents a formative multi-method evaluation on future gaming systems. Following a scenario-driven approach, quantitative and qualitative methods are employed to elicit feedback from different target user populations. Based on the results of the different evaluation parts, a set of design requirements for future home entertainment systems is derived. These requirements are then used to guide the development process of a ubiquitous computing gaming platform. To demonstrate the usefulness of the gaming platform, a sample application is discussed, which is described in the last section of this paper.

Keywords: User Interfaces, Pervasive Games, Evaluation, System Development, Tangible User Interfaces, Human Computer Interaction.

1 Introduction

With the emergence of ubiquitous computing technologies, our physical work and leisure spaces are augmented with computing functionality that unobtrusively assists its inhabitants [12]. While early projects focused mainly on supporting productiveness and efficiency in work environments, most current projects aim to foster long-term and low-pace communication and interaction between people in home environments. For example, the *ASTRA* project investigated an asynchronous awareness system that helped related and distributed households to stay in touch with each other [11]. A similar approach was taken in the *interLiving* project [13], which aims at developing technologies that facilitate communication between different generations of family members living in different households. Other projects as, e.g., *EasyLiving* [1] and *Aware Home* [5] concentrate on more fundamental challenges of intelligent home environments.

In addition to these communication-related aspects, future home environments also address fun and entertainment as important driving forces for the permeation of

C. Stephanidis and M. Pieper (Eds.): ERCIM UI4ALL Ws 2006, LNCS 4397, pp. 352–368, 2007.
© Springer-Verlag Berlin Heidelberg 2007

ubiquitous computing technologies in the home. As mentioned above, ubiquitous computing is concerned with the integration of information technology into our everyday lives, thus bringing the computer back to the real world. This inclusion of real-world aspects in entertainment applications opens up a large space of possibilities to create novel interaction experiences that bridge the gap between virtual and physical worlds.

However, it still has to be investigated if future users of such technologies will adopt their full potential or if contemporary forms of entertainment and gaming are already sufficient. From a user interface perspective, we can clearly perceive that computer games focus the users' attention mainly on the computer screen or 2D/3D virtual environments, and players are bound to using keyboards, mice and gamepads while gaming, thereby constraining interaction. By bringing more physical movement and social interaction into games, we might be able to utilize the benefit of computing systems while at the same time make the games accessible for ordinary people including elders, who were not socialized with playing computer games and who, consequently, do not participate significantly in contemporary computer entertainment. The formative study presented in this paper hence investigates, if there is a demand for future home entertainment technologies that emphasize the physical realities of the players, and if yes, how such technologies will have to be designed in order to have a maximal impact with different target groups.

2   The Formative Evaluation

2.1 Introduction

The evaluation described in this chapter was part of an empirical cross-cultural study [9] conducted at six different sites in five European countries in the context of the EU IST-IP project Amigo, Ambient Intelligence for the Networked Home Environment (http://www.amigo-project.org). While the goal of this evaluation was to elicit feedback from a target user population on concepts for intelligent home environments, this paper concentrates on novel game concepts. It is aimed to obtain feedback from potential users on the usefulness and attractiveness of different game concepts for smart home environments.

2.2 Materials and Methods

In order to get quantitative as well as qualitative feedback, the evaluation was subdivided into two parts with distinct methods and measures. For both parts, a scenario-driven approach was chosen to elicit feedback from a target user population. In the first part, the participants had to evaluate a fictitious scenario regarding its usefulness and attractiveness. In the second part, single aspects of the scenario were discussed in a structured focus group session. To explain individual components of future innovative game concepts to the target users a scenario was used (see Table 1 for core scenario elements).

Table 1. Scenario elements describing the functionality of a future gaming system

a) It asks for parental permission.	e) It lets the game player interact with body movements.
b) It downloads and shows game play lists.	
c) It adapts the lights and the sounds of the home to the environment of the game.	f) It recognizes friends at the front door and lets them join in the game.
d) It displays a video wall to show the game and other players.	g) It recognizes and integrates the game devices of the friend.
	h) It downloads the profile of the friend.

Scenario Evaluation. To collect quantitative feedback on the different concepts, the scenario was visualized and shown to the participants in an exhibition-like setup. The participants were asked to rate each scenario element regarding its usefulness and attractiveness and to list the advantages as well as disadvantages of each concept. The stimulus material consisted of visualizations of the scenarios, with a corresponding text as an introduction. Two neighboring rooms were furnished as a reception room with tables and chairs, refreshments, paper, pencils and as an exhibition room showing the visualization of the scenarios. In the reception room, the participants received a general introduction and a short instruction on the tasks that they had to perform in the exhibition room.

Fig. 1. Presentation of stimulus material (left) and assessment of scenario elements (right)

The participants were instructed to form small groups with 2 to 4 people. When they entered the exhibition room, each group was instructed to assess the scenario and its elements. After fulfilling these tasks the group moved to the next scenario. The participants were asked to rank the elements for each scenario according to their perceived usefulness and to list advantages and disadvantages of the elements.

Focus Group. The goal of the focus group discussion was to get qualitative feedback on the concepts described in the scenario and to investigate the expectations and needs for future gaming applications. The discussion was guided by structured questions focusing on the specific aspects of the scenario. The participants first were asked about their current entertainment preferences and then they were asked to develop ideas on how to improve the entertainment experience in the future. The discussion was supported by a metaplan technique. All ideas and comments of the participants were collected on cards, than clustered and labeled by the participants, and finally rated concerning importance.

2.3 Participants and Schedule

The evaluation was conducted with N=10 participants of two different age classes (see Table 2). One group consisted of three men and two women aged between 16 and 25 and the other group consisted of two men and three women aged between 32 and 38.

Table 2. Overview over participants

Group	Participants	Gender	Age
Group 1	1	male	15
(15 – 25 years)	2	female	24
	3	male	23
	4	female	15
	5	male	25
Group 2	6	male	35
(32 – 38 years)	7	female	32
	8	male	35
	9	female	32
	10	female	37

The overall schedule for the quantitative and qualitative evaluation session is shown in Table 3.

Table 3. Schedule for the evaluation (3 hours)

Duration	Activity
5 min	Arrival, introduction and explanation
10 min	Warming up
15 min	Presentation of scenarios
20 min	Questionnaires
40 min	Lunch break
50 min	Focus group discussion
10 min	Coffee break
20 min	Clustering and rating of the focus group results
10 min	Unwinding, cooling down, debriefing

3   Results

3.1   Quantitative Results

The questionnaires provided different types of data. In the following sections, the results of the ranking tasks are presented, first regarding the usefulness of the scenario elements, and then regarding their attractiveness. In the subsequent section the general feedback as well as the list of advantages and disadvantages are illustrated.

Usefulness. In the first part of the questionnaire, the participants had to rank the scenario elements regarding their usefulness (1 being the most useful scenario element, 8 the least useful). Table 4 gives an overview over the ranking results.

Table 4. Ranking of scenario elements regarding their usefulness

Element	Sum	Average	Median	SD
A	28	2,8	2	2,300
B	53	5,3	4,5	1,829
C	36	3,6	3	2,319
D	51	5,1	5,5	2,558
E	42	4,2	4	2,098
F	64	6,4	6,5	1,430
G	40	4	3,5	2,625
H	43	4,3	4	1,767

Table 5 shows the number of participants, which rated each scenario element in one of the first three ranks.

Table 5. Frequency of participants who rated each element in one of the first three ranks

Element	Rank 1		Rank 2		Rank 3	
	Freq.	Perc.	Freq.	Perc.	Freq.	Perc.
a	4	50%	2	25%	1	12,5%
b	0	0%	0	0%	1	12,5%
c	2	25%	2	25%	3	37,5%
d	1	12,5%	1	12,5%	0	0%
e	1	12,5%	1	12,5%	1	12,5%
f	0	0%	0	0%	1	12,5%
g	2	25%	3	37,5%	0	0%
h	0	0%	1	12,75%	3	37,5%

The evaluation of the ranking task showed that the standard deviation for most scenario elements is rather high. In order to get valid results, the ratings of the first three ranks were accumulated, before prioritizing the scenario elements.

Table 6. Prioritization of scenario elements regarding usefulness

Priority	Scenario Element	Top3
1	a) It asks for parental permission. c) It adapts the lights and the sounds of the home to the environment of the game.	70%
2	g) It recognizes and integrates the game devices of the friend.	50%
3	h) It downloads the profile of the friend.	40%
4	e) It lets the game player interact with body movements.	30%
5	d) It displays a video wall to show the game and other players.	20%
6	b) It downloads and shows game play lists. f) It recognizes friends at the front door and lets them join in the game.	10%

Attractiveness. In the second part, the participants had to rank the same scenario elements regarding their attractiveness. See Table 7 for an overview of the results.

Table 7. Ranking of scenario elements regarding their attractiveness

Element	Sum	Average	Median	SD
A	48	4,8	6	3,155
B	50	5	5,5	2,160
C	25	2,5	2,5	1,354
D	48	4,8	4	2,486
E	37	3,7	4	2,163
F	62	6,2	6	1,549
G	45	4,5	5	2,121
H	45	4,5	5	1,900

Similar to the previous part, Table 8 shows the number of participants, which rated each scenario element in one of the first three ranks.

Advantages and Disadvantages. The discussion of advantages and disadvantages mainly reflected the quantitative results from the ranking tasks. The feedback on the different scenario elements could be clustered into three domains:

Table 8. Frequency of participants who rated each element in one of the first three ranks

Element	Rank 1		Rank 2		Rank 3	
	Freq.	Perc.	Freq.	Perc.	Freq.	Perc.
a	2	25%	1	12,5%	0	0%
b	0	0%	2	25%	1	12,5%
c	3	37,5%	3	37,5%	3	37,5%
d	0	0%	2	25%	4	50%
e	2	35%	0	0%	1	12,5%
f	0	0%	0	0%	0	0%
g	2	25%	0	0%	0	0%
h	1	12,5%	2	25%	1	12,5%

Table 9 shows the prioritization of scenario elements, based on the accumulated ratings of the first three ranks.

Table 9. Prioritization of scenario elements regarding attractiveness

Priority	Scenario Element	Top3
1	c) It adapts the lights and the sounds of the home to the environment of the game.	90%
2	d) It displays a video wall to show the game and other players.	60%
3	h) It downloads the profile of the friend.	40%
4	a) It asks for parental permission. b) It downloads and shows game play lists. e) It lets the game player interact with body movements.	30%
5	g) It recognizes and integrates the game devices of the friend.	20%
6	f) It recognizes friends at the front door and lets them join in the game.	0%

Adaptiveness of the Environment. The idea of adapting light and sound to the current game situation was the concept most often addressed by the participants of both age groups. Adapting the physical environment to the virtual game atmosphere was regarded as one of the major building block for an enhanced gaming experience and increased realism.

Enhancement of the Social Situation. The idea of extending traditional video games into the real world and thereby enabling rich social interactions between the players was regarded as an attractive feature for new gaming applications. In this context, easy integration mechanisms for additional players and devices were widely appreciated. Being used to the small effort necessary to participate in traditional board games, the integration of players and control devices into current video games, seems to be a major problem for the average user.

Automatic Control and Security Mechanisms. Although the topic of automatic security and control mechanisms was addressed quite often, the expressed opinions regarding the usefulness of such mechanisms varied considerably. Most users, and especially those with children, liked the idea of automated age control, and regarded this feature as useful assistance in protecting children from inappropriate game content. In contrast, others feared that such autonomous control mechanisms this might lead to a depletion of social contacts and an erosion of parental authority. Although automation was widely appreciated in order to minimize the installation effort for game devices and players, the majority of participants feared that too much automation might lead to a loss of control. Especially functions like the automated access control (scenario element f) raised serve concerns among the participants.

3.2 Qualitative Results

For clarity, the feedback gained during the focus group discussion is subdivided into five groups.

Needs and Requirements. Most participants felt satisfied with existing entertainment devices and remarked that it would be hard to convince them of the benefits of a new entertainment system. Both groups were rather satisfied with traditional board games and therefore quite reserved concerning the need for new entertainment systems. Especially the group of older participants mentioned, that new systems has to be really innovative to be of any interest. A simple improvement of existing features would not be enough to convince them. The younger group was more open for innovations, but noted that existing systems cover all their needs. Hence, the acceptance of future entertainment systems will strongly depend on their functional quality. The older participants further remarked that new systems are likely to be interesting in the first moment, but that classical board games might be favored in the long run.

Basic Qualities. The participants cared most about the compatibility, extensibility and usefulness of the system. They clearly want a flexible system with upgrade options. Both groups remarked that it has to be possible to take the system with them if they move into another house. They would only buy a new system if it offers various functions and a possibility to extend it, so that they will be able to use it for a long time. During the rating task, both groups generated a cluster labeled "extensibility". This cluster included multiple items claiming options to add new functionality, possibilities to integrate further game parts, as well as an update opportunity for the operating system. All participants agreed that future entertainment system must combine various functions. Similar to modern game consoles, which offer possibilities to watch DVDs, to communicate and to listen to music, a new entertainment system must also combine various functions related to entertainment. The group with the older participants also remarked that the system must save power. They asked for low power consumption in general as well as an automatic stand-by function, which automatically turns off the system if it is not used for a certain period of time. There was also a common agreement, that such systems must not be too expensive. A price comparable to the price of today's games consoles was considered as appropriate.

System Design Goals. All participants agreed that there has to be a simple way to disable automatic control mechanisms completely. Generally, it was regarded as very important that the user is always in control of the system and never the other way round. Most participants emphasized that the interaction must be easy, quick and intuitive. Some suggested an interface with speech input and output. Therefore, intuitive interaction mechanism mentioned for all situations, ranging from the setup of the system, over its configuration to the daily interaction. In addition, the system shall save time by supporting activities the user would do anyway. Another requirement was to have service persons to deliver and install the system, to give some basic training on how to configure and use each feature, and to be available afterwards to help if problems occur. Furthermore, the system shall not require any maintenance after being installed. Both groups used traditional tabletop games as a benchmark to judge new entertainment systems. Participants in both groups noted that the game board should remain as a physical object. This requirement was explained with the rich social situation while using tabletop games. The participants claimed that they want to play together with their friends, although the system shall offer the opportunity to function as an additional player. One participant explained that real game pieces and game boards would enable a haptic experience and generated an atmosphere on their own, which he appreciated very much. Another participant suggested that the system could add sound or special effects to traditional board games or represent the game board in form of a projection. Another topic, which was addressed by many participants, was security and safety. Most participants were concerned about (software) attacks from outside as well as about potential accidents caused by malfunctions of the system.

Content Design Goals. As mentioned above, both groups emphasized the social aspects of playing games. Generally, the system should help to foster a sense of community between users. This must be considered for each application, no matter if it is a game, a communication system or a movie. Games must offer a single-player mode as well as a multi-player mode for various numbers of players. The system must be able to replace missing human players as well as an option to control non-player characters. All participants expect that future entertainment systems provide better graphics and a more realistic game world than current systems do. Although this was mentioned as a clear requirement, one participant remarked the ambivalence. On the one hand the participants would appreciate an immersive game world, but on the other hand they fear that this may cause losing contact to reality.

Features. Generally, the participants want a useful combination of features realized in independent components. The users should be able to decide on their own, which features they need and than be able integrate them into the system. But the system should only focus on entertainment. Completely different features of smart home environments, like for example housekeeping functionalities, should not be integrated in the system. Future gaming applications should be able to control the physical environment, e.g. light or sound, in order to adapt the room to the current game situation. The system should also include new technologies, like 3D projections and speech interfaces. Furthermore, the systems should improve traditional board games with additional feedback in form of acoustical and visual effects, and provide an option to simulate additional players. Finally, the applications should represent remote players, who play from a different location, like they were in the same room.

3.3 Resume of the Evaluation

The focus groups showed that an entertainment system must be designed with care to convince people of all ages. Furthermore, all features must be useful and the system must provide an added value to existing entertainment systems. Mediating personal communication and connecting people is regarded as a very sensitive topic. A feature to connect distributed people is only appreciated if the contact would be less intensive or non-existing without the system. But if a direct interaction between people is possible, the system must never replace that. The major goal of an entertainment system is to support a rich social situation with as much direct interaction between users as possible. Additionally, the system should provide a more realistic entertainment experience for games as well as for movies or other content.

4 Derived Design Implications

Given the results of both parts of the evaluation, implications for the design of a future home entertainment system can be derived. These requirements form the basis of the development of a ubiquitous computing gaming platform [7] that evolves from the work within the aforementioned Amigo EU project.

Support for Graphical and Physical User Interfaces. Entertainment applications traditionally make strong use of graphical output to support the immersion into the game. Many of the innovations both in 3D rendering algorithms and rendering hardware are in fact driven by the highly competitive games market. As the participants of the study noted, game applications need to provide both rich graphical output to appeal to the users and additionally integrate non-standard physical interfaces that support the social dynamics of the involved players and link between physical and virtual worlds without requiring exclusive attention. Hence, different forms of interaction, different user interface concepts, and multiple and heterogeneous devices are required as well as a content-adapted presentation including the ambient light and sound condition in the immediate environment.

Flexible Device Configuration. As indicated by the participants of the formative evaluation, the setup of interaction devices in a future game session can vary greatly, depending on what is available at a user's site. Solutions tailored to one specific site that is mostly static in its configuration might make sense in a business context, but since home entertainment naturally aims at mass market deployment the developer of a ubiquitous computing game cannot anticipate the device setup of the end user. One user might possess a certain interaction device, while another user owns a different one. When both participate in the same game session, they should be able to bring their own devices and make use of them. As the participants of the study note, this should involve basically no integration overhead. Accordingly, the game application should be able to operate on a minimal device setup, e.g. a single desktop PC, and adapt to a myriad of additional input and output devices.

Runtime Adaptability. In a home entertainment setting, interaction situations are very little structured with participants joining and leaving at any time. Due to this dynamic nature of the interaction situations, interaction devices need to be flexibly integrated and be added and removed at any point in time, which the participants of the study explicitly point out. Since it cannot be taken for granted that private devices are always available in sufficient quantities (see flexible device configuration), the gaming application must also be capable of dynamically reassigning private devices to different users. In addition to the device configuration, also the game applications themselves need to be adaptable during runtime regarding their modeled rules and game mechanics. This relates to the notion of "house rules" that allow participants of the game to change certain game mechanics as a result of their own playing history. The runtime adaptability of traditional tabletop games is one of the reasons for their continuing success despite the technical superiority of computer entertainment. This point clearly relates to the participants' notion of traditional board games as benchmarks for future gaming systems.

User Interface Orchestration. Lights and sound should be adaptable to the contents of the current entertainment application. Obviously, the orchestration of user interfaces is a crucial point in ubiquitous computing gaming applications. For dramatic reasons, it is important to make effective use of the various mostly output devices in a smart space. For instance, story-telling elements such as the infamous cut-scenes from contemporary computer games demand for large public displays to have the intended immersive effect. When heterogeneous interaction devices with different interaction characteristics are integrated in a smart home environment, it is essential to utilize each single device in accordance with its interaction affordances. Hence, a coordination infrastructure needs to be aware of device characteristics in order to distribute user interfaces among interaction devices.

Appropriate Modeling of the Social Space. As the participants of the study remarked, it is essential for a future entertainment system to support the interaction between humans in their natural environments, instead of forcing humans to communicate via a computer. Consequently, when dealing with multiple users, an inherent distinction between private and public information must be made. Notes taken in a negotiation meeting, for instance, must not be directed to a public display. For entertainment applications, it is often favorable to further introduce multiple degrees of privacy for game events, so that different degrees of shared, public and individual knowledge in the social space can be utilized by a game application to foster cooperation and competition between human participants. The gaming platform must therefore inherently address information representation and information flow to ensure that the social space is appropriately provided with information form the virtual domain (cf. user interface orchestration).

5   A Platform for Future Home Entertainment Applications

The requirements deducted from the user evaluation that were discussed in the previous section, inform the development of a smart home gaming platform that integrates various physical interaction devices and adapts the ambient parameters of the players' rooms accordingly. This allows the realization of immersive, stimulating entertainment applications without having to deal with the complexities that ubiquitous computing environments introduce to the development of interactive applications.

Fig. 2 demonstrates how the ambient parameters of the players' environment are adapted to the atmosphere conveyed by the gaming application. This alteration of the physical reality enhances the immersion of the gaming experience. According to the preferences of the subjects in the study, this is an important feature beyond traditional computer and video games needed to convince the more hesitant population of older consumers (group 2).

Another prominent requirement found in the study was the easy integration of various physical interaction devices in a game session. Since board games were nominated in the study as references and benchmarks, the physical devices supported by the platform mainly relate to interaction metaphors found in board games. In the following sections, two such devices are discussed.

5.1   The Smart Dice Cup

A heavily augmented version of a traditional dice cup called Smart Dice Cup is used for representing the central act of rolling dice in a ubiquitous computing game. Dice are crucially important components of a wide range of games. They are used for creating variations in the game flow. By rolling dice, an element of chance is introduced to an otherwise static and deterministic flow of game actions. The chance in the dice, however, is not equal to the generation of a random number. Rolling dice involves both a physical act and skill (some people and some dice roll better results

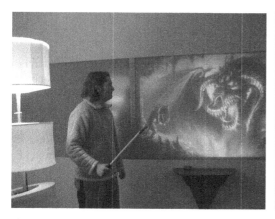

Fig. 2. Adaptation of light and sound for immersive experiences (left) and the Smart Dice Box (right)

than others) as well as a social mechanism to supervise and control the physical act, because cheating is a common phenomenon associated with this particular way of adding variability to games. The Smart Dice Cup is shown in Fig. 2.

The interaction was designed to be as similar to a traditional dice box as possible. To generate random numbers, the device is lifted, shaken, put on a plain surface upside down, and then finally lifted again to see the results. However, in contrast to traditional dice, the sum of the spots is not counted from the physical dice after being tossed on the surface of the table. Instead, the spots are displayed via light emitting diodes (LEDs) on the surface of the dice box top. Shaking the device also emits a sound mimicking the sound of shaking a traditional dice box, although the integrated sound hardware does hardly deliver sound of acceptable quality. Since the smart dice box is capable of communicating with the environment via radio transmission, it is more preferable to let another sound source outside the device perform the respective audio output. In addition to the basic interface of shaking, dropping and turning the device, there is also a conventional button interface with a graphical display integrated in the top surface of the dice box. The button interface is used for advanced configuration of the device when no other, more sophisticated interface such as a respective GUI application (running on a nearby PC) is available or when single dice are to be "held" or "released", i.e. when they are to be included or excluded from tossing. Each of the five dice displayed on the surface of the dice box consists of seven red LEDs that represent the spots of the respective die. Whenever the device is shaken, the respective light patterns change in accordance to the tossed result. A small green LED is used to indicate whether the respective die is held or released, i.e. if its face changes when the device is shaken. To toggle between holding and releasing a die, a small button is associated with each die that turns the respective green LED on or off with each press, thus ensuring an intuitive way of changing the individual held states by providing visual feedback. The Smart Dice Cup is an important physical building block for ubiquitous computing games. Since rolling dice is a central component in many tabletop games, the transition between the physical act of rolling dice and the respective virtual processing is crucial for realizing effective hybrid games.

5.2 Sentient Game Boards

Another class of custom-built interaction devices also relate directly to the domain of board and tabletop games. The interaction design of board games is proven to support social group situations effectively [8], partly due to the horizontal orientation of the display. This facilitates direct face-to-face communication among players. The common turn-taking, slow-paced game styles let the board interface only briefly and infrequently demand exclusive attention from individual players. The interaction with a sentient game board that conveys its physical state to a virtual application should be as natural and simple as with a traditional game board. Physical objects should simply be put on a dedicated horizontal area and hereby represent their own positions. Due to the augmentation with information technology, it might be possible to achieve additional benefits to the mere sensing of the physical artifacts. For instance, in contrast to a traditional game board, a smart board might be used as an additional output device and display dynamically changing game boards, if it includes a screen, or convey information via LEDs or other means. Likewise, playing pieces might be equipped with additional functionalities. This includes a simple memory or unique identification capabilities by e.g. integrating RFID tags or even integrating entire particle computers. Some platforms such as Smart Dust are only a cubic millimeter in diameter, thus allowing for being integrated into small-scale artifacts such as typical playing pieces. There are multiple potential realizations for sentient game boards each having unique advantages and drawbacks. In the following sections, two examples are presented.

Magnetic Fields. Magnetic game objects can be sensed very inexpensively by magnetic field sensors built into a game board. These simple reed sensors are triggered, whenever a magnetic field of a certain strength is sensed. Building a respective game board thus comes down to finding the matching relation between the strength of the magnets integrated in the playing pieces and the sensitivity of the reed sensors. While a position recognition based on a grid of reed sensors works robustly, such sensors can not be used to determine an object's identification, i.e. objects would have to be identified by the strength of their magnets, however, as the field strength decreases with the distance to the sensor, variations in positioning would result in different field strengths at the sensors. This lack of object identification capabilities is, of course, a severe drawback to the technology. As an augmentation to the simple and inexpensive reed sensors, Hall Effect sensors can be applied that measure magnetic fields perpendicular to the Hall element, i.e. a single magnetic object results in differing sensor magnitudes depending on its orientation. Thus, the orientation of playing pieces can be sensed in addition to their positions. This allows for interesting new game elements as e.g. in spy games, where players can try to sneak past guards that face to a different direction unable to "see" them.

Electric Resistance. One of the benefits of magnetic field sensors is their wireless operating mode. It is sufficient to put or hold a piece near a sensor in order to detect it. This advantage cannot be realized with any solution involving electric current. However, when electricity flows through playing pieces, varying resistors built into them allow for a cheap, robust and fine-grained identification of an arbitrary amount of pieces. The real strength of electric current however lies in the extreme simplicity of providing playing pieces with discrete states that change within individual pieces. For instance, as shown in the prototype board in Fig. 3, the chest piece is currently open. By closing it, the virtual representation of the physical piece would change from an open to a closed state. Similarly, continuous state changes such as pieces' orientations are possible. The wizard and the blue creature are facing towards distinct directions as visualized in the virtual counterpart application. By turning the physical objects, the virtual representations would rotate accordingly. Such discrete and continuous state changes are simply implemented by integrating switches and potentiometers into the pieces that alter the objects' resistances.

Apart from the disadvantage of the necessary physical contact of the pieces, the technology offers significant advantages over magnetic solutions including object identification and the unique feature of having discrete object states. Otherwise, its features are comparable to magnetic solutions, both are cheap, can interoperate with simple output mechanisms such as LEDs, mobile boards can be realized, and they work robustly enough.

6   Sample Application

With physical interaction devices such as game boards and dice boxes, one can develop future home entertainment applications that provide the features asked for by the participants of the study. One such gaming application called "In Search for the Amulet" [6] was created as a proof-of-concept demonstrator.

Fig. 3. A Sentient Game Board (left) and sample application 'In Search for the Amulet' (right)

With this prototype, the aim was to develop a simple, yet challenging game that average visitors in an open house situation can grasp immediately. It should show the potential of hybrid games by presenting a believable and beneficial distribution of game elements along virtual, physical, and social dimensions. The game prototype revolves around a physical game board on which a map of 64 fields is shown. The game board functions as an interface between real and physical world in that an array of integrated RFID sensors transmits the positions and identities of playing pieces to a software application. Two players move their physical playing pieces over the map to search for shards of broken amulets and other items hidden on the map. Once a player collects all the shards of a single amulet, she wins. Several events and also virtual characters aggravate this endeavor. For instance, a wicked kobold moves around the virtual representation of the game board and talks to the players from time to time, e.g. telling one player what items the other player has collected so far or stealing items from one player and selling them to the other. Apart from the physical game board and the dice box, each player has a small display that shows private information the other player is not allowed to perceive, such as the content of her bag or the effects of private events (meeting with virtual non-player characters, being caught in a trap, etc). To further underline the integration of both virtual and physical elements, the weather conditions present in the game world (players can take less steps in storm or lightning), are also represented as physical effects. For instance, in sunny weather, a lamp shines directly on the game board, whereas real wind is created via a fan controlled by the game logic. To ensure the game play to profit by the provision of direct face-to-face interaction between the players, trading items between both players is a central element of the game, since one player might have found an item the opponent is in need of and vice versa. It requires a great deal of negotiation and pretence skills to convince the other player to give away her shards without arousing suspicion that exactly these shards might mean sudden victory for the opponent.

7 Conclusions

In this paper presented a formative evaluation on future home entertainment systems. A scenario describing a future gaming environment was used to illustrate new game concepts and interaction techniques. In a two-step evaluation process, the scenario was presented to a target user population of two age groups. In order to elicit from the participants on the different scenario elements, questionnaires as well as a structured focus group discussion were employed. The user feedback was used to define a set of design requirements for future home entertainment systems, which were than materialized in form of a ubiquitous computing gaming platform. The usefulness of this gaming platform was confirmed through the development of a sample application.

The approach taken to develop pervasive gaming applications that are comprised by a distributed set of heterogeneous interaction devices has the implication that the single components, such as the dice cup or the game board, are interchangeable. By decoupling UI components from the actual gaming applications, it becomes irrelevant, if e.g. a physical game board, a 3D rendered display of the board, or a simple magnified 2D GUI control e.g. for visually impaired people is used to control the movements of the playing pieces. In this sense, the approach follows the notion of "universally accessible games" brought up by Grammenos et al. [4]. By explicitly taking tangible interaction devices into account that go beyond traditional graphical user interfaces, accessibility among non-computer gamers should be improved, as e.g. the affordance of a dice cup is to simply shake it, which requires no previous computer interface knowledge. Ullmer and Ishii [10] point out the inherent feature of a tangible interface to unify representation and control, which makes a TUI faster and more intuitive to use than most graphical interfaces. This applies also to game related interfaces such as [2], which discusses a magic wand, or [3] which deals with smart playing cards as supportive interfaces.

So far, we have developed the platform from the requirements of our evaluation' subjects with the flexibility to support different interaction devices for different user groups. The next step will be to evaluate the platform with different user groups in order to gain more insights on which kinds of gaming interfaces appeal most to which user groups.

Acknowledgements. The work presented in this paper was partly supported by the European Commission as part of the IST-IP AMIGO project (contract IST–004182). We would like to thank our colleagues and friends Timo Engelke, Norbert A. Streitz, Wolfgang Hinrich, and Dan Grollman who contributed to this work.

References

[1] Brumitt, B., Meyers, B., Krumm, J., Kern, A. Shafer, S. (2000) EasyLiving: Technologies for Intelligent Environments. In: *Proceedings of the International Conference on Handheld and Ubiquitous Computing*, pp. 12 – 27.

[2] Ciger, J., Gutierrez, M., Vexo, F., Thalmann, D. (2003) The Magic Wand. In: *Proceedings of the 19th Spring Conference on Computer Graphics*, Budmerice, Slovakia, April 24 - 26, pp. 119 – 124.

[3] Floerkemeier, C., Mattern, F. (2006) Smart Playing Cards – Enhancing the Gaming Experience with RFID. In: *Proceedings of PerGames 2006*, pp. 27 – 36.

[4] Grammenos, D., Savidis, A., Georgalis, Y., Stephanidis, C. (2006) Access Invaders: Developing a Universally Accessible Action Game. In: K. Miesenberger, J. Klaus, W. Zagler, A. Karshmer (Eds.): *Computers Helping People with Special Needs, Proceedings of the 10th International Conference, ICCHP 2006*, Linz, Austria, 12 – 14 July, pp. 388 – 395

[5] Kidd, C.D., Orr, R.J., Abowd, G.D., Atkeson, C.G., Essa, I.A., MacIntyre, B., Mynatt, E., Starner, T.E., Newstetter, W. (1999) The Aware Home: A Living Laboratory for Ubiquitous Computing Research. In: N.A. Streitz, J. Siegel, V. Hartkopf, S. Konomi (Eds.) *Proceedings of the Second International Workshop on Cooperative Buildings* (CoBuild'99), pp. 191 – 198.

[6] Magerkurth, C., Memisoglu, M., Hinrich, W. (2005). Entwurf und Umsetzung Hybrider Spielanwendungen. In: *Proceedings of Mensch & Computer 2005* (M&C'05), pp. 211 – 220.

[7] Magerkurth, C., Engelke, T., Grollman, G. (2006). A Component Based Architecture for Distributed, Pervasive Gaming Applications. In: DVD *Proceedings of the ACM Conference on Advancements in Computer Entertainment Technology* (ACE'06).

[8] Mandryk, R. L., Maranan, D. S., Inkpen, K. M (2002). False Prophets: Exploring Hybrid Board/Video Games. In: *Extended Abstracts of the Conference on Human Factors in Computing Systems* (CHI'02), pp. 640 – 641.

[9] Röcker, C., Janse, M., Portolan, N., Streitz, N. A. (2005). User Requirements for Intelligent Home Environments: A Scenario-Driven Approach and Empirical Cross-Cultural Study. In: *Proceedings of Smart Objects & Ambient Intelligence* (sOcEUSAI'05), pp. 111 – 116.

[10] Ullmer, B., Ishii, H. (2000) Emerging Frameworks for Tangible User Interfaces. In: *IBM Systems Journal*, 39(3), pp. 915 – 931.

[11] van Baren, J., Romero, N. (2003) *ASTRA: Design of an Awareness Service and Assessment of its Affective Benefits*. MTD Thesis, ISBN 90-444-0291-9. User System Interaction, Technical University of Eindhoven, The Netherlands.

[12] Weiser, M. (1991). The Computer for the 21st Century. In: *Scientific American*, 265(3), pp. 66 – 75.

[13] Westerlund, B., Lindqvist, S., Sundblad , Y. (2003) Co-designing with and for Families. In: *Proceedings of the Conference COST269, User Aspects of ICTs: Good / Bad / Irrelevant*, pp. 290 – 294.

Mobile Messenger for the Blind

Jaime Sánchez and Fernando Aguayo

Department of Computer Sciences
University of Chile, Chile
+56 2 673 1280
{jsanchez, faguayo}@dcc.uchile.cl

Abstract. An increasing number of studies have used technology to help blind people to integrate more fully into a global world. We present software to use mobile devices by blind users. The software considers a system of instant messenger to favor interaction of blind users with any other user connected to the network. Input/Output implementation modules were emphasized creating a 9-button virtual keyboard and associated Text-to-Speech technology (TTS). The virtual keyboard helps to write into the pocketPC without needing external devices, representing a real challenge for novice blind users. The TTS engine was adapted to blind users by adjusting the engine. Usability evaluation of these modules was iteratively applied to end-users. As a result, the integration of the designed modules into a communication system helped us to create a messenger system specially tailored to people with visual disabilities.

1 Introduction

A number of sound-based applications [8, 12, 13, 14, 15, 16] have been developed to assist the learning of children with visual disabilities, obtaining significant results in the development of tempo-spatial, memory, and logic- mathematics skills. However, these applications are limited to a static context of use such as the school classroom and home. This has lead authors to find out how technology can support mobile activities of children with visual disabilities and related issues.

PocketPC mobile devices emerged as a consequence of diverse efforts to create more portable PCs. Thus, computer peripherals are replaced depending on associated mobile user needs such as the traditional keyboard that is substituted by text recognition and on-screen keyboard; and the stereo sound is replaced by mono sound. This series of adjustments has modeled user expectations ending up with an efficient mobile device. In many respects the design of these devices did not consider users with special needs. Actually, most mobile devices do not model the mental strategies of these users.

Diverse efforts have been made in order to adapt the PocketPC to users with impairments, achieving the design of somehow physically different devices but oriented only to specific users. An example of this is the creation of a PocketPC specially designed for blind users with a screen reader and replacing the tactile screen by a series of functional buttons all over the surface [1].

C. Stephanidis and M. Pieper (Eds.): ERCIM UI4ALL Ws 2006, LNCS 4397, pp. 369 – 385, 2007.
© Springer-Verlag Berlin Heidelberg 2007

Some external devices have been created to facilitate the interaction of users with special needs that also can help blind users to use the pocketPC. The problem is that they force users to use an additional device [17] debilitating mobility, the main attribute of mobile devices.

Our work is focused on the use of standard pocketPC together with software specially designed for users with visual impairments, without requiring additional hardware. This leads users with visual impairments to use the pocketPC not including special requirements, facilitating their integration into a global world. To fully use the device blind users only need adequate software and little initial training as it happens with sighted users when using new software in their mobile devices.

The purpose of this study was to create software to enhance communication between different types of users [6], blind and sighted, by using a standard pocketPC. The software used was designed together with blind people in an iterative process to facilitate the integration user-device, and the communication between the user and messenger contacts.

Due to the fact that this software was designed together with end-users from the very beginning, multiple usability evaluation tests were applied to successively designed prototypes before coming up with the final product. This situation pushed us to present this work in a nontraditional way, because the implementation is threaded with the end-user usability testing. It also helped us to observe how the initial software product suffered changes to better adapt and fit the needs of end-users. During usability testing a sample of users from different ages participated to obtain a product shaped for different needs.

One of the most significant proposals of our study is the design of a virtual keyboard, specially designed for blind people. The model used for the keyboard is discussed in different studies that use the same model as an alternative to the traditional keyboard, but it is only applicable to users without disabilities [3, 4, 5].

2 Design, Development, and Testing

In order to improve the design, implementation, and re-design of the software, the implementation was divided into 4 stages:

1. Keyboard
2. Text-to-Speech (TTS)
3. Instant Messenger Systems (IMS)
4. Instant Messenger System with Audio (IMSA)

These stages, tightly related to the interaction between the user and device, were constantly tested in order to arrive to a real solution for users with visual impairments. The comments and suggestions made by users during testing were fully implemented by redesigning the prototype and thus improving the software.

The tools used for the development of both pocketPC and PC were Microsoft Visual Studio .NET 2003, programming language C#, and a TTS engine that is an external library from ACAPELA. We also used audio files with numbers and letters recorded in our research center.

2.1 Sample Participants

During testing, a group of people with visual impairments participated, ranging from users with residual vision to totally blind users. All of them were legally blind. The sample consisted in 8 participants, ages 12 to 25 years old.

2.2 Keyboard

The most interesting advantage of some mobile devices is the capacity of handwriting recognition on the tactile screen. This type of writing has being improved through the time due to the lack of keyboard embedded in mobile devices. Event though this input mode is very useful for sighted users, it is too complicated to be used by users with visual impairment, because they can not see the arrangement of strokes neither the areas where these strokes can be drawn.

Our research team searched a solution to supply the absence of a physical keyboard. We discarded voice recognition due to the fact that it requires a specific training for each user besides to an excessive use of pocketPC functioning resources. We then arrived to the idea of using a virtual keyboard on the screen, specially oriented to these users. This is not the traditional keyboard composed by 108 keys. Rather, we first designed a keyboard with only 12 buttons such as in mobile phones, and then we ended up with only 9 buttons. Some studies analyze this type of writing in different devices [4, 5].

Table 1. Button distribution on the screen

1	2	3
4	5	6
7	8	9
*	0	#

Our goal was to create an interface that could be used by blind users and at the same time, be efficient for writing. The first step was to study the use of virtual keyboards by blind users. In the first approach, a keyboard composed of 12 buttons (Fig. 1a) was used, similar to mobile phones with numbers from 1 to 9, including 0, # and *, covering the whole screen of the mobile device. During testing this keyboard users hardly found the central buttons (4, 5, 6, 7, 8 and 9, see Table 1), but corner buttons from upper and lower rows were very easy to operate due to the fact that for them it was very easy to represent keyboard corners that matched screen corners. Users also succeeded at localizing buttons 2 and 0 by using the technique of middle points. We then conclude that this first prototype was useless because it was complex to use.

After experimenting with the 12-keys keyboard we created another prototype by using just 9 buttons (Fig. 1 b).

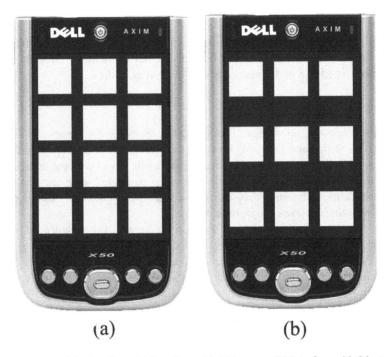

Fig. 1. Evolution of the interface: (a) Interface with 12 buttons, (b) Interface with 9 buttons

By using only numerical buttons from 1 to 9, users could localize buttons 1,3,7,9 through the screen corners; buttons 2,4,6,8 through the middle points of the screen sides; and button 5 through the projection of middle points (see Table 2). When this prototype was tested with blind users, preliminary encouraging results were obtained.

The next step was the creation of a functional prototype to test the new keyboard interface with blind users. A TTS was embedded into this prototype to provide feedback to their writing.

Table 2. New button distribution on the screen

1	2	3
4	5	6
7	8	9

Different functionalities were added to these 9 buttons by following a known scheme as with mobile phones. The functionalities were designed as follow:

- Button 1: space and delete
- Button 2: keys (a, b, c)
- Button 3: keys (d, e, f)
- Button 4: keys (g, h, i)

- Button 5: keys (j, k, l)
- Button 6: keys (m, n, o)
- Button 7: keys (p, q, r, s)
- Button 8: keys (t, u, v)
- Button 9: keys (w, x, y, z)

In order to find the desired letter users have to press multiple times the button that contains such letter. To find the desired letter the user has to wait one second and then it is accepted as valid. This is the same period utilized in cellular writing, and we detected that it is an appropriate time. Also, if after finding the desired letter the user presses another button, the letter is accepted immediately. Consequently, a word is constructed in a similar way as in mobile phones (Fig. 2).

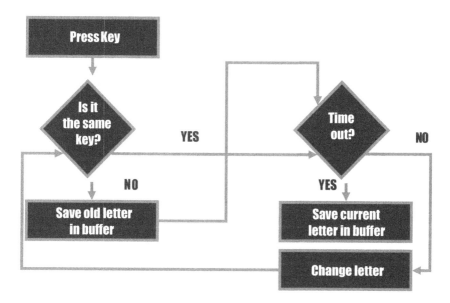

Fig. 2. Functioning of the virtual keyboard

The visual interface is also relevant for users with residual vision, but legally blind, that were also our target population. This is the reason why the selection of colors for the interface was based on previous studies that use high contrast colors to distinguish shapes for users with residual vision [11, 15].

When this new prototype was designed, another usability test for buttons use and acceptance was implemented to determine if users could write words efficiently. Usability testing was implemented as a case study (individually) by providing pocketPCs to users to familiarize them with both the device and the new software. Then, users were informed about software basic operations and the functions of each button. End-users had free time to use the software and later they performed predefined tasks such as writing their complete name using the software tools. This testing was carried out with users of different ages and different degrees of blindness. During the test we found out that the time the user spent to choose a letter was very short for younger users, but it was adequate for older ones. Thus, in order to make the testing easier for young users, the time for letter acceptance was increased by modifying the initial time from 1 to 1.5 seconds. If the letter chosen was not the desired, the user had to press the button again until finding the desired letter. If the letter is not set on the pressed button the user had to delete and look for it in another button.

Another important detail was the latency between the time elapsed from the moment a user pressed a button to the TTS reply saying the corresponding letter. When solving this we found ourselves in a crossroad because the TTS architecture did not provide options for an efficient processing. A solution was sought in the field of keyboard prediction in order to send the requirement to the TTS before the user pressed a button and thus providing an efficient feedback. This solution did not work due to the degrees of freedom of the user when writing. Then we decided to adopt a mixed solution when providing feedback to the user depicted in the use of sound [2]. The solution consisted of using pre-recorded sounds and the TTS in the following way:

1. Pre-recorded sounds are composed by letters and numbers.
2. The TTS is used for pronunciation of words and sentences. When a user presses a button the corresponding sound to a letter is played, avoiding the TTS processing and thus providing an efficient feedback to the user.

Later, a new testing was implemented in order to validate the changes made and to search for new improvements. When evaluating the use of the virtual keyboard we observed that:

1. Users could easily use the keyboard for writing sentences without difficulties. This was clearly observed in users with residual vision and adult users.
2. Users who had more difficulties in the use of the virtual keyboard were children less than 12 years old and those totally blind. This can be explained because they had never used a mobile phone and they did not have any experience with the use of multiple function buttons. In addition to this, buttons are virtual on the screen implying that they do not have relieves, making harder the keyboard representation.

The implementation team searched for a mechanism for users to adapt to the new input created. A solution was the use of a grid with relieves over the virtual keyboard to help users to understand button distribution and functioning. This mechanism did not work because the tested grids did not provide the desired tactile feedback. We redesigned again the problem of physical representation of buttons splitting users in two groups:

a. Users that understand the operation of a mobile phone keyboard but did not find the position of buttons.
b. Users that had not used a mobile phone keyboard so it was harder for them to understand the use of the virtual keyboard.

The solution for group "a" was very simple and consisted of placing marks around the screen that highlighted the middle points where the buttons of the virtual keyboard were placed. In case "b" we arrived to the solution of putting a rubber keyboard from a mobile phone on top of the pocketPC screen (Fig. 3) to help blind users to feel the buttons before pressing them. The idea with this keyboard was to use it in an intermediate stage before using a keyboard with 9 virtual buttons. We obtained important results after testing. After a short time of interaction with the rubber keyboard, users got along with the virtual keyboard without any problems. The user in Fig 3 has the device close to his ear due to the low volume provided by the device, but this was later solved by using headphones.

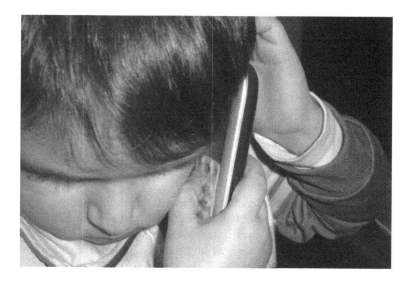

Fig. 3. Interaction with a rubber keyboard

An anecdotic situation during testing was that buttons did not have a label describing different associated letters because it was obviously not necessary for blind users and users with residual vision (they only discriminate shapes). But, to testing facilitators labels were essential to recognize the letter distribution on buttons, especially when the tasks were performed with novice users using the keyboard. To solve this situation we labeled buttons displaying their functionality (Fig. 4) and thus supporting the work of the facilitator.

Once we implemented relevant changes in the interface a new testing was applied obtaining results that were completely satisfactory. Users wrote quickly due to the lack of latency between the moment of pressing of a virtual button and the pronunciation of a letter by the pocketPC. They also started to memorize the letter location in the buttons, decreasing the error rate when searching for a letter.

The implementation of a mobile phone physical keyboard for the pocketPC was also relevant because users used this keyboard for writing and after a while, they were capable of using the virtual keyboard without the aid of the physical interface.

The marks put over the mobile device to signaling middle points had also a positive effect on users because the location of central buttons was much easier.

Fig. 4. Interface with labels on the buttons

End-users found an interface feedback problem during testing because there was no audio reply when they pressed out of the buttons, in the space between buttons. Another important observation was that they were not comfortable with the voice and volume used by the TTS. The changes implemented included additional feedback suggested by users during testing. This is the reason why we implemented a sound that plays each time users pressed between buttons. Suggested changes were not implemented directly to the TTS used, but in a parallel work we developed a module to take full advantage of the TTS effectiveness.

We finally implemented a new testing but this time users did not suggested changes to the interface.

2.3 Text-to-Speech (TTS)

This stage started in parallel with the design of the input interface and consisted basically of finding an engine that could translate words into audio waves, a TTS (Text-to-Speech). A search was made for available solutions on developed products. Compatibility and performance tests were implemented later focusing mainly on voice clarity, in Spanish with English support, and without consuming all resources of the pocketPC, because the TTS was just an additional tool used for a higher objective.

Another essential requirement was the complexity of programming the TTS. We did not want TTS programming to be a problem but rather an easily adjustable tool. The search started with freely distributed products. After diverse testing we arrived to the conclusion that products that include the Spanish language had low performance because they used excessively the pocketPC processor, decreasing the performance of our software.

A second search for a TTS was extended to commercial software. We found ACAPELA which came up with an excellent performance without consuming excessive pocketPC resources and includes easy-to-use API.

This TTS was embedded during the first keyboard testing, validating the performance obtained in the preliminary TTS testing. When users used the TTS they made comments related to the volume and tone of the voice.

We have to consider that when we design for sighted users we centered on the graphical interface by making it pleasant to for the user through the correct selection of colors and forms. For users with residual vision the graphical interface is simpler because the use of colors is not excessive, only high contrast colors are used. Shapes have not details because they can distinguish at most general shapes. But sound interfaces play a main role providing feedback to users with visual impairment. This is the reason why we confer so much importance to their comments and observations about the TTS. We have to consider that TTS is very valued in mobile devices without considering the type of user because of their potential to empower interfaces [9].

In order to improve the TTS we decided to search the real possibilities to modify it through manipulation of the API. After a while we were able to modify three main aspects of the API: Volume, tone and voice speed. The changes to the API allowed

Fig. 5. Testing the TTS

manipulating in real time these three parameters. This is the reason why we decided to implement exclusively a voice testing of the TTS. Thus we created software that only uses the TTS to speak a sentence multiple times, fixing the volume but varying the tone and voice speed.

The voice testing consisted of end-users hearing the same sentence multiple times but with variations in tone and voice speed. Users had to mention which voice was more pleasant and the observer wrote down the corresponding parameters. Then the observer played the TTS voice again but this time controlling the parameters in order to validate the information gathered initially (Fig. 5).

Another aspect evaluated during testing was the feelings of end-users concerning the different voices emerged from TTS. We tested if the voice heard could be related to some person or to a characteristic of a person. This aspect is very important because it could easily characterize users with the TTS.

The testing was carried out with blind users finding the parameters that modified the voice and making it more pleasant to them. These parameters were constant in most users with little variation to the rest of the users.

The characterization of different voices produced when modifying tone and speed parameters was successful. End-users were capable of characterizing the voices heard such as differentiating a girl, an old woman, a slim man, and a tall man. These results leaded us to create sound-based emoticons on the messenger for blind users using different voices. Once the voice was defined we could continue implementing our main software, a messenger system for blind users.

2.4 Instant Messenger System with Audio Server (IMSAS)

During the development of this module diverse projections were made concerning the solution we should offer and what could provide a pocketPC. If we try projecting an instant messenger system in a mobile device we arrive to the conclusion that the main features of these systems are completely opposite. On the one hand, online connection needs an Instant Messenger System (IMS), and, on the other hand, mobile devices are not capable of being permanently connected at a reasonable cost.

In order to solve this problem we had to modify the features of one of them. One option was to get the pocketPC permanently connected to Internet through cell phone technology. This approach has the disadvantage of being highly expensive which could lead us to failure. Another approach is using an Instant Messenger System with Audio Server, IMSAS, asynchronously. This means to modify one of the most distributed and used system protocols, MSN Messenger, which would let us in an irreconcilable position with the rest of users, making the solution unpractical.

An important goal of our project was the integration of visual impaired users to massive communication systems such as MSN Messenger, which forced us to use the actual protocol utilized by this system, without making any modification. This guaranteed us that our users can communicate with other users who use traditional MSN Messenger system capable to be executed in PCs and pocketPCs.

In order to change the synchronous way of working in the IMS, we created an intermediate server between IMS users and the Instant Messenger System with Audio (IMSA). We designated the IMSA server as IMSAS with the following features:

1. To allow the creation of a synchrony state for IMSA users, since they interact with IMSAS, in charge of creating sessions that will keep the synchrony with the rest of our contacts.
2. The IMSAS supports the fact that the contacts of our users can see them as connected to the messenger system, but absent, in such a way that contacts know that their messages will not be answered immediately.

The IMSAS operation mode is the following:

1. The user starts a session through the IMSA created in the IMSAS, which keeps a permanent connection of the user with the IMS network.
2. The IMSAS stores sent messages to our users and deliver them when connected to the IMSAS through the IMSA. Thus the IMSA is able to communicate the received messages. Users can write messages while they are disconnected of the IMSAS, which are stored in the IMSA and delivered when the connection is reestablished. The IMSAS is in charge of providing queued messages to the corresponding contacts if they are connected to the network; otherwise the messages are stored until the contacts connect to the IMS again.

At the moment, MSN Messenger does not allow this type of asynchronous communication, however it has been announced that the next version of Messenger will bring an asynchronous communication implementation to leave messages to offline users. When IMSA and IMSAS are connected they behave as a conventional IMS, receiving and delivering instant messages. The interaction is shown in Fig. 6.

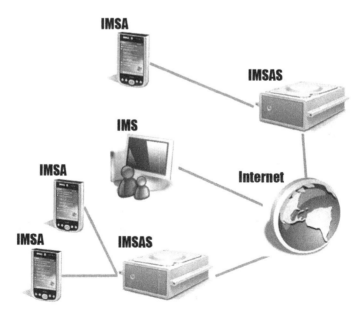

Fig. 6. A communication scheme for the messenger system

At the end of the IMSAS implementation we designed an independent evaluation of the IMSA by using a basic communication application between messenger users. Testing results of IMSAS were very positive favoring the communication with different type of contacts, being fully transparent that an intermediate server was being used. The next step in the implementation was the integration of the implemented solutions (keyboard, TTS, IMSAS) to end with the IMSA development.

2.5   IMSA

The purpose of this module was the integration of previous modules joined to a synchronous/asynchronous communication system, which maintains the user's state and the conversations with contacts, besides to allowing navigation through contacts. The integration of the implemented solutions was very simple since they were considered from the beginning of the development. First, we created a base-program to communicate to IMSAS by using a WI-FI TCP/IP connection, allowing that whenever users find an Internet access-point, they can communicate to IMSAS and therefore being able to put together the required synchronizations. The data flow between IMSA and IMSAS is made by encrypting the data, so they cannot be listened in the network. By having this final platform we proceeded to integrate the virtual keyboard with the TTS. Until then we only had integrated solutions separately, but we did not have a solution capable to manage resources efficiently: Users, contacts and conversation management.

This module was in charge of capturing the user input and executing the right actions. For instance, if the user navigates the list of contacts is not necessary to activate the virtual keyboard, but it requires activating the physical buttons of the pocketPC. This module helps to maintain different conversations with different

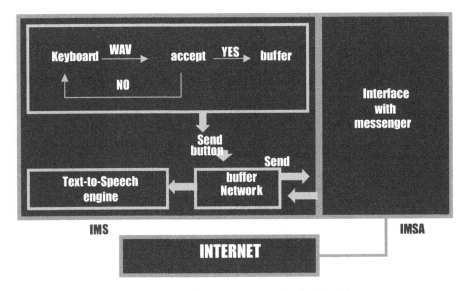

Fig. 7. IMSA and IMSAS communication Model

contacts and provides feedback to the user when receiving information concerning a conversation either made previously with a contact or a new conversation demanded by another contact. This module also maintains the logs of conversations to synchronize them with the IMSAS.

The diagram (Fig. 7) displays the process of choosing letters to make up words, stored in a buffer. When the send button is pressed, the buffer is taken and delivered to the network manager. This manager sends the buffer to IMSAS which sends it to the messenger system. The IMSA is constantly listening to what it gets from the IMSAS and thus when a message is received the user is immediately notified (Fig. 7).

After the integration between communication modules we implemented end-user evaluation with users utilizing the pocketPC to establish a conversation. During this evaluation IMSA and IMSAS were used synchronously, facilitating the conversation flow. All conversations were established between only two users. The following is an extract of a conversation between a user and his instructor in the first session:

Teacher: Hello
User: Hello
Teacher: What it's your name?
User: Marcos
Teacher: What do you think about the keyboard?
User: Difficult and slow
Teacher: Do you like the writing system?
User: I have to get used to it

During this stage users showed writing problems, mainly when looking for a letter, since they did not press the button with the right character, thus having to delete it several times. Next, there is an example obtained from the virtual keyboard logs, concerning the writing of a user:

dj[delete]m[delete]ifid[delete]cil[space]t[delete]y[space]la[delete]enj[delete]to.

The way to interpret this log is deleting the last character whenever the [delete] command appears and adding a blank space when a [space] command does it. By applying this rule the sentence "dificil y lento" ("difficult and slow") appears, meaning that the user had to delete it 6 times, causing frustration. As users learned the letter positions in the buttons they made fewer mistakes and frustration was diminished. We could also see that the used sentences were short, due to a fast-answer self-pressure imposed by users, and as they made plenty of errors, they needed to answer shortly and precisely.

After some sessions end-users maintained conversations with a testing guide using the IMSA and the essence of the conversation was about its usability. We provide next an outline of a conversation with the same user of the previous example:

User: Hi fernando
Guide: Hi marcos
Guide: I need your help
User: Tell me what you need
Guide: I need you to tell me what you think about the software that you're using

User: First, I thought that it was complicated
User: But now it is easier writing with it
User: Because I don't make mistakes when writing
Guide: What do you think about the usefulness of this software?
User: Now I can communicate with my friends because I have messenger.

An analysis of this conversation help us to realize that the sentences utilized by the user are remarkably longer, this is because the user was able to work efficiently with the virtual keyboard, and making fewer errors in a faster writing. When evaluating virtual keyboard logs we observed that the mistakes made by the user were minimal with less than one average error by sentence. This indicates that the learning curve of the keyboard was exponential, helping us to draw future projections on the use of this type of interfaces for enhancing the writing in mobile devices by people with visual impairments. The error rate of users reduced remarkably as they got used to the virtual keyboard (Fig. 8).

The TTS did not receive any comments from end-users. This can be seen as a positive fact since it became a transparent tool that was pleasant to them. Whenever the technology is pleasant and functional to users, it becomes invisible. The results of

Fig. 8. Interaction with IMSA

the final evaluation of the IMSA were very positive allowing users that had never utilized an instant messenger system, to become able to communicate without difficulties. From the point of view of users that were familiarized with instant messenger systems, the results were also positive, since they appreciated the features of the IMSA that were not currently provided by the MSN Messenger system, combined with a typical screen reader for blind people such as the alert message reception.

Users made favorable comments after usability evaluation regarding the reasons why the liked this tool:

- "Because of its novelty. Because as a visual impaired person I can talk to another person from another country, from another place".
- "The letter's order, which it is just like the ones on a cell phone".
- "It's fast, messages arrive immediately".
- "Communicating with other people is fun".

3 Conclusions

The main result of our study was to enable blind users to use standard pocketPC by using custom made software to map their mental models. The possibility that users with visual disabilities can write on the screen of a mobile device opens a critical opportunity for these users by closing the interaction gap between blind users and pocketPCs. Even though in the beginning of our study this writing method presented some complexities, especially in novice users writing on the screen of cell phones, after a while it became a usable system that facilitated the interaction between the device and the user.

The learning curve of the proposed use of the virtual keyboard was exponential and clearly noticeable during the different testing stages. At the beginning, users made many errors because they did not know the exact location of each letter on the keyboard inducing delays in the writing time. We have to consider that it is very different to make an error when typing in a conventional keyboard than when doing it with a pocketPC, because when the user makes a error typing a letter in a conventional keyboard it implies that presses only one key, while in a pocketPC the user has to go through all letters of the button and then realize that it is not the correct button. Let us consider that for a current keyboard the errors take a t time. If the keys have an average of 3 letters on the virtual keyboard, the time consumed by the error will be $3*t$.

Another important issue when evaluating the writing time is the process of deleting a letter. In the case of a normal keyboard this action is executed by pressing a key; in our virtual keyboard it implies pressing a button twice. Therefore, compared to a normal keyboard the keyboard introduced in this study strongly penalizes the fact of making an error because the t factor in a normal keyboard can be multiplied by 3 in our virtual keyboard. This explains why at the beginning of the use of virtual keyboards, the words written by users were short and precise, revealing that they felt that it took too much time to write.

During the testing period users became familiarized with the use of the proposed keyboard achieving the memorization of the location of letters which made the writing easier. After some sessions of using the device, our users found themselves writing at a faster speed due in part to few errors made on writing. The writing speed using the virtual keyboard was increased evidencing a better use of the keyboard for writing longer sentences than in previous sessions.

We believe that TTS technology has a critical impact among these users. This makes TTS a fundamental tool for system output. For this reason the results obtained during testing variations of voice parameters played an important role when creating sound-based emoticons.

Usability testing indicated that end-users accepted well the type of audio used (TTS) to reproduce the messages, even though they wanted to listen natural instead of synthetic voices. Audio comprehension by using the software was also very high and meaningful. IMSA allow users that had never utilized an instant messenger system, to become able to communicate without difficulties. The users that were familiarized with instant messenger systems, appreciated the features of the IMSA that were not currently provided by MSN Messenger system, combined with a screen reader.

Future work should include a system for text prediction similar to the systems used in some mobile devices [7, 10].

Finally, the possibility that blind users can interact with users from different places through these devices help them to be integrated and included in a global world without physical frontiers. We believe that mobile applications such as the one presented in this study can help to diminish those frontiers.

Acknowledgments. This report was funded by the Chilean National Fund of Science and Technology, Fondecyt, Project 1060797.

References

1. http://www.geekzone.co.nz/content.asp?contentid=2976, 12 May, 2006
2. Gong L., Lai J.: Shall We Mix Synthetic Speech and Human Speech? Impact on Users' Performance, Perception, and Attitude. Proceeding of the ACM CHI '01, Seattle, Washington, USA, March 31 - April 5, 2001, pp 158- 165
3. Green N., Kruger J., Faldu C., Amant R.: Late breaking result papers: A reduced QWERTY keyboard for mobile text entry. CHI '04 extended abstracts on Human factors in computing systems, Vienna, Austria, April 24-29, 2004, pp 1429-1432
4. Hwang S., Lee G.: Qwerty-like 3x4 Keypad Layouts for Mobile Phone. Proceeding of the ACM CHI '05, Portland, Oregon, USA, April 2-7, 2005, pp 1479-1482
5. Hwang S., Lee G., Jeon B., Lee W., Cho I.: FeelTip: Tactile input Device for Small Wearable Information Appliances. Proceeding of the ACM CHI '05, Portland, Oregon, USA, April 2-7, 2005, pp 1475-1478
6. Isaacs, E., Walendowski, A., Ranganathan, D.: Hubbub: A wireless instant messenger that uses earcons for awareness and for "sound instant messenger". Proceeding of the ACM CHI '01, Seattle, Washington, USA, March 31 - April 5, 2001, pp 3-4
7. Kronlid F., Nilsson V.: TreePredict Improving text entry on PDA's. Proceeding of the ACM CHI '01, Seattle, Washington, USA, March 31 - April 5, 2001, pp 441-442
8. Lumbreras, M., Sánchez, J.: Interactive 3D sound hyperstories for blind children. Proceedings of the ACM-CHI '99, Pittsburgh, USA, pp. 318-325

9. Pakucs B.: Butler: A Universal Speech Interface for Mobile Environments. Human Computer Interaction with Mobile Devices and Services MobileHCI04, LNCS 3160, University of Strathclyde, Glasgow, Scotland, September 13-16, 2004, pp. 399-403

10. Pavlovych A., Stuerzlinger W.: Model for non-expert text entry speed on 12-button phone keypads. SIGCHI conference on Human factors in computing systems, Austria, April 24-29,2004, pp 351 – 358

11. Rigden   C.: 'The Eye of the Beholder'—Designing for Colour-Blind Users. Human Factors. British Telecommunications Engineering, Vol. 17, Jan. 1999

12. Sánchez, J., Lumbreras, M., Cernuzzi, L.: Interactive virtual acoustic environments for blind children: Computing, Usability, and Cognition. Proceedings of ACM CHI 2001, pp. 65-66. Seattle, Washington, April 2-5

13. Sánchez, J., Baloian, N., Hassler, T., Hoppe U.: AudioBattleship: Blind Learners Collaboration through Sound. Proceedings of ACM CHI 2003, Fort Lauderdale, Florida, April 5-10, pp. 798-799.

14. Sánchez, J., Aguayo, F.: (2005). Blind Learners Programming Through Audio. Proceedings of ACM CHI 2005. Portland, Oregon, April 2-7, 2005, pp. 1769-1772

15. Sánchez, J., Sáenz, M.: 3D Sound Interactive Environments for Problems Solving, The Seventh International ACM SIGACCESS Conference on Computers and Accessibility , ASSETS, Baltimore, Maryland, USA, 2005, pp 173-179

16. Sánchez, J., Sáenz, M. (2006). 3D sound interactive environments for blind children problem solving skills. Behaviour & Information Technology, Vol. 25, No. 4, July – August 2006, pp. 367 – 378

17. Wobbrock J., Myers B., Aung H.: Writing with a joystick: a comparison of date stamp, selection keyboard, and EdgeWrite. Proceedings of the 2004 conference on Graphics interface GI '04, Canadian Human-Computer Communications Society, pp.1-8

Subway Mobility Assistance Tools for Blind Users

Jaime Sánchez and Eduardo Maureira

Department of Computer Science
University of Chile
{jsanchez, emaureir}@dcc.uchile.cl

Abstract. In this study, we introduce software for blind users that represents a subway system in a desktop computer. A user can organize and prepare a travel with the assistance of the software before riding the subway. After a usability study and cognitive evaluation, we detected the need for creating a mobile solution with similar goals as the desktop application. This software for mobile devices has also the capacity to help the user to solve mobility and orientation problems in real subway stations. In order to design a handheld version it was necessary to consider new features such as travel duration, tickets fare, and the estimated time duration of the travel. Conclusions from the usability study revealed the importance of using interface elements such as the audio-based hierarchy menu, the travel simulation, and the information about the subway network, stations and their surroundings. The cognitive study results revealed important gains in the development of orientation and mobility skills to use the subway system in blind users, which help them to be more integrated to the society.

1 Introduction

Biological beings have the inherent necessity of autonomous and effective ways of mobilizing. Human beings depend on their particulars qualities to meet these goals. Users with visual disabilities differ in their capacity of learning autonomy and mobilizing effectively to sighted people, mainly because the latter understand the world through vision. People with visual disabilities use orientation and mobility techniques to learn the capacities to recognize the environment, the spatial relation between objects and themselves, and tactile, auditory and olfactory stimuli. Once blind people acquire the ability to use orientation and mobility techniques, they increase their capacity to use ways of moving efficiently.

Through discrimination and localization of audio cues the auditory sense convey information to people with visual disabilities, becoming one of the most critical senses to them. Along with this, the auditory sense favors the perception of points of reference, the description of some physical places, the development of abstract thinking, the capacity of concentration, and the creation of mental schema of diverse physical environments [10, 11, 13, 14, 15, 16, 17].

Sighted users tend to utilize increasingly technological devices in different contexts. They can also interact with applications without graphical interfaces. For

C. Stephanidis and M. Pieper (Eds.): ERCIM UI4ALL Ws 2006, LNCS 4397, pp. 386–404, 2007.
© Springer-Verlag Berlin Heidelberg 2007

example, telephone-based interfaces are designed to facilitate the access to a telephone service such as voice-mail, electronic bank, and web sites [1, 3].

The navigation through real environments by blind users exposes them to higher risks than sighted users because the physical cane cannot help them to identify all objects in the space. For this reason, it is necessary to provide cues to users with visual disabilities to get a more reliable mobility, allowing them to access to more information from the environment. Providing excessive information to the user in an unnecessary way may have a counter effect leading to confusion [6, 7, 8].

Today the use of sound as support mean to graphical interfaces is a fundamental requirement in diverse interactive tools for sighted users. Technology advancement is allowing better capabilities in sound representation of different environments such as greater and better immersion of users into virtual environments. Thus, entertainment and communication requirements demand the use of better sounds. Blind users need audio-based interfaces because they use the sense of hearing as the principal source of awareness and knowledge construction for learning purposes [9]. Sound conveys information to know reference points, receive place descriptions or visualizations, develop abstraction and concentration capabilities, and create a mental schema of the surrounding.

Audio-based interfaces may include a speech or a non-speech audio. Non-speech audio facilitates the interaction with information and the representation through different devices. This helps blind users to concentrate on navigation of the physical environment, being aware that the information is perceived through their ears [12].

In the case of supporting mobility in the subway for sighted people, Métro is proposed as a solution. This software designed for handheld devices, considers an interactive visual interface. Métro is a free guide of subway networks around the world to know the ways of making a travel and to get contextual information of stations to orient users in a mobile way during their travel [19].

Users with visual disabilities have many mobility problems. One of them is the specific case of mobilizing through a subway network. In Santiago city, the subway is a highly used public transport on way of expansion, providing better comfort and faster travels than other types of public transportation. Then it is very important to take into account these benefits for blind users.

The ways of learning, entertaining and communicating are rapidly changing thanks to new wireless technologies. Currently, handheld devices functionality is not only a high priority, but also their access capabilities to diverse applications such as games, messages, and office tools, allowing users to stay connected, with greater mobility but at the same time, depending more on the technology. Thanks to these new devices, the promise "anytime, anywhere" is becoming a reality for users, to get freedom from the desk work, and make the interactive work more dynamic, mobile, and active [2].

2   Research Problem

The lack of knowledge about some aspects of the subway network is the principal difficulty for subway users. To obtain a complete knowledge of the subway network a person has to reach three levels of knowledge:

1. *Conceptual*: To understand subway network concepts such as subway lines, stations and platforms. This level refers mainly to basic and general concepts of a subway network in any city of the world. Once the concepts are learned, the user continues to the next level.
2. *Knowledge*: To comprehend specific information about a particular subway network such as the subway station name, surroundings, location, lines names that identify a route or path, and the type of station (transfer and local).
3. *Articulation*: To utilize different knowledge and concepts learned by the user for an efficient use of the subway network. It includes mainly the planning, estimation cost, and spatial orientation of the travel.

When these three levels are accomplished, the user has also to be able to master the orientation into the space to become independent. When the user looses spatial orientation, also looses autonomy.

Users with or without visual impairments that understand and use the subway network as a transportation vehicle have different problems with their level of knowledge and spatiality. Spatial problems are easier to solve for sighted users because they can visually order and classify the physical environment taking advantage of their visual memory, thanks to the use of visual references such as stores, colors, and signals of a subway network. Users with visual disabilities orient themselves through sound interpreting the surrounding world and learning to localize sounds that serve as signals for orienting and mobilizing with greater autonomy.

In the real world, sounds are not necessarily fixed; nevertheless, visual references are fixed. For this reason, it is necessary to have available better tools to support and solve orientation problems. Blind people can face a major knowledge issue because vision can be used as an imitation channel to learn how to use a certain tool, together with the affordance of related interface elements.

3 Purpose of the Study

The main purpose of this study was to create, improve, and evaluate the usability of audio-based software to stimulate and develop tempo-spatial sensory, cognitive skills, and specific mobility and orientation techniques in people with visual disabilities. All of these processes allow users safe and independent mobility favoring their autonomy when using different transportation systems such as the subway.

In this study, we also implemented a usability study during the design and development of software to assist the mobilization and orientation in a subway system. In order to determine the cognitive impact of using the software, learners practiced with cognitive tasks specially tailored for this purpose.

4 Model

We designed a software model that incorporates diverse functionalities in order to evaluate and identify an appropriate feedback, and to establish differences when developing educational software for either blind or sighted people [18].

Our software has a metaphor that represents a simulation of a subway travel through a wagon. Travels are implemented in a logical way because the software does not consider spatial representations of virtual spaces. The metaphor considers notions of consecutive, transfer, and terminal stations.

In the particular case of the Chilean subway network in Santiago, wagons travel between two stations from one extreme to the other, through a specific line that covers both directions. The stations have two platforms, one on each side of the rail. In these platforms, passengers wait for subway wagons at specific directions. Transfer stations consist of different levels; each level has a specific line and each line crosses to the other, allowing to associate each line to a level.

In a typical software simulation session, the user has to choose previously the departure and arrival stations of the travel. In order to be aware at any moment the state of the game and to provide the functionalities to be implemented in a virtual travel, the software utilizes object-oriented programming techniques to model the stations, lines, network lines, and travels. The model calculates the optimal route from the current station to the arrival station in order to take strategic decisions during simulations.

The application displays information to the user through an interactive menu hierarchy to transfer information to the three levels of knowledge. This menu is presented through audio and can be complemented with contextual help to interact with the software.

User actions are saved in a session log file for later analysis to evaluate learning when using the software.

5   Software Description

A work session with the software consists of two stages. During the first stage, the user prepares a travel by defining the departure and arrival stations. In the second stage, the user virtually moves through the subway network, starting at the departure station.

At the beginning, the software does a random selection of values for each of the three main variables in a travel through the subway network. These variables are subway line, travel platform (direction), and starting station (transfer or local).

Fig. 1 shows a travel from the Pedro de Valdivia station (line 1) to Toesca station (line 2) of the Santiago's subway network.

The software was programmed in Java using the Swing library. The software code is divided into four main packages:

1. *Metro*: Defines the objects that represent a subway network
2. *DomArea*: Groups all classes related to XML document management
3. *Navegacion*: Represents the navigation through menu hierarchies, feedback, sound coordination, and other functionalities of the software
4. *Sonido*: Groups all methods related to the use of sound

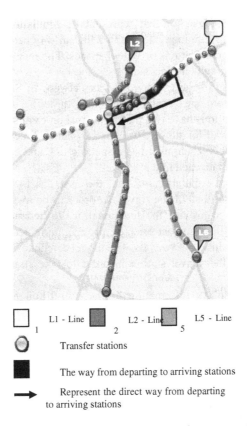

L1 - Line 1   L2 - Line 2   L5 - Line 5

Transfer stations

The way from departing to arriving stations

Represent the direct way from departing to arriving stations

Fig. 1. A travel through the Santiago's subway network

The *Navegacion* package behaves as an API that allows a quick structuring of hierarchic menus for audio-based software. Although this API was designed and developed for this software, we believe that the API logic may be re-used in other audio-based software, independently of the programming language, framework, final user, and objectives of the software.

The menu hierarchy of this API contains a header and a group of items. These items can be linked to other menus to create menu hierarchies and menu networks. The messages associated to the header and each item of the menu, are displayed as a sequence of sound files.

The logic of the sound sequence is managed by the *Sonido* package. This logic let a message to belong to either: (1) Always the same sound sequence, (2) A sound sequence chosen randomly from a set of sound sequences, or (3) A sound sequence chosen from a play list (not randomly).

5.1 User-Software Interaction

The graphical objects of the interface are organized into three panels. When starting the software the user has to input personal information in the first panel. This information is saved into the session registry for later analysis. Then, in the second panel, the user chooses both the departure and arrival stations. Finally, in the third panel, the user explores the subway network and associated contents in the three levels of knowledge (see Fig. 2).

The software has a sequential and unidirectional flow. In the third panel, the user can choose to begin a new simulation and select the departure and arrival stations in the second panel. The main graphical objects are text boxes, combo boxes, and buttons, using the keyboard as input. The software provides audio feedback to users with visual disabilities when using these visual components. When navigating by using menu hierarchies, at the third panel, the user interacts exclusively with a text box. This box captures keyboard events without changing the focus between different graphic components.

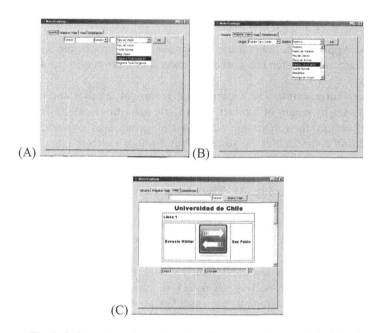

(A)   (B)

(C)

Fig. 2. Software interfaces. (A) User. (B) Prepare the travel. (C) Travel.

6   Cognitive Evaluation

6.1   Participants

The study was designed with a sample of 10 users from the rehabilitation level of the School for the Blind "Santa Lucía" in Santiago, Chile, ages ranging from 20 to 32 years old. This group was divided into two equal subgroups, a control subgroup, that did not interact with the software, and an experimental group. The subgroups were created in such a way that the age and the number of users with residual vision were balanced.

6.2 Concrete Materials

To model the mental image that users created about the geographic distribution of the Santiago Subway, we worked with two types of materials:

- Cardboard base and LEGO© bricks. The use of this material allows users to represent in detail the stations of the Santiago subway network by building them with different bricks, which vary according to whether it is a local or a transfer station.
- Cardboard base with stakes. By using this material, users represent the geographical distribution of the Santiago Subway network lines, by joining different stakes through rubber bands.

6.3 Methodology

The activities were divided into four steps:

1. **Pre-test Application.** Users made a real travel route through the Santiago subway to evaluate and register the actions of users and their control in an independent journey.
2. **Software Interaction.** The experimental group got familiar and interacted with the software by means of interactive concrete activities to assimilate, generalize, and reflect on their learning. The control group was exposed to the same information embedded in the software but through a lecture class with a teacher teaching the main concepts and helping students to prepare the travels through the subway.
3. **Cognitive Tasks** (see Fig. 3). There were four cognitive tasks to observe the development of the following skills: To know and apply tempo-spatial concepts, to make an efficient use of senso-perceptive organs, and to select and apply concepts provided by the software for independent mobilization through the Santiago subway network.
   - _Task 1_: To know and apply tempo-spatial orientation and mobility concepts by modeling the subway network with concrete materials, according to the mental representation that each user had about the subway
   - _Task 2_: To make another modeling representation of the Santiago subway network by using concrete materials. In order to develop this task the experimental group had to attain the activities of step 2
   - _Task 3_: To make virtual travels. The experimental group made them by using the software and the control group performed them verbally. These travels had to be accomplished in two stages. In the first one, there were three predefined routes to perform; in the second one, the route was defined by the user
   - _Task 4_: To take a defined route in the real world using the subway network
4. **Post-test Application.** In the same way as in the pre-test, users made a real travel route in the Santiago subway to evaluate and register the actions of learners and control in an independent journey.

Fig. 3. Users solving cognitive tasks

6.4 Instruments

- **Pre-test and post-test,** the Specific Route Displacement Test, SRD, was used. A particular route was elaborated to test the participants. We evaluated their performance in a given subway route using appreciation scales consisting in a group of statements describing actions and skills used. In order to elaborate both the route and the evaluation scale, we considered: 1. The user orientation and mobility skills, 2. The same route for everyone, 3. Departure time, 4. Number of transfers, 5. Number of stations, 6.Visual degree, and 7. Knowledge of real displacements through the Santiago subway.

- **Cognitive task evaluation test,** for each cognitive task an evaluation test was created to observe and register orientation and mobility skills to be developed, stimulated or enhanced through the activities. This test consisted in statements that evaluate mobility and orientation skills involved in the tasks.

- **Record graphs**, the software record graphed actions performed by learners during their interaction.

6.5 Procedure

Cognitive testing was carried out during four months. As the stages of the applied methodology were attained, and depending on the group to which each user belonged, cognitive testing was carried out in different places. Pre-tests and post-tests were applied on site. Users from the experimental group interacted with the software in a computer room whereas the users from the control group attended classes in a lecture-type classroom. Both groups performed cognitive tasks with concrete materials. In order to avoid distortions in the results of the cognitive testing, only the experimental group interacted with the software and all users utilized the same version of the software.

6.6 Results

These results analyzed correspond to the experimental subgroup, which obtained a better performance than the control subgroup.

Results are divided in three areas: behaviors, skills, and competences. Behaviors refer to the specific handling of techniques with the white cane, which correspond to the orientation and mobility program applied to environments of medium complexity. Skills include aspects needed to perform an independent movement. Finally, competences describe the level of development of a user in each described skill.

The results show that the highest gain took place in the competence domain (20% out of the total), followed by the skills domain (16%), and the behaviors domain (6%). Nevertheless, all areas obtained gains after using the software and cognitive tasks.

From this study, some questions emerged about the impact that a mobile-device application would have on mobility and orientation in a subway system. For this reason, we later developed mBN (Mobile Blind Navigation), a pocketPC version of our former software. We believed that this mobile software should not be just a portable version of the former software. We should also redefine and study both the interface and the information displayed. We had to define the functionality to be exploited in the mobile version and the cognitive impact. Although this new software aims to the same users, it is subtly different since it is oriented to a different context of use, and thus complementing the desktop version. The primary goal of the mobile version was to help to solve unexpected problems and issues during mobilization through the subway that cannot be anticipated in the desktop version.

7 Software Description of mBN

Our software was also developed for a pocketPC device. We used Microsoft Windows Mobile 2003 operating system compatible framework. mBN software contents are presented in a hierarchy of menus displayed into the screen and also as audio cues. A menu has a heading and a set of items, the number of elements in each set has to meet the usability cognitive restriction of 7 ± 2 elements. Menus can be defined as circular or normal according to the way to explore them.

Navigating through the menu of the software creates the need to offer the following command set: *Next*, a command to go forward in the item of the menu list; *Back*, a command to go backwards in the menu; *Enter*, a connected item to enter to a submenu; *Quit*, to return to a container from its submenu; *Know Current Item*, to provide to the user and the program, the option to recognize and capture the name of the item available at a certain time; *Know Title*, to recognize and capture the name of a current menu title.

When a menu is not circular, the software provides audio interfaces with information about starting and finishing the menu. When identifying a menu that contains submenus, the software has to provide feedback to the user to interact naturally with the displayed menu structure.

When using mBN software users have to execute commands through the touch screen of a pocketPC. The interface was designed and developed "with" and "for" users with visual impairments. The interaction is achieved using the corners of the pocketPC screen by joining the adjacent corners. Thus, the software registers, analyzes, and interprets the movements and jumps of the pointer. With this information, the software knows whether a command was executed. Blind user's interaction with the touch screen is performed without needing the pointer pen by using the tact to map the relief of the four corners needed to construct and execute a command.

The input interface allows the user to execute eight different commands by displacing the pointer to adjacent corners. When the user needs to select a specific command, the software presents the user three specific feedback sounds. The first one identifies the initial selected corner; the second one identifies the corner to the left; and the last sound refers to the command represented by the second corner sequence. In order to select a command, the user has a fixed time. If the time ends, the software reproduces a fourth sound. The names of corners are related to the names of the six dots used in the Braille code (see Fig. 4).

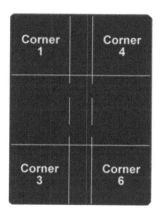

Fig. 4. mBN corner's names

The commands for the input interface are next, last, mute, repeat, quit, enter, title and help. The combination of corners to follow in order to achieve the desired command is shown in Fig. 5.

The information managed by mBN is represented internally by strings transmitted to the user via spoken audio texts and high contrast color text on the screen. A Text-to-Speech engine does the translation of the written information to speech audio messages (TTS). These messages are complemented by earcons for a better attention and motivation when interacting with the software.

The information about the subway network is stored in XML files (eXtensible Markup Language). Thus, it is possible to add stations and lines to the system. Desktop software was created in order to update mBN by adding, editing, and deleting the information about the context of each station.

Command	Initial Corner	Final Corner	Side/Direction
Next	4	6	Right/Vertical
Last	6	4	Right/Vertical
Mute	6	3	Down/Horizontal
Repeat	3	6	Down/Horizontal
Quit	3	1	Left/Vertical
Enter	1	3	Left/Vertical
Title	1	4	Up/Horizontal
Help	4	1	Up/Horizontal

Fig. 5. Commands and sequences of mBN

7.1 Menus Map

The main menu has four items: Travel, ticket fee, subway network, and quit.

1. *Travel*: The user must choose both departure and arrival stations. Once the stations are chosen, the user enters into a new schema of menus where a real travel around the subway network is simulated.
2. *Ticket Fee*: This menu displays the current time, schedule, and the ticket fee depending on the time of purchasing.
3. *The subway network*: This menu has three submenus with lines, terminal stations, and transfer stations.

8 Usability Evaluation of mBN

8.1 Participants

The sample for the usability evaluation of mBN consisted in 5 people, aged 19 to 28 years old, from the Blind School "Santa Lucía" in Santiago, Chile. Four of them had residual vision and one was blind. It is important to mention that these users did not have experience interacting with PDA devices.

8.2 Methodology

The development of mBN software was planned around three goals. For each one, it was necessary to have completely validated the preceding objective before going to the next one. The validation of each of them was implemented with a series of specific usability tests. The objectives were the following:

1. **Input Interface.** This evaluates the interaction of the user with the software, so that the software favors actions to be expressed on it.

2. **Hierarchy of menus based on Audio.** The idea is to achieve a prototype where the user, based on commands learned in the *Input Interface*, can navigate through a familiar concept map of contents.
3. **mBN.** This is a hierarchy of menus based on audio including contents that mBN has to transfer to the user.

The first two goals were evaluated in a laboratory and the last goal was evaluated in a real setting by using the subway as a transportation vehicle. In laboratory testing, users interacted with a tutorial to introduce them to the software and hardware, and performed a guide of activities with the prototype.

The field-testing consisted in analyzing and applying the functions provided by the tool in a real setting. During the field-testing users were provided with extra earphones to interact with the pocketPC.

8.3 Instruments

1. **End-user questionnaire,** consisted in two sections: 1. A set of 29 closed questions with a 1 to 5 scale, and 2. A set of five open-ended questions taken from a usability questionnaire by Sánchez [13, 14]. Questionnaires were read and explained by facilitators to users, and then answered by them.
2. **Anecdotic record,** consisted in recording the information captured through observation while the user was interacting with the software.
3. **Automatic record,** consisted in data structured in XML format that is internally stored by the software while the user interacts with it, registering every used key, the stations taken, and the time used to perform every action.

To support the process of gathering data in the usability testing, complementary software was created (AnalisisSesion). This software checks the session recorded during sessions of mBN (automatic record) to calculate statistical values.

8.4 Procedure

Laboratory testing was implemented during 5 sessions in two months. Field-testing was done during 4 sessions in one month. Different interface features were evaluated during sessions of laboratory testing (see Fig. 6).

Laboratory Test ID	Prototype
PL1	Input Interface
PL2	Input Interface
PL3	Menu Hierarchy
PL4	mBN
PL5	mBN

Fig. 6. Prototype testing in each session

The objective of sessions PL1 and PL2 was to determine the understandability of the input interface. There was a dictation of each command with the objective of determining the following aspects: The ability of the user to identify corners, the ability of the user to memorize the eight commands and their associated lines, the timeline required to execute a command, and the border space for a good functioning of the interface.

In session PL3, input interface commands were associated to real actions. A simple prototype was designed including a set of connected menus with familiar information to users, measuring the affordance of commands in the context of a hierarchy of menus. Sessions PL4 and PL5 consisted in having a more advanced prototype embedded with all contents for end-users of mBN. The work done during testing corresponded to guided activities with the prototype.

8.5 Results

The first sessions (PL1 and PL2) provided information that validated the events and sound feedback, the logic of the interface, the design, and the programming strategy. It also favored the improvement of the design and coding for the following milestones. It reflected the mapping of commands and the associated lines for execution. From PL3 session, information was gathered about the time spent by one user when utilizing functionalities through the proposed input interface, by dragging the pointer from one corner to another.

In the testing of the menu hierarchy there was a need for implementing circular menus due to their size. The screen of the device could be used as support for the audio interface in the case of users with residual vision and teachers involved in the testing. As a result, we got the same restrictions for mBN software, functions that should be implemented in the logic of the menus, requirements, organization, and the debugging of contents presented in the software, such as including a menu with the value of a ticket in accordance with the time, and including relevant information about the surroundings of the station.

9 Cognitive Testing of mBN

9.1 Participants

In order to implement the cognitive testing we selected a sample of six users from the School for the Blind "Santa Lucía" of Santiago, Chile, ages 19 to 28. Four people in the sample had residual vision and two of them had total blindness.

9.2 Methodology

Four cognitive tasks to evaluate the interaction with the software were developed. All of them pursued the use of tempo-spatial, cognitive, psychomotor, and specific orientation and mobility skills to allow people with visual disabilities secure and independent displacements through different places of interest, improving their autonomy when riding the subway transportation and mobilizing through its surrounding area. In the first task, we used scaled representations of the city. For the rest of the tasks, we used mBN software:

a. *Task 1, Let's get to know the city through the Metro:* The goal was to mentally represent the surroundings of the subway network, stimulating senso-perceptive organs, exercising the analysis of the information given and recognizing the four cardinal points along with associating them to reference points.

b. *Task 2, Let's travel to a known place:* The objective was to support secure autonomous movement towards a point of interest close to the subway network, to use the information given by mBN, in order to arrive at the destination place and select relevant information.

c. *Task 3, I want to know new places:* The idea behind it was to analyze the information given, in order to, afterwards, select what is relevant, apply the contents embedded in the software, and discriminate the information for an efficient path.

d. *Task 4, What do I do if I have a problem?:* The objective was to use tempo-spatial references given by the software, achieve autonomy and efficiency when mobilizing through the subway network in Santiago to arrive at a point of interest to and react positively towards unexpected problems.

Two special education teachers with experience with people with visual disabilities participated in the cognitive testing along with users. There were three stages in the implementation of the cognitive study:

1. The application of a pre-test to evaluate skills, competences, and initial behaviors.
2. The implementation of cognitive tasks.
3. A post-test to evaluate skills, competences, and behaviors at the end of the study to contrast them with initial results in order to determine the impact of the use of mBN on users.

9.3 Instruments

Three evaluation tests were applied during the process:

1. Pre-test and post-testing including 43 statements to be answered by end-users and special education teachers. The section for end-users was completed with statements related to behaviors in the subway and when using mBN. The section for the teacher consisted of three domains: skills, competences, and social and personal aspects.
2. A test for the first cognitive task, consisting in 25 statements divided in psychomotor, cognitive and social/affective areas. The motor area was related to the manipulation of the concrete materials used. The cognitive area was related to the use of concrete material (recognition of lines, main streets, transfer stations, etc.). Finally, the social/affective area was related to behaviors and attitudes during the implementation of the activity.
3. Tests for cognitive tasks 2, 3, and 4. The statements included behaviors observed in the subway and the use of mBN software. These statements considered behaviors, skills, and social and personal competences.

9.4 Procedure

Depending on the type of activity, two places were used for cognitive testing. The first one was the computer laboratory where we developed cognitive task 1 and users interacted with the software for the rest of the activities. The second place used was the real subway network along with the surrounding area of one station. The testing was developed during two months with two-hour sessions per week.

9.5 Results

One of the variables evaluated was the behavior of users in the subway, meaning the handling with different elements such as the ticket offices and turnstiles. We have observed that there was a significant gain between pre-test and post-test results in the evaluation of the interaction with these elements, with a gain of six points in average over a total of 30 points (see Fig. 7). Users also evaluated themselves in the control of activities and their behavior when using different areas of the subway.

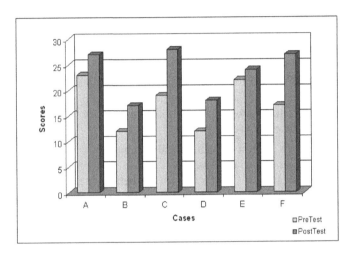

Fig. 7. Pre-test/post-test user's behavior in the subway network

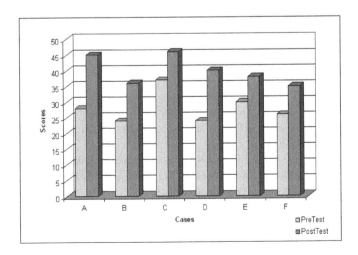

Fig. 8. Pre-test/post-test skills

Users achieved independent mobilization. There also was an improvement in areas such as processing of sensory-perceptual information, observation of their surroundings, classification of auditory information, and obtaining information from mBN software embedded in the pocketPC (see Fig. 8).

In relation to competences, users showed considerable improvements in areas such as spatial orientation, time orientation, verbal interaction, autonomy, choose a route, and achievement of a travel through a planned route. At a smaller scale, there was also improvement in problem solving (see Fig. 9).

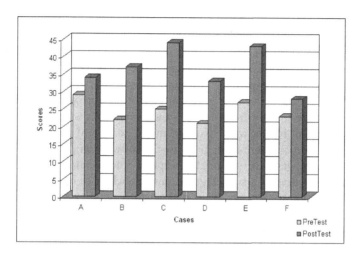

Fig. 9. Pre-test/post-test competences

In social and personal aspects, there was a consensus in the increase in trust and security of users when facing the subway network, evidencing gains when using mBN. When a user dominated a function, the security and trust also increased when facing this type of transportation. Additional information provided by the software related to the ticket cost and estimated time of the travel was very useful because they did not manage these terms correctly.

10 Discussion

At a conceptual level, the glossary embedded in the software allowed users to familiarize with basic concepts about the subway as a transportation source. The most important concepts such as transfer stations, platforms, end stations, consecutive stations, and lines, were reinforced by the affordance created by interacting with travel simulations.

The desktop application was more useful for blind users in a pre-cane stage. At the beginning, users did not have the autonomy to move throughout the subway network. However, after they interacted with the application they were able to understand the subway network as a transportation source in the three levels of knowledge implemented without the need of a guide. Teachers also valued the application as an aid to apply, reinforce, and complement their lessons.

The variation in the mastering of behaviors by the user obtained the lower indicators because learners needed to understand certain prerequisites related to this type of transportation and know how to apply them. Among these concepts, there were behaviors such as using the stairs to have access to the stations, the ability to move inside the stations, identify ticket offices, turnstiles, platforms, recognition of textures, and staying in a safe place when getting in and out of the subway wagon. These behaviors did not vary significantly because they are pre-requisites for independent movements. However, there was an improvement in the learning of the names of the stations, their sequence, and their relation to a corresponding line.

The execution of some actions needed certain skills such as spatial orientation, observation of the surroundings, and classification of auditory information. These aspects increased significantly after using the software and performing the cognitive tasks. Users were able to construct a mental idea of the spatial distribution closer to reality and were able to mobilize in a secure and autonomous way.

The most relevant results were observed in the domain of competences of users, explained by the use of information given by the software and its immediate transfer to reality, favoring gains in sensorial-perception information processing, problem solving without the need of a sighted guide, and a much more independent movement in and out of the subway network. This, undoubtedly, represents a contribution to the development of blind users and one-step towards real social integration.

mBN software helped users to travel through the subway network and access to nearby places and streets. However, we need to find out more information about the mobilization inside the stations, because it is difficult to identify exits, line changes, access, and the like. In this sense, the help provided by the software should be improved by using our data. In spite of this, there were improvements in the independent mobilization of users and their orientation skills, providing them more security when using the subway.

The use of mBN allows the displacement of users because it provides specific information to guide them during their travel. Because it is a new device, there were some dificulties at the very beginning, but users slowly began to adjust ways of using it. They found solutions such as using it from their pockets, using an earphone in order to avoid losing the auditory reference in their surroundings, and choosing a safe and comfortable place to handle them.

The testing showed satisfactory results when using different elements around the subway transportation, and thus assuring a better performance of end-users in a given station, and in the use of turnstiles, platforms, wagons, and ticket offices.

Finally, it was very relevant that users achieved independence and autonomy in management and displacement throughout the subway network. This evidenced that the software displayed in a mobile device, as the pocketPC, provided them certain keys and helped to improve independent ways of moving in the subway network, emerging new ideas such as the possibility to extend this tool to other transportation systems.

Acknowledgments. This report was funded by the Chilean National Fund of Science and Technology, Fondecyt, Project 1030158.

References

1. Brewster, S., Raty, V., Kortekangas, A.: Using Earcons to Provide Navigation Cues in Telephone-Based Interfaces, ACM Interactions, 1996, pp 9-10.
2. Brewster, S., Capriotti, A., Hall, C.: Using Compound Earcons to Represent Hierarchies, Publishing in BCS HCI'97 Conference Companion HCI Letters, 1997, pp 19-22.
3. Brewster, S.: Using Earcons to Provide Navigation Cues in Telephone-Based Interfaces, ACM Interactions 6, 1999, pp 9-10.
4. Dowling, J., Boles, W.: Mobility assessment using simulated Artificial Human Vision. 2005 IEEE Computer Society Conference on Computer Vision and Pattern Recognition, CVPR'05 - Workshops p.32
5. Gaudissart, V., Ferreira, S., Mancas-Thillou, C., Gosselin, B.: Sypole: a Mobile Assistant for the Blind, Proceedings of European Signal Processing Conference, EUSIPCO 2005, Antalya (Turkey).
6. Koruda, T., Sasaki, H., Tateishi, T., Maeda, K., Yasumuro, Y., Manabe, Y. & Chihara, K.: Walking aids based on wearable/ubiquitous computing – aiming at pedestrian's intelligent transport systems. Proceedings of the IV International Conference Disability, Virtual Reality & Associated Technologies, 2002 ICDVRAT 2002. Veszprém, Hungary, pp 117-122.
7. Lahav, O., Mioduser, D.: Multisensory virtual environment for supporting blind persons' acquisition of spatial cognitive mapping, orientation, and mobility skills. In Proceedings of the 4th International Conference on Disability, Virtual Reality and Associated Technologies, ICDVRAT 2002, Veszprém, Hungary, 2002. pp. 213-220.
8. Lahav, O., Mioduser, D.: Blind Persons' Acquisition of Spatial Cognitive Mapping and Orientation Skills Supported by Virtual Environment. In Proceedings of the 5th International Conference on Disability, Virtual Reality and Associated Technologies, ICDVRAT 2004, Oxford, UK, 2004. pp. 131-138.
9. Mereu, S., Kazman, R.: Audio enhanced 3D interfaces for visually impaired users. In Proceedings of CHI'96, ACM Press.
10. Sánchez, J.: Interactive Environments for Blind Children: Computing, Usability, and Cognition. Proceedings of the International Conference on New Technologies in Science Education (I), Aveiro, Portugal, 4-6 July, 2001. pp. 17-27.
11. Sánchez, J., Zuñiga, M.: Evaluating the Interaction of Blind Learners with Audio-Based Virtual Environments. 11th Annual CyberTherapy 2006 Conference: Virtual Healing: Designing Reality. June 13 - 15, 2006 . Gatineau, Canada, pp. 66
12. Sánchez, J.: Blind Children Centered Technology. Human Centered Technology Workshop 2006. Pori , Finland , June 11-13, 2006, pp. 104-112
13. Sánchez, J., Sáenz, M.: 3D Sound Interactive Environments for Problem Solving. Proceedings of The Seventh International ACM SIGACCESS Conference on Computers and Accessibility, Assets 2005, Baltimore, Maryland, USA, October 9-12, pp. 173-178
14. Sánchez, J., Sáenz, M.: Sound Immersed Virtual Environments for Blind Children. Proceedings of The Fourth International Workshop on Virtual Rehabilitation IWVR '05. Catalina Island, California, USA. September 19-21, 2005, pp. 192-202

15. Sánchez, J., Flores, H.: Training Blind Children to Develop Mathematics Skills Through Audio. Proceedings of the Cybertherapy 2005, Basel, Switzerland, June 6-10, 2005, pp. 123-124

16. Sánchez, J., Sáenz, M.: Developing Mathematics Skills through Audio Interfaces. Proceedings of 11 th International Conference on Human-Computer Interaction, HCI 2005. Las Vegas , Nevada , USA , July 22-27, 2005 .

17. Sánchez, J., Sáenz, M.: Three-Dimensional Virtual Environments for Blind Children. CyberPsychology and Behavior, CP&B, Apr 2006, Vol. 9, No. 2, pp. 200-206.

18. Sánchez, J., Baloian, N., Flores H.: A methodology for developing audio-based interactive environments for learners with visual disabilities. Proceedings of the World Conference on Educational Multimedia, Hypermedia & Telecommunications ED-MEDIA 2004, Lugano, Switzerland , (June 21-26, 2004), pp. 124

19. Van Caenegem, F., Bernard, P.: Métro, The ultimate public transport guide for your PDA or Smartphone. http://nanika.net/Metro

An Accessible Multimodal Pong Game Space

Anthony Savidis[1], Apostolos Stamou[1], and Constantine Stephanidis[1,2]

[1] Foundation for Research and Technology – Hellas (FORTH)
Institute of Computer Science
GR-70013, Heraklion, Crete, Greece
{as,stamou,cs}@ics.forth.gr
[2] University of Crete, Department of Computer Science, Greece

Abstract. *King Pong* is an accessible remake of the classic Pong game, supporting a spatially localized audio environment and force feedback (transforming sound into haptic feedback). It may be played either by one player and the computer as opponent, or by two players. In the two-player mode, the opponents can share the same computer, or alternatively play the game over the network. King Pong also supports recording (logging) and playback of game play activities with time stamps for off-line analysis and evaluation. The game is fully configurable, regarding the auditory grid, the behavior of the force feedback, the graphical appearance and various sound effects. Moreover, different levels of difficulty are supported, affecting speed and the game arena (i.e., circular top-bottom sides). This paper reports the design methodology regarding the spatial auditory grid, as well as the use of force feedback, and discusses issues related to the game-play itself, such as the simulation of an artificial opponent.

Keywords: Universally accessible games, Non-visual interaction, Auditory displays, Spatially localized audio, Force feedback.

1 Introduction

Today, there are about 180 million people worldwide who have a visual impairment, and it is estimated that 40 to 45 million of them are blind (World Health Organization, 2001). Additionally, ageing is another factor that further aggravates the above numbers in the sense that it adversely affects vision. As recent surveys showed, the worldwide population is ageing, making a greater number of people unable to play mainstream computer games. Today, the game industry is investing on 3D games, with content conveyed entirely through 3D inaccessible artwork. The audio part of these games is auxiliary, aiming to better set-up the overall game atmosphere, and this is not expected to change in the near future.

In the context of the above, this paper discusses the development of an accessible pong game space, named King Pong, targeted to blind and visually-impaired people. Additionally, the departure from the typical desk-top set-up of a computer game towards media-rich game spaces is emphasized, introducing and experimenting with the methods of view fusion, i.e., combining and synchronizing auditory grids with graphical projected displays. Therefore, apart from being originally designed to

C. Stephanidis and M. Pieper (Eds.): ERCIM UI4ALL Ws 2006, LNCS 4397, pp. 405–418, 2007.

accommodate accessibility requirements, the King Pong game is also enjoyable by sighted users as well.

A pong game was chosen because it is very simple to play, with rules and mechanics mostly obvious to anyone. Additionally, the pong game is based on spatially-oriented attention within an inherently simple game scene, enabling to investigate augmented auditory representations.

2   Related Work

Currently, there is a significant trend towards employing games for training and learning, known as game-based learning [6], in order to take advantage of the unparalleled motivation and engagement that computer games can offer to learners of all ages. University departments are gradually introducing computer games in their curricula to support alternative learning styles, attract student interest and help reinforcing learning objectives [4]. Games are also promoted as policy education, exploration, and management tools (e.g., the Serious Games Initiative).

Unfortunately, computer games are usually quite demanding in terms of motor, sensor and mental skills needed for interaction control, and they often require mastering inflexible and quite complicated input devices and techniques. These facts often render games inaccessible to a large percentage of people with physical or situational [7] disabilities. So far, little attention has been paid to the development of computer games that can be played by all players, independently of their personal characteristics, requirements, or (dis)abilities. Furthermore, as long as it concerns human-computer interaction issues, computer games have fundamental differences from all the other types of software applications for which accessibility guidelines and solutions are already becoming widely available.

In contrast to Web accessibility, up to now, relatively few efforts have been devoted to game accessibility. Currently, there are no related official guidelines or standards, nor any world-wide initiatives comparable to W3C-WAI in the domain of game accessibility, as well as no related governmental or legislative actions. Game accessibility is mainly a concern of organised groups of disabled people (e.g., the Audyssey on-line gaming magazine[1] and AudioGames.net[2] for the blind, DeafGamers[3] for the deaf), or of companies producing related products (e.g., GamesForTheBlind.com[4] and BSC GAMES[5] for the blind, Arcess[6] and Brillsoft[7] for the motor-impaired). Public awareness is generally quite low and limited to a handful of Web articles (e.g., [1], [2], [3], [5]). In September 2005, the "Big Toe"[8] show of BBC7 broadcasted a short radio piece on accessible gaming, while, in the context of the 3rd International Conference on Universal Access in Human-Computer

---

[1] http://www.angelfire.com/music4/duffstuff/audyssey.html
[2] http://audiogames.net
[3] http://www.deafgamers.com
[4] http://gamesfortheblind.com
[5] http://www.bscgames.com
[6] http://arcess.com
[7] http://www.brillsoft.com
[8] http://www.bbc.co.uk/bbc7/bigtoe

Interaction[9] a session entitled "When Computer Games Meet Universal Access" was dedicated to the development of accessible games. Also, in 2005, the Retro Remakes web site[10] hosted a single-switch game programming competition, where the submitted games had to be playable through a single keyboard key, and thus could potentially be accessible to people with motor impairments.

Currently, the most prominent organized international effort related to game accessibility is the *Game Accessibility Special Interest Group*[11] of the prestigious International Game Developers Association (IGDA). The Game Accessibility SIG was formed in 2003 with the aim *"to develop methods of making all game genres universally accessible to all, regardless of disability"*. Another, more recent effort is the Accessible Game Developers (AGDev) Wiki[12], which aims to set up a community of developers in order to advance the state of accessible gaming.

3 Game Design

3.1 Game Play

Regarding game play, King Pong resembles the classic Pong game, simulating table tennis (ping pong) through a small ball which travels across the screen. Additionally, there are two paddles which are controlled by one player each. The players control their respective paddle, only in the vertical direction, using a keyboard or joystick. When the ball hits the borders of the playing field or one of the paddles, it bounces, and its vector velocity changes according to the angle of the impact. In contrast, if one player's paddle misses the ball, the other player scores a point. In addition to that, King Pong offers another variation of the classic pong game, the circular pong. In fact, circular pong has just one main difference with the classic one, which is the shape of the game field. Circular pong has a circular, rather than rectangular, game field, and paddles move in a circle around the game field. Except that, players can not rely on the borders to keep the ball in play. It is beyond doubt that circular pong has far greater difficulty level in comparison to classic pong and is mainly aimed at advanced players.

King Pong can be played either by a single player against a computerized opponent or by two players, each controlling a paddle. The two–player game can be played not only by sharing the same computer, but also over network.

3.2 Game Media Space

3.2.1 Dual Game Space

The design of the game was targeted to delivering an enhanced game-play experience for both blind and sighted users, primarily emphasizing accessibility and interaction quality. In this context, it was decided to design a dual game space, providing a concurrent visual (graphical) and non-visual (auditory) realization. To this end,

---

[9] http://www.hci-international.org
[10] http://www.retroremakes.com
[11] http://www.igda.org/accessibility
[12] http://www.agdev.org

following initial scenario-based conversations with blind users, it quickly came out that they were very much attracted by the idea of an auditory media space, providing spatially-localized audio, in comparison to the use of typical head-phones simulating 3D audio. Initial experiments were carried out with the use of typical 3D head-phones, but the results were less satisfactory than expected. Therefore, a multimodal game space was designed, comprising an auditory grid, on top of which the graphical game arena was to be projected in real-time. The design was based on the active synchronization of the auditory display with the graphical display. Clearly, this offers far more than multiple views, as it reflects a type of *view fusion* where the two alternative views are concurrently combined to provide an enriched display experience; naturally, this additional benefit concerns only sighted users, for which the graphical display seems to have localized auditory capabilities. Initially, the potential topology of the spatial augmented displayed was investigated, leading to three alternative concept sketches, as shown in Fig. 1.

From the three alternatives, it was decided to start working on the "planar" prototype, mainly because it has been considered as easier to construct so as to quickly initiate the experiments; it is assumed that the results may be transferred to the other two alternatives in a straightforward manner, if those are to be eventually implemented.

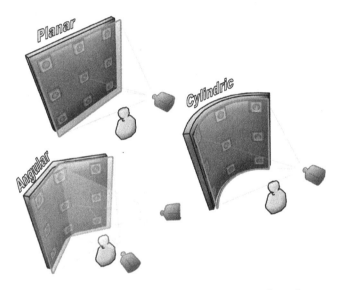

Fig. 1. Early concept sketches of three alternative media space configurations, supporting *view fusion*, combining an auditory grid with graphical projection

3.2.2 Emphasizing Cross-Modal Equivalence

The goal of this work is to design and evaluate multimodal navigation tools for the Pong game, enabling children who face severe visual impairments to interact with it. To achieve this objective, a 3D audio environment and haptic devices are used. Although, ideally, disabled people should be able to experience the information as fluently as able-bodied people, it is beyond dispute that this is not entirely possible. Despite that, disabled people should be able to interact with the application without encountering obstacles and difficulties. In this context, alternative methods to present information (concerning the position and the velocity of the ball, the position of paddles, etc.) for visually impaired players were investigated. For this purpose, the auditory and haptic modalities have been effectively combined and collaborate in such a way as to provide the players with a clear overview of the game space.

3.3 Auditory Space

3.3.1 Planar Auditory Grid

In order to provide auditory navigational aids to players, an auditory planar media space structure is being constructed, approximately 2W x 1.5H meters, supporting spatially localized audio. The laboratory prototype version currently consists of a lattice of nine (9) loudspeakers, as a 3x3 grid, with distinct loudspeakers; the input devices for non-visual interaction, in particular a vibrating joystick and the Phantom™ force-feedback (see Fig. 2).

The eventual auditory display will encompass twenty four (24) auditory cells, arranged in four (4) rows, six (6) cells each, with a loudspeaker per cell, thus resulting in an auditory media space with twenty four independent channels. The idea is that

Fig. 2. The current auditory grid (3x3), as it has been prototypically set-up for the King Pong media-space game; a flexible special-purpose construction is underway to encompass the loudspeaker grid (supporting 6x4)

every distinct game object occupies at any point in time at least one primary auditory cell, associated with a distinct dynamic sound. The choice of the sound sample used to represent the pong ball is personalized, since it is to be heard continuously, requiring the user to concentrate on it to so as to effectively track the current ball position. Additionally, when the ball bounces on the terrain borders (top and bottom) a "wooden" sound is reproduced at the hit location, while, similarly, if the ball hits any of the two paddles, a "metallic" sound is reproduced.

When the paddle reaches the upper or lower borders of the game area, a "collision" sound is reproduced to indicate that the paddle cannot move further in the same direction. All such sounds are configurable via a configuration file according to individual user preferences.

3.3.2 Auditory Feedback Method

The default behavior is to activate two (2) loudspeakers, each one with a different volume, to indicate the ball position, following the technique illustrated in Fig. 3. More specifically, according to the current ball position, the *primary region* is calculated as the one in which the ball entirely resides. Apart from the primary region, secondary regions are identified according to the intersection of the ball direction vector with the neighbor cells (see Fig. 3). In this context, three *secondary regions* are distinguished: (a) $R(+1)$ is the one with which the direction vector intersects more; (b) $R(-1)$ is the cell not overlapping with the direction vector; and (c) $R(0)$ is the cell intersecting less than $R(+1)$. Notably, the $R(+1)$ cell is expected to become the next primary region after the particular current one. The characterization of regions is adopted to identify the type of dynamic auditory feedback for the auditory cells close to the ball. In the default style, only the loudspeakers for the *primary region* and the $R(+1)$ are activated, with relative volumes defined in a configuration files (e.g., the primary region may have twice the volume of the secondary region).

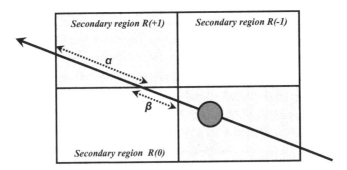

Fig. 3. Identifying the primary and the three secondary regions for auditory feedback according to the current ball position and the direction vector

Theoretically, this method suffers from two problems: firstly, it is possible that two secondary $R(+1)$ regions are identified (i.e., equivalent intersection lines with two cells); secondly, the primary region may not be uniquely identifiable, as the ball may overlap concurrently with multiple cells. The latter scenario is observed only when the intersection line is smaller than a T threshold (close to the diameter of the ball). To overcome such ambiguities, the following rules have been introduced:

- If there are two candidates $R(+1)$ regions, then, if the ball is moving upwards, choose the top $R(+1)$ cell, else choose the bottom $R(+1)$ region;
- The next primary region is always set to be the current $R(+1)$ region, only if its intersection line is above the T threshold; else, the primary region remains unchanged.
- The ball diameter is bounded in a way that T (*diameter* + ε) is always less than the width and height of the auditory cells.

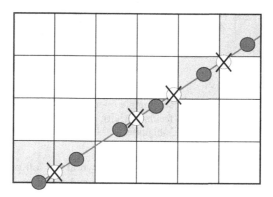

Fig. 4. An example showing the active primary auditory regions for the ball positions and the ignored primary positions (with an "x") when intersection lines are below T; intuitively, the resulting auditory path better traces the ball in comparison to activating all primary regions

An example where the above rules are applied is shown in Fig. 4. For all types of regions, the audio feedback and the volume is fully configurable, supporting the selection among alternatives with varying patterns regarding frequency, pitch and duration. Additionally, the presence of feedback for $R(0)$ and $R(-1)$ regions is optional (it may be enabled or disabled).

Even when the previous rules are applied, there are scenarios in which the resulting sampled-path over the auditory grid is awkward in comparison to the real ball movement. In any case, this is inherent in the fact that the auditory grid resembles in resolution a 4Hx6W raster display. Actually, when initially studying the feedback method, the visual raster display was considered as a proper analogy, and a typical line scanning algorithm was adopted for the auditory rasterization of the ball path. However, it quickly became evident that the auditory grid is fundamentally different from a raster display, since, on the one hand, there is a moving ball with real dimensions that identifies the overlapping and crossings, while, on the other hand, neighbor cells may have to contribute to the temporal auditory feedback, so that a larger part of the path than a single cell can be provided at any point in time.

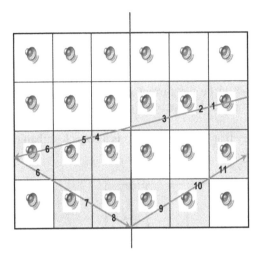 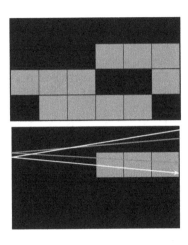

Fig. 5. The crossed primary regions on an example round of the ball, indicating: (a) the issue of low auditory resolution with localized feedback (left); and (b) the need for paddle size above the auditory resolution (right) to avoid ambiguities

An example of primary auditory regions is shown at the left part of Fig. 5. Due to the fact that the resolution of the display is reduced to an auditory grid element, apparently the most accurate information that the blind user may be given regarding the ball position is at the auditory region area. Consequently, the height of the paddle (moving vertically) should not be less that the height of auditory cells, else the blind user will have no way to perceive if the ball is going to hit the paddle or not within a single target auditory cell. For instance, as shown at the right side of Fig. 5, although there are two distinct ball paths targeting to the same auditory cell, with a paddle of height less than the height of the cell, it is possible that the ball hits at different points of a single cell, not covered by the paddle. Hence, even if the blind user correctly positions the paddle within the target cell, the ball may still be missed. For this reason, the paddle height for the blind user equals the cell height. Clearly, for the sighted user the same does not hold, meaning that there are two paddles of different size when a sighted and a blind user play together.

3.3.3 Enhanced Directional Auditory Feedback

In pong games, the performance of the player is related to the ability of dynamically projecting and predicting the ball position, so that the paddle can be positioned accordingly. Typically, a player will follow the movement of the ball, repositioning the paddle continuously as the target hit spot is predicted. In this game-play style, it is inevitable that the direction of the ball is easily perceived by players at any point in time. However, although this is obvious in a graphical display context, in a temporal auditory representation it is hard to conceive the particular direction vector of the ball. To enable blind users effectively project the direction vector, the concurrent auditory feedback of the *current target* position was introduced, i.e., the auditory cell at the sides of the terrain where the ball is going to hit next (see Fig. 6).

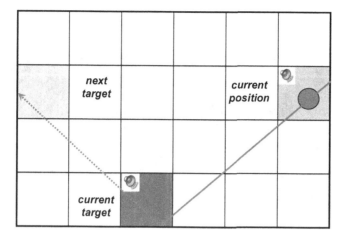

Fig. 6. Supporting auditory directional feedback through configurable target position indication; once the current target is reached, the feedback for the next target is immediately activated

In this method, there are always two independent audio sources (active cells) over the auditory grid, through which the direction vector can be identified. In practice, this required blind users to be trained and play for a small period of time with the game, so that they can become familiar with this method. However, once they managed to interpret this type of feedback, they became capable of quickly identifying the target cell, enabling them to react more precisely in repositioning the paddle.

3.3.4 Circular Terrain

This set-up concerns the top and bottom sides of the grid that are considered as "folded". Hence, once the ball hits the top side, it automatically emerges from the bottom side and vice versa. This scenario requires that blind players are more familiar with the game, since the ball-path is "broken" as the ball is instantly displaced every time the sides of the terrain are crossed. Additionally, the feedback for the *current* target, as previously discussed, is only activated once the ball passes the opposite side of the terrain. Other than that, terrain circularity did not require any particular modifications or adjustments of the auditory feedback methods previously discussed.

3.4 The Graphical Interface

The graphical User Interface is a typical Pong style dynamic visualization, supporting configurability of all game-related bitmaps, such as paddle, background, score digits, ball, terrain split and direction indicators. Additionally, the split into auditory cells may be displayed, serving mainly evaluation and configuration purposes. The game scenery has been designed for projection on a large display, over the auditory grid, rather than to be played in front of a computer screen.

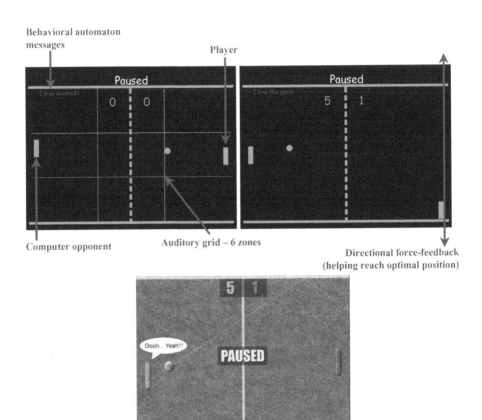

Fig. 7. Snapshots of the graphical interface (top: "retro" profile, bottom: "golf" profile), with some explanatory annotations; bitmaps regarding user / computer paddle, ball, scene boundaries and background, are configurable

This decision is aligned with the objective of delivering view fusion, where the visual display is augmented with localized audio. In this sense, some textual messages, such as those displayed by an automated computer opponent (a behavioral automaton actually), are displayed in small sized fonts (see Fig. 7), more appropriate for large projected display areas.

3.5 Directional Force-Feedback

The prototype versions employ a vibration feedback controller, the Logitech RumblePad™ 2. Through this device, continuous hints are provided to the blind user regarding the correct positioning of the paddle. Since in the auditory grid the height is four cells, the paddle is allowed to perform discrete movements in a column of four cells (see left part of Fig. 8). Hence, at any point in time, the maximum distance between the current paddle position and the target required position so that the ball can be hit is three (3). Consequently, three discrete levels of increasing force feedback were identified, which are applied to indicate the distance of the paddle form the correct position (if the paddle is not eventually positioned at the target, the player will miss the ball, resulting in losing the current game session). At any position of the paddle, the force applied is shown in Fig. 8, depending on the relative distance of the cell with the correct paddle position. Once the user positions the ball correctly and hits the ball, and while the ball travels to the opposite side of the terrain, force feedback is disabled. Hence, during this small period of time, the blind user may move the paddle, not being supported by force-feedback as to where the paddle should be positioned. This feature may be configured so that force feedback is constant for novice gamers, even when the ball has left the blind-user terrain side.

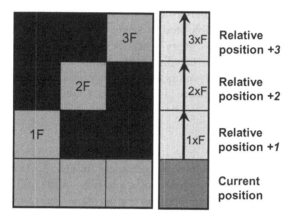

Fig. 8. Applying discrete directional forces at three levels to indicate where the direction and offset that the paddle has to move to reach the correct target position

4   Additional Features

4.1   Recording and Playback

An essential part in the development cycle of an accessible game is the evaluation process. To this end, King Pong supports recording and playback of game play, in the form of interaction events with relative time stamps, so as to facilitate rehearsal and evaluation. This way, any recorded game session can be precisely reproduced so as to detect potential problematic issues. Notably, video recording is not adequate for the evaluation of the adopted *view fusion* method, since in many cases it was necessary to sit in front of the auditory grid, while an interaction session was being played-back, to realize exactly the way the auditory feedback was delivered to the blind-user. This type of inspection is also not possible with real-life monitoring, since the type of auditory feedback received by the blind-user is significantly different than that received by an inspector sitting at a position different than that of the end-user.

4.2 Intelligent Opponent

In the Pong game, the player may normally compete with the system in a single-play mode. In this context, a trivial solution is to make the computer-opponent unbeatable, since the optimal positioning of the paddle is trivially computed and applied. To overcome this difficulty, features of artificial behavior were added to the computer opponent, so as to make the simulation of the second player more realistic, since the opponent may loose, making the single-player mode more appealing. To this purpose, the computerized opponent may have one of the following moods: enthusiastic, bored, tired or angry. A behavioral state machine controls the transition from one state to another. The initial state is "enthusiastic" and is altered according to game progress. For instance, the opponent is "enthusiastic" if the score of both players is very close, gets "bored" if it has a considerable lead in score, or becomes "tired" when a game session takes a long time, or gets "angry" once the human player has a considerable lead in score. The state affects the handling of the computer paddle. For example, in an "angry" state, the paddle is moved nervously, while in a "tired" state, the paddle performs relatively slow movements. The state transitions are indicated through spoken and written messages.

4.3 Two Player Modes

The King Pong game allows for two-player games, as follows: (a) Local competition. The two players share the same computer, sitting in front of the grid (left and right). Both players may use haptic interfaces, as far as there are two force feedback controllers available. (b) Remote competition. In this case, the input from one machine is transmitted to the other over the network. Due to the very low bandwidth and latency requirements, the game state is always identical during time.

4.4 Implementation Details

King Pong has been fully implemented in C++, using Microsoft DirectX technology, the SDL (Simple Direct-media Layer) multimedia library and the BASS audio library. SDL is a low-level cross-platform graphics and input library. It is used for rendering the graphics on the screen and getting data from the input devices supported by the game. BASS is a cross-platform 3D audio library and it is used for implementing the auditory interface. Finally, DirectInput (portion of DirectX) is used for controlling the force-feedback device. Currently, the game can be played only on a computer that runs Microsoft Windows.

Alternatively to multi-channel audio, HRTF-based audio can be used. This is a technique that simulates the presence of a sound-emitting object in any position within the listener's environment and reproduces the simulation on a pair of headphones. The main advantage of this method is that it is more economical compared to the first one (big number of speakers, advanced audio card). On the other hand, HRTF-based audio is less powerful.

5   Evaluation

The game has been evaluated with the involvement of nine (9) blind users. Each user was asked to play the game for 20 to 30 minutes using varying profiles that they considered better to suited to their needs (like auditory feedback details, sound effects, volume, speed of ball, etc.). During this time, the user could pause or start over again the game as many times required. When they finished playing, users were interviewed so as to fill-in an adapted version of the IBM Usability Satisfaction Questionnaires. The evaluation results are summarized in Fig. 9. A small post-evaluation questionnaire was used to collect information on the background of the participants.

The overall scores are considered to be very good, but this may also be attributed to the fact that the game was simple to play. Furthermore, after several conversations with the participants, it came out that the social value of the concept of accessible games created a very positive attitude and increased the motivation of players to play, compete and socially interact. The main complaints reported were related to the speech and sound quality, as well as to the game difficulty when the speed of the ball was increased. This problem could probably been alleviated by conducting user profiling sessions prior to the evaluation process, and then adequately adapting all difficulty-related game parameters.

Participant	ASQ	OVERALL	SYSUSE	INFOQUAL	INTERQUAL
Player 1	2,33	3,00	2,75	3,60	3,00
Player 2	3,00	3,06	3,00	3,40	2,67
Player 3	3,33	3,29	3,25	3,60	3,33
Player 4	2,33	2,53	2,50	2,40	2,67
Player 5	2,33	2,18	2,25	2,00	2,33
Player 6	3,00	2,76	2,88	2,60	2,67
Player 7	1,67	1,59	1,13	1,60	2,67
Player 8	2,00	1,94	1,38	2,00	2,67
Player 9	1,33	1,71	1,13	2,00	2,33
Average	**2,37**	**2,45**	**2,25**	**2,58**	**2,70**

Fig. 9. The results of the subjective usability evaluation of King Pong (The range is from 1 to 7, where 1 is the highest / best possible score)

6   Summary and Conclusions

This paper has reported the design and implementation of an accessible game realizing a media space that supports fused views, in particular a graphical display augmented with spatially localized audio. It is an accessible variation of pong game, which can be also concurrently played by two players either locally or remotely. The game supports directional auditory and haptic feedback to enable blind users better perceive the position of moving targets, such as the pong ball.

It is planned to extend the current version of the game so as to support accessibility by people with severe impairments of upper limbs, through binary switches for input control. Additionally, since the fine tuning of the auditory aspects of the game was proved to be a very demanding process, the incorporation of interactive configuration facilities for therapists is also planned, thus enabling them to fine-tune or alter the auditory parameters dynamically, while the user is actually playing.

Acknowledgements. This work has been partially funded by the European Commission in the context of the MICOLE project (IST-2003-511592 STP) of the Information Society Technologies Program, DG Information Society. The partners in the MICOLE consortium are: University of Tampere (Finland); University of Glasgow (U.K.); University of Metz (France); Uppsala University (Sweden); Lund University (Sweden); Royal Institute of Technology KTH (Sweden); Siauliai University (Lithuania); Institute of Computer Science FORTH (Greece); University of Pierre and Marie Curie (France); France Telecom (France); Reachin Technologies AB (Sweden).

References

1. Bierre, K.: Improving Game Accessibility. Gamasutra (2005). Retrieved 14 October 2005, from: http://www.gamasutra.com/features/20050706/bierre_01.shtml
2. D'Amico, C.: Gaming With A Disability. 3DAction planet (2001). Retrieved 14 September 2004, from: http://www.3dactionplanet.com/features/editorials/disabledgamers/index2.shtml
3. Ellis, B.: Ouch Guide to... Switch Gaming. BBC's Ouch! web site (2005). Retrieved 14 October 2005, from: http://www.bbc.co.uk/ouch/closeup/switchgaming_guideto.shtml
4. Giguette, R.: Pre-Games: Games Designed to Introduce CS1 and CS2 Programming Assignments. ACM SIGCSE, Vol. 35 Issue 1 (2003) 288–292
5. O'Modhrain, S.: Accessible gaming. BBC's Ouch! web site (2004). Retrieved 14 September 2004, from: http://www.bbc.co.uk/ouch/closeup/gaming.shtml
6. Prensky, M.: Digital Game-Based Learning. McGraw-Hill, New York, NY (2000)
7. Sears, A., Lin, M., Jacko, J., Xiao, Y.: When Computers Fade... Pervasive Computing and Situationally-Induced Impairments and Disabilities. In Jacko, J., Stephandis, C. (eds.): Human - Computer Interaction: Theory and Practice, Proceedings of the 10th International Conference on Human-Computer Interaction, Crete, Greece, 22-27 June 2003. Lawrence Erlbaum Associates, Mahwah, New Jersey (2003) 1298-1302

Web Compliance Management: Barrier-Free Websites Just by Simply Pressing the Button? Accessibility and the Use of Content-Management-Systems

Martina Schulz[1] and Michael Pieper[2]

[1] complexx.com GmbH, Reuschenberger Mühle
Alte Garten 60-62, 51371 Leverkusen, Germany
martina@complexx.com
[2] Fraunhofer Institute for Applied Information Technology – FIT
Schloss Birlinghoven, D-53754 Sankt Augustin, Germany
michael.pieper@fit.fraunhofer.de

Abstract. The World Wide Web has become an important instrument of social participation, equal opportunities and self-determination. Especially for disabled people and the elderly, the Internet offers the possibility to take care of their affairs by themselves and to compensate lost mobility to a certain degree. Therefore information on the Internet should be easy to access, easy to use as well as easy to understand. However, disabled people, unpracticed users and the elderly - because of their specific functional limitations and needs - encounter barriers and restrictions in accessing many websites. In order to refresh contents of a website, many software producers have put an effort in developing easy-to-use content-management-systems (CMS) which most recently address the topic of accessibility as well. The central aim of the study presented in this paper was to find out whether certain CMSs in fact do offer a technology which allows for an editor to refresh a barrier-free website without special knowledge in accessibility by simply "pressing the button" of a CMS integrated tool, which claims to automatically offer compliance with standard accessibility guidelines.

1 Design of the Study and Method of Resolution

This paper offers an overview of the results of an extensive questionnaire-based study which has been conducted as part of a Master Thesis at Duisburg-Essen University in 2006 [1].

The paper starts with a description of the term barrier-free, defining the understanding of this term as basis for the whole survey.

In a next step, the paper gives a short overview on CMSs, their function and their relevance for commercial and public use, followed by a synopsis of the results of the questionnaire, presenting which requirements of accessibility can be served automatically, by "simply pressing the button", when using a CMS. The limitations and drawbacks of the examined systems are listed and discussed.

C. Stephanidis and M. Pieper (Eds.): ERCIM UI4ALL Ws 2006, LNCS 4397, pp. 419–426, 2007.
© Springer-Verlag Berlin Heidelberg 2007

Finally, the paper summarizes some ideas concerning how these shortcomings of CMSs might be faced in the future in order reduce them.

2 Barrier-Free Web design

Barrier-free web design is a topic frequently discussed in many groups, forums, essays and surveys. The term barrier-free is subject to a heterogeneous interpretation depending on and changing with the needs of users and the circumstances of use.

2.1 The Internet as Communication and Information Medium

Due to the primarily visual design of the Internet as communication medium, most approaches focus on the problems and barriers that blind people and people with impaired vision face when accessing a website. But people with other types of disabilities, as well as Internet users who, due to their age or other health problems, are disabled or are temporarily disabled face a variety of problems when accessing the web, too.

The different effects of impaired vision, hearing disabilities and dysfunction in movements, as well as the technical equipment used to equalize these disabilities, have been extensively discussed in the literature. Further information on this is presented in the original survey.

The broad collective term of cognitive disorders embraces all kinds of mental disabilities. These are rather undefined within the research so far. The term 'cognitive disorders' includes people with Down Syndrome, people suffering from dyslexia or brain lesions, as well as persons with a poor short-term-memory and spatial sense or with a low intelligence quotient.

Age-related problems account for further disabilities which for seniors most often means suffering from several of the limitations described above. But the elderly population is the one which uses the Internet extensively with new users discovering the possibilities of the Internet every day. This population group is the most economically healthy, and thus seen from an economical perspective it is very interesting for commercial websites and web shops. Marketing experts agree that there is a huge need for meeting the consumer needs of the so-called "Silver-Surfers" by reducing barriers for elderly web users. Apart from physical disabilities, the generation 50+ takes a longer time to get used to the Internet, as this generation has not learned to navigate in complex, non-linear information systems.

A lack of foreign language skills can become a barrier on the Internet, too. People who do not know the English language or do not understand certain Anglicism which are often used in websites of other native languages (e.g., sitemap, about us, submit, faq, etc.) might be excluded from the use of these websites.

2.2 Definition of a Barrier-Free Website

Legal guidelines, as for example the BITV in Germany, often do not find acceptance as general policy for defining useful accessibility with experts and the associations of handicapped people, since they are regarded as insufficient or limited in many cases. Hence, the question arises of which guidelines can give a better orientation in order to ensure that a website is barrier-free for as many people as possible. Here alternative test procedures and contest conducted by stakeholder groups might be an interesting way to come to terms with accessibility. For example, the BIENE AWARD granted for barrier-free web design.

BIENE is the abbreviation for „Barrierefreies Internet eröffnet neue Einsichten" (barriere-free internet offers new perspectives). Since 2003, the BIENE AWARD is awarded by the *Aktion Mensch* and the *Stiftung Digitale Chancen* to the best barrier-free website on the Internet.

There are quite a few different reasons, why the test procedure of the BIENE AWARD is suitable for defining what barrier-free websites are all about. For once, the project is supported by groups and associations which do not only support people with a certain type of disability. The *Deutsche Behindertenhilfe – Aktion Mensch e.V.* is an organization which cares for social issues in general and which follows the ideal of social justice, the right of self determination and participation of everyone in society. Thus *Aktion Mensch* cares for people with a wide variety of disabilities and works for equal rights for them. The second association behind the BIENE AWARD, the *Stiftung Digitale Chancen,* even goes one step further and defines as the goal of its work is to get people interested in the possibilities that the Internet has to offer and help them to take part and access the World Wide Web, in order to make them find out what prospects the digital world keeps for them. In result the BIENE AWARD is based on a broad definition of its target groups and an idea of accessibility which goes with this definition. On the other hand, the BIENE AWARD involves disabled people for the testing of the websites in the contest – this validation conducted by experts is considered as the best way to get relevant results for accessibility testing.

In order to extract the definition of barrier-free webdesign as implied in the methodology and underlying rationale of the BIENE AWARD, all the questions and testing instructions of the contest have been evaluated in an extensive analysis.

Many of the testing instructions deal with questions concerning a better digest of the presented information and granting a better understanding of the contents. Aspects which affect people with certain disabilities are to be tested only by people who suffer from such disability.

Overall it can be stated that the BIENE AWARD not only concretizes the legal guidelines of the German BITV, but aims to grant a barrier-free access to a broader group of users. The testing of the BIENE AWARD does not concentrate on accessibility for people using technical equipment in order to use the web, but in addition strives to facilitate an intellectual access to the presented information. This is done by defining certain criteria for navigation, structure as well as design and depiction of contents.

According to these criteria, accessibility means more than just a barrier-free and valid source code, which matches the technical requirements of the WCAG and guidelines of the BITV. Following the idea of the BIENE AWARD, accessibility starts with the concept of the website and embraces the depiction and structure of contents as well. Accessibility does not only mean to optimize a website for disabled persons using technical equipment to access the web, but to grant an intellectual access to information for people with cognitive and educational problems as well as inexpert users.

3   Content-Management-Systems

Despite the fact that the Internet is the youngest medium to transmit and distribute information, it has grown faster than all other new media and has become one of the most popular sources for information around the world. Since the number of websites and consequently the number of linked HTML-documents on the World Wide Web increase constantly, and as eBusiness becomes a necessity for success in business in general, enterprises are forced to manage their activities on the web in a professional way.

There is no standardized official definition of CMS and even the software producers have different answers to the question what web content management is.

One way to explain the concept is to derive the meaning by looking at the different terms. Content means all the information published on a website, e.g., text, pictures, graphics or data like videos, sounds etc.

The term management points out the fact that there is a process involved. A CMS plans, manages and controls the collection, production and administration of information until it is published on the web. Information is transferred in a workflow within the CMS on which the process of publication is based upon – thus a CMS can be described as a tool to gather, produce, process, manage and publish information and content on the World Wide Web.

The main advantage of CMSs derives from the separation of content, structure and layout. Contents are produced independently from their presentation by the author and are provided with information concerning the structure (headline, picture, plain text) through pre-built patterns of structure. Thus the author does not necessarily know HTML, since the system automatically transforms the content into the designated presentation. The information on the presentation and design on the website is predefined in patterns. These so-called templates define the structure and the presentation of contents on the website and they contain certain static elements which are used frequently (header, footer, navigation and for example free variable parameters for dynamic contents). A template represents the framework of a website. The CMS transfers the content into the templates, processes various sites and links these automatically to a consistent website.

3.1   The Use of CMS and Its Economical Relevance

For enterprises, the World Wide Web offers an instrument to address a broad target group beyond regional or national borders. Even small business units have the chance to compete with large enterprises through virtual size and global presence. Flexibility and customer orientation gain an enormous significance in the digital age. The quantity and most of all the quality of information, as well as its up-to-dateness and customized focus on the target group, become the decisive criteria for business and enterprises in times of digital communication. In view of the dramatically increasing amounts of information and its shortening life-cycle (caused for example by shortening life-cycles of products), an effective management of information and content without a CMS will not be possible.

Surveys show that the market for web-content-management-systems, which in 2003 obtained a turnover of 100 millions US-Dollar, will grow up to 10% each year. According to analysts, the external as well as the internal web presence (intranet) is a must which most enterprises calculate for in their economical plans. If there is no effective management of the website, the business might suffer from negative effects. On the one hand, there is the threat that the corporate message does not reach the costumer in a substantial way which results in decreasing turnover. Additionally, there is the need for more manpower in order to administer the website, which means increasing operating costs and higher economical risk.

As a result, it can be concluded that parallel to the increasing impact of information as a resource for economical success, the importance of CMS will increase as well. The same is true for the distribution of information and communication of the public administration, for which the Internet has become an important medium, too. Projects, as for example the eGovernment initiative BundOnline 2005, by which in 2002 the German Government committed itself to offer about 400 Internet compatible services of the Federal Administration as online services, cannot be handled without the use of professional CMS.

Towards the important objective of developing an information society and building up a modern administration, CMS is a core component.

3.2 Questionnaire for Software Producers

The selection of the CMSs for the conducted survey was based upon the products listed on www.contentmanager.de. All products based upon a licence model offered by commercial software producers that stated in their product description that the CMS is capable of processing barrier-free websites were selected for the survey. In total, there were 37 systems which matched the criteria set for the selection. These criteria can be found in [1].

Setting up an extensive questionnaire, the producers of CMSs were asked how their system ensures that new content is refreshed automatically on the websites and how it manages to refresh these contents in accordance with the guidelines for barrier-free web design. The questions were limited to the process of refreshing contents only, taking for granted that the original website is set up barrier-free in general. After finishing the survey, there were 8 complete questionnaires which can be taken as exemplary for this kind of product.

3.3 Results of the Questionnaire

The survey has shown that in general all the systems analyzed support the editor in refreshing contents according to the rule sets of the guidelines for accessibility. By checking if certain information or elements exist (such as description for pictures or titles for paragraphs) and offering data fields, dialogs and templates the editor has helpful tools at hand, which enable refreshing the website in a barrier-free way.

Under this perspective, all tested CMS offer tools and assistance like automatic checks, workflows and compulsory data fields or restrictions in order to guarantee a valid and barrier-free output of refreshed information. Producing a barrier-free website without knowing HTML and having special knowledge about accessibility while publishing new contents on a website "simply by pressing the button" is possible. The systems manage to transfer the new contents into valid and barrier-free source code.

Furthermore, the systems offer tools which check automatically if the new source code complies with the guidelines of W3V, BITV and other rule sets before publishing the new web contents. Websites with barrier-free source code offer undisturbed access to web contents for users who rely on the usage of technical equipment by publishing additional information in the source code. These might be alternative text for the description of pictures, which can be displayed technically for blind people (e.g., by Braille or a screenreader) or the marking of quotes so that screenreaders read them as a quote, as well as titles for tables and paragraphs which give additional orientation marks for users with impaired visibility using technical devices to overcome these disabilities.

But it is important to realize that by using the checks and tools of the CMS, it can be only controlled whether certain additional information and elements exist, whereas the system cannot control if they are reasonable and helpful for the disabled user. A check regarding the content cannot be done by the CMS. Furthermore, the system only produces warnings for the editor when the source code is not barrier-free and it sets up a task to correct the detected error. Basically, the CMS is only capable of asking for filling in additional data and checking on codes. "Soft" elements such as the reasonable meaning of alternative texts for pictures cannot be controlled and judged by the system. It is able to give out a warning or even to refuse publication if the editor did not fill in an alternative text, but it is not capable of knowing whether the required text does help the user to grasp the meaning of the content or if the text describes the pictures adequately. The compulsory filling in of the mainly used language on a website helps a screenreader to pronounce the text correctly, but if this text is spammed with foreign terms and complicated in structure and grammar, not only the blind person who uses a screenreader faces a problem finding intellectual access to that information. Some systems even offer assistance to give a better intellectual access to contents by splitting up long text paragraphs into smaller with separate headlines – but they cannot check whether the editor has formulated the text in a way that is easy to understand (BITV 14).

Hence all systems in the survey offer technical prerequisites which enable them to publish new contents according to the accessibility guidelines „simply by pressing the button", as long as these guidelines relate to the use of additional information and the correct usage of the markup-language. They are not capable of checking automatically up the "soft" elements of accessibility, not even those of the legal guidelines (BITV 14).

4 Deficiencies of CMSs and Possible Approaches to Produce Barrier-Free Websites Using CMSs

The results of the questionnaire show that the systems are not capable of checking up the so-called "soft" elements of accessibility. Some software producers stated explicitly that only trained and professionally sensitized administrators and editors have the skills to create a barrier-free website.

The survey has shown that CMSs are ready to almost automatically produce websites that can be accessed with technical devices as they are used by many disabled people. A comprehensive barrier-free refreshment of web content which also takes into account the intellectual access to the information, as for example for the needs of seniors and people with cognitive disorders, can only be accomplished by skilled editors. Only trained persons are able to administer the "soft" elements which create a barrier-free website for all types of disabilities – this work cannot be done by the system.

On the edge of the pure technical aspects of accessibility, there is the question of which are the specific skills and knowledge the editor or administrator needs in order to account for fully barrier-free websites. Which are the needed qualifications for web administrators and editors? How can they be sensitized to the problems and needs of disabled people? The following paragraph shows in brief a few ideas about how an approach to comprehensive barrier-free web design, using technical systems like CMSs, might be possible.

4.1 Validation by Experts

One method to validate a barrier-free presentation especially for people with certain disabilities, is to check the website together with „expert"– users who access the web with the same functional limitations as the focused target group. The involvement of such "experts" guarantees a consistent and lasting quality check and helps to collect a helpful pool of "expert-knowledge" which can be shared and used by editors. Working together with "experts" the editor gets to know the needs and requirements of disabled users better, is sensitized to these problems and learns to take these factors into consideration for future work.

4.2 Empathic Modeling

If the involvement of „experts" is not possible, which in practice will often be the case due to the wide variety of possible disabilities, validation by "experts" can be replaced by empathic modelling. The concept of empathic modelling means that the editor tries to put herself in the position of the disabled user, in order to thus serve all requirements of accessibility. This method will be most effective if it is preceded by a close collaboration and exchange of knowledge with disabled users.

4.3 Research for New Communication Concepts

The results and concepts of research might serve the editor as helpful guidelines for daily work. In order to come up with new concepts and guidelines for accessibility, it is necessary to set up multidisciplinary research projects. Web experts, people with disabilities and scientists such as communication experts, psychologists and linguists should work on models and concepts for barrier-free web content.

4.4 Training for Editors and Administrators

The survey has shown that the CMS and the checking tools for accessibility make it compulsory to fill in additional information which is supposed to fulfil the requirements of accessibility and that these systems only warn the editor if the processed source code is not valid to the guidelines. To properly react to these warnings and to be able to produce web content which is easy to understand and easy to access for as many users as possible, the editor need special training. This training is a sine qua non for a successful empathic modeling and should be accompanied by a close collaboration with communication experts and disabled users.

5 Conclusion

The evaluated data of the presented survey have shown that Web Compliance Management [1] is not only a technical topic, but regards communication theory as well, and due to the increasing impact of the Internet and CMS, Web Compliance Management will be of great significance to enterprises and organizations. As a summarizing conclusion, it can be said that barrier-free websites might be processed by technical systems by "simply pressing the button" in theory – in order to create a web presentation that is barrier-free from the perspective of disabled users this "button" has to be pressed by an editor who knows about the specific needs and requirements of disabled people.

Reference

1. Schulz, M. (2006). Web Compliance Management: Barrier-free Websites just by simply pressing the button? - Accessibility and the Use of Content-Management-Systems. Master Thesis (in German). Duisburg-Essen University.

Inclusive Design of Ambient Knowledge Transfer

Chris Stary, Edith Stary, and Stefan Oppl

University of Linz, Freistädterstraße 315, A-4040 Linz
Christian.Stary@jku.at, Stefan.Oppl@jku.at
VS Pantzergasse, AG Individualised Learning, A-1190 Vienna
EdithStary@gmx.at

Abstract. Inclusive Design of knowledge transfer aims to involve different learners and coaches into the transfer process of knowledge in a way that actively supports learning. In this paper we elaborate some benefits for learners and coaches when applying major principles of Maria Montessori along the transfer process of knowledge. Benefits stem from learners' self control and individualised learning experiences. We motivate the immersion of learners into physical and ambient transfer environments, and reveal first insights from testing those ideas. The results of our work should guide further developments of inclusive knowledge-transfer environments.

1 Introduction

Inclusive design (cf. [17]) focuses on cognitive barriers to inclusiveness as well as on Human Factors Engineering [20]. As such, the relationships between user capabilities and product demands in general have become central (see figure 1) for developing User Interfaces for All [49].

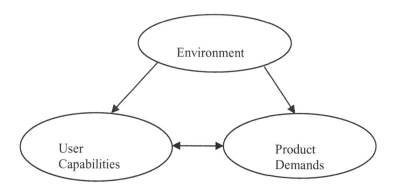

Fig. 1. The relationship between user capabilities and product demands (cf. [20])

When shifting the focus towards knowledge transfer user capabilities become central for learning and the transfer process (see figure 2). Maria Montessori has established one of the most integrative approaches to transfer knowledge addressing learner capabilities explicitly (cf. [25], [26], [27], [28], [29], [30], [31]; [37]; [16];

C. Stephanidis and M. Pieper (Eds.): ERCIM UI4ALL Ws 2006, LNCS 4397, pp. 427–446, 2007.
© Springer-Verlag Berlin Heidelberg 2007

[22]). Her credo can be mapped to the conveyed meaning of figure 2: Effective learning can only occur in situations (her so-called prepared environments) where individual knowledge-transfer demands can be met. On one hand, learner capabilities determine the individual way and extent of grasping information. On the other hand, the design of the environment has to address learner capabilities directly or indirectly, since learners have to interact with elements of that environment.

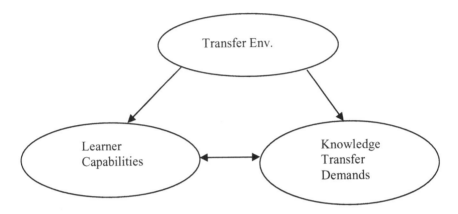

Fig. 2. The relationship between user capabilities and knowledge transfer demands in learner-centred transfer settings

With the advent of digital Montessori-inspired Manipulatives (MiMs) in elementary educational settings the effectiveness of knowledge transfer could be increased (cf. [55]). Their major task is to facilitate understanding through grasping and manipulating relevant information, thus reducing the cognitive load when learning. The latter seems to be crucial, since high cognitive work load might lead to *metacognitive miscalibrations* [47]. Such miscalibrations might hinder learning, in particular when grasping complex information (p. 115). The key to avoid miscalibrations seems to lie in the provision of a proper representation technique of knowledge (cf. [7]). As Dori [9] points out it should differ from the format used for computers (p.121). In order to support learners it should capture domain content (cf. [12]). Both aspects, and the interactive access to (domain) knowledge are addressed through MiMs, as they provide concepts for visualization and hands-on experience.

In our work we focus on the design of ambient knowledge-transfer settings that allow learner-centred access to domain structures and content through MiMs. Our first results presented here are in line with the successful hands-on organisation of discrete pieces of abstract information [15], and discrete physical object manipulation representing digital information [52]. The approach follows the idea of Task Blocks by Terry [50], since physical blocks can be used to represent computational functions. It encourages hands-on, active experimentation and vision-based acquisition including graphical interpretation of knowledge (cf. [1]; [5]).

The paper is organized as follows: We briefly set the stage for Montessori-oriented education and learning to ground our conceptual inputs in section 2. In this section we also revisit the concept of immersion, since it allows to bridge the gap between physical and virtual worlds. We review existing experiences with immersive transfer environments that allow to conceptualise learner-centred settings. In section 3 we exemplify learner-oriented settings from the transfer perspective and provide some results from applying Montessori-oriented immersion in virtual and face-to-face settings. Section 4 gives an overview of the implementation of a proper ambient environment providing generic capabilities for the immersive settings developed in section 3. Section 5 concludes the paper.

2 Immersion as a Key Concept

We introduce the learner-centred design of knowledge transfer and learning according to Maria Montessori (section 2.1), before identifying immersion as key for individual and social engagement in learning activities (section 2.2).

2.1 Maria Montessori's Principles

In her work Maria Montessori has integrated several principles towards inclusive design of knowledge transfer and individualised knowledge acquisition (cf. [25], [26], [27], [28], [29], [30], [31]; [22]):

- The acquisition of knowledge has to be *tuned to individual types of learners.* Learning should be an individualised process that might also occur in group settings.
- Learning is oriented towards *doing* (‚Hilf mir, es selbst zu tun' – 'Help me in doing it on my own'). Learners should acquire competence and skills while directly working with subject elements or manipulating content.
- Learners should *control* the process of knowledge acquisition by *themselves,* including stage setting for sensible learning phases.
- Learning should *lead to and be built on visible structures* (‚Innere Ordnung bedingt äußere Ordnung' – 'Inner structure requires external structure') with a maximum degree of freedom for the learner. Elements relevant for learning should be positioned and manipulated under the learner's control.
- Learning should be *based on material or pre-structured content* to focus the attention of learners.
- Learning should occur *in a comprehensive, but focussed way* (‚Sich-Vertiefen auf den Lerngegenstand' – 'in-depth concentration on the subject of acquisition'). Subject-specific elements should be complemented by *transformation tasks.* For instance, business process modelling using event-driven process chains in ARIS [44] should be complemented by UML (Unified Modelling Language)-models or modelling tasks, since the latter provide a different perspective on process modelling elements.
- Learning should be *observed* by coaches, however, without active intervention, even in the case of faulty or misleading procedures, e.g., caused by opinion leaders in group settings.

From her observations Maria Montessori concluded that any learning process should be facilitated by allowing learners to manipulate learning objects in a self-managed way. This process should be implemented in a prepared environment allowing to handle manipulatives in an individualised way. The environment is supervised and designed by the coach or teacher, whereas the acquisition of knowledge is in the responsibility of each learner. The role of the learner is defined to handle the material according to inherent properties of the content and, in this way develop skills. The coach should provide few inputs when requested by the learner or attracting the learner's attention. Ideally, the prepared environment guides the learner to domain-specific properties and tasks that can be accomplished in a self-managed way using the elements of the environment.

Knowledge is assumed to be generated when providing activity-oriented design of the elements for learning. For instance, the constituents of a technical communication system are introduced by a set of elements or a template, starting with messages, packets, frames and layers, before entering the stage of integrating those elements in a service provided by a communication layer of the ISO (International Standard Organisation) model. Semantic correctness should be checkable visually or achieved through role playing.

The tasks that are traditionally performed in Montessori-oriented settings start on a straightforward level and become increasingly complex:

1. *Structuring (Ordering) elements*: Montessori considers (mathematical) structuring as a training in exact thinking. She considers the domain-specific grouping of elements, the correct assignment of phenomena, and the multi-dimensional capturing of things in the world to be substantial for further acquisition processes. Exact working, however, requires the combination of motor- and sensor experience.

2. *Communication* of models or concepts and transformation processes by means of language: The verbal handling and the semantic correct application of domain ontologies are at the centre of knowledge transfer. Language has to be materialized and embodied in cognition.

3. *Cosmic education* through comprehensive and symbolic application of knowledge – ‚Der ‚konstruierende' Geist kann viel mehr enthalten als der, in den die Kenntnisse künstlich wie in einen Sack gestopft werden; in ihm sind die Gegenstände wie in einem Haus gut voneinander getrennt, harmonisch aufgestellt und nach ihrem Gebrauch unterschieden.' (‚The constructionist mind might contain more than an artificially packed bag full of information; the constructionist mind separates things in a well-structured 'house', arranges them harmonically and in accordance to their utility.'). Montessori's constructionist approach envisions learning to occur in a well-structured and well-organized 'home' with harmonized arrangements and objects that can be recalled according to their inherent properties and scope of use.

For Maria Montessori, individual exploration of the environment and self-managed handling of learning elements are the keys to in-depth and holistic understanding. Learners should (re)construct information or knowledge in an accordingly prepared environment - ‚Die Umgebung muss also die Mittel zur Selbsterziehung enthalten ... Was tun wir als erstes, um den [Lernenden] zu einer Rekonstruktion zu verhelfen? Wir bereiten eine Umgebung vor, die reich an interessanten Aktivitätsmomenten ist.' (‚The environment has to contain all means for self-education ... What do we initially do to guide learners to (re)construction? We prepare an environment full of compelling moments for activity.') Providing means for self-education requires the preparation of objects attracting the interest of learners for manipulation, rather than pieces of information or objects without indication of their usage or utility.

Coaches should motivate the acquisition, facilitate the transfer process and leaning, and be able to resolve conflicts. They serve as mediators between elements and learners in the transfer environment. Learning centres around these elements and their manipulation by the learners.

2.2 Immersion for Individual and Social Engagement

Computer-generated settings might enrich human perceptual capabilities, in particular through the embodiment of metaphors. With their help information spaces can be constructed that do not only require computer systems to be accessed, but are also intertwined with human-computer interaction ([51]; p. 291). Users do not interact as a separate part of the artificial world, they are part of it. This phenomenon is also termed immersion. Immersion facilitates active participation in processes (rather than consumption of graphical information) through direct manipulation of objects.

Given immersion, another factor moves also to the centre of interest: the capability to share experiences and to interact in a common context even over large distances. It is the idea of structural and dynamic networking. Focusing on networking and context-sensitive interaction allows for more than the reproduction of predefined sequences of interaction with a limited set of features. It allows for exploration, self-management, and social process support (cf. [48]). These are issues that allow to progress toward human-centred knowledge transfer, for instance to move forward from 'simple' training mechanisms in the sense of reproducing activities and facts in a predefined domain toward collaborative knowledge exploration in an open space.

With respect to content, Norman and Spohrer [33] have found out that high quality educational material should provide a high degree of confidence in its (i) usefulness, (ii) interest (which is particularly in line with Maria Montessori – see section 2.1), and (iii) effectiveness. They have elaborated their principles of 'learner-centered education' in terms of individual engagement, effectiveness, and viability. Engagement means collaboration among highly motivated learners in the course of education. It is enabled through 'rapid, compelling interaction, and feedback' (*ibid.*, p. 26). Effectiveness in the sense of Norman and Spohrer denotes the depth of understanding and the skills learners acquire. The viability addresses the seriousness of the problems tackled, the relevance of the topics, and the accuracy of tools for the process of knowledge transfer.

One way to meet these objectives even in virtual settings has been to recognise the multiple dimensions of knowledge transfer and tackle them explicitly. For instance, Resnick et al. [40] have observed: 'Educational technology has too heavily emphasized the equivalent of stereos and CDs and not emphasized computational pianos enough' (*ibid.*, p.42). The researchers' goal was to develop computational construction kit development 'enabling people to express themselves in increasingly ever-more complex ways, deepening their relationships with new domains of knowledge' (*ibid*, p.42).

The theory of constructional design focuses on a constructionist approach to learning. Constructional design of material is a type of meta design (designing for designers) to support learners in their own design activities and thus leading to hands-on experience in construction. Papert [38] argues for constructionist approach to learning: In design-based learning, things that people design (such as Lego® constructions) 'serve as external shadows of the designer's internal mental models. These external creations provide an opportunity for people to reflect on – and then revise and extend – their internal models of the world.' ([40], p.42)

Engagement, as demanded by Norman and Spohrer, is implemented through something more than learning-by-doing, since, in contrast to learning-by-doing little attention has been given to the 'general principles governing the kinds of "doing" most conductive to learning' ([40], p.42). Two general principles should guide the design of construction kits and activities binding the learner to the object: personal and epistemological connection. They are defined as follows:

– *'Personal connections.* Constructions kits and activities should connect to users' interests, passions, and experiences. The point is not simply to make the activities more "motivating". When activities involve objects and actions that are familiar, users can draw on their previous knowledge, connecting new ideas to their pre-existing intuitions.

– *Epistomological connections.* Construction kits and activities should connect to important domains of knowledge – and, more significantly, encourage new way of thinking (end even new ways of thinking about thinking). A well-designed construction kit makes certain ideas and ways of thinking particularly salient, so that users are likely to connect with those ideas in a natural way in the process of designing and creating.' ([40], p. 42)

Materials enabling rich learning experience should provide both types of connections. Two ways of implementations have been pursued: enrichment of existing objects, and virtualising the core material. In the 'Things That Think' initiative (MIT's Media Lab) everyday objects should embed computational capabilities, not only to accomplish particular tasks more cheaply or easily or intelligently, but to 'enable people to think about things in new ways' ([54]; p. 44). One solution were programmable bricks. Structures and mechanisms have been developed using programmable Lego®-bricks for cars and castles building *including* behaviours. Actually, a brick is a very personal computer. In this way, a strong *personal connection* can be established, since the brick is part of the learners' culture and lifes. Such bricks allow to compare artificial with natural beings (e.g., robots and animals) as well as to understand complex systems' behaviour, e.g. feedback strategies. In this way an *epistemological connection* can be set up.

NICE's underlying theoretical framework 'combines constructivist educational theory with ideas that emphasize the importance of collaborative learning and narrative development' ([42]; p.62). Constructivist pedagogy is one 'by which learners actively construct and interrelate knowledge and ideas' (*ibid.*). These findings lead us to the conclusion the more objects are available in a concrete form and way, and the more focused communication occurs, the more effectively (and efficiently) learning can be supported in knowledge-transfer environments.

The involvement of learners seems to play a central role for knowledge acquisition and throughout the process of knowledge transfer, redefining the role of developers: 'The process of constructional design is not a simple matter of "programming in" the right type of connections' ([40]; p.49), since student behaviour is not predictable by developers. 'Developers of design-oriented learning environments need to adopt a relaxed sense of "control" ' (*ibid.*) in the sense of creating "spaces" for *possible* activities and experiences rather than limiting the interaction space. However, developers have to make those spaces dense with personal and epistemological connections. Then, there will emerge learning spaces, both appealing and intellectually interesting (as demanded by Norman and Spohrer).

The context of learning (situations) has to be kept and made transparent in the course of knowledge transfer. One way to establish transparent context is to structure material for interactive use and link it to communication and collaboration facilities, as e.g., proposed for Scholion [3]. In such an approach, a data models have to be enriched with information about the state of affairs on particular elements of the material. For instance, an explanatory remark of the coach for the learners has to be directly linked to both, frequently asked questions, and the term that is defined in the material. The state of affairs might either concern the stage of knowledge transfer in a virtual class room, the level of learning, or the state of discussing material. The individual access to materials and additional information, such as links to fundamental work in a particular discipline, as well as commonly shared content, such as the discussion board, have to become integral part of the virtual learning environment.

Understanding immersion in the sketched sense of *individual and social engagement* in the knowledge transfer process enables more than scanning and retrieving information. Both, constructionist, and constructivist knowledge transfer and acquisition support the personal and epistemological connection of learners to subjects. In table 1 the vectors and phases of maturity for immersion have been summarized according to the results from experimenting in virtual spaces (cf. [40], [42], [48]). Interactions address the delivery of superior value. Competency leverage concerns the obtainment and coordination of critical competencies. Work configuration targets towards the design of value-adding processes.

Those vectors also provide some rationales for transfer-system design, ranging from transfer encountering via transfer sourcing to learning. The first vector focuses on the relationship between content and actors. Starting with remote interaction procedures actors should be qualified to handle objects with minimal semantic distance to the addressed content. Encountering knowledge transfer in traditional settings is mainly related to passive consumption of content. In an intermediate step content can be individualised, e.g., by marking elements of content. In an advanced setting the individualisation of content is extended to re-arranging information and browsing content according to individual structures. The latter might become public and shared with other learners.

Table 1. Vectors of immersion in knowledge transfer and phases of development

Immersion	Interactions Transfer Encounter	Competence Leverage Transfer Sourcing	Work Configuration Transfer Activities Learning
Initial step	Download of material and passive consumption	Searching and finding material	Maximising input for building up individual expertise, coaches in the domain, learners with respect to learning techniques
Intermediate step	Customisation of content	Definition of core competencies, for coaches with respect to knowledge transfer, for learners with respect to learning techniques	Making explicit individual strengths and capabilities, e.g., structuring material (coaches), preparing for intensive study of material (learners)
Advanced step	Designing customised material through patterns for navigation and sharing	Creation of new competencies, e.g., team teaching or collaborative learning	Building community expertise through defining shared knowledge pools

The second vector addresses the allocation of tasks between users and transfer environments. Efficient sourcing of information and elements has the goal to bind users tighter to the environment. In an initial step, all processes for gathering information to act in a given domain are concerned. They should contribute to more effective learning. In an intermediate step the identification of core competencies is emphasized. Tasks and functions among users and between technical system components and users might have to be rearranged, in order to increase the effectiveness of learning procedures. Finally, new competencies can be created.

The third vector addresses the actual activities to be set, and the processes to be performed for actual task accomplishment or problem solving. Initially, some standard procedure is followed along defined interfaces according to a task at hand. All routine parts (including interactions) can be automated to maximise individual learning effects. As soon as activities become part of task chains the transfer environment involves other users – learning becomes a collaborative endeavour. It might lead to novel forms of learning communities. Those expertise can finally become a proactive part of the transfer environment.

Since each vector has to contribute so successful transfer, information and communication technology has to support both, each vector in its evolutionary development, and their interfaces, and intertwining.

According to Scardamalia and Bereiter ([43]; p.37), high level processes, such as building communities for learning pro-actively, can be termed second-order knowledge processing, since they focus on understanding and fostering capacity building, rather than on storing, retrieving, and displaying information (first order knowledge processing). Widening this concept towards self-organized and –managed learning gives way to intentional learning, where the acquisition and exploration process is under the control of the learner: 'Intentional learning is how learners of varying ability choose to empower and transform themselves by making wise decisions, setting goals, and using strategies and processes to ensure learning' ([24]; p.174). In order to guide learners to this challenging stage of learning ability, mixed-initiative learning as suggested in Lester et al. [21] should help to bridge the gap between totally supervised and totally unsupervised procedures of knowledge transfer and learning (cf. section 2.1).

3 Inclusive Design of Knowledge Transfer Environments

In this section we review a virtual and physical transfer case we have developed at the University of Linz in the course of teaching Communications Engineering. About 30 students have been involved in several scenarios in Business Informatics and Geographical Information Sciences. We report on the development of immersive environments, both for virtual and physical settings, and reflect the procedure to be followed for the inclusive design of knowledge transfer. The virtual setting (section 3.1) is explained through handling client-server communication in distributed environments. The physical case (section 3.2) is shown to develop an understanding of the inherent logic of protocols for communication in distributed information systems.

3.1 A Virtual Case: Handling Requests in Distributed Computing Environments

This case has been developed using traditional learning elements. Figure 3 shows basic communication blocks requiring specific patterns (Request - Processing - Reply) involving a sender (client) and a receiver (server) for successful distributed computing.

This logic can be applied to the Distributed Computing Environment (DCE) for Unix applications (transformation): The communication between client and server requires several steps (see figure 4). After the server has registered using a directory service, the address of each server becomes available to all network clients ①. Any client can look up into the directory service for possible service requests by one or more servers ②,③. Then the client retrieves a security key from a security server to address the server ④,⑤. After having received a key the server can be contacted using that key ⑥,⑦. Traditionally, this initialisation works via remote procedure calls that split communication from business logic requests. As soon as the addressed server is able to handle the request of the client the respective results are passed on to it ⑧,⑨.

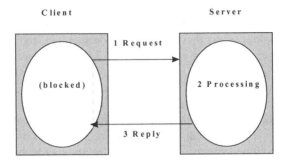

Fig. 3. Client-Server Communication

Distributed Computing Environment DCE (Unix)

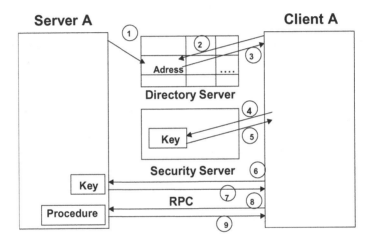

Fig. 4. A sample application

The immersive setting requires several phases for successful knowledge transfer: preparation, activation, self assessment. The preparation is performed by one or more coaches who identify and select the learning material and arrange the transfer environment. In this case we used Scholion, a virtual transfer environment [3], to support setting interactive tokens by learners along the directed arcs within the emptied architectures (see also figure 5) in the activation phase. In doing so, learners follow the logic for setting up communication and exchanging data the same way a distributed computing environment does. The structure of the content guides the learners, without active intervention by coaches.

The learners are provided with basic explanations concerning the setting and the rationale of the client-server principle. During knowledge acquisition the (virtual

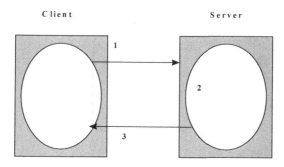

Fig. 5. Client-Sever Communication Scheme for Interactive Exploration

and/or physical) coach is able to follow the activities set by the learner and provide feedback on demand. In the showcase the learners should both grasp the idea of splitting communication for setting up the communication and handling the business logic of an application in distributed software systems.

The self assessment is also triggered by the learners. After having developed a basic understanding of client-server communication, sample applications like the one presented in figure 4 can be presented as empty shell similar to the initial example (figure 3 and 5), and should be completed by the learner. Such trainings can be repeated many times, including a reset, starting with a simple Request-Processing-Reply sequence before handling the more complex cases of computing environments.

3.2 A Physical Case: Protocols and Services in Distributed Systems

Distributed systems require a layered architecture for setting up communication and providing a variety of services, such as naming or remote procedure calls. Services are required for interaction in distributed systems on the level of data management, business logic, and user interfaces. Traditionally, learners have difficulties to grasp the idea of abstraction and layering as well as to apply this idea for constructing distributed software systems. In order to overcome those difficulties we have used Nikitin cubes (cf. [32]). This material has differently coloured surfaces which allow to encode different types of information.

One of those encodings concerns the decomposition of messages into frames and packages for transmission over a communication channel, and thus, the representation of both, communication overhead, and application data for different communication layers. Learners should recognise that passing information from one layer to another generates substantial communication overhead. This overhead becomes larger the more layers are involved for transmission. For each layer a colour has been determined. Split encodings, e.g., white/red on one cube, are used to mark the communication overhead for each layer, e.g., in white with red indicating application data.

Learners might then arrange and move the cubes with the relevant colour-coded surface upfront between the layers to simulate communication processes. In this way they become part of the setting (immersion) and experience the complexity of message passing between layers and finally, between communication partners.

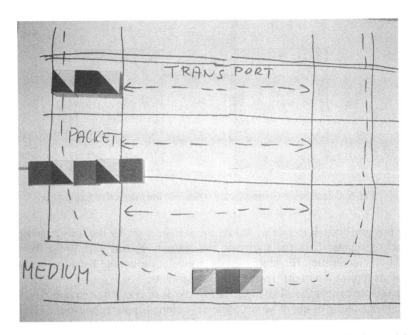

Fig. 6. Immersive setting to understand technical communication, given the intertwining of protocol layers and the medium for transmission (net) in distributed systems

The preparation for this showcase (figure 6) requires paper and pens as well as a scheme to encode the cubes. In the shown case the message content is encoded red on the transport layer, the communication part for the transport layer white, and on the lower levels blue and yellow, respectively. The activation phase allows the learner to start playing with the cubes and try to grasp the idea of layered communication. In order to start, the layers have to be drawn on paper by the learner, identifying sender and receiver. Then, using the cubes, the generation of communication overhead has to be visualized through encoding the content (in the figure the red part at the transport layer) and the corresponding communication part (the white part at the transport layer) for messaging. It becomes self-evident that the data transmitted via the medium contain a variety of communication overhead generated by each layer. The learners might repeat this sequence, either to actively grasp the idea and/or assess their knowledge in the self assessment phase.

Using such type of learning elements learners train to structure and embody knowledge according to that structure. They get trained to derive concrete results from abstract settings through comparison, sorting different types of information, and similar tasks. Learners can keep 'the big picture' in the course of acquisition, while going in–depth for task accomplishment. Immersion is enabled through the context-sensitive provision of learning elements. It fosters the integrative conceptual and practical transfer of information. In this way, it facilitates knowledge creation. Most of those settings allow for group work and active sharing of acquisition or transfer experience (cf. [5]). One party of such settings should be the coach, providing feedback to learners and input on demand.

4   Ambient Intelligence Enabling Inclusive Knowledge Transfer

Recently, several attempts have been made to develop technology to support individual and collaborative support technologies enabling inclusive knowledge transfer in the aforementioned sense ([35], [36]). Besides manifold approaches to reduce the cognitive effort for expressing individual views and concepts at the notational level (cf. [8]; [46]) and to provide contextual modelling support (cf. [13]), empirical evidence ([10]; [55]) reveals that tangible artefacts (manipulatives) can lead to improved intelligibility of the individual learning objects and other pieces of abstract information.

In the following we first give the conceptual design (section 4.1) and then detail the technical implementation (section 4.2).

4.1 Conceptual Design

As it turns out, once a proper codification of knowledge has been achieved (see section 3), e.g., providing consensual meaning to Nikitin block parts through assigning white parts to communication overhead for protocol simulations, an ambient environment needs to encode and process this information in a straightforward way. In addition to the physical interface of such an environment, a virtual interface might be required to work with traditional applications, such as modelling tools. In that case the two surfaces have to be kept synchronised using implicit interfaces (e.g., the underlying sensor infrastructure) – see [36]. Data that are only available on the virtual surface but are required on the physical surface (e.g., context symbols) have to become physically available through explicit interfaces.

The Design of the Manipulatives. For the creation of educational immersive environments, like shown in the example in section 3.2, a set of several building blocks is needed: communication data, and application data. These building blocks are presented though differently shaped and distinct colour-coded items. As tangible physical blocks – manipulatives – support the hands-on experience, the lateral surfaces of these blocks are used to indicate possible connections to other block types by dynamically colouring them using the respective colour. In order to model the connections between blocks, connectors of different types (upper/lower level) are needed. As arbitrary connections between building blocks are not valid in every case, the connectors on the physical surface provide tactile and visual feedback, in particular with respect to the legitimacy of using a certain connector.

Figure 7 shows a sample set of networked building blocks of our Tangible Modelling Demonstrator. The blocks are used to encode domain-specific knowledge, e.g., packets in Communications Engineering. Each tangible can be opened and might contain further tangibles (cf. container metaphor). In the figure the synchronised digital representation of the tangibles is also displayed. Nested elements are handled by corresponding mouse clicks.

Fig. 7. Sample Setting for virtual and tangible ambience in knowledge transfer

Tangible Context. The various aspects of the (distributed) processing context are visualized using a *container* metaphor. Assuming that the current elements are located on a certain level of abstraction, a higher abstract representation of the entire set of elements can be modelled as a container. A similar approach can be applied to the processing neighbourhood, where related elements can be visualized as neighbouring containers.

The refinement of elements is visualized by physically applying the container metaphor to the basic building blocks. These blocks are built as physical containers with a lid that can be opened to access its interior. Due to physical constraints the elements to be put into these containers are built differently. Although they are shaped and coloured like the respective building blocks, they have a smaller form factor and are massive with perceivable weight. These elements are referred to as *artefact*s. Consequently following the container metaphor, the 'amount of data' contained in a block is proportional to its weight and thus can be perceived directly by grasping it.

Moreover, the sound created by shaking a block indicates additionally available information. The analogies used here were also inspired by the ideas of Maria Montessori [31] and will be further elaborated in future work.

Before an artefact can be put into a building block, the actual information has to be assigned (i.e. bound) to it. This information can either be specified in advance and retrieved from the virtual surface, or it can be defined just-in-time on the physical or virtual surface. It is bound to the artefact using an explicit data-binding interface. As artefacts are too small to be displayed directly, the information bound to them can be accessed (displayed) upon explicit request by users.

4.2 Technical Implementation

The physical manipulation environment has to provide the following non-functional features to enable (collaborative) knowledge acquisition as described above:

- Determining a building block's position
- Determining contained artefacts
- Determining connectors from and to a block
- Visualizing designators of building blocks and connectors
- Binding of information to artefacts
- Helping to reconstruct stored situations

Although both, a straightforward *Smart Thing* approach (with IT-infrastructure merely in the manipulatives), and a corresponding *Smart Space* approach (with IT-infrastructure only in the physical surface) can be pursued for implementation, existing solutions (e.g., as presented in [15] or [39]) show that a combined approach allows for more degrees of freedom when choosing mature and accessible technologies.

Currently, visual tracking and projecting information is under development, although the rather high complexity of building blocks due to the features required will lead to IT-augmentation of the blocks. In order to enable evolutionary development, a sensor/actuator abstraction layer will be introduced. We are currently working on this layer of abstraction. It is based on concepts of existing frameworks in this domain, such as Papier-Mâché [19] or MUSE [6].

The *physical modelling interface* has to be considered as a complex system *per se*: It does not only include the actual modelling area but also the infrastructure providing the desired functionality. The latter basically includes means to retrieve and display information related to basic building blocks.

The support infrastructure has to be able to locate and identify building blocks placed on the surface and to enable the transmission of data from building blocks to the coordinating background system and vice versa (for data retrieval). We favour a visual tracking system as it requires the least complex infrastructure for building blocks and thus scales well for larger representations. A visual approach is feasible, since no real time tracking capabilities are required - in fact the current state of the setting is captured as a snapshot every time, as changes of settings occur in the time frame of seconds (approx. 5-10).

Data transmission from and to building blocks is implemented using the connector-wires. They span a meshed network which – with the appropriate IT-infrastructure in the containers – can be used to identify the connections between containers, for data transmission and for power supply.

However, additional functionality is needed to display information related to any element or structure placed on the surface. Basically there are two cases in which data have to be displayed: (i) a previously stored model has to be reconstructed on the physical surface; (ii) elements on the surface have to be augmented with additional information. Both cases are implemented by projecting the respective data. Using mirror systems increases the readability. Moreover, it allows for a more compact design.

A *Modular Container System.* The building blocks are implemented as containers. They can hold several artefacts, display labelling text and are capable of being connected to a number of other building blocks. This functionality implies several features that have to be provided by any of the four types of building blocks. For reasons of flexibility we thus propose a modular system consisting of a common ITC-enabled basic platform module and a container module for each type of building block (shaped and coloured accordingly).

From an infrastructure point-of-view, the basic platform module merits attention. As a central element, it holds a Micro-Controller (based on the Intel 8x51-series - Intel, [14]) which provides a link between display, sensor and communication modules. Communication with other building blocks will be implemented using the CAN-Bus-System [4]. Display functionality will be based on a Dot-Matrix-LCD-Panel.

Artefacts. Artefacts are designed to represent data. This data is not stored directly as part of the artefacts. It is available in a repository. Each artefact has to be uniquely identifiable, in order to associate it with the respective data. We achieve unique identification using an UIN (unique identification number) based on RFID-technology.

In order to facilitate the communication between the virtual surface, the physical surface, and the storage of settings, some kind of standardized data representation is crucial. To additionally allow the transfer of models to external tools and keep our system open for extension towards remote modelling, we have defined a data format compliant to the XMI-standard (XML Metadata Interchange – [34]). It is used to represent the structure of the model (formally as well as layout).

Related Systems. Using the application domains of tangible user interfaces identified by Ullmer et al. [53], our system could be classified to be suitable for information visualisation and modelling (and simulation). A variety of attempts have been made to develop tangible user interfaces for these areas. We sketch those that achieve similar goals or use a similar technological approach. Jacob et al. [15] have presented a tangible user interface for organising information using a grid. While their system is designed to support planning tasks, it also uses physical blocks to represent abstract data with additional information projected onto the modelling surface. This system has been one of the first that has been empirically tested against GUI- and paper-based modelling approaches.

A system with a similar technological approach but different objectives is 'The Designers' Outpost' [10]. It which aims at enabling (remote) collaboration for website design. It uses physical and virtual (projected) elements for data representation which are used side by side (interchangeably) on a physical modelling surface. In that context, Klemmer et al. [18] have also introduced the idea of tracking and providing the design history of models built using tangible interfaces.

Zuckerman et al. [55] use tangible interfaces for educating children abstract structures of dynamic behaviour. Their 'Digital Montessori-inspired Manipulatives' can be used to physically construct models of abstract processes and simulate them. Both input and output are implemented through the tangible building blocks. This system is similar in terms of the pedagogical concepts lying behind our design decisions. However, it does not aim at providing fully featured modelling capabilities, since it allows modelling only control flows. The technological approach shows similarities on the hardware layer, but does not include facilities for storage and retrieval of representations, including the history from creation.

5 Conclusion

Striving for inclusive design of knowledge transfer requires an integration of findings from educational psychology as well as e-learning. Inclusive design approaches embody learners and teachers into the transfer and generation process of knowledge, regardless of being in a physical or a virtual learning environment. We have reviewed essential inputs from Montessori- and virtual settings. Immersion seems to be crucial, since it allows learners to become an integral part of a transfer environment in their individual way to perceive reality and interact with objects in that reality. Prerequisites for successful knowledge acquisition are the structured preparation of learning elements (performed by the coaches), and the inherent motivation to accomplish tasks using that material in a self-managed way.

Our experiences in both worlds show that both, learners and coaches can benefit from inclusively designed environments. Learners acquire knowledge under self control and individualised learning settings in an active way. Of major importance seems to be the direct access to learning elements and their intuitive use, as suggested by Maria Montessori (cf. [25], [26], [27], [28], [29], [30]) as well as virtual reality designers (cf. [45]; p. 20). Meeting this objective, this type of setting can lead to a significant increase in the effectiveness of the knowledge transfer from learner-to-learner, e.g., when preparing for exams, and from coaches to learners, e.g., in the course of lectures (cf. [23]), and from coach-to-learner: 'It's very difficult to get your views across unless you have something physical to show to explain what you're saying' (cited in [11] p.126, see also [2]).

With respect to technology, our system spans across multiple levels. Viewing the embodiment dimension we can find full embodiment for the physical modelling elements, which are also used for output of supportive information. Nearby embodiment is used for placement and display of contextual information elements. Distant embodiment is used for displaying information held by artefacts. With respect to the metaphor dimension, we can find 'noun' for the definition of new contextual information types, and 'noun and verb' for the container metaphor. We have to think about higher use of metaphors in order to further reduce the cognitive overhead for handling manipulatives.

Due to the differences in the tangible codification of data, various embodiment levels seem to be necessary to meet our demands for supporting collaborative transfer or learning processes. We intend to introduce a development method that incorporates sharing of knowledge as well as generating capacities in a collaborative way. Such a method might need several coding schemes to guide coaches as well as learners in a homogeneous way.

Consequently, our future activities will focus on both, capacity building and knowledge generation in a more human-centred and natural way, and exploring technological capabilities for the (re)presentation of the didactically encoded knowledge in an interactive transfer setting.

References

[1]   Anderson, D.; Frankel, J.L.; Marks, J.; Agarwala, A; Beardsley, P.; Hodgins, J.; Leigh, D.; Ryall, K.; Sullivan, E.; Yedidia, J.S.: Tangible Interaction and Graphical Interpretation: A New Approach to 3D Modeling, in: Proceedings of 27th Ann. Conf. on Computer Graphics and Interactive Techniques, July 2000.

[2]   Astrachan, O.: Concrete Teaching: Hooks and Props as Instructional Technology, in: Proc. ITiCSE'98. ACM, pp. 21-24, 1998.

[3]   Auinger, A.; Stary, Ch.: Didaktikgeleiteter Wissenstransfer. Interaktive Informationsräume für Lern-Gemeinschaften im Web, Deutscher Universitätsverlag, Wiesbaden, 2005.

[4]   Bosch: Controller Area Network (CAN), http://www.can.bosch.com (08.02.2006).

[5]   Buchenau, M:; Suri, J.F.: Experience Prototyping, in: Proc. DIS'00, ACM, pp. 424-433, 2000.

[6]   Castro, P.; Greenstein, N.; Muntz, R.; Bisdikian, C.; Kermani, P.; Papdopouli, M.: Locating Applciation Data Across Service Discovery Domains, in: 7th International Conf. on Mobile Computing and Networking, Rome, July 2001.

[7]   Crapo, A.W.; Waisel, L.B.; Wallace, W.A.; Willemain, Th.R.: Visualization and the Process of Modeling: A Cognitive-theoretic View, in: Proc. KDD'00, ACM, pp.218-226, 2000.

[8]   Dann, H.D.: Variation von Lege-Strukturen zur Wissensrepräsentation, in: B. Scheele (Ed.): Struktur-Lege-Verfahren als Dialog-Konsens-Methodik. Ein Zwischenfazit zur Forschungsentwicklung bei der rekonstruktiven Erhebung subjektiver Theorien, Aschendorff, Münster, pp. 2-41, 1992.

[9]   Dori, D.: ViSWeb – The Visual Semantic Web: Unifying Human and Machine Knowledge Representations with Object-Process Methodology, VLDB-Journal, Vol. 13, pp. 120-147, 2004.

[10] Everitt, K.M.; Klemmer, S.; Lee, R.; Landay, J.: Two Worlds Apart: Bridging the Gap Between Physical and Virtual Media for Distributed Design Collaboration, in: Proc. CHI'03, ACM, pp. 553-560, 2003.

[11] Gasen, J.: Encouraging Social Responsibility through Collaborative Team Learning, in: Proc. CHI'96, ACM, pp. 125-126, 1996.

[12] Goldman, N; Balzer, R.; Wile, D.: The Inference of Domain Structure from Informal Process Descriptions, SIGART Newsletter 63, ACM, pp. 75-82, 1977.

[13] Herrmann, Th.; Hoffmann, M.; Loser, K.U.; Moysich, K.: Semistructured Models are Surprisingly Useful, in: Proc. Coop 2000, pp. 313-323, 2000.

[14] Intel: MCS 51 Microcontrollers, http://www.intel.com/design/mcs51/cf_51.htm (08.02.2006).

[15] Jacob, R.J.K.; Ishii, H.; Pangaro, G.; Patten, J.: Hands-On Interfaces: A Tangible Interface for Organizing Information Using a Grid, in: Proc. CHI'02, ACM, 2002.

[16] Heiland, H.: Maria Montessori, Rowohlt, Reinbeck, 1991

[17] Keates, S.; Clarkson, P.J.: Countering Design Exclusion: An Introduction to Inclusive Design, Springer, London, 2003.

[18] Klemmer, S.; M. Thomsen, E. Phelps-Goodman, R. Lee, J. A. Landay, Where Do Web Sites Come From? Capturing and Interacting with Design History, in: Proc. CHI'02, ACM, pp. 1–8, 2002.

[19] Klemmer, S.; Li, J.; Lin, J.; Landay, J.: Papier-Mâché: Toolkit Support for Tangible Input, Proc. CHI'04, ACM, pp. 399-406, 2004.

[20] Langdon, P.; Adams, R.: Cognitive Inclusion: Cognitive Design Considerations, in: Proc. HCII'05, 2005.

[21] Lester, J.C.; Stone, B.A.; Stelling, G.D.: Lifelike Pedagogical Agents for Mixed-Initiative Problem Solving in Constructivist Learning Environments, in: User Modeling and User-Adapted Interaction, Vol. 9, No. 1, pp. 1-44, 1999.

[22] Ludwig, H.; Fischer, Ch.; Fischer, R. (ed.): Montessori-Pädagogik in Deutschland. Rückblick – Aktualität – Zukunftsperspektiven: 40 Jahre Montessori-Vereinigung e.V., Lit, Münster, Hamburg, London, 2002.

[23] Marchionini, G.; Crane, G.: Evaluating Hypermedia and Learning: Methods and Results from the Perseus Project, in: Transactions on Information Systems, ACM, Vol. 12, No. 3, pp. 5-34, January 1994.

[24] Martinez, M.: Designing Intentional Learning Environments, in: Proc. SIGDOC, ACM, pp. 173-180, 1997.

[25] Montessori Maria, Kinder sind anders, Hoffmann, Stuttgart, 1988.

[26] Montessori Maria, Kosmische Erziehung, Herder, Freiburg, 1988.

[27] Montessori Maria, Das kreative Kind, Herder, Freiburg, 1989.

[28] Montessori Maria, Die Macht der Schwachen, Herder, Freiburg, 1989.

[29] Montessori Maria, Schule des Kindes, Herder, Freiburg, 1989.

[30] Montessori Maria, Die Entdeckung des Kindes, Herder, Freiburg, 1991.

[31] Montessori, Maria: The Montessori Method, Kessinger Publishing, New York, 2005.

[32] Nikitin, B.; Nikitin, L.: Das Nikitin Material. Aufbauende Spiele zum Erziehungsmodell der Nikitins, Logo, Bremen, 2002.

[33] Norman, D.A.; Spohrer, J.C.: Learner-Centered Education, in: Communications of the ACM, Vol. 39, No. 4, pp. 24-27, April 1996.

[34] OMG: Object Management Group, MOF 2.0, XMI Mapping Specification 2.1., http://www.omg.org/technology/documents/formal/xmi.htm (08.02.2006).

[35] Oppl. St.; Stary, Ch.: Towards Human-Centered Design of Diagrammatic Representation Schemes, in: Proc. TAMODIA'05, ACM, 2005.

[36] Oppl, St.: Towards Intuitive Work Modeling with a Tangible Collaboration Interface Approach, in: Proc.WETICE'06, TICE-Workshop, IEEE, 2006.

[37] Oswald, P.; Schulz-Benesch, G.: Grundgedanken der Montessori-Pädagogik, Herder, Freiburg, 1990.

[38] Papert, S.: The Children's Machine, Basic Books, New York, 1993.

[39] Patton, J.; Ishii, H.; Hines, J.; Pangaro, G.: Sensetable: A Wireless Object Tracking Platform for Tangible User Interfaces, in: Proc. CHI'01, ACM, pp. 253-260, 2001.

[40] Resnick, M.; Bruckman, A.; Martin, F.: Pianos, not Stereos. Creating Computational Construction Kits, in: interactions, Vol. 3, No. 8, ACM, pp. 41-50, september+october 1996.

[41] Rheingold, H.: Virtuelle Welten. Reisen im Cyberspace, Rowohlt, Reinbeck, 1995.

[42] Roussos, M.; Johnson, A.E.; Leigh, J.; Vasilakis, Ch.A.; Barnes, C.R.; Moher, Th.G.: NICE: Combining Constructionism, Narrative and Collaboration in a Virtual Learning Environment, in: Computer Graphics, pp. 62-63, August 1997.

[43] Scardamalia, M.; Bereiter, C.: Technologies for Knowledge-Building Discourse, in: Communications of the ACM, Vol. 36, No. 5, pp. 37-41, May 1993.

[44] Scheer, A.W.: ARIS – Business Process Modeling, Springer, 2003.

[45] Sherman, B.; Judkins, Ph.: Virtual Reality. Cyberspace-Computer kreieren synthetische Welten, Scherz, München, 1995.

[46] Siau, K.; Tan, X.: Improving the Quality of Conceptual Modeling using Cognitive Mapping Techniques, in: Journal of Data & Knowledge Engineering Vol. 55, Elsevier, pp. 343-356, 2003.

[47] Smith, D.K.; Moores, T.; Chang, J.: Prepare Your Mind for Learning, in: Communications of the ACM, Vol. 48, No.9, pp. 115-118, 2005

[48] Stary, Ch.: Exploring the Concept of Virtuality – Technological Approaches and Implications from Tele-Education, in: Virtual Reality - Cognitive Foundations, Technological Issues & Philosophical Implications, eds: Riegler, A.; Peschl, F.-M.; Edlinger, K.; Fleck, G.; Feigl, W., Schriftenreihe des Wiener Arbeitskreises für Systemische Theorie des Organismus. Organismus und System Band 3, pp. 113-128, Peter Lang, Frankfurt/Main, 2001.

[49] Stephanidis, C. (ed.): User Interfaces for All. Concepts, Methods, Tools, Lawrence Erlbaum, Mahwah, NJ, 2001.

[50] Terry, M.: Task Blocks: Tangible Interfaces for Creative Exploration, CHI Extended Abstracts, ACM, 2001.

[51] Turkle, Sh.: Leben im Netz. Identitäten in Zeiten des Internet, Rowohlt, Reinbeck, 1998.

[52] Ullmer, B; Ishii, H.; Jacob, R.J.K.: Token+Constraint Systems for Tangible Interaction with Digital Information, in: TOCHI, ACM,Vol. 12, March 2005.

[53] Ullmer, B.; Ishii, H.: Emerging Frameworks for Tangible User Interfaces, in: J. M. Carroll (Ed.): Human-Computer Interaction in the New Millenium, Addison-Wesley, pp. 579-601, 2001.

[54] Weiser, M.: Some Computer Science Issues in Ubiquitous Computing, in: Communications of the ACM, Vol. 36, No. 7, pp. 75-84, 1993.

[55] Zuckerman, O.; Arida, S.; Resnick, M.: Extending Tangible Interfaces for Education: Digital Montessori-inspired Manipulatives, in: Proc. CHI'05, pp. 859-868, ACM, 2005.

Web Mediators for Accessible Browsing

Benjamin N. Waber, John J. Magee, and Margrit Betke

Computer Science Department, Boston University,
111 Cummington St. Boston, MA USA
{bwabes,mageejo,betke}@cs.bu.edu

Abstract. We present a highly accurate method for classifying web pages based on link percentage, which is the percentage of text characters that are parts of links normalized by the number of all text characters on a web page. We also present a novel link grouping algorithm using agglomerative hierarchical clustering that groups links in the same spatial neighborhood together while preserving link structure. Grouping allows users with severe disabilities to use a scan-based mechanism to tab through a web page and select items. In experiments, we saw up to a 40-fold reduction in the number of commands needed to click on a link with a scan-based interface. Our classification method consistently outperformed a baseline classifier even when using minimal data to generate article and index clusters, and achieved classification accuracy of 94.0% on web sites with well-formed or slightly malformed HTML, compared with 80.1% accuracy for the baseline classifier.

Keywords: Web mediators, link grouping, web page classification, k-means clustering.

1 Introduction

People who cannot physically use a mouse, for example because of quadriplegia, often rely on an assistive device that moves the mouse pointer by tracking the user's head or eyes. Computer access with such devices is difficult because they typically do not provide the same selection accuracy as a mouse pointer. Moreover, since the user cannot type with a physical keyboard, text entry, for example of a web address, requires the use of an on-screen keyboard. Selection of a letter on this keyboard or a small text link in a web page may be particularly difficult on traditional browsers for users who experience tremors or other unintentional movements that prevent them from holding the mouse pointer still. One possible solution is to change (1) the display of a web page and (2) how the interface navigates the information based on its content. A page can be rendered and navigated differently depending on the "type" of page. Such classification allows us to create a variety of customizations to occur in interaction mode and display depending on the intended application and user. We could also allow the user to select not just a single link, but a group of links. This would allow the web browser to either enlarge the single group of links on the page or, for users who only have control of a binary interface, allow them to scroll through individual links within that group.

C. Stephanidis and M. Pieper (Eds.): ERCIM UI4ALL Ws 2006, LNCS 4397, pp. 447–466, 2007.

The principal technical contributions of this paper are a clustering method to accurately determine the type of a web page based on a technique that examines the text characters on a page and a link grouping method that respects the structure of the web page while providing groupings that substantially increase the effectiveness of browsing.

The clustering method computes the *link percentage*, the percentage of text characters that are parts of links as compared to all text characters on a web page. We posit that there are only two types of pages – articles and index pages – on web sites that deal with news media: article pages contain mostly text and index pages contain mostly links to articles and other indices. This classification may be helpful to allow people with disabilities to browse the web in an effective and efficient fashion. After determining the content of a web page as an index or article, our method can render the page to meet the needs of users with disabilities, for example, by increasing the size of links on index pages. This makes the links easier to read, but more importantly, it makes them easier to select. All text on article pages is enlarged to increase readability.

We also present a novel link grouping algorithm that preserves link structure to enable disabled users to browse web pages orders of magnitude faster than current systems allow.[1] Our link grouping method proceeds in two stages: first it builds a *link tree*. The leaves of the link tree are the links on a web page. The parents of these leaves are the first common parent between different links in the HTML Document Model (DOM) tree [1]. Our method then leverages this structure by moving up from the leaves of the link tree, attempting to group links at their parent node. If all links could not be merged subject to the constraint that the sum-of-squared differences (SSD) error of the new grouping is less than a thresholding function.

Our method for classifying web pages based on link percentage is highly accurate. We used k-means clustering [10] to automatically create unique thresholds to differentiate index pages and article pages on individual web sites. We also used web page classification to alter web page display on an accessible web browser that we developed for users with disabilities. Our method consistently outperformed a baseline classifier even when using minimal data to generate article and index clusters, and achieved classification accuracy of 94.0% on web sites with slightly malformed HTML, compared with 80.1% accuracy for the baseline classifier.

2 Related Work

Previous work on classification of web pages into specific types has been limited. It is hoped that this paper will spur interest in the use of web context and computer context in general and to improve accessibility in particular. In the research community, "context" has too often referred to the *physical* context of the user, such as location. Little research has been done on the context of the *computer* environment, which is crucial to understand so that users with disabilities and mobile users can effectively utilize applications. For example, references [22] and [26] discussed this notion of computer context.

---

[1] The link grouping algorithm is implemented in Javascript and can run on any web browser that supports the Document Object Model.

A notable exception to this is the AVANTI web browser of Stephanidis et al. [24], which utilizes user profiles to modify web pages for individual users. It also incorporated a link review and selection acceleration features, which is particularly relevant to our work.

For mobile users, computer context may be as simple as the currently open applications, while for a person with disabilities computer context includes their disability, the human-computer interface system they are using, the applications they normally use, and numerous other factors. Harnessing the power of context in the web, when we have detailed information on the current state of the application, is a good place to start the investigation of this concept.

We define *web context* as the type of web page the user is currently viewing. Extending this concept to include pages that the user previously browsed in the current session is beyond the scope of this paper, but was examined by Milic-Frayling et al. [18]. Methods for determining context or content of web pages vary widely. Cimiano et al. [7, 8] proposed a system called PANKOW (pattern-based annotation through knowledge on the Web) and its derivative C-PANKOW (context-driven PANKOW). Larson and Gips [16] created a web browser for people with quadriplegia that reads web page text and provides other accessibility options for people with disabilities. Gupta et al. [13] determined web site context (in their case genre, such as news or shopping) in order to facilitate content extraction.

Fig. 1. Left: The rendering of an index page in our web browser. Notice that the link text is enlarged relative to the plain text to address the problem of mouse clicks generated by dwell time in mouse substitution devices. Right: The rendering of the same page in Internet Explorer.

Kim et al. [15] described a method for segmenting topics in discussion boards in order to help blind users more effectively browse the web. Particularly important is that the authors also identified navigational context as an important cue for web browsing, especially for users with disabilities.

Mobile devices usually have small screens and therefore have difficulty fully displaying traditional web pages. Classification of web pages could assist methods that use text summarization to facilitate web browsing on these devices ([4] and [21]) or aid text summarization methods that drive user interfaces for people with disabilities [21]. Index pages, for example, typically display text snippets that are summaries of larger articles, and thus further summarizing these snippets is probably unnecessary. For text extraction and news delivery purposes knowing the type of pageis necessary and an accurate classification method would further enhance the accuracy of these systems. Reis et al. [23] clustered pages by layout features to attempt to distinguish between "section pages" and article pages to facilitate news extraction. It is evident that classification of a web page as an article would aid this methodology

Fig. 2. Left: The rendering of an article page in our web browser. All text has been enlarged to enhance readability. Right: The rendering of the same page in Internet Explorer.

Various previous work has been performed in re-rendering web pages for mobile devices. Buyukkokten et al. [4] presented a number of text summarization methods for display on personal data assistants (PDAs) or mobile phones. The web pages are broken into segments of text that can be displayed or hidden. Summaries are constructed from keyword extraction or a determination of significant sentences.

Chen et al. [5] detect and organize a web page into a two-level hierarchy. Each section of a page is displayed as a thumbnail that the user can zoom in to view more closely. For pages that are not able to be split, an intelligent block scrolling method is used to present the web page. Hornbæk et al. [14] analyzed the effectiveness of these zoomable interfaces for the user's navigation experience. While these results are for navigating a map interface, similar conclusions may be drawn for navigating a zoomable web page display interface. This result supports the technique that we chose to alter web page display. Our method essentially "zooms-in" on a web page.

Many alternative user interfaces limit the number of ways the user can interact with a computer. Various mouse substitution devices, for example, have been developed both for people with disabilities and for other purposes. The EagleEyes [9] project uses electrodes placed around a user's eyes to detect eye movements and translate them into mouse pointer movements on a screen. The Camera Mouse [2] tracks a user's face or other body part to control the mouse based on the user's movements. These interfaces have proven very successful with many users with severe disabilities, however fine "pinpoint" control of the mouse is difficult. Generating a mouse click requires the user to dwell the mouse pointer over the item to be selected for a short period of time. Given the small size of a link in a regular web page, users may have difficulty navigating web sites as they are normally presented.

The accessibility problem for web pages comes with the openness of the web. Web designers are generally free to present their information in whatever layout they find appealing. Drop down menu bars or clickable image maps may aid in the navigation of a web site with the traditional user interface of a mouse, but may hinder the usefulness of the web site for alternative accessibility interfaces. Sullivan and Matson [25] surveyed accessibility on some of the web's most popular sites, while Chi et al. [6] presented a method that automatically generates a web site usability report. Leporini and Paternò [17] introduced blind user accessibility criteria for web sites. They identify link grouping as an important part of this accessibility, and they stress that automatic recognition of such a feature is crucial since web designers will typically not put in the required effort to make a page conform to their criteria.

Duda et al. [10] summarize a number of point clustering algorithms and implementation techniques. Particularly relevant to this work is their description of agglomerative hierarchical clustering and clustering in the presence of unknown data structure. Agglomerative hierarchical clustering creates clusters by merging the closest clusters together until the desired number of clusters is reached, thus giving the result a minimum variance flavor. They also describe methods for evaluating the validity of cluster splitting by examining the behavior of a fitness function as the number of clusters are increased, stopping splitting only if the split results in a fitness function increase that falls below that found by a thresholding function.

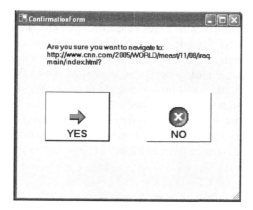

Fig. 3. Interface window to confirm that the user wanted to select a link

3 Web Browser

In our IWeb Explorer web browser [20], we addressed several problems that users with disabilities had with traditional web browsers such as Microsoft Internet Explorer and on-screen keyboards. Perhaps the most glaring problem of conventional web browsers is the lack of an opportunity for the user to confirm that a link was selected correctly. Our confirmation window, shown in figure 3, has yielded a positive response in preliminary tests with users with disabilities, and we hope to further improve this browser by allowing users and their caretakers to change the way that different pages are displayed to suit their individual needs.

Screenshots of our browser for both an article and index page compared to the rendering provided by Internet Explorer are shown in figures 1 and 2. The link text clearly stands out on index pages much more in our browser since it is enlarged to address the problem of mouse clicks generated by dwell time in mouse substitution devices, while article text is enlarged to enhance readability. This is done automatically using our web context recognition method, which is described below.

When people with disabilities used this web browser without our web context component, effective web browsing was not attainable [20]. It therefore became clear that to make web browsing applications viable for all users, web context needed to be leveraged.

4   Web Context Recognition

4.1   Page Classification

The key observation of our technique is that by examining link percentage we can accurately determine the "type" of a web page. The link percentage is the percentage of text characters that are parts of links as compared to all text characters on a web page. We posit that on sites dealing with news media that there are only two types of pages: articles and indices, where articles contain mostly text and indices contain mostly links to articles and other indices. Below we refer to pages as "dynamic" if their contents change from day to day.

While the idea to classify web pages based on link percentage seems intuitive, the question is, is it actually feasible to break down pages into categories by this one-dimensional characteristic? Figure 4 gives an example where a dynamic index page and multiple article pages are clearly separable over time. Does this mean that a single threshold on link percentage will be an accurate classifier for all web sites? From the graphs of the link percentage of article and index pages drawn from four popular web sites over a period of two weeks shown in figure 5, it is clear that a single threshold does not suffice. Index pages have a higher link percentage than articles in most cases, but a single threshold cannot separate these two types of pages across the web.

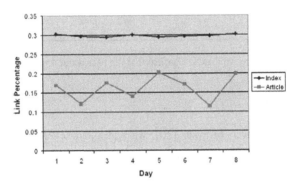

Fig. 4. The link percentage the BBC web site over a period of 8 days. The index page that was chosen was the same, but different articles were chosen at random every day. Observe that there is a clear distinction in link percentage between the index page and the article pages.

For the 50 web sites that we tested, the average ratio of link percentage in index pages to link percentage in article pages was approximately 3, including malformed HTML characters (for the interested reader, the web site that had the highest link percentage ratio in our corpus was that of the Real Madrid football team, with an average index page link percentage of 95.3% and an average article page link percentage of 0.001%). To find these link percentages, we use an HTML parsing mechanism that works on most web pages. HTML is often not well-formed, however, so we perform some further processing after the link text and plain text has been extracted from the HTML code by removing as many extraneous tags as possible.

Once we have parsed a web page's HTML code and determined the link percentage, the issue of determining a proper threshold arises. If the user has not other web pages

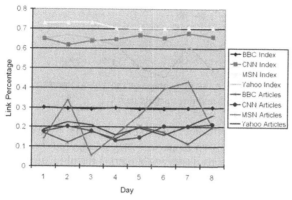

Fig. 5. The link percentage for various sites over a period of 8 days. The examined index pages are dynamic and typically change every day. Different articles at these sites were chosen at random every day. While it is apparent that index pages have higher link percentages than articles, there is not one threshold that can separate these two types of pages for all web sites, as shown by the MSN article link percentage rising above the link percentage for the BBC index page. It is also important to notice that, except for the Yahoo index page, the dynamic index pages' link percentages do not change by more than 3%. The behavior of the Yahoo index page's link percentage is due to malformed HTML.

from this site, then we can only use generic thresholds to determine the type of a page. An initial threshold of 0.4 was used in experiments and found to perform reasonably well. After the user has visited at least one page of each type, however, we can begin to discover how the link percentage values of index pages and article pages are clustered. Using the k-means clustering algorithm for each web site, with k = 2, one cluster for article pages and one cluster for index pages, we can accurately classify future web pages from this site. We use as the initial mean points of the cluster the pages with the lowest and highest link percentage for the article and index clusters, respectively. We then run the k-means algorithm to determine the final clusters. Using these clusters, we choose as our decision threshold the value midway between the link percentage of the page with the highest link percentage in the article cluster and the link percentage of the page with the lowest link percentage in the index cluster. An example where clusters are separated by a threshold computed in this way is given in figure 6. The k-means algorithm can be viewed as a method to approximate the maximum-likelihood estimates for the means of the clusters.

We observed that even dynamic web pages' link percentages do not fluctuate very much over short periods of time. We studied four popular websites over the course of seven months and found that the link percentages for the same index pages had a total range of less than eight percent. Therefore, once a page is visited its link percentage is stored in a database and is retrieved if the page is visited again and no HTML parsing is performed. This saves computational effort and can easily be overridden by the user if the classification results falter because of a change in the web site structure.

4.2 Customized Page Display

Our web browser enlarged link text on index pages to support mouse substitution interfaces that use dwell time to generate mouse clicks. The browser also enlarged plain

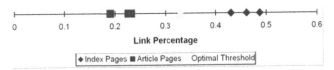

Fig. 6. The optimal threshold for link percentage on the Yahoo Sports web site given the link percentages of three index pages and three article pages

text on article pages to enhance readability. This is just one possible display modification, and for certain web pages this may or may not be useful. The user can undo these display modifications if they wish, putting the ultimate decision of the page's display in their hands (see figures 1 and 2 for a comparison of our browser's rendering of a web page using web context to that of Internet Explorer).

We could further enhance the user's interaction experience by changing the way that keyboard or mouse commands are issued depending on the type of web page that the user is viewing in order to facilitate navigation. Moreover, we could provide the user with tools to create their own rules for modifying web page display based on page type. This kind of control is extremely crucial for people with disabilities. With many of the currently available assistive interface systems web browsing is still difficult. For example, using an interface system such as the Camera Mouse [2] to select links or scroll down a page is hard even for users without disabilities. With our method, these users could scroll down an article web page merely by moving the mouse pointer to the left half of the screen, or iteratively cycle through links by performing the same action on an index page. It is our hope that this method can alleviate some of the accessibility problems that people with disabilities have with current interface systems. We also hope that future work will place more emphasis on the context of their actions to enrich the interactive experience and make it more effective and efficient.

Another aspect of customized page display is the use of manual corrections if a user has a preference for a different display than provided by our method or if the web page was misclassified, which occurs when pages were created with malformed HTML (see below). We decided that the best course of action is to omit the page in question from the clustering algorithm altogether.

5   Link Grouping

Link grouping allows users with severe disabilities to use a scan-based mechanism to tab through a web page and select item. This can substantially improve the user's rate of communication, and could be applied to mouse substitution interfaces by allowing users to click on a group of links so they can more easily select the desired single link.

5.1   Link Tree Creation

The link tree creation step of our link grouping algorithm creates the framework under which we can cluster points according to their location on the web page as well as their location in the HTML code. Essentially our method leverages the structure of the HTML code, which can be quite nicely represented in tree form by allowing an element to be a node in a tree and the elements that it encapsulates to be its children.

An example link tree along with the HTML code that it was created from is picture in figure 7. The tree representation allows us to employ a divide-and-conquer method from grouping as described below. Our method can also use this tree to constrain link grouping so that groups do not span inappropriately across the web page. Note that it is not that such across-page grouping is incorrect per se, rather that it would create a very unnatural grouping consisting of circles of links that did not respect the structure of the web page. In addition, this would leave us with a very unconstrained clustering problem, and we certainly prefer an approach that can apply the divide-and-conquer paradigm to the grouping problem.

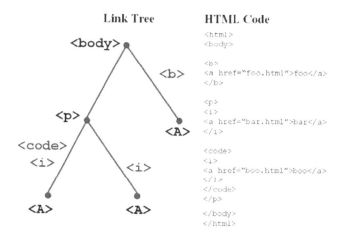

Fig. 7. The left figure represents the link tree for the HTML code on the right. At the leaves are the link nodes, and the internal nodes are the first common parent of its children in the DOM tree. The parents of each node in the DOM tree that are not represented as internal nodes of the link tree are shown in blue. This example can best be understood by examining the HTML code and viewing the structure of the DOM tree. Observe that the first common parent of the link to "bar.html" and the link to "boo.html" is the "<P>" node. Therefore this is their parent in the link tree. Next, note that the first common parent of the link to "foo.html" and the "<P>" node is the "<BODY>" element, which is the root of the tree.

The pseudocode for link tree creation is shown in algorithm 1. Our algorithm, *CreateLinkTree*, takes as input an HTML DOM tree and outputs the link tree. The algorithm starts at the links of the DOM tree and traverses it until it reaches the root node of the document, marking every node that it visits along the traversal (line 9). If, however, it comes across an already marked node, our algorithm converts that node into an internal node in the link tree, connected to the link nodes that already marked it (lines 5 and 6). If that link node has already been incorporated into a subtree of the link tree, that subtree becomes the current node's child. Traversal of the DOM tree then stops. The last case that can occur is that a link traversal will arrive at a node that is already an internal node in the link tree. Here the link will simply add itself as another child to that node and stop traversal.

In the worst case, the links do not intersect until the "<BODY>" node of the DOM tree (since this node must encapsulate all links). If there are n links, and the height of the DOM tree from the link nodes is *log(q)*, where *q* is the number of elements in the DOM tree, it is clear that the link tree creation algorithm is bounded by *O(nlog(q))*, since our method must make n traversals of length *log(q)*. Note that typically *n<<q*.

```
Algorithm 1 CreateLinkTree:
Input: HTML DOM Tree T, Output: Root of the link tree
   1: for each link a in T
   2:       traverser = a
   3:       while traverser.parent != root
   4:         traverser.parent.child = a
   5:         if marked(traverser.parent)
   6:           make node(traverser.parent)
   7:           break
   8:         end if
   9:         mark(traverser.parent)
  10:         traverser = traverser.parent
  11:       end while
  12: end for
  13: return root
```

5.2 Link Grouping

The link tree creation step of our algorithm has now given our method the machinery to perform link grouping. For all of the clustering steps below, our algorithm, GroupLinks, uses a set of points defined by the position of the links on the rendered web page in Cartesian coordinates. In general, our algorithm traverses the link tree from the top down and attempts to merge the clusters of link points of one of its child nodes with those of another child node if each child has only one link cluster. The optimal number of clusters is chosen by the criterion function defined below. Pseudocode for the link grouping algorithm is given in algorithm 2.

```
Algorithm 2 GroupLinks:
Input: Link Tree Node R, Significance p
Output: Link Groupings
   1:  if isLeaf(R)
   2:        return R.position
   3:  end if
   4:  for each child c of R
   5:        groups(c) = GroupLinks(c)
   6:  end for
   7:  mergeGroups = {groups(c)} s.t.
   8:  num_clusters(groups(c)) = 1
   9:  create_hierarchical_clusters(mergeGroups)
  10:  current_clusters = 1
  11:  while equation 1 is not satisfied
  12:        current_clusters++
  13:  end while
  14:  return clusters(current_clusters) +
                Σ[num_clusters(groups(c)) |
                num_clusters(groups(c))    1]
```

More specifically, using the link tree as a structural guide, the algorithm recursively breaks down the clustering problem into that of merging the link point clusters of children nodes together, starting at the root node, by a criterion function. If our method cannot merge all of the children of some internal node together, then, intuitively, these link groups should be excluded from merging with other groups at higher levels in the tree. As stated earlier, doing so would violate our constraint of respecting the structure of the web page.

At the current node, call it node i, the method first runs the link grouping algorithm on all of its children (line 4). If node i has no children, it is a link and thus simply returns its position to its parent as a single cluster (line 2). Otherwise, the algorithm checks which of node i's children can be merged (line 7), which is the case if each child returned only a single cluster of points. For all of node i's children that can be merged, our method runs the agglomerative hierarchical clustering algorithm on the mean points of each of its children's clusters (line 8). This algorithm essentially merges the closest clusters at every step. As stated above it is for this reason that we can expect the clusters to have low variance. Assuming that there are c children of node i, this gives our algorithm a total of c clusters before i is processed.

The next step is to determine the optimal number of clusters. We do this using the equations (due to [10]):

$$J(k+1)/J(k) = 1 - 2/d\pi - \alpha \; 2(1 - 8/\pi^2 d)/nd \; . \tag{1}$$

where $J(k)$ is the SSD error for k clusters, d is the distance between the means of the clusters that were split to create $b + 1$ clusters from b clusters, and n is the number of points in all clusters.

The parameter α is determined by solving the equation:

$$\alpha = \; 2 * \mathrm{erf}^{-1}(1 - p/2) \; . \tag{2}$$

where erf is the Gauss error function, defined by the equation:

$$\mathrm{erf}(x) = 2/ \; \pi \int_0^x e^{-t^2} \, dt \; . \tag{3}$$

Here, p is the significance level at which we believe that we have at least $k + 1$ clusters. Our algorithm starts with $k = 1$, stopping once the inequality in equation 1 is violated. It then returns the resulting clusters.

Naturally, having k+1 clusters will yield a lower SSD error than k clusters. Essentially, what equation 1 does is model the clusters as k different normal distributions and check that the error reduction that we see is not due to chance at the p significance level, since if there actually were only k clusters we would expect any other clusters that formed to be formed by chance.

Once the final clusters have been returned to the root node, we can modify the web page to make it more accessible to users with disabilities. While this modification mechanism can be accomplished by various parameterized functions, in our implementation we choose to use color to identify links in the same group, using different colors for different groups. This is shown in figures 8 and 9. Other options include link enlargement when the mouse cursor hovers over a link group, making all links in a group lead to a page where the links are made very large for easy navigation, and many other possibilities which we will explore further in the Future Work section.

Background   [edit]

Heimaey before the eruption

Iceland is a region of frequent volcanic activity, due to its location astride the Mid-Atlantic Ridge, where the North American and Eurasian Plates are moving apart, and also over the Iceland hotspot, which greatly enhances the volcanic activity. It is estimated that a third of all the basaltic lava erupted in the world in recorded history has been produced by Icelandic eruptions.

The Vestmannaeyjar (Icelandic for Westman islands) archipelago lies off the south coast of Iceland, and consists of several small islands, all formed by eruptions in the Holocene epoch. Heimaey, the largest island in the group and the only inhabited one, also contains some material from the Pleistocene era. The most prominent feature on Heimaey before 1973 was Helgafell, a 200 m (650 ft) high volcanic cone formed in an eruption about 5,000 years ago.

The Vestmannaeyjar archipelago was settled in about 874 AD, originally by escaped Irish slaves belonging to Norse settlers on the mainland. These settlers gave the islands their name, Ireland being west of mainland Scandinavia. Although plagued by poor water supplies and piracy during much of its history, Heimaey became the most important centre of the Icelandic fishing industry, having one of the few good harbours on the southern side of the country, and being situated in very rich fishing grounds.

Since the settlement, no eruptions had been known to occur on the islands until   , when a new member of the archipelago, Surtsey, was formed by a four year eruption which began offshore about 20 km (12 mi) south-west of Heimaey. However, offshore eruptions may have taken place in 1637 and 1896. Scientists have speculated that volcanic activity in the archipelago may be increasing due to the southward propagation of the rift zone which crosses Iceland.

Fig. 8. A Wikipedia (http://www.wikipedia.org) web page that has been processed by our link grouping algorithm. The different link groups are in different colors so that the user can easily pick out different groups. In this page, shown only partially here, 66 clusters were found.

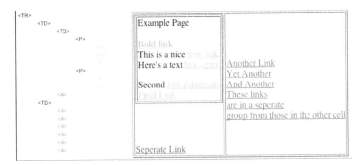

Fig. 9. Left: The link tree for the web page on the right. The links in the tree have the color that they were given in the web page after they were processed by our link grouping algorithm. Right: An example web page processed by the link grouping algorithm.

The link grouping creation algorithm is bounded by $O(n^3)$ in the worst case, where n is the number of links, since our method must find the closest group at every step of hierarchical clustering, for n steps. Note that this worst case is only realized if every link has only one common parent at the root of the link tree, which does not happen in practice since that would require essentially no other content on the web page. Since the link tree exhibits the structure of a tree with branching factor b in the average, the algorithm is bounded by $O(b^2 log_b(n))$, since the height of the link tree is $log_b(n)$ and the algorithm needs to create b clusters at each level of the tree. If no links can be merged, the algorithm stops at the leaves of the link tree and is bounded by $O(b^2)$. In practice, we measured a runtime that falls somewhere in between the last two bounds that we derived, since typically we can merge only some of the link point clusters at each node. Note that the runtime depends heavily upon the p used in equation 2, since p essentially bounds the size of a cluster in 2D space. The complete algorithm, including the creation of the link tree, then, for the bound on the link grouping algorithm of $O(b^2 log_b(n))$, is simply $O(nlog(q))$, as long as we have $b<<n$, which is again normally the case.

Suppose that our user is using a simple tab interface which requires the user to press the tab button once to move to the next link and enter to click on the link. Using our grouping algorithm, this user could select a specific group and then an individual link. Assuming that there are c final clusters and that each group has an average of s links, the average number of tabs required to click on a link would be $c+s/2$. In comparison, the tab-based interface that is currently employed on commercial web browsers has an average number of tabs of $n/2$. Therefore, our method improves the communication rate of users by a factor of $n/(c+s)$. Note that if s is too large, we could simply split each cluster into subgroups in order to minimize the number of tabs required and maximize $n/(c+s)$, but that is left to future work. As a precaution, if only one cluster is created then the grouping is not used, since this would result in requiring the user to press the tab button once just to be able to perform the original selection task. Clearly, in the worst case, where the number of clusters equals the number of links, our method performs as well as the current tab-based implementations on web browsers, and due to the trivial computational cost of our grouping algorithm (the highest number of links in our web corpus of 300 pages was 1250, and the link grouping program ran in under a second), our method could be an integral component for an accessible web browser, or any web browser in general

6   Experiments

To test our web context method we used it to classify web pages from a corpus of the top 25 news and top 25 sports web sites as rated by Alexa Web Search (URL: www.alexa.com). For each web site, three index pages and three article pages, as categorized by a human observer, were used for testing for a total of 300 web pages. One index page and one article page from each web site were randomly chosen to create an index cluster and an article cluster in the web context program, and these pages were not included in the test set. Since users often only browse a small number of web sites [19], we expect that in practice our method will eventually have enough data to find the true link percentage distributions of article and index pages.

We compared our method to a static threshold technique, which used a predetermined global threshold (a link percentage of 0.4) to differentiate between index pages and articles. We treat this classifier as the baseline in our discussion of results, since it is the simplest solution to the classification problem. We also compared our method to an "optimal" classifier, which chooses the best possible classification threshold for each web site. This is merely a theoretical classifier; given complete knowledge of what the correct classifications are, it finds the optimal classification threshold.

There were many web pages that contained severely malformed HTML, as evidenced by the fact that even the optimal classifier did not generate 100% accuracy on every web site. The results are shown in figure 10, broken down by site category (news or sports). The average classification accuracy for each method is shown in table 1, and a graph comparing the static threshold method and the clustering method is shown in figure 11. In figure 10 and 11 accuracy of 100% implies that all pages in the test set for a particular web site were classified correctly, while 83% implies that five out of the six pages in the test set were classified correctly, and so on.

Table 1. Classification accuracy of three classifiers as the fraction of the number of correctly labeled web pages out of 300 test web pages

Page Type	Static Threshold	Clustering	Optimal Classifier
News Pages	0.734	0.840	0.946
Sports Pages	0.700	0.760	0.866
All Pages	0.717	0.800	0.906

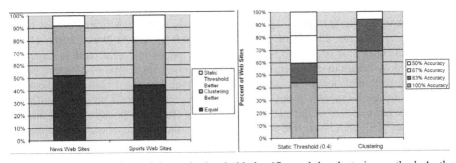

Fig. 10. The classification accuracies for the three different classifiers. Left: Accuracies on 25 news web sites, containing a total of 150 web pages. Right: Accuracies on 25 sports web sites, containing a total of 150 web pages.

Fig. 11. Left: A comparison of the static threshold classifier and the clustering method. As the

HTML parsing improves, evidenced by the higher accuracy of the optimal classifier for the news web site data set, so does the performance of our clustering method. Right: The classification accuracy for the static threshold and clustering methods on sites for which the optimal classifier achieved 100% accuracy. Our clustering method correctly classified 94% of web pages, while the static threshold method only classified 80% correctly.

To evaluate our link grouping method, we tested it on a number of web pages from our original corpus using a significance level p = 0.001, which kept the link groups to a reasonable size. We discuss the results of these experiments below.

7   Results and Discussion

7.1   Web Context

In our experiments, the clustering method gave higher performance than the static threshold method, correctly classifying 80.0% of the test pages compared to the static threshold's 71.7%. Our method's accuracy, however, is clearly not equivalent to the optimal classifier, which classified 90.6% of the pages correctly. The other 9.4% of pages had highly malformed HTML code, since when the experimenter hand labeled the link and plain text, these pages were found to cluster in the expected fashion and often the hand labeled link percentages differed from those given by the parsing program by over 40%.

It is also interesting that our method achieved better results than the static threshold 38% of the time, while only having poorer performance in 14% of our experiments. This result is encouraging because it shows that we are consistently outperforming the baseline classifier and reaching a level of performance that is close to that of the optimal classifier.

It also makes sense to ask how the static threshold and clustering methods compare when all web sites where the optimal classifier did not achieve 100% accuracy are removed. Then we see the clustering method achieved 94.0% accuracy, while the static threshold technique rose to only 80.1% accuracy. These results are shown in figure 11. The clustering method performed better than the static threshold on 47% of the web sites, and the static threshold method performed better on only 9.4% of sites. This indicates that as HTML parsing accuracy increases, our clustering method gets closer to 100% accuracy. Indeed, there are still some parsing errors left over in this group of sites, only less of them and of smaller magnitude. It seems clear that combining our method with an "HTML cleaning technique" such as that introduced in [27] would yield extremely high levels of accuracy.

The strength of our method is that it finds the proper threshold between index and article pages in a web site given little data. The fact that we do not know a priori which web pages are indices and which are articles poses a problem if the user visits only pages of a single type. The algorithm will then assume that one of the pages is in fact an index and thus erroneous clusters will emerge until the user visits a page of the other type. This is not a problem if the user can turn off our web page classification method for certain sites that do not have different kinds of pages. It is important to make the user aware of this caveat, lest they prematurely turn off the algorithm for sites where it would work appropriately if it had more information.

Note that, in general, users will collect more data from each site over the course of normal browsing, so we would expect even better results than those reported here. Our experiments are meant to show merely the bare minimum of what our method is capable of.

It also may be unsettling that we ignore images, display markup, and position information. While we realize that these are important parts of a page's content, it is difficult to develop rules that would generalize to the entire web, since some articles have many images while index pages have very few. Some images, however, are used as links in place of text. It is unclear exactly how influence should be computed for these images, but these images may prove useful as an additional cue in a future extension of our system, although currently they are ignored during processing.

In addition, text markup is used in many different ways with rather loose rules governing their use, and given that our classification performance is extremely high, it does not seem that the extra processing required would generate large gains in accuracy.

7.2 Link Grouping

The results for link grouping varied widely, with the reduction in tabbing by the factor of $n/(c+s)$, spanning from a factor of 40 to an improvement of only 1.5, with a mean of 12. In addition, our algorithm on average took 0.2 seconds to run, with the longest time at 0.8 seconds. Thus our method clearly runs in real time and provides real performance gains for the user.

Our link grouping algorithm has shown itself to be quite versatile and effective, working across web pages in multiple languages with a myriad of layouts. While is difficult to state what the "correct" link grouping would be in an objective manner, personal experience with the algorithm has shown that it does indeed respect the layout of the page and provides very intuitive groupings on most pages. As a bonus, our method is easy to plug in to any web browser, since it was built entirely in code that can be inserted directly into a web page by a browser.

Actual modification of web page display, however, did not receive as much attention as the algorithm itself. There are innumerable possibilities for modifications, and these vary drastically with the intended audience. We will explore some of these possibilities below.

8 Future Work

Extracted HTML text characters can clearly be used to form a very accurate classification algorithm, but in order to push accuracy higher we may need to use other cues. Using rendering data to weight text according to its centrality in the displayed page (i.e. weighting text that is closer to the top and middle higher than text that is more towards the sides and bottom) appears to be an attractive extension, although it is not clear if a general rule can be developed that works for a broad segment of web sites.

We may also wish to handle pages that contain a high volume of images used as links rather than text links. While not encountered in our test corpus, handling of such pages is crucial, and perhaps assigning a default weight to each image-link would further improve results.

Detecting web pages and sites that are merely Java applets or Flash programs is also important, since we can no longer determine the optimal mode of interaction with the web page. If, however, we allow the user to specify what mode of interaction to use when they visit this page, then we can contact the interface system each time this page is visited again and instruct it to output commands according to the user's specification. This is a very useful feature that will likely be implemented in our web browser in future work.

It may also be useful to segment the rendered page into different regions using a decomposition method such as that introduced by Chen et al. [5] and then classify each of the regions using our method. The classification of the entire page could come from a weighted sum of the classifications of each region. This decomposition could also aid in interaction modification, since we can imagine displaying regions of different types in different ways and changing the user interaction method if they select a particular region. This would incur a higher computational cost, but it may be a necessary extension to further utilize web context on PDA-class devices.

We could extend our approach to web page classification into the image processing realm by using a bitmap image of the rendered page to classify text regions and other regions using pixel information only. This would be insulated from many of the problems of parsing malformed HTML, but this type of algorithm would be computationally expensive and require the page to be rendered before it is altered, placing further burden on the user. It may be useful to combine this image-based method with our current classification scheme, however, to yield a more robust estimate of page type.

One issue that we touched upon earlier was sites that have only one page type or web sites where only pages of one type are visited. To handle this case automatically it may be necessary to first attempt to fit a single cluster to all web pages on a site and then see if the fit is acceptable. If not, then the regular algorithm can resume. Characterizing what constitutes a "good" fit may prove troublesome and complicates this technique.

There are also web sites which do not fall within the domain of sports or news web sites that may have multiple types of pages. A major component of future work is to identify these page types and examine if they generalize across a wide range of web sites as the article and index types do. If it appears that new page types provide a nice fit for a wide range of web sites, incorporating these types into a future algorithm would be a definite possibility. It may be, however, that beyond the basic article-index distinction different interaction modes and display modifications are not useful. This issue clearly demands further research.

We also wish to extend our web browser to give more control to the user in displaying web pages. We are experimenting with ways to offer this functionality, and it will surely create a greatly enhanced interaction experience for the user. Detailed experiments on how page display modification and changes in the interaction mode positively impact the user interface experience will also be performed to further validate our results. This is particularly relevant to our link grouping algorithm, which could allow users to click on a link group to enlarge that group of links, or to highlight a link group in a different color as it's selected. What options are most user-friendly and intuitive would make for interesting future research.

Our work is a preliminary step into the larger investigation of computer context. In later work we would also like examine other types of computer context and investigate whether or not extending web context to include previously browsed pages is feasible. Work in this area has only just begun.

9 Conclusion

We have presented a highly accurate method for classifying web pages based on link percentage. Our k-means clustering method created unique thresholds to differentiate index pages and article pages on individual web sites. Accuracy increased when we removed web sites from the corpus that had extremely malformed HTML, and it is expected that more robust HTML parsing will yield even more accurate results. Our method consistently outperformed a baseline classifier even when using minimal data to generate initial article and index clusters.

Our link tree creation algorithm and link grouping method have been shown to be quite effective and guaranteed to outperform or at least stay at the same level as the functionality offered by current web browsers, leading to a possible improved communication rate for users with disabilities. This method is fast and is portable to nearly all available web browsers, giving it promise to become an integral tool for web accessibility.

We also used web page classification and link grouping to alter web page display on a web browser, and future work will center around giving the user more control in determining how different types of web pages are displayed and choosing intuitive ways to change interaction modes of an interface system based on web page classification and link grouping.

References

1. Document object model (dom) level 1 specificiation version 1.0. W3C Recommendation, 1998.
2. Betke, M., Gips, J., Fleming, P.: The Camera Mouse: Visual tracking of body features to provide computer access for people with severe disabilities. IEEE Transactions on Neural Systems and Rehabilitation Engineering, 10(1):1–10, Mar. 2002.
3. Bharat, K., Chang, B., Henzinger, M., Ruhl, M.: Who links to whom: Mining linkage between web sites. In International Conference on Data Mining (ICDM), pages 51–58, 2001.
4. Buyukkokten, O., Garcia-Molina, H., Paepcke, A.: Seeing the whole in parts: text summarization for web browsing on handheld devices. In Proceedings of the 10th International World Wide Web Conference (WWW), pages 652–662, Hong Kong, 2001.
5. Chen, Y., Ma, W.-Y., Zhang, H.-J.: Detecting web page structure for adaptive viewing on small form factor devices. In Proceedings of the 12th International World Wide Web Conference (WWW), pages 225–233, Budapest, Hungary, 2003.
6. Chi, E. H.-H., Rosien, A., Supattanasiri, G., Williams, A., Royer, C., Chow, C., Robles, E., Dalal, B., Chen, J., Cousins, S.: The bloodhound project: automating discovery of web usability issues using the infoscent simulator. In Computer-Human Interaction 2003 Conference on Human Factors in Computing Systems (CHI), pages 505–512, 2003.

7. Cimiano, P., Handschuh, S., Staab, S.: Towards the self-annotating web. In Proceedings of the 13th International World Wide Web Conference (WWW), pages 462–471, New York City, 2004.

8. Cimiano, P., Ladwig, G., Staab, S.: Gimme' the context: Context-driven automatic semantic annotation with C-PANKOW. In Proceedings of the 14th International World Wide Web Conference (WWW), pages 332–341, Chiba, Japan, 2005.

9. DiMattia, P., Curran, F. X., Gips, J.: An Eye Control Teaching Device for Students without Language Expressive Capacity – EagleEyes. The Edwin Mellen Press, 2001.

10. Duda, R., Hart, P., Stork, D.: Pattern Classification. Wiley-Interscience, 2001.

11. 11.Fogaras, D., Rácz, B.: Scaling link-based similarity search. In Proceedings of the 14th International World Wide Web Conference (WWW), pages 641–650, Chiba, Japan, 2005.

12. Gupta, S., Kaiser, G.: Extracting content from accessible web pages. In Proceedings of the 14th International World Wide Web Conference (WWW), pages 26–30, Chiba, Japan, 2005.

13. Gupta, S., Kaiser, G., Stolfo, S.: Extracting context to improve accuracy for html content extraction. In Proceedings of the 14th International World Wide Web Conference (WWW), pages 1114–1115, Chiba, Japan, 2005.

14. Hornbæk, K., Bederson, B.B., Plaisant, C.: Navigation patterns and usability of zoomable user interfaces with and without an overview. ACM Transactions on Human-Computer Interaction, 9(4):362–389, Dec. 2002.

15. Kim, J.W., Candan, K.S., Dönderler, M.E.: Topic segmentation of message hierarchies for indexing and navigation support. In Proceedings of the 14th International World Wide Web Conference (WWW), pages 322–331, Chiba, Japan, 2005.

16. 16.Larson, H., Gips, J.: A web browser for people with quadriplegia. In 10th International Conference on Human-Computer Interaction, Crete, Greece, 2003.

17. 17.Leporini, B., Paternò, F.: Increasing usability when interacting through screen readers. In Universal Access in the Information Society, Volume 3, Number 1, pages 57-70, 2004.

18. Milic-Frayling, N., Jones, R., Rodden, K., Smyth, G., Blackwell, A., Sommerer, R.: SmartBack: Supporting users in back navigation. In Proceedings of the 13th International World Wide Web Conference (WWW), pages 63–71, New York City, 2004.

19. Montogmery, A., Faloutsos, C.: Indentifying web browsing trends and patterns. Computer, pages 94–95, 2001.

20. Paquette, M., Betke, M., Magee, J.: IWeb Explorer: A web browser designed for use with an eye controlled mouse device. Boston University Computer Science MA Thesis Report, 2005.

21. Parmanto, B., Ferrydiansyah, R., Saptono, A., Song, L., Sugiantara, I.W., Hackett, S.: AcceSS: Accessibility through simplification & summarization. In Proceedings of the Second International Cross-Disciplinary Workshop on Web Accessibility (W4A2005), pages 18–25, Chiba, Japan, 2005.

22. Pitkow, J., Schutze, H., Cass, T., Cooley, R., Turnbull, D., Edmonds, A., Adar, E., Breuel, T.: Personalized search. Commun. ACM, 45(9):50–55, 2002.

23. Reis, D., Golgher, P.B., da Silva, A.S., Laender, A.H.F.: Automatic web news extraction using tree edit distance. In Proceedings of the 13th International World Wide Web Conference (WWW), pages 502–511, New York City, 2004.

24. 24.Stephanidis, C., Paramythis, A., Karagiannidis, C., Savidis, A.: Supporting Interface Adaptation: The AVANTI WebBrowser. In Proceedings of the 3rd ERCIM Workshop on User Interfaces for All, Obernai, France, 1997.

25. Sullivan, T., Matson, R.: Barriers to use: Usability and content accessibility on the web's most popular sites. In Proceedings of the 2000 Conference on Universal Usability, pages 139–144, Arlington, Virginia, USA, 2000.
26. Winograd, T.: Architectures for context. Human-Computer Interaction, 10(24):401–419, 2001.
27. Yi, L., Liu, B., Li, X.: Eliminating noisy information in web pages for data mining. In KDD '03: Proceedings of the ninth ACM SIGKDD international conference on Knowledge discovery and data mining, pages 296–305, Washington, D.C., USA, 2003.

Author Index

Lecture Notes in Computer Science

For information about Vols. 1–4297

please contact your bookseller or Springer